FACES OF ANTHROPOLOGY

A READER FOR THE 21ST CENTURY

THIRD EDITION

KEVIN RAFFERTY, PH.D.

DOROTHY CHINWE UKAEGBU, PH.D.

COMMUNITY COLLEGE OF SOUTHERN NEVADA (CHEYENNE)

Pearson
Custom
Publishing

Printed in the United States of America

10 9 8 7 6 5 4 3 2 1

Please visit our web site at www.pearsoncustom.com

ISBN 0–536–60997–7

BA 992201

 PEARSON CUSTOM PUBLISHING
75 Arlington Street, Suite 300, Boston, MA 02116
A Pearson Education Company

CONTENTS

SECTION ONE

Changing Faces of Anthropology:
The Subfields

TALKING THE TALK ON INDIGENOUS RADIO

Donald R. Browne

Thirty years ago, indigenous peoples throughout the world had little, if any, opportunity to hear their languages over the radio. Majority cultures dominated the airwaves and most nations saw little value in supporting indigenous cultures in any form. But the late 1960s proved to be a time of social upheaval throughout much of the Western world and various minority groups began to stake their claims to air time—often through community radio stations. As the 20th century comes to a close, we find indigenous radio services in almost all the larger industrialized nations, as well as in many of the smaller ones. A few even have limited amounts of time on nationally networked services.

One major reason for interest in indigenous radio was the opportunity it presented to bring fresh life to indigenous languages, and possibly to rescue some from extinction. Because radio is an oral medium, it appeared to be suited ideally for this purpose. And it certainly seems to have worked for the Welsh, the Sami, and the Maori; and a number of North American indigenous language services have encouraged many indigenous youth to take their languages seriously. However, the languages have been impacted in a number of unexpected ways as well.

Restoring or Preserving the "Purity" of Indigenous Languages

When radio services came into existence and were used by minority groups, most of their staff wanted to show listeners that their languages were alive. Not only could they be heard over radio, but they could be heard presenting current events. This demonstrated that indigenous languages weren't simply museums for the preservation of songs, folk tales, and myths. However, as soon as local or indigenous stations began to present newscasts, discussions, and talks about current affairs, their staff often discovered that the terminologies of those languages were inadequate to deal with AIDS, space travel, and other 20th century phenomena. Sometimes it was possible to create appropriate terms by fusing two or more existing words, as in the Maori term for computers, *rore hiko* or "electric brain." Sometimes listeners sug-

gested new uses for older terms, as did a number of Irish Gaelic speakers who called Raidio na Gaehachta (RNG), or "Radio for the Irish Speaking Region," to suggest that *staighrbeo*, meaning "living stairs," would be appropriate for *escalator*. But it was a far more frequent practice to give a majority culture term an indigenous ending or even to simply use the term as it was.

This practice poses a dilemma. If indigenous electronic media hope to restore or preserve the purity of their languages, aren't they defeated before they begin, at least where the worlds of technology, medicine, perhaps sports, and possibly societal problems, are concerned? Does any truly alternative indigenous term stand a chance when majority culture media quickly and broadly establish the "appropriate" terminology? If the indigenous media seek a compromise solution by borrowing Western terminologies and "indigenizing" them with prefixes, suffixes, and pronunciations, what then? Should that become a common practice, how much of the "true" indigenous language remains? Granted, all languages change over time, but the mass media seem to possess the capacity to bring about such change more rapidly and more comprehensively than any older media-bards, poets, singers, traders, etc.—ever were able to do. If French purists rail against the franglicization of their language when France is a media-rich nation, what chance does Maori, Sami, Basque, or Lakota stand?

Fortunately for speakers of those languages, enough true language has survived through the centuries so that there's a solid and sizable foundation upon which to build as we move into the 21st century. For all their complaints, the French purists would have to admit that the vast majority of their native tongue remains intact, despite the incursions of *le prime time* or *le hamburger*.

There are even cases of indigenous terms being picked up by majority cultures. The Maori "hello," or *kia ora*, appears to be in increasing use among New Zealand *pakeha* (Europeans). Australia's famous symbols—the koala, the kookaburra, and the kangaroo—all bear Aboriginal names. The Inuit igloo is familiar to most North Americans, many of whom don't realize that they use at least one Inuit word when they refer to it. Certainly there isn't anything like a two-way street in which the flow of linguistic traffic is the same in both directions. But prospects for the future viability and purity seem good for most indigenous languages now available through radio—if purity isn't taken too literally or pushed too far.

Employing Indigenous Dialects

The role of dialects in the indigenous electronic media often is a delicate issue. Many indigenous languages feature a fair amount of dialect variation. Indigenous language radio stations sometimes face difficult decisions regarding the choice of dialects, if they choose to use any at all. The problem isn't just a lack of common terminology. Dialect variation can be a matter of intense pride. In the Tainui-dominated areas of New Zealand, most Tainui radio stations cite the superiority of the Tainui dialect form of Maori as one reason for them not using the Maori national newscasts of Mana Maori Media. (Another reason is that enough coverage of Tainui activities doesn't exist.) If linguistic areas are reasonably definable to geographic terms, if the indigenous language service includes local stations, and if the areas themselves are configured so that the station signals fit the geographical-linguistic boundaries more or less perfectly (which is rare), dialect broadcasts may present few problems. Each dialect then will have its own self-contained broadcast outlet. A number of indigenous language services, however, are largely or wholly national and operate from a single or limited number of locations (Ireland's RNG is such an operation). In those cases, deciding whether to broadcast in dialects at all, and if so, which ones, can be a major problem.

The problem rarely is one of comprehension. Most dialect speakers can understand other dialects at least well enough to extract the basic meaning. The effort may be considerable, especially with certain Sami dialects that have evolved to the point where they might be considered as separate languages. In such instances, it's doubtful that most audience members would bother to make any accommodation.

The emotional overtones connected with dialects can pose a far greater barrier. The Tainui example just cited may be extreme in its exclusiveness, but speakers of various Irish dialects still criticize some RNG announcers for their "dreadful" Kerry accents (or Donegal, or Connemara); north Welsh speakers may have similar reactions to south Welsh speakers. Related examples appear in many minority language broadcasting situations. Still, radio can help in breaking down some of these emotional barriers. For example, the staff at RNG and Radio Cymru have

told me that they hear far fewer complaints about dialects now than they once did, and even some grudging acceptance along the lines of "But I do find what she/he has to say quite interesting."

There's yet another dimension to the dialect issue. If an indigenous radio service often makes use of localized dialects, might that deter the indigenous population from coalescing as a force to be reckoned with on a national level? My conversations with aboriginal broadcasters in Australia often touched upon that issue. Dozens of Aboriginal languages and dialects exist, most of them spoken by a few hundred to a few thousand individuals. While some aboriginal broadcasters are committed to providing services to those languages and dialects, their ability to carry more than a half dozen or so is severely limited. Aside from ability, however, those broadcasters wonder how a strong Aboriginal presence could be established at a national level without working through a common language, which turns out to be English. Using English as the common language not only injures their cultural pride, but it seems to be the only practical solution for gaining access to political power.

Reshaping Communication Practices

Radio follows a set of almost universally understood practices. Programs usually start and end at hour and half-hour intervals. Voices are supposed to be "on mike" and clearly audible to the audience. In interviews and discussions, pauses between sentences and speakers should be brief. Announcers speak the broadcast languages correctly, or at least according to the majority culture's standards of correctness. In general, those practices coincide, more or less closely, with practices in everyday life. But some indigenous practices differ. Discussions among Native Americans in North America and among Aborigines in Australia often are characterized by long pauses. Formal Maori discussions are held according to a strict protocol, in which the sometimes random give-and-take of a formal discussion in North America or Europe would be out of place. However, as radio becomes an integral part of indigenous culture, does it bring a set of expectations as to practices that might be at variance with indigenous practices?

Consider the matter of pauses. Will indigenous radio staff consciously or unconsciously reshape practices, such as having long pauses, and quicken the pace in order to match the practices of majority culture radio? If they don't, will they face pressure from listeners used to majority culture radio who may entertain similar expectations for the new indigenous stations? And if the traditional leaders within minority cultures are accustomed to providing deliberative, detailed statements in responding to questions, how will they fare if indigenous radio follows the majority culture journalistic preference for "sound bites" or at least concise, compact statements?

Evidence indicates that Aboriginal groups already have experienced some changes in notions of how leadership is communicated. From my observations, city dwellers, many of them unable to speak aboriginal languages, appear more ready to ascribe leadership to individuals who are able to accommodate themselves to media demands. Rural dwellers may be less inclined to do so, although younger individuals seem more open to the possibility that leadership may come from something other than ancestry, longevity, or other traditional hallmarks.

Michael Manlev, a Tasmanian Aboriginal with blond hair and blue eyes, has become a prominent national Aboriginal figure, in part because both Aboriginal (but especially city-based) and white Australian media have provided him with considerable exposure. He is eloquent, dramatic, controversial, and seems highly adept at presenting himself—in English—through the media, sound bites and all. However, he also has attracted the criticism of a number of older, more traditional leaders of rural Aboriginal groups who claim that he "doesn't represent anyone." That's quite true since he has no tribal ties. Tasmanian Aboriginal groups were wiped out well over a century ago. And he certainly doesn't communicate in ways that they recognize as valid. But he *has* attracted a considerable Aboriginal following.

Ireland's RNG has daily Irish (Gaelic) broadcasts of discussions, talks, and disc jockey patter. They feature a discursive approach: speakers take plenty of time to say whatever it is they have to say, just as they would in everyday life. But the national English language radio services of Radio Telefis Eirann have picked up their pace and have reduced the amount of talk, partly in competitive response to the "more music, less talk" approach of the newer local commercial radio stations in Ireland. RNG also has reduced the amount of talk, but is divided over the degree of reduction needed. Part of that division stems from concern about the effect such a reduction would have on what some staff members regard as an essential element of the Irish language—its discursive quality. In fact, it's perfectly possible to speak briefly in Irish, even if it isn't what Irish speakers usually do. Here lies the heart of the problem: should RNG take upon itself the role of "change agent" where style of discourse is concerned? Or, if it

remains faithful to Irish custom, does it risk losing listeners, particularly among the younger people, who are vital to the future of the station itself?

Speaking Languages Correctly

There often is a real shortage of individuals capable of speaking indigenous languages fluently and correctly. Recruiting them to appear on indigenous radio can be especially difficult when a number of indigenous media outlets appear within a short time span, as they've done in Aboriginal, Maori, and Native American (especially Canadian) media. Often, there aren't enough native-speaking individuals to meet the demand for their services. At the same time, many of those who have struggled to keep the language alive are almost certain to press for high standards of performance through the media. However, most of the individuals who themselves have struggled to develop indigenous media realize the importance of involving younger people, both as audiences and as performers. Yet the younger generation is apt to be sorely lacking in indigenous language skills. When the media use them as announcers, disc jockeys, and journalists, as most media operations do, there's very likely to be an outcry from skilled language speakers. A Welsh community radio station, Radio Maldwyn, discovered as much when their young English-speaking announcers attempted to pronounce Welsh place names.

Most media managers seem willing to risk broadcasting in less-than-perfectly delivered indigenous languages. Still, even if younger speakers improve their command of the indigenous language, they're likely to be less respectful of its purity. They also are likely to include more majority culture influences, not only in choice of terminology, but also to styles of presentation. Ole Henrik Magga, President of the Sami Parliament, was concerned that Sami radio didn't always serve older listeners as well as it should. He felt that newscasts in Sami were prepared and delivered more to the manner of majority culture newscasts: fast-paced and abbreviated. Older Sami listeners, he contended, associate newslike items delivered in Sami with a slower and more discursive approach, and sometimes find Sami radio's presentations hard to follow.

Whether younger Sami listeners would welcome a slower, more discursive style is another question. Radio Cymru decided in 1994 that its Welsh newscasts were too discursive. A major self-study, supported by the work of an outside consultant, led the station's newsroom to conclude that its news writing style needed a bit of slimming. Part of the assumption guiding the decision was that younger (including middle-aged) Welsh speakers, whether they realized it or not, were using the language less discursively than their forebearers did.

Interviews could pose similar dilemmas. Indigenous radio can stimulate language learners to use the languages, especially in the course of interviews. If those media were to follow rigid policies of speech correctness, the numbers of potential interviewees would shrink dramatically, especially among younger people. Very few stations are that rigid, but some don't make much effort to seek out and to encourage less-than-fully fluent speakers to serve as interviewees. However, most stations have at least a few staff members who aren't fluent so there often is some degree of encouragement by example.

Stations also have begun to take more initiative in developing programs that require the participation of language learners. Radio Cymru has a Saturday morning program in which teenagers talk about events of special importance to them. The various levels of fluency are apparent even to a non-Welsh speaker. The program's producers encourage just about everyone to "have a go," and seem to make a deliberate effort to display a wide range of language skills in each broadcast. RNG, one of the more purist indigenous language services, is working harder with schools, sports clubs, and other organizations to bring language learners to the microphone. In 1993, the station began to offer secondary school Irish language learners the opportunity to prepare and present mini-documentaries about their own lives and concerns. They were to tape a roughly 20-minute program and send it to RNG. The station announced the winning entries, which didn't always feature perfect Irish. When Ireland's soccer team played in the 1994 World Cup, the RNG sports announcers covering the event sought the few Irish speaking players on the team, encouraged them to speak in Irish, coached them where necessary, and came out with several very effective, if less than "Irish perfect," interviews.

The advantages to such practices seem obvious enough. Whether the disadvantage of sanctioning incorrect language use is outweighed by the encouragement it seems to give to language learners is a matter of opinion But the very presentation of such models could potentially reshape the use of indigenous languages by a wider audience.

Virtually no hard scientific evidence exists to indicate that the initiation of an indigenous language radio service helps to restore or revive its use, but stations broadcasting substantial amounts of such languages certainly have that hope and expectation. There is some anecdotal evidence, such as increased interest on the part of young people (and their parents), in taking formal study courses in their languages and increased amounts of popular music—live and recorded—in their languages. It's also quite likely that each medium of communication using indigenous or non-majority languages has its effect on every other medium. Language classes stimulate listening to indigenous media; indigenous media provide an important outlet for popular music; popular music heightens interest in learning the language. While I've sounded some cautionary notes above, there are grounds for optimism in the challenging and vital task of helping indigenous languages to live and even flourish. Those languages will change, of course, and not all the changes or the ways in which speakers use the languages will be to everyone's taste. That's true of all languages, and, after all, what's most important is that the languages *live*.

References

Browne, Donald R. 1992. "Raidio na Gaeltachta." *European Journal of Communication.* Vol. 7.

Carmen Marquez, Lucia. 1993. "The Uses of Radio by Ethnic Minorities in Mexico: A Study of a Participatory Project." Unpublished Ph.D. dissertation, University of Texas at Austin.

Cotter, C. M. 1996. "Irish on the Air: Media, Discourse, and Minority Language Development." Unpublished Ph.D. dissertation, University of California at Berkeley.

Davies, John. 1994. *Broadcasting and the BBC in Wales.* Cardiff: University of Wales Press.

Jones, Lyn. 1994. *Te Reo Aotearoa Idrangi: Maori Language Broadcasting Development in New Zealand.* London Commonwealth Relations Trust.

Keith, Michael. 1995. *Signals in the Air: Native Broadcasting in America.* Westport, CT: Greenwood.

Michaels, Eric. 1993. *Bad Aboriginal Art.* Minneapolis: University of Minnesota Press.

Molnar, Helen. 1993. "The Democratization of Communications Technology in Australia and the South Pacific: Media Participation by Indigenous Peoples." Unpublished Ph.D. dissertation. Monash University, Victoria. Australia.

Sauvagcau, Florian, Pierre Trudel, and Marie-Helene Lavoie. 1995. *Les Tribunes de la Radio Echos de la Crise d'Oka Quebec.* Institut Québecois du Récherche sur la Culture.

"TALKING THE TALK ON INDIGENOUS RADIO"

Donald R. Browne

1) What are some of the reasons for indigenous people's interest in radio and radio broadcasting?

2) How do changes in indigenous expressions to accommodate modern concepts (space travel, AIDS, etc.) pose a dilemma for the speakers of those languages?

3) How do the standard practices of radio broadcasting and traditional forms of oral language usage interact with and affect one another?

4) How does broadcasting in an indigenous language affect the viability and survival of these languages, if at all?

CHILDREN'S LINGUISTIC AND SOCIAL WORLDS

Marjorie Harness Goodwin

Calling for the study of language as "a mode of social action," Malinowski directed explicit attention to the importance of children's groups:

> In many communities we find that the child passes through a period of almost complete detachment from home, running around, playing about, and engaging in early activities with his playmates and contemporaries. In such activities strict teaching in tribal law is enforced more directly and poignantly than in the parental home. ["The Problem of Meaning in Primitive Languages" (1923), *The Meaning of Mean*ing, C. K. Ogden and I. A. Richards, eds., 1973, p. 283]

Despite Malinowski's early plea for documentation of children's life-worlds, few anthropologists have taken as their mission the study of the linguistic, cultural, and social life of children: children as subjects, actors, and creators of culture. Far more anthropological emphasis has been placed on children's interaction with adults than with other children, partly because socialization is treated as a fundamentally *psychological*, rather than social, process. Children are believed to gradually *internalize* adult values and to be in need of "integration into the social world." The child is defined by what she is subsequently *going to be* rather than what she presently is. Because traditional social science views the child's world as a defective version of the more important adult world into which she eventually will be socialized, studies of children's life-worlds have been neglected. Remarkably, at a time when the call for moving women and other minorities to the center of social thought is commonplace among feminists, children have been left at the margins and treated as invisible.

British anthropologists neglected the study of children's worlds (apart from the study of age-sets and initiation ceremonies) because they associated the study of children with psychological paradigms, which they considered reductionist. In contrast, during the 1970s in the US, edited volumes such as *Socialization as Cultural Communication* (1976) and *From Child to Adult* (1970), the *Case Studies in Education and Culture* series (with 16 ethnographies!) and the work of the Whitings featured children and adolescence as important domains of anthropological inquiry.

I approach the *Anthropology Newsletter* theme on limits to knowledge in anthropology by focusing on what is known and unknown about children's linguistic and social worlds.

The Known: Diversity Across Cultures

One subfield that has devoted insightful analytic attention to children is linguistic anthropology. Language is a defining feature of the human species. Radically different theories have been proposed for how language is acquired. Researchers working within linguistic and psychological frameworks focus most of their research on children's innate knowledge of language structures, an approach that divorces the child from cultural settings and frameworks for interaction. In contrast, during the past 20 years linguistic anthropologists have developed a major perspective and focus for the study of language acquisition. E. Ochs and B. B. Schieffelin ("Language Socialization: Three Developmental Stories," *Culture Theory: Essays on Mind, Self, and Emotion*, R. A. Shweder and R. A. LeVine, eds., 1984) deal with diverse ways children acquire language within the endogenous scenes that compose the life-world of a society and simultaneously become competent social actors using language appropriately. Language and the social self mutually create one another. Recognizing that the human brain is essential to language, this perspective brings together aspects of the child's social, cultural, and linguistic worlds, realms treated as separate domains of inquiry outside anthropology. Children's use and understanding of grammar is tied to basic practices of interaction within culturally specific settings as well as culturally specific understandings about how to think, feel, know, and act in concert with others.

Cross-cultural studies show that children's grammatical or communicative competence does not necessarily depend on the way Euro-American middle-class mothers organize their communication with infants and children through simplified conversation (using short sentences, slowing their pace, and exaggerating intonation contours) in intense

Reprinted from *American Anthropologist Association Newsletter*, Vol. 38, No. 4, April 1997. Copyright © 1997 by the American Anthropologist Association.

dyadic exchanges. Among such societies as Western Samoans, the Kaluli of Papua New Guinea, K'iche Mayan, rural and urban Javanese, and African American working-class families, children develop linguistic competence without having talk directed explicitly to them. Many societies do not consider infants and very young children intentional beings and do not initially treat them as viable conversational partners. Colwyn Trevarthan's studies demonstrate how infants in middle-class British society can socialize their parents, through their vocalizations, looks, and gestures. Such patterns, however, do not constitute a cultural universal. Among the Walpiri and Inuit, for example, children's vocalizations are not treated as communicative. Although interpretation of children's babbling through expansions and clarifications by caretakers occurs routinely in Japanese and Euro-American middle-class society, this is not the case in such societies as the Kaluli or the Western Samoa, where it is believed that one party cannot know another's intentions. Unlike linguists and psychologists, linguistic anthropologists treat the acquisition of language as embedded within a social matrix. Recognizing that a child's language acquisition is shaped by a particularly human biological endowment and universal features of talk-in-interaction, linguistic anthropologists study the culturally situated scenes of social practice that produce competent language users and social actors.

The Unknown: Children's Language Socialization

Although psychologists have theorized that child to child interaction provides the most appropriate setting to investigate the fullest elaboration of social processes among children, children's interaction with other children has not been a focus in child language studies. Cross-culturally, 4-to-9-year-old children participate widely in nurturant, caretaking interactions. Despite the fact that sibling caretaking characterizes many societies worldwide, we know very little about the interaction because the focus has been on adult caretaker/child roles.

Psychologists and psycholinguists believe that the preschool period is the most important transitional period for various aspects of cognitive development. Thus children over the age of 4 usually are ignored. Anthropological research on children above this age has focused on the school, documenting language practices in the classroom, studying class and ethnic conflicts, and addressing how schools make it possible for children to fail. Moving beyond the classroom, we have virtually no ethnographic studies of peer interaction in the neighborhood or on the playground. When children's peer groups or language practices have been studied, the focus has usually been on urban, Western males, often in groups treated as deviant and marginal, such as gangs. With respect to the study of African American Vernacular English, a focus on unemployed males' street talk as the authentic language variety for African Americans has reified a dangerously inaccurate stereotype: "young men, with nothing to do, doing nothing, talking trash, going nowhere," effectively marginalizing other African American groups, and especially females (M. Morgan, "No Woman No Cry: The Linguistic Representation of African American Women," *Cultural Performances: Proceedings of the Third Berkeley Women and Language Conference,* M. Bucholtz et al., eds., 1995, p. 527).

Thanks to careful work of the Opies and numerous folklorists, we have collections of the verbal art of children—their jump rope and "counting out" rhymes, hand-clap songs, jokes, riddles, and chants—and their games. These folklore traditions are passed by children to other children, usually outside adult awareness. Unfortunately, we know very little about how children interact in the midst of actual play activities, subverting the rules for their own strategic interests. This is a very serious gap. Perpetuating Piaget's argument that the "legal sense" is less developed in girls' games than those of boys, social scientists characterize girls' games as cooperative, passive, and lacking in complex social structure. In my own studies of girls playing such games as hopscotch and jump rope, however, I find moves are fiercely challenged as violations. Games provide a locus for intense political debate and orientation to the complexity of rule use. Such embodied practices constitute a locus for the acquisition of stances and argumentative moves that make political actors.

At Work and Play

Research during the 1970s on women's language proliferated stereotypes, positing deficit views of female interaction patterns and supporting the notion that the "essential nature" of females is apolitical. Research I have done over the past 20 years with preadolescent African American and Latina girls contradicts such a position. First, rather than having a single essential nature, females speak with many different voices. Here anthropology has a distinct contribution to make by investigating ethnographically the diverse settings in which girls and women live their lives. Models of female interaction based on an "innately pacifist" cooperative female personality fall apart when the full spectrum of girls' language practices is observed. Girls' language choices build different social organizations, adapted in detail to the social situations that constitute their life-world. Second, females are capable of intricate and powerful forms of political activity. Indeed, among the African American children with whom I have worked, the girls' he-said-she-said dispute processes were far more elaborate, complex, consequential, and enduring than anything I have found among the boys.

Although we have begun to investigate children's interaction during play, we know far less about interaction during their work activities. We know that children's work is significant in many countries for family survival and national economy. A 1996 UNICEF report estimates that there are 250 million child workers, between 5 and 14, with the majority of 10-to-14-year-old children working 6 days a week for at least 9 hours a day. Cross-culturally, children between 5 and 7 are expected to assist with caretaking and domestic tasks. How children organize their interaction in the midst of work activities, such as running errands, trading for their mothers, or collecting and processing food, has not been investigated.

Power of the Peers

Sociolinguists have argued since the 1970s that children's peer groups provide far more powerful influences on their language structure than parents; although we know little about the development of children's language variation patterns, we do know that adolescents lead all other age groups in sound change and use of vernacular. Youths are innovators in many forms of experimentation with identity in today's multiethnic, multicultural cities. Adolescents, through their selection of semiotic resources, such as hair style, clothing, dance style, movement pattern, music, gestures, eyeliner and lipstick color, space use, demeanor, and language varieties, affirm, contest, and play with ethnic roles and class affiliation during leisure time.

Youths also have had an important political voice in society: during literacy campaigns in revolutionary Cuba and Nicaragua; in dramatic public demonstrations demanding equal education and the right to organize in South Africa in the mid-1970s and 1980s; as part of the First National Street Children's Congress in Brasilia (1986), where children demanded an end to institutional and police violence

and full citizenship; and in 12-year-old children's rights activist Iqbal Masih's bold public exposures of bonded labor in Pakistan, which eventually led to his death. We know little about the speech registers youths use during their political activity or across a range of situations. Although we might know about the phonological, prosodic, and lexical features of the language variety youths select, we know little about these speakers' language ideologies of speech activities. We don't know much about how ethnicity, class, age, and gender become relevant in interaction or consequential for the deployment of alternative language choices by bilingual, multilingual, or multidialectal speakers. We know little about the nature of multiethnic communication during mundane interactions between new immigrants and established residents in important mediating institutional settings (such as schools) where they come together. We know almost nothing about how autistic, physically challenged, blind, or deaf children acquire language and become members of discourse communities (although the Nicaraguan sign-language project constitutes an important exception). Without a longitudinal study we cannot know how individuals of any social group change their language variety, ethnic, class, or gender identification of interactive strategies across developmental time.

Making the Unknown Knowable

To study children as social actors, we need detailed longitudinal ethnography study of their activities and language practices in a variety of consequential settings. Linguistic anthropology has provided a rigorous methodology for documenting such practices. Ethnographic recordings of extended interactions can be examined again and again with new research questions. These records constitute more than informant narratives told to (and elicited by) the anthropologist. Through them we can hear the voices of people we study in the midst of their everyday conduct articulating for each other what constitute important events of their lives.

Usually viewed as a symbolic medium, language constitutes a core form of social organization. Children acquire what it means to be human in their society through participating in diverse culturally situated social practices and linguistic routines. Through language, children of diverse ethnicities, social classes, ages, abilities, and genders orchestrate their social organization and socialize one another across a range of activities. Without longitudinal ethnographic studies of children from different ethnic backgrounds in diverse structural settings, we cannot know how children's lives are shaped by their encounters with family, peers, adults, and others expressing various language ideologies, in neighborhoods, schools, and after school, or how children change developmentally over time.

We need to move children from the margins to the center of anthropological inquiry. Today, more than 40 percent of the world's urban population are children 15 and younger, many of whom are especially vulnerable. More than 15 million children in refugee camps face the special dangers of high infant mortality, exposure to violence, separation from families, sexual violence, and militarization. In societies undergoing rapid social, economic, or political change—whether due to urbanization, colonialism, apartheid, or war—children create groups apart from adult supervision for emotional support and physical survival, as they experience the world differently from their parents and grandparents. It is time we take children seriously and use the distinctive practices of anthropology to give voice to their social worlds and concerns.

"Children's Linguistic and Social Worlds"

Marjorie Harness Goodwin

1) According to Goodwin, how has contemporary social science tended to view the world of children?

2) How do different cultures impart grammatical and communicative competence to children?

3) What influences do socialization practices and peer interactions have on a child's linguistic development and abilities?

A Tale of Two Obsessed Archeologists, One Ancient City, and Nagging Doubts about Whether Science Can Ever Hope to Reveal the Past

Robert Kunzig

The land around Konya in south-central Turkey is flat now, a checkerboard of wheat and barley, but 9,000 years ago it was flatter still. Nine thousand years ago there were no mounds. Today, on a map of the area, the word *höyük,* Turkish for "mound," is all over the place. Twenty miles southeast of Konya, one of the biggest mounds of all, Çatalhöyük, rises 65 feet above the plain. If you stand on its grass-covered summit with archeologist Ian Hodder and look past the white tent that shields some of his diggers from the sun, your view is unbroken for tens of miles. Nine thousand years ago, Çatalhöyük was alone in this vastness, and it had only just begun to grow. This was in the Neolithic Period, the end of the Stone Age: People had only just come down from the mountains to build one of the first large settlements on the planet.

For six summers straight, Hodder, a professor at the University of Cambridge, has brought a large team here to study the mound of ruins that is Çatalhöyük (CHAH-tahl-HU-yook). He hopes to continue for the next 19 years, until he retires. Other sites document the Neolithic revolution—when humans gave up a hundred thousand years of wandering to farm and begin building a civilization. But none are as rich as Çatalhöyük.

Between 7000 and 6000 B.C., as many as 10,000 people lived here in boxes of mud brick, with roofs made of wood beams and reeds. Surrounded by open space, they built a town so dense it lacked streets and doorways; the residents climbed over their neighbors' roofs to their own, and then dropped in through a hole that also served as a chimney. Just generations away from a nomadic lifestyle, they chose to live in extremely crowded conditions. No one really knows why.

In those rank and smoky houses, on white plaster walls, the people of Çatalhöyük created art, lots of art. They painted strange pictures of small men confronting outsized beasts; they molded plaster reliefs of leopards, bulls, and female breasts. Under the plaster floors they buried their dead, wrapped in shrouds and accompanied by clay rings and beads and mirrors of glassy obsidian from nearby volcanoes. For generations they lived on top of their ancestors, and then at some point—again, no one knows why—they abandoned the house. They swept it clean, they cleaned out the grain bins and even the fireplace, and they knocked down the walls. Then they built another house just like it on the ruins, and the mound grew another layer.

Hodder is not the first to dig into this mound. He heard about Çatalhöyük in the late 1960s, as a student attending lectures at the University of London. The lecturer, James Mellaart, was famous for discovering the site: He had shattered the old idea that civilization had begun only in the Fertile Crescent, the arc of land from Mesopotamia to Egypt. Mellaart's lectures were memorable. "He was hugely enthusiastic about the past, he taught without notes, and he remembered every single carbon 14 date that came out of the Near East," a former student, Louise Martin, recalls. Mellaart's story of Çatalhöyük was the kind that made students want to become archeologists. But he could not take them there to dig: In 1965, he had fallen into a dispute with the Turkish government.

So for 30 years the site languished. "It was clear it ought to be excavated again," Hodder says. "There was terrible erosion, and so many questions left unanswered. It's always been felt that it was a duty of the British to come back and resolve the mess. But that was never possible while Mellaart still wanted to come back himself." Now Mellaart has retired and given a blessing to Hodder's excavation—if not to his methods and results. "He's an extraordinary mind and a great archeologist," Hodder says. "We disagree about some of the interpretations." Of Hodder's project, Mellaart says: "I wouldn't call it an excavation. Scientific research, perhaps."

In the 30 years that separated Mellaart's Çatalhöyük from Hodder's, archeology changed radically. By his last season, even Mellaart was out of date: Scientific archeology had arrived, and with it a preference for the quantifiable over the symbolic, for testable hypotheses over stories. Then in the 1980s, some archeologists began to question their whole enterprise, to dismiss as naive the view that you could ever know what really happened in the past, and as Eurocentric the interpretations that people like Mellaart had applied to ancient cultures. Having barely become modern and scientific, archeology suddenly became postmodern.

One of the most widely respected leaders of that second revolution is Hodder. At Çatalhöyük, he is getting a chance to rewrite Mellaart's story—and to put his postmodern theories into practice.

James Mellaart is 73 now, on the short side, a bit pear-shaped, a bit jowly, a bit short of breath. He wears his roomy trousers hiked high and a tartan tie when the occasion demands it. (Mellaart is of Dutch extraction, but three centuries ago his family were MacLartys from Scotland.) Large glasses frame eyes that squeeze down to small slits of mirth as he talks. Were he standing on a windswept mound, the thin gray hair would quickly come unkempt, but he is not: He is sitting in a comfortable chair in his flat in north London. The flat, located in an unremarkable block, is richly Turkish, all dark wood and kilims and glass cabinets filled with out-of-the-ordinary curios. As Mellaart tells the story of the dig of his life, his Turkish-born wife and colleague, Arlette, intervenes with small cups of muddy coffee and occasional explanations.

Mellaart first saw Çatalhöyük up close in 1958. Within minutes, in the last light of a November evening, he discovered it was littered with obsidian tools. The site was Neolithic from top to bottom. Few Neolithic sites had been found before in Anatolia, and none that size—hundreds of yards long—had been found anywhere.

The importance of the site was obvious. When Mellaart finally started digging there in 1961, though, he didn't expect it to be beautiful too; the potsherds he had found at the surface were undecorated fragments of cooking vessels. His doubts lasted about three days into the dig. "We had a narrow little trench," Mellaart says, "and one of my workmen called me and said, 'Sir, look.' On the wall, a piece of plaster had fallen off. And there were paintings. That changed the whole thing."

Much older paintings had been found before in European caves, such as Lascaux in France. Those paintings dated from the Paleolithic, the Old Stone Age, when humans were nomadic hunter-gatherers. What Mellaart had found at Çatalhöyük were the oldest paintings from the Neolithic, the oldest paintings made by humans on the walls of houses they had built themselves. The first was of a hunter and a stag. More hunting scenes followed, but also pictures of men sporting with all sorts of animals, pulling their tails and tongues and riding on their backs. There were pictures of men dancing in leopard skins and of headless men being pecked by giant vultures. There was even what looked to Mellaart like an erupting volcano: probably Hasan Däg he decided, which is visible from the mound on a clear day, 80 miles to the northeast. Under the volcano, the artist had painted a strange pattern of rectangles that could be taken for the terraced town of Çatalhöyük itself. Mellaart said it was the first landscape painting in history.

Working with a team of fifty over four seasons of furious digging, Mellaart also uncovered plaster wall reliefs of leopards butting heads and of splayed human figures he interpreted as women giving birth. In some cases, they were giving birth to plaster bulls' heads sporting real bulls' horns, called bucrania. Some walls were festooned with those, and some plaster benches were ringed with upright bulls' horns. But perhaps the strangest pieces of art were the plaster breasts that protruded from numerous walls; some were burst open to reveal the skulls of vultures or weasels. "Death in the midst of life?" Mellaart wondered.

Of the scads of statuettes Mellaart found, few were male. Most of the recognizable ones showed big-breasted, corpulent women. They were representations of the Mother Goddess, Mellaart said, artifacts of the earliest human religion. (These days Goddess worshippers visit Çatalhöyük by the busload.) The most famous statuette, which has become a symbol of the site, shows the Goddess astride two leopards, apparently giving birth.

Mellaart dug up some 200 houses in a 13-layer cake slice cut from one of the mound's 32 acres. All the buildings were roughly the same size—300 square feet or so, with a single large room sometimes flanked by smaller storerooms. But 40 of them were so heavily decorated that Mellaart thought them shrines rather than houses. By chance, he decided, he had excavated the priestly quarter of the town, in which priestesses dressed as vultures worshipped the Goddess. With what purpose in mind? "Fertility, of course," he says now. "Fertility! For themselves, for their animals." Although the people of Çatalhöyük still hunted, in Mellaart's view, they got most of their meat from domesticated cattle, and they planted a variety of crops. Thanks to the fertile earth, they had conquered hunger. That is what allowed them to create so much art.

Mellaart loved to interpret that art. There was a story that went with the volcano painting: Çatalhöyük was the center of a far-flung trade in volcanic obsidian, Mellaart said. The artist was depicting the source of the town's wealth, of its tools, and of the polished black mirrors into which women must have gazed with dawning self-consciousness. There was a story, too, for an even more obscure painting, one with symbols that looked like atomic radiation warnings (flowers, to Mellaart's eyes), little triangles floating nearby (butterflies), and four forklike figures arranged in a cross (humans with outstretched arms). "Does this wall painting symbolize an act of homage to the great goddess on a spring morning in the Konya Plain amid fields of flowers and humming insect life nearly eight thousand years ago," Mellaart wrote, "or is this too fanciful an interpretation?"

"Jimmy Mellaart is like a man who went to the moon," says Louise Martin, an archeozoologist at the University of London who took Mellaart's courses there and now works with Hodder at Çatalhöyük. "He came to this place and he hasn't been able to get over it. The wonderful stories just roll off his tongue."

Ian Hodder—tall, blond, slender, a very youthful man of 50—likes stories too, and in that sense he is Mellaart's soul mate. The scientific archeology that was just coming along as Mellaart left Çatalhöyük tended to neglect stories, and to neglect art and symbolic artifacts, which aren't amenable to scientific analysis. This approach was called "processual archeology" in some circles because it focused on the processes by which people adapted to their environment—what crops they planted, say, and how many calories they extracted from them. Hodder's postmodern archeology, on the other hand, is "post-processual." It emphasizes art and artifacts as clues to what people in the past were thinking. "People have to adapt to their environment," Hodder says, "but their ideas and beliefs about the world have an impact on the way they adapt to it." Hodder's goal, like Mellaart's, is to understand how prehistoric individuals acted at individual moments—like those spring mornings on the Konya Plain.

But two deep canyons separate the men. For one, Hodder can't ignore the scientific advances that have made it possible to wring a lot more data from archeological ground. Mellaart dug with shovels, picked artifacts and bones out of the dirt with his hands, and threw the rest into an enormous spoil heap. In Hodder's dig, much of the dirt itself is analyzed. It is sieved for tiny remains, and then it is dropped into barrels of water to separate out yet tinier ones; slivers of obsidian, for example, sink to the bottom, whereas seeds float. And as the diggers dig, sometimes for a month on a single corner of a single house, they leave strips of each mud layer intact so that a micromorphologist can come by and take samples and examine them under a microscope—to find things that escape even the sieve and the flotation tank.

The other canyon between Hodder and Mellaart is Hodder's theory. Mellaart's dig was pretheoretical, straightforward, optimistic. "We dug a large hole and got out things," explains Arlette Mellaart. The Mellaarts thought those things might tell them what really happened at Çatalhöyük which is not at all the postmodern spirit. "Postmodernism is difficult to define," says Hodder. "But one definition people use is the 'end of grand narrative'—the end of the idea that there is one answer to the world. Postmodernism is much less optimistic, less certain. It focuses much more on 'multivocality': there are many different voices in the world and different perspectives, not just the Western one."

Another word thrown around Çatalhöyük these days is *reflexivity*. The archeologists watch themselves; they even have anthropologists watching them and studying how they are perceived by nearby villagers who are also, presumably, watching them. Scientific specialists like Martin—zoologists, botanists, micromorphologists, and stone-tool specialists—tour the trenches regularly to watch the diggers. Hodder says all this watching is necessary because objective archeological facts—bones, seeds, stone tools can never be separated from the subjective meanings that archeologists assign to them based on the context in which they are found. Because the context is destroyed by digging, interpretation has to begin "at the trowel's edge" and so Hodder wants a lot of people looking over the shoulder of the person with the trowel. Hodder's archeology involves a lot of talking.

The talk does not stop in the trenches. It continues in the pleasant dig house Hodder had built at the site, where discussions of methodology often take precedence over the study of artifacts. It continues too on the project's Web site, where Hodder can be seen "dialoguing" with a representative of the "Goddess community." Although Hodder, unlike Mellaart, thinks there is scant evidence that goddesses were ever worshipped at Çatalhöyük, he feels it is his duty to discuss the site with anyone and make his data available. When Goddess adepts tell Hodder they don't want his data, because it is already contaminated by his own white-male subjectivity—well, Hodder *loves* that criticism. It gives him an anecdote he can use in lectures, papers, and interviews. It supports his main point: that there is no one objective reality at Çatalhöyük, no single story as Mellaart hoped—but many stories, all with a tentative connection to reality at best.

The talk, the tentativeness, the microscopic analysis, the constant self-analysis—these things make for slow digging. That is the biggest difference between Mellaart and Hodder. Mellaart excavated 200 houses in four seasons; Hodder, with a much larger team, has uncovered 3 houses in six seasons. As long as time and money are unlimited, the advantages of his approach are obvious. When Wendy Matthews, the micromorphologist on his team, examines small pieces of wall, floor, or trash heap under her microscope, she sees things Mellaart dug right through, and she comes close to evoking scientifically the historical moments he could only imagine. She sees the tens of layers of plaster the Çatalhöyük people applied to their walls, annually or even seasonally, covering up soot but also their own murals. She sees the small pile of bone and obsidian splinters swept into a corner by some Neolithic toolmaker—perhaps it was on a spring morning.

Hodder's great hope is that such painstaking analysis will produce a richer interpretation of Çatalhöyük. The great risk he runs is that the lack of quantity in his work will translate into a lack of quality: that he will never find enough evidence to say much of anything.

In 1997, Hodder's team made an amazing find in a house called Building 1, on the opposite side of the mound from Mellaart's dig. Under the floors were the skeletons of at least sixty-four human beings. Mellaart had found bones under platforms too, but never so many. Analysis of the bones by Peter Andrews and Theya Molleson of the British Natural History Museum suggests the bodies were buried intact—and not, as Mellaart thought, only after they had been picked clean by vultures. The smoke from the open fire in the house may have helped mask the stench.

The bones and teeth suggest that the people of Çatalhöyük were rather healthy, insofar as they survived childhood: half the sixty-four skeletons were those of children, seventeen of them under two years old. Andrews and Molleson believe all the skeletons may have belonged to a single extended family. They couldn't have all lived in that same house, but for some reason they were all buried there. Perhaps it was the house of a patriarch.

Even if those sixty-four people didn't crowd into a single small house, Çatalhöyük was a crowded place. The site was on a river called the Çatalhöyük and around it lay marsh, fertile alluvial plain, and woods and steppe that were probably teeming with big game. Why humans would settle there is no great mystery. The mystery is why 5,000 to 10,000 of them chose to settle on the same spot, when there was plenty of space around them.

If anything, the Hodder excavation has only deepened the mystery by calling into question the assumption that the decision to settle was triggered by the emergence of agriculture. Hodder's team has found evidence—it's only suggestive, given how little they've excavated—that the Çatalhöyük people relied less on farming than Mellaart thought. Analyzing much smaller bits of animal bone than Mellaart ever found, Martin has determined that most of them did not come from cattle; most came from sheep and goats. She thinks the Çatalhöyük people had probably domesticated sheep, but it is not clear they had domesticated cattle. A lot of the bones come from wild animals.

The plant remains point to a similar conclusion. Like Mellaart, paleobotanists Christine Hastorf and Julie Near of the University of California at Berkeley have found wheat, barley, lentils, and peas at Çatalhöyük. "Mellaart assumed that those domesticated plants were their staples," says Near. "But he didn't do flotation, which is the only way you see a wider variety of plants." By putting dirt from the house floors and rubbish heaps in her flotation tank, Near has found that the residents of Çatalhöyük were energetic collectors of wild plants as well. They were particularly fond of the tuberous roots of a marsh reed called *Scirpus*.

All this adds up in Hodder's mind to the view that the people of Çatalhöyük were hunters and gatherers at least as much as they were farmers. "You've got this enormously varied environment," he said one day late last summer, standing on top of the mound, gazing out over a seamless spread of modern farm fields. "And that allows you to sustain what is a staggering population of five or ten thousand. Imagine this whole mound a sea of pueblo-like buildings, and whole families getting up and going out to try to hunt and gather plants and dirt for plaster—it's a massive use of the landscape. Although they're hunter-gatherers, they're also living on a very large site. That challenges the imagination—how do you organize an enormous group of people; how do you manage to feed them all?"

Mellaart saw Çatalhöyük as the ancestor of much more elaborate Bronze Age civilizations, such as Knossos on Crete, and he assumed it too must have been ruled by an elite—perhaps the priests whose shrines he thought he had uncovered. Only central leadership, in his view, could explain the orderliness of Çatalhöyük, with its buildings all constructed to the same specifications—hearths always on the south side, burials on the north—one right on top of the other over many generations.

A Tale of Two Archeologists

James Mellaart says the reason the Turkish government withdrew his permit to dig at Çatalhöyük after the 1965 season was that he was discovering too many paintings. True, the Turks did not have the resources to preserve all his priceless findings: some of the slabs of plaster he sent to the Anatolian Civilizations Museum in Ankara have never even been unwrapped. "I suppose people panicked," Mellaart says. "There are disadvantages to finding too much." But the reason for his rift with the Turks seems to have more to do with a woman named Anna, whom he met by chance on a train to Izmir in the 1950s.

When Anna entered his compartment, she was wearing a striking gold bracelet. Mellaart recognized it as Bronze Age. He remarked on it, and Anna said she had a lot more of that at home if he cared to come have a look. Mellaart did. Getting off the train in Izmir, they drove through a foggy night to an old house whose location remained murky thereafter. Anna showed him a stash of gold artifacts that ostensibly came from a place nearby, called Dorak. She said that this priceless ancient treasure belonged to her family. Mellaart had no camera, so he spent several days and nights feverishly drawing the things.

That, at least, is how the story is told in *The Dorak Affair*, a 1967 account of the matter by Kenneth Pearson and Patricia Connor of the London *Sunday Times*. Neither they nor anyone else was ever able to locate Anna's house in Izmir, and the lady herself had vanished. She never provided Mellaart with promised photographs of the treasure, but she did authorize him to publish his drawings. He finally did in 1959, in the *Illustrated London News*. A few years later, when Mellaart was digging at Çatalhöyük, newspapers in Istanbul got wind of the article. They created a scandal about the foreign archeologist who had looted Turkey of a treasure no one had ever seen. Mellaart's relations with the government never recovered.

Pearson and Connor, after an energetic investigation, concluded that the *film noir* scenario must have happened more or less as Mellaart related it. They suggested he may have been duped by Turkish antiques smugglers who used him to hype their wares abroad.

Hodder, on the other hand, thinks Knossos is the wrong analogy. It was a complex city-state that came along 4,000 years after Çatalhöyük, he points out. If the Çatalhöyük folk were hunter-gatherers, Hodder argues, the way to understand them is to compare them with simple societies today, like the African tribes he has studied, or like the Tikopia of Polynesia: they too live in small dark houses, and they still bury their dead under the floors.

Because the Çatalhöyük buildings are all about the same size—no obvious palaces or temples—Hodder believes there was no central leadership. Because just about every building has some type of decoration, Hodder believes there were no shrines; some houses were just more decorated than others. The difference between a building with a patch of red paint on one wall, and a building of the kind Mellaart found, with elaborate murals on all four sides, a plaster wall relief of a splayed human figure, and bulls' horns everywhere—to Hodder that difference is merely one of degree. And if there were no distinct shrines, then there was no priestly elite or organized religion. The people may have been ruled by clan chiefs, like the Tikopia, or by no chiefs at all; their lives may have been governed by ritual and taboo. They probably venerated the ancestors buried under the floors, as the Tikopia do.

As for the "Mother Goddess," whom Mellaart saw as the forerunner of classical goddesses like Demeter—there are only a few recognizable statuettes from Çatalhöyük, says Hodder, and even they weren't always treated like deities. Mellaart found the fat-lady-with-leopards in a grain bin. "It's obviously a goddess—no human being sits on two leopards!" says Mellaart. ("Especially when she's having a baby!" adds Arlette.) Hodder is unimpressed: He allows only that women at Çatalhöyük had "a powerful symbolic role." What they symbolized, he believes, was not divinity but domesticity. Whereas the art that Mellaart found shows men doing active things, the women are generally sitting down, and not always on leopards.

"People at that time needed to domesticate themselves, to become stable, to stop moving around, to sit," Hodder says. "I think the woman as the mother is a metaphor of being sedentary—the hearth, the house, the home." Although the origin of settlements and of agriculture is usually seen in economic and environmental terms—as the discovery of a new process whereby human beings could extract a living from their surroundings—Hodder sees it postprocessually. Before people could domesticate plants and animals, they first had to "domesticate the wild within," to tame "the wild dangers associated with death, reproduction, and female sexuality." This most important transition in human prehistory, then, was first of all a cultural and psychological one.

That interpretation is one Hodder has been pushing for years. He is hoping that new art unearthed at Çatalhöyük will produce more evidence for it. It seems doubtful that a theory so subtle and inward could ever be convincingly documented by art so prone to divergent interpretation; what Mellaart saw as a volcano looming over Çatalhöyük, after all, Hodder thinks might be only a leopard skin. But anyway, Hodder's team hasn't yet found any new art worth mentioning.

By the end of 1998, year the excavation at Çatalhöyük had reached a crisis. Hodder had been planning not to dig at all in 1999, to give his team time to write a book describing their methodology. But then he learned that, thanks to an irrigation project, the water table around the mound has sunk five meters in just the past few years. At the bottom of the mound, which Mellaart's dig never reached, are the artifacts of the first people to settle at Çatalhöyük. Having been wet for millennia, they are now dried out and are being destroyed. Hodder found himself asking his corporate sponsors for extra cash to fund a "rescue" operation, eight months of digging instead of the usual two. His hope is to get to the bottom of the mound before the year is out.

"Since Mellaart's work here, we've had a lot of other sites which are big and earlier," Hodder says. "But, Çatalhöyük has remained absolutely significant and different; it stands out because of the art. There's nowhere else that has this density and richness of painting and creative production, sculpture and statuettes and modeling—everything from little spoons to enormous bucrania. It's an extraordinary outpouring of art. Many of us had thought that people would find more and more of these sites elsewhere, but it just hasn't happened. So the question becomes even more, 'Why here? What is it that creates that?' We still have no understanding.

"That's why we want to dig to the beginnings of the site. We'd like to get to the bottom of it."

"A Tale of Two Obsessed Archeologists, One Ancient City, and Nagging Doubts about Whether Science Can Ever Hope to Reveal the Past"

Robert Kunzig

1) Describe the organization and the architecture of Çatalhöyük between 7000 B.C. and 6000 B.C. as described in the article.

2) What methodological changes have occurred in the field of archaeology from the time Mellaart began his research at the site of Çatalhöyük to Hodder's time at the same site?

3) What are the basic differences in theoretical orientation between Mellaart's interpretation of the site and Hodder's interpretation?

4) How do Mellaart's and Hodder's explanations of female statuary and female roles at Çatalhöyük differ? Do you think that the nature of cultural beliefs about women in the 1960s and the 1990s may have anything to do with these differing interpretations?

WHEN WE WERE VERY YOUNG

Samuel M. Wilson

Among the artifacts left behind by the Iroquois people who lived in southern Ontario in late prehistoric times was a miniature pot made from a lump of clay. A tiny thumb or finger, too small to be a grown-up's, had shaped the inside of the pot, leaving the impression of a tiny fingernail. Archaeologists also have recovered small clay versions of smoking pipes, impractical because they lack holes. These were children's toys—small and ephemeral, easily overlooked in the refuse of the past. Just as male scholars were typically once blind to the presence of women in the archaeological record, grown-up archaeologists often don't look for children in the past.

The inhabitants of Cerén, a Mayan site in western El Salvador, fled in A.D. 595, leaving everything in place—crops in the field, pots of food, their most cherished goods. A nearby volcanic eruption covered the whole settlement with ash. Carefully excavated by archaeologist Payson Sheets and his colleagues, this site gives us a remarkable glimpse of life in the Mayan Classic period. One of the houses at Cerén contained a complete inventory of the artifacts of everyday life. Next to an interior doorway, just (in my view) where a kid would sit, was a diminutive pot and a scattering of twenty small shards of pottery. Reporting on these finds, Christian J. Zier remarks (with due scholarly caution) that they "may be the playthings of a child and could indicate that this is a child's room. This statement is tentative at best and will remain so."

In my own excavations in North America and the Caribbean, I have found odds and ends that did not fall into any obvious category: a collection of colored rocks, a few fossilized casts of the inside of shellfish, a half-burned lump of clay with a hole in it, poorly made little arrowheads. Not until I had children and saw their piles of treasure did the finds start to make sense. At times, I have come close to throwing away something my children prized, thinking it was a piece of junk, and as an archaeologist I might have done just that with the artifacts of children who lived long ago.

Various unusual things are relegated to the category of "enigmatic finds" and get stuck at the end of archaeological reports. Going over the artifacts from the Israeli site of Tell Jemmeh, Smithsonian archaeologist Gus Van Beek noticed some rounded disks an inch or two across. They were made from pieces of broken pottery and had two holes drilled through them. Earlier archaeologists had taken them for buttons or had simply described them as "perforated disks." But Van Beek saw in them a "buzz," a simple toy he recalled from childhood. To play, you loop string through the two holes and hold one end of the loop in each hand. When the string is wound up and you pull the two ends of the loop apart, the disk in the middle spins and makes a buzzing sound. Van Beek identified archaeological examples of this toy at other sites in the Near East, as well as in Pakistan, India, China, Japan, and Korea. Buzzes have been found in the sites of Native American peoples in North and South America, and even in the remains of British army camps from the Revolutionary War.

Children's toys today include many low-tech items that are common around the world. Rattles, whistles, bull-roarers (a slat of wood tied to the end of a thong and whirled around the head), balls, tops, and buzzes are fun to play with by themselves. There are also the pieces and markers that go along with games. The most common kinds of toys, however, allow children to do things that grown-ups do, but on a miniature scale: small versions of hunting and fishing gear, model boats, baskets, dolls, pots, and plates.

In his *Laws*, Plato argued that "the man who is to make a good builder must play at building toy houses, and to make a good farmer he must play at tilling land; and those who are rearing them must provide each child with toy tools modeled on real ones" (translation by R. G. Bury). I wonder whether Plato ever gave a boy or girl an "educational" toy and then watched as the child made a temple to Dionysus out of the box it came in.

In the dry shelters of the Lower Pecos region on the Texas-Mexico border, normally perishable artifacts made of wood, fiber, and leather have been well preserved. Archeologist Ken Brown studied more than a hundred such artifacts, identifying child-size versions of digging sticks, wood and fiber snares, and netted backpack frames. He sees these as tools for teaching children how to behave and survive in the world and, perhaps, even make a small contribution to the group's quest for food.

In 1879, a famine wiped out the village of Kukulik on Saint Lawrence Island, south of the Bering Strait between Alaska and Siberia. Excavation of the site in the 1930s brought to light an extraordinary range of artifacts made of wood, bone, and other materials. Among the objects were dolls, miniature kayaks, and small carved bears and seals. Similarly, the prehistoric Thule of Canada and Greenland left behind numerous dolls and miniatures of adult artifacts. In a recent study, archaeologist Robert W. Park, of the University of Waterloo, Ontario, compared these to the traditional toys of the Inuit, the Thule's descendants.

A great many archaeologists are justifiably wary of viewing any given miniature artifact as a plaything. Miniature versions of everyday objects can have potent ritual significance. An exhibit at the Idaho State Historical Museum in Boise ("Backtracking: Ancient Art of Southern Idaho") included a number of human figurines identified as possible dolls. Some Shoshone people who visited the exhibit, descendants of makers of the artifacts, saw them as the powerful representations of the supernatural character Nu'-numbi and perhaps taken from a shaman's paraphernalia.

Probably the most famous of prehistoric artifacts that are thought to be toys are the wheeled dogs and other animals from pre-Conquest tombs in Mexico. They have attracted a lot of attention because they show that ancient Mesoamericans understood the principle of the wheel—even though they put it to no practical application, perhaps because they lacked draft animals and lived in mountainous terrain. Archaeologist Francisco Javier Hernandez argued in an extensive study that these were ritual objects (of now unknown meaning) made to be used in burials. This is probably also the case with the elaborate dioramas buried with Egyptian royalty in the third and fourth millennia B.C., in which miniature figures carried the things people would need in the next world.

The idea that artifacts we identify as toys might once have had deeper meanings connects with the influential argument put forward by French historian Philippe Ariès in his 1960 classic, *Centuries of Childhood*. He contended that the Western conception of childhood as a distinct stage of human development and as a protected time of make-believe and play has emerged only in the past few centuries.

A child's early years would indeed have been different in the past, if only because mortality rates and demographics were generally different. In Roman society, for instance, infant mortality may have been as high as one-third of live births, and half the population was under the age of twenty. Some have argued that in prehistory, and even in recent centuries, parents showed relative indifference toward younger children precisely because so few survived. But burials of children with grave goods show that children were cherished as early as Upper Paleolithic times. At the Russian site of Sungir, for example, a man, a girl, and a boy were buried together with ivory spears, stone tools, small animal carvings, and thousands of beads carved from the tusks of mammoths. The grave dates to about 23,000 years ago. Such deliberate burials became more common during the Upper Paleolithic, and through them, children become more visible in the archaeological record.

Although Upper Paleolithic peoples may not have considered childhood to be a carefree and innocent stage of life, they apparently did distinguish it from adulthood and marked the transition through ritual. Some of the painted caves of northern Spain and southwestern France, including the recently discovered caves of the Ardèche in France, preserve footprints of young people. And the cavern called Gargas, in the Pyrenees, has hundreds of handprints stenciled onto the walls—some, judging by their size, the hands of adolescents or children. These traces may have been left by young people at the time of their initiation into adulthood.

An awareness of childhood can contribute to the more general effort, current in archaeology, to look for individuals in prehistory, to trace families and lineages through time and to discover what motivated people to behave the way they did. Formerly, archaeologists tended to view past societies as composites of integrated subsystems—economy, demography, politics, social organization, and so on. By focusing more on individuals and the choices they confronted, we come face to face with the concrete agents of change in human prehistory. In doing so, perhaps we shall even discover that children were among their societies' most important innovators.

"WHEN WE WERE VERY YOUNG"

Samuel M. Wilson

1) Why do possible children's artifacts often get relegated to the "enigmatic finds" category of archaeological definition and interpretation?

2) How would a child's life in the past and a child's life of today differ?

3) What is the potential importance for archaeology and other social sciences of examining the lives of children in the past?

A Reverence for Cows

Doranne Jacobson

"In America, what do they do to someone who murders a cow?" Some thirty years ago, as an anthropologist visiting the village of Nimkhera, in central India, I faced this loaded question. A local farmer, Sidha Singh, stood accused of murdering his calf. He had whacked it with a stick to drive it out of his granary, and it had died shortly thereafter. A council of village elders had convened to consider the case. Fortunately, my interrogator, an earnest Hindu youth, knew nothing of the flagrant U.S. trade in hamburgers and T-bone steaks. "Oh," I said, "in my country, murderers are sent to jail." My young friend nodded approvingly.

Thus I evaded discovery, but Sidha Singh did not. The council found him guilty of cow murder—*gao hatya*—a significant sin within Hinduism. They sentenced him to pay a substantial fine and host a banquet for all the villagers. Until he met these obligations, Sidha Singh and his family would be excluded from all local social events, and no parents would consider allowing their children to marry his. A man of modest means, he surely intended his valuable animal no harm, but his misfortune meant a lengthy period of religious and social purgatory, as well as severe economic strain for himself and his family.

The case of the murdered calf brought home to local youngsters the importance of treating their cattle well. Throughout India, Hindus revere these humped and dewlapped animals (*Bos indicus*, known to Westerners as zebu cattle) and refrain from harming them. People love their cattle, give them pet names, feed them special foods, adorn them for festivals, and worship them in rituals. The finest feasts include dishes made with milk and ghee (clarified butter), cooked over fires fueled by cakes of dried cow dung. For observant Hindus, eating beef is anathema, much as eating dog meat is to most Europeans and North Americans. However, by consuming a few drops of a mixture of the five products of the cow—milk, curd (yogurt), ghee, urine, and dung—ritual purity can be enhanced. And for rituals in the home, cow-dung paste is applied to a small area of the floor to purify a sacred space before the deities are invited to provide their blessings.

To Western observers, this reverence for cows may seem illogical. Why should McDonald's have to serve mutton burgers in India, when beef burgers sell by the billions elsewhere? Why are those scrawny creatures allowed to roam city streets and impede trucks, cars, and motorcycles? As milk producers, they can hardly compete with Wisconsin's hefty beasts. And think about all that beefsteak going to waste. Meanwhile, environmentalists ponder whether or not India's 200 million cattle—one-quarter of the world population—cause environmental degradation through overgrazing.

The place of the sacred cow in Indian culture and ecology has been intensely debated for decades among social scientists and animal husbandry experts. Some argue that Hindu practices regarding cattle are large irrational and have led to excessive numbers of animals. Anthropologist Marvin Harris has challenged this view strongly, demonstrating that religious prohibitions against killing and eating cattle are of crucial material benefit in India. Such taboos, he points out, help preserve essential draft and milk animals, not only in times of plenty but also in times of famine (see *Cows, Pigs, Wars, and Witches: The Riddles of Culture,* Vintage Books, 1990). Zebu cattle often appear scrawny, but these animals are extremely disease-resistant and hardy. In harsh conditions, they can survive on surprisingly little, including garbage and scrub vegetation. When fodder is more plentiful, they regain their robust condition, pulling the plows so necessary to feeding India's multitudes.

Cattle have been important to South Asians since prehistoric times. Humped cattle appear with other animals in hunting scenes on the walls of central Indian rock-shelters, probably painted in the Late Stone Age. Cattle bones at a few archaeological sites in Pakistan and central India suggest the keeping and possible domestication of cattle more than seven thousand years ago. The great Indus valley civilization (sometimes called the Harappan culture), which flourished from approximately 2600 to 1900 B.C. in an area now part of both India and Pakistan, depended heavily on domesticated animals—predominantly zebu cattle—as well as on wheat and barley. Indus valley farmers and traders yoked cattle to plows and carts and transported cargo in long caravans of pack oxen. Carved stone seals from that time prominently feature beautiful images of sacred bulls—precursors to today's widely found statues of Nandi, the bull ridden by the god Shiva.

The debate on the Indian cow remains lively. Recent research by anthropologist Carol Henderson and others suggests that Hindu attitudes and fluctuating cattle demographics reflect complex interactions between ideology, ecology, politics, population levels, and land usage rights (see "The Great Cow Explosion in Rajasthan," by Carol Henderson, in *Advances in Historical Ecology*, edited by William L. Balée; Columbia University Press, 1998). Today, as in past millennia, Indian cattle continue to provide milk, as well as cow dung for fertilizer and cooking fuel (in the form of the traditional dried cakes or, increasingly, as bio-gas generated from composted dung). Even in a nation that is building nuclear capability, cattle remain a crucial source of power for drawing plows and carts. And as the animals browse on crowded city streets, their ability to recycle garbage is phenomenal.

Although Hindu ideology is uncompromising, Indians are practical people. Cattle population figures vary according to local historical and ecological conditions, hinting at a quiet culling. Even as stray dogs in the United States somehow disappear, unwanted Indian cattle also vanish. Some are allowed to roam free until they die naturally, their meat consumed by dogs and vultures and their hides claimed by low-status Hindu leatherworkers. Other surplus cattle are sold to Muslim traders, who are not averse to slaughtering them. Some Indian Muslims and Christians and a few Hindus, Sikhs, and Parsis occasionally eat beef.

As India's population grows, more families need animals. At the same time, more tractors and trucks are being purchased by those who can afford them, and many farmers are giving up their bullocks.

Pasture lands are shrinking as irrigated agriculture takes over previously uncultivated areas, making it harder to maintain large animals. In cities, too, the situation continues to evolve. To keep traffic flowing smoothly, cattle have been banished from the main streets of Mumbai (formerly Bombay). In New Delhi, home of politicians sensitive to conservative backlash, municipal cow catchers gently kidnap stray cattle from downtown areas to save them from traffic accidents and from killing themselves by eating plastic bags. The revered bovines are then delivered to a comfortable suburban refuge to live out their days.

Thirty years have passed since Sidha Singh was sentenced for cow murder. On a recent visit to his village of Nimkhera, I met Hindu farmers proud of their new prosperity, gained from Green Revolution crops, chemical fertilizers, and electric—or diesel—pump-powered irrigation. Several local farmers had purchased tractors with which to plow their fields, worked until recently by teams of oxen. The farmers informed me that they had increased profits by reducing the number of cattle they owned. In Nimkhera and other settlements throughout India, prosperous farmers and dairymen now increasingly favor water buffalo over zebu cattle as milk animals. Buffaloes do cost more to purchase and maintain, but they yield greater quantities of richer milk—and greater profits.

I learned that it took Sidha Singh nearly a decade to save up enough to pay his fine and feast hundreds of his neighbors. He had also succeeded in arranging proper marriages for his son and daughter. I noted that his cattle seemed healthy and that their horns sparkled with tinsel, remnants of their Diwali holiday decorations. But when Sidha Singh's name happened to come up in conversation with a group of women, one of them turned to me. "You remember him," she said. "He was the one who murdered his calf."

"A Reverence for Cows"

Doranne Jacobson

1) What is the religious importance of cattle to Indian society?

2) What are the religious and economic explanations offered for the importance of cattle to India?

3) What were the legal and social consequences to Sidha Singh as a result of his inadvertent killing of his calf?

4) What are the various uses cattle are put to in modern Indian society?

5) What would the potential impacts be on Indians if they were to decide to eat cattle? Consider some of the economic, social, and religious impacts.

TEMPLES OF DOOM

Heather Pringle

Few things so unnerved the Spanish conquerors of the New World as the prospect of death on a sacrificial stone. On one summer afternoon in 1521, while laying siege to the Aztec capital of Tenochtitlán, what is now Mexico City, Hernán Cortés and his army watched in horrified silence as Aztec priests on the opposite lakeshore struggled up the stairs of a temple with 66 Spanish captives. Stretching them one at a time across a narrow stone, the priests carved out their beating hearts, then swiftly butchered their bodies so their flesh could be eaten ritually. Four decades later, one of Cortés's lieutenants wrote: "We were not far away from them, yet we could render them no help, and could only pray to God to guard us from such a death."

For the Aztecs, human sacrifices were ironically the stuff of life. Only human blood, they later told Spanish priests, could give the sun strength for its daily climb from the underworld. Other societies shared their belief in the power of the human heart. As Spanish armies ventured into the small Mayan villages of the Guatemalan rain forests and marched over the paved Incan roads of the Andes, they returned with tales of similar terrifying bloodbaths.

But for all the grisly accounts of the early Spanish chroniclers, archeologists have exhumed surprisingly little evidence of these rituals. Even in excavations at Templo Mayor, the most important temple in Tenochtitlán and the place where, according to the Aztecs' own books, some 20,000 war captives were sacrificed in a single ceremony in 1487, archeologists have yet to turn up any mass graves or any of the massive skull racks constructed by Aztec priests from the craniums of their victims. One reason, says John Verano, a physical anthropologist at Tulane University in New Orleans, is that the racks were simply "broken up, burned probably, and thrown out." As a result, scientists have failed to gather even basic data on the origins and the practice of human sacrifice in the Americas.

But now, thanks to a series of stunning archeological discoveries, researchers are gaining a clearer glimpse of these ancient rituals. The picture comes not from the most famous civilizations encountered by the Spanish armies but from a much earlier and lesser known Andean people—the Moche (pronounced MO-chay) of Peru's northern coastal desert. A sophisticated society of farmers and fishers, the Moche flourished from A.D. 100 to 800 in the narrow river valleys that slice down from the Andes to the Pacific near the modern city of Trujillo. The Moche so prospered from their irrigated cornfields and the cold, nutrient-rich waters of the nearby Pacific that they had time to raise ten-story pyramids, rub shoulders in settlements of 50,000 people, and nurture great artists.

For decades, archeologists puzzled over the paintings on Moche pots. Many portrayed knife-wielding gods holding human heads, and owl-headed priests presiding over human sacrifices, but few researchers believed they reflected actual practices. Over the past five years, however, researchers have uncovered startling forensic evidence of human sacrifice—from mass graves of ritually slaughtered and dismembered victims to giant wall murals incorporating butchered human bones. By comparing skeletal remains with painted scenes, they are now assembling what is arguably the most detailed portrait of sacrifice in the ancient world yet to emerge.

The grim finds promise to shed new light on many aspects of Moche culture, from religion to warfare to politics. Although the clearest evidence of human sacrifice had come from a crumbling temple pyramid in what many suggest was the Moche capital, Verano and others have now found tantalizing hints of similar sacrifices at another important Moche center, suggesting that several ruling houses, perhaps each governing a major river valley, could have held sway over the Moche.

The new discoveries raise a host of questions, not the least of which is why the Moche performed human sacrifices. Experts, such as Elizabeth Benson, turn for answers to the Andean peoples' religious beliefs and their abiding concern with the fertility of the land. "Blood was like rain; it was like water," says Benson, an independent scholar living in Maryland and the author of several books on the Moche. "It made things grow. It nourished the earth." Other researchers disagree, pointing out that religious beliefs only justified actions taken for other reasons.

The ecology and politics of human sacrifice were a long way from most researchers' minds when a little-known Canadian archeologist, Steve Bourget, began searching five years ago for sites where the Moche performed their slaughter. Bourget, who now teaches at the University of East Anglia in Norwich, England, had just finished his Ph.D. dissertation on Moche art and sacred geography at the University of Montreal. During his studies, he had found several depictions of mountaintop rituals in which priests seemed to fling humans to their death down steep slopes. Such scenes, he knew, fit with ancient beliefs in the region: the Incas had regarded mountain peaks as sacred. If the Moche pots showed real events, reasoned Bourget, then the sacrifices could have taken place very near several major Moche temples that stood at the feet of small mountains.

At a sprawling site just a few miles southeast of Trujillo, he spent days clambering up and down the steep, rocky flanks of Cerro Blanco, a small mountain directly above one of the most important Moche temples, called the Pyramid of the Moon. But while Bourget found a likely prominence for sacrifices, he could not find bones or other evidence of such rites. The same disappointment awaited him at a second Moche settlement, Huancaco.

Back home, Bourget began poring over Moche depictions of a different sacrifice ritual, one that had been studied in detail in the 1970s and 1980s by Christopher Donnan, an archeologist at UCLA. The gruesome ritual, which Donnan called the warrior narrative, was a favorite theme of Moche artists, appearing on ancient pots and wall murals. "It starts with Moche warriors going off to combat," says Donnan. "Then there's the combat itself, and some of the warriors are captured. All their weapons, ornaments, and clothing are taken from them. What follows is a stage where the captors make them bleed—very deliberately, I think. They slap their faces and they tear the warriors' nose ornaments out. They put ropes around their necks and parade them. The sacrifice follows." Under the watchful eyes of ritualists—three high priests and a high priestess, each in distinctive ritual finery—attendants slit the captives' throats and catch their blood in ceremonial goblets. Later they dismember the bodies.

Donnan, like other Moche experts, assumed that the warrior narrative owed more to fiction than fact. But in 1987, while excavating a tomb at the site of Sipán, Peruvian archeologist Walter Alva and his colleagues exhumed the body of a great Moche lord, dressed sumptuously for death and dating to approximately A.D. 300. The man wore large circular earspools and an immense gold headdress, a nose ornament, and a back flap, all crescent-shaped like the blade of a sacrificial knife. By his side lay a scepter with a bladelike handle. These were the insignia of the warrior priest. "I never imagined that we would find this stuff," says Donnan. "I didn't even mention it to the [research] team for a few days, because I thought the probabilities were so remote that I must be losing my grip." Further excavations uncovered the tombs of two high priestesses.

But if the sacrifices were actual events, where were all the victims? Back in England, Bourget studied depictions of the warrior narrative for clues. In a few, the ancient artists had painted lines of captured prisoners being led to pyramid-shaped temples. Were they slaughtered there? The more Bourget thought about it, the more likely it seemed. And he even had a hunch about where to look in the rambling temple complexes. At the Pyramid of the Moon, he had noticed a plaza about the size of four tennis courts surrounded by a high adobe wall, built around 500: in one corner of the plaza rose a large outcrop of rock— a mini-mountain. "I extrapolated that if there was a human sacrifice practice in the mountains, and if rocks are a symbolic extension of the mountains themselves, the sacrifices might have been performed in front of these rock altars," he says.

In 1995, Bourget put together a small team of researchers and began excavating the plaza. Peeling back layers of sediment, he was soon surrounded by whitened human skeletons. Splayed and tangled like a truckful of rag dolls tossed into a pit, the dead bore little resemblance to most Moche cadavers, which were laid out neatly on their backs. Near some were fragments of smashed clay figurines of naked men bound about the neck with a rope. Bourget was jubilant. "We'd never found a real sacrificial site before," he says. "We had iconographic representations of sacrificial practices. We had indirect evidence from funerary contexts and some evidence of decapitation. But we never had a real sacrificial site. For the first time, we could really see how the Moche performed human sacrifice."

Such a rare and complex burial site called for a specialist: a physical anthropologist who had studied the Moche and would approach the tangled bodies with all the fastidiousness of a modern crime investigator. John Verano fit the bill perfectly. An osteologist occasionally called in to assist with present-day forensic cases in the United States, Verano had worked with archeological teams on Peru's north coast since the mid-1980s. He set up an impromptu morgue in the Archeology Museum at the University of Trujillo.

As Bourget trucked in box after box of human remains from the dig over the next two field seasons, Verano and two assistants examined the

Why Did the Gods Demand Blood?

"To the people who say the Moche or the Aztecs did sacrifices because their gods demanded it, I would say, 'Why did their gods demand it and other peoples' gods did not?'" observes Michael Winkelman, an anthropologist at Arizona State University in Tempe. "I think there are good ecological, social, and political reasons people end up in these practices and predicaments."

In the 1980s, Winkelman delved through thousands of pages of published scientific accounts of forty-five societies around the world, searching for human sacrifice. He came up with seven sacrifice-performing societies, from the Marquesans of the South Pacific to the Romans. Other research teams had ranked the groups for a multitude of variables, from risk of famine to the adequacy of food-storage systems. By correlating the rankings with human sacrifice, Winkelman detected several traits that distinguished the societies.

Although all seven groups were agricultural, only one suffered a high risk of famine and none were notably short of meat protein. But nearly all suffered from relatively high population densities, exceeding twenty-six people per square mile. And all fought wars over land and scarce resources. "So even if these societies have a very good food availability, the large population creates a lot of pressure because it places them all at risk if something happens to the food supply. So people are sacrificing each other partly to reduce the impact on existing food supplies," says Winkelman.

Moreover, all seven of the sacrificing societies were ruled locally by a leader from a powerful family and regionally by one lord who successfully wooed the support of local leaders. In such a system, treachery and betrayal were constant threats. To intimidate those contemplating betrayal, Winkelman says, leaders naturally gravitated toward human sacrifice.

Although some Moche experts call Winkelman's work thought provoking, few are ready to accept that his analyses apply to the Moche, because not enough is known about their population density or political organization. Still, Verano says of the tortured and executed Pyramid of the Moon warriors: "I could imagine that it would solidify the power of the leaders by terrifying the population. No one really saw what was happening, but they heard screams and the men never came back."

collections for indicators of age and sex, and then pored over each bone, recording all traces of injury, violence, or illness. Nothing could be taken for granted. Although some skulls were separated from their bodies, for example, it was entirely possible that gravity had tugged them down a slight slope in the plaza floor as the skeletons decomposed. Only a clear pattern of cut marks could be accepted as evidence of decapitation. "You don't want to accuse anyone of murder if it's an accidental death," says Verano. "And you don't want to accuse someone of mutilating a body if it's just decomposition."

At least seventy corpses had once littered the ground of the temple plaza. All who could be identified belonged to a select demographic group: young, healthy, physically active males. Indeed, the mean age at death was just 23. Many, it turned out, were old hands at combat. One in every four bore healed rib, arm, leg, and skull fractures.

In addition, many of the men had fractures just beginning to knit at the time of death. These confirmed the story. Some of the dead, for example, had broken their arms in a specific spot, the midshaft of the ulna as if from parrying a blow. Others exhibited tiny fractures radiating from their nasal apertures: These corresponded eerily to scenes from the warrior narrative. "In Moche art," Verano says, "the artists often show prisoners being smacked on the nose so their noses will bleed, and that's often done at the time of capture."

Judging from the healing of wounds, the battered men survived for nearly two weeks after their capture, their last weeks mired in misery. Some endured torture in the form of deeply slashed fingers and toes, others suffered worse. "I had someone who had something inserted between the toes up into the arch of his feet and repeatedly pushed back and forth," says Verano, "so it was like a grooved injury."

Death, when it finally arrived, came swiftly. Among the men whose cervical spines were still intact, most bore cut marks that slashed across the front and sides of the neck vertebrae. Someone had slit their throats with a sharp knife. Others had perished from massive skull injuries; it looked as if someone armed with a heavy blunt weapon—perhaps a Moche war club—had bashed in their craniums.

Executioners abandoned most of the corpses to the elements. The soil surrounding the bodies, says Verano, was strewn with the Rice Krispie-like pupa shells of insects that feed on carrion and are incapable of digging for their dinners. This brutal treatment, he suggests, could have been intended to send a message to others. "Proper burial was very important in the Andes for people in the Inca period," says Verano. "One of the worst punishments that you could face was to be denied proper burial."

A few of the victims were set aside for a different fate. In a small enclosure next to the temple plaza, Bourget and his team exhumed the scattered remains of seven men. Cut marks striped their bones, often just where muscles once attached. "People were clearly taking the muscle off the bones for some reason," says Verano. "I think it's as good an argument for cannibalism as you'd find anywhere."

Taken together, Verano's data suggest that the bodies at the Pyramid of the Moon belonged to Moche warriors wounded and captured on the field of battle. It is entirely possible, he says, that the ancient desert dwellers, like the Aztecs, fought at least some battles specifically to capture young males for sacrifice. Little evidence of European-style warfare, which often left razed settlements and ruined defensive works in its wake, has ever surfaced in Moche territory. And most war scenes from Moche paintings show pairs of nobles dueling until one warrior is defeated.

What happened after capture is still unclear, but Verano suspects prisoners were marched back to the victors' home villages, where some were tortured, perhaps to prove them worthy of the ritual ahead. Like the Aztecs, notes Verano, the Moche may have considered death on the sacrificial stone an honorable way to go. "And you can see that surviving torture and proving that you were brave throughout the whole episode would have been crucial. You can imagine that it would be critical right up to the point of the sacrifice, because if you are screaming and being dragged up to have your throat slit, you won't look very honorable."

The sacrifice itself was cloaked in high pageantry. Dressed in full regalia, the ritualists watched as the captives were brought forward, naked but for the ropes. As the prisoners perished, the high priestess collected their blood in a goblet and passed it to the warrior priest—with a small addition. In many depictions, Moche artists portrayed a small wineskin-shaped fruit known as the ullucu. Native to the Amazon, the ullucu contains an anticoagulant agent, "which gives you a spooky idea that perhaps its juice was added to keep the blood from coagulating," Verano says.

Just how often the Moche conducted sacrifices and how many lives they took has yet to be determined. Only a small portion of the Pyramid of the Moon has been excavated, and Verano and others now believe that similar sacrifices took place in other Moche settlements. At El Brujo, a Moche community just 40 miles northwest of the Pyramid of the Moon, excavators from the University of Trujillo recently found what appears to be another mass grave. And last summer, Verano discovered something strange about an enormous mural on the site.

The pre-Columbian equivalent of a billboard, the mural was once visible for miles across the valley. Painted in brilliant crimson and electric yellow, it shows a row of Moche nobles dancing hand in hand above the heads of war captives stripped naked and bound with ropes around the necks. While studying the mural, researchers found a fallen chunk of mud plaster from one of the dancer's feet. A piece of bone protruded from one end. Examining it carefully, Verano could see that it was the rounded end of a human femur. It had been chopped from a cadaver, stripped of flesh, and incorporated into the giant mural. "The dancers are stepping on the bones of their enemies," he says, "or they're dancing on the bones of their victims."

Although new evidence explains much about how sacrifices were performed, it falls far short of answering why. The dead have little to say on this score, and for clues, most Moche researchers have turned to early Spanish accounts of Incan religion. In the manuscripts of priests living among the Incas, researchers, such as Elizabeth Benson, have traced an intimate link between the offering of human lives and agricultural fertility. "I think that in the past, people thought they could change the world by ritual," says Benson. "We think we can change it with technology, so we've lost a lot of the sense of the importance of ritual. But in the past, people thought that this was how you controlled the world, how you had enough food for your people. And a human being was the most important offering you could make."

For all their importance, the men at the Pyramid of the Moon knew little kindness in their final moments. Only now, a millennium and a half later, concludes Verano, have they received the respect due to the dead. "When I was brushing them off and cleaning the bones and putting them in boxes, I thought, 'The last time anybody touched you, they were cutting your throat or sticking sticks up your feet.' I treated them kindly, but it was a little late."

"TEMPLES OF DOOM"

Heather Pringle

1) What documentary (written) evidence do we have for the Aztec practice of human sacrifice? How does (or did) the archaeological data support or contradict the written accounts?

2) What evidence do we have concerning the Moche practice of human sacrifice? Where is it found and how is it interpreted?

3) What archaeological evidence did Bourget uncover to support the idea of Moche human sacrifice?

4) What does the archeological evidence reveal about the methods of human sacrifice and the intensity of the practice among the Moche?

5) What were the possible political, religious, and economic reasons behind human sacrifice in various cultures?

EPISTEMOLOGY:
HOW YOU KNOW WHAT YOU KNOW

Kenneth L. Feder

Knowing Things

The word *epistemology* means the study of knowledge —how you know what you know. Think about it. How does anybody know anything to be actual, truthful, or real? How do we differentiate the reasonable from the unreasonable, the meaningful from the meaningless—in archaeology or in any other field of knowledge? Everybody knows things, but how do we really know these things?

I know that there is a mountain in a place called Tibet. I know that the mountain is called Everest, and I know that it is the tallest land mountain in the world (there are some a bit taller under the ocean). I even know that it is precisely 29,028 feet high. But I have never measured it; I've never even been to Tibet. Beyond this, I have not measured all the other mountains in the world to compare them to Everest. Yet I am quite confident that Everest is the world's tallest peak. But how do I know that?

On the subject of mountains, there is a run-down stone monument on the top of Bear Mountain in the northwestern corner of Connecticut. The monument was built toward the end of the nineteenth century and marks the "highest ground" in Connecticut. When the monument was built to memorialize this most lofty and auspicious of peaks—the mountain is all of 2,316 feet high—people knew that it was the highest point in the state and wanted to recognize this fact with the monument.

There is only one problem. In recent times, with more accurate, sophisticated measuring equipment, it has been determined that Bear Mountain is not the highest point in Connecticut. The slope of Frissell Mountain, which actually peaks in Massachusetts, reaches a height of 2,380 feet on the Connecticut side of the border, eclipsing Bear Mountain by about 64 feet.

So, people in the late 1800s and early 1900s "knew" that Bear Mountain was the highest point in Connecticut. Today we *know* that they really did not "know" that, because it really was not true—even though they thought it was and built a monument saying so.

Now, suppose that I read in a newspaper, hear on the radio, or see on television a claim that another mountain has been found that is actually ten (or fifty or ten thousand) feet higher than Mount Everest. Indeed, recently, new satellite data convinced a few, just for a while, that a peak neighboring Everest was, in actuality, slightly higher. You and I have never been to Tibet. How do we know if these reports are true? What criteria can we use to decide if the information is correct or not? It all comes back to epistemology. How indeed do we know what we think we "know"?

Collecting Information: Seeing Isn't Necessarily Believing

In general, people collect information in two ways:

1. Directly through their own experiences.

2. Indirectly through specific information sources, such as friends, teachers, parents, books, TV, etc.

People tend to think that number 1—obtaining firsthand information, the stuff they see or experience themselves—is always the best way. This is unfortunately a false assumption because most people are poor observers.

For example, the list of animals alleged to have been observed by people that turn out to be figments of their imaginations is staggering. It is fascinating to read Pliny, a first-century thinker, or Topsell, who wrote in the seventeenth century, and see detailed accounts of the nature and habits of dragons, griffins, unicorns, mermaids, and so on (Byrne 1979). People claimed to have seen these animals, gave detailed descriptions, and even drew pictures of them. Many folks read their books and believed them.

Some of the first European explorers of Africa, Asia, and the New World could not decide if some of the native people they encountered were human beings or animals. They sometimes depicted them with hair all over their bodies and even as having tails.

Neither are untrained observers very good at identifying known, living animals. A red or "lesser" panda escaped from the zoo in Rotterdam, Holland, in December 1978. Red pandas are very rare animals and are indigenous to India, not Holland. They are distinctive in appearance and cannot be readily mistaken for any other sort of animal. The zoo informed the press that the panda was missing, hoping the publicity would alert people in the area of the zoo and aid in its return. Just when the newspapers came out with the panda story, it was found, quite dead, along some railroad tracks adjacent to the zoo. Nevertheless, more than one hundred sightings of the panda *alive* were reported to the zoo from all over the Netherlands *after* the animal was obviously already dead. These reports did not stop until several days after the newspapers announced the discovery of the dead panda (van Kampen 1979). So much for the absolute reliability of firsthand observation.

Collecting Information: Relying on Others

When we explore the problems of secondhand information, we run into even more complications. Now we are not in place to observe something firsthand; we are forced to rely on the quality of someone else's observations, interpretations, and reports—as with the question of the height of Mount Everest. How do we know what to believe? This is a crucial question that all rational people must ask themselves, whether talking about medicine, religion, archaeology, or anything else. Again, it comes back around to epistemology; how do we know what we think we know, and how do we know what or whom to believe?

Science: Playing by the Rules

There are ways to knowledge that are both dependable and reliable. We might not be able to get to absolute truths about the meaning of existence, but we can figure out quite a bit about our world—about chemistry and biology, psychology and sociology, physics and history, and even prehistory. The techniques we are talking about to get at knowledge that we can feel confident in—knowledge that is reliable, truthful, and factual—are referred to as *science*.

In large part, science is a series of techniques used to *maximize* the probability that what we think we know really reflects the way things are, were, or will be. Science makes no claim to have all the answers or even to be right all the time. On the contrary, during the process of the growth of knowledge and understanding, science is often wrong. The only claim that we do make in science is that if we honestly, consistently, and vigorously pursue knowledge using some basic techniques and principles, the truth will eventually surface and we can truly know things

about the nature of the world in which we find ourselves.

The question then is, What exactly is science? If you believe Hollywood, science is a mysterious enterprise wherein old, white-haired, rather eccentric bearded gentlemen labor feverishly in white lab coats, mix assorted chemicals, invent mysterious compounds, and attempt to reanimate dead tissue. So much for Hollywood. Scientists don't have to look like anything in particular. We are just people trying to arrive at some truths about how the world and universe work. Although the application of science can be a slow, frustrating, all-consuming enterprise, the basic assumptions we scientists hold are really very simple. Whether we are physicists, biologists, or archaeologists, we all work under four underlying principles. These principles are quite straightforward, but equally quite crucial.

1. There is a real and knowable universe.

2. The universe (which includes stars, planets, animals, and rocks, as well as people, their cultures, and their histories) operates according to certain understandable rules or laws.

3. These laws are immutable—that means they do not, in general, change depending on where you are or "when" you are.

4. These laws can be discerned, studied, and understood by people through careful observation, experimentation, and research.

Let's look at these assumptions one at a time.

There Is a Real and Knowable Universe

In science, we have to agree that there is a real universe out there for us to study—a universe full of stars, animals, human history, and prehistory that exists whether we are happy with that reality or not.

The Universe Operates According to Understandable Laws

In essence, what this means is that there are rules by which the universe works: stars produce heat and light according to the laws of nuclear physics; nothing can go faster than the speed of light; all matter in the universe is attracted to all other matter (the law of gravity).

Even human history is not random but can be seen as following certain patterns of human cultural evolution. For example, the development of complex civilizations in Egypt, China, India/Pakistan, Mesopotamia, Mexico, and Peru was not based on random processes (Lamberg-Karlovsky and Sabloff 1979; Haas 1982). Their evolution seems to reflect similar general patterns. This is not to say that all these civilizations were identical, any more than we would say that all stars are identical. On the contrary, they existed in different physical and cultural environments, and so we should expect that they be different. However, in each case the rise to civilization was preceded by the development of an agricultural economy. In each case, civilization also was preceded by some degree of overall population increase as well as increased population density in some areas (in other words, the development of cities). Again, in each case we find monumental works (pyramids, temples), evidence of long-distance trade, and the development of mathematics, astronomy, and methods of record keeping (usually, but not always, in the form of writing). The cultures in which civilization developed, though some were unrelated and independent, shared these factors because of the nonrandom patterns of cultural evolution.

The point is that everything operates according to rules. In science, we believe that, by understanding these rules or laws, we can understand stars, organisms, and even ourselves.

The Laws Are Immutable

That the laws do not change under ordinary conditions is a crucial concept in science. A law that works here, works there. A law that worked in the past works, today and will work in the future.

For example, if I go to the top of the Leaning Tower of Pisa today and simultaneously drop two balls of unequal mass, they will fall at the same rate and reach the ground at the same time, just as they did when Galileo performed a similar experiment in the seventeenth century. If I do it today, they will. Tomorrow, the same. If I perform the same experiment countless times, the same thing will occur because the laws of the universe (in this case, the law of gravity) do not change through time. They also do not change depending on where you are. Go anywhere on the earth and perform the same experiment—you will get the same results (try not to hit any pedestrians or you will see some other "laws" in operation). This experiment was even performed by U. S. astronauts on the moon. A hammer and a feather were dropped from the same height, and they hit the surface at precisely the same instant (the only reason this will not work on earth is because the feather is caught by the air and the hammer, obviously, is not).

We have no reason to believe that the results would be different anywhere, or "any-when" else.

If this assumption of science, that the laws do not change through time, were false, many of the so-called historical sciences, including prehistoric archaeology, could not exist.

For example, a major principle in the field of historical geology is that of *uniformitarianism*. It can be summarized in the phrase, "the present is the key to the past." Historical geologists are interested in knowing how the various landforms we see today came into being. They recognize that they cannot go back in time to see how the Grand Canyon was formed. However, because the laws of geology that governed the development of the Grand Canyon have not changed through time, and because these laws are still in operation, they do not need to. Historical geologists can study the formation of geological features today and apply what they learn to the past. The same laws they can directly study operating in the present were operating in the past when geological features that interested them first formed.

The present that we can observe is indeed the "key" to the past that we cannot. This is true because the laws or rules that govern the universe are constant—those that operate today operated in the past. This is why science does not limit itself to the present, but makes inferences about the past and even predictions about the future (just listen to the weather report for an example of this). We can do so because we can study modern, ongoing phenomena that work under the same laws that existed in the past and will exist in the future.

This is where science and theology often are forced to part company and respectfully disagree. Remember, science depends on the constancy of the laws that we can discern. On the other hand, advocates of many religions, although they might believe that there are laws that govern things (and which, according to them, were established by a Creator), usually (but not always) believe that these laws can be changed at any time by their God. In other words, if God does not want the apple to fall to the ground, but instead, to hover, violating the law of gravity, that is precisely what will happen. As a more concrete example, scientists know that the heat and the light given off by a fire results from the transformation of mass (of the wood) to energy. Physical laws control this process. A theologian, however, might agree with this ordinarily, but feel that if God wants to create a fire that does not consume any mass (like the "burning bush" of the Old Testament), then this is exactly what will occur. Most scientists simply do not accept this assertion. The rules are the rules. They do not change, even though we might sometimes wish that they would.

The Laws Can Be Understood

This may be the single most important principle in science. The universe is knowable. It may be complicated, and it may take years and years to understand even apparently simple phenomena. However, little by little, bit by bit, we expand our knowledge. Through careful observation and objective research and experimentation, we can indeed know things.

So, our assumptions are simple enough. We accept the existence of a reality independent of our own minds, and we accept that this reality works according to a series of unchanging laws or rules. We also claim that we can recognize and understand these laws or at least recognize the patterns that result from these universal rules. The question remains then: how do we do science—how do we explore the nature of the universe, whether our interest is planets, stars, atoms, or human prehistory?

The Workings of Science

We can know things by employing the rules of logic and rational thought. Scientists—archaeologists or otherwise—usually work through a combination of the logical processes known as *induction* and *deduction*. The dictionary definition of induction is "arguing from specifics to generalities," whereas deduction is defined as the reverse, arguing from generalities to specifics.

What is essential to good science is objective, unbiased observations—of planets, molecules, rock formations, archaeological sites, and so on. Often, on the basis of these specific observations, we induce explanations called *hypotheses* for how these things work.

For example, we may study the planets Mercury, Venus, Earth, and Mars (each one presents specific bits of information). We then induce general rules about how we think these inner planets in our solar system were formed. Or, we might study a whole series of different kinds of molecules and then induce general rules about how all molecules interact chemically. We may study different rock formations and make general conclusions about their origin. We can study a number of specific prehistoric sites and make generalizations about how cultures evolved.

Notice that we cannot directly observe planets forming, the rules of molecular interaction, rocks being made, or prehistoric cultures evolving. Instead, we are inducing general conclusions and principles concerning our data that seem to follow logically from what we have been able to observe.

This process of induction, though crucial to science, is not enough. We need to go beyond our induced hypotheses by testing them. If our induced hypotheses are indeed valid—that is, if they really represent the actual rules according to which some aspect of the universe (planets, molecules, rocks, ancient societies) works—they should be able to hold up under the rigors of scientific hypothesis testing.

Observation and suggestion of hypotheses, therefore, are only the first steps in a scientific investigation. In science, we always need to go beyond observation and hypothesizing. We need to set up a series of "if . . . then" statements; "if" our hypothesis is true "then" the following deduced "facts" will also be true. Our results are not always precise and clearcut, especially in a science like archaeology, but this much should be clear—scientists are not just out there collecting a bunch of interesting facts. Facts are always collected within the context of trying to explain something or of trying to test a hypothesis.

As an example of this logical process, consider the health effects of smoking. How can scientists be sure that smoking is bad for you? After all, it's pretty rare that someone takes a puff on a cigarette and immediately drops dead. The certainty comes from a combination of induction and deduction. Observers have noticed for about three hundred years that people who smoked seemed to be more likely than people who did not to get certain diseases. As long ago as the seventeenth century, people noticed that habitual pipe smokers were subject to tumor growths on their lips and in their mouths. From such observations we can reasonably, though tentatively, induce a hypothesis of the unhealthfulness of smoking, but we still need to test such a hypothesis. We need to set up "if . . . then" statements. If, in fact, smoking is a hazard to your health (the hypothesis we have induced based on our observations), then we should be able to deduce some predictions that must also be true. Sure enough, when we test specific, deduced predictions like

1. Smokers will have a higher incidence than nonsmokers of lung cancer

2. Smokers will have a higher incidence of emphysema

3. Smokers will take more sick days from work

4. Smokers will get more upper respiratory infections

5. Smokers will have diminished lung capacity

6. Smokers will have a shorter life expectancy

We see that our original, induced hypothesis—cigarette smoking is hazardous to your health—is upheld.

That was easy, but also obvious. How about an example with more mystery to it, one in which scientists acting in the way of detectives had to solve a puzzle in order to save lives? Carl Hempel (1966), a philosopher of science, provided the following example in his book *The Philosophy of Natural Science*.

The Case of Childbed Fever

In the 1840s, things were not going well at the Vienna General Hospital, particularly in Ward 1 of the Maternity Division. In Ward 1, more than one in ten of the women brought in to give birth died soon after of a terrible disease called "childbed fever." This was a high death rate even for the 1840s. In one year, 11.4 percent of the women who gave birth in Ward 1 died of this disease. It was a horrible situation and truly mystifying when you consider the fact that in Ward 2, another maternity division in the *same* hospital at the *same* time, only about one in fifty of the women (2 percent) died from this disease.

Plenty of people had tried their hand at inducing some possible explanations or hypotheses to explain these facts. It was suggested that more women were dying in Ward 1 due to "atmospheric disturbances," or perhaps it was "cosmic forces." However, no one had really sat down and considered the deductive implications of the various hypotheses—those things that would necessarily have been true if the proposed, induced explanation[s] were in fact true. No one, that is, until a Hungarian doctor, Ignaz Semmelweis, attacked the problem in 1848.

Semmelweis made some observations in the maternity wards at the hospital. He noted some differences between Wards 1 and 2 and induced a series of possible explanations for the drastic difference in the mortality rates. Semmelweis suggested:

1. Ward 1 tended to be more crowded than Ward 2. The overcrowding in Ward 1 was the cause of the higher mortality rate there.

2. Women in Ward 1 were from a lower socio-economic class and tended to give birth lying on their backs, while in Ward 2 the predominant position was on the side. Birth position was the cause of the higher mortality rate.

3. There was a psychological factor involved; the hospital priest had to walk through Ward 1 to administer the last rites to dying patients in other wards. This sight so upset some women already weakened by the ordeal of childbirth that it contributed to their deaths.

4. There were more student doctors in Ward 1. Students were rougher than experienced physicians in their treatment of the women, unintentionally harming them and contributing to their deaths.

These induced hypotheses all sounded good. Each marked a genuine difference between Wards 1 and 2 that might have caused the difference in the death rate. Semmelweis was doing what most scientists do in such a situation; he was relying on creativity and imagination in seeking out an explanation.

Creativity and imagination are just as important to science as good observation. But being creative and imaginative was not enough. It did not help the women who were still dying at an alarming rate. Semmelweis had to go beyond producing possible explanations; he had to test each one of them. So, he deduced the necessary implications of each:

1. If hypothesis 1 were correct, then cutting down the crowding in Ward 1 should cut down the mortality rate. Semmelweis tried precisely that. The result: no change. So the first hypothesis was rejected. It had failed the scientific test; it simply could not be correct.

2. Semmelweis went on to test hypothesis 2 by changing the birth positions of the women in Ward 1 to match those of the women in Ward 2. Again, there was no change, and another hypothesis was rejected.

3. Next, to test hypothesis 3, Semmelweis re-routed the priest. Again, women in Ward 1 continued to die of childbed fever at about five times the rate of those in Ward 2.

4. Finally, to test hypothesis 4, Semmelweis made a special effort to get the student doctors to be more gentle in their birth assistance to the women in Ward 1. The result was the same; 10 or 11 percent of the women in Ward 1 died compared to about 2 percent in Ward 2.

Then, as so often happens in science, Semmelweis had a stroke of luck. A doctor friend of his died, and the way he died provided Semmelweis with another possible explanation for the problem in Ward 1. Although Semmelweis's friend was not a woman who had recently given birth, he did have precisely the same symptoms as did the women who were dying of childbed fever. Most importantly, this doctor had died of a disease just like childbed fever soon after accidentally cutting himself during an autopsy.

Viruses and bacteria were unknown in the 1840s. Surgical instruments were not sterilized, no special effort was made to clean the hands, and doctors did not wear gloves during operations and autopsies. Semmelweis had another hypothesis; perhaps the greater number of medical students in Ward 1 was at the root of the mystery, but not because of their inexperience. Instead, these students, as part of their training, were much more likely than experienced doctors to be performing autopsies. Supposing that there was something bad in dead bodies and this something had entered Semmelweis's friend's system through his wound—could the same bad "stuff" (Semmelweis called it "cadaveric material") get onto the hands of the student doctors, who then might, without washing, go on to help a woman give birth? Then, if this "cadaveric material" were transmitted into the woman's body during the birth of her baby, this material might lead to her death. It was a simple enough hypothesis to test. Semmelweis simply had the student doctors carefully wash their hands after performing autopsies. The women stopped dying in Ward 1. Semmelweis had solved the mystery.

Science and Nonscience: The Essential Differences

Through objective observation and analysis, a scientist, whether a physicist, chemist, biologist, psychologist, or archaeologist, sees things that need explaining. Through creativity and imagination, the scientist suggests possible hypotheses to explain these "mysteries." The scientist then sets up a rigorous method through experimentation or subsequent research to deductively test the validity of a given hypothesis. If the implications of a hypothesis are shown not to be true, the hypothesis must be rejected, and then it's back to the drawing board. If the implications are found to be true, we can uphold or support our hypothesis.

A number of other points should be made here. The first is that in order for a hypothesis, whether it turns out to be upheld or not, to be scientific in the first place, it must be testable. In other words, there must be clear, deduced implications that can be drawn from the hypothesis and tested. Remember the hypotheses of "cosmic influences" and "atmospheric disturbances"? How can you test these? What are the necessary implications that can be deduced from the hypothesis, "More women died in Ward 1 due to atmospheric disturbances"? There really aren't any, and therefore such a hypothesis is not scientific—it cannot be tested. Remember, in the methodology of science, we ordinarily need to

1. Observe

2. Induce general hypotheses or possible explanations for what we observe

3. Deduce specific things that must also be true if our hypothesis is true

4. Test the hypothesis by checking out the deduced implications

If there are no specific implications of a hypothesis that can then be analyzed as a test of the validity or usefulness of that hypothesis, then you simply are not doing and cannot do "science."

For example, suppose you observe a person who appears to be able to "guess" the value of a playing card picked from a deck. Next, assume that someone hypothesizes that "psychic" ability is involved. Finally, suppose the claim is made that the "psychic" ability goes away as soon as you try to test it (actually named the "shyness effect" by some researchers of the paranormal). Such a claim is not itself testable and therefore not scientific.

Beyond the issue of testability, another lesson is involved in determining whether an approach to a problem is scientific. Semmelweis induced four different hypotheses to explain the difference in mortality rates between Wards 1 and 2. These "competing" explanations are called *multiple working hypotheses*. Notice that Semmelweis did not simply proceed by a process of elimination. He did not, for example, test the first three hypotheses and—after finding them invalid—declare that the fourth was necessarily correct because it was the only one left that he had thought of.

Some people try to work that way. A light is seen in the sky. Someone hypothesizes it was a meteor. We find out that it was not. Someone else hypothesizes that it was a military rocket. Again this turns out to be incorrect. Someone else suggests that it was the Goodyear Blimp, but that turns out to have been somewhere else. Finally, someone suggests that it was the spacecraft of people from another planet. Some will say that this must be correct, since none of the other explanations panned out. This is nonsense. There are plenty of other possible explanations. Eliminating all the explanations *we* have been able to think of except one (which, perhaps, has no testable implications) in no way allows us to uphold that final hypothesis. . . .

It's like seeing a card trick. You are mystified by it. You have a few possible explanations: the magician did it with mirrors, there was a helper in the audience, the cards were marked. But when you approach the magician and ask which it was, he assures you that none of your hypotheses is correct. Do you then decide that what you saw was an example of genuine, supernatural magic? Of course not! Simply because you or I cannot come up with the right explanation does not mean that the trick has a supernatural explanation. We simply admit that we do not have the expertise to suggest a more reasonable hypothesis.

Finally, there is another rule to hypothesis ranking and testing. It is called *Occam's Razor* or *Occam's Rule*. In essence, it says that when a number of hypotheses are proposed through induction to explain a given set of observations, the simplest hypothesis is probably the best.

Take this actual example. During the eighteenth and nineteenth centuries, huge, buried, fossilized bones were found throughout North America and Europe. One hypothesis, the simplest, was that the bones were the remains of animals that no longer existed. This hypothesis simply relied on the assumption that bones do not come into existence by themselves, but always serve as the skeletons of animals. Therefore, when you find bones, there must have been animals who used those bones. However, another hypothesis was suggested: the bones were deposited by the Devil to fool us into thinking that such animals existed (Howard 1975). This hypothesis demanded many more assumptions about the universe than did the first: there is a Devil, that Devil is interested in human affairs, he wants to fool us, he has the ability to make bones of animals that never existed, and he has the ability to hide them under the ground and inside solid rock. That is quite a number of unproven (and largely untestable) claims to swallow. Thus, Occam's Razor says the simpler hypothesis, that these great bones are evidence of the existence of animals that no longer exist—in other words, dinosaurs—is better. The other one simply raises more questions than it answers.

The Art of Science

Don't get the impression that science is a mechanical enterprise. Science is at least partially an art. It is much more than just observing the results of experiments.

It takes great creativity to recognize a "mystery" in the first place. In the apocryphal story, countless apples had fallen from countless trees and undoubtedly conked the noggins of multitudes of stunned individuals who never thought much about it. It took a fabulously creative individual, Isaac Newton, to even recognize that herein lay a mystery. Why did the apple fall? No one had ever articulated the possibility that the apple could have hovered in midair. It could have moved off in any of the cardinal directions. It could have gone straight up and out of sight. But it did not. It fell to the ground as it always had, in all places, and as it always would. It took great imagination to recognize that in this simple observation (and in a bump on the head) rested the eloquence of a fundamental law of the universe.

Further, it takes great skill and imagination to invent a hypothesis in this attempt to understand why things seem to work the way they do. Remember, Ward 1 at the Vienna General Hospital did not have written over its doors, OVERCROWDED WARD or WARD WITH STUDENT DOCTORS WHO DON'T WASH THEIR HANDS AFTER AUTOPSIES. It took imagination first to recognize that there were differences between the wards and, quite importantly, that some of the differences might logically be at the root of the mystery. After all, there were in all likelihood many, many differences between the wards: their compass orientations, the names of the nurses, the precise alignment of the windows, the astrological signs of the doctors who worked in the wards, and so on. If a scientist were to attempt to test all these differences as hypothetical causes of a mystery, nothing would ever be solved. Occam's Razor must be applied. We need to focus our intellectual energies on those possible explanations that require few other assumptions. Only after all these have been eliminated, can we legitimately consider others. As summarized by that great fictional detective, Sherlock Holmes:

> It is of the highest importance in the art of detection to be able to recognize, out of a number of facts, which are incidental and which are vital. Otherwise, your energy and attention must be dissipated instead of being concentrated.

Semmelweis concentrated his attention on first four, then five possible explanations. Like all good scientists, he had to use some amount of what we can call "intuition" to sort out the potentially vital from the probably incidental. Even in the initial sorting, we may be wrong. Overcrowding seemed a very plausible explanation to Semmelweis, but it was wrong nonetheless.

Finally, it takes skill and inventiveness to suggest ways for testing the hypothesis in question. We must, out of our own heads, be able to invent the "then" part of our "if . . . then" statements. We need to be able to suggest those things that must be true if our hypothesis is to be supported. There really is an art to that. Anyone can claim there was a Lost Continent of Atlantis, but often it takes a truly inventive mind to suggest precisely what archaeologists must find if the hypothesis of its existence were indeed to be valid.

Semmelweis tested his hypotheses and solved the mystery of childbed fever by changing conditions in Ward 1 to see if the death rate would change. In essence, the testing of each hypothesis was an experiment. In archaeology, the testing of hypotheses often must be done in a different manner. There is a branch of archaeology called, appropriately enough, "experimental archaeology" that involves the experimental replication and utilization of prehistoric artifacts in an attempt to figure out how they were made and used. In general, however, archaeology is largely not an experimental science. Archaeologists more often need to create "models" of some aspect of cultural adaptation and change. These models are simplified, manipulable versions of cultural phenomena.

For example, James Mosimann and Paul Martin (1975) created a computer program that simulated or modeled the first human migration into America some 12,000 years ago. By varying the size of the initial human population and their rate of growth and expansion, as well as the size of the big-game animal herds in the New World, Mosimann and Martin were able to test their hypothesis that these human settlers caused the extinction of many species of game animals. The implications of their mathematical modeling can be tested against actual archaeological and paleontological data.

Ultimately, whether a science is experimentally based or not makes little logical difference in the testing of hypotheses. Instead of predicting what the results of a given experiment must be if our induced hypothesis is useful or valid, we predict what new data we must be able to find if a given hypothesis is correct.

For instance, we may hypothesize that long-distance trade is a key element in the development of civilization based upon our analysis of the ancient Maya. We deduce that if this is correct—if this is, in fact, a general rule of cultural evolution—we must find large quantities of trade items in other parts of the world where civilization also developed. We might further deduce that these items should be found in contexts that denote their value and importance to the society (for example, in the burials of leaders). We must then determine the validity of our predictions and, indirectly, our hypothesis by going out and conducting more research. We need to excavate sites belonging to other ancient civilizations and see if they followed the same pattern as seen for the Maya relative to the importance of trade.

Testing a hypothesis certainly is not easy. Sometimes errors in testing can lead to incorrectly validating or rejecting a hypothesis. Some of you may have already caught a potential problem in Semmelweis's application of the scientific method. Remember hypothesis 4? It was initially suggested that the student doctors were at the root of the higher death rate in Ward 1, because they were not as gentle in assisting in birthing as were the more experienced doctors. This hypothesis was not borne out by testing. Retraining the students had no effect on the mortality rate in Ward 1. But suppose that Semmelweis had tested this hypothesis instead by removing the students altogether prior to their retraining. From what we now know, the death rate would have indeed declined, and Semmelweis would have concluded incorrectly that the hypothesis was correct. We can assume that once the retrained students were returned to the ward (gentler, perhaps, but with their hands still dirty) the death rate would have jumped up again because the students were indeed at the heart of the matter, but not because of their presumed rough handling of the maternity patients.

This should point out that our testing of hypotheses takes a great deal of thought and that we can be wrong. We must remember: we have a hypothesis, we have the deduced implications, and we have the test. We can make errors at any place within this process—the hypothesis may be incorrect, the implications may be wrong, or the way we test them may be incorrect. Certainty in science is a scarce commodity. There are always new hypotheses, alternative explanations, and more deductive implications to test. Nothing is ever finished, nothing is set in concrete, nothing is ever defined or raised to the level of religious truth.

Beyond this, it must be admitted that scientists are, after all, ordinary human beings. They are not isolated from the cultures and times in which they live. They share many of the same prejudices and biases of other members of their societies. Scientists learn from mentors at universities and often inherit their perspectives. It often is quite difficult to go against the scientific grain, to question accumulated wisdom, and to suggest a new approach or perspective.

For example, when German meteorologist Alfred Wegener hypothesized in 1912 that the present configuration of the continents resulted from the breakup of a single inclusive landmass and that the separate continents had "drifted" into their current positions (a process called *continental drift*), most rejected the suggestion outright. Yet today, Wegener's general perspective is accepted and incorporated into the general theory of *plate tectonics.*

Philosopher of science Thomas Kuhn (1970) has suggested that the growth of scientific knowledge is not neatly linear, with knowledge simply building on knowledge. He maintains that science remains relatively static for periods and that most thinkers work under the same set of assumptions—the same *paradigm.* New ideas or perspectives, like those of Wegener or Einstein, that challenge the existing orthodoxy, are usually initially rejected. Only when scientists get over the shock of the new ideas and start testing the new frameworks suggested by these new paradigms are great jumps in knowledge made.

That is why in science we propose, test, tentatively accept, but never prove a hypothesis. We keep only those hypotheses that cannot be disproved. As long as an hypothesis holds up under the scrutiny of additional testing through experiment and/or is not contradicted by new data, we accept it as the best explanation so far. Some hypotheses sound good, pass the rigors of initial testing, but are later shown to be inadequate or invalid. Others—for example, the hypothesis of biological evolution—have held up so well (all new data either were or could have been deduced from it) that they will probably always be upheld. We usually call these very well supported hypotheses *theories.* However, it is in the nature of science that no matter how well an explanation of some aspect of reality has held up, we must always be prepared to consider new tests and better explanations.

We are interested in knowledge and explanations of the universe that work. As long as these explanations work, we keep them. As soon as they cease being effective because new data and tests show them to be incomplete or misguided, we discard them and seek new ones. In one sense, Semmelweis was wrong after all, although his explanation worked at the time—he did save lives through its application. We now know that there is nothing inherently bad in "cadaveric material." Dead bodies are not the cause of childbed fever. Today, we realize that it is a bacteria that can grow in the flesh of a dead body that can get on a doctor's hands, infect a pregnant woman, and cause her death. Semmelweis worked in a time before the existence of such things was known. Science in this way always grows, expands, and evolves.

Science and Archaeology

The study of the human past is a science and relies on the same general logical processes that all sciences do. Unfortunately, perhaps as a result of its popularity, the data of archaeology have often been used by people to attempt to prove some idea or claim. Too often, these attempts have been bereft of science.

Archaeology has attracted frauds and fakes. Myths about the human past have been created and popularized. Misunderstandings of how archaeologists go about their tasks and what we have discovered about the human story have too often been promulgated. As I stated . . . my purpose is to describe the misuse of archaeology and the non-scientific application of the data from this field . . .

References

Byrne, M. St. Clere, ed. 1979. *The Elizabethan Zoo: A Book of Beasts Fabulous and Authentic.* Boston: Nonpareil Books.

Haas, J. 1982. *The Evolution of the Prehistoric State.* New York: New York University Press.

Hempel, C. G. 1966. *Philosophy of Natural Science.* Englewood Cliffs, NJ: Prentice-Hall.

Howard, R. W. 1975. *The Dawn Seekers.* New York: Harcourt, Brace, Jovanovich.

Kuhn, T. 1970. *The Structure of Scientific Revolutions.* Chicago: University of Chicago Press.

Lamberg-Karlovsky. C. C., and J. Sabloff. 1979. *Ancient Civilizations: The Near East and Mesoamerica.* Prospect Heights, Ill.: Waveland Press.

Mosimann, J., and P. Martin. 1975. Simulating Overkill by Paleo-Indians. *American Scientist* 63: 304–313.

Van Kampen, H. 1979. The Case of the Lost Panda. *The Skeptical Inquirer* 4(1): 48–50.

"EPISTEMOLOGY:
HOW YOU KNOW WHAT YOU KNOW"

Kenneth L. Feder

1) What are the two ways people generally collect information? Why or why aren't they generally effective? Give examples from the article and American culture.

2) What are the four major rules concerning the operation and the functioning of science?

3) How did Semmelweiss exemplify how science should be conducted? What innovations did he institute and what possible pitfalls could he have encountered in his experiments?

4) How can errors creep into scientific methodology?

5) Define the following terms and give an example: multiple working hypotheses, Occam's Razor, paradigm.

6) Consider a popular belief (UFOs, Atlantis, Bigfoot, etc.) that you are interested in or find a fascinating possibility. Using science's rules of functioning, how would you go about dispassionately examining this belief?

ONCE WE WERE NOT ALONE

Ian Tattersall

Homo sapiens has had the earth to itself for the past 25,000 years or so, free and clear of competition from other members of the hominid family. This period has evidently been long enough for us to have developed a profound feeling that being alone in the world is an entirely natural and appropriate state of affairs.

So natural and appropriate, indeed, that during the 1950s and 1960s a school of thought emerged that, in essence, claimed that only one species of hominid could have existed at a time because there was simply no ecological space on the planet for more than one culture-bearing species. The "single-species hypothesis" was never very convincing—even in terms of the rather sparse hominid fossil record of 35 years ago. But the implicit scenario of the slow, single-minded transformation of the bent and benighted ancestral hominid into the graceful and gifted modern *H. sapiens* proved powerfully seductive—as fables of frogs becoming princes always are.

So seductive that it was only in the late 1970s, following the discovery of incontrovertible fossil evidence that hominid species coexisted some 1.8 million years ago in what is now northern Kenya, that the single-species hypothesis was abandoned. Yet even then, paleoanthropologists continued to cleave to a rather minimalist interpretation of the fossil record. Their tendency was to downplay the number of species and to group together distinctively different fossils under single, uninformative epithets such as "archaic *Homo sapiens*." As a result, they tended to lose sight of the fact that many kinds of hominids had regularly contrived to coexist.

Although the minimalist tendency persists, recent discoveries and fossil reappraisals make clear that the biological history of hominids resembles that of most other successful animal families. It is marked by diversity rather than by linear progression. Despite this rich history—during which hominid species developed and lived together and competed and rose and fell—*H. sapiens* ultimately emerged as the sole hominid. The reasons for this are generally unknowable, but different interactions between the last coexisting hominids—*H. sapiens* and *H. neanderthalensis*—in two distinct geographical regions offer some intriguing insights.

A Suite of Species

From the beginning, almost from the very moment the earliest hominid biped—the first "australopith"—made its initial hesitant steps away from the forest depths, we have evidence for hominid diversity. The oldest-known potential hominid is *Ardipithecus ramidus*, represented by some fragmentary fossils from the 4.4-million-year-old site of Aramis in Ethiopia. Only slightly younger is the better-known *Australopithecus anamensis*, from sites in northern Kenya that are about 4.2 million years old.

Ardipithecus, though claimed on indirect evidence to have been an upright walker, is quite apelike in many respects. In contrast, *A. anamensis* looks reassuringly similar to the 3.8- to 3.0-million-year-old *Australopithecus afarensis*, a small-brained, big-faced bipedal species to which the famous "Lucy" belonged. Many remnants of *A. afarensis* have been found in various eastern African sites, but some researchers have suggested that the mass of fossils described as *A. afarensis* may contain more than one species, and it is only a matter of time until the subject is raised again. In any event, *A. afarensis* was not alone in Africa. A distinctive jaw, from an australopith named *A. bahrelghazali*, was found recently in Chad. It is probably between 3.5 and 3.0 million years old and is thus roughly coeval with Lucy.

In southern Africa, scientists have just reported evidence of another primitive bipedal hominid species. As yet unnamed and undescribed, this distinctive form is 3.3 million year old. At about 3 million years ago, the same region begins to yield fossils of *A. africanus*, the first australopith to be discovered (in 1924). This species may have persisted until not much more than 2 million years ago. A recently named 2.5-million-year-old species from Ethiopia, *Australopithecus garhi*, is claimed to fall in an intermediate position between *A. afarensis*, on the one hand, and a larger group that includes more recent australopiths and *Homo*, on the other. Almost exactly the same age is the first representative of the "robust" group of australopiths, *Paranthropus aethiopicus*. This early form is best known from the 2.5-million-year-old "Black Skull" of northern Kenya, and in the period between about 2 and 1.4 million years ago the robusts were represented all over eastern Africa by the familiar *P. boisei*. In South Africa, during the period around 1.6 million years ago, the robusts included the distinctive *P. robustus* and possibly closely related second species, *P. crassidens*.

I apologize for inflicting this long list of names on you, but in fact it actually underestimates the number of australopith species that existed. Furthermore, we don't know how long each of these creatures lasted. Nevertheless, even if average species longevity was only a few hundred thousand years, it is clear that from the very beginning the continent of Africa was at least periodically—and most likely continually—host to multiple kinds of hominids.

The appearance of the genus *Homo* did nothing to perturb this pattern. The 2.5 to 1.8-million-year-old fossils from eastern and southern Africa that announce the earliest appearance of *Homo* are an oddly assorted lot and probably a lot more diverse than their conventional assignment to the two species *H. babilis* and *H. rudolfensis* indicates. Still, at Kenya's East Turkana, in the period between 1.9 and 1.8 million years ago, these two species were joined not only by the ubiquitous *P. boisei* but by *H. ergaster*, the first hominid of essentially modern body form. Here, then, is evidence for four hominid species sharing not just the same continent but the same landscape.

The first exodus of hominids from Africa, presumably in the form of *H. ergaster* or a close relative, opened a vast prospect for further diversification. One could wish for a better record of this movement, and particularly of its dating, but there are indications that hominids of some kind had reached China and Java by about 1.8 million years ago. A lower jaw that may be about the same age from Dmanisi in ex-Soviet Georgia is distinctively different from anything else yet found (see "Out of Africa Again . . . and Again?" by Ian Tattersall; *Scientific American*, April 1997). By the million-year mark, *H. erectus* was established in both Java and China, and it is possible that a more robust hominid species was present in Java as well. At the other end of the Eurasian continent, the oldest-known European hominid fragments—from about 800,000 years ago—are highly distinctive and have been dubbed *H. antecessor* by their Spanish discoverers.

About 600,000 years ago, in Africa, we begin to pick up evidence for *H. heidelbergensis*, a species also seen at sites in Europe—and possibly China—between 500,000 to 200,000 years ago. As we learn more about *H. heidelbergensis*, we are likely to find that more than one species actually is represented in this group of fossils. In Europe, *H. heidelbergensis* or a relative gave rise to an endemic group of hominids whose best-known representative was *H.*

neanderthalensis, a European and western Asian species that flourished between about 200,000 and 30,000 years ago. The sparse record from Africa suggests that at this time independent developments were taking place there, too—including the emergence of *H. sapiens*. And in Java, possible *H. erectus fossils* from Ngandong have just been dated to around 40,000 years ago implying that this area had its own indigenous hominid evolutionary history for perhaps millions of years as well.

The picture of hominid evolution just sketched is a far cry from the "*Australopithecus africanus* begat *Homo erectus*; begat *Homo sapiens*" scenario that prevailed 40 years ago—and it is, of course, based to a great extent on fossils that have been discovered since that time. Yet the dead hand of linear thinking still lies heavily on paleoanthropology, and even today many of my colleagues would argue that this scenario overestimates diversity. There are various ways of simplifying the picture, most of them involving the cop-out of stuffing all variants of *Homo* of the last half a million or even two million years into the species *H. sapiens*.

My own view, in contrast, is that the 20 or so hominid species invoked (if not named) above represent a minimum estimate. Not only is the human fossil record as we know it full of largely unacknowledged morphological indications of diversity, but it would be rash to claim that every hominid species that ever existed is represented in one fossil collection or another. And even if only the latter is true, it is still clear that the story of human evolution has not been one of a lone hero's linear struggle.

Instead, it has been the story of nature's tinkering: of repeated evolutionary experiments. Our biological history has been one of sporadic events rather than gradual accretions. Over the past five million years, new hominid species have regularly emerged, competed, coexisted, colonized new environments, and succeeded—or failed. We have only the dimmest of perceptions of how this dramatic history of innovation and interaction unfolded, but it is already evident that our species, far from being the pinnacle of the hominid evolutionary tree, is simply one more of its many terminal twigs.

The Roots of Our Solitude

Athough this is all true, *H. sapiens* embodies something that is undeniably unusual and is neatly captured by the fact that we are alone in the world today. Whatever that something is, it is related to how we interact with the external world: it is behavioral, which means that we have to look to our archaeological record to find evidence of it. This record begins some 2.5 million years ago with the production of the first recognizable stone tools: simple sharp flakes chipped from parent "cores." We don't know exactly who the inventor was, but chances are that he or she was something we might call an australopith.

This innovation represented a major cognitive leap and had profound long-term consequences for hominids. It also inaugurated a pattern of highly intermittent technological change. It was a full million years before the next significant technological innovation came along: the creation about 1.5 million years ago, probably by *H. ergaster,* of the hand axe. These symmetrical implements, shaped from large stone cores, were the first to conform to a "mental template" that existed in the toolmaker's mind. This template remained essentially unchanged for another million years or more, until the invention of "prepared-core" tools by *H. heidelbergensis* or a relative. Here, a stone core was elaborately shaped in such a way that a single blow would detach what was an effectively finished implement.

Among the most accomplished practitioners of prepared-core technology were the large-brained, big-faced, and low-skulled Neanderthals, who occupied Europe and western Asia until about 30,000 years ago. Because they left an excellent record of themselves and were abruptly replaced by modern humans who did the same, the Neanderthals furnish us with a particularly instructive yardstick by which to judge our own uniqueness. The stoneworking skills of the Neanderthals were impressive, if somewhat stereotyped, but they rarely if ever made tools from other preservable materials. And many archaeologists question the sophistication of their hunting skills.

Further, despite misleading early accounts of bizarre Neanderthal "bear cults" and other rituals, no substantial evidence has been found for symbolic behaviors among these hominids, or for the production of symbolic objects—certainly not before contact had been made with modern humans. Even the occasional Neanderthal practice of burying the dead may have been simply a way of discouraging hyena incursions into their living spaces, or have a similar mundane explanation, for Neanderthal burials lack the "grave goods" that would attest to ritual and belief in an afterlife. The Neanderthals, in other words, though admirable in many ways and for a long time successful in the difficult circumstances of the late Ice Ages, lacked the spark of creativity that, in the end, distinguished *H. sapiens.*

Although the source of *H. sapiens* as a physical entity is obscure, most evidence points to an African origin perhaps between 150,000 and 200,000 years ago. Modern behavior patterns did not emerge until much later. The best evidence comes from Israel and environs, where Neanderthals lived about 200,000 years ago or perhaps even earlier. By about 100,000 years ago, they had been joined by anatomically modern H. *sapiens,* and the remarkable thing is that the tools and sites the two hominid species left behind are essentially identical. As far as can be told, these two hominids behaved in similar ways despite their anatomical differences. And as long as they did so, they somehow contrived to share the Levantine environment.

The situation in Europe could hardly be more different. The earliest *H. sapiens* sites there date from only about 40,000 years ago, and just 10,000 or so years later the formerly ubiquitous Neanderthals were gone. Significantly, the *H. sapiens* who invaded Europe brought with them abundant evidence of a fully formed and unprecedented modern sensibility. Not only did they possess a new "Upper Paleolithic" stoneworking technology based on the production of multiple long, thin blades from cylindrical cores, but they made tools from bone and antler, with an exquisite sensitivity to the properties of these materials.

Even more significant, they brought with them art, in the form of carvings, engravings, and spectacular cave paintings; they kept records on bone and stone plaques; they made music on wind instruments; they crafted elaborate personal adornments; they afforded some of their dead elaborate burials with grave goods (hinting at social stratification in addition to belief in an afterlife, for not all burials were equally fancy); their living sites were highly organized, with evidence of sophisticated hunting and fishing. The pattern of intermittent technological innovation was gone, replaced by constant refinement. Clearly, these people were *us.*

In all these ways, early Upper Paleolithic people contrasted dramatically with the Neanderthals. Some Neanderthals in Europe seem to have picked up new ways of doing things from the arriving *H. sapiens,* but we have no direct clues as to the nature of the interaction between the two species. In light of the Neanderthals' rapid disappearance, though, and of the appalling subsequent record of *H. sapiens,* we can reasonably surmise that such interactions were rarely happy for the former. Certainly the repeated pattern at archaeological sites is one of short-term replacement, and there is no convincing biological evidence of any intermixing in Europe.

In the Levant, the coexistence ceased—after about 60,000 years or so—at right about the time that Upper Paleolithic-like tools began to appear. About 40,000 years ago, the Neanderthals of the Levant yielded to a presumably culturally rich *H. sapiens*, just as their European counterparts had.

The key to the difference between the European and the Levantine scenarios lies, most probably, in the emergence of modern cognition—which, it is reasonable to assume, is equivalent to the advent of symbolic thought. Business had continued more or less as usual right through the appearance of modern bone structure, and only later, with the acquisition of fully modern behavior patterns, did *H. sapiens* become completely intolerant of competition from its nearest—and, evidently, not its dearest.

To understand how this change in sensibility occurred, we have to recall certain things about the evolutionary process. First, as in this case, all innovations must necessarily arise *within* preexisting species—for where else can they do so? Second, many novelties arise as "exaptations," features acquired in one context before (often long before) being coopted in a different one. For example, hominids possessed essentially modern vocal tracts for hundreds of thousands of years before the behavioral record gives us any reason to believe that they employed the articulate speech that the peculiar form of this tract permits. Finally, we need to bear in mind the phenomenon of emergence whereby a chance coincidence gives rise to something totally unexpected. The classic example here is water, whose properties are unpredicted by those of hydrogen and oxygen atoms alone.

If we combine these various observations, we can see that, profound as the consequences of achieving symbolic thought may have been, the process whereby it came about was unexceptional. We have no idea at present how the modern human brain converts a mass of electrical and chemical discharges into what we experience as consciousness. We do know, however, that somehow our lineage passed to symbolic thought from some nonsymbolic precursor state. The only plausible possibility is that with the arrival of anatomically modern *H. sapiens*, existing exaptations were fortuitously linked by some relatively minor genetic innovation to create an unprecedented potential.

Yet even in principle this cannot be the full story, because anatomically modern humans behaved archaically for a long time before adopting modern behaviors. That discrepancy may be the result of the late appearance of some key hardwired innovation not reflected in the skeleton, which is all that fossilizes. But this seems unlikely, because it would have necessitated a wholesale Old Worldwide replacement of hominid populations in a very short time, something for which there is no evidence.

It is much more likely that the modern human capacity was born at—or close to—the origin of *H. sapiens*, as an ability that lay fallow until it was activated by a cultural stimulus of some kind. If sufficiently advantageous, this behavioral novelty could then have spread rapidly by cultural contact among populations that already had the potential to acquire it. No population replacement would have been necessary.

It is impossible to be sure what this innovation might have been, but the best current bet is that it was the invention of language. For language is not simply the medium by which we express our ideas and experiences to each other. Rather it is fundamental to the thought process itself. It involves categorizing and naming objects and sensations in the outer and inner worlds and making associations between resulting mental symbols. It is, in effect, impossible for us to conceive of thought (as we are familiar with it) in the absence of language, and it is the ability to form mental symbols that is the fount of our creativity, for only after we create such symbols can we recombine them and ask such questions as "What if. . . ?"

We do not know exactly how language might have emerged in one local population of *H. sapiens*, although linguists have speculated widely. But we do know that a creature armed with symbolic skills is a formidable competitor—and not necessarily an entirely rational one, as the rest of the living world, including *H. neanderthalensis*, has discovered to its cost.

References

Bickerton, Derek. 1990. *Language and Species*. University of Chicago Press.

Howells, William. 1997. *Getting Here: The Story of Human Evolution*. Updated edition. Compass Press.

Jablonski, Nina G. and Leslie C. Aiello, editors. 1998. *The Origin and Diversification of Language*. University of California Press.

Stringer, Christopher and Robin McKie. 1997. *African Exodus: The Origins of Modern Humanity*. Henry Holt.

Tattersall, Ian. 1995. *The Fossil Trail: How We Know What We Think We Know About Human Evolution*. Oxford University Press.

Tattersall, Ian. 1995. *The Last Neanderthal: The Rise, Success and Mysterious Extinction of Our Closest Human Relatives*. Macmillan. (Second edition by Westview Press due December 1999.)

White, Randall. 1986. *Dark Caves, Bright Visions: Life in Ice Age Europe*. W. W. Norton/American Museum of Natural History.

"ONCE WE WERE NOT ALONE"

Ian Tattersall

1) In the 1950s and 1960s, what was the prevailing idea regarding the possibility of multiple species of hominids existing at the same time? What reasons lay behind this thinking?

2) What is unusual in a biological sense about modern man (*Homo sapiens*)?

3) What were the essential differences between modern man (*Homo sapiens*) and Neanderthals, both physically and cognitively? How did these differences lead to modern man's biological ascendancy over the Neanderthals?

4) Why does Tattersall believe that his estimate of twenty hominid species having once existed may actually be an underestimate?

SECTION TWO

Fieldwork Among the Familiar and the Strange

Kenya, Land of My Fathers: A Time Traveler in Kenya

Chapurukha M. Kusimba

Thirty-five years ago, I was born and given the name Cullen, in honor of an Irishman who was then my father's boss at the Kilembe mines in Uganda. My parents were from western Kenya, but I spent the first five years of my life in Uganda, where Father had found work as a civil engineer. After the two neighboring nations failed to resolve the labor migration crisis, Kenyans were forced to leave Uganda, and we settled in Father's village of Kaptola, where my parents had a modest two-bedroom house. This is where my two brothers, my sister, and I first became acquainted with our extended family. Having been born and raised in Uganda, we spoke Luganda, Lutoro, and some English, but none of our family's mother tongue, Lubukusu. Mother and Father decided that we should spend some time in the village to learn the ways of our people.

Our home was about one hundred yards from my grandparents' huge, six-bedroom house, which always seemed to be a beehive of activity. Here, in the evenings after school and dinner, all the grandchildren gathered to complete their homework, listen to Bible stories or fairy tales, sing traditional and Christian hymns, and, quite often, take refuge from irritated parents. For the next twelve years, in the great house that Grandfather built and Grandmother managed, I and my expanding family of cousins and siblings were raised. We were growing up in a recently independent and fast-changing society, little realizing that our generation enjoyed a unique link to the past.

Occasionally, one of us would bring home an arrowhead or stone tool, and our grandparents would patiently explain how people lived in former times. The Bukusu, to which I belong, are a Bantu-speaking people and inhabit the area around Mount Elgon on the Kenya-Uganda border. Traditionally, the Bukusu lived in large fortress villages, farming and grazing cattle in scattered meadows. They were surrounded by the Nilotic-speaking Iteso, Sabaot, and Nandi; by other Bantu groups; and by the Ndorobo, who were hunter-gathers. In times of peace and prosperity, these peoples engaged in trade and intermarried. In times of famine, they competed for land and stole from one another's herds. Skirmishes, raids, and counterraids were somehow accepted as a way of life.

Born in 1904, Grandfather was a skilled hunter, wonderful teacher, and excellent farmer. He became a Quaker in 1916 and was one of the first local missionaries to set up a meetinghouse among the pastoral Sabaot people of western Kenya. Our grandparents made it clear that we were in one way or another connected with our neighbors, including the hunter-gatherers, who brought us baskets, mats, dried meats, honey, and dried bamboo shoots in exchange for grains (mostly millet, sorghum, and maize).

Grandfather spoke all the languages of his neighbors, among whom he preached the Quaker message of peace and brotherhood. Few Kenyans can now speak more than four indigenous languages, in addition to English and Kiswahili. That people were traditionally multilingual is testimony to the interactions that existed among them. At the time I was growing up, however, the history of African groups was little known, and what we were taught in school was that African cultures were static until European missionaries and colonists arrived in the late nineteenth century.

Kenyan peoples that I learned about in childhood included the Swahili of the coast, whose Arab ties and history as slave traders gave them a less than favorable reputation. Grandfather remembered that Swahili caravans used to stop and trade in western Kenya on their way to Uganda. On one such visit, Grandfather, then five years old, approached one of the Swahili men, borrowed his rifle, and carried the heavy object for a few minutes to the amazement of all those present. One Swahili man declared, *Huyu mtoto ana nguvu kama ya simba*, "This child is as powerful as a lion." Grandfather then got the nickname Kusimba, or Big Lion, a name that he later formalized.

The history of the Swahili also came up when I accompanied Grandfather on a hunting expedition on the slopes of Mount Elgon. There I saw many rock shelters and caves, some with paintings. Because we were learning in school that ancient people used to live in caves, I asked Grandfather whether our people lived in some of them. His response was that people took refuge in the mountains and caves from the slave trade and slavery, which continued at least into the 1880s. He explained that Islamic Swahili people from the coast would attack whole villages and take people away. He also said that one of our ancestors, who had been engaged as a porter by Swahili traders when Grandfather was a young man, had never returned. It was widely believed that he had been taken into slavery. Even in my own childhood there were stories of lost children who were believed to have suffered a similar fate, and the books we used in school were replete with images of caravans led by ferocious, bearded Arab and Swahili men, wielding whips over emaciated slaves tied together and carrying ivory to the coast.

Grandfather's stories helped me understand that the cultural diversity of African people preceded European colonization; that trade, friendships, and alliances among different communities led to the exchange of ideas, information, and often genes. At the same time, Grandfather laid much of the blame for the destruction of East African societies on the slave trade and slavery. As a Quaker and a product of a missionary school, he laid that blame on the Muslim peoples of the coast.

When I got older, I began to learn about the Swahili firsthand. In 1984, I was in a group of one hundred students from Kenyatta University in Nairobi who traveled to the coast to see historical and archeological sites. I was greatly impressed by the great palace and main mosque at Gede (Gedi), built more than 700 years ago. Our guides attributed this and other significant sites to seafaring Arabs and Arabized Persians who came to East Africa to trade and to colonize the coast. Archeologists and historians thought that although these seafaring people intermixed with Africans, their coastal settlements developed in isolation from the up-country African settlements that surrounded them and with which they traded. In the words of archeologist Neville Chittick, then director of the British Institute of Eastern Africa, the coastal settlements were economically dependent on Africa but "it was seawards that they faced, looking out over the great maritime region constituted by the Indian Ocean."

This view did not seem convincing to me, and I determined to delve into the question of Swahili origins. I returned to Mombasa to begin archeological research in the autumn of 1986. There I met Mohammed Mchulla, a curatorial assistant in the department of archeology at the Fort Jesus Museum. Mohammed invited me to live with his family—his wife, Maimuna, and their two young boys, Abubakr and Abdillatif. Over the next ten months, before I left

for graduate school in the United States, Mohammed's house was my home away from home, and I have returned every year since. Through this personal contact, I have been helped to understand Swahili society today and have enjoyed enlightening conversations with sages, poets, midwives, blacksmiths, potters, boat makers, tourist guides, and friends.

The resources of the Swahili coast, which extends from Somalia through Kenya, Tanzania, Mozambique, Madagascar, and the Comoros, have attracted many different peoples. Although most coastal inhabitants speak Kiswahili, a Bantu language, other ethnic groups also inhabit the area, including the hunter-gatherer Dahalo, Waata, and Boni (Sanye); the pastoral Orma and Somali; and the agricultural Malakote, Pokomo, and Mijikenda. To understand the roots of Swahili culture requires more than sorting through all these groups. Five hundred years of colonization also have to be unscrambled. This includes conquest by the Portuguese, who first rounded the Cape of Good Hope in search of a trade route to India; rule by the Omani Arabs, who followed in the eighteenth century after the coast enjoyed a brief period of independence; and finally, occupation by the Western European industrial powers, which met in Berlin in 1884 and partitioned Africa.

Influenced in part by local explanations of Swahili origins and by the abundance of Arabic loan words, the colonizing European intellectual community was convinced that Swahili peoples, especially the elite, were not African, even when they grudgingly accepted that Kiswahili was a Bantu language. All the monuments found in East Africa were assigned to various foreign societies—Phoenicians, Sabaens, Persians, Egyptians, Indians, Omanis—but never to the indigenous Africans. In recent years, however, historians and linguists have begun to question the common assumptions. And since 1980 several major archeological excavations and more than ten doctoral research projects have been carried out, mostly by African archeologists, that have shed new light on the complex origins and development of the Swahili states.

For an archeologist, understanding a place that has seen so many political changes can be a nightmare. But a chronology of the Swahili coast has been constructed based upon radiocarbon dates, coins, imported ceramics, and local pottery. The earliest sites that have been excavated date to the second century A.D. These finds suggest that coastal people lived in village communities, where they fished, farmed, kept domestic animals (chickens, donkeys, camels), and smelted and forged iron. Shards of Partho-Sassanian ware at some of these sites suggest that Egyptians and Ethiopians would round the Horn to trade with communities along the Somali coast. Such contact is mentioned in *Periplus of the Erythraean Sea*, written about A.D. 50, and Claudius Ptolemy's second-century *Geography*.

In the absence of earlier sites, archeologists speculate that the coast was settled sometime between 500 B.C. and A.D. 1. Based on linguistic evidence, Derek Nurse and Thomas Spear believe that Bantu-speaking people spread to the coast from what is now Zaire. The rivers and sea yielded fish and shellfish; the forested floodplains could be cleared, providing both fertile farmland and wood fuel for smelting and forging the region's abundant iron ore; and the clay deposits in the swamps were suitable for pottery making.

Chris Ehret and other linguists suggest that when the Bantu speakers arrived on the coast, the ancestors of present-day Eastern Cushites, Somali, Boni, and Aweera inhabited the hinterland and may also have been rapidly settling along the northern coast of Kenya and Somalia. The Cushites were mostly hunter-gatherers and nomadic pastoralists. Interactions among the various groups, each exploiting specific resources, would have promoted friendships, alliances, gift exchanges, barter, and occasional skirmishes.

Sites dating from the eighth century on are better known, and among their artifacts are local cowries and shell beads, evidence of trade with neighboring and interior groups by such craft specialists as potters, ironworkers, shell bead makers, and boat and canoe builders. By the ninth century, the annual monsoon winds were bringing foreign merchants bearing cloth, clothing, ceramics, and beads in exchange for ivory, rhino horns, hides and skins, ebony, ostrich feathers, ambergris, *bêche-de-mer*, copal, iron, gold—and slaves. As shown by archeologist Mark Horton, Islamic influence began to leave a mark in the ninth century, when a timber mosque was built at Shanga. But Horton found no evidence of foreign settlement at the site in terms of burials or monumental architecture.

Between 1000 and 1200, trade between the coast and the interior, Madagascar, and the Middle East increased. Along the length of the coast, pots were traded for sorghum, millet, rice, and other cereals. Pots, cowrie shells, shell beads, textiles, and cereals were exchanged with hinterland peoples up the rivers for honey, cattle, hides, ghee, and such luxuries as gold, copper, and ivory. Cereals, especially rice, were among the export items from East Africa, bringing in such maritime trade goods as beads and ceramics (primarily from India and China). According to a twelfth-century account by the Arab geographer

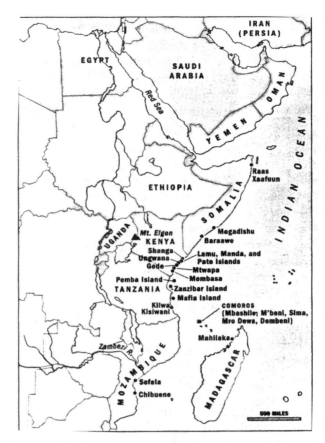

Major archeological sites and historic cities of the Swahili civilization have long been attributed to traders and colonists from the Middle East and elsewhere overseas. New research is helping to clarify the indigenous contributions to East African coastal settlement.

Idrisi, Indians preferred iron from East Africa over their own because of its malleability. (Galu, a village site I excavated, produced the world's oldest crucible steel, a high-carbon steel dated to the seventh century. Before the Galu discoveries, crucible steel was known only from tenth-century India, Sri Lanka, and Arabia.)

As the population grew and settlements became more permanent, an emerging elite began to exercise control over resources, crafts, and trade. By 1300, Islam had become a widespread part of coastal culture. Islam provided a connection between the local elite and other Muslim elites and traders that helped catapult the East African coast into international commerce. The next two centuries witnessed the importation of Chinese porcelain, Islamic pottery, glass beads, and other trade goods. At the same time, local manufacturing surged, not only of pottery and iron but also of new products, notably cotton and kapok clothing.

While early inhabitants built their dwellings of wattle and daub or unfired mud brick on a wooden frame, buildings of unfired mud brick with coral mortar foundations and of coral blocks in lime mortar began to appear after 1200. The buildings, including distinct mosques, were clustered by type of construction, suggesting that place of residence was determined by wealth, social status, and perhaps religious affiliation. Many of the elite, including merchants and political leaders, interred their dead in monumental tombs that show ranking among the townspeople. Nineteenth-century accounts by missionaries and explorers suggest that individuals of lower rank were prohibited from wearing daggers and silk dresses, building coral houses, learning to read the Koran, and buying and displaying expensive jewelry and porcelain.

The civilization of East Africa reached its zenith between 1300 and 1500. Many towns, including Mogadishu, Pate, Lamu, Mombasa, Kilwa, and Mahilaka, burgeoned into major cosmopolitan centers. Traders and merchants began to wrest more political and economic power from the farmers, fishers, potters, and ironworkers. They forged alliances and connections outside the community through contracts (including intermarriage) with potential trading partners and, in general, were the ones to welcome innovations. As the coast became more involved in trade, more and more people from the interior and abroad settled among the coastal people, creating a society that was dynamic, tolerant, and enterprising.

The question that intrigues scholars who study these developments is the extent to which Swahili civilization was an indigenous phenomenon. The vital role of local production and trade with interior African peoples argues for a strong indigenous basis. In contrast, foreign influence is represented in the spread of Islam. The identity of the Swahili elite is harder to ascertain. Nevertheless, important clues suggest that the intermediary between the hinterland and the foreign merchants was an indigenous business community.

In *Islamic Architecture on the East African Coast* (1966), British archeologist Peter Garlake examined the structures generally regarded as evidence of a Middle Eastern or Arabic colonial presence. He concluded that in basic features, such as construction techniques, ornamental and decorative detail, and composition and planning of mosques and domestic buildings, Swahili architecture evolved from local patterns. Also suggestive of the indigenous identity of coastal elites are fourteenth- and fifteenth-century tombs with circular, rectangular, or polygonal pillars and paneled façades. Called phallic pillars by the

locals, they are decorated with porcelain bowls and Arabic scripts, often citations from the Koran. Unknown in the Middle East, these structures are widespread among the Oromo of Somalia and Kenya, where they symbolize manhood and show that those interred are men.

Dutch anthropologist A. H. J. Prins has argued that the traditional Swahili system of land tenure would have established a land-owning elite among the original settlers and their descendants, enabling them to control vast tracts of land, labor, and goods through a council of elders. According to their system, virgin land that an ancestor had cleared and walled in for cultivation was inherited and owned communally by patrilineal descendants. The landowners could thus levy taxes on commoners and immigrants; forge patronage relationships that provided labor for fishing, craft production, and other enterprises; and deny immigrants from the interior and abroad the right to own land.

Whatever the nature of the elite, Swahili civilization as a whole was never politically unified. When the Portuguese arrived in 1500, the region put up little organized resistance. The conflict was unlike any that East Africans had experienced. Instead of occasional raids, this conquest saw the burning and destruction of whole villages, with the vanquished often taken wholesale into slavery. Many of these people were shipped to Portuguese colonies in the New World or sold to other European and Arab slavers. Local as well as foreign mercantile traders lost control of the Indian and Red Seas and stopped coming to East Africa. Long-established trade relationships between the coast and hinterland were destabilized.

Colonization brought increased immigration of Europeans, Arabs, and Asians into East Africa. Swahili towns were composed of numerous and diverse clans claiming different ethnic origins, ranging from the African mainland, the Arabian Peninsula, Persia, India, Portugal, and the Far East. Members of the former elite, no longer in a position of control, conspired against one another, allying with colonizers through marriage and becoming political puppets. Those who revolted were defeated and hanged or took refuge in the hinterland in hill fortresses.

The loss of independence and freedom drove many coastal people to seek the safety of the interior. This period of separation must have fostered cultural, linguistic, and ethnic differentiation between coastal and hinterland peoples. The exile continued until slavery was abolished at the end of the nineteenth century. Then, many coastal peoples and others began to move more freely and to reestablish alliances. After some sixteen generations, they had a lot to relearn, including an understanding of cultural ties. In present-day Kenya, centered on the national capital of Nairobi, there is a tendency to regard the Swahili as an alien people. Unfavorable stereotypes of them as lazy urbanites who neglect their rich lands are being used to justify land grabbing and destruction of coastal archeological sites.

This summer marks the final season of my excavations at Mtwapa, a coastal settlement nine miles north of Mombasa. Inhabited from 1100 to 1750, it was, at its height in the fifteenth century, a port town with several wards, each with its own wells, mosques, and cemeteries. Imported beads, textiles, and iron tools passed through Mtwapa in exchange for such hinterland products as cereals, ivory, rhino horns, iron, hides, and skins. Salinization of the wells, together with the Portuguese conquest of the region and a southward expansion of the Oromo, eventually led to abandonment of the town, whose ruins cover about nine acres. My next project, beginning this fall, is to survey and excavate sites in the hinterland of Mtwapa in order to understand their relationship to the coastal settlement.

I hope my work will help unravel the myths that exclude the Swahili from participation in Kenya's post-colonial national identity. Grandmother may think I'm a well-paid gravedigger, but I have managed to convince some of the folks back home that the Swahili are our brothers. Grandfather passed on in 1982 but, as an ancestor, continues to inspire my work.

"KENYA, LAND OF MY FATHERS: A TIME TRAVELER IN KENYA"

Chapurukha M. Kusimba

1) Who were the Swahili, and what were their importance in eastern African history?

2) What were African students taught about the early history and prehistory of eastern Africa?

3) What political, cultural, economic, and ideological reasons were behind the European interpretation of remains and sites in eastern Africa?

4) What were the earliest dates of settlement in eastern Africa, and what type of lifestyle did the earliest settlers of the region practice?

5) What groups were in contact with each other through eastern African prehistory and history? What impact did they have on the settlement of the region?

6) What cultural changes occurred in the last 100 years as a result of European colonization of eastern Africa?

7) How has archaeological research changed our ideas regarding eastern African history?

ARE ETHNOGRAPHIES "JUST SO" STORIES?

E. Paul Durrenberger

Some anthropologists think that ethnographies are "just so" stories, not necessarily to be believed as true. I don't agree. Here is why.

> Skarp-Hedin leapt across the river, kept his footing as he hit the ice on the other side, went into a glide, and swooped down on Thrain, swinging an axe to split his head open to the jaw bone and spill Thrain's back teeth onto the ice. Skarp-Hedin didn't even slow down. One man threw a shield at him, but he jumped up and over it and just kept on going. Then Skarp-Hedin's four brothers came running up and killed three of Thrain's friends.
>
> They let four of the young people who were in Thrain's group go because Skarp-Hedin couldn't bring himself to kill them. (Skarp-Hedin and his brothers were irritated at Thrain and his followers for insulting them.) Later on, the young men Skarp-Hedin didn't want to kill helped burn Skarp-Hedin and his brothers and father and mother in their house, but not before Skarp-Hedin had gouged out one man's eye with Thrain's back tooth, which he had saved from that day on the ice.

This story could be from a tabloid newspaper you see at the checkout counter at the grocery store or from a slasher movie. But it isn't. Here is another story.

> There is a beautiful girl named Helga. When she is twelve, her father takes in a boy of the same age who doesn't get along with his own father. Helga and the boy, Gunnlaug, fall madly in love with each other. When Gunnlaug turns eighteen, he goes abroad to make his name and fortune, and Helga's father agrees that he won't make her marry anyone else for three years. Gunnlaug travels all over northern Europe composing poems for kings and raiding and pillaging. Because of a dispute over poetry, he makes a lifelong enemy of another poet, named Hrafn. Gunnlaug gets delayed, and by the time he gets home more than the three years have passed and his enemy has married Helga.
>
> Their families won't let them kill each other in a duel, so they agree to fight it out somewhere else. Gunnlaug manages to visit Helga a few times and gives her a cloak that a king had given him. He and Hrafn travel around until finally they meet, have a long and bloody fight, and both die. Helga now has no husband and no boyfriend. Her father finds another poet for her to marry, and she has some children with this man but never really loves him because she can never get her first love, Gunnlaug, out of her mind. Finally, she catches an epidemic disease. One day she lays her head in her husband's lap, has someone get the cloak Gunnlaug had given her, and dies holding it.

Are these true stories? Nobody knows. They are stories that Icelanders wrote in the thirteenth century as part of their sagas about things that were supposed to have happened two or three hundred years before. The first is from Njal's saga and the second is from Gunnlaug's saga.[1] Nobody even knows who wrote the sagas. All we know is that they were written in Icelandic. If these slasher-romances aren't true stories—and nobody can tell if they are true—why should we pay attention to them, especially in anthropology?

Whatever else these stories are, they are cultural artifacts, just as much as a 1965 Chevy, a hand axe, or an episode of *Days of Our Lives* is a cultural artifact. If we want to learn about a culture, we study its artifacts, especially the ones that say something about social relations and the culture itself. But if someone made up the stories, what can they tell us about the culture or the society?

The imagination cannot go beyond culture. All of us are limited by our cultures. Our cultures define who we are and how we are, what we do, what we think and how we think. So, if you work this equation backward, you can learn a lot about a culture from looking at its artifacts, especially artifacts such as literature that talk about the culture itself.

We learn, for instance, that Icelandic people would kill each other over an insult, or even an imagined insult. We learn that they traveled abroad, raided, traded, made poetry, and fell in love. We learn that fathers could make daughters get married against their will, and many other details of the culture of medieval Iceland.

These are stories in books, and I like them as stories as well as for what they can tell us about medieval Iceland. I believe that we can use fiction for ethnography. If you want to learn about people, read their stories and you will see their culture reflected in the authors' imaginations. This is one of the things Ruth Benedict did in her perceptive study of Japanese culture "at a distance," *The Chrysanthemum and the Sword*.[2] This is what you do in your literature classes. Read Shakespeare's plays and you see a different culture. The manufactured parts of stories are names and events; the culturally given parts are motivations, emotions, judgments, social relations, and settings. To be good, fiction has to be true. The reason we can use fiction for ethnography is that everyone's imagination is a product of his or her culture, a reflection of the culture, so we can see the culture through the fictions.

The wrenching part of anthropology, what some people call culture shock, is being in places where people are doing things that we cannot imagine. You cannot imagine something you have never heard about or seen or done. But all of a sudden there you are, as anthropologist Bronislaw Malinowski was in the second decade of the twentieth century, in a canoe with a bunch of men blowing smoke and making magic to make things work out right.[3] The reason you are on this dangerous voyage in the middle of the ocean in a dugout canoe is that these men want to trade some shell bracelets for some necklaces on another island. To you it is all some kind of costume jewelry, but to them every individual piece has a history and a value. Their sense of prestige hangs on the trades they make, just as a medieval Icelander's prestige hung on never tolerating an insult, or yours hangs on the kind of car you drive, your credit rating, the clothes you wear, the music you listen to, who you date, and how you smell.

Blowing smoke and making magic to get a canoe across the ocean does not make sense to us. But it made sense to Trobriand Islanders when Malinowski was there early in the twentieth century. It was beyond his imagination, but it was an ordinary part of Trobriand culture.

Sometimes it is even more wrenching to come back to your own country and see that everything you thought was "just the way people do things" is really just another culture, another kind of imaginary construct that doesn't make that much sense.

When you think about it, many of the things we take for granted are pretty silly. Think about money, for example. Paper? Backed by the U.S. government? The only reason we can use money is that we all agree to believe that it has value. These days you can't even trade it for silver or gold, and when you think about it, what is the use of gold except for making wire and jewelry? Money is an incredible leap of the

imagination, but an everyday part of our culture. And it gets even weirder than that. There are a lot of people who make a living just by pushing money from one place to another. And even stranger, they don't even push the actual money; they just enter figures in computers and things happen, and for this they make a nice living—making fictions of fictions. Stocks and bonds are stranger yet. You can take whole courses on how this stuff works in your school of business or economics department; you can learn all of the esoteric language and how to make a living doing this kind of magic. You can get a degree in it. It might seem strange to think of getting a B.A. in magic, but that's what business schools do. To anthropologists, it is just another kind of blowing smoke.

When people's assumptions are different from ours, we don't understand their motives, judgments, or sense of propriety. That is where anthropology comes in—trying to understand other people as well as ourselves.

So everything is a cultural artifact. That is one of the important lessons of anthropology. But if everything is a cultural artifact, isn't anthropology just another cultural artifact, like money, a 65 Chevy, a soap opera, or an Icelandic saga?

Whatever you can say about sagas, soap operas, and anthropology, a 65 Chevy will run. If it doesn't you can fix it so it will. There is a bottom line with some things: They work or they don't. You can try teleportation all you want, but if you want to get some place fast you will buy an airplane ticket. Airplanes work. So do computers. Cars, computers, and airplanes are all the result of scientific knowledge. So scientific knowledge must be "culture-free," right?

Wrong. Even science is a cultural artifact—something we make up, something we imagine. How do we know that? Because science changes from time to time and place to place. European science used to tell us that the earth was at the center of the universe and the sun went around it. European scientists didn't record any new stars. They couldn't. God made the heavens and the earth as they were and they did not change. Everyone knew that. If you saw what you thought was a new star, it was just one you had missed before. The Chinese, on the other hand, were looking at the heavens for signs and portents. They did not assume the heavens were changeless; they were looking for changes, and they saw and recorded new stars that astronomers today classify as novas.

Then an astrologer with strange religious ideas, a man named Copernicus, had the idea that the sun was at the center of the system. Everyone thought he was nuts until it turned out he could make a calendar that kept track of holidays better than the

Ptolemaic system could. Easter stayed in the spring and Christmas stayed in the winter instead of straying all over the seasons. The Church wanted a consistent calendar, so they liked this calendar and the rest of the solar system came in on its coat tails. Evidence? There wasn't any evidence one way or the other. In terms of observations you could make at the time, the Copernican system didn't work any better than the old Ptolemaic one that put the earth at the center of everything. Facts did not determine the choice. Imagination—culture—is stronger than facts.

But people who navigated with the Ptolemaic system could get where they wanted to go. It worked. It probably couldn't get them to the moon, but it could get them from Europe to America or Asia and that is what counted in those days. It will work as well today as it did then for navigation—as long as you don't leave our planet. The point is that just because something works does not necessarily mean that the ideas it is based on are correct. Even the pragmatic test of "working" is not always a good guide to truth. So what is left?

The answer is uncomfortable, but one that you might as well get accustomed to: Nothing is left. Everything we can think of, including science, is a cultural artifact. We cannot escape that. Culture is part of our being just as surely as is walking on two feet and talking and having an opposable thumb. It is built and bred into us and has been part of our evolutionary history since we walked out of Olduvai gorge or wherever we originated in our homeland in Africa.

What we try to do in anthropology is to move beyond our own cultures and understand other cultures. We try to do that in a scientific way. So what kind of artifact is science? It strives for reliable and valid knowledge. Valid means that we observe and measure what we think we are observing and measuring. Do Scholastic Aptitude Tests or entrance examinations really predict your college grades? If they do, they are valid. What do grades measure? Reliability means that anyone else would see and describe the same things if they did the same things. Science is cultural because the very terms for judging reliability and validity are cultural, thus anthropology is a cultural artifact.

This is not surprising when you think about it. But some anthropologists were very surprised when they figured it out. A long time ago, Aristotle wrote about rhetoric. These anthropologists discovered that all arguments are rhetorical, that they are all cultural artifacts. They discovered that Malinowski used rhetoric—that he was a writer. They acted like this was a big discovery and were very proud of

themselves for making it, like the character in Moliere's play who learns that he has been speaking prose all his life.

In 1922, Malinowski said he was constructing interpretations of the kula, the trading of necklaces and shell arm bands; he made the analogy to a physicist constructing a theory from experimental data that everyone can understand but that falls into place when the physicist makes a consistent interpretation, a story. Malinowski was implying that he, like the physicist (a scientist), was constructing interpretations to help people understand things.[4]

In 1973, Clifford Geertz said he discovered that anthropological writings are interpretations, cultural artifacts, something anthropologists make, and he said they were fictions because they are cultural constructs.[5] (You should read some of Geertz's writings, just because anthropologists talk about him a lot. But be warned that Geertz gets confusing. If you find yourself scratching your head and wondering what he means, don't worry. He writes as if he wants to confuse you. And so he does.) He went on to say that these fictions are not untrue; they are just cultural artifacts, something someone makes, and in that sense they are just like any other kind of cultural artifact.

About ten years later, James Clifford and George Marcus got some anthropologists and other people together to talk about these things, and published a book of their essays in 1986.[6] In the introduction, Clifford discusses the idea of ethnographies as fiction, something made, and says they are not false, just incomplete—not unreal, just culturally determined. Some of the words he and the other anthropologists use are "irony," "hegemonic," "discourse," "trope," "interpretation," "hermeneutics," "subjectivity," "conflate," "elide," and "privilege" (as a verb).

Some of these anthropologists call themselves postmodernists. Don't worry if you haven't figured out exactly what that means; they don't want you to, so you are not likely to. Think of it as more of a riddle than a question, or a zen koan whose answer you aren't supposed to understand anyway. The difference is that a zen master will promise you enlightenment if you stick with it and think about the riddle. Enlightenment is another cultural construct. But the postmodernists only promise more confusion. They are in the business of making confusion, not trying to understand it. When they pose you a riddle, if you know it, you know it, and if not, then you are in outer darkness. I am telling you that outer darkness is an "OK" place to be, and that we have to remember now and then to ask whether the emperor has any clothes.

In 1990, Katherine Hayles wrote a book about chaos theory.[7] She had studied chemistry and then

English, so she knew something about scientific subjects as well as literature. Talking about postmodernists in literature, she asked about what she called the political economy of their discipline, the political and economic conditions of the people who write literary criticism. If there is only one correct view, she pointed out, these people would be out of business in no time flat. But if there are many equivalent views, none any better than the others, then they can keep on cranking out literary criticism and debating about how to do it until the cows come home. Maybe it is the same for postmodernism in anthropology.

Geertz recognizes the problem. You cannot be systematic about interpretations; if you can't be systematic, you can't evaluate them. It's like trying to figure out how to get an "A" in a course if nobody will tell you how you are being graded. Nobody wants to talk about how to grade interpretations. So they are all equally good. Listen to Geertz:

> For a field of study which, however timidly (though I, myself, am not timid about the matter at all), asserts itself to be a science, this just will not do. There is no reason why the conceptual structure of a cultural interpretation should be any less formulable, and thus less susceptible to explicit canons of appraisal, than that of, say, a biological observation or a physical experiment.

So far so good, and we think Geertz is right on track, but now comes the punch line to his joke:

> . . . no reason except that the terms of which such formulations can be cast are, if not wholly nonexistent, very nearly so. We are reduced to insinuating theories because we lack the power to state them.[8]

Allow me to interpret. It would be nice to know how to grade interpretations, but we don't know how. So we don't. Instead of having theories, we guess.

If all stories are equivalent, how can we choose among them? Comparing personal interpretations is fundamentally undemocratic because, as Geertz suggested, the way to choose is to yield to the authority of the person who presents the interpretation. This person presents the interpretation and he or she is . . . what? The most powerful? The loudest? The most fashionable? However, while Geertz's suggestion at first looks very liberal—it seems to say "entertain every point of view"—it really means "take my word for it and don't be critical or ask questions." On the other hand, if all interpretations are equally legitimate, then they might as well all be fiction.

If fiction can be ethnography and ethnography is fiction, can there be fictional ethnographies? There can be and there are, and it is something anthropologists talk about and even argue about. Maybe the

most famous of these are the writings of Carlos Castaneda, who started with *The Teachings of Don Juan, A Yaqui Way of Knowledge*, which was published in 1968.[9] This was such a success that he went on to publish several others in the same vein. For a while there was a debate about whether Castaneda's books were "true."

Some people pointed out that he must have copied from well-known books about shamans and mysticism because of parallels in the texts. Others argued that the correspondences were universals of shamanic experience. Richard De Mille collected a number of assessments of Castaneda's work in 1980.[10] De Mille distinguishes between validity and authenticity. Validity means that a story corresponds to what we think we know, similar to the idea of validity for judging scientific work. New stars were not valid to early European astronomers, but they were to Chinese astronomers because of their different systems of reference—frameworks for validity, which are culturally variable. Authenticity means whether the events happened the way the stories say they did.

Did Skarp-Hedin really chop Thrain's teeth out of his head on the ice? The story is valid because it matches what we know about medieval Iceland and other such societies, but we don't know if it is authentic. Were Galileo's telescopic observations of the heavens accurate (authentic)? Check them for yourself. Anyone can do it. Science is democratic; it doesn't hide or confuse things.

Were Castaneda's stories authentic? It is more difficult to determine whether he really knew Don Juan. It isn't as simple as repeating an experiment or observation.

Because there are many authentic and valid ethnographic reports in libraries and books, De Mille suggested that people can use them to concoct valid but inauthentic reports. When you write a term paper, you cite your sources and do not pretend that you are the one who studied diet in China, or marriage customs in India, or religion in Peru. You and your professor are probably equally glad just to have the paper handed in by the due date without a five-year delay for you to go to the place, learn the language, and do the study yourself. You would have to take an incomplete for half a decade. That is what books are good for. But they require honest use. You get an "F" on your term paper if you plagiarize—another one of those cultural things.

When you read an ethnography, how do you know it is true? How do you know the author didn't make it up, as Castaneda did? The main reason is that the writer says, "I was there; this is based on my experience, on what I saw and heard." That experience is the writer's authority, the reason to believe what the writer says. But that is what Castaneda said to claim ethnographic authority, and he was not writing ethnography. In the 1986 book that Clifford and Marcus edited is a piece by Mary Louise Pratt of Stanford's Spanish and Portuguese Department. Pratt points out that you can write an accurate account of life in another culture without ever having been there.[11] Ruth Benedict did. And I have never been to medieval Iceland, but I wrote a book about it.[12] Pratt wonders why there was a big flap in anthropology journals over a book, by Florinda Donner, *Shabono*, published in 1982.[13] Was it fiction based on ethnographies and other sources like Castenada's works, or was it ethnography?

Pratt sees the threat to anthropologists in the missing link, the "being there" that gives ethnographers the "authority" to say they have given you an authentic account. I think the use of the word "authority" for this meaning is interesting, because an appeal to authority, in a somewhat different sense, is the only way to judge stories that are not scientific.

Pratt goes on to talk about how anthropologists establish that they were there, that their accounts are authentic. This is what all scientists do. Galileo said he looked through a telescope and this is what he saw. His authority, his claim to authenticity, came from his having looked through the telescope. If you don't believe him, you can read other books by other people who have looked through telescopes, look at their photos or drawings, or look through a telescope yourself. If other people cannot see the same things, the observations are not reliable. And so it is for ethnography.

Pratt says that ethnographic writing is boring. How, she wonders, could such interesting people doing such interesting things produce such dull books? Boredom, of course, is self-generated. It isn't in what we see but in how we respond to it. Have you ever tried to explain why you were fascinated by an experiment you did in chemistry lab to someone who was so bored with science that he didn't even want to discuss it? If people are bored with something, we can't change their minds about it. It's like what they say about trying to teach pigs to sing. It is a waste of your time and it irritates the pig. People of the English persuasion have tried to explain cricket to me, but I would just as soon watch paint dry.

I must confess that I find some art and some ethnography boring and some exciting. I never could get into *Gravety's Rainbow*, though my wife swears by it. I know Joyce's *Ulysses* is a great work, but I can't get into it. Or Jane Austen. But I once spent an afternoon absorbed in an ethnography of Timbuktu.

Fiction writers are obliged to try not to bore their readers; ethnographers can be irritatingly indifferent to their audience and use the most atrocious obfuscatory language. Among the most obfuscatory and boring writers of modern anthropology, by the way, are those who discovered that they were writing rhetoric. Richard de Mille suggests that Castaneda perpetrated his hoaxes because the competition was too great in the fiction market. Castaneda's stories are short on plot, lack detail, have unconvincing characters who never develop and who show stereotyped emotions, and have nothing in the way of human relations. That is not good fiction—it would never sell—but it makes pretty good reading as fact because readers love supposedly true adventures, even if they aren't well written.

In fiction, the ideas of truth are a little different, and that is why Pratt didn't understand the big flap about authenticity in anthropology. John Gardner, in his book about writing, *The Art of Fiction*,[14] suggests that telling truth in fiction can mean one of several things: being factually correct, being coherent so that it does not feel like lying, or affirming a moral truth about human existence. Like Pratt, he considers authenticity to be trivial, except in creating an appearance of truth that makes a story interesting and compelling (what literary people call "verisimilitude"). He regards validity—making the story fit a cultural framework—as more important. Universal morality he appreciates as the highest form of truth, the goal of art.

This highest truth, as any anthropologist will tell you, is cultural. But reality is just there. Science is the job of trying to match the two. Skarp-Hedin was affirming a truth when he chopped out Thrain's teeth, but his actions would not be considered quite so praiseworthy today. Skarp-Hedin would wind up pleading insanity and hoping to get committed to an asylum rather than death row. But to know that, we have to know something about our culture and other cultures; and to know those things, we have to describe and understand them; and to do that, we have to tell truth as best we can, as Galileo did. Other people and their actions, thoughts, words, and deeds are realities that anthropologists try to understand.

Ethnographers, if they are honest and authentic, must be willing to say, "If you don't believe our stories, you can go there yourself and see for yourself." They have to believe that if you do what they did you will see the same things. So the stories to establish authenticity are more than just figures of speech or rhetorical tactics or ploys—tropes, as they say— or they are no less so than any other such rhetoric of any scientific report. And to say that everything is a trope is about as enlightening as to say that we speak in prose. Sometimes people do go and check others' work, and sometimes, though not all the time, it leads to disputes about who was using the better telescope because different people may present equally valid and equally authentic but different pictures of what they saw.

Try it out sometime. You and two of your friends each get cameras and all go to an event like a wedding or a carnival or a graduation—anything at all. Then compare the pictures you took. You all will have been at the same place with the same people, but I will bet that you each took different pictures to emphasize different things. This is one reason different anthropologists can tell different stories—they concentrate on different things. (This may be what was at stake in the differences between Oscar Lewis and Robert Redfield in their understandings of Mexican peasant life.)[15] On the other hand, maybe you went to different weddings and one was in Texas and the other in New Jersey. Or maybe you are comparing pictures from this year's wedding with your grandfather's wedding. There can also be differences of time and location.

The more precisely you can tell people what you did, the better they can try to see things the way you saw them. That is the reason anthropologists have to spend some time on methodology—talking about how they know what they are talking about (to establish reliability), as well as theory. Methodology is the framework for validity.

If everything is a cultural construct and all ethnographic accounts are stories like any other kind of science, does it make any difference whether we make them up in libraries or in some foreign place? Isn't one story as good as another?

Remember that inauthentic ethnographies depend on authentic ones. The only reason people can make up ethnography in a library is that someone did the real job of description before. Without that kind of aid they could not move beyond the imaginative limits of their own culture and would have to write poor fiction rather than fake ethnography.

How you judge a story depends on what you want it for. If its only job is to amuse you, then popular television writing will win over any academic or scientific writing any day of the week. That is what makes popular writing and television popular. Maybe that is why academic writers are so poorly paid. If you are trying to get from Europe to America or Asia, or from the earth to the moon, you need a different kind of story. If you want the kind of story that makes a computer work, you don't ask how amusing it is, you ask how well it works.

And so it is for understanding other cultures and your own culture. That which leaves you with the most authentic and valid account is the best ethnography. That is the ethnography upon which you can

base a sound search for those higher truths. Ask anyone who has tried to understand your culture and its moral truths. Talk to some foreign students as they are getting used to American ways and see what they tell you. You will be surprised at what surprises them.

One young woman confided to me her amusement on hearing at an orientation session that Americans were very conscious of smells in their love lives. She laughed as she regaled me with stories she had heard and this whole new dimension of social relations she had never thought about before. In the United States, that is the foundation for a whole neurosis and the industry based on it. While Icelanders think Americans silly to bathe every day, Thai think Americans uncouth for bathing only once a day.

When you see yourself through others' eyes, you never see what you thought you would see, what you see through your own eyes. Watching yourself in a video is an alienating experience. You don't look like you thought you would. The person holding the camera didn't see things the way you saw them.

Horace Miner wrote an essay called "Body Ritual among the Nacirema," which was published in 1956 in the *American Anthropologist*.[16] "Nacirema" is "American" spelled backwards. In the article, he describes how Americans brush their teeth as he imagines an anthropologist might describe this ritual. It seems strange because he puts it in a different context than we do when we brush our teeth. So ethnographic accounts often have an air of strangeness about them to the people they describe. Different people see things differently—that is one of the great lessons of anthropology. Texans, for instance, didn't much like Michener's treatment of their state in his novel. But Texans didn't like Ferber's *Giant* either. Only a Texan, they argue, can really understand the uniqueness of that people and that land. Anything that doesn't agree with our own self images, anything that doesn't confirm the rightness of our own prejudices and opinions, we are likely to dismiss as wrongheaded at worst or innocent fiction at best. Texans say they are heirs to a proud historical tradition, while others see this kind of attitude as boorish, ethnocentric bigotry.

If you are an athlete and your coach tells you how to improve your stroke, your serve, the swing of your golf club, your gait when you are running, or how to hold the bat to hit the ball, you can view the tapes, concede that you don't look to others as you imagined you did, and listen to your coach's advice. Your game will improve. Or you can insist that your view is the only right one and suffer the consequences. It is your choice. It is the same in music, writing, art, computer science, engineering . . . you name it. And it is our choice. We may not like what de Toqueville said about America, but it might help us to listen, whether we like the story or not, whether it is amusing or not.

Three of my favorite writers died on motorcycles. One of them, C. Wright Mills, was a sociologist. He wrote that ordinary people felt they were living in traps because of large social forces beyond their control. To understand a person's life or the history of his or her society, you have to understand both together.[17] Another, John Gardner, wrote fiction and also wrote about writing fiction. He wrote that fiction seeks out truth. We cannot sort universals into moral codes, but fiction interests us because it helps us learn how the world works, how we and all other human beings can resolve conflicts we share, what values we agree with, and what the moral risks are. He said that a writer who cannot distinguish truth from a peanut butter sandwich can't write good fiction.[18] The third, T. E. Lawrence, wrote something that was sociology, fiction, history, and autobiography as well.[19] All three of these men met the same end. Maybe we should learn to wear helmets when we get on motorcycles.

Some of my favorite writers are still alive. Halldor Laxness is an Icelandic novelist who wrote with such precision that I once despaired that he left nothing for anthropologists to do—regarding Iceland, at least.[20] Like Texans, Icelanders didn't much like his writing, until he won a Nobel prize. Then it was OK because foreigners thought it was good. Richard Condon wrote the definitive work on economics in his novel *Money Is Love*.[21] Miles Richardson is an anthropologist who captured what it is to be an anthropologist.[22]

Richardson talks about how he became an anthropologist and how anthropologists accuse each other of every imaginable sin. He wonders how to explain such accusations when they contrast so with the image of anthropologists as people who are sympathetic to differences. He talks about doing fieldwork and the conditions of fieldwork—that we have to drop the idea that the world is the same as it was for Malinowski seventy years ago. We have to accept the contemporary world on its own terms. When we do this, we can begin to see clearly, we can listen carefully, and we can hear what we must. There are different ways to listen, as there are different ways to take photographs. We can be detached; we can be revolutionaries, bureaucrats, apologists. There are a lot of ambiguities because of the differences in power among people and among peoples and countries.

How can we get anything out of this enterprise besides a bunch of equally good if not equally entertaining "just-so" stories? Richardson says that there is another way to think of anthropology—something like what Gardner had in mind for writers: They are myth-tellers, people who stand on the edge of the society in the outer darkness, away from the hot glow of the campfires that comfort us, and tell the myth of humanity with skill and passion. We cannot falsify what we are. We work with all the pieces of the puzzles we have: what we can develop, what our predecessors developed, what our students are developing. We try to understand it all. We stand between the most and the least powerful social orders and feel the tensions. To tell the story well, Richardson says, we need the passion of the radical, the detachment of the scientist, and the practicality of the liberal. That is our job, he concludes—to tell the human story, to tell it well, to tell it truly.

But why does Richardson call it a myth, this story of our selves and our fellow humans? Isn't it a "just so" story, along with all the other myths science banishes with its valid and reliable analyses? He calls the story of humanity a myth not because it is untrue but because it reaches for that higher truth that Gardner spoke of. Such myths are true. Anthropology tells those stories, and it is up to us to tell them well and truly.

Notes

1. Anonymous, *Njal's Saga*, trans. Magnus Magnusson and Hermann Pálsson (New York: Penguin, 1960); Anonymous, *The Saga of Gunnlaugur Snake's Tongue with an Essay on the Structure and Translation of the Saga*, trans E. Paul Durrenberger and Dorothy Durrenberger (Rutherford, NJ: Fairleigh Dickinson University Press, 1992).

2. Ruth Benedict, *The Chrysanthemum and the Sword* (Boston: Houghton Mifflin, 1946).

3. Bronislaw Malinowski, *Argonauts of the Western Pacific: An Account of Native Enterprise and Adventure in the Archipelagoes of Melanesian New Guinea* (Prospect Heights, IL: Waveland Press, 1984; originally published in 1922).

4. Ibid.

5. Clifford Geertz, *The Interpretation of Cultures* (New York: Basic Books, 1973).

6. James Clifford and George E. Marcus, eds., *Writing Culture: The Poetics and Politics of Ethnography* (Berkeley: University of California Press, 1986).

7. Katherine N. Hayles, *Chaos Bound: Orderly Disorder in Contemporary Literature and Science* (Ithaca: Cornell University Press, 1990).

8. Geertz, *The Interpretation of Cultures*, p. 24.

9. Carlos Castaneda, *The Teachings of Don Juan: A Yaqui Way of Knowledge* (Berkeley: University of California Press, 1968).

10. Richard De Mille, *The Don Juan Papers: Further Castaneda Controversies* (1980; reprint Belmont, CA: Wadsworth Publishing, 1992).

11. Mary Louise Pratt, "Fieldwork in Common Places," in James Clifford and George E. Marcus, eds., *Writing Culture: The Poetics and Politics of Ethnography* (Berkeley: University of California Press, 1986), pp. 27–50.

12. E. Paul Durrenberger, *The Dynamics of Medieval Iceland: Political Economy and Literature* (Iowa City: University of Iowa Press, 1992).

13. Florinda Donner, *Shabono: A True Adventure in the Remote and Magical Heart of the South American Jungle* (New York: Laurel Books, 1982).

14. John Gardner, *The Art of Fiction* (New York: Alfred A. Knopf, 1984).

15. Robert Redfield, *Tepoztlán, a Mexican Village: A Study of Folk Life* (Chicago: University of Chicago Press, 1930); Oscar Lewis, *Life in a Mexican Village: Tepoztlán Restudied* (Urbana: University of Illinois Press, 1951).

16. Horace Miner, "Body Ritual among the Nacirema," *American Anthropologist* 58 (1956): 503–507.

17. C. Wright Mills, *The Sociological Imagination* (New York: Oxford University Press, 1959).

18. Gardner, *The Art of Fiction*.

19. T. E. Lawrence, *The Seven Pillars of Wisdom: A Triumph* (Garden City, NY: Doubleday, 1938).

20. Halldor Laxness, *Salka Valka*, trans. F. H. Lyon (London: George Allen & Unwin Ltd., 1936); Halldor Laxness, *Independent People* (New York: Alfred A. Knopf, 1946).

21. Richard Condon, *Money Is Love* (New York: Dial Press, 1975).

22. Miles Richardson, *Cry Lonesome and Other Accounts of the Anthropologist's Project* (Albany: State University of New York Press, 1990).

Suggested Readings

Condon, Richard. *Money Is Love*. New York: Dial Press, 1975. A novel that treats the mysteries of money and economic systems. Many of Condon's other novels are equally interesting.

Durrenberger, E. Paul. *The Dynamics of Medieval Iceland: Political Economy and Literature*. Iowa City: University of Iowa Press, 1992. Discusses the relationships between politics, economics, and literature in medieval Iceland.

Geertz, Clifford. *The Interpretation of Cultures*. New York: Basic Books, 1973. Not a very good book, definitely not well written, but anthropologists talk about it a lot. Read it some time if you want to see what they are talking about.

Hayles, Katherine N. *Chaos Bound: Orderly Disorder in Contemporary Literature and Science*. Ithaca: Cornell University Press, 1990. Discusses chaos theory.

Kuhn, Thomas S. *The Copernican Revolution: Planetary Astronomy in the Development of Western Thought*. New York: Vintage Books, 1957. Accessible discussion of astronomy in European cultures. Shows how Ptolemaic astronomy made sense with the observations they had at that time and how sun-centered theories made no more sense than earth-centered ones. This is a good portrayal of the relationship between facts and theories and how ideas about astronomy influenced other areas of thought. Kuhn later wrote the influential book *Structure of Scientific Revolutions*. Chicago: University of Chicago Press, 1962.

Malinowski, Bronislaw. *Argonauts of the Western Pacific: An Account of Native Enterprise and Adventure in the Archipelagoes of Melanesian New Guinea*. 1922; reprint Prospect Heights, IL: Waveland Press, 1984. Better than you might guess as a book just to read and a classic of anthropology. Good summer vacation book.

Mills, C. Wright. *The Sociological Imagination*. New York: Oxford University Press, 1959. Mills is a good writer. His work is generally accessible, no nonsense, to the point, sensible, and necessary reading for anyone going on in anthropology or any social science.

Richardson, Miles. *Cry Lonesome and Other Accounts of the Anthropologist's Project*. Albany: State University of New York Press, 1990. The best account of what it is like to be an anthropologist.

"Are Ethnographies 'Just So' Stories?"

E. Paul Durrenberger

1) What is a cultural artifact? How is anthropology possibly a cultural artifact?

2) Is science a culture-free enterprise? Why or why not?

3) What does the author and western science mean by the terms validity, reliability, and authenticity?

4) How do anthropologists establish the validity and authenticity of their research?

5) What is "myth" and what purpose does it serve in all cultures?

6) Why does the author call anthropologists "myth tellers"? What does he mean by this expression?

7) Define and discuss an American or western myth. How would you interpret that myth in the light of Durrenberger's article?

SPOILED SPORTS

Sports Centered: Why Our Obsession Has Ruined the Game, and How We Can Save It

Jay Weiner

How far back must we go to remember that sports matter? How deeply into our personal and national pasts must we travel to recall that we once cared?

Do we have to return to 1936? Adolf Hitler tried to make the Olympics into a propaganda machine for anti-Semitism and racism. In that case, American track star Jesse Owens, demonstrating that the master race could be mastered at racing, stole Hitler's ideological show. Were not sports a vehicle of significant political substance then?

Or should we return to 1947 and Jackie Robinson? A baseball player integrated our "national pastime" a year before the U.S. Army considered African Americans equal. Robinson's barrier-break may have been largely based on ticket-selling economics for the Brooklyn Dodgers' owners, but didn't sports do something good?

Their fists raised, their dignity palpable, track stars Tommie Smith and John Carlos spread the American black power and student protest movements to the world when they stood on the victory stand at the 1968 Olympics in Mexico City. Politics and sports mixed beautifully then.

Remember when tennis feminist Billie Jean King took on an old fart named Bobby Riggs in 1973, boldly bringing the women's movement to the playing fields? That moment of sports theater stirred up sexual politics as much as any Betty Friedan essay or Miss America bra burning could ever do.

Sports had meaning. And sports were accessible.

Remember when your grandfather or your uncle—maybe your mother—took you to a game when you were a little kid? The hot dog was the best. The crowd was mesmerizing. The colors were bright. The crack of the bat under the summer sun, or the autumn chill wrapped around that touchdown run, was unforgettable. Back then, some nobody became your favorite player, somebody named Johnny Callison or Hal Greer or Clarence Peaks or Vic Hadfield, someone who sold cars in the off-season and once signed autographs for your father's men's club for a $50 appearance fee. Those "heroes" were working-class stiffs, just like us.

Now you read the sports pages—or, more exactly, the business and crime pages—and you realize you've disconnected from the institution and it from you. Sports is distant. It reeks of greed. Its politics glorify not the majestic drama of pure competition, but a drunken, gambling masculinity epitomized by sports-talk radio, a venue for obnoxious boys on car phones.

How can we reconcile our detachment from corporatized pro sports, professionalized college sports—even out-of-control kids' sports—with our appreciation for athleticism, with our memories? And how, after we sort it all out, can we take sports back?

Part of the problem is that we want sports to be mythological when, in our hearts, we know they aren't. So reclaiming sports requires that we come to grips with our own role in the myth-making. Owens, Robinson, Smith, Carlos, and King played to our highest ideals and so have been enshrined in our sports pantheon. But we've also made heroes of some whose legacies are much less clearcut. Take Joe Namath, the 1960s quarterback who represented sexual freedom, or Bill Walton, the 1970s basketball hippie who symbolized the alienated white suburban Grateful Dead sports antihero. Neither deserves the reverence accorded Owens or Robinson or even King, but both captured the essence of their era. Or how about relief pitcher Steve Howe, who symbolized the evils of drug addiction in the 1980s, or Mike Tyson, who currently plays the archetypal angry black male? No less than Tommie Smith and John Carlos, these anti-icons were emblematic of their age.

It may be discomfiting, but it's true: The power of sports and sports heroes to mirror our own aspirations have also contributed to the sorry state of the institution today. The women's sports movement Billie Jean King helped create proved a great leap forward for female athletes, but it also created a generation of fitness consumers, whose appetite for Nikes and Reeboks created a new generation of Asian sweatshops.

Fans applauded the courage of renegade Curt Flood, the St. Louis Cardinals outfielder who in 1969 refused to be traded, arguing that baseball players should be free to play where they want to play. We cheered—all the way to the Supreme Court—his challenge to the cigar-smoking owners' hold on their pinstripe-knickered chattel. Now players can sell their services to the highest bidder, but their astronomical salaries—deserved or not—alienate us from the games as much as the owners' greed.

The greed isn't new, of course. The corporate betrayal of the fan is as traditional as the seventh-inning stretch. The Boston Braves moved to Milwaukee in 1953, and the Dodgers and New York Giants fled to

California in 1958, for money, subsidized facilities, and better TV contracts. But what has always been a regrettable by-product of sports has suddenly become its dominant ethos. Our worship of sports and our worship of the buck have now become one and the same. So it shouldn't surprise us that we get the heroes we expect—and maybe deserve.

So how do we as a society reclaim sports from the corporate entertainment behemoth that now controls it? Some modest proposals:

Deprofessionalize college and high school sports.

Let's ban college athletic scholarships in favor of financial aid based on need, as for any other student. And let's keep high school athletics in perspective. Why should local news coverage of high school sports exceed coverage given to the band, the debating society, or the science fair? Sports stars are introduced to the culture of athletic privilege at a very young age.

Allow some form of public ownership of professional sports teams.

Leagues and owners ask us to pay for the depreciating asset of a stadium but give us no share of the appreciating asset of a franchise. Lease agreements between teams and publicly financed stadiums should also include enforceable community-involvement clauses.

Make sports affordable again.

Sports owners call their games "family entertainment." For whose family? Bill Gates? Owners whose teams get corporate subsidies should set aside 20 percent of their tickets at prices no higher than a movie admission. And, like any other business feeding at the public trough, they should be required to pay livable wages even to the average schmoes who sell hot dogs.

Be conscious of the messages sport is sending.

Alcohol-related advertising should be banned from sports broadcasting. Any male athlete convicted of assaulting a woman should be banned from college and pro sports. Fighting in a sports event should be at least a misdemeanor and maybe a felony, rather than a five-minute stay in the penalty box.

Let's take the sports establishment by its lapels and shake it back toward us. Because even with all the maddening messages of male dominance, black servility, homophobia, corporate power, commercialism,

and brawn over brains, sports still play an important role in many lives. When we watch a game, we are surrounded by friends and family. There are snacks and beverages. We sit in awe of the players' remarkable skills. We can't do what they do. They extend our youth. The tension of the competition is legitimate. The drama is high.

And therein lies the essence of modern American sport. It's a good show, albeit bread and circuses. And we just can't give it up. So why not take it back for ourselves as best we can, looking for ways to humanize an institution that mirrors our culture, understanding that those who own sport won't give it up without a fight, knowing that we like it too much to ever just walk away.

Religion? Science? Or Just Plain Fun?

Gerald Early

The appeal of sports, especially of high-performance athletics, is that they permit us to judge people precisely by what they do. This greatly simplifies life because it greatly simplifies the search for meaning. We might be interested in motives—the athlete's, the spectator's—but our primary interest is in a moment of action that either fails or succeeds. That the action is not merely physical but is indeed an extremely strenuous, intensely ritualized rendition of a highly developed physical skill makes it all the more definitive because meaning becomes, in this way, strikingly specific and discernible, explicit and self-evident. The body is given not simply an artistry, an expression, as in dance, but rather a goal. Sports do not etherealize the body but make it more concrete.

Sports are about the finality of the consequences of an action or a set of actions, the immediate, intractable drama of making a physical but deliberative choice upon which one's fate rests. Thus, sports make human life a metaphysical expression intelligible both as a higher purpose and as an absurd futility in ways that religion, for instance, cannot.

But even more important is the connection between sports and science. Sports provide a context for demonstrating the rationally engineered human body. This suggests something about the values that sports represent and reflect in the modern world. Sports are not a science, but they could not be played and enjoyed today without science. Sports are all the things religion and science as mystery and measurement aspire to be in the realm of the human imagination; and so, in many ways, for purposes of expression, sports are better than either. They are magnificent junctures of spectacle and explanation, of ritual and reason.

Sports, finally, are about our hope for order and, paradoxically, our realization that our hope will be dashed. This is why, ultimately, sports are such powerful attractions. What attracts us is the contradiction of trying to find a sense of permanence in an ephemeral, contrived, minor expression of the human will. Buried in the activity of play are innocence and experience, triumph and tragedy.

If we train like athletes, we believe, we can protect our bodies against the relentlessly encroaching chaos of decline and unbeing. The body, after all, is the last frontier, and our history has been merely the projection of insecurities about our physical presence. If this is so, sports may be the greatest religious experience, the most refined and profound encounter we can ever hope to have with the reality and the unreality of ourselves.

Sold Out, From Team Booster to TV Backdrop: The Demise of the True Fan

Susan Faludi

On the evening of December 17, 1995, Big Dawg staggered through the door, past his wife, Mary, and collapsed on the couch in their tiny living room. An hour earlier, Mary had seen him on television. Now, she described how the cameras moved in for close-ups when he started crying. He shrugged. "I don't mind it," he said, his voice a monotone.

All day long, the reporters had been on him. They had "mugged" him in the parking lot and followed him into the bleachers. "There were so many out-of-town reporters," he said. "Gary Myers from HBO, and the *Daily News, The New York Times*, the top guys from ESPN. It took me an hour to get a hundred yards." In the stands, three reporters sat with him the entire game, monitoring his every emotion, and wherever he looked, he found himself staring down the barrel of a camera lens. When they asked for his feelings on this, the final day, he stuck with an appropriately updated version of his trusty reply: "Today, it all ended and my best friend died." This was how Big Dawg, aka John Thompson, described the final game that his beloved Cleveland Browns were ever going to play in Municipal Stadium.

The football team's owner, Art Modell, was moving the languishing 50-year-old franchise to Baltimore, where he had struck a sugar plum deal dripping with juicy perks, tax breaks, and government subsidies that guaranteed him an income of $30 million a year regardless of the team's performance or the size of the crowds. The "employees"—the players—would come with him. But he was leaving the fans behind.

Big Dawg was not just any Browns fan. He was the self-avowed leader of the Dawg Pound, a rabid pack of men who had turned the decrepit bleachers by the stadium's east end zone into a barking kennel, a howling Greek chorus accompanying the action on the field. "I like to think that the Dawg Pounders are the 12th man," Big Dawg liked to say. Big referred to his weight, which hovered around 385 pounds, setting him apart from D. Dawg and Junkyard Dawg, Jam Dawg, Sick Dawg, and Ugly Dawg. For years, most of these men (they were almost all men) had presided over every home game in dog masks and floppy, fake-fur dog ears, greeting every play with a brandishing of foam and rawhide bones, raining dog biscuits onto the field, and offering up a perpetual cacophony of woofs and yelps. Displaying "how they felt," you might say, was their *raison d'être*. And this had been their last performance.

"We won the game," Big Dawg recalled later, "but I sat around after like we had lost." He was hard-pressed to put a name to the nature of his particular loss, although he knew that it was irrevocable and, in some strange way, the source of unspeakable personal shame. He was certain of only one thing. "I want to win," he said, and he looked up at the ceiling wringing his hands as if imploring some deity on high. "I want to win so bad."

Football has been a part of American male ritual since the 1890s. It was first embraced on the college gridiron during the great imperial and masculine anxieties of the turn of the century. Its founding father, Walter Camp, was a clock company executive for whom the new sport represented, according to historian Michael Oriard, "the ideal training ground for a managerial elite" who would run a new business world of trusts and combines.

But in those prewar days, football had another face as well, one more familiar on the factory floor than in the company boardroom. Pro football, as opposed to college football, was the sport of the steelworker, the ironworker, and the miner, whose faces, long before they were helmeted and smeared with anti-reflective face paint, had been covered with the soot and sweat of manual labor. This version of the game emerged on the soggy, snowbound fields of America's heavy-industrial belt, in gritty contests between underfunded teams with names like the Ironton Tanks and the Providence Steam Roller. In the imaginations of their fans, the players on these gridirons were right out of WPA murals, monumental stone-faced workers come to life and playing out a gruntlike drama on a muddy swath of land under the frosted skies of smokestack America.

Conventional wisdom said that spectators flocked to football stadiums precisely because the drama there celebrated an ascendant American power and authority that they identified with. They were reveling in their nation's empire building, and the more they saw, the more it whetted their appetites. But the fans' relationship to the game was never that conveniently straightforward. For the working-class spectator, "supporting" his team was also a way of fighting against marginalization, a way of clinging to the idea that national destiny was still something played out by common men on a muddy field, even in an era dominated by skyboxes, television, and Astroturf.

"One of the great mistakes of superficial observers is to believe that players do all the work while fans merely sit passive and 'vicariously' have things done for them," philosopher and sports devotee Michael Novak has written, describing his own experience watching football as "an ordeal, an exercise, a struggle lived through." Football was a workingman's way of resisting being sidelined, even as he sat in the stands. Here he might still believe himself a central "player" in one of his culture's central dramas. He would be ill-prepared for his ultimate marginalization when the transformation of a sport pumped up by TV and ad revenues, and geared largely to America's sports bars and living rooms, revealed just how passive and insignificant a force he was to his team's fortunes.

The Cleveland Browns were hardly the first team to pull up stakes, but their fans had especially good reasons to dread "The End," as Big Dawg called it. The Browns represented a pro football tradition grounded in loyalty, stoicism, and industry, and conceived in the rivalry of two steelworker communities 50 miles south of Cleveland. The American Professional Football Association, the direct forerunner of the National Football League, was organized in a garage in Canton, Ohio, now home to the Pro Football Hall of Fame. Paul Brown, the founding coach of the Browns, was raised in neighboring Massillon, his father a dispatcher on the railroads that hauled the fruits of industrial labor out of town. At Massillon's Washington High School, in the depths of the Depression, coach Brown created a brand of play that would earn him the title "father of modern pro football." He also created something else at Massillon: the modern football fan.

The meaning of that creation was made clear to me by a 62-year-old Massillonian named Phil Glick.

A 1951 Washington High School graduate, Glick had been a lifelong parts sizer at Timken Roller Bearing Company in Canton until 1992, when he opted for early retirement over the risk of being laid off: He was also a fan extraordinaire whose devotion to his high school football team, the Massillon Tigers, led to his election as president of the Massillon Tigers Football Booster Club.

His vintage boosterism had less to do with spectatorship or expropriation of the players' fame than with community service—being known for doing something useful and supportive. The Massillon boosters weren't "fans" as we now understand the word; they were care providers, and the recipients of their care were young athletes. "It's sort of like Big Brothers, except with a player," Glick explained of the Sideliners, the first Massillon booster club he helped guide. Each Sideliner "adopts" a player, becoming a surrogate father who is responsible for the boy's needs and there to help him when he is in trouble. Some Sideliners help with homework; some make sure their players are properly clothed and provided for; others offer postgraduation advice.

Sports fans as paternal providers was Paul Brown's notion. When the town fathers were invested in the young men's welfare, Brown calculated, they also would be invested in the team's future, and he was right. Brown had given the men of Massillon a special paternal stake in the game. Every Monday night, he would show the Booster Club films of the previous game and ruminate with them about the upcoming contest. At one point, interest was so great that 2,500 fans showed up for an outdoor briefing.

The team repaid fan devotion with a legendary record that elevated Massillon to "the capital of high school football in the nation." In the nine years Paul Brown coached them, the Tigers won 80 games and lost only 8. Six times the Tigers prevailed in the Ohio State championships and twice they were named national champions. When Brown finally left in 1940 for a coaching job at Ohio State, it was on the wings of a 33-game winning streak.

While the townsmen reclaimed their breadwinning roles with the Depression's end, supporting the team gave them something assembly-line jobs at the steel mills didn't: a sense that they were more than cogs in a corporate machine. To the Tigers Boosters, the team belonged to them—its triumphs were legitimately theirs. It put their small town on the map at a time when national manufacturers, national brands, and national entertainment were beginning to erase small-town identities. "The proprietors in town explain it this way," a local accountant commented: "Some poor guy might work eight hours a day down the street at the steel mill and be a nobody, but for 10 weeks every fall, he's a king because he's from Massillon."

For a man to have a hand in the making of a team's fortunes, at a time when the making of everything else was fast slipping out of his grasp, was the root of what it meant to be a "fan." He could, in the common parlance, help "build a winner." The field became an artisan's workshop where products could still be made locally and custom crafted.

In 1946, Brown took his winning formula to Cleveland, and fans there would prove as intensely devoted and ecstatically loyal as those he left in Massillon. But as the years passed, a painful role reversal would take place. It was evident in a large photograph framed and hanging behind the desk of Robert Gries, Jr., who was, like his father before him, a minority owner of the Browns. A passionate Clevelander whose family's philanthropic and civic commitment to the city spans five generations, Gries divested himself of his holdings in the team rather than profit from the move to Baltimore. While we spoke in his office one afternoon, Gries rose and turned to study a photograph on the wall—a black-and-white shot from a 1953 game at Municipal Stadium. "This was the first time the stadium was full for a football game. And look at it. What do you see? There's something here that's very different."

The hats? I ventured. Because every man—and the stands were virtually all male—was wearing a fedora, along with a suit and tie.

"Yes, it's the hats," Gries said, eyes still fixed on the photo. "Hats and suits. And this was in the end zone." The very seats to which the Dawg Pounders would eventually lay claim.

Gries' father was part of the original group of men who first organized in 1936 to bring football to Cleveland. His father's motives, Gries recalled, were "civic, totally civic. My father was not a 'fan'". Nor were his motives fiscal. "There wasn't money in football in those days. It was the idea of bringing something to Cleveland."

Much later, a crucial difference between those fedoras and the bill caps of today would strike me. The fedora was the haberdashery of a man in a position to give an adult man with some sense of his value and purpose in a civic society into which he blended seamlessly. The cap was the garb of a boy, a manchild still waiting for his inheritance, still hoping to be ushered in by the male authorities and given a sign, a badge, perhaps a fedora, to indicate his induction into adult society. The Massillon boosters had

backed their team with such enthusiasm because it was a way literally to give a boost, a leg up, to the next generation; they had embraced their role as supporters because it allowed them to father a team. A generation later, fans like Big Dawg were seeking exactly the opposite; they were looking for a team to father them. For these new-era fans, the hope was that the team would be their boosters.

The members of the original Browns team had entered football older, many of them already experienced in the world of work, not to mention the cauldron of war. They weren't depending on football to be their masculine crucible. But a younger generation joining the Browns in the late 1950s and early 1960s had come of age under the shadow of the postwar corporation, and they had a more vulnerable, more uneasy relationship to a "master organizer" like Paul Brown. They didn't feel like good soldiers, they felt like impotent yes-men. They came directly from school, not war, and resented Brown's acting *in loco parentis*. Most of them had arrived at training camp expecting that inside its gates lay the key to adult recognition, which the coach would deliver.

So the players rebelled against and eventually overthrew Paul Brown, and adopted a big brother in his place: Art Modell, who bought the Browns in 1961 for the then-unheard-of price of $4 million. He was only 35, and his claim to fame heretofore had been producing, in 1949, New York's first daytime television show, *Melodies*, which played on TV sets installed in supermarkets to whet the consumer appetites of female shoppers.

Modell was thrilled to be in the presence of these young American centurions and, unlike Paul Brown, he was accessible and adoring, more like one of the boys than a father figure. He acted at first like a boy with an autograph book—"a goggle-eyed fan," as Bernie Parrish put it, "overly impressed with us as players."

As a TV producer, Modell understood that the future of football lay in the medium that would eventually command every team owner's loyalties. Modell would become a key player in brokering the ascendance of football as a televised sport; he chaired the National Football League's television committee for 31 years. He helped create *Monday Night Football*. He was in on the breakthrough $14 million sale of TV rights to CBS in 1964, and helped to negotiate a four-year, $656 million deal with the networks in 1977—the first time the league earned more from television than from ticket sales.

The new media culture changed the way the game was played and the relationship not only between the sport and its players but also between the sport and its fans. In the new relationship, the players would be the superstars and the fans their wide-eyed idolizers. The players were to become the flyboys, the astronauts, and all that was left for the average fan to do, it seemed, was watch from his living room couch.

In the process, the players—not just in football but in baseball and basketball as well—would gain much. No longer could owners keep them for their short careers in a state of near peonage, controlling their every move. Now, players found themselves in a lively labor market where they could bargain and negotiate.

Television and ad money had decoupled them from servitude, but also from the very idea of "the team," from any concept of loyalty to anything except perhaps their own agents, their own careers, their own images. But the freer many of them became, the less independent they often felt. To market themselves, after all, they were forced to market images of themselves in a culture where sports was increasingly just that—a series of images played and replayed between all the car and beer ads in the living rooms of America. It was no mistake that the new sports "stars" like Browns fullback Jim Brown would sometimes go on to act in Hollywood movies or would become TV sports announcers and personalities introducing the next generation of stars—and their media—wise quirks—to the public.

Much has been written about how televised football sliced the game into consumable bits sandwiched between commercials, forced the use of injurious Astroturf because it was prettier to look at, turned the sport into a big-stakes money machine, and so forth. But what did it do to the fans?

At first, the only "fans" who seemed to have a visible role were the cheerleaders. It was no coincidence that at the same time football began to be televised, the male "yell captains" of college football were replaced with pom-pom girls. By the late 1970s, most pro football teams had a corps of cheerleaders, none so extravagantly unclothed as the Dallas Cowboys', who became a business institution in their own right, complete with a line of costume jewelry and trading cards. The yell captains had connected the fans with the action on the field, but the pom-pom girls became an entertainment concession at the service of the cameras. Meanwhile, the new male fans, the ones the advertisers salivated over, were increasingly not in the stands. By the 1980s, many of them would be huddled at sports bars, gazing up like so many worshippers at the TV pulpit posted over their heads, framed by Bud Lite signs. The boosters were long gone. Reshaped in Modell's own image would be the "goggle-eyed fan." Which is to say that, in the end,

the fans would be betrayed by one of their own.

The stadiums would increasingly become the preserves of an upper crust as ticket prices rose out of the range of the average working-class salary. The men pro football had originally promised to speak for and glorify—the hardworking factory workers of what was now becoming the rust belt—were the ones most shut out and turned off in the transition to an electronic age. Football's television viewers were more white-collar, middle-management, and suburban—more likely to have the wherewithal to buy the high-ticket items being advertised on-screen than the traditional working-class ethnic audience. Paul Brown had started out seeking to elevate pro football into a "high-class" realm. From the beginning in Massillon, class transformation had been a tacit part of the program of the boosters who were football's founding fans. But instead of pulling up the working-class community that football represented, the Modells of the sport left those who belonged to that world behind.

This betrayal of the sports boosters did not, however, come without a fight—especially in Cleveland, where the fans were unwilling to relinquish a longstanding relationship. But, as the team entered the 1990s, the fans who had donned dog faces and hard hats found themselves face to face with a truth they had been desperately trying to dodge. The battle now was for the camera's attention. The show of hard hats, of dog suits, of toughing it out in the rain and the snow, in the end became exactly that—a show, a beauty contest of sorts, where the object was to attract the camera with bizarre caricatures of working stiffs. They, too, had become just more entertaining images for the real fans of this new age, the consumers watching TV.

Take Me Out of Their Ball Game: Too Many Parents Spoil the Play

Maria Guhde Keri

My son's baseball team had just lost their last game of the season—they were out of the tournament. We losing parents tried our best to look glum, while the winning parents attempted to hide their jealousy. By the time we arrived at our cars, the lucky losers were excitedly discussing vacations we could take, projects we could begin, and friends we could finally see. Baseball season was over! We were free!

"At least until soccer season," one mom reminded us. "We're playing football this year," another added, rolling her eyes, and I couldn't block an image of parents and children all suited up in matching football uniforms, complete with pads. As a veteran sports mom, I knew exactly why she had used the plural we.

When one child in the family plays a sport, it is indeed a family affair. I think maybe the team photos should include us parents, derrieres parked in lawn chairs, arms laden with water bottles, diaper bags, and Barbie carry-alls.

We want to be there for our kids, to take an interest in what's important to them. This is what good parents do, right? Maybe. When I was young, kids rode their bikes or were dropped off for their games and practices. Only later would Mom or Dad ask how it went. My father was a coach, but I don't remember being dragged along to my brother's games. In fact, the kids on my dad's teams would converge on our house to be driven to the games in our 12-seater station wagon. No parents required.

Sometimes I think that by being so involved in our kids' sports, we dilute their experience. After all, it's not *their* win, it's *our* win. Do all the valuable lessons—losing, striking out, missing the winning shot—have the same impact when Mom and Dad are there to immediately say it's OK?

Of course, we need to make sure Michael is listening to the coach and the coach is listening to Michael, and to ensure that Lauren is getting off the bench but not being pushed too hard. And psycho sports parents are obviously a problem: the dad who screams at his son for every fumble, the mom who reacts to the 14-year-old umpire's bad call as if it were a threat to world peace. We know they are wacko.

But then there are the rest of us, the good parents. Are we cramping our kids' style? Maybe they just want to get together and play a game.

Did you ever walk into a room where kids are playing, say, a board game? They're animated, excited, totally focused on what they're doing. When you appear, they stiffen, grow quiet, and appear confused. An adult is watching, and suddenly the game and the rules are changed—maybe even ruined. Now imagine 40 of us adults descending on a ball game. Do we really believe we make it more fun for our children?

I'm essentially a non-athlete; my only "sport" was cheerleading. I don't remember my mother ever coming to my games, much less shouting from the stands "Good, honey, but smile more!" or "Doing great, but you were late on that last turn." I think I would have told her to either shut up or stay home.

And don't the siblings deserve a well-balanced, un-rushed dinner once in a while? To play in their own neighborhood, their own yard? What are they learning when life revolves around Lauren's soccer games, and family harmony ranks a distant second?

Maybe we parents should be doing more constructive things: cutting the lawn, painting the dining room,

volunteering, writing a book—in short, getting a life instead of just driving our children to theirs. Our time is important, too; we need to show our children that moms and dads can and need to do more than watch. Certainly, our involvement depends on our children's ages and personalities. My 5-year-old T-ball player will surely not be so enthusiastic about my seeing his every hit when he is 15. My 8-year-old daughter, on the other hand, already seems relieved when we miss one of her soccer games. Somewhere there is a perfect balance between not caring at all and caring too much. As parents, we know that at some point we need to make it *their* game, *their* recital, *their* grades. If we share every element of their lives, we're cheating them out of part of it.

We need to shut up. And sometimes—not always—we need to stay home. As hard as it is to risk missing her first home run, or not being there to comfort him after the missed foul shot, at some point we need to take ourselves out of their ball game. Because this is what good parents do.

Can Women Save Sports?: As the Prices Rise, the Passion Could Fade—Or Maybe Not

Mary Jo Kane

When the U.S. women's soccer team won the World Cup last summer, *People* magazine gushed about the refreshing contrast these "clean-cut and entirely charming" young women with "unmistakable passion" provide to often chemically enhanced, money-hungry, professional male athletes. Even *Sports Illustrated,* noting with sexist surprise how quickly the team became a national conversation piece, dubbed them "Queens of the World."

Female stars are emerging in basketball, too. And female college athletes earn better grades and get into less trouble than their male counterparts. But can women save sports? Writer Lynette Lamb posed this and other questions to Mary Jo Kane, director of the University of Minnesota's Tucker Center for Research on Girls & Women in Sport.

Women seem more interested in athletic thrill than money, which may make them better role models for fans and children. Will this change once women earn salaries and endorsement fees commensurate with men?

There will be some changes, but I don't think women will ever totally mimic male athletes, not because they are morally superior but because of sexism. We don't allow women the same degree of freedom. Will women athletes become less pure? Absolutely. But will four women players gang rape a young boy? Of course not. Money will corrupt to some degree, but the culture won't ever tolerate the same behavior from women that it tolerates from men.

Sports analyst Mariah Burton Nelson recently wrote a book about how fear of competition works to women's disadvantage. Why do you think that so many women—even some feminists—dislike competition?

Women have not been trained to be as competitive as men. Many women are comfortable with competition that honors self and opponent and in which the process is as important as the outcome. What most reject is competition as a zero-sum game in which the object is not just to win but to subdue, destroy, and humiliate the opponent. Women know what it is like to be degraded and humiliated. As norms change and being a female athlete is not only accepted but encouraged, women will become increasingly competitive.

What has been the greatest impact of Title IX, the 1972 law mandating equal access to sports for girls and women?

Title IX has given young women a sense of entitlement to sports. In one generation, the infrastructure, expectations, and values have changed so that if a girl is a good athlete and is willing to pay the price, there's a sport for her to play. But that sense of entitlement also has made young women forget their history. They don't know about the blood that has been shed and the careers that have been put on the line to get them where they are today.

Is Title IX in jeopardy today?

Everyone who has sued under Title IX has won. In 1998, the U.S. Supreme Court refused to hear a case appealing a Title IX decision, thus letting stand all previous decisions in favor of women. The only way to fight it is to change the law, which Title IX opponents are trying to do, using the language of affirmative action. It's true that some schools have dropped minor men's sports, such as gymnastics or wrestling, to pay for women's sports, but those decisions are not mandated by Title IX. Instead of cutting the outrageous expenditures they make on football and basketball, athletic directors claim they don't have enough money to add women's sports. By cutting minor men's sports, they succeed in pitting women against men, in distracting the public from looking at the outrageous expenditures in major men's sports, and in creating hostility against Title IX.

Why do women's sports inspire fury in some men?

That anger is the same felt by any group that has historically held a monopoly on an activity and is being asked to relinquish it. Men grow up believing that sport is the inherent birthright of being male, and that women need to earn the right to play. Their keen sense of ownership is behind their fierce resistance.

You frequently point out how the media portrays women athletes not as athletes but as sex symbols or nonthreatening moms and wives. Some women athletes are complicit in this. How can this troublesome aspect of women's sports coverage be changed?

To change that would be to strike at the very heart of sexist and homophobic attitudes in our culture. Sport is one of the most powerful institutions in this culture, because of its status and economic and political clout. There's a great deal at stake in sports participation, and the group that has monopolized sport doesn't want to give that up. They know that the best way to maintain control is to perceive the challenger as a second-class citizen. And the best way to discredit women athletes is to trivialize or marginalize their accomplishments—to focus on them as sexy or as moms. After all, if females are great athletes, then it's harder to say as a society that they shouldn't get press coverage, money, scholarships. But if they are portrayed as people who do sports in their spare time, or as merely pretty girls, it's much easier to deny them access and to maintain the status quo. It's obvious why women like (soccer player) Brandi Chastain agree to pose nude for magazines. She and others who participate this way are heavily rewarded by the culture. But in the final analysis, they aren't the ones responsible—those who produce the images are responsible. Why is it so important for *Gear* magazine, for example, to portray Chastain as a sex object? To say it's just about her is a simplistic analysis.

A recent Women's Sports Foundation report found that underfunding and gender inequities persist, demoralizing female athletes. What can concerned individuals do?

Our center's 1998 research found that because of the notion that sport belongs to men, there remain deep-seated and persistent barriers to girls in sport: gender stereotyping, sexism, and homophobia. Be aware of this in the media; call those editors and reporters, and pressure them to be more sensitive. Don't shortchange the women in your life by saying that men's sports are more important. And be sensitive to the decisions made at the local level. Women are not asking for a handout, we're asking for an investment. Just put the same investment in us that you put into men. Then we'll see what happens.

Playing for Keeps

Linda Mastandrea. Sprinter Linda Mastandrea holds two Olympic medals, but she didn't start racing until she was in her 20s. In fact, for the first part of her life, no one, including herself, thought she could ever be athletic.

"As a kid growing up with cerebral palsy, I couldn't run, I couldn't jump, I couldn't even walk very well," Mastandrea, 35, says. "So I spent a lot of time on the sidelines. People assumed sports were out of the picture for me."

Today, she's leading a campaign to raise the profile—and funding—of Paralympic athletics. An attorney and advocate in the Chicago office of the nonprofit America's Athletes with Disabilities, Mastandrea has been a member of the United States Olympic Committee (USOC) board of directors since 1998, and is using her position to be a "thorn in the side" of the other members, pushing and prodding them to provide equal funding and recognition for Paralympic athletes.

Her goals are numerous, but she's convinced they're attainable. They include securing funding and training facilities for disabled athletes, providing Paralympians with the option of joining the health insurance plan provided to able-bodied Olympians, and encouraging media attention and exposure for Paralympic events, which are currently held immediately following the closing ceremonies of the "real" Olympic Games.

"Paralympic athletes have struggled under the USOC leadership for years," Mastandrea says. "In many ways, it comes down to money. There's a perception that athletes with disabilities are not marketable, and therefore supporting us is a charity thing. But I think a lot of people—able-bodied or not—identify with people with disabilities. An athlete is an athlete is an athlete. If you love sports, you love sports. I'm here to attest that the thrill of the game can change your life. It doesn't matter if you're in a wheelchair or if you are standing."

Her own life changed when the coach of her university's wheelchair basketball team encouraged her to join the squad. On wheels, Mastandrea discovered that she was an athlete. "Before college, sports was something for everybody else," she says. "But once I got in a chair and on the basketball court, it was like, 'Wow. I've never felt this great before. I'm playing basketball even though my legs don't work very well.' Once I realized I could be an athlete, I never looked back."

Track and field was next, and soon Mastandrea was competing—and winning—in 100-, 200-, and 400-meter races against other disabled athletes. In 1992, she joined the U.S. Paralympic team, traveling to the summer games in Barcelona, and later to Atlanta (where she earned her gold and silver medals) in 1996.

The Paralympic experience was exciting, but it was also expensive. Mastandrea, like her teammates, had to pay for her own coaches, rent her own training facilities, and find her own health insurance. Since 1994, the USOC has provided travel, housing, and uniforms for Paralympic athletes, but those benefits pale in comparison to the perks dished out to able-bodied competitors.

"It's a lot like where the women's sports movement was 25 years ago," Mastandrea says. "Disabled athletes are up against a lack of recognition, a lack of funding, a lack of opportunity."

—*Andy Steiner*

Bruce Stern. Bruce Stern likes professional basketball about as well as the next guy. He likes college ball even better. He's just not one of those diehard junkies.

"People will come in talking about who was traded to whom, and it goes right over my head," says the Washington, D.C.–based lawyer.

But you don't have to be a basketball fanatic to understand opportunity and options, two things the 35-year-old Los Angeles native is selling these days as he prepares to launch the National Rookie League (NRL), an unaffiliated minor league for the National Basketball Association. He likens the system to professional baseball and hockey minor leagues. Stern's league, open to young men ages 17 to 24, will be based in six East Coast cities (Washington, D.C.; Philadelphia; Baltimore; Boston; New York City; and Hampton Roads, Virginia), playing from June to August to avoid conflicts with NBA and major college games.

Mainly, though, the NRL is Stern's answer to two things he thinks are ailing college and professional basketball, both on and off the court: the academic obstacle course athletes must run to get to the NBA, and growing public alienation from the professional game.

For now, college basketball remains the main path to the NBA, a club already so exclusive that the chances of getting in are on a par with winning the lottery or being struck by lightning—twice. NCAA academic standards have shut out many would-be players, a disproportionate number of them African American. And too many athletes who do get into college aren't there to learn, he says: "Top athletes coming out of [high] school don't go to college to get a college education. . . . Many are there for as long as it takes them to make it into the NBA or NFL. I don't blame them. I just think there should be a better way."

Stern's "better way" includes something like a GI Bill for NRL players. In addition to paying yearly salaries of $20,000 to $25,000, the NRL will set aside $7,500 for college for each year an athlete participates, he says. The league also will offer life skills training and has already established a link with the University of Colorado at Denver to offer courses there.

But this high-stakes, high-powered money game is also about business, a fact that doesn't escape Stern. He has about 100 investors, has put up nearly $200,000 of his own savings, and gave up a chance to be a law firm partner to pursue the NRL. "Nobody's expecting to get rich, but this is a business," he explains. Through stock ownership and cheap seats—$5 to $12—that families can afford, he hopes the league will break even in three years.

Finally, in a game that sometimes seems to be as much about race as it is about competition and money, the fact that Stern is a white lawyer trying to build a league that almost certainly will be fueled by African American talent has posed some interesting questions. "I'm white, there's no getting around that," Stern says, adding that several league boards have a majority of black members, and he expects many of the coaches to be African American.

Stern hopes the NRL will provide young men with more options than ever before. If he sounds idealistic, that's OK, he says. If he doesn't, he challenges his critics to wait and see what happens. High school baseball and hockey players can choose to play in the minor leagues, he says, and "if you play tennis in high school, you can turn pro or you can go on to college. But basketball players don't have that option. All we want to do is provide athletes with an option, and they can make a choice."

—*Marcia Davis*

Pat Griffin. She says that in the world of sports, closets have no place. Maybe it was because she had a job, or because she felt it was time for her to step forward and become a role model. But more likely it was because she couldn't stand being quiet about her life any longer. Whatever the reason, in 1987, triathlete and educator Pat Griffin told an audience at a national sports conference in Las Vegas that she is a lesbian.

For most people, coming out publicly takes guts, but for Griffin, it was especially risky. Besides being a professor at the University of Massachusetts at Amherst, she was also coach of the women's swim team, and she was afraid her announcement would spark negative fallout from team members or their parents.

But in the end, Griffin's desire to tell the truth once and for all outweighed her concerns. "The closet gets pretty cramped," she says now. "Eventually I had to come out in order to make room for myself to grow."

And Griffin couldn't have picked a better moment: The sponsoring organization had asked her to give a speech on homophobia and women's sports, a topic dear to her heart. Using her own career as an example made perfect sense.

"When I first started coaching, I was very closeted, except eventually to a few of my swimmers," Griffin says, recalling that during her early years as a competitive athlete and coach, she constantly worried that her sexual preference would be discovered and she would lose her job. "As I got older and settled in one place, I made myself known to some of the women on the basketball and lacrosse teams, and told them that they could come talk to me about issues they were facing in their lives. It made me bolder."

Emboldened by her speech, and buoyed by support from friends and colleagues, Griffin eventually wrote *Strong Women, Deep Closets: Lesbians and Homophobia in Sport* (Human Kinetics 1998). The book includes interviews with lesbian athletes and coaches, highlighting the complex relationship between perceptions of female athleticism and sexual preference.

Perhaps because physically strong, powerful women call into question the concept of male dominance, athletic women throughout history have been characterized as less feminine or more "mannish" than their less sporty sisters, Griffin says. In Western society at least, the word *lesbian* can be a dangerous label, especially for women athletes, many of whom have famously avoided raising questions about their sexuality. Crossing the delicate border between *gay* and *straight* can threaten careers (Babe Didrikson), raise hackles (Billie Jean King), or at least limit endorsement dollars (Martina Navratilova).

"In women's sports, it's more than just lesbians, it's about the lesbian label," Griffin explains. "When you call an athlete a lesbian, the beauty goes out of the game. It's a way to make a person back down, to keep quiet."

Griffin, for one, isn't going to keep quiet anymore. In the years since her announcement, she's helped produce a video on homosexuality and sports called *Out for a Change*, and has consulted with the NCAA and the Women's Basketball Coaches Association about ways their groups can counter discrimination against gay and lesbian athletes. She's even competed in the Gay Games, winning a bronze in the triathlon in 1994, and a gold in the hammer throw in 1998.

By making herself an example, Griffin hopes to get a conversation going, to provide other gay and lesbian athletes with the inspiration they need to come forward, and to build support among heterosexual teammates. These are high hurdles, she knows, but, like any true competitor, she's never been able to turn her back on a challenge.

"These are big changes I'm talking about," she says. "And you can't put all the responsibility on lesbians and gay men. If we want true athletic equity, we're going to need more heterosexual allies in this fight. Once that starts happening on a larger scale, we'll just see one victory after another."

—*Andy Steiner*

Philip Bess. Urban ballparks are his pleasure and his goal. Despite spending his California boyhood listening to the dulcet lullabies of Los Angeles Dodgers play-by-play man Vin Scully on his transistor radio, Philip Bess became a lifelong fan of baseball's hapless Chicago Cubs. A cynic might call Bess' long-distance embrace of the Cubbies an early sign of a doomed contrarian. Instead, the 47-year-old architect, author, and college professor half-seriously prefers to describe himself as "an Aristotelian Catholic communitarian"—a person who believes that "the best life for individual human beings is the disciplined life of moral and intellectual virtue lived with others in communities."

This, quite naturally, has put Bess at odds with the owners of major league baseball teams and the designers of the ballparks in which they play.

Bess' thin but incisive 1989 book, *City Baseball Magic*, has become a cult classic among those who want to do more than just grumble about eating $5 tube steaks in the nosebleed sections of new $500 million "baseball entertainment complexes." In the book, Bess details how huge stadiums have torn the fabric of urban neighborhoods, distanced fans from the game they love, and fostered the inflationary spiral that has enabled greed to permeate baseball. Then he offers a solution: his design for a "traditional urban ballpark" (named Armour Field in the book) complete with club seating and luxury boxes, but on a smaller site with fewer frills and more intimacy than modern ballparks other. The price tag, even adjusting for 1999 dollars, is less than half the cost of most stadium projects.

With a new preface its only update, this year's 10th anniversary reprint by St. Paul's Knothole Press feels as fresh and relevant as ever. Many believe *City Baseball Magic* influenced the recent spate of "old-fashioned" ballparks constructed in Baltimore, Cleveland, and Denver, a trend Bess contends is little more than a marketing gambit designed, literally, to provide megaparks with the veneer of tradition. He argues that not since Yankee Stadium was constructed in the 1920s has a park conformed to the traditional street-and-block gridwork that enhances pedestrian traffic and the social character of the surrounding neighborhood. Instead, stadiums are plunked down on sprawling "superblocks," sealing them off from their urban environment and enabling owners to capture ancillary revenues on everything from parking to restaurants. Site and construction costs are almost always borne by taxpayers.

Bess, who loves urban living as much as he loves baseball, maintains that a traditional urban ballpark enhances the team's identity and blends it with the city's character, as happens at Fenway Park in Boston, Wrigley Field in Chicago, and other older stadiums. So long as team owners are minimally invested in the cost of ballparks and architect fees are a set percentage of the total tab, it is up to the public sector, Bess says, to make teams "just a player in the conversation" while compelling owners to be responsible corporate citizens.

As a professor of architecture at Andrews University in Berrien Springs, Michigan, and the head of Thursday Architects, Bess doesn't need baseball as much as the game needs his ideas. But he lives just two and a half miles from Wrigley, so he'll continue to patronize his beloved Cubs.

—*Britt Robson*

A League of Our Own: The Thrill of Victory Doesn't Have to be Vicarious

Mark Cooper

"I felt a rush like I had personally just won the World Series!" said Al Glanz, a paunchy 51-year-old attorney. "Only in bowling can an out-of-shape middle-aged short guy win that kind of victory." Glanz, a college-days SDS comrade and current lead-off man of my five-person bowling team, Al's Animals, was remembering our 1997 league championship.

After thirty-eight Tuesday nights of competition against seventeen mixed-gender teams, we Animals found ourselves in the final roll, matched against some big bruisers. Miraculously, we split the first two games. And, going into the 10th and last frame, we were neck and neck. Al bowled two strikes and finished over 150. In the anchor position, I beat my 198 average.

As 100 league members looked on, the opposing team's anchor, Big Kahuna, was shooting his tenth frame. Apparently he miscalculated the narrow difference between us and—grossly overconfident—

Reprinted from *The Nation*, August 10, 1998.
Copyright © 1998 by The Nation.

whipped his 16-pound Code Red ball out toward the lone 10-pin standing on the back right-hand corner of the alley. Hubris has a price: The Kahuna's ball angled sharply to the 5-board and, skidding in the conditioning oil, failed to stabilize, then plunked unceremoniously into the gutter three feet short of the pin.

The electronic tote board flashed our one-point victory as we basked in applause and cheers. After the awards ceremony we left elated, with armfuls of trophies and $287 in prize money. A year later, we still talk excitedly of our razor-close win.

Such are the wonders of organized, serious bowling. I'm the only team member with a high average. At the time of our championship, Al hadn't bowled in 25 years and had worked himself up to 125. Team member and printer Miki Jurcan was a first-year bowler averaging 137. Bookkeeper Kim Yoh shot in the high 150s, and her developmentally disabled brother, Dale, in the 140s.

But bowling is the most democratic of sports. You play in your own neighborhood, with teams drawn from networks of friends or co-workers; the squads often are mixed gender and usually mixed generation. It's relatively inexpensive and easy to learn (at least the basics). But most important, 95 percent of bowling leagues rely on the socialist notion of handicap—a formula that adjusts for differences between teams. We won the championship against much better bowlers not because we outbowled them but because first they had to "spot" us 65 pins a game, and, this time, we outbowled ourselves. From each according to his ability. . . .

Bowling is a literate sport. In a two-team matchup, you must follow 10 evolving narratives through three games and 30 frames. Much as in baseball (and unlike soccer or basketball), in bowling virtually every moment of play can be studied, analyzed, regretted, or celebrated. Even on a losing night, you might pick up two different splits, or, finally perfect your conversion of a troublesome spare. Bowling also requires basic mathematical skills. Even with automatic scoring, you still have to calculate quickly in your head to know where you stand.

Maybe this is why a younger generation seems to be giving up on bowling. Many claim it's too boring, too square. But maybe for a culture that is becoming allergic to narrative and sequential logic, it's just too demanding. With alarming frequency, bowling alleys are converting to places with names like Cosmic Bowl, where irony has replaced competition and acquired skill, and where black lights, fluorescent pins, pounding disco music, and cheap beer induce a crowd of kids to come "bowling"—in quotes.

Make no mistake. I harbor no nostalgia for retro bowling, at alleys untouched since V-J Day, with hand pinspotters, scoring pads and pencils, lacquered wood lanes, and hard rubber balls. These are museums, if you ask me. My love affair is with brightly lit, well-scrubbed, air-conditioned, suburban 48- and 52-lane palaces. I like the new technology that has, in the past 15 years, redefined the game.

Like the handicap, technology is a great leveler for those not born with raw bowling talent. To reduce fire hazard, urethane replaced lacquer as the protective coating over wooden lanes; it soaked up less conditioning oil and made the lanes "faster." The old balls wouldn't hook well on the new surfaces and so were replaced by highly engineered "reactive" urethane balls, which made the "break point" of your shot—where the ball would start curving into the pocket more stable and predictable. Depending on the urethane and resin mix, the hardness of the shell, the placement of the weight block, and the angle of the finger grips, you can get a ball that "breaks" hard or easy, short or long; one that performs well in oil or is better suited to dryer lanes.

There is a downside: Bowling balls have gotten expensive—as much as $200. Their specialization encourages fleet ownership (I have six active bowling balls and buy about two a year). League play—$10 to $12 a week for three games of competition—is still cheap for a night's entertainment, and everyone gets back some prize money. But as leagues have declined, bowling alleys need to charge, on average, an outrageous $3.50 a game for open play. An hour's worth of practice can cost you $20 or more.

And yet, that unmistakable smell of conditioning oil and the rumble and crack of the pins still hold the same allure for me that they did when I was a child in the 1950s. I would watch in wonderment as Dick Weber hung out a string of seven or eight strikes at the Hollywood Legion Lanes. In no other organized sport is the line between amateur and pro so blurred. Almost every bowling alley pro shop is staffed by a *pro*—a major-league bowler. When my mentor, Rick Polzien, isn't fitting me for a new ball or working with me out on the lanes to keep my head up and shoulders straight, he's likely to be on tour competing for the big bucks. Next time Mike Piazza's in town, try calling him and asking if he's got a few moments to play catch with you.

At my neighborhood bowling alley, there are, apart from Rick, half a dozen other card-carrying members of the Professional Bowlers Association playing side by side with bookkeepers, teachers, and mechanics in the Thursday-night singles league. To enter the PBA, you need to average only 200 for any two years of amateur league play—for me, a wholly attainable goal. Into mid-middle age, I still toy with the notion of going on tour. I might even be a contender.

SPOILED SPORTS

1) How do sports reflect American society?

2) How does Weiner suggest we de-emphasize the impact of sports on our culture? Do you agree that such a de-emphasis is necessary, and if so, why?

3) Why does Faludi describe sports, particularly football, as being part of American male ritual in the twentieth century?

4) How does Faludi contrast the meaning of the word "fan" in the early 20th century with the concept of the "fan" in present-day sports?

5) What is the relationship of sports, children, and family in modern American society?

6) How are men's and women's sports and athletes viewed in modern American society?

7) Discuss some of the various attitudes and approaches taken to sports in the "Playing for Keeps" article in this section.

Professional Football:
An American Symbol and Ritual

W. Arens

O, you sir, you! Come you hither, sir. Who am I, sir?

OSWALD: My lady's father.

LEAR: 'My lady's father'! my lord's knave! you whoreson dog! you slave! you cur!

OSWALD: I am none of these, my lord; I beseech your pardon.

LEAR: Do you bandy looks with me, you rascal? [striking him.]

OSWALD: I'll not be strucken, my lord.

KENT: Nor trip'd neither, you base football player.
—*King Lear,* Act I, Scene 4

"A school without football is in danger of deteriorating into a medieval study hall."
—*Vince Lombardi*

Attitudes toward football players obviously have changed since Shakespeare's time. Today, the once "base football player" occupies the throne and rules the land. In fact, to have played too many games without a helmet seems to be a prerequisite for high office in our country. The prominent role football assumes in our society deserves comment. I would contend that although only a game, it has much to say about who and what we are as a people.

Although I am a professional anthropologist by training and have carried out field work in another culture, this essay owes its impetus to the years I have sat in front of a television watching hundreds of football contests. Out of a feeling of guilt, I began to muse in a more academic fashion about this game and turned to the numerous books written by players and to the rare anthropological accounts of sport in other societies. This has led me to believe that if an anthropologist from another planet visited here, he would be struck by the American fixation on this game and would report on it with the glee and romantic intoxication anthropologists normally reserve for the exotic rituals of a newly discovered tribe. This assertion is based on the theory that certain significant symbols are the key to understanding a culture. It might be a dreadful thought, but nonetheless true, that if we understood the meaning of football, we might better understand ourselves.

I emphasize a symbolic analysis because this game that intrigues us so much is engaged in by relatively few, but highly skilled individuals. Most of us at one time or another have played golf, tennis, basketball, softball, or even baseball, but only the "pros" play football. Touch football must be discounted because it lacks the essential ingredients of violent physical contact and complexity of game plan. The pleasure derived from football therefore is almost totally vicarious. This sport's images and messages satisfy our collective mind, not our individual bodies.

An appreciation of this argument requires an initial short detour in time to examine the evolution of this American sport from its European origins. The enshrined mythology states that the game was first played by a group of English soldiers who celebrated their victory over a Viking settlement by entering the losers' burial ground and using the skulls of the enemies' dead in a kicking match. Sometime later, an animal's inflated bladder was substituted for the skull, and the sport of "Dane's Head" became known as football. During the early Middle Ages, the game was a disorganized all-day competition between neighboring towns. The ball was placed midway between two villages and the object was to kick it along the countryside into the village and finally onto the green of the opposing community for a score. The game became so popular with the English peasantry that Henry II banned the pastime in the twelfth century because it interfered with the practice of archery. The sport was not reinstated until the seventeenth century, by which time the longbow had become an obsolete weapon.

According to Reisman and Denny (1969), who have charted the game's evolution, the kicking aspect remained dominant until 1823 when, as popular legend has it, a scoundrel named William Ellis, of Rugby School, "with a fine disregard for the rules of football, as played in his time, first took the ball in his arms and ran with it." This innovation on soccer was institutionalized at the school, and shortly thereafter was adopted by others; hence the name "rugby"—and the association of this sport in England with the educated elite.

Although both games were exported to America, only rugby was modified in the new setting. The claim

Reprinted from *Gendered Voices: Readings from the American Experience,* by Karin Bergstrom Costello, 1996. Harcourt Brace and Company.

has been made by the participants, and officially adopted by the National Collegiate Athletic Association, that the first intercollegiate game took place between Rutgers and Princeton in 1869. However, because that contest followed soccer rules, the honor of having played the first game of what was to emerge as American football rightly should go to Harvard and McGill in 1874, when rugby regulations were the order of the day. In the remaining decades of the nineteenth century, the sport began to take on a more American form as a definite line of scrimmage and the center snap, replaced the swaying "scrum" and "heal out" of English rugby. This meant that possession of the ball was now given to one team at a time. However, the introduction of the forward pass in the early years of this century signaled the most radical break with the past. These revisions on rugby resulted in greater structure and order, but at the same time more variety and flexibility, because running, kicking, and forward passing were incorporated as offensive maneuvers. Football had become an American game.

As a result of this process, football has emerged as an item of our cultural inventory that we share with no other country but Canada, where it is not nearly so popular. Does football's uniqueness and popularity say something essential about our culture? Rather than dismiss this question as trivial, we should be aware that we share our language, kinship system, religions, political and economic institutions, and a variety of other traits with many nations, but not our premier spectator sport. This is important when we consider that other societies have taken up baseball, a variation of cricket, and basketball, a homegrown product. Like English beer, the American brand of football is unexportable, even to the colonies. No one else can imagine what the natives see in it. On the other hand, soccer, the world's number one sport, has not been a popular success in America. In a peculiar social inversion, though, the educated and well-traveled American middle class has taken some interest in this sport of the European working classes. Nonetheless, football is uniquely American and little else can be included in this category.

Also, football as compared to our language and many values, is not forced upon us. It is an optional aspect of our culture's inventions, which individuals choose to accept. Our society, like any other complex one, is divided by race, ethnicity, income, political affiliation, and regionalism. However, seventy-nine percent of all the households in the country tuned in to the first Super Bowl on TV, implying that the event cut through many of the divisive factors just mentioned. Personally, I can think of precious little else that I have in common with our former or current president, with a rural Texan, or an urban black man other than a mutual passion for this game. Football represents not only "Middle America," as is so often claimed, but the whole of America. When we consider football, we focus on one of the few things we share with no one outside our borders, but do share with almost everyone within it.

The salient features of the game and the society that created and nourishes it reflect some striking similarities. The sport combines the qualities to an extent, but in football the process has surely reached the zenith. Every professional and major college team finds it necessary today to include a player whose only function is place kicking, and another for punting. Some have individuals whose sole responsibility is to center or hold the ball for the point after touchdown. Football is also a game in which success now demands an extensive reliance on spophisticated electronic technology from telephones to computers while the match is in progress. In short, football, as opposed to its ancestor, rugby, epitomizes the spirit and the form of contemporary American society.

Violence is another of our society's most apparent features. This quality of American life and its expression in football clearly accounts for some of the game's appeal. That football involves legitimate bodily contact and territorial incursion defines it as an aggressive sport par excellence. It is hardly surprising therefore that books by participants are replete with symbolic references to war. For example, Jerry Kramer, a Green Bay Packer during their glory years of the 1960s, divides his book, *Instant Replay*, into the following sections: Preliminary Skirmishes; Basic Training; Mock Warfare; Armed Combat; War's End. Frank Leahy, a former coach of Notre Dame and in his time a living symbol of America, wrote in his memoirs:

> . . . the Stars and Stripes have never taken second place on any battlefield. With this in mind, we ask you to think back and ask yourself where our young men developed the qualities that go to make up a good fighting man. . . . These rafts are something that cannot be found in textbooks nor can they be learned in the lecture room. It is on the athletic fields that our boys acquire these winning ways as much a part of the American life as are freedom of speech and of the press (1949: 230).

Mike Holovak (1967), a former coach of the New England Patriots, waxed even more lyrical in reminiscing about his World War II military service. He refers to those years as the time he was on "the first team" in the "South Pacific playground" where the tracers arched out "like a long touchdown pass" and the artillery fired "orange blobs—just like a football."

To single out violence as the sole or even primary reason for the game's popularity is a tempting oversimplification. There are more violent sports available to us, such as boxing, which allows for an even greater display of legitimate blood spilling. Yet, boxing's popularity has waned over the last few decades. Its decline corresponds with the increased interest in professional football, in which aggression is acted out in a more tactical and sophisticated context. Football's violence is expressed within the framework of teamwork, specialization, mechanization, and variation, and this combination accounts for its appeal. A football contest more adequately symbolizes the way in which our society carries out violence than does a sport that relies on naked individual force. An explanation of football's popularity on the basis of violence alone also overlooks the fact that we are not unique in this respect. There have been many other violent nations, but they did not enshrine football as a national symbol.

Although the "national pastime" may not have suffered the same fate as boxing, interest in baseball also has ebbed. If my analysis of football is correct, then baseball is not in step with the times either. The action in baseball does not entail the degree of complexity, coordination, and specialization that now captures our fancy. I think this is what people mean when they say that baseball is boring. The recent introduction of the designated hitter and the occasional base-running specialist who never bats or fields are moves to inject specialization and to heighten the game's appeal to modern America. In essence, baseball belongs to another era, when life was a bit less complicated.

To return to our original interest, one final point must be made on the symbolism of football. Earlier, I wrote that football represented the whole of America and overcame traditional differences in our society. However, the importance of the division between the sexes, which has more recently become part of our consciousness, was not mentioned. Football plays a part in representing this dichotomy in our society because it is a male preserve that manifests and symbolizes both the physical and cultural values of masculinity. Entrance into the arena of football competition depends on muscle power and speed possessed by very few males and beyond that of most females. Women can and have excelled in a variety of other sports, but football generally excludes them from participation. It was reported in a local newspaper that during a game between female teams the players' husbands appeared on the sidelines in women's clothes and wigs. The message was clear: If the women were going to act as men then the men were going to transform themselves into women.

These "rituals of rebellion" involving an inversion of sex roles have been recorded often by anthropologists. It is not surprising that this symbolic rebellion in our culture was aimed at a bastion of male supremacy.

If this argument seems farfetched, consider the extent to which the equipment accents the male physique. The donning of the required items results in an enlarged head and shoulders and a narrowed waist, with the lower torso poured into skin-tight trousers accented only by a metal cod-piece. The result is not an expression, but an exaggeration of maleness. Dressed in this manner, the players engage in handholding, hugging, and bottom patting, which would be ludicrous and disapproved of in any other context. Yet, this is accepted on the gridiron without a second thought. Admittedly, there are good reasons for wearing the gear, but does that mean we must dismiss the symbolic significance of the visual impression? The game could just as easily be played without the major items, such as the helmet, shoulder pads, and cleats. They are as much offensive as defensive in function. Indeed, in comparison, rugby players seem to manage quite well in the flimsiest of uniforms.

The preceding discussion puts us in a better position to ask the question hinted at earlier—are we in effect dealing with an American ritual of some meaning? The answer depends upon how ritual is defined. A broad anthropological view suggests that it is a standardized, repetitive activity carried out for the purpose of expressing and communicating basic cultural ideals and symbols. A ritual therefore does not necessarily imply communication with the supernatural. The inauguration of a president or the playing of the national anthem are common examples of nonreligious rituals in America. An objective evaluation of the problem also demands recognizing that an act can have a sacred and a secular character at the same time. Consequently, at one level, football can be viewed simply as a sport and at another level as a public ritual. Considering some of the players' activities from this perspective furnishes some interesting and supportive observations.

If we view the game as a ritual and, therefore, in some respects as a sacred activity, we would expect the participants to disengage themselves from the profane world of everyday affairs. This is a common aspect of ritual behavior in any part of the world. Especially relevant for the participants is the avoidance of what anthropologists refer to as "pollution"—an impure ritual state—as the result of contact with contaminating acts or situations. Association with this profane realm renders a participant symbolically unfit to engage in a sacred performance.

In many rituals performed entirely for and by males, sexual contact with females must be avoided. Abstinence under these conditions is almost a cultural universal because the sexual act is an expression of man's animal or profane nature. In many a rite of passage for boys about to enter adulthood, the participants are taken out of the community, isolated from the opposite sex, and may not be seen by them. In other societies, prior to a significant activity such as the hunt or warfare, the community members are admonished to refrain from sexual behavior for fear of disastrous consequences. Is it really surprising then that in the world of sport, and with football in particular, sex before the event is viewed with suspicion? In this context, I am reminded of Hoebel's (1960) statement that "The Cheyenne feeling about male sexuality is that it is something to be husbanded and kept in reserve as a source of strength for the great crises of war." This compares well with the attitude at the virtually monastic world of football training camps. At these facilities, all the players, including those married, are sequestered together during practice days. They are allowed to visit their wives, who must be living off the grounds, on Saturday night only, because there is no practice on Sunday. As is to be expected, they must return to the all-male atmosphere on Sunday evening in consideration of Monday's activities. The result is that sex and football, the profane and the sacred, are segregated in time and space. During the season, a variation of the procedure prevails. The players and staff spend Saturday night together because the contest takes place on Sunday. In each instance there is a clear-cut attempt to avoid the symbolic danger of contact with females prior to the event.

This was impressed on me when I traveled with my university's team by chartered bus to a game to be played at the opponent's field. Because there were a few unoccupied seats, two of the players asked the coach if their girlfriends could ride along. He said in all seriousness that they could not ride to the game with us, but that they could join us on the bus on the way home. A writer who spent the season with the Rice University football squad mentioned a similar instance (Tippette 1973). When the team bus pulled up in front of the dormitory where they would spend the night on the opponent's campus, a number of the girls from the college entered the vehicle and began to flirt with the players. The Rice coach, who was in an accompanying car, stormed onto the bus and ordered the girls off immediately. He then told the players that they should have known better—the incident was a dirty trick instigated by their foe. Dirty trick or not, somebody planned the exercise, well aware of the unsettling effect that it would have on the team.

One further example is from the professional arena. Describing the night before the first Super Bowl, when the Green Bay Packers were allowed to bring along their wives as a reward for championship play, Jerry Kramer wrote: "My wife's been here for the past few days, and so has Chandler's. Tonight we're putting the girls in one room, and Danny and I are sharing one. It's better for the girls to be away from us tonight. We're always grumpy and grouchy before a game" (1968).

There are, of course, some perfectly reasonable arguments for segregating the players prior to a game. For one, the coaches argue that they are assured that the team members get an undistracted night's sleep. Thus it is assumed that the players will be better able to concentrate on the upcoming event. At the same time, when these vignettes are considered, the theme of possible pollution through contact with females is not altogether absent. In any event, the inhibition of sexual activity prior to an athletic event has no apparent scientific rationale. The latest position based on research argues that sex is actually beneficial, because it induces a more restful night's sleep.

The *New York Times* recently reported that a British physician who has advised and interviewed his country's Olympic competitors mentioned that one informant admitted setting the world record in a middle distance track event an hour after sexual intercourse. Another confessed that he ran the mile in less than four minutes an hour and a half after the same activity. One must look beyond rationality for an explanation of the negative attitude toward sex on the part of the elders who control professional football. However, if we grant that the sport involves a significant ritual element, then the idea does make some sense. From this standpoint, scientific reasoning is not relevant.

Accounts of rituals in other cultures also indicate the prevalent belief in symbolic contamination through contact with illness or physical imperfection. Examples of this sort of avoidance also crop up in football. Players report that those who become sick to their stomachs in the summer heat of training camp are avoided and become the objects of ridicule. In a similar vein, participants are rightfully admonished to stay away from an injured player so that the trainer can attend to him. However, they do not appear to need the advice because after a momentary glance they studiously avoid a downed colleague. Injured, inactive players on the team I was associated with as a faculty sponsor were not allowed to mingle with the active participants during the game. The loquacious professional Jerry Kramer also writes that when he was hurt and disabled, he felt like an "outsider," "isolated" and "separated" from the rest of the group. Others have written that they were ignored during these times by their teammates and coaches. I do not want to push this argument too far because there are many sound reasons to explain this patterned reaction. At the same time, I can think of similar arguments for the behavior of people in other cultures after having come into contact with illness or death.

Eating is another profane act, because it is a further indication of our animal nature. As in every society, contact with certain foods renders an individual unfit to participate in rituals. However, in contrast to sexuality and physical imperfection, nourishment cannot be avoided for any length of time. Instead, under controlled conditions, the act of eating is incorporated into the ritual, and the food becomes charged with a sacred character. Consequently, not just any type of food is acceptable, but only specified types with symbolic significance may be ingested by ritual participants. What would be more appropriate in our society than males eating beef prior to the great event? Imagine the scorn that would be heaped upon a team if it were known that they prepared themselves for the competition by eating chicken.

The problem with a purely functional interpretation is that this meat, which, it is believed, must be eaten on the day of the competition, is not converted into potential energy until hours after the game has ended. Although the players must appear for this meal because it is part of the ritual, actually very few eat what is presented to them. Instead, in contradiction to the ritual experts, the participants prefer a high-energy snack, such as a pill, which they realize has more immediate value. Nevertheless, those who control the players' behavior, as in the other instances, adhere to a less functional course by forcing their charges to confront a meaningful symbolic substance. If this situation were presented to an anthropologist in the heart of the Amazon, I wonder how long it would take to suggest ritual cannibalism on the part of the natives.

I have tried to make it clear that I am well aware that there are a number of secular, functional explanations for the behavior that has been described. However, it bears repeating that a ritual has a variety of levels, components, and consequences. The slaughter of a white bull during a rite of passage for males among cattle-keeping people in Africa has an obvious nutritional benefit for those who consume it. At the same time, though, this does not obviate the ritual significance of the act. If I am making too much of the symbolic element of American football, then perhaps we ought to reconsider the ease with which we accept this type of analysis for other supposedly simpler cultures. Accounts of team log racing among the Shavante Indians of Brazil as an attempt to restore harmony to a social order beset by political divisions (Maybury-Lewis, 1967) and the analysis of cock fighting in Bali (Geertz, 1972) as an expression of national character have caused little stir. Unless we consider ourselves something special, our own society is equally suited to such anthropological studies. It is reasonable that if other people express their basic cultural themes in symbolic rituals, then we are likely to do the same.

References

Geertz, Clifford. 1972. "Deep Play: Notes on a Balinese Cockfight." *Daedalus* Winter.

Hoebel, E. Adamson. 1960. *The Cheyenne.* New York: Holt, Rinehart and Winston.

Holovak, Mike. 1967. *Violence Every Sunday.* New York: Coward-McCann.

Kramer, Jerry. 1968. *Instant Replay.* New York and Cleveland: World Publishing Company.

Leahy, Frank. 1949. *Notre Dame Football.* New York: Prentice-Hall.

Maybury-Lewis, David. 1967. *Akwe-shavante Society.* Oxford: Clarendon Press.

Reisman, David, and Reuel Denny. 1969. "Football in America: A Study in Cultural Diffusion." In J. W. Lory, Jr. and G. S. Kenyon, eds., *Sport, Culture and Society.* New York: Macmillan.

Tippette, Giles. 1973. *Saturday's Children.* New York: Macmillan.

"PROFESSIONAL FOOTBALL: AN AMERICAN SYMBOL AND RITUAL"

W. Arens

1) Why does Arens claim that football is the quintessential American sport?

2) What essential American values does football reflect and reinforce?

3) How does Arens suggest that football enhances "maleness" in American culture?

4) Can any aspect of football be defined as ritual in the cultural or the religious sense?

5) Using Aren's article and class discussion material, why can the Superbowl be seen as the ultimate American secular (and perhaps religious) ritual?

SECTION THREE

Solving Human Problems

RACE WITHOUT COLOR

Jared Diamond

Science often violates simple common sense. Our eyes tell us that the Earth is flat, that the sun revolves around the Earth, and that we humans are not animals. But we now ignore that evidence of our senses. We have learned that our planet is in fact round and revolves around the sun, and that humans are slightly modified chimpanzees. The reality of human races is another commonsense "truth" destined to follow the flat Earth into oblivion. The commonsense view of races goes somewhat as follows. All native Swedes differ from all native Nigerians in appearance: there is no Swede whom you would mistake for a Nigerian, and vice versa. Swedes have lighter skin than Nigerians do. They also generally have blond or light brown hair, while Nigerians have very dark hair. Nigerians usually have more tightly coiled hair than Swedes do, dark eyes as opposed to eyes that are blue or gray, and fuller lips and broader noses.

In addition, other Europeans look much more like Swedes than like Nigerians, while other peoples of sub-Saharan Africa—except perhaps the Khoisan peoples of southern Africa—look much more like Nigerians than like Swedes. Yes, skin color does get darker in Europe toward the Mediterranean, but it is still lighter than the skin of sub-Saharan Africans. In Europe, very dark or curly hair becomes more common outside Scandinavia, but European hair is still not as tightly coiled as in Africa. Since it's easy then to distinguish almost any native European from any native sub-Saharan African, we recognize Europeans and sub-Saharan Africans as distinct races, which we name for their skin colors: whites and blacks, respectively.

What could be more objective?

As it turns out, this seemingly unassailable reasoning is not objective. There are many different, equally valid procedures for defining races, and those different procedures yield very different classifications. One such procedure would group Italians and Greeks with most African blacks. It would classify Xhosas—the South African "black" group to which President Nelson Mandela belongs—with Swedes rather than Nigerians. Another equally valid procedure would place Swedes with Fulani (a Nigerian "black" group) and not with Italians, who would again be grouped with most other African blacks. Still another procedure would keep Swedes and Italians separate from all African blacks but would throw the Swedes and Italians into the same race as New Guineans and American Indians. Faced with such differing classifications, many anthropologists today conclude that one cannot recognize any human races at all.

If we were just arguing about races of nonhuman animals, essentially the same uncertainties of classification would arise. But the debates would remain polite and would never attract attention outside the halls of academia. Classification of humans is different "only" in that it shapes our views of other peoples, fosters our subconscious differentiation between "us" and "them," and is invoked to justify political and socioeconomic discrimination. On this basis, many anthropologists therefore argue that even if one *could* classify humans into races, one should not.

To understand how such uncertainties in classification arise, let's steer clear of humans for a moment and instead focus on warblers and lions, about which we can easily remain dispassionate. Biologists begin by classifying living creatures into species. A species is a group of populations whose individual members would, if given the opportunity, interbreed with individuals of other populations of that group. But they would not interbreed with individuals of other species that are similarly defined. Thus all human populations, no matter how different they look, belong to the same species because they do interbreed and have interbred whenever they have encountered each other. Gorillas and humans, however, belong to two different species because—to the best of our knowledge—they have never interbred despite their coexisting in close proximity for millions of years.

We know that different populations classified together in the human species are visibly different. The same proves true for most other animal and plant species as well, whenever biologists look carefully. For example, consider one of the most familiar species of bird in North America, the yellow-rumped warbler. Breeding males of eastern and western North America can be distinguished at a glance by their throat color: white in the east, yellow in the west. Hence they are classified into two different races, or subspecies (alternative words with identical meanings), termed the myrtle and Audubon races, respectively. The white-throated eastern birds differ from the yellow-throated western birds in other charac-

Reprinted by permission from *Discover*, November 1994. Jared Diamond/© 1994.

teristics as well, such as in voice and habitat preference. But where the two races meet, in western Canada, white-throated birds do indeed interbreed with yellow-throated birds. That's why we consider myrtle warblers and Audubon warblers as races of the same species rather than different species.

Racial classification of these birds is easy. Throat color, voice, and habitat preference all vary geographically in yellow-rumped warblers, but the variation of those three traits is "concordant"—that is, voice differences or habitat differences lead to the same racial classification as differences in throat color because the same populations that differ in throat color also differ in voice and habitat.

Racial classification of many other species, though, presents problems of concordance. For instance, a Pacific island bird species called the golden whistler varies from one island to the next. Some populations consist of big birds, some of small birds; some have black-winged males, others green-winged males; some have yellow-breasted females, others gray-breasted females; many other characteristics vary as well. But, unfortunately for humans like me who study these birds, those characteristics don't vary concordantly. Islands with green-winged males can have either yellow-breasted or gray-breasted females, and green-winged males are big on some islands but small on other islands. As a result, if you classified golden whistlers into races based on single traits, you would get entirely different classifications depending on which trait you chose.

Classification of these birds also presents problems of "hierarchy." Some of the golden whistler races recognized by ornithologists are wildly different from all the other races, but some are very similar to one another. They can therefore be grouped into a hierarchy of distinctness. You start by establishing the most distinct population as a race separate from all other populations. You then separate the most distinct of the remaining populations, and separating distinct populations or groups of populations as races or groups of races. The problem is that the extent to which you continue the racial classification is arbitrary, and it's a decision about which taxonomists disagree passionately. Some taxonomists, the "splitters," like to recognize many different races, partly for the egotistical motive of getting credit for having named a race. Other taxonomists, the "lumpers," prefer to recognize few races. Which type of taxonomist you are is a matter of personal preference.

How does that variability of traits by which we classify races come about in the first place? Some traits vary because of natural selection: that is, one form of the trait is advantageous for survival in one area, another form in a different area. For example, northern hares and weasels develop white fur in the winter, but southern ones retain brown fur year-round. The white winter fur is selected in the north for camouflage against the snow, while any animal unfortunate enough to turn white in the snowless southern states would stand out from afar against the brown ground and would be picked off by predators.

Other traits vary geographically because of *sexual* selection, meaning that those traits serve as arbitrary signals by which individuals of one sex attract mates of the opposite sex while intimidating rivals. Adult male lions, for instance, have a mane, but lionesses and young males don't. The adult male's mane signals to lionesses that he is sexually mature, and signals to young male rivals that he is a dangerous and experienced adversary. The length and color of a lion's mane vary among populations, being shorter and blacker in Indian lions than in African lions. Indian lions and lionesses evidently find short black manes sexy or intimidating; African lions don't.

Finally, some geographically variable traits have *no* known effect on survival and are invisible to rivals and to prospective sex partners. They merely reflect mutations that happened to arise and spread in one area. They could equally well have arisen and spread elsewhere—they just didn't.

Nothing that I've said about geographic variation in animals is likely to get me branded a racist. We don't attribute higher IQ or social status to black-winged whistlers than to green-winged whistlers. But now let's consider geographic variation in humans. We'll start with invisible traits, about which it's easy to remain dispassionate.

Many geographically variable human traits evolved by natural selection to adapt humans to particular climates or environments—just as the winter color of a hare or weasel did. Good examples are the mutations that people in tropical parts of the Old World evolved to help them survive malaria, the leading infectious disease of the old-world tropics. One such mutation is the sickle-cell gene, so-called because the red blood cells of people with that mutation tend to assume a sickle shape. People bearing the gene are more resistant to malaria than people without it. Not surprisingly, the gene is absent from northern Europe, where malaria is nonexistent, but it's common in tropical Africa, where malaria is widespread. Up to 40 percent of Africans in such areas carry the sickle-cell gene. It's also common in the malaria-ridden Arabian Peninsula and southern India, and rare or absent in the southernmost parts of South Africa, among the Xhosas, who live mostly beyond the tropical geographic range of malaria.

The geographic range of human malaria is much wider than the range of the sickle-cell gene. As it happens, other antimalarial genes take over the protective function of the sickle-cell gene in malarial Southeast Asia and New Guinea and in Italy, Greece, and other warm parts of the Mediterranean basin. Thus human races, if defined by antimalarial genes, would be very different from human races as traditionally defined by traits such as skin color. As classified by antimalarial genes (or their absence), Swedes are grouped with Xhosas but not with Italians or Greeks. Most other peoples usually viewed as African blacks are grouped with Arabia's "whites" and are kept separate from the "black" Xhosas.

Antimalarial genes exemplify the many features of our body chemistry that vary geographically under the influence of natural selection. Another such feature is the enzyme lactase, which enables us to digest the milk sugar lactose. Infant humans, like infants of almost all other mammal species, possess lactase and drink milk. Until about 6,000 years ago most humans, like all other mammal species, lost the lactase enzyme on reaching the age of weaning. The obvious reason is that it was unnecessary—no human or other mammal drank milk as an adult. Beginning around 4000 B.C., however, fresh milk obtained from domestic mammals became a major food for adults of a few human populations. Natural selection caused individuals in these populations to retain lactase into adulthood. Among such peoples are northern and central Europeans, Arabians, north Indians, and several milk-drinking black African peoples, such as the Fulani of West Africa. Adult lactase is much less common in southern European populations and in most other African black populations, as well as in all populations of east Asians, aboriginal Australians, and American Indians.

Once again races defined by body chemistry don't match races defined by skin color. Swedes belong with Fulani in the "lactase-positive race," while most African "blacks," Japanese, and American Indians belong in the "lactase-negative race."

Not all the effects of natural selection are as invisible as lactase and sickle cells. Environmental pressures have also produced more noticeable differences among peoples, particularly in body shapes. Among the tallest and most long-limbed peoples in the world are the Nilotic peoples, such as the Dinkas, who live in the hot, dry areas of East Africa. At the opposite extreme in body shape are the Inuit, or Eskimo, who have compact bodies and relatively short arms and legs. The reasons have to do with heat loss. The greater the surface area of a warm body, the more body heat that's lost, since heat loss is directly proportional to surface area. For people of a given weight, a long-limbed, tall shape maximizes surface area, while a compact, short-limbed shape minimizes

it. Dinkas and Inuit have opposite problems of heat balance: the former usually need desperately to get rid of body heat, while the latter need desperately to conserve it. Thus natural selection molded their body shapes oppositely, based on their contrasting climates.

(In modern times, such considerations of body shape have become important to athletic performance as well as to heat loss. Tall basketball players, for example, have an obvious advantage over short ones, and slender, long-limbed tall players have an advantage over stout, short-limbed tall players. In the United States, it's a familiar observation that African Americans are disproportionately represented among professional basketball players. Of course, a contributing reason has to do with their lack of socioeconomic opportunities. But part of the reason probably has to do with the prevalent body shapes of some black African groups as well. However, this example also illustrates the dangers in facile racial stereotyping. One can't make the sweeping generalization that "whites can't jump," or that "black's anatomy makes them better basketball players." Only certain African peoples are notably tall and long-limbed; even those exceptional peoples are tall and long-limbed only on the average and vary individually.)

Other visible traits that vary geographically among humans evolved by means of sexual selection. We all know that we find some individuals of the opposite sex more attractive than other individuals. We also know that in sizing up sex appeal, we pay more attention to certain parts of a prospective sex partner's body than to other parts. Men tend to be inordinately interested in women's breasts and much less concerned with women's toenails. Women, in turn, tend to be turned on by the shape of a man's buttocks or the details of a man's beard and body hair, if any, but not by the size of his feet.

But all those determinants of sex appeal vary geographically. Khoisan and Andaman Island women tend to have much larger buttocks than most other women. Nipple color and breast shape and size also vary geographically among women. European men are rather hairy by world standards, while Southeast Asian men tend to have very sparse beards and body hair.

What's the function of these traits that differ so markedly between men and women? They certainly don't aid survival: it's not the case that orange nipples help Khoisan women escape lions, while darker nipples help European women survive cold winters. Instead, these varying traits play a crucial role in sexual selection. Women with very large buttocks are a turn-on, or at least acceptable, to Khoisan and Andaman men but look freakish to many men from other parts of the world. Bearded and hairy men readily find mates in Europe but fare worse in Southeast Asia. The geographic variation of these traits, however, is as arbitrary as the geographic variation in the color of a lion's mane.

There is a third possible explanation for the function of geographically variable human traits, besides survival or sexual selection—namely, no function at all. A good example is provided by fingerprints, whose complex pattern of arches, loops, and whorls is determined genetically. Fingerprints also vary geographically: for example, Europeans' fingerprints tend to have many loops, while aboriginal Australians' fingerprints tend to have many whorls.

If we classify human populations by their fingerprints, most Europeans and black Africans would sort out together in one race, Jews and some Indonesians in another, and aboriginal Australians in still another. But those geographic variations in fingerprint patterns possess no known function whatsoever. They play no role in survival: whorls aren't especially suitable for grabbing kangaroos, nor do loops help bar mitzvah candidates hold on to the pointer for the Torah. They also play no role in sexual selection: while you've undoubtedly noticed whether your mate is bearded or has brown nipples, you surely haven't the faintest idea whether his or her fingerprints have more loops than whorls. Instead it's purely a matter of chance that whorls became common in aboriginal Australians, and loops among Jews. Our rhesus factor blood groups and numerous other human traits fall into the same category of genetic characteristics whose geographic variation serves no function.

You've probably been wondering when I was going to get back to skin color, eye color, and hair color and form. After all, those are the traits by which all of us members of the lay public, as well as traditional anthropologists, classify races. Does geographic variation in those traits function in survival, in sexual selection, or in nothing?

The usual view is that skin color varies geographically to enhance survival. Supposedly, people in sunny, tropical climates around the world have genetically dark skin, which is supposedly analogous to the temporary skin darkening of European whites in the summer. The supposed function of dark skin in sunny climates is for protection against skin cancer. Variations in eye color are also supposed to enhance survival under particular conditions, though no one has ever proposed a plausible hypothesis for how those variations might actually enhance survival.

Alas, the evidence for natural selection of skin color dissolves under scrutiny. Among tropical peoples, anthropologists love to stress the dark skins of African blacks, people of the southern Indian peninsula, and New Guineans and love to forget the pale skins of Amazonian Indians and Southeast Asians living at the same latitudes. To wriggle out of those paradoxes, anthropologists then plead the excuse that Amazonian Indians and Southeast Asians may not have been living in their present locations long enough to evolve dark skins. However, the ancestors of fair-skinned Swedes arrived even more recently in Scandinavia, and aboriginal Tasmanians were black-skinned despite their ancestors' having lived for at least the last 10,000 years at the latitude of Vladivostok.

Besides, when one takes into account cloud cover, peoples of equatorial West Africa and the New Guinea mountains actually receive no more ultraviolet radiation or hours of sunshine each year than do the Swiss. Compared with infectious diseases and other selective agents, skin cancer has been utterly trivial as a cause of death in human history, even for modern white settlers in the tropics. This objection is so obvious to believers in natural selection of skin color that they have proposed at least seven other supposed survival functions of skin color, without reaching agreement. Those other supposed functions include protection against rickets, frostbite, folic acid deficiency, beryllium poisoning, overheating, and overcooling. The diversity of these contradictory theories makes clear how far we are from understanding the survival value (if any) of skin color.

It wouldn't surprise me if dark skins do eventually prove to offer some advantage in tropical climates, but I expect the advantage to turn out to be a slight one that is easily overridden. But there's an overwhelming importance to skin, eye, and hair color that is obvious to all of us—sexual selection. Before we can reach a condition of intimacy permitting us to assess the beauty of a prospective sex partner's hidden physical attractions, we first have to pass muster for skin, eyes, and hair.

We all know how those highly visible "beauty traits" guide our choice of sex partners. Even the briefest personal ad in a newspaper mentions the advertiser's skin color, and the color of skin that he or she seeks in a partner. Skin color, of course, is also of overwhelming importance in our social prejudices. If you're a black African American trying to raise your children in white U.S. society, rickets and overheating are the least of the problems that might be solved by your skin color. Eye color and hair form and color, while not so overwhelmingly important as skin color, also play an obvious role in our sexual and social preferences. Just ask yourself why hair dyes, hair curlers, and hair straighteners enjoy such wide sales.

You can bet that it's not to improve our chances of surviving grizzly bear attacks and other risks endemic to the North American continent.

Nearly 125 years ago, Charles Darwin himself, the discoverer of natural selection, dismissed its role as an explanation of geographic variation in human beauty traits. Everything that we have learned since then only reinforces Darwin's view.

We can now return to our original questions: Are human racial classifications that are based on different traits concordant with one another? What is the hierarchical relation among recognized races? What is the function of racially variable traits? What, really, are the traditional human races?

Regarding concordance, we *could* have classified races based on any number of geographically variable traits. The resulting classifications would not be at all concordant. Depending on whether we classified ourselves by antimalarial genes, lactase, fingerprints, or skin color, we could place Swedes in the same race as either Xhosas, Fulani, and Ainu of Japan, or Italians.

Regarding hierarchy, traditional classifications that emphasize skin color face unresolvable ambiguities. Anthropology textbooks often recognize five major races: "whites," "African blacks," "Mongoloids," "aboriginal Australians," and "Khoisans," each in turn divided into various numbers of sub-races. But there is no agreement on the number and delineation of the sub-races, or even of the major races. Are all five of the major races equally distinctive? Are Nigerians really less different from Xhosas than aboriginal Australians are from both? Should we recognize 3 or 15 sub-races of Mongoloids? These questions have remained unresolved because skin color and other traditional racial criteria are difficult to formulate mathematically.

A method that could in principle overcome these problems is to base racial classification on a combination of as many geographically variable genes as possible. Within the past decade, some biologists have shown renewed interest in developing a hierarchical classification of human populations—hierarchical not in the sense that it identifies superior and inferior races but in the sense of grouping and separating populations based on mathematical measures of genetic distinctness. While the biologists still haven't reached agreement, some of their studies suggest that human genetic diversity may be greatest in Africa. If so, the primary races of humanity may consist of several African races, plus one race to encompass all peoples of all other continents. Swedes, New Guineans, Japanese, and Navajo would then belong to the same primary race; the Khoisans of southern Africa would constitute another primary race by themselves; and African "blacks" and Pygmies would be divided among several other primary races.

As regards the function of all those traits that are useful for classifying human races, some serve to enhance survival, some to enhance sexual selection, while some serve no function at all. The traits we traditionally use are ones subject to sexual selection, which is not really surprising. These traits are not only visible at a distance but also highly variable; that's why they became the ones used throughout recorded history to make quick judgments about people. Racial classification didn't come from science but from the body's signals for differentiating attractive from unattractive sex partners, and for differentiating friend from foe.

Such snap judgments didn't threaten our existence back when people were armed only with spears and surrounded by others who looked mostly like themselves. In the modern world, though, we are armed with guns and plutonium, and we live our lives surrounded by people who are much more varied in appearance. The last thing we need now is to continue codifying all those different appearances into an arbitrary system of racial classification.

"RACE WITHOUT COLOR"

Jared Diamond

1) What is "race" from both the vernacular and scientific meanings of the word?

2) Why do humans classify the world, including other peoples?

3) What does Diamond suggest are possible reasons that physical human traits vary?

4) What alternate ways does Diamond suggest "races" could be defined? What unusual combinations can you define in this manner?

5) What does Diamond suggest are the reason(s) that human skin color varies across the world?

6) How do "common sense" classifications and knowledge contribute to modern human problems surrounding "race" in this country and around the world?

TO CONTACT OR NOT?:
THE JARWAS OF THE ANDAMAN ISLANDS

Vishvajit Pandya

A cluster of 306 islands in the Bay of Bengal makes up India's territory of the Andaman and Nicobar Islands. Planeloads of tourists come to the airport at Port Blair to see the tropical rain forests and the coral reefs in a place that is rapidly becoming the ecotourism hotspot of India. As the tourists disembark, they pass pictures showing a historical prison that once housed many Indian freedom fighters. The display evokes a sense of the crucial role this island played in India's colonial history.

Elsewhere on the walls of the airport and in the photo studios of the local bazaar one can see images of a small, dark-skinned, tribal people in a semi-naked state. These are the hunting and gathering negrito tribes of the Andaman Islands, who live on tribal reserves off-limits to tourists and today make up approximately 0.32 percent of the total population of the islands.

History of Contact

In 1857, Captain John Campbell, a senior British Officer and consultant for the Council of Indian Government, wrote in favor of selecting the Andaman Islands as a penal settlement. "Convicts cannot be prevented from escaping when working on the mainland, but they . . . cannot get away from the Andamans, as the savages are far too hostile to allow one to escape." J. Walker, reporting to C. Beadon, Secretary to the Government of India, stated that within ten months, 240 of the first shipload of 733 convicts had been found killed by native arrows in the vicinity of the penal settlement. Seventy prisoners were reported to have escaped and disappeared without trace (Portman 1899).

In the early twentieth century, Port Blair was developed as an administrative seat and the region around it was developed using prisoners from mainland India. The forest was cleared with the aid of Andamanese tribal people (of the Aka Bea and Kol groups) who were employed as guides. The Jarwas, the tribal group discussed in this essay, frequently attacked the people they saw as invading their territory. In retaliation, Andamanese and Burmese forest workers and sepoys were often ordered to undertake "punitive expeditions." Vacant Jarwa campsites in the

deep forest were invaded by armed people, ransacked, and set alight. Various objects, such as metal implements, arrows, pots, and baskets, were seized and removed, mostly to establish if any escaped convicts were living among the Jarwas, a fact that was never really established. Reports suggest that face-to-face confrontation led to fatalities on both sides and to the capture of Jarwa women and children, who were then taken to Port Blair.

Frequently, gunfire and arrows were exchanged at close range. Not only did this result in a loss of life on both sides, but "a great deal of blood" was found on the trail after the firing had ceased—but seldom were the Jarwas themselves traced. In a 1925 expedition, 37 dead Jarwas were accounted for, reflecting the intense nature of such punitive expeditions. Similar contact, violence, and destruction occurred on Little Andaman Island between the Ongee and the settlers until the mid-1880s (Portman 1899).

Today, beyond the boundary of Port Blair, forest still covers 87 percent of the land. This resource is attracting boatloads of people, mainly from poorer parts of southern and eastern India, and the islands are gradually being cleared for small homes and cultivation (Saldanha 1989). These immigrants often are described as encroachers who evade administrative regulations. There is growing concern about preserving the island at a level that can sustain the present population and achieve economic growth without damaging the ecology. This view is shared by the early settlers, some administrators, and environmental lobbyists. However, the problem is compounded by the presence of tribal populations, such as the Jarwas, who have lived in the forests of the South and Middle Andaman Islands since before the earliest colonizers, prisoners, or settlers.

Jarwas are one of the last remaining tribes in this part of the world not to be assimilated to any degree with the outside society. Jarwas are confined to 765 square kilometers of forest, an area that has been declared a Jarwa reserve. This area was set apart by the Tribal Act of 1956 for the Jarwas' use and to keep them contained and protected. Around its perimeter, the number of settlers continues to increase. Whether these tribal groups should be kept isolated in a "human zoo" or encouraged to become part of the cultural mainstream is a long-standing question for

India. The issue is complicated by the question of whether the Jarwas really know that a boundary exists between their forest and the forest beyond, which is being invaded by the world. It is beyond doubt that Jarwas frequently experience non-Jarwas extracting wood and other forest resources, including wild pigs, a prime Jarwa food. The only indication that a boundary exists between them is a series of signs indicating the limits of Jarwa territory. Both Jarwas and non-Jarwas frequently cross over and the boundary remains a misunderstood notion, despite the presence of police to enforce it.

Contact Encounters

Since the completion of the Andaman Trunk Road in 1988, private and commercial traffic has begun passing through the Jarwa reserve. The 23-kilometer stretch of road has brought an increasing number of outsiders close to the Jarwas. Busloads of people travel northward from Port Blair along this road accompanied by armed escorts from the Andaman Nicobar Police Force. During construction of the road, workers often were targeted by the Jarwas, and a police escort now is provided in case the Jarwa attack or try to stop vehicles passing through their territory. Drivers of all vehicles are expected to refrain from sounding their horns so as not to disturb any Jarwas hunting in the forest.

In the last 10 years, police camps have been established within the Jarwa reserve to serve as warning posts and to protect settlers by scaring the Jarwas away with gunfire. The police, who originally intended to protect the Jarwas, today are seen as a force for the protection of settlers. In October 1991, Jarwas attacked the police camp at Jhirkatang and one policeman was killed. In defense (or retaliation), the police claimed to have fired three hundred rounds "in the air." According to the Jarwas, the individual killed in this attack was a poacher of wild pigs within the Jarwa territory. Settlers, on the other hand, tell of brave individuals who defended themselves against the "wild savages" in the forest.

In 1970, the Jarwas were contacted officially by the Indian government. Since 1974, contact with the Jarwas on the western coastline has been regular, systematic, and increasingly friendly. These contacts are organized by the government-administered agency for tribal welfare known as Andaman Adim Jan Jati Vikas Samiti (AAJVS). Every full moon and depending on the weather, AAJVS organizes a team of people who travel by boat to the western coast of Middle Andaman via Kadamtalla. The team includes administrators, a doctor, an officer from the statistics department, and an anthropologist from the local anthropological survey office.

As the ship reaches the coastline, it starts sounding its horn, searching for Jarwas moving out from the forest. Upon sighting the Jarwas, the ship is brought to a halt and smaller motorboats are loaded with raw bananas, coconuts, strips of cloth, metal pots, and nails. While members of the contact party make their way to the sandy coastline, in another boat members of police, not allowed to land on the beach, remain on alert for any undesirable events. On average, about 20 people are contacted at any given spot. Sometimes only women and children are contacted. At other times a large group of 50 to 60 appear.

As the boat loaded with gifts approaches the beach, the Jarwas, with their woven baskets, come out to meet it, scrambling for the gifts brought by the contact party. The Jarwas try to pick up what they can and fill their baskets. Often, the other members of a family help: picking up what they can and filling baskets, depositing their contents on the beach, and returning to collect the next load. Running between the boat and the beach the Jarwas sing in a repetitive chant-like tone. As gift items are unloaded and distributed among the Jarwas, the contact party disembarks and cautiously moves among the Jarwas congregated at the beach. On occasions, the distributed food is shared between the Jarwas and the contact party. During this time, the contact party makes audio and photographic records, notes the number of Jarwas present, whether there are any visible signs of sickness, injury, or if there is anyone needing medical attention.

The Jarwas also are involved in their own observation of the contact party. Variations in body size and shape, the clothes and skin of the contact party are carefully scrutinized by the Jarwas. Sometimes they mimic the sounds most often repeated by the contact parties. Over time, the Jarwas have learned that the contact party has instruments like tape-recorders, cameras, and video cameras. The Jarwas have heard the tapes played back to them; they have seen what the world looks like through the viewfinder of a camera. On some occasions, Jarwas have shown the contact party objects like eyeglasses, metal pots, clothing, and camera cases procured on the previous contact event. Generally, within three to four hours the event is brought to an end. Slowly the Jarwas begin picking up their loads of gifts and start moving into the forest. The contact party waves goodbye to the Jarwas and returns to the ship.

Many of the observations made in this way have confirmed what was known about the Jarwas since the days of British occupation of the islands, and much of the basic information has remained constant (Temple 1903, Portman 1899, Sarkar 1990). But information gathered in the span of a short contact encounter repeated three to five times a year is subject to a range of interpretations and misrepresentations. There is no systematic record of the people contacted, even the number of Jarwas living in the region is not definite. It is even questionable whether the Jarwas refer to themselves as Jarwas or not. Some administrators have questioned the benefit of these contacts to the Jarwas. Most of the people involved in the contact event regard it as an extremely tiring and risky chore that they have to do and that they would like to get it over with quickly. After the event, a radio signal is sent to Port Blair that the mission was successfully accomplished under the leadership of the senior government staff member accompanying the team. The estimated number of Jarwas contacted is relayed. This information is broadcast on the radio news across the whole island.

The contact event and the contact team's role have changed over time, as has the Jarwas' response to them. In the early contact phase, items like cooked rice and plastic trinkets were distributed. Soon it was realized that such items were a health hazard and a cultural imposition, and such distributions were stopped. Also, the right to join the contact party is now strictly controlled. Gone are the days when any visitor of importance was allowed to accompany the contact team in order to see the "exotic primitives living in harmony with nature." Those involved with the Jarwas over long periods of time are split among themselves about the objective of the mission: Some feel that regular contact instills mutual trust and encourage the Jarwas to join the mainstream of society; others feel that nothing is accomplished or learned by any involved.

A policy that is no longer encouraged is the embarkation of Jarwas on board the contact ship. This was reviewed after an incident in 1977 when two Jarwa men, having spent time in Port Blair, were returned with the hope that they would carry the message of trust and goodwill. Soon after, five poachers were killed by Jarwas in the region where the visitors to Port Blair had been dropped. Eventually the contact parties stopped bringing Jarwas to the Uttara Jetty of Kadamtalla where they, and the non-Jarwas, had become a curious exhibition for each other (AAJVS 1994). Yet, as late as 1983–84, the Jarwas exhibited eagerness to come on board the main ship and, if possible, take more gift items, including any piece of metal they could disconnect from the ship's decking. Some veteran members of the contact party remember that in the earlier days of contact the Jarwas were like mischievous children who would not hesitate to take things from the contact party members and hide them away. Incidents like these raise questions about boundaries, authority, and power relations. The evidence suggests that the Jarwas understand the relations of power but not the boundaries that, from the authorities' point of view, limit them.

What Has Been Achieved?

The news of successful Jarwa contact often raises the question: What has been achieved by such events? Some islanders feel that more vigorous efforts should be made to transform the Jarwa; that they should be made to give up their wilderness existence and be civilized quickly. Some from Ferargunj in the Andaman Islands said to me, "Giving little gifts here and there is not achieving anything. It is just a slow and corrupt way of scheming off money in the name of tribal welfare! In fact, it is making the Jarwas learn to depend on all assistance being given by the outsiders." A school teacher in Tirur said, "Look there is a lesson of history that we are ignoring: outsiders continued to give help and all forms of assistance to the Great Andamanese and made them settle down in Strait Island. Are they self-sufficient and happy today?" The Great Andamanese is a group of 20-odd individuals of conflicted cultural identity: Caught between being citizens of India and expecting special treatment, they are descended from a significant tribal group that has dramatically dwindled.

Some students at Tirur settlement pointed to the overlooking hills and said that they were aware of the fact that Jarwas can come out from the forest. In 1991, the Jarwas came out and killed an eight-year-old boy who was playing at the edge of the fields while his sister watched the family's cattle. The school children, on being asked what they thought Jarwas were, narrated a story about the de-evolution of trained elephants that were left behind by timber contractors after the Second World War, eventually becoming feral in the forest. "The Jarwas are like the elephants: They came from some kingdom across the sea and got stranded in the forest here, and over a period they forgot all their civility and shame. They became wild."

Although many villagers feel that the nature of the contact with the Jarwas should be changed and accelerated to civilize and discipline them, Port Blair residents, many with a commitment to environmental heritage, feel very differently. In their view, contact is not only useless, it is destroying the autonomous, healthy, natural existence of the Jarwas as hunters and gatherers. They feel that all contact with the tribes like Jarwas should be completely stopped.

Even if it were decided that contact with the Jarwas should cease, the question remains: Will the Jarwas stop contacting non-Jarwas? One of the major concerns of the growing number of settlers around the Jarwa reserve forest is the occurrence of incidents associated with Jarwa hostility. Jarwas come out to the small settlements and carry away clothes hanging outside, metal utensils, and tools; consume fruits from planted banana and coconut trees; destroy fences and the thatching of the houses; and kill dogs or livestock with arrows. To a degree, the settlers around the Jarwa reserve forest are now used to these incidents. They report them to the local administration when they happen and claim compensation. Each person killed by Jarwa results in a government payment of about $350 as compensation for the loss. All hostile attacks involving death are registered as crimes under the Indian Police Code. However, in practice, the courts tend to accept the final report of the police that the accused could not be traced or arrested and the criminal case against Jarwas often is abandoned. What settlers fear most are the occasions on which Jarwas appear to have selectively killed individuals in the settlement. People believe that those who are targeted by the Jarwas often have been spotted by the Jarwas in the forest trying to hunt or extract forest products, both of which are prohibited activities.

The folk notion that Jarwas punish settlers involved in illegal activities is questionable however, because it implies that the Jarwas seek out these culprits. It is not even clear that the Jarwas recognize the boundaries that separate them from the settlers and contacts with the Jarwas are such that their version of these events cannot be elicited.

Yet it cannot be denied that Jarwas resent outsiders exploiting their forest. Occasionally, a settler's body is recovered from the Jarwa reserve; whereas bodies mutilated with Jarwa arrows have been recorded at local police stations as "killed by the Jarwas within the reserve forest." The settlements that the Jarwas are most likely to raid are those nearest the Jarwa forest, and settlers have chased Jarwas away by firing guns or have been shot at by Jarwas arrows. Available records for 1983–88 indicate that 28 hostile incidents were reported to administration. Of these, 20 attacks were in settlements and eight in the reserve forest. In the period from 1946–61, 76 encounters were registered at the district headquarters and 15 settlers were killed, no records exist of Jarwa losses for this period. In most of the reported incidents of Jarwas entering settlements, death is infrequent

(Mann 1973). It must be noted that damages and losses sustained by the Jarwas are not recorded. Nothing is recorded or reported about how the settlers may have hurt or killed the Jarwas while conducting prohibited activities in the Jarwa reserve forest. Historically, Jarwas never leave behind an injured or dead body and contact parties often have reported observing Jarwas with bullet wounds.

Failure of Contact?

What, then, is the nature of contact between Jarwas and outsiders? Has distribution of "gift items" accomplished any specific goals? From the settlers' point of view, what objectives are being achieved? After all, settlers still experience hostility. From November 1993 to January 1994, 11 individuals were reported to have been killed by the Jarwas. Is it possible that the administratively sanctioned contact events are, in fact, instilling in the Jarwas a sense of themselves as "gift takers"? The contact party lets the Jarwas take whatever they bring and this taking is seen as a step toward "friendliness." But when Jarwas "take" the very same items at the settlement, they are regarded as conducting a "hostile attack." Is this misunderstanding generated by the very ritualized contacts conducted by administration? Just because the Jarwas are now recipients of "gifts," should the settlers be allowed to take things out of the Jarwa forest? After all, "hostility" and "friendliness" are relative notions. Perhaps the Jarwas don't see themselves as becoming friendly or turning around and becoming hostile.

Can contact solve this problem? Have there been any insights made into Jarwa culture or of the problem as it is perceived by the Jarwas themselves? One might take the stand that they are entitled to their land and dignity and should not be pushed out by the forces imposed on them by the outside world. Perhaps the Jarwas should be left alone with strict enforcement of the law that would restrict intrusions in their reserve forests. But would that include the restriction on the use of the road going through the forest? Perhaps it too could be controlled. But can they remain isolated? And for how long? Should we not make an effort to understand systematically what the Jarwas have to say about the situation? But where is the voice of the Jarwas? It is a problem that needs to be solved before it is too late.

Conclusion

Have the Jarwa always been as isolated and hostile as they have been made out to be in the literature or is their current position a construct of the government's administrative view of how the tribe should remain? Much of what is known about the "hostile" and "isolated" Jarwas is derived from contact expeditions. Contacts through which "outsiders" visit the Jarwas create a particular event, referred to as "friendly contact," which is characterized by specific forms of interactions and meanings. Friendly contact, which happens on the west coast, although its meaning becomes undecipherable when considered in relation to the events where the Jarwas come out eastward of their assigned reserve forest, and make contact with non-tribal settlers. Do moments of contact between tribal and non-tribal participants create a notion of boundary, making historically constructed boundaries redundant? Much of the verbal/linguistic categories in events of contact remain untranslated and misunderstood while the actions of tribal and non-tribal participants, particularly in conjunction with observations made by those involved with contact, construct a space within which relations of contact are "culturally translated."

Since 1998, the Jarwas have taken a lead on their own in doing the translation of contact relations and events for themselves. It is reported that frequently the Jarwas now walk out of the forest and come into the Kadamtalla region and they contact the settlers and the administration in daytime. According to settlers, this is not regarded as hostility, but the Jarwas trying to become like "us." It is now a dramatic situation on the streets of Kadamtalla's bazaar that the "naked" Jarwas are provided by the settlers with clothes, treated to tea and snacks, and entertained by loud film music. What is going to be the outcome of this contact is a matter of concern. After all, in colonial times, ancestors of the remaining twenty Great Andamanese used to come out to the streets of Port Blair where they were treated to opium and liquor and were sexually used. Things have changed as far as awareness among the outside world is concerned

but we need to know why the Jarwas have finally decided to be represented as contactors with the outside world now.

Note

For other Andaman Islanders, like the Ongees and the Great Andamanese, different kinds of changes have taken place. One hundred and one Ongees continue to live on Little Andaman with various forms of government aid and welfare programs. Twenty-odd Great Andamanese are still settled on Strait Island. Both Ongees and Great Andamanese maintain a lifestyle different from the old ethnographic accounts, learning to count in Hindi and occasionally watching the video monitor. In comparison, the world of the Jarwas remains relatively unchanged.

References

AAJVS. 1994. *Records of the Jarwa Contacts 1980–1991.* Secretariat, Port Blair.

Mann, R. 1973. "*Jarwas of Andamans—An Analysis of Hostility.*" *Man in India* 53:2 201–20.

Portman, M. 1899. *A History of Our Relations with the Andamanese.* Calcutta: Office of the Superintendent of Government Printing, India.

Saldanha, C. 1989. *Andaman, Nicobar, and Lakshadweep: An Environmental Impact Assessment.* New Delhi: Oxford and IBH Publishing Company Ltd.

Sarkar, J. 1990. *The Jarwas.* Calcutta: Seagull Books and Anthropological Survey of India.

Temple, R. 1903. *Census of India, 1901: Andaman and Nicobar Islands.* Calcutta: Superintendent of the Government Printing.

"To Contact or Not?: The Jarwas of the Andaman Islands"

Vishvajit Pandya

1) Discuss the history of contact between aboriginal groups on the Andaman Islands and Western culture.

2) What methods have the Jarwas employed to defend what they see as their land rights and political autonomy?

3) What recent peaceful means have been attempted to peacefully contact the Jarwas? Have they been successful?

4) What are the ethical and practical concerns that can and should be considered when dealing with contact with the Jarwas, or any relatively isolated peoples?

5) In your opinion, what should be the proper relationship between the Jarwas and the outside world? Should they be contacted, left alone, incorporated into a large modern state, or are there other alternatives that can and should be considered?

Isn't This My Soil?: Land, State, and 'Development' in Somali Ethiopia

Christina Zarowsky

Conventional development discourse generally does not incorporate a historical perspective; instead it uses a project or, at best, a program-oriented approach. In contrast, a historical and openly political framework is present in the Somali Ethiopian village of Hurso. Land, or the lack of it, was the central issue of Hurso testimonials about the life of grinding poverty that I collected in 1996 and in 1998. The absence of any sustainable means of production is considered the core problem, leading to hunger, disease, lack of social cohesion and cooperation, and both individual and collective demoralization. Although the problems attributed to lack of land are immediate, however, their origin and resolution are historical and political. "Development" emerges as an important pragmatic and rhetorical strategy in this community's struggle for survival. Underlying their appeals for development and development assistance is the memory of their dispossession and an unresolved claim for justice—for land.

Hurso, in eastern Ethiopia, is home to about 5,000 Somali of the Gurgura clan, formerly fruit farmers and agropastoralists. Hurso's lands were seized by the Derg, the Marxist government of Mengistu Haile Mariam, which ruled Ethiopia from 1974 to 1991 in the aftermath of the 1977–78 Ogaden War. In this war, Somalia unsuccessfully attempted to annex the ethnically Somali lands of Ethiopia. These lands consisted of the semi-arid Ogaden, the rich pastures of the Haud, and other lowlands off the eastern edge of the Ethiopian highlands.

Hurso is now known (if it is known at all) as the site of a large military training center of the newly refederated Ethiopia. It is remembered by its inhabitants as an almost heavenly place of permanent water, good grazing, and bountiful orchards. Today, it is a desolate stop on the railway from Addis Ababa to Djibouti, where people eke out an existence gathering and selling firewood (considered one step above begging), running tiny shops and teahouses, and selling meager amounts of onions, potatoes, and bananas. According to one elder:

> "Hurso was a big village, with many, many kinds of fruit—lemons, oranges, papayas, mangos. We have a proverb: Hurso—the Rome of the Gurgura. Today the people are returnees and refugees.

Women sell firewood. The life of the children is so hard. I was born here and lived 25 years before I left here. Today I see only empty land."

The story of the peoples' flight and return was told by men, women, elders, as well as youth who had been infants at the time. Most villagers fled into the surrounding countryside during the Ogaden War, and then returned to their lands. In the aftermath of the war, the Ethiopian government decided to expand the military base near the village and began to expropriate farmlands. Some families were offered compensatory lands in Sodere, hundreds of kilometers away, but the majority refused to leave. One day, the military arrived and surrounded the villagers. They were told to evacuate within 12 hours. Bulldozers arrived and destroyed homes and shops. People fled, some to Djibouti, others to Somalia, depending on their contacts and available transportation at crossroads towns. A few stayed in the area and lived in the scrub forest or stayed with pastoralist kin. These individuals would return to their lands and attempt to farm them. They were repeatedly beaten until, according to the villagers, the army concluded these individuals were mad and harmless. A few families were allowed to stay to service the military base and the train that stops in the village; these faced very strict controls on travel, visiting, and other activities between 1979 and 1991. The majority fled to Djibouti, where they stayed in UNHCR (United Nations High Commissioner for Refugees) camps.

Beginning in 1986, there was increasing pressure from the Djibouti government for Ethiopian refugees to leave the country, or at least the camps, as food aid from overseas had decreased dramatically. Some Hurso residents returned to Ethiopia in 1988, but the majority stayed in Djibouti, either in the capital, Djiboutiville, or in the border area with Ethiopia. When the Derg fell in 1991, they hoped the lands would be returned. Tens of thousands of Ethiopians, including some Hurso residents, stayed in Djibouti until a final repatriation program was completed in 1996.

With the fall of the Derg in 1991 came promises from the new government under the leadership of the Tigrean People's Liberation Front (TPLF), that farmlands would be restored and most of the refugees returned. To this day, the population is still waiting, negotiating, and trying to survive. The main sources of income are gathering and selling firewood, petty trade, and portering bundles of goods for traders who board the train at Hurso. A woodseller spends one day collecting and carrying firewood, which he or she can sell the next day for about 5 birr—less than US$1; a day laborer can earn 7 birr per day; and women selling tiny amounts of vegetables in the marketplace earn about 5 birr per day. In comparison, the one way fare to Dire Dawa, on a decrepit pickup truck that carries twenty-four passengers at a time, is 7 birr. Most people eat one or two meals a day and chronic malnutrition is endemic. During the rainy season, epidemics of malaria regularly break out and the health workers at the clinic do their best to manage in the face of sporadic delivery of medication and long periods without receiving their government-paid salaries.

The military base itself is critical to the village's survival; it is the main source of demand for the shops. Behind the clinic is a string of huts, separate from the rest of the village. These are the brothels—the home and the workplace to about fifty women frequented by the soldiers at the base. These women need to eat and cook and they buy a significant proportion of the food and firewood that Hurso residents try to sell.

Claiming Rights to Land, Claiming a Human Life

According to Gurgura tradition, firm claims to farming lands can be established on two grounds: traditional use over several generations and cultivation by individuals or lineages. This method of claiming land corresponds to the Somali, whose traditional use of lands for grazing and as a source of water are the two main sources of legitimate claims to territory. The lands around the village of Hurso are claimed by the Gurgura on several grounds: traditional use over at least seven generations; grants by various Ethiopian and Italian government; military conquest; and extensive planting of mango, citrus, papaya, and other fruit orchards. The farms were held by families, although the individual whose name is mentioned as "owner" of the larger farms or gardens are trustees of land considered to be available for the subsistence purposes of extended families or entire lineages.

People speak of the land as if they still own it; "This is Ahmed's garden;" "This is Amina's garden." Although the lands were taken almost 20 years ago, the community is still intensely loyal and passionate about them. People cling to the lands both because they are good, fertile lands, and because they still

consider them to be their lands. Until there is an option for creating ties to other lands or other livelihoods, both identity as well as survival are associated to them. I asked dozens of people why they returned to Hurso. People patiently told me that the government had changed and they were promised that the lands would be returned; there was no longer a way to make a living in Djibouti and lands surrounding Hurso could not support a significantly larger population—the land looks empty but is, in fact, full to its carrying capacity. Also, the original owners of the lands near Sodere (where some Hurso residents had been resettled) had returned after the fall of the Derg and had thrown out the resettled Hurso families. One man was less patient:

> Q: "Why did you return to Hurso?"
> A: "What do you mean? Isn't this my soil?"

Survival, Development, Identity, and State

The relationships among and between community members, government, military, and the workers hired by the military to guard the expropriated lands are complex. Resentment against the military base and the workers was minimal; the community's anger is directed not at the soldiers, but at the government. Some Gurgura men from the village itself, former members of the Gurgura Liberation Front, were also being trained at the base. The men guarding the farmlands chewed a mild stimulant, chat, (also an appetite or hunger suppressant) to maintain cordial relationships with the villagers in case of an eventual return of farmlands.

Responsibility for the initial dispossession and current poverty is placed on the government and the Ministry of Defense—believed to be holding on to the lands out of greed—both for revenue (which a local member of the federal parliament estimated at US$3–4 million per year) and simply possession. However, the district and regional governments shared some of the blame because it was felt they mishandled the negotiations for their return. Two trips to Addis by Hurso elders exhausted funds that could have been used for direct negotiation by the community. Future progress depended on action by district, regional, and federal officials.

Relationships between Somali Ethiopians and the Ethiopian state are ambivalent—clearly illustrated in Hurso. The history of relations between Somalis and the Ethiopian state is long and generally negative from both the Somali and the Ethiopian perspectives.

The current Hurso situation is clearly the result of acts by the Ethiopian state against a predominantly Somali population. In the newly refederated Ethiopia, however, Somalis now speak and go to school in Somali, have their own regional government (albeit corrupt and inefficient, in the view of many), and are for the first time, potentially equal to other Ethiopians as citizens. Many of my Somali interlocutors were cautiously optimistic about the possibilities for Somalis in the new Ethiopia.

Loyalty and identity, however, were invested in the clan, the land, and Somali ethnicity. What becomes clear through examining the history of land claims in Hurso is that the state is not seen as an oppressive and unitary force, but rather as a feature of the environment, currently a powerful actor with a tendency to swallow all other players, but with whom it is possible to make certain tactical alliances. In Hurso and elsewhere, among both men and women, national politics are now seen as crucial to development and survival.

Currently, both necessity and the tentative opening of the Ethiopian state to regional autonomy and full participation by all citizens lead Hurso and other Somali Ethiopian communities to conclude that the potential benefits are worth the risk of aligning themselves with the state. Nevertheless, it is always better to keep as many options open as possible. "Development" puts the state's role into a broader framework, where it is often the *de facto* final arbiter, but where the poor also have other potential advocates.

In 1998, a UNICEF-funded water project was working well, a new district government was in place, and other ties to the state and regional economy gave Hurso more power to press their claims for survival and restitution. International relief assistance, where the refugee relief system is the dominant organizing institution, is no longer the only tie between the community and the rest of the world. However, the channels of communication represented by both humanitarian aid and development must be kept open, in part as a check on the abuse of power by the state.

In his 1994 book, *The Anti-Politics Machine*, James Ferguson documents how the depoliticizing discourse and practice of development facilitates the encroachment of the state and its bureaucracy into more places and dimensions of life. For example, even though most development projects are deliberately apolitical, building a school, clinic, or agricultural extension office also brings employees who are ultimately responsible, not to the community nor to the donors, but to the government. The interests of the government are fundamentally political.

In Hurso, this same encroachment is visible, but the current and former residents of Hurso see this encroachment in historical, political, and pragmatic terms. My criticisms of development were greeted with impatient dismissal: "Yes there is plenty of corruption, abuse, and ineptitude of which we are well aware, but we want schools, clinics, and a water supply." Villagers openly admitted that they no longer had the skills—or more importantly—the desire to live off the land. Development was now integral to their notion of what constitutes a decent, human life. Contrary to the general findings of post-development critics, they did not want less development, but more; not less integration into the state, but more.

Their reasons for wanting more links to the state are pragmatic. In interviews about the larger context of Somali-Ethiopia relations, respondents stressed the importance of the clause in the new constitution permitting secession as a last resort. In the current circumstances, both union with Somalia and outright independence seem decidedly inferior to active participation in the Ethiopian state, which offers at least the possibility of political power and economic advancement, while safeguarding Somali autonomy should the situation become unacceptable. However, as the changing Hurso discourse on basic human needs demonstrates, it may not be easy to opt out of new ways of thinking about identity, survival, and what constitutes a human life.

Concretely, development in Hurso means both economic independence (ideally, by acquiring farmlands) and a combination of standard development and relief programs that address health care, water supply, education, childcare, and nutrition problems. Criticisms of these same programs were sharp. For example, Halcho, a community where 58 of the poorest families were resettled, needed extensive and expensive irrigation systems that involved drilling deep wells. But in the meantime, what were the farmers supposed to eat? Women involved in a revolving funds program stated that although it was a great idea, there were a number of basic problems: The market was already saturated with petty traders in milk and vegetables and there was no accessible market for other goods at the moment. Cash, especially this small a sum, was problematic because in Hurso, there is tremendous social pressure against refusing outright requests for financial assistance. If it were known that you had received 500 birr, then relatives and neighbors would approach you to repay small loans they had made to you, or to "lend" them money to take a sick child to the hospital; the money would soon be gone. The best development program of all would be to allocate land, making survival possible with fewer direct ties to the state or to development agencies. Nevertheless, promises of development programs—health care, clean water, and education—are likely to remain important for this community, even if the lands are returned.

Ultimately, development in Hurso means a sustainable and decent livelihood, and unfortunately the state's involvement is also essential for this to occur. To achieve a decent, human life or *nolol adaaminiimo*, it is necessary to have avenues through which to press claims—for justice, restitution, and short term assistance. Hence local, regional, national, and international politics, and telling the story of dispossession and its implied remedy, restitution, have become very important. Development was also a rhetorical strategy to possibly diversify the range of groups and individuals on whom one could make justice, compassion, or rights-based claims.

Story telling and history are valued for their own sake among the Somali, so it was generally easy for me to talk to people. However, given what I knew about the political importance of story telling, poetry, and history in Somali societies, it was clear that I was meant to hear these stories with a view to *action*.

"The owner must fight for his property."
—*Muusa Omar's* gabay *(poem)*

"I am asking you—what are you going to do for us?" —*Ali Yusuf's testimony*

"The main point is to help each other. To talk is fine, but let's get to the main point. You see our problems with your own eyes, as an eyewitness—they don't need much explanation."
—*Haawa Omar's testimony*

History, politics, development, and the state are key elements in this community's story of dispossession, poverty, and living an inhuman life. However, although the state is accorded a certain legitimacy and even respect as a worthy opponent, it should not be confused with the loyalty and sense of belonging that was built by using the land and maintained through the story of dispossession. Human life, a decent life, is not only a matter of calories and clean water, human life implies justice, beauty, and belonging. Aasha, the midwife, summarizes their passion towards the land, and the bitterness, sadness, and contempt that characterize the Hurso view of the state: "They are not careful of the land. It becomes hyenas' houses." This suggests a love relationship with the land, and hence an imperative to tend it and care for it. "Hyena's houses" suggests barren land, wasteland, even a rubbish heap, in implied contrast to the beautiful, fertile, beloved land that it was.

The story of Hurso, then, is a love story as well as a story of injustice. The Hurso Somali were ejected from their land during the war. They returned as refugees, their lands still in the hands of the Ministry of Defense. They survive, but are far from what they consider to be a decent, human life. Development projects and development rhetoric are important ways of coping, but the fundamental problem, in their eyes, is not a question of charity, but of simple justice.

"I am 15 years old. I was born in Turkaylo, near Hurso village. I had farmland in Hurso before 1977. After the Derg took my farmland I went to Serkama. Hurso! Before the Derg, there was no place better than Hurso. Anybody who knows how it was before will be in *wareer* [mad with worry and distress] when he *sees* it now. And still now I think it is the Derg or those who remained from the Derg government who are eating our gardens. Now my morale is not good, because still my properties are in the hands of the enemy. I think Hurso seems as if it is getting some air, but unfortunately the Derg remainders are still present. Hurso people need to get a balanced life, *nolol adaaminiimo*—food, health, education and so on. And to get their farmlands. I think if the government wants to develop Hurso's life, they have to give back their farms. I wish to add: you asked me many things and I am asking you, what are you going to do for us?"—*Ali Yusuf*

References

Ferguson, James. 1994. *The Anti-Politics Machine.* Minneapolis: University of Minnesota Press.

"Isn't This My Soil?: Land, State, and 'Development' in Somali Ethiopia"

Christina Zarowsky

1) Compare the remembered conditions in the village of Hurso to the conditions that exist in the present time.

2) What is the main source of income for the remaining villagers of Hurso?

3) What are the methods, traditional and otherwise, used by the Gurgura to establish ownership of farming lands?

4) Describe the state of the relationship between the Gurgura villagers and the current Ethiopian government.

5) How is "development" viewed by the Gurgura in economic, social, and political terms?

Law, Custom, and Crimes Against Women: The Problem of Dowry Death in India

John Van Willigen and V. C. Channa

This routinely reported news story describes what in India is termed a "bride-burning" or "dowry death." Such incidents are frequently reported in the newspapers of Delhi and other Indian cities. In addition, there are cases in which the evidence may be ambiguous, so that deaths of women by fire may be recorded as kitchen accidents, suicides, or murders. Dowry violence takes a characteristic form. Following marriage and the requisite giving of dowry, the family of the groom makes additional demands for the payment of more cash or the provision of more goods. These demands are expressed in unremitting harassment of the bride, who is living in the household of her husband's parents, culminating in the murder of the woman by members of her husband's family or by her suicide. The woman is typically burned to death with kerosene, a fuel used in pressurized cook stoves, hence the use of the term "bride-burning" in public discourse.

Dowry death statistics appear frequently in the press and parliamentary debates. Parliamentary sources report the following figures for married women 16 to 30 years of age in Delhi: 452 deaths by burning for 1985; 478 for 1986 and 300 for the first six months of 1987 (Bhatia 1988). There were 1,319 cases reported nationally in 1986 (*Times of India*, January 10, 1988). Police records do not match hospital records for third degree burn cases among younger married women; far more violence occurs than the crime reports indicate (Kumari 1988).

There is other violence against women related both directly and indirectly to the institution of dowry. For example, there are unmarried women who commit suicide so as to relieve their families of the burden of providing a dowry. A recent case that received national attention in the Indian press involved the triple suicide of three sisters in the industrial city of Kanpur. A photograph was widely published showing the three young women hanging from ceiling fans by their scarves. Their father, who earned about 4000 Rs. [rupees] per month, was not able to negotiate marriage for his oldest daughter.

The grooms were requesting approximately 100,000 Rs. Also linked to the dowry problem is selective female abortion made possible by amniocentesis. This issue was brought to national attention with a startling statistic reported out of a seminar held in Delhi in 1985. Of 3000 abortions carried out after sex determination through amniocentesis, only one involved a male fetus. As a result of these developments, the government of the state of Maharashtra banned sex determination tests except those carried out in government hospitals.

The phenomenon of dowry death presents a difficult problem for the ethnologist. Ethnological theory, with its residual functionalist cast, still does not deal effectively with the social costs of institutions of what might be arguably referred to as custom gone bad, resulting in a culturally constituted violence syndrome.

This essay examines dowry and its violent aspects, and some of the public solutions developed to deal with it in India. Our work consists of a meta-analysis of some available literature. We critique the legal mechanisms established to regulate the cultural institution of dowry and the resultant social evils engendered by the institution, and argue that policies directed against these social evils need to be constructed in terms of an underlying cause rather than of the problem itself. We consider cause, an aspect of the problem infrequently discussed in public debate. As Saini asserts, "legal academicians have shown absolutely no interest in the causal roots of dowry as practiced in contemporary India" (1983: 143).

The Institution

Since ancient times, the marriage of Hindus has required the transfer of property from the family of the bride to the family of the groom. Dowry or *daan dehej* is thought by some to be sanctioned by such religious texts as the *Manusmriti*. Seen in this way, dowry is a religious obligation of the father of a woman and a

Reprinted by permission from *Human Organization,* Vol. 50, No. 4, 1991.

matter of *dharma* (religious duty) whereby authority over a woman is transferred from her father to her husband. This transfer takes different forms in different communities in modern India (Tambiah 1973). In public discussion, the term "dowry" covers a wide range of traditional payments and expenses, some presented to the groom's family and others to be retained by the bride. Customs have changed through time. The financial burdens of gifts and the dowry payments per se are exacerbated by the many expenses associated with the marriage celebration itself, but dowry payment is especially problematic because of its open-ended nature. As Tambiah notes, "marriage payments in India usually comprise an elaborate series of payments back and forth between the marrying families" and "this series extends over a long period of time and persists after marriage" (1973: 92). Contemporary cases such as the death of Mrs. Sunita, often revolve around such continued demands.

A daughter's marriage takes a long time to prepare and involves the development of an adaptive strategy on the part of her family. An important part of the strategy is the preparation for making dowry payments; family consumption may be curtailed so as to allow accumulation of money for dowry. Seeing to marriage arrangements may be an important aspect of retirement planning. The dowries that the family receives on behalf of their sons may be "rolled over" to deal with the daughter's requirements. Families attempt to cultivate in both their sons and daughters attributes that will make them more attractive in marriage negotiations. Many things besides dowry are considered in negotiations: "non-economic" factors have demonstrable effect on the expectations for dowry and the family's strategy concerning the dowry process.

Education is a variable to be considered in the negotiation process. Education of young women is somewhat problematic because suitable husbands for such women must also be college educated. The parents of such young men demand more dowry for their sons. A consideration in sending a young woman to college will therefore be her parents' capacity to dower her adequately so as to obtain an appropriate groom. In any case, education is secondary to a man's earning power and the reputation of a woman's family. Education is, however, important in the early stages of negotiation because of the need to coordinate the level of the education of the men and women. Education qualifications are also less ambiguously defined than other dimensions of family reputation. Physical attractiveness is a consideration, but it is thought somewhat unseemly to emphasize this aspect of the decision.

Advertisements in newspapers are used for establishing marriage proposals (Aluwalia 1969, Niehoff 1959, Weibe and Ramu 1971), but contacts are more typically established through kin and other networks. Some marriages may be best termed "self-arranged," and are usually called "love marriages." In these cases, young men and women may develop a relationship independent of their families and then ask that negotiations be carried out on their behalf by family representatives.

Analysis of matrimonial advertisements shows some of the attributes considered to be important. Listed in such advertisements are education, age, income and occupation, physical attributes, *gotra* (a kind of unilineal descent group) membership, family background, place of residence, personality features, consideration of dowry, time and type of marriage, and language.

Consideration of dowry and other expenditures are brought out early in the negotiations and can serve as a stumbling block. Dowry negotiations can go on for some time. The last stage is the actual "seeing of the groom" and the "seeing of the bride," both rather fleeting encounters whose position at the end of the process indicates their relative lack of importance.

Marriage is a process by which two families mutually evaluate each other. The outcome of the negotiations is an expression of the relative worth of the two persons, a man and a woman, and, by extension, the worth of their respective families. This estimation of worth is expressed in marriage expenditures, of which dowry is but a part. There are three possible types of expenditures: cash gifts, gifts of household goods, and expenditures on the wedding celebration itself. The cash gift component of the dowry goes to the groom's father and comes to be part of his common household fund. The household goods are for use by the groom's household, although they may be used to establish a separate household for the newlyweds. When separate accommodations are not set up, the groom's family may insist that the goods do not duplicate things they already have.

Dates for marriages are set through consideration of horoscopes; horoscopy is done by professional astrologers (*pandits*). This practice leads to a concentration of marriage dates and consequent high demand for marriage goods and services at certain times of the year. During marriage seasons, the cost of jewelry, furniture, clothes, musicians' services and other marriage related expenditures goes up, presumably because of the concentration of the demand caused by the astrologers.

The expenditures required of the woman's family for the wedding in general and the dowry in particular are frequently massive. Paul reports, for a middle-class Delhi neighborhood, that most dowries were over 50,000 Rs. (1986). Srinivas comments that dowries over 200,000 Rs. are not uncommon (1984).[1]

Ethnological Theories About Dowry

Dowry had traditionally been discussed by ethnologists in the context of the functionalist paradigm, and much theorizing about dowry appears to be concerned with explaining the "contribution" that the institution makes to social adaptation. The early theoretician Westermarck interpreted dowry as a social marker of the legitimacy of spouse and offspring, and as a mechanism for defining women's social roles and property rights in the new household (Westermarck 1921: 428). Murdock suggests that dowry may confirm the contract of marriage (1949). Dowry is interpreted by Friedl as a means to adjust a woman to her affinal home as it rearranges social relationships including the social separation of the man from his parents (1967). Dowry payments are public expressions of the new relationship between the two families, and of the social status of the bride and groom.

Dowry is seen in the social science literature as a kind of antemortem or anticipated inheritance by which a widow is assured of support, and provision for her offspring (Friedl 1967; Goody 1973, 1976). It transfers money to where the women will be and where they will reproduce; as a result, resources are also placed where the children will benefit, given the practice of patrilineal inheritance of immovable, economically valuable property like farm land.

In India, dowry is also seen as an expression of the symbolic order of society. According to Dumont, dowry expresses the hierarchal relations of marriage in India and lower status of the bride (Dumont 1957). The amount of dowry given is an expression of prestige. The capacity to buy prestige through dowry increases the potential for social mobility (Goody 1973). Dowry is a kind of delayed consumption used to demonstrate or improve social rank (Epstein 1960).

There is a significant discontinuity between discussions of dowry in the ethnological theory and in public discourse. Certainly the dowry problem does appear in the writing of contemporary ethnologists, but it is simply lamented and left largely uninterpreted and unexplained.

The Extant Solutions to the Problem

The Dowry Prohibition Act of 1961, as amended in 1984 and 1986, is the primary legal means for regulating the dowry process and controlling its excesses. The laws against dowry are tough. Dowry demand offenses are "cognizable" (require no warrant) and nonbailable, and the burden of proof is on the accused. There are, in fact, convictions under the law.

The act defines dowry as "any property of valuable security given or agreed to be given either directly or indirectly—(a) by one party to a marriage to the other party to a marriage; or (b) by parents of either party to a marriage or by any other person, to either party to the marriage or to any other person" (Government of India 1986: 1). The act makes it illegal to give or take dowry, "If any person after the commencement of this act, gives or takes or abets the giving or taking of dowry, he shall be punishable with imprisonment for a term which shall not be less than five years; and with fine which shall not be less than fifteen thousand rupees or the amount of the value of such dowry which ever is more" (Government of India 1986: 1). While this section unambiguously prohibits dowry, the third section allows wedding presents to be freely given. Thus the law does not apply to "presents which are given at the time of marriage to the bride (without demand having been made in that behalf)" (Government of India 1986:1). Identical provisions apply to the groom. Furthermore, all such presents must be listed on a document before the consummation of the marriage. The list is to contain a brief description and estimation of the value of the gifts, name of presenting person, and the relationship that person has with the bride and groom. This regulation also provides "that where such presents are made by or on the behalf of the bride or any other person related to the bride, such presents are of a customary nature and the value thereof is not excessive having regard to the financial status of the person by whom, or on whose behalf, such presents are given" (Government of India 1986: 2). Amendments made in 1984 make it illegal for a person to demand dowry with the same penalty as under the earlier "giving and taking" provision. It was also declared illegal to advertise for dowry, such an offense being defined as not bailable, with the burden of proof on the accused person.

This legislation was coupled with some changes in the Indian Penal Code that legally established the concept of "dowry death." That is, "where the death of a woman is caused by any burns or bodily injury or occurs otherwise than under normal circumstances within seven years of her marriage and it is shown that soon before her death she was subjected to cruelty or harassment by her husband or any relative or her husband for, or in connection with, any demand for dowry, such death shall be called 'dowry death,' and such husband or relative shall be deemed to have caused her death" (Government of India 1987: 4). The Indian Evidence Act of 1871 was changed so as to allow for the presumption of guilt under the circumstances outlined above. Changes in the code allowed for special investigation and reporting procedures of deaths by apparent suicide of women within seven years of marriage if requested by a relative. There were also newly defined special provisions for autopsies.

To this point, however, these legal mechanisms have proved ineffective. According to Sivaramayya, the "act has signally failed in its operation" (1984: 66). Menon refers to the "near total failure" of the law (1988: 12). A similar viewpoint is expressed by Srinivas, who wrote, "The Dowry Prohibition Act of 1961 has been unanimously declared to be an utterly ineffective law" (1984: 29).

In addition to the legal attack on dowry abuses, numerous public groups engage in public education campaigns. In urban settings, the most noteworthy of these groups are specialized research units such as the Special Cell for Women of the Tata Institute of Social Sciences (Bombay), and the Center for Social Research (New Delhi). Also involved in the effort are private voluntary organizations such as the Crimes Against Women Cell, Karmika, and Sukh Shanti.

These groups issue public education advertising on various feminist issues. The anti-dowry advertisement of the Federation of Indian Chambers of Commerce and Industry Ladies Organization exemplifies the thrust of these campaigns. In the following advertisement, which was frequently run in the winter of 1988 in newspapers such as the *Times of India*, a photograph of a doll dressed in traditional Indian bridal attire was shown in flames.

> Every time a young bride dies because of dowry demands, we are all responsible for her death. Because we allow it to happen. Each year in Delhi hospitals alone, over 300 brides die of third degree burns. And many more deaths go unreported. Most of the guilty get away. And we just shrug helplessly and say, "what can we do?" We can do a lot.
>
> Help create social condemnation of dowry. Refuse to take or give dowry. Protest when you meet people who condone the practice. Reach out and help the girl being harassed for it. Act now.
>
> Let's fight it together.
>
> As parents, bring up educated, self-reliant daughters. Make sure they marry only after 18. Oppose dowry; refuse to even discuss it. If your daughter is harassed after marriage stand by her.
>
> As young men and women, refuse marriage proposals where dowry is being considered. As friends and neighbors, ostracize families who give or take dowry. Reach out to help victims of dowry harassment.

> As legislators and jurists, frame stronger laws. Ensure speedy hearings, impose severe punishments. As associations, give help and advice. Take up the challenge of changing laws and attitudes of society. Let us all resolve to fight the evil. If we fight together we can win.
>
> SAY NO TO DOWRY.

Also engaged in anti-dowry work are peasant political action groups such as Bharatiya Kisan Union (BKU). BKU consists of farmers from western Uttar Pradesh whose political program is focused more generally on agricultural issues. The group sponsored a massive 25-day demonstration at Meerut, Uttar Pradesh, in 1988. The leadership used the demonstration to announce a social reform program, most of it dealing with marriage issues. According to news service reports, "The code of social reforms includes fixing the maximum number of persons in a marriage party at 11, no feasts relating to marriage and no dowry except 10 grams of gold and 30 grams of silver" (*Times of India*, February 11, 1988). Buses plying rural roads in western Uttar Pradesh are reported to have been painted with the slogan "The bride is the dowry." Private campaigns against dowry occur in the countryside as well as among the urban elites, although it is likely that the underlying motivations are quite different.

Policy Analysis

Our argument is based on the assumption that social problems are best dealt with by policies directed at the correction of causative factors, rather than at the amelioration of symptoms. While current legal remedies directly confront dowry violence, the linkage between cause and the problematic behavior is not made. Here we develop an argument consisting of three components: women's access to production roles and property; delocalization of social control; and economic transformation of society. The pattern of distribution of aspects of the institution of dowry and its attendant problems is important to this analysis. Although dowry practices and the related crimes against women are distributed throughout Indian society, the distribution is patterned in terms of geography, caste rank, socioeconomic rank, urban/rural residence, and employment status of the women. In some places and among some people there is demonstrably more violence, more intensity of dowry practices, and more commitment to dowry itself. Much of the distributional data are problematic in one way or another. The most frequent problem is that the studies are not based on national samples. Furthermore, the interpretation of results is often colored by reformist agendas. There is a tendency to deemphasize differences in frequency from one segment of the population to another so as to build support of dowry death as a general social reform issue. Nevertheless, while the data available for these distributions are of inconsistent quality, they are interpretable in terms of our problem.

Women's Access to Production Roles and Property

Dowry violence is most frequent in north India. Some say that it is an especially severe problem in the Hindi Belt (i.e., Uttar Pradesh, Haryana, Punjab, Delhi, Bihar) (Government of India 1974: 75). It is a lesser, albeit increasing problem in the south. There is also a north/south difference in the marriage institution itself. To simplify somewhat, in the north hypergamy is sought after in marriage alliances, in which case brides seek grooms from higher rank descent groups within their caste group (Srinivas 1984). In the south, marriages are more typically isogamous.

The literature comparing north and south India indicates important contrasts at both the ecological and the institutional levels. Based on conceptions developed by Boserup (1970) in a cross-cultural comparative framework on the relationship between the farming system and occupational role of women, Miller (1981) composed a model for explaining the significant north-south differences in the juvenile sex ratio [the ratio of males to females ten years of age and below]. The farming systems of the north are based on "dry-field plow cultivation," whereas in the south the farming systems are dominated by "swidden and wet-rice cultivation" (Miller 1981: 28). These two systems make different labor demands. In the wet rice or swidden systems of the south, women are very important sources of labor. In the north, women's involvement in agricultural production is limited. According to Miller, women in the north are excluded from property holding and receive instead a "dowry of movables." In the south, where women are included in the production activities, they may receive "rights to land" (Miller 1981: 28). In the north, women are high-cost items of social overhead, while in the south, women contribute labor and are more highly valued. In the north there is a "high cost of raising several daughters" while in the south there is "little liability in raising several daughters." There is thus "discrimination against daughters" and an "intense preference for sons" in the north, and "appreciation for daughters" and "moderate preference for sons" in the south. Miller thus explains the unbalanced-toward-males juvenile sex ratios of the north and the balanced sex ratios of the south (Miller 1981: 27–28). The lower economic value of women in the north is expressed in differential treatment of children by sex. Females get less food, less care, and less attention, and therefore they have a higher death rate. In general the Boserup and Miller economic argument is consistent with Engles's thesis about the relationship between the subordination of women and property (Engels 1884, Hirschon 1984: 1).

Miller extended her analysis of juvenile sex ratios to include marriage costs (including dowry), female labor participation, and property owning, and found that property owning was associated with high marriage costs and low female labor force participation, both of which were associated with high juvenile sex ratios. That is, the death rate of females is higher when marriage costs are high and women are kept from remunerative employment. Both of these patterns are associated with the "propertied" segment of the population (Miller 1981: 156–159). Her data are derived from the secondary analysis of ethnographic accounts. The literature concerning the distribution of dowry practices and dowry death is consistent with these results.

Miller's analysis shows a general pattern of treatment of females in India. Their access to support in various forms is related to their contribution to production (Miller 1981). This analysis does not explain the problem of dowry violence, but it does demonstrate a fundamental pattern within which dowry violence can be interpreted.

The distribution of dowry varies by caste. In her study of dowry violence victims in Delhi, Kumari found that members of the lower-ranking castes report less "dowry harassment" than do those in higher ranking castes (Kumari 1988: 31). These results are consistent with Miller's argument since the pattern of exclusion of women from economic production roles varies by caste. Women of lower castes are less subject to restrictions concerning employment outside the realm of reproduction within the household. These women are often poor and uneducated, and are subject to other types of restrictions.

In the framework of caste, dowry practices of higher-caste groups are emulated by lower-caste groups. This process is known as "Sanskritization" and it may relate to the widely held view that dowry harassment is increasing in lower-ranking castes. Sanskritization is the process by which lower-ranked caste groups attempt to raise their rank through the emulation of higher-rank castes. The emulation involves discarding certain behaviors (such as eating meat or paying bride price) and adopting alternatives (Srinivas 1969). Attitudinal research shows that people of the lower socio-economic strata have a greater commitment to dowry than do those of higher strata (Hooja 1969, Khanna and Verghese 1978, Paul 1986). Although the lower and middle classes are committed to dowry, the associated violence, including higher death rates, is more typically a middle class problem (Kumari 1988).

Employment status of women has an effect on dowry. In her survey of dowry problems in a south Delhi neighborhood, Paul (1986) found that the amount of dowry was less for employed middle-class women than it was for the unemployed. This pattern is also suggested by Verghese (1980) and van der Veen (1972: 40), but disputed by others (Murickan 1975). This link is also manifested among tribal people undergoing urbanization. Tribal people, ranked more toward the low end of the social hierarchy, typically make use of bride price (i.e., a payment to the bride's family) rather than dowry (Karve 1953). As these groups become more integrated into national life, they will shift to dowry practices to emulate high castes while their women participate less in gainful employment (Luthra 1983). Croll finds a similar relationship in her analysis of post-revolutionary China. She says, "it is the increased value attributed to women's labor which is largely responsible for the decline in the dowry" (1984: 58).

Both Kumari (1988) and Srinivas (1984) developed arguments based on non-economic factors. Kumari in effect indicated that if dowry could be explained in economic terms, marriage would be simply a calculation of the value of a woman: if the value were high, bride price would be paid, and if the value were low, dowry transactions would occur. This formulation was presented as a refutation of Madan's dowry-as-compensation argument (Kumari 1988). We agree that reducing this practice to purely economic terms is an absurdity. The argument is not purely economic, but it is certainly consistent with a cultural materialist perspective (Harris 1979) in which symbolic values are shaped by an underlying material relationship that is the basis for the construction of cultural reality.

Delocalization of Social Control

Dowry violence is more frequent in cities (Saini 1983). Delhi has the reputation of having a high frequency of problems of dowry (Srinivas 1984: 7). The urban-rural distribution pattern may be a manifestation of the effects of the delocalization of dowry. Dowry, when operative in the relationships among local caste groups in related villages, was to an extent self-regulating through caste *panchayats* (councils) and by the joint families themselves. These groups easily reach into peoples' lives. By contrast, the national level laws

have inadequate reach and cannot achieve regulation. While in some areas caste groups continue to function to limit abuses, these groups are less effective in urban settings. Population movements and competition with state level social control mechanisms limit the effectiveness of self-regulation. A government commission study of women's status argues "that because of changed circumstances in which a son generally has a separate establishment and has a job somewhere away from home, the parents cannot expect much help from him, and so they consider his marriage as the major occasion on which their investment in his education can be recovered" (Government of India 1974: 74). These views are consistent with the research results reported by Paul, who demonstrates that dowry amounts are higher among people who have migrated to Delhi and those who live in nuclear families, because the families in general and the women in particular are less subject to social constraints (Paul 1986). New brides do not seem to have adequate support networks in urban settings.

Economic Transformation of Society

The custom of dowry has been thrown into disarray by inflationary pressures. The consumer price index for urban non-manual workers has increased from its reference year of 1960 value of 100 to 532 for 1984–85 (Government of India 1987). The media of dowry exchange have changed dramatically because of the increasing availability of consumer goods. It has become increasingly difficult to prepare for giving dowry for a daughter or sister. Sharma argues that, in part, dowry problems are caused by rapid change in the nature of consumer goods which made it no longer possible to accumulate gift goods over a long period as the latest styles in material goods could not be presented (1984: 70–71).

The current regime of individual dowry seeking and giving is constituted as a kind of rational behavior. That is, it is achieved through choice, is consistent with certain values, and serves to increase someone's utility. There are a number of things sought by the groom's family in these transactions. Wealth and family prestige are especially important. The family prestige "bought" with marriage expenditures, which is relevant to both the bride and groom's side in the transaction, is no doubt very much worth maximizing in the Indian context. From the perspective of the bride's family, dowry payments involve trading present consumption for future earning power for their daughter through acquiring a groom with better qualities and connections. In a two-tier, gender-segregated, high-unemployment, inflationary economy such as that of India, one can grasp the advantage of investing in husbands with high future earning potential. It is also possible to argue that in societies with symbolic mechanisms of stratification, it is expected that persons will attempt to make public displays of consumption in order to improve their overall performance and so to take advantage of the ambiguities of the status hierarchy system. The demand for both symbolic goods and future earnings is highly elastic. Family connections, education, and wealth seem especially important in India, and they all serve as hedges against inflation and poverty. With women having limited access to jobs and earning lower pay, it is rational to invest in a share of the groom's prospects. If you ask people why they give dowry when their daughters are being married they say, "because we love them." On the other hand, grooms' families will find the decision to forgo dowry very difficult.

Summary

The distributional data indicate that the relationship between the way females are treated in marriage and their participation in economic production is consistent with Miller's development of the Boserup hypothesis. It is assumed that the pattern of maltreatment of females has been subject to various controls operating at the levels of family, caste, and community. Urbanization reduces the effectiveness of these mechanisms, thus increasing the intensity of the problem. This trend is exacerbated by the economic transformations within contemporary Indian society. It is our viewpoint that policies developed to reduce dowry-related violence will fail if they do not increase the economic value of women.

The criminalization of dowry may have been a politically useful symbol, but it has not curtailed the practice. As dowry is attacked, the state has not adequately dealt with the ante-mortem inheritance aspect of the custom. If dowry continues to provide a share of the family wealth to daughters before the death of the parents, then legally curtailing the practice is likely to damage the economic interests of women in the name of protecting them. One might argue that the primary legal remedy for the dowry problem actually makes it worse because it limits the transfer of assets to women. Perhaps this is why research on attitudes toward dowry indicates a continued positive commitment to the institution (Mathew 1987). India is a society in which most people (most particularly the elite) have given and received dowry; most people are even today giving and taking dowries. Declaring dowry a crime

creates a condition in which the mass of society are technically criminals. The moral-legal basis of society suffers, and communal, parochial, and other fissiparous forces are encouraged.

To be effective, anti-dowry legislation must make sure that the social utility provided by dowry practices be displaced to practices that are less problematic, and that the apparent causes of the practice be attacked. To do so would mean that attempts to eradicate the social evils produced by the dowry institution need to be based on an examination of women's property rights so as to increase their economic access. Traditional Hindu customs associated with inheritance give sons the right from birth to claim the so-called ancestral properties. This principle is part of the Mitakshara tradition of Hindu law, which prevails throughout India except in Bengal, Kerala, Assam, and northern parts of Orissa. These properties are obtained from father, paternal grandfather, or paternal great-grandfather. According to Sivaramayya (1984: 71), "The Hindu Succession Act (the law which controls inheritance) did not abrogate this right by birth which exists in favor of a son, paternal grandson and paternal great grandson. The availability of the right in favor of these male descendants only is a discrimination against daughters." The right is derived from ancient texts. According to Tambiah (1973: 95), the Dharmasastras provide that it is "essentially males who inherit the patrimony while women are entitled to maintenance, marriage expenses and gifts." While the Hindu Succession Act abrogates much traditional law, it specifically accepts the principle of male birth right to the property of the joint family. That is, "When a male Hindu dies after the commencement of the Act, having at the time of death an interest in a Mitakshara coparcenary property, his interest in the property shall devolve by survivorship upon the surviving members of the coparcenary and not in accordance with this Act" (Government of India 1985: 3). The Hindu Succession Act in its most recent form provides for the intestate or testamentary inheritance of a female of a share of the family property. Yet the prior right of males at birth is not abrogated. Hindu males own a share of the family rights at birth; females can inherit it. Testamentary succession overrides the principle of intestate succession, and therefore the interests of females can be usurped simply by writing a will. The other procedures for a female to renounce an interest in family property are very simple. Moreover, according to Sivaramayya (1984: 58), "no specific formality is required for the relinquishment of the interest beyond the expression of a clear intention to that effect." Instruments of relinquishment can be and are forged.

The ante-mortem inheritance function of dowry has been eroded or perhaps supplanted by transfer of goods to the grooms' family for their consumption and the expression of the so-called prestige of the family. Indeed social science commentary on dowry in India suggests that this aspect of dowry is relatively unimportant in any case because only a small portion of the total marriage expenditure is under the bride's control. There is evidence that even the clothing and ornaments and other personal property of the bride are being usurped (Verghese 1980). Implementation of a gender-neutral inheritance law as advocated by the Government of India Committee on the Status of Women may serve to increase the economic value of women in general, while it serves as an alternative to the ante-mortem inheritance aspect of dowry. Since dowry constitutes a kind of ante-mortem inheritance, it is logical to change the inheritance laws in conjunction with the restrictions on dowry behavior. Sisters as well as brothers need to have a share in the family wealth from birth, and that right should be associated with legal procedures that increase the difficulty of alienation of property rights. There is no question that such a procedure would serve to erode the stability of the patrilineal family by diluting its economic base.

The Government of India has passed legislation such as the Hindu Succession Act (1955) and the Hindu Adoption and Maintenance Act (1956), both of which inter-alia provide for a woman's right of inheritance from her father. For example, under the Adoption and Maintenance Act, a woman has a claim of rights of maintenance from her husband's father in case she is widowed. Moreover, she has the right to claim inheritance from her deceased husband's estate. In spite of these changes, inheritance provisions are quite different for males and females. The Chief Justice of the Supreme Court of India, Honorable Mr. Justice Y. V. Chandrachud wrote that in spite of changes, "some inequalities like the right of birth in favor of a son, paternal grandson and paternal great grandson still persist" (1984: vii). Provision of females with equal rights to inherit ancestral property from birth, or from a bequest, or at the death may reduce dowry problems. Furthermore, property that is allowed to remain in the name of the deceased for any length of time, as is frequently the case in India, should revert to the state. As it stands, property may remain in the name of a deceased ancestor, while his descendants divide it informally among themselves.

The establishment of a gender-neutral inheritance law represents a significant shift in public policy. We argue that there is a link between pro-male property laws and violence toward women. While we assert this position, we also need to recognize that the property laws give coherence and stability to an essential Indian institution, the joint family. The Mitakshara principle of male inheritance rights is both a reflection and a cause of family solidarity. Modifying this principle in an attempt to reduce violence toward women could have a deleterious effect on family coherence. In addition, the fundamental nature of these institutions makes it inconceivable that there would be substantial resistance to these changes. Yet if one considers this issue in historic terms, it is apparent that during the 20th century, legal change is in the direction of gender neutrality, a process that started with the Hindu Law of Inheritance (Amendment) Act (1929) and the Hindu Succession Act (1956), and continues through judicial decisions to the present (Diwan 1988: 384). As Diwan notes in reference to the changes brought by the Hindu Succession Act of 1956, "the Mitakshara bias towards preference of males over females and of agnates over cognates has been considerably whittled down" (1988: 358). Such change is not easy. The changes brought with the Hindu Succession Act in 1956 were achieved only after overcoming "stiff resistance from the traditionalists" (Government of India 1974: 135). The same report states, "The hold of tradition, however, was so strong that even while introducing sweeping changes, the legislators compromised and retained in some respects the inferior position of women" (Government of India 1974: 135). It must be remembered that the texts that are the foundations of contemporary law include legislation (such as the Hindu Succession Act itself), case law, and religious texts, so that the constitutional question is also a question for religious interpretation, despite the constitutional commitment to secularism.

We are advocating further steps toward gender neutrality of the inheritance laws so that women and men will receive an equal share under intestate succession, and have an equal chance to be testamentary heirs. The law should thus be gender-neutral while still permitting a range of decisions allowing property to stay in a male line if the holder of the property so chooses. The required social adjustment could be largely achieved through the decisions of a family, backed by the power of the state. Families could express their preferences, but the state would not serve to protect the economic interests of males. The process could involve the concept of birthright as well as succession at death. We do not choose to engage those arguments, but do point out that the rapid aging of the Indian population may suggest that a full abrogation of the Mitakshara principle of birthright would be the best social policy because doing so would give older people somewhat greater control over their property in an economy virtually devoid of public investment in social services for older people (Bose and Gangrade 1988, Sharma and Dak 1987).

There are precedents for such policy at the state level. In Andhra Pradesh, the Hindu Succession Act was amended to provide for a female's birthright interest in the Mitakshara property. In Kerala, the Mitakshara property concept was legally abrogated altogether. Other gender asymmetries in the laws of India need to be attacked. The overall goal of policy should be to increase the economic value of women.

Ethnological theory directs our attention to social recognition of marriage and property transfer as functionally important features of the institution. The state can provide a means of socially recognizing marriage through registration and licensure. The law expresses no explicit preference for traditional marriage ritual, and it is possible to have a civil marriage under the provisions of the Special Marriage Act (1954) through registration with a magistrate. Nevertheless, this system co-exists parallel with the traditional system of marriage, which is beyond the reach of state control. Other marriages may be registered under this act if the persons involved so choose, and if a ceremony has been carried out. These special marriages are an alternative to an unregistered marriage.

We conclude that a useful mechanism for state control of dowry problems is the establishment of universal marriage registration, which does not exist at the present time. Marriage registration is also called for by the first Round Table on Social Audit of Implementation of Dowry Legislation (Bhatia 1988), which may serve to provide some monitoring of dowry abuses and perhaps to manifest the state's interest in an effective marriage institution. It would be naive to assume that such a policy would be widely honored, but as it is, low-income persons do not get married because they do not have the resources for marriage under the traditional non-state controlled regime. There are numerous reform groups that organize mass marriage ceremonies of village people so as to help them escape the burden of marriage expenditures. The point is that compliance is a large problem even under current circumstances.

In conclusion, we feel that the causes of the dowry problems are a product of the low economic value of women, loss of effective social control of abuse through delocalization, and pressures caused by economic transformation. The traditional family, caste group, and community controls which have been reduced in effectiveness should be replaced by state functions. The foundation of state control is universal marriage registration and licensure. The

impact of the economic value of women on the problem is indicated by the transition from bride price to dowry among tribal people. It is also associated with a reduction in the extent of gainful employment and lower dowry amounts demonstrated for employed women. A broad program to increase the economic value of women would be the most useful means of dealing with the problem of dowry. Further restrictions on dowry without providing for a radically different property right for females are probably not in the interests of Indian women, since dowry represents ante-mortem inheritance. This underlying paradox may explain the commitment to dowry revealed in attitudinal research with Indian women, even though it is also an important feminist issue. The alternatives include the abolishment of the legal basis for the joint family as a corporate unit as has been done in Kerala, or the legal redefinition of the joint family as economically duolineal, as has occurred in Andhra Pradesh.

Note

1. For purposes of comparison, a mid-career Indian academic might be paid 60,000 Rs. per year.

References

Aluwalia, H. 1969. Matrimonial Advertisements in Panjab. *Indian Journal of Social Work* 30:55–65.

Bhatia, S. C. 1988. Social Audit of Dowry Legislation. Delhi: Legal Literacy Project.

Bose, A. B. and K. D. Gangrade. 1988. *The Aging in India, Problems and Potentialities*. New Delhi: Abhinav.

Boserup, Ester. 1970. *Women's Role in Economic Development*. New York: St. Martin's Press.

Chandrachud, Y. V. 1984. Foreword. In *Inequalities and the Law*. B. Sivaramayya, ed. Pp. iv–vi. Lucknow: Eastern Book Company.

Croll, Elisabeth. 1984. The Exchange of Women and Property: Marriage in Post-revolutionary China. In *Women and Property—Women as Property*. Renee Hirschon, ed. Pp. 44–61. London/New York: Croom Helm/St. Martin's Press.

Diwan, Paras. 1988. *Modern Hindu Law, Codified and Uncodified*. Allahabad: Allahabad Law Agency.

Dumont, Louis. 1957. *Hierarchy and Marriage Alliance in South Indian Kinship*. London: Royal Anthropological Institute.

Engles, Fredrich. 1884. *The Origin of Family, Private Property and the State*. New York: International.

Epstein, T. Scarlett. 1960. Peasant Marriage in South India. *Man in India* 40:192–232.

Friedl, Ernestine. 1967. *Vasilika, A Village in Modern Greece.* New York: Holt, Rinehart and Winston.

Goody, Jack. 1973. Bridewealth and Dowry in Africa and Eurasia. In *Bridewealth and Dowry.* Jack Goody and S. J. Tambiah, eds. Pp. 1–58. Cambridge: Cambridge University Press.

_____. 1976. *Production and Reproduction, A Comparative Study of the Domestic Domain.* Cambridge: Cambridge University Press.

Government of India. 1974. *Towards Equality: Report of the Committee on the Status of Women.* New Delhi: Government of India, Ministry of Education and Social Welfare.

_____. 1985. The Hindu Succession Act. New Delhi: Government of India.

_____. 1986. The Dowry Prohibition Act, 1961 (Act No. 28 of 1961) and Connected Legislation (as on 15th January, 1986). New Delhi: Government of India.

_____. 1987. *India 1986, A Reference Manual.* Delhi: Ministry of Information and Broadcasting.

Harris, Marvin. 1979. *Cultural Materialism: The Struggle for a Science of Culture.* New York: Random House.

Hirschon, Renee. 1984. Introduction: Property, Power and Gender Relations. In *Women and Property—Women as Property.* Renee Hirschon, ed. Pp. 1–22. London/New York: Croom Helm/St. Martin's Press.

Hooja, S. L. 1969. *Dowry System in India.* New Delhi: Asia Press.

Karve, Irawati. 1953. *Kinship Organization in India.* Bombay: Asia Publishing.

Khanna, G. and M. Verghese. 1978. *Indian Women Today.* New Delhi: Vikas Publishing House.

Kumari, Ranjana. 1988. Practice and Problems of Dowry: A Study of Dowry Victims in Delhi. In *Social Audit of Dowry Legislation.* S. C. Bhatia, ed. Pp. 27–37. Delhi: Legal Literacy Project.

Luthra, A. 1983. Dowry Among the Urban Poor, Perception and Practice. *Social Action* 33:207.

Mathew, Anna. 1987. Attitudes Toward Dowry. *Indian Journal of Social Work* 48:95–102.

Menon, N. R. Madhava. 1988. The Dowry Prohibition Act: Does the Law Provide the Solution or Itself Constitute the Problem? In *Social Audit of Dowry Legislation.* S. C. Bhatia, ed. Pp. 11–26. Delhi: Legal Literacy Project.

Miller, Barbara D. 1981. *The Endangered Sex, Neglect of Female Children in Rural North India.* Ithaca, NY: Cornell University Press.

Murdock, George P. 1949. *Social Structure.* New York: Macmillan.

Murickan, J. 1975. Women in Kerala: Changing Socioeconomic Status and Self Image. In *Women in Contemporary India.* A. de Souza, ed. Pp. 73–95. Delhi: Manohar.

Niehoff, Arthur H. 1959. A Study of Matrimonial Advertisements in North India. *Eastern Anthropologist* 12: 37–50.

Paul, Madan C. 1986. *Dowry and the Position of Women in India. A Study of Delhi Metropolis.* New Delhi: Inter India Publishers.

Saini, Debi. 1983. Dowry Prohibition Law, Social Change and Challenges in India. *Indian Journal of Social Work* 44(2):143–147.

Sharma, M. L. and T. Dak. 1987. *Aging in India, Challenge for the Society.* Delhi: Ajanta Publications.

Sharma, Ursula. 1984. Dowry in North India: Its Consequences for Women. In *Women and Property—Women as Property.* Renee Hirshcon, ed. Pp. 62–74. London/New York: Croom Helm/St. Martin's Press.

Sivaramayya, B. 1984. *Inequalities and the Law.* Lucknow: Eastern Book Company.

Srinivas, M. N. 1969. *Social Change in Modern India.* Berkeley, CA: University of California Press.

_____. 1984. *Some Reflections on Dowry.* Delhi: Oxford University Press.

Tambiah, S. J. 1973. Dowry and Bridewealth and the Property Rights of Women in South Asia. In *Bridewealth and Dowry.* Jack Goody and S. J. Tambiah, eds. Pp. 59–169. Cambridge: Cambridge University Press.

van der Veen, Klaus W. 1972. *I Give Thee My Daughter—A Study of Marriage and Hierarchy Among the Anavil Brahmins of South Gujarat.* Assen: Van Gorcum.

Verghese, Jamila. 1980. *Her Gold and Her Body.* New Delhi: Vikas Publishing House.

Weibe, P. O. and G. N. Ramu. 1971. A Content Analysis of Matrimonial Advertisements. *Man in India* 51:119–120.

Westermarck, Edward. 1921. *The History of Human Marriage.* London: MacMillan and Co.

"Law, Custom, and Crimes Against Women: The Problem of Dowry Death in India"

John Van Willigen and V. C. Channa

1) What is a dowry? What legal, social, economic, and religious purposes does it serve?

2) What is a "dowry death"? How do such deaths occur?

3) Why does the Indian government downplay the problem of "dowry death" in India?

4) What current legal remedies are in place to combat the problem of "dowry death"? Are they effective?

5) What social solutions do the authors argue for to help reduce or eliminate dowries and "dowry deaths"?

TREATING THE WOUNDS OF WAR

Carolyn Nordstrom

I use these tin cans when I do my healing ceremonies. I take an empty can and put in some rocks and then seal it. I shake the can when I am working, and the rocks clatter—it makes quite a noise. This can with the rocks in it, that is what someone's head is like when they have *been* affected by war.—
Traditional medical practitioner, Mozambique

With the October 1992 ceasefire, the 15-year war in Mozambique is over. Or is it? There is more to consider than ongoing military control in a country trying to reconstruct order from chaos. Cultures of violence and trauma are legacies of an extremely brutal war. To understand them, it is necessary to look back at the fighting that marked the war in Mozambique during the 1980s.

Mozambique's "internal" war was developed and guided externally. It began when Frelimo (Frente de Libertação de Moçambique) came to power after Mozambique achieved independence from Portugal in 1975. Rhodesia and then South Africa instigated and led the rebel group RENAMO (Resistência Nacional Moçambicana) in an attempt to undermine the model that a black majority Marxist-Leninist–led country offered to resistance fighters of other countries. Although RENAMO supporters and opportunists do exist in Mozambique, essentially the rebel group has little popular support. With destabilization, rather than any coherent political ideology, as the defining factor in forming RENAMO, dirty war tactics—using terror in the targeting of civilian populations—predominated. Its human-rights violations have been among the worst in the world.

The extent of the violence in Mozambique can be captured in a few statistics:

- More than one million people, the vast majority of them noncombatants, lost their lives in the war.

- The war orphaned more than 200,000 children. (Some estimates are much higher.) Adequate assistance is more a wish than a reality in a country where one-third of all schools and hospitals were closed or destroyed by RENAMO and only a single orphanage operates.

- The war displaced nearly a quarter of the 15 million people in Mozambique from their homes. More than half of all Mozambicans were affected directly by the violence, famine, and destruction unleashed by the war.

- Ninety percent of Mozambicans live in poverty, 60 percent in extreme poverty. Forty percent are malnourished, and in the last year of the war more than half of the country's inhabitants were in need of direct food aid. Famine, limited resources, inadequate infrastructure, and fighting hindered aid efforts and took the lives of many.

- We can only guess at the numbers who were raped; beaten, tortured, and maimed; burned out of villages and homes; kidnapped by RENAMO for forced labor and concubinage; or forced into fighting—not to mention those who were forced to watch this happen to loved ones.

Definitions of Violence

The people who theorize about and wage war tend to try to control its definitions. These definitions, however, are narrow ones that focus predominately on military engagements and troop interactions. Even if civilians and communities are recognized casualties of a war, the military apparatus, and by extension the war itself, is seen as something apart from the ebb and flow of everyday life and cultural vitality. The Mozambicans cited in this article challenge the traditional assumption of political and military science that war's violence applies only to soldiers, political ideologies, and governments. Violence comes unbidden and unexplained into the heart of the civilian population, the center of war's destructiveness.

Since World War II, when civilian wartime casualties began to far outpace combat casualties, modern wars have only vaguely resembled the formal "textbook" definitions of war. This is nowhere more apparent than in an armed conflict, such as Mozambique's, in which the use of terror against noncombatants—as a way to enforce political acquiescence—was a primary strategy of warfare. Civilian life and society not only become the battleground in these wars, they become the targets. Violence spills out across the social and cultural landscape to affect the country's entire population.

It is the abhorrent brutality that has most captured the attention of those investigating RENAMO's war of terror: journalistic reports, government analyses, and international nongovernmental organizations (NGOs) all focus on physical acts of brutality, especially RENAMO's. Stories that most violate notions of human decency—gruesome mutilations, rapes, murders—tend to circulate most widely. Yet when I listened to average Mozambicans discuss the war, these barbarous accounts, although present, weren't the focal point of the violence. People were concerned with a deeper, more enduring type of violence: the destruction of home and humanity, of hope and future, of valued traditions and community integrity. Psychological, emotional, and cultural violence rank equally with, and in many cases outrank, physical violence.

Consider the words of an old traditional healer in a town in the center of Zambezia Province that had been the site of intense conflict for several years:

> "Wounds [from the war] can be easily treated. That is, the physical wounds. Some of these kids have wounds because they have seen things they shouldn't see, that no child should have to see— like their parents being killed. They change their behavior. This is not like being mad; that we can treat. No, this is from what they have seen: it is a social problem, a behavioral problem, not a mental problem. They beat each other, they are disrespectful, they tell harsh jokes and are delinquent. You can see it in their behavior toward each other: more violence, more harshness, less respect— more breaking down of tradition."

Mozambicans consistently pointed out that not all severely disruptive wounds stem from direct physical violence:

> "The war brings many types of violence, and some we can deal with better than others. The physical mutilation and massacres are horrible: the women raped, the ears and lips cut *off*, the friend chopped to death with a machete. . . . There is no excuse for this, no easy solution to the suffering it causes. But you want to know what I think is the worst thing about this war? It is sleeping in the bush at night. [Because RENAMO often attacked at night, many people slept in the bush.] Animals live in the bush, not humans. My marriage bed is the center of my family, my home, my link with the ancestors and the future. This war, the *Bandidos Armados* ["armed bandits"—RENAMO], have broken my marriage bed, and with that they try to break my spirit, break what makes me who I am, make me an animal. This is the worst violence you can subject someone to."

The war also kills hope and any sense of normality. One day I was speaking to a child of five or six who had walked hundreds of miles with his family after RENAMO had attacked and burned his village. He had the countenance of an adult and the weakened body of a child half his age, and he spoke about the violence he had witnessed with a detached seriousness, much as an old man might speak. Asked about a small wound on his leg, the type of injury children are prone to get, he answered:

> "The wound? I will die of it. We walked here many days, and we had nothing while we walked. I watched my brother starve to death during that time. We had to leave our home because the bandits attacked it, and I saw them kill my father. Now we are here and I watch my mother dying slowly, because we have nothing. I will die too."

These forms of violence are only marginally recognized in traditional conflict studies, and solutions to these types of problems are seldom even broached. Among those most affected by war, however, finding solutions to these kinds of violence are paramount. This is not only because violence is so crippling to the sustainability of life, limb, and community, but because Mozambicans who have seen violence first hand recognize the dangers of the growth of a culture of violence. Virtually every Mozambican I spoke with agreed with the wisdom captured by the healer who said:

> "People have just seen too much war, too much violence—they have gotten the war in them. We treat this, we have to—if we don't take the war out of the people, it will just continue on and on, past RENAMO, past the end of the war, into the communities, into the families, to ruin us."

The idea that violence can, as one person said, "stick on a person like a rash on the soul" is pervasive in Mozambique.

Healing War's Wounds

What is fairly unique about Mozambicans is their conviction that cultures of violence that can be built up can also be broken down. In fact, in many heavily affected areas, people asked that every new arrival touched by the war's violence—including those who had seen people die of starvation—be treated by a traditional healer who specialized in war trauma to "take the violence out of them."

Traditional healers have incorporated conflict resolution into their healing arts. They counsel marginalized or renegade soldiers (predominately RENAMO) to give up fighting and return to their communities and a peaceful way of life. The healers focus on severing the person from the soldier mentality. They act to reintegrate the person into community life, and they can teach community members to accept the ex-soldier (who may well have committed atrocities there). Healers have even encouraged others to kidnap RENAMO soldiers to "help them get over the war." Conversely, many citizens criticize UN schemes to demobilize soldiers and move them to camps isolated from the community—a situation that could continue the cycle of violence.

Average citizens on the front lines are far more involved in the mitigation of conflict than outsiders might suspect. Granted, the situation at the local level is complex and often contradictory. There are people working in the political, military, and economic spheres who seek to benefit from the fractures caused by war. Others, like the traditional healers, are trying to solve the inequalities, injustices, and abuses caused by war and those who exploit violence for their own gain. These positive forces include local-level political groups (both legal and proscribed) who meet across conflict lines to defuse tensions; traders who carry goods, messages, and refugees across no-man's-lands; religious leaders who sponsor peace talks in the thick of the battle; teachers who work with traumatized children in battle-scarred villages.

Ongoing narratives weaving violence, isolation, treachery, and hope are often at the heart of discussions by average civilians as they search for better solutions to the culture of violence wrought by the war. These discussions, unlike those concerned only with the physical destructiveness of violence, emphasize the long-term problems, those that will last well beyond ceasefires, that can grow out of the current conflict.

The reverberating effects of violence on uncertain futures are nowhere more evident than with women who have been kidnapped and raped by soldiers, and who have, in many instances, borne children from these assaults. As Joaquim Segurada, a Portuguese anthropologist working with a private organization in Mozambique, noted:

> "So what happens when these women go back to their homelands? Still they are missing their husbands, their families, and who will want them? Maybe they return to find their lands missing—that they have lost the rights to them when they lost their husband, or maybe some avaricious person or enterprise has taken their land over, and the women have no means, no strength to fight this. But worse than that, they will have lost "normalcy": the context of their family and home can never be the same again—it has been irreparably destroyed. Healthy culture, as they knew it, is gone."

Women working for the Organization for Mozambican Women in Zambezia, one of the provinces most severely affected by the war, were more graphic in assessing this problem. They frequently lamented the many times that women who were forced to have sex with soldiers returned home to find husbands who had taken other wives or who despised them for having been with other men, families who marginalized them for having lived with the enemy, and communities who called the children produced by rapes *lixo* (garbage).

In Mozambique, many educators, religious and community leaders, healers, and citizens recognize that violence is "formative," that it shapes people's perceptions, self-images, and outlooks on life. That this situation need not exist motivates the work of many who want to change the reality of the front lines.

Local solutions attempt to deal not only with immediate traumatization, but with disrupted social and cultural systems that can linger long after the last bullet has been fired. Many people at the epicenter of a war realize it is often cyclical: it deposits seeds of conflict that will germinate at a later date. But many are optimistic that specific actions can break this cycle of violence. Few accept that conflict is natural to humans. They have seen that a few soldiers can wreak brutal havoc on an entire society.

Resolution and Transformation

One of the most unfortunate barriers to healing cultures of violence is the fact that national and international agencies too often neither support nor recognize much of the local-level work conducted to identify and treat the legacies of violent conflict. These agencies lose the insights of those at the "ground" level, dooming good intentions to failure as local people go without the sponsorship that could carry their ideas to fruition on a large scale. As one old Mozambican villager, recently burned out of his home and village, summed up, "If the governments and all those other outsiders who think they know what is going on would just get out of this, we could cure this country in no time."

As the destructive legacies of cultures of violence become recognized, the wounds of war that can spark new conflicts over time can be healed. The old Mozambican quoted above might be encouraged by some of the programs the government is instituting. In the hope of curtailing the reverberations of war's violence, the Ministry of Education has begun a program to assist traumatized youth in primary schools, and the Organization for Mozambican Women has projects to help women who are grappling with the effects of rape, dislocation, and chronic poverty. And, as of 1989, the government has elected to incorporate indigenous healers into the health-care system to benefit from the range and depth of healing knowledge they offer—knowledge that heals societies as well as bodies.

"TREATING THE WOUNDS OF WAR"

Carolyn Nordstrom

1) War was a constant factor in Mozambique for more than 15 years. What were the costs, in human lives and in cultural disruption, of the conflict?

2) What types of violence does the article refer to in regard to the Mozambique war?

3) How do traditional healers deal with the internalized violence of the survivors of the war? How do they treat these "walking wounded"?

4) How do average citizens help to normalize the social and political situations and begin to heal the wounds of war?

5) How have women, in particular, been impacted by the war?

RESOURCE RIGHTS AND RESETTLEMENT AMONG THE SAN OF BOTSWANA

Robert K. Hitchcock

In March, 1996, Roy Sesana, a G//ana headman from Molapo in the Central Kalahari Game Reserve of Botswana, and John Hardbattle, a Nharo from Buitsavango in the Ghanzi Farms region, spoke before the Human Rights Commission of the United Nations in Geneva, Switzerland. As representatives of an indigenous San non-government organization (NGO), Kgeikani Kweni (First People of the Kalahari), they stressed that the San, the indigenous peoples of southern Africa, were facing some major human rights problems, including forced resettlement out of their traditional areas and legislation which restricted their rights to hunt and gather. These situations, they argued, resulted in San losing their land, resources, and cultural identity.

San in Botswana have been required to move out of areas that they had occupied, to some cases, for hundreds of years. The resettlement process has had significant effects on their well-being: it reduces their access to natural resources with which they are familiar, restricts the amount of land they have to reside to and use, and puts them in positions where they are impinging on other groups, a process that has led sometimes to social conflicts.

In 1997, the government of Botswana chose to resettle several hundred residents outside the Central Kalahari Game Reserve (CKGR), the second largest game reserve in Africa. The justification for this involuntary resettlement was that it would promote conservation and development and would improve the standards of living of the San. The Central Kalahari case provides an excellent example of how international, national, and local pressures have affected the well-being of local people in Africa and how recommendations from environmental organizations and development agencies have influenced policies at the state level.

Botswana's Land Management Policies

An argument made by Hardbattle and Sesana was that San had been removed from areas in the past to establish freehold farms. Beginning in the early 1970s, the World Bank funded projects that resulted in the resettlement and the loss of resource access rights of stable numbers of San, especially in the western sandveld regions of the country. People originally residing in these commercial ranches were required to relocate, and relatively little compensation was provided to the households that were resettled. The government of Botswana dealt with the land rights of the people removed from the commercial ranches by establishing so-called communal service centers. But these areas were generally small in size and did not contain sufficient resources to sustain the populations residing there either as hunter-gatherers or as mixed forager-agropastoralists.

Later, it was found that there was little land that could be set aside as reserves, so an alternative land category was created: Wildlife Management Areas (WMAs). These areas are portions of the country in which natural resource use, both consumptive and non-consumptive (e.g. game viewing), is to be the primary economic activity. By 1992, some 66,750 square kilometers were gazetted legally as WMAs under the Wildlife Conservation and National Parks Act. Other land was designated as state land, including national parks and game reserves. The largest of these conserved areas was the CKGR, which was established in 1961 with the help of anthropologist George Silberbauer to accommodate the needs of several thousand G/wi, G//ana, and Bakgalagadi, people who had lived in the region for generations.

In the 1960s, people in the reserve were primarily hunter-gatherers who depended on a wide range of plant and animal species. Mobility was relatively high, with annual camp moves occurring as often as 10 to 15 times per year. Group sizes were small, averaging between twenty-five and eighty, and they consisted of people related primarily through kinship, marriage, long-standing friendship, and socioeconomic ties. In the 1960s, the people of the Central Kalahari tended to range over large areas that averaged between 900 and 4,000 square kilometers. Over time, there has been a general reduction in range sizes to the point where they averaged less than 450 square kilometers in the late 1980s and early 1990s. Specific groups had long-standing customary rights to specific territories, which they passed from one generation to the next. People were able to obtain rights to territories on the basis of birth, marital (affinal) ties, and by asking the areas traditional occupants. There also were cases where people established customary land rights through colonization, that is, moving into areas that were either uninhabited or that had experienced population reductions due to drought, disease, or out-migration for employment.

There have been significant changes over time in the economic systems of resident populations in the CKGR. Whereas the people of the region were mobile foragers in the 1960s, in the 1990s, the majority of the people living in the reserve depended on domestic foods obtained through drought relief or national feeding programs, or by purchasing it. Some residents kept goats, dogs, donkeys, and horses, but—it should be noted—no cattle. Horses and dogs were used sometimes in subsistence hunting activities and nearly all the hunting in the reserve was done with traditional weapons, including spears, bows and poisoned arrows, clubs, and snares. After 1979, local hunters were allowed to obtain a specified number of wild animals legally as long as they had in their possession a Special Game License (SGL), a license that was, in effect, a subsistence hunter's license. Some environmental researchers argued vociferously that local people should not be allowed to hunt at all in the reserve. They sought the assistance of the European Union to put pressure on Botswana to remove the people from the CKGR and to declare the area as a game reserve along the lines of those outlined by the World Conservation Union (IUCN).

Between 1986 and the present, various pressures on people inside the reserve encouraged them to move outside the reserve. "Freezing" development in the CKGR was one effective method. When the borehole at !Xade, the largest community in the reserve, broke down, it took months before it was fixed. Buildings and roads were not maintained in the reserve, except for those going to Department of Wildlife and National Parks camps and mining exploration camps. According to local people, the drought relief food programs were implemented more slowly and less effectively in the Central Kalahari than elsewhere in Botswana, a situation that threatened the well-being of people in several parts of the reserve.

The Department of Wildlife also was accused of intimidating the local people in the Central Kalahari and selectively enforcing wildlife conservation laws. Local people maintained that they were detained and arrested more frequently than other (non-San) people and they pointed out that they often received higher fines and stiffer jail sentences than did people who resided in towns and villages. This was the case, they argued, in spite of the fact that people from towns

were much more involved in hunting for meat and skins for sale than the people in the Central Kalahari.

Even more disturbing than the high rates of arrest were the charges that people were mistreated by game scouts and other officials. There were a number of incidents where people claimed that they were tortured or received inhumane or degrading punishment when suspected of poaching or when being questioned about other people who might be engaged in illegal hunting. According to one report, the most common form of torture included the use of a rubber ring placed tightly around the testicles and a plastic bag placed over the face of a person. There were cases where people died of injuries inflicted upon them by Department of Wildlife and National Parks officials. Such an incident allegedly occurred at !Xade in August, 1993, when a 40-year-old man died after being detained and questioned at length by game scouts. Community leaders in the Central Kalahari have argued that authorities have stepped over the line from anti-poaching to persecution.

The government of Botswana maintained that the CKGR should become a game reserve and, as such, people living there should be resettled outside the boundaries of the reserve. Their reasoning was that people and wildlife were incompatible in a game reserve; people in the Central Kalahari were no longer traditional because they now hunted with dogs and horses; it was too expensive to provide services to such a remote and scattered population; and more effective development assistance could be provided in a location that was closer to roads, air strips, and other infrastructure.

To encourage the people of the Central Kalahari to move to a location outside the reserve, the government of Botswana offered compensation to people. Although rumors concerning the large amounts of compensation that would be provided were widespread, including "enough for a new four wheel drive vehicle," most payments made thus far have been, at most, a few thousand Pula (around U.S. $1,000). Given the resources that people have had to give up when they moved out of the reserve, this amount is, according to local people, far below what would be required to reestablish themselves at a level at least equivalent to what they had while living in the reserve (something that is required in World Bank guidelines on involuntary resettlement).

International assistance for projects in the Central Kalahari was recommended both by local people and by agencies working with them. In the early 1990s, efforts were made to get the IUCN, based in Switzerland, to declare the CKGR a Biosphere Reserve or a World Heritage Site in order for people to continue living there.

As a result of the planned resettlement proposals, the San and the Bakgalagadi began to organize at the grassroots level to protest the plans and to recommend alternative scenarios, including ones in which local people would be allowed to continue to reside in the reserve and engage in community-based natural resource management and ecotourism activities. They sought international attention through going to meetings and holding press conferences. They also allied themselves with both local and outside organizations, including Ditshwanelo, the Botswana Center for Human Rights, and the Survival International in London.

In March 1997, the Botswana Minister of Local Government, Lands, and Housing requested a budget of 6 million Pula (about U.S. $1.5 million) to resettle people outside the CKGR. Some of these funds were to be used in the development of New !Xade, a resettlement location outside the CKGR in the Okwa Wildlife Management Area in Ghanzi District. The resettlement of several hundred people out of !Xade to New !Xade was carried out in May, 1997. New !Xade consisted of little more than lines of tents and a water storage tank: There was no functioning borehole in the area and water had to be piped from some 60 kilometers away. According to people who were moved, little if any attention was paid to local patterns of kinship and social organization in the move, and the distribution of people in the settlement was such that relatives and friends were sometimes separated from one another, something that was not the case in their former home.

There were numerous complaints about New !Xade. One of the most poignant of these was the fact that there were practically no trees at the new settlement and people had to walk long distances to obtain fuel wood and wild food plants. There also were complaints about the Land Board's slow response to the applications of resettled people for arable and residential plots in the settlement area. An additional problem, they point out, is the high level of alcohol sales by outside agencies and individuals in the settlement, which allegedly has contributed significantly to fights and to spouse and child abuse problems.

The people of the Central Kalahari have argued vociferously that their needs and the conservation goals of Botswana were not being met as a result of the policies being pursued. They pointed out that large numbers of tourists in four-wheel drive vehicles were now coming into the reserve and that the fragile pan and fossil river bed surfaces were being destroyed. They noted that more cattle were now seen in the reserve than was the case previously. They also expressed that the reason that they were being removed was so that well-to-do private citizens could set up lucrative safari camps to the reserve. Their worst fears began to be realized when they learned that a large-scale mining venture was being established at Gope in the southeastern corner of the CKGR and that a paved road from the DeBeers diamond mine at Orapa was being constructed.

It is ironic, local people argue, that the land and resources of the Central Kalahari are now being exploited not by the people who had lived there and managed the resources for generations, but rather by outsiders, including sizable numbers of tourists and mining companies. The question that local people ask is whether or not the government of Botswana actually intends to promote conservation of the CKGR, or whether it is using the conservation and sustainable development rhetoric as a means of getting other governments to go along with their efforts to promote the interests of large-scale, well-to-do agencies and individuals at the expense of the local communities.

Community-Based Natural Resource Management Projects in Botswana

One of the ways that Botswana has attempted to deal with the problems of wildlife losses and environmental degradation is to establish community-based natural resource management programs (CBNRMPs) that aim to benefit local people. Various NGOs and development agencies, including the United States Agency for International Development and SNV (the Netherlands Development Organization), have worked with district authorities and local communities in Botswana to set up and run projects that combine conservation and development. As of 1998, there were nine CBNRM projects in Botswana, some of which had been in place for a decade. In some cases, these projects had generated sizable amounts of income, several hundred thousand Pula per year, and the members of the communities received training and other kinds of technical assistance.

In the 1980s, the Kalahari Conservation Society, a Botswana-based NGO, provided assistance to a local group that wanted to establish a conservation area in a picturesque region of northeastern Botswana. Located on the northern tip of Sua Pan in the Makgadikgadi Pans region, what was to become the Nata Sanctuary is a picturesque area that consists of undulating plains, pans of clays and salts (45 percent of its surface area), and a strip gallery forest along the Nata River, which flows seasonally off the Zimbabwe Plateau. The area is known for its large numbers of migratory birds, especially flamingos and pelicans, which use the area as a feeding ground and breeding area. The area also supports a variety of antelopes, including springbok, impala, and kudu.

From the time the sanctuary idea was conceived in the mid-1980s, it was visualized as a biological reserve area where people other than tourists and staff members would be excluded. Planning the sanctuary did include some discussions with people in the immediate area, including Nata Village, which is 6 kilometers to the northwest, but it did not include consultations with the people from villages along the lower and middle stretches of the Nata River where some 2,000 people reside.

The Nata Sanctuary, which is 230 square kilometers in size, is located in an area that has long been used for a variety of purposes by Tyua foragers and Bamangwato and Kalanga agropastoralists. Besides Nata Village, which is close to the sanctuary, there are small villages and dispersed extended family compounds ranging in size from 10 to 120 people. The area was largely cattle post or *meraka* grazing land in the past, but some people also fished in the lower reaches of the Nata River in addition to hunting and collecting salt.

Foraging continued to play a role in the diet and economies of local people, hence the importance of the sanctuary area to local communities. A wide range of fauna and flora were exploited, and some of these resources were important sources of income for local people. For example, palm leaves were used by women to make and then sell baskets.

A useful aspect of this project, according to the various organizations that supported it, was that it involved local and non-local people in land use and resource management decisions. However, questions were raised by people living in communities along the Nata River about access to the salt deposits in the Nata Delta that are now contained within the boundaries of the sanctuary. There also have been ongoing conflicts about the collection of thatching grass and firewood and the grazing of livestock inside the sanctuary's boundaries.

The Nata Lodge is nearby and benefits from the presence of the sanctuary and, in turn, supplies a restaurant and petrol station. Some local people work at the lodge, but few other benefits and no compensation have been provided to those people who lost access to resources within Nata Sanctuary. New tarred roads have been completed in the northern Kalahari linking Nata with Maun and Kasane. As a result, the numbers of tourists have increased significantly in what had been a fairly remote part of Botswana. These tourists are camping, using scarce firewood, and purchasing crafts, and thus impacting the environment and economies of local people.

Expanding the number of CBNRM projects, including the one in the Gweta area to the west of Nata, has resulted it an increased exploitation and sale of various wild plant products, including *marula*, a sweet fruit. Local groups have argued that the commercialization of these items has led to a reduction in the availability of these resources for use by the poor, especially San. Like a number of other community-based natural resource management programs in Africa, the Nata Sanctuary and the Gweta marula exploitation programs have served to undermine the degree to which local people have access to resources.

Conclusion

International development agencies, such as the World Bank, and governments of states like Botswana often have used rhetoric like "integrated conservation and development" to justify establishing programs that change the nature of land tenure from communal to either private (freehold or leasehold) or reserved. Environmental NGOs have used similar kinds of arguments to reduce the exploitation of natural resources by local communities or to have them removed from land that they deem should be preserved "for posterity." All too often, the goals of conservation and development are lost in efforts to promote large-scale tourism or other kinds of capital-intensive development.

Braam LeRoux, a founding member of Kuru Development Trust (a development organization aimed at helping the Nharo San and other people of western Botswana), has argued that it is important to carry out "community-owned development" in which local people have control over all aspects of development, from needs assessments to project planning, and from implementation to monitoring and evaluation. Building on the cultural values of the group or community is essential. Among San populations, there are basic principles by which these societies operate: respect for the land, sharing and reciprocal use and exchange of resources, consensus-based decision making, and social equity. By incorporating these indigenous principles into a holistic development approach, it would be possible to bring about local empowerment and to promote sustainable, community-owned development rather than the kind of top-down, socially and environmentally destructive kinds of development that has characterized the livestock and conservation projects in Botswana.

References

Ditshwanelo. 1996. *When Will This Moving Stop? Report on a Fact-Finding Mission of the Central Kgalagadi Game Reserve.* April 10–14, 1996. Gaborone, Botswana: Ditshwanelo, the Botswana Center for Human Rights.

Hitchcock, Robert K. and Rosinah Rose B. Masilo. 1995. *Subsistence Hunting and Resource Rights in Botswana* Gaborone, Botswana. Natural Resources Management Protect and Department of Wildlife and National Parks.

LeRoux, Braam. 1996. *Community-Owned Development: Exploring an Alternative Rural Development Support Program.* Ghanzi, Botswana: Kuru Development Trust and Working Group of Indigenous Minorities in Southern Africa.

Matloff, Judith. 1997. "Rootless in the Kalahari." *Christian Science Monitor.* September 5–11. p. 10.

Ministry of Commerce and Industry. 1986. *Report of the Central Kalahari Game Reserve Fact Finding Mission.* MCI Circular No. 1. Gaborone, Botswana: Ministry of Commerce and Industry.

Mogwe, Alice. 1992. *Who Was (T)here First? An Assessment of the Human Rights Situation of Basarwa in Selected Communities in the Gantsi District, Botswana.* Gaborone, Botswana: Botswana Christian Council.

Republic of Botswana. 1975. *National Policy on Tribal Grazing Land.* Government Paper No. 2. Gaborone: Government Printer.

———. 1992. *Wildlife Conservation and National Parks Act.* Act No. 28. Gaborone, Botswana: Government Printer.

———. 1997. *Community-Based Natural Resources Management Policy* (Draft). Gaborone, Botswana: Government of Botswana.

Silberbauer, George B. 1981. *Hunter and Habitat in the Central Kalahari Desert.* Cambridge: Cambridge University Press.

Survival International. 1997. *Botswana Squeezes Kalahari Peoples Out.* Urgent Action Bulletin. London: Survival International.

Tanaka, Jiro. 1980. *The San, Hunter-Gatherers of the Kalahari.* Tokyo: University of Tokyo Press.

World Bank. 1990. *Involuntary Resettlement.* Operational Directive 4.30: Washington, D.C.: The World Bank.

"Resource Rights and Resettlement Among the San of Botswana"

Robert K. Hitchcock

1) What were the resettlement policies of the Botswana government, and what were the initial consequences to the San?

2) Compare the lifestyle and the subsistence practices of the San before and after the resettlement program.

3) What methods, both blatant and subtle, have been employed by the authorities to induce people to leave the Central Kalahari Game Reserve (CKGR)?

4) What reasons have the Botswana government given to argue for the removal of people from the CKGR?

5) What are "Community-Based Natural Resource Management Programs," and how do they operate?

SECTION FOUR

Subsistence and Economics

Yanomamö: Varying Adaptations of Foraging Horticulturalists

Raymond B. Hames

The documentation of behavioral variation in cultural anthropology is key to scientific description and explanation. Early ethnographers were content to describe typical patterns of behavior to give readers an idea of what was expected or customary in a given culture. To understand variation in cultural practices, anthropologists who are engaged in cross-cultural comparison use individual societies as data points or exemplars of particular traits. Although comparative or cross-cultural approaches have been enormously productive, they are not the only useful approach to a scientific understanding of cultural variation. Within each society, individuals or even whole regions may vary enormously in how they conduct their social, economic, and political lives. Accurately documenting this intracultural variation and attempting to associate it with explanatory factors is an important alternative approach. This is not to say that intracultural comparisons are superior to or in competition with cross-cultural approaches. In fact, I would expect them to complement each other. For example, one might demonstrate cross-culturally that warfare is strongly associated with a particular environmental variable. This then might lead us to test that proposition within a particular cultural group if that environmental variable had enough variation.

The goal of this chapter is to describe variation in Yanomamö economic activities at cross-cultural, regional, and individual comparative levels. I will first compare Yanomamö horticultural adaptation to other horticultural groups. The striking finding here is that compared to other horticulturalists the Yanomamö spend an enormous amount of time in the foraging activities of hunting, gathering, and fishing. In many ways, they behave like hunters and gatherers, peoples without agriculture. I will then turn to a regional comparison of Yanomamö economic adaptations by comparing how highland and lowland Yanomamö adapt to the rain forest. Here we will find that highland Yanomamö are much more dedicated to a sedentary horticultural life than lowland Yanomamö. Finally, I will turn to an analysis of individual Yanomamö to describe how sex and age

determine the division of labor and the amount of time that individuals work.

Demography, Geography, and Environment

The Yanomamö are a tribal population occupying the Amazonian border between Venezuela and Brazil. In Venezuela, the northern extension of the Yanomamö is delimited to the north by headwaters of the Erebato and Caura rivers, east along the Parima mountains, and west along the Padamo and Mavaca in a direct line to the Brazilian border. In Brazil, they concentrate themselves in the headwaters of the Demini, Catrimani, Araca, Padauari, Urari Coera, Parima, and Mucajai rivers. In both countries, the total area inhabited by the Yanomamö is approximately 192,000 square kilometers. Dense tropical forest covers most of the area. Savannas are interspersed in forests at high elevations. In general, the topography is flat to gently rolling, with elevations ranging from 250 to 1,200 meters.

Area Exploited

The area village members exploit in the course of their economic activities is probably best characterized as a *home range*. Home ranges differ from territories because they are not defended, but like territories they tend to be used exclusively by a single group. This exclusiveness is not determined by force but by the following simple economic considerations. Important food resources tend to be evenly distributed in the tropical forest. When Yanomamö establish a new village they intensively exploit and deplete resources near the village. Through time, they must travel greater distances where higher return rates compensate for greater travel costs needed to reach areas of higher resource density. At a certain point, they will begin to reach areas that are exploited by neighboring villages and if they were to travel still further they would begin to enter areas close to neighboring villages that have been depleted. At this point, it is not economic to travel further since the costs of gaining resources increases (more travel time) while resource density decreases. Thus, the borders of home ranges are established with some overlap with the home ranges of adjacent villages. The point to understand here is that a village has near-exclusive use of its home range but that exclusivity is determined by economic factors and not by aggression or threat of aggression.[1]

Where warfare is intensive home, ranges may become more like territories if enemy villages are neighbors. In such cases, exclusive use of an area is maintained through aggression or threat of aggression. However, it is difficult to determine what is being defended. It may be that the Yanomamö want to keep enemies out of their foraging areas so that they may hunt and gather without the worry of meeting a raiding party; or it may be that a powerful village decides to press its advantage over a weaker neighbor by expanding its range into a neighbor's area to monopolize all the resources in the area. The way in which Yanomamö verbally rationalize their reasons for warring complicates this matter further. Yanomamö may claim that they go to war in order to avenge an insult, a previous killing, an abduction of a woman, or the illness-causing spells cast by a neighboring shaman. Therefore, Yanomamö explain war in terms of vengeance for harm caused by an enemy. The problem here is that neighboring villages invariably have members who have done one or more of the above to a neighbor or a neighbor's ancestor. Why some past wrongs are ignored or acted upon may be determined by economic (territorial) and political (opponent's strength or perceived threat) factors. Further complexities of Yanomamö warfare are described in the section on conflict below.

We have little comparative data on sizes of the home ranges of Yanomamö villages. Differences in home range may be the result of ecological differences in resource density or the distribution of neighboring villages. The limited data we have indicate that home ranges vary from three hundred to seven hundred square kilometers, roughly a circular area with a radius of ten to fifteen kilometers. This radius is approximately the distance one can easily walk through the forest in less than a day.

Demography and Settlement Pattern of Yanomamö Villages

Although ethnographers have done extensive and excellent demographic research on some Venezuelan and Brazilian Yanomamö, a complete census for Venezuelan and Brazilian Yanomamö is lacking. Current estimates are 12,500 and 8,500 Yanomamö in Venezuela and Brazil, respectively, for a total of 21,000. However, the figures for Brazil may be significantly less because of epidemics and white-Yanomamö fighting caused by incursions of Brazilian gold miners starting about 1987. I discuss this problem later. In Venezuela and Brazil, there are approximately 363 villages ranging in size from 30 to 90 residents each. But some Venezuelan villages in the Mavaca drainage may reach two hundred or more. Napoleon A. Chagnon[2] provides evidence that warfare intensity is associated with village size: Where warfare is intense, villages are large. People are forced to associate in large villages both to deter attackers and enable themselves to mount effective counterattacks. Population density ranges from about 6.7 square kilometers per person to 33.5 square kilometers per person.

Anthropologists consider stable settled life one of the important consequences of the agricultural revolution. Although the Yanomamö are agriculturists, villages are unstable in duration, location, and membership. A typical Yanomamö village (*shabono*) has the shape of a giant circular "lean-to" with a diameter of fifty meters or more depending on the number of people living in the village. Each house or apartment section of a village has a roof and a back wall but no front or side walls. Individual family lean-tos are joined in a circle. When a Yanomamö sits in his hammock and looks left or right he sees his next-door neighbor; if he looks straight ahead he sees a broad plaza and the dwellings of neighbors on the other side of the village. A village structure rarely lasts more than a few years before the roof thatch begins to rot and the entire village becomes filled with vermin. On such occasions, a new village may be constructed adjacent to the old one.

Aside from the reasons stated above, Yanomamö villages are relocated about every five years because of economic and political considerations.[3] The practice of shifting cultivation forces the Yanomamö to use extensive tracts of land. This is because garden land is used for only two to three years, and then, abandoned to the encroaching forest. Through time gardens become increasingly distant from the village. When gardens or easily accessible garden land become too distant, the village may move several kilometers to be in the midst of good garden land. Raiding provides a political cause for village relocation. When a village is repeatedly raided by a more powerful enemy, the entire village may be forced to relocate. Such moves are designed to put as much distance as possible between themselves and an enemy and may cause great privation due to loss of easy access to productive gardens.

Highland and Lowland

There is good reason to suspect that there are fundamental differences in environmental quality for Yanomamö who occupy highland and lowland elevations. Defining a precise boundary between the highlands and lowlands is impossible at this point. However, I tentatively define highland populations as villages found in areas higher than 500 to 750 meters of elevation and occupying areas of highly dissected and hilly terrain with small fast flowing streams and occasional savannas. The lowland environment is flatter with slowly moving, larger streams and rivers. This highland-lowland distinction appears to have important implications for the fundamental economic activities of gathering, hunting, fishing, and agriculture.

General ecological research provides considerable evidence that plant biomass and diversity decrease with increases in altitude. Detailed ethnographic research on the Yanomamö points to a similar conclusion. For example, ethnobotanical research by Lizot[4] shows a greater variety of edible plants are available to lowland groups, more plants are restricted to lowland environments, and, on average, more edible plants are available on a monthly basis for lowland groups. In addition, the cultural geographer William Smole[5] notes a decrease in edible plants with increasing elevation. Although it cannot be positively concluded that gathering is more productive in lowland areas because plants differ enormously in food value, processing costs, density, and seasonal availability, available data show that the rate of return in gathering wild forest resources is much greater in lowland than in highland areas.[6]

It is well established that fish are more abundant and larger in the wider, slower moving rivers in lower elevations.[7] A comparison of sites reveals that groups living along large streams or rivers consume twice as much fish and other aquatic prey (frogs, caimans, and crabs).[8] In addition, these lowland groups gain fish at efficiencies two to three times higher than highland groups.[9]

The evidence on game density is less direct. However, it is my impression (based on Yanomamö statements and direct observation) and that of other Yanomamö researchers[10] that game animals are much less abundant in higher elevations. In terms of kilograms of game killed per hour of hunting, Colchester shows that the highland Sanema Yanomamö hunt much less efficiently than lowland Yanomamö.[11] Because both highland and lowland groups use the same bow and arrow technology and are equally adept hunters, it can be concluded that the greater hunting success of lowlanders is the result of greater game densities in the lowlands. A review of the ecological and biogeographical literature on altitude and animal biomass gradients suggests that huntable biomass declines with increasing elevation.[12]

We have no convincing comparative data to indicate significant differences between highland and lowland areas for agricultural pursuits. Agricultural productivity is a complex interplay of many factors, such as soil quality, quantity and distribution of rain, and temperature extremes. It is clear, as I show below, that significant differences in garden size correspond to a highland and lowland divide. What is not clear, however, is whether these differences are the result of environmental, economic, or socio-political factors to be discussed below.

Yanomamö Economics

Economically, the Yanomamö, along with most other tribal peoples living in the tropics, are classified as shifting cultivators because most of their dietary calories come from horticulture. However, a significant amount of time is allocated to the foraging activities of hunting, gathering, and fishing. In fact, as we shall see later, the Yanomamö allocate more time to foraging activities than they do to agriculture. Their dedication to foraging is greater than any other Amazonia group and any other horticultural group that we know of.[13] Given this huge investment in foraging activities it might be more accurate to refer to the Yanomamö as "foraging horticulturalists." In this section, I describe the basic productive components of the Yanomamö economy.

Technology

Until the mid-1950s, the Yanomamö relied on a locally produced "stone age" technology, which was dependent on local, non-metal resources. For example, axes were made of stone, knives of bamboo, fish hooks of bone, and pots of clay. Since that time, much of their traditional technology has been replaced by steel cutting tools (machetes and axes), aluminum pots, and other industrial items given or traded to the Yanomamö primarily by missionaries. The main impact of such introductions has been to reduce labor time and increase Yanomamö dependence on non-Yanomamö to satisfy these new needs.[14] In many instances the Yanomamö no longer possess the skills to make or use traditional technology, such as clay pots or fire drills.

Gardening

In shifting cultivation, forest is cleared with machetes, axes, and fires. The newly opened forest is then planted with plantains, root crops (manioc, sweet potatoes, and taro) and a large variety of plants that serve as relishes, medicines, and technology sources. After about two to three years of cultivation, the garden is abandoned to the encroaching forest. In most years, Yanomamö add to the size of a current garden by clearing adjacent forest. As yields begin to diminish and weeding becomes time consuming, they cease to work old areas of the garden and let them naturally revert to scrub and, later, to forest. Men do nearly all the heavy work involved in clearing, such as slashing the undergrowth and felling large forest trees. Men and women work together to plant the garden and women are responsible for the nearly daily trips to the garden to harvest and weed.

There is considerable variation, as Figure 1 clearly indicates, in the amount of land under cultivation per capita in Yanomamö villages. Per capita land cultivated in highland villages averages five times as much as in lowland villages, a difference that is statistically significant. At least two possible ecological and economic explanations exist for these differences. Garden land may not be as fertile in higher elevations, or basic crops may not be as productive because of the cooler temperatures in highland areas.[15] As a result, highlanders are forced to increase garden size to produce the same quantity of plantains as lowlanders. A second reason to cultivate less land in lowland areas is that foraging success (efficiency) is greater in lowland areas, therefore lowlanders may gain a larger fraction of their diet from foraging, which lessens their dependence on garden food.

There is a basic contrast in subsistence crops relied upon by highland and lowland groups that may have far-reaching consequences in helping us understand their economic differences. Lowland groups rely on plantains and bananas as the basic subsistence crop while some highland groups rely more heavily on manioc, a very productive root crop. Where either crop is a staple, it contributes up to forty percent or more of all dietary calories. This difference leads us to ask why some highland groups depend on manioc and what impact dependence on one or the other has on the overall Yanomamö economy. Colchester suggests that manioc is a recent introduction from neighboring groups such as the Ye'kwana.[16] Where manioc has been introduced, the Yanomamö have taken it up because it appears to be a forty percent more efficient source of calories than plantains. However, this alleged advantage may disappear because the comparative data on efficiency do not consider processing costs. Some varieties of manioc become poisonous ("bitter") soon after harvesting and must be detoxified. In addition, many varieties require a laborious process of peeling, grating, and baking before consumption. Plantains, in contrast, are easily peeled and quickly cooked by roasting or boiling. Chagnon makes an opposite argument by suggesting that manioc was aboriginal with the Yanomamö and it was replaced by plantains (an Old World crop introduced by the Spanish more than four hundred years ago) because plantains were a more efficient producer of calories.[17] Unfortunately, neither Colchester or Chagnon have quantitative data to back up their claims. Clearly, relatively simple research could help settle this issue.

Figure 1
Garden Land Per-Capita (m²) in Nine Villages,
and Low-land /Highland Contrasts

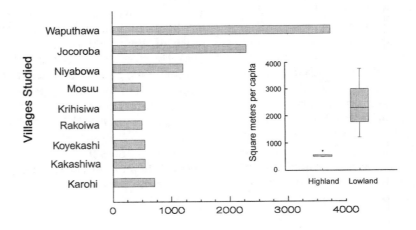

Whether or not manioc or plantains are ancient or recent introductions, dependence on one or the other may have a strong impact on the Yanomamö economy. The key issue here is not one of efficiency but of reliable and predictable yield. Tropical forest peoples tend to rely on crops that can be harvested over a long time. In contrast to temperate horticulturalists, many tropical peoples who grow root crops or plantains do not harvest their entire field during a single harvest period and do not store the crop to tide them through seasons when crop growth is impossible or risky. Instead, tropical cultivators stagger-plant throughout the year so that what is needed can be harvested from the field every few days or weeks. For example, one can harvest manioc six, twelve, or eighteen or more months after it is planted. This allows the manioc cultivator considerable flexibility in insuring a steady and reliable yield. Plantains, in contrast, have much less flexibility. Although Yanomamö attempt to stagger-plant plantains to gain a reliable weekly or half-weekly yield, a variety of environmental factors thwart this strategy. Dry spells can hasten maturation while prolonged wet spells slow maturation. Also, heavy winds that accompany violent thunderstorms may blow down plantains with heavy maturing racemes (bunches). Yanomamö can salvage blown down bunches of plantains (if they're close to maturation) by hanging them in the village. When the plantains ripen there will be a momentary glut of food, but there will be a lack of plantains in the near future when they would have otherwise matured.

Heavy dependence on plantains by lowland groups may help us to understand their greater reliance on gathering compared to manioc-producing highland groups. Since plantains are far less reliable than manioc, lowland Yanomamö may be forced to gather because of periodic underproduction of plantains. Evidence consistent with this idea is presented in Table 1. The only highland group on which we have time allocation (Sanema, in the table) shows that the average adult spends only twenty-six minutes each day gathering, which is the lowest figure in the table and fully one-half of the average time allocated to this task in lowland villages.

If manioc is more reliable than plantains we must ask why plantain-growing lowlanders do not grow more manioc than they currently do. Because lowland gathering is about twice as efficient as highland gathering, it may mean that unreliable plantain production is buffered by highly productive gathering. Because the overall work effort for the highland Sanema is essentially identical to the average level of work for lowland villages (see the Total column in Table 1), I suggest that this is clear evidence that plantain gardening coupled with a high reliance on gathering causes no discernible hardship in overall work effort.

Foraging

Foraging is the simple extraction of resources from the environment without any attempt to modify the environment (as agriculture does) to increase the

Table 1
Time Allocation in Eight Yanomamö Villages (Minutes per Day)[25]

Village	Hunt	Fish	Garden	Gather	Cook	Manufacture	Misc	Total	Source
Bisaasi	83	86	29	51	42	43	33	367	2
Hasubë	65	19	40	100	ND	ND	ND	[a]	4
Koyekashi	42	85	85	66	26	36	17	357	3
Krihi	32	108	32	54	26	58	65	375	2
Mishi	13	109	81	53	37	149	17	459	1
Rakoi	12	109	44	24	27	68	76	360	2
Sanema	70	15	52	26	59	118[b]	ND	350	5
Toropo	61	56	43	55	41	69	35	359	1
Yanomami	38	40	38	45	54	52	84	357	2
Mean	50	64	45	52	37	62	49	359	

Sources: 1 = Hames, 1989; 2 = Hames, b; 3 = Lhermillier, 1974; 4 = Good, 1989; 5 = Colchester, 1984. ND = no data.

[a] total not given because of incomplete data

[b] technology and maintenance activities are combined and column mean ignores these figures

yield of that which is harvested. Hunting, gathering, and fishing are the basic foraging activities. Foraging is the most ancient technique humans use to exploit the environment and is an adaptation that humans share with all other animals. What is interesting about Yanomamö foraging is the large amount of time they allocate to it. As time allocation statistics in Table 1 indicate, Yanomamö allocate more than twice as much time to foraging as they do to gardening.

Given the amount of time the Yanomamö spend foraging on a daily basis, the term *foraging horticulturalists* might be an apt designation for their economic adaptation to the tropical forest. The logic of this designation is reinforced further by the Yanomamö practice of *waiyumö*, or trekking. Trekking is camping in the forest and subsisting mostly by foraging. It usually occurs in the dry season when there is an abundance of forest fruit and the dryness makes walking and camping out pleasant. The probable motivation behind most trekking is to save travel time by taking advantage of abundant vegetable resources distant from the village. However, trekking may also be stimulated by a shortage of garden food or the presence of powerful enemies. If the latter is the cause, then trekking is an adaptation designed for concealment against enemies. Treks may last a week to more than a month and normally include all village members. Dependence on wild resources is not total; young men are sent from forest camps to gardens to harvest plantains if the wild resources are scarce.

Hunting

Hunting is the main source of dietary protein for the Yanomamö. As we shall see in the time allocation statistics, hunting is essentially a male activity with important social and ritual functions. Bows and arrows, which measure approximately two meters in length, are the main weapons of the hunt. The long arrow is not accurate beyond about thirty meters. This is of little significance in dense tropical forest where it is rare to have a clear shot at a greater distance.[18] Skills in locating game and stalking it to a short distance are abilities that differentiate good from poor hunters. Game sought ranges from 1-kilogram birds, to 25-kilogram peccaries, and to the occasional 175-kilogram tapir (the largest terrestrial animal in South America). Yanomamö quivers contain large lancelotate (spear shaped) tips for big game, poisoned pencil-shaped tips for monkeys, and harpoon points for birds and small terrestrial game. Because arrows are two meters long, a hunter can carry no more than three arrows on a hunt;

however, hunters carry a case that contains a repair kit of thread, resin, and a hand tool to repair damaged arrows.

Although most hunting is done by individuals or pairs, organized group hunts occur under two important circumstances. If a hunter discovers a herd of white-lipped peccaries (a distant relative of the pig weighing twenty to thirty kilograms), he carefully notes the location and immediately returns to the village to alert other hunters who return to cooperatively hunt the herd. To prepare for a feast *(reahu),* organized hunting parties travel great distances and may continuously hunt for a week in order to amass a large quantity of game to provide high-quality meals for visiting allies on a variety of social occasions (reahu and *braiai* rituals). During these excursions hunters especially seek highly esteemed game, such as peccaries, turkey-like birds, and monkeys.

Gathering

The harvesting of wild plant resources is an activity that includes all ages and sexes and is commonly organized by families and groups of families. Important resources include honey, palm fruits, brazil nuts, palm heart, and cashew fruit. Men specialize in the risky task of climbing trees to shake loose fruit or to sever fruit-laden branches. The peach palm is especially important. It is planted in gardens but it only begins to yield several years after a garden has been abandoned and it continues to bear for a decade or more. The Yanomamö assert that peach palms are owned by those who planted them and it is not uncommon for disputes to arise over ownership. With the exception of the peach palm, the Yanomamö make little or no effort to harvest fruit trees or palms so they may be harvested on a sustained basis. The Yanomamö fell small, fruit-ladened trees to make harvesting easier, but never such forest giants as Brazil nut or cashew trees because of the enormous labor required.

Fishing

Most Yanomamö villages occupy areas between major rivers that are crossed by small streams. Fish found here are seldom larger than a few kilograms. Nevertheless, fishing is widely and avidly pursued by all ages and sexes, especially in the dry season through hand catching, stream poisoning, and archery. In the dry season, small streams begin to shrink, leaving fish in large ponds or cutoffs. The Yanomamö will use a vegetable poison to stun fish and cause them to rise to the surface where they can be grabbed or shot with a miniature bow and arrow. Women sometimes will jointly push a long, broad palm frond through the water to herd fish towards a bank where they can be trapped.

Marriage and Family

Yanomamö marriage rules prescribe that marriage partners ought to be cross-cousins. Ideally, mates are double cross-cousins, a result of the practice of sister exchange. Soon after their first menses, women typically marry men in their early twenties. Although women are required to reside in their husband's village after marriage (patrilocal marriage), a husband must initially live with his in-laws for several years and work diligently for them, performing what is known as bride service. This requirement may be relaxed for high-status males. Polygyny (a man having more than one wife) is permitted; ten to twenty percent of all males at any time are polygynists. Ideally, polygynists marry sisters (sororal polygyny) because the Yanomamö believe that sisters get along better. If a woman's husband dies, she may be required to marry his brother (levirate marriage) and if a man's wife dies he may claim her sister as a bride (sororate marriage). Men and women average 2.8 marital partners during their lifetime, with about seventy-five percent of those marriages ending as a result of divorce with the balance as a result of death of one of the partners.[19]

Monogamous or polygynous nuclear families are the rule among the Yanomamö. Deviations from this pattern occur when aged parents live closely associated with married children or when newlyweds dwell with one or the other's parents. Each family has a garden or gardens and is responsible for basic subsistence activities.

Political Organization

Each Yanomamö village is an autonomous political entity, free to make war or peace with other villages. Coalitions between villages are important: nevertheless, such coalitions tend to be fragile and ephemeral. Although the Yanomamö are an egalitarian people, age, sex, and personal accomplishments are important in status differentiation. Yanomamö men acquire high status through valor in combat, accomplished oratory, and expertise in shamanism. However, high status cannot be inherited—it must be earned. Mature men dominate positions of political authority and religious practice. Local descent groups play important roles in regulating marriages and settling disputes within the village.

The village headman is the dominant political leader and comes from the largest local patrilineage (a kin group whose members trace descent through male relatives). When a village is large or when two local descent groups are approximately equal in size, a village may have several headmen. The headman must rely on demonstrated skills in settling disputes, representing the interests of his lineage, and successfully dealing with allies and enemies. Styles of leadership vary: some headmen lead through practiced verbal skills while others resort to bullying. Concerted action requires the consensus of adult males. However, an individual is free to desert collective action if it suits him.

Villages range in size from about forty residents to more than two hundred. As a village increases in size it has a tendency to break into two groups of approximately equal size, which form new villages. As villages become large, kinship relationships become weaker and village headmen are less able to amicably settle disputes.[20] In addition, local resources tend to be more quickly depleted, which causes an increase in work effort.[21] However, if warfare is intense village members are more likely to realize the value of large size as a deterrent against enemies and are more likely to tolerate irksome co-villagers and increased work loads.

Social Control

Conflicts typically arise from accusations of adultery, failure to deliver a betrothed woman, personal affronts, stinginess, or thefts of coveted garden crops such as tobacco and peach palm. For men, if such conflicts move past a boisterous shouting match, a variety of graded, formal duels may occur. If a fight becomes serious, respected men may intervene to cool tempers and prevent others from participating. Frequently, duels end in a draw, which allows each contestant to preserve his dignity. For women, dueling is rare. Instead, a direct attack is made by the aggrieved woman using hands and feet or makeshift weapons.

Conflict

Warfare between villages is endemic among the Yanomamö. While the initial cause of a conflict may be frequently traced to a sexual or marital issue, conflicts are self-perpetuating since the Yanomamö lack any formal mechanisms to prevent aggrieved parties from exacting the amount of vengeance or counter-vengeance they deem sufficient once a conflict has started. The primary vengeance unit is the lineage, but co-resident non-kin have some obligation to assist, because co-residence with a feuding faction is seen as implicit support of the faction by the faction's enemies. Most combat is in the form of stealthy raids. The goal is to quickly kill as many of the enemy as possible (who frequently are found on the outskirts of the other village engaging in mundane activities), abduct nubile women if possible, and return quickly home. Although the primary goal is to kill mature men and their kin believed to be responsible for a previous wrong, unrelated co-villagers may be killed if there is no safe opportunity to kill primary targets. Endemic warfare has a profound effect on politics and settlement size and location. Each village needs at least one allied village it can call upon for assistance if it is overmatched by a more powerful enemy; and village size and distance between villages tend to increase with the intensity of conflict. Peace between villages may develop if conflict has remained dormant for a long period and there is a mutual need for an alliance in the face of a common enemy. It begins with a series of ceremonially festive visits. If old antagonisms do not flare, visits may lead to joint raids and intermarriage between villages that strongly solidify an alliance. Proximity of missions and government agencies has had little impact on warfare.

Major Changes

Over the last twenty years, most Yanomamö have become totally dependent on outside sources of axes, machetes, aluminum cooking pots, and fish hooks and line. These metal goods have replaced much of their stone-age technology. Most of these items have come from missionaries as gifts and wages. Through mission-organized cooperatives, the Yanomamö recently have begun to market baskets and arrows and some agricultural products.

Missionary presence also has distorted the traditional Yanomamö settlement pattern. Yanomamö attempt to gain easy access to mission outposts by moving their villages near a mission. As a result, the normal spacing of about a day's walk between villages has diminished dramatically. For example, around the Salesian mission at Mavaca there are five villages and numerous small settlements with a total population of about nine hundred people within one day's walk. This population density is unprecedented for the Yanomamö and has led to severe depletion of wild resources. In addition, a significant fraction of that population no longer lives in traditional round communal villages but rather in small settlements of two to three houses occupied by a few

families. Despite these changes, missionaries have failed to gain significant numbers of Yanomamö converts to Christianity. The Yanomamö have enormous pride in their culture and have strong doubts about the authenticity or superiority of Christian beliefs.

However, the greatest change and threat to the Yanomamö are the thousands of Brazilian gold miners who have infiltrated Yanomamö territory in Brazil and who have again (July 1993) illegally entered into Venezuela and this time killed seventeen men, women, and children. The situation in Brazil is similar to the situation in the United States in the 1800s when whites expanded into the lands of Native Americans. Miners bring epidemics of measles and influenza that lead to high mortality rates among the Yanomamö. Gold processing pollutes streams with mercury, killing fish and ruining a village's water supply. And open warfare between miners and Yanomamö has killed numerous Yanomamö and disrupted village life.[22]

Time Allocation

In the West, we tend to think of work as something done away from the home for forty hours a week. In subsistence-based tribal populations, this sort of definition is as inadequate for them as it is for us. Although it is true that the Yanomamö, for example, leave the village to travel to garden, forest, and stream to acquire resources, much work takes place in the village. But the same thing is true in the West. Driving to work, mowing the lawn, shopping for food, washing clothes, and all those other household chores that must be done are not what we would call leisure time activities. We do these tasks to maintain our material well-being. I believe that most of us would define leisure time activities as including dining out, going to the movies, visiting friends, and playing sports. Therefore, one can define work as all those other activities we must do to maintain or enhance our material existence. Clearly, adults in the West work more than 40 hours per week if we use this expansive definition of work. Researchers who have investigated time allocated to work in the West show that urban European and North Americans work on average 55 to 65 hours per week, or 7.8 to 9.3 hours per day, seven days a week.[23]

Table 1 presents time allocation data for adults in eight Yanomamö villages on a basic set of work activities. The table reveals that the Yanomamö work about 6 hours per day (360 minutes) or 42 hours per week. This is significantly less than the 55 to 66 hours of work in modern societies. Furthermore, if we compare Yanomamö and related simple tropical horticulturalists to other types of economies (hunters and gatherers, pastoralists, agriculturists, etc.), we find that they are among the most leisured people in the world.[24]

Although Table 1 shows little variation in overall labor time (mean 359, SD 7.88), considerable variation exists among villages in time allocated to various subsistence tasks. Much of the variation can be attributed to local conditions, such as the season in which the researcher collected the data, the degree to which a village is associated with missionaries, or special environmental conditions. Nevertheless, the only highland site, Sanema, shows some interesting patterns. This village allocates the third-most time to gardening, the least time to fishing, the second-least amount of time to gathering, and the second-most amount of time to hunting. Gathering and gardening times are probably related, as I suggested earlier. Because the density of wild sources of plant food is lower in the highlands, foraging is not as productive, which leads highlanders to spend more time gardening. Related to this is the higher reliability of manioc gardening, which makes gathering less of an important alternative source of vegetable foods. Another way of expressing the contrasting dependence on foraging (hunting, gathering, and fishing) and gardening in highland and lowland locales is to note that the highland population spends the least amount of time foraging and has the lowest ratio of foraging time to gardening time (2.13:1.0 compared to a mean of 4.43:1.0 for the lowlanders).[25]

The extremely low amount of time highlanders allocate to fishing and the relatively high amount of time they allocate to hunting are also related.

Highlanders do little fishing because of difficulties exploiting steep and narrow highland streams. Because fishing and hunting are the only ways of gaining sufficient high-quality protein to the diet and fishing is unprofitable, highlanders are forced to hunt more intensively.

Division of Labor

As Figure 2 indicates, women spend significantly more time in cooking, fishing, gathering, and caring for children than men do, whereas men spend more time hunting than women. From what we know about the division of labor cross-culturally, these differences in time allocation are not surprising. In all cultures, hunting is either predominately or wholly a male activity. Although the data indicate that Yanomamö women do almost no hunting, some qualifications are necessary. Yanomamö women occasionally accompany men on hunting forays to act as spotters and to assist in the retrieval of game. Rarely do they ever make kills while with men. However, they occasionally make fortuitous kills of their own while gathering or fishing. Such kills are made without the use of bows and arrows.

Although the data show no significant difference between men and women in gardening, there are important differences in garden tasks performed. Men almost exclusively do the heavy work of felling large trees, slashing the undergrowth, and burning the resulting debris prior to planting. Both sexes share in planting, whereas the daily tasks of weeding and harvesting fall almost exclusively to women. The

Figure 2
Male and Female Time Allocation to Basic Economic Tasks

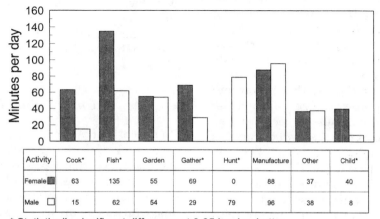

Male and female time allocation to basic economic tasks

Activity	Cook*	Fish*	Garden	Gather*	Hunt*	Manufacture	Other	Child*
Female	63	135	55	69	0	88	37	40
Male	15	62	54	29	79	96	38	8

* Statistically significant difference at 0.05 level or better

pattern of men doing tasks which are dangerous and/or take them far from home is consistent with Judith Brown's model of the division of labor.[26] Brown suggests that women tend to dominate tasks that are compatible with simultaneous child care. Such tasks are not dangerous, can be accomplished near to home, and can be interrupted and resumed with no loss of efficiency.

While Brown's model usefully captures much of the variation in the division of labor among the Yanomamö and other groups, it does not explain why women who are post-menopausal or otherwise unencumbered with intensive child care do not, for example, engage in hunting or tree felling. For dangerous and arduous activities, such as tree felling, it is probable that models that focus on physical strength differences may be useful. Or perhaps task linkages are required to complement Brown's model.[27] However, lack of female participation in hunting may require yet another explanation. Hunting is a highly skilled activity that is not easily learned and requires frequent practice to maintain proficiency. On average, little Yanomamö boys spend sixty to eighty minutes per day playing with bows and arrows and spotting, tracking, and stalking small birds and other tiny game near the village. It may be the case that women don't hunt because they never acquired the skills necessary to become proficient hunters.

The question of whether men or women work more can be answered only if we have a reasonable definition of work. Generally, economic anthropologists define work as all of those activities required to directly maintain and enhance survival and reproduction. Thus, it includes rather obvious activities such as the provisioning and preparing of food, construction and repair of tools and shelter, and the acquisition and management of fuel (or firewood, in the case of the Yanomamö). If we use this definition of work, Yanomamö women work about twelve minutes per day more than men, but the difference is not statistically significant. This finding is rather interesting because, in the vast majority of horticultural tribal populations on which we have time allocation data, women work significantly more than men.[28] The only societies in which men work significantly more than women are hunters and gatherers. That Yanomamö men and women work approximately equally is therefore consistent with the point made earlier: That they can be best characterized as foraging horticulturalists because their time allocation patterns fall between horticulturalists and hunter-gatherers.

Some may consider this definition unnecessarily restrictive because it ignores a task that is critical for the long-term survival of the Yanomamö: child care. The tropical forest harbors many sources of environmental trauma that are very dangerous to infants and small children. Inside and outside the village there are stinging and biting insects, dangerous plant spines, and poisonous plants, snakes, and insects. Infants and small children are protected from these threats by being carried in slings much of the time and actively watched when they are set down.[29] Although caring for infants and small children in this way may be pleasurable, it is also exhausting and difficult. And recall that I defined work as those things we do to enhance or maintain our physical well-being. Just as the Yanomamö labor to provide food for their children, they also physically care for them. To assess the impact of child care on overall labor time differences, I must restrict my analysis to data I collected on four Yanomamö villages (Mishimishimaböwei, Rakoiwä, Krihisiwä, and Bisaasi) because none of the other studies collected child care data. When I include direct child care activities (carrying, feeding, nursing, holding, etc.),[30] female work time increases by forty-three minutes per day while male work time increases by only eight minutes per day. If child care activities are added to conventionally defined labor, then Yanomamö women work more than men.

Status and the Allocation of Labor

The Yanomamö, like all people, exhibit strong individual differences in the amount of labor they perform that are independent of sex. Factors such as age, number of dependents, and marital status should logically help us to understand much of the variation. For example, one would expect that a married couple with numerous dependent children to labor more than newlyweds with no dependents. Such a prediction is based on a number of assumptions, such as each family is wholly responsible for supplying its economic needs and economic resources are freely available. Although this latter assumption is correct for the Yanomamö, the former is suspect, as I will later explain. In this section, I will examine the degree to which age determines individual labor time allocation.

Child Labor Trends

On the basis of our own experiences we expect that the amount of work one does will increase with age and that it eventually begins to diminish when one retires or becomes physically incapacitated. We also tend to believe that childhood should be a carefree time with little in the way of work responsibilities—a time for play, exploration, and learning. An examination of Yanomamö time allocation data will allow us to evaluate all of these ideas; and, because the Yanomamö are relatively typical representatives of the tribal world, we can get a sense of whether our Western experience is in any way typical over the history of humankind.

Figure 3 shows the amount of time children from ages five through eighteen allocate to labor time activities.[31] As can be easily seen, labor time does generally increase with age of the child. The rate of increase is uneven only because of small sample sizes in some of the age groups. Over the chart, I have superimposed adult male and female labor time. You will note in this graph that adult females work significantly more (421 min./day) than males (372 min./day). These figures differ from the ones given earlier in the ten-village comparison because they derive from the four villages I studied. I use this smaller data set here because it is the only one broken down by age. As the figure indicates, boys and girls begin to achieve adult labor time levels by the time they become teenagers.

The data presented seem to indicate that childhood is brief and children are quickly recruited into the family work force. To some extent these figures are an artifact of the method I used to collect time allocation data. If I could not observe someone when I was sampling behavior, I had to rely on reports of what they were doing. For example, someone would tell me that all the members of a particular family were in the forest gathering wild palm nuts or weeding the garden. When I was able to accompany families on their economic activities, I found that children did work but not as hard or as constantly as adults: They worked about forty to eighty percent as much as adults when, for example, a garden was being weeded. Nevertheless, the data tell us something important about work and family life that provides a strong contrast to what occurs in the urban West. Yanomamö children work alongside their parents and are important to the household economy. The family unit does not separate in the morning; children and adults do not go their separate ways to school and work only to rejoin each other in the evening. "School" for a Yanomamö child is in the context of the family economy where they learn how to hunt, gather, garden, fish, and perform all the other activities necessary for them to become competent adults.

Adult Labor Trends

If we extend the analysis of time allocated to work across the entire life span, we expect to see labor time increase to a point and then decrease. This pattern, an inverted U-shaped curve, is evident for both men and women in Figure 4. However, the shapes of the curves are quite different. Male allocation of labor time begins at a lower level but increases rapidly until it peaks around age thirty-five, and then rapidly decreases thereafter. Females, in contrast, begin at initially higher levels, ascend more slowly to a peak at age fifty and then decrease their efforts much more slowly. The last point is rather interesting: the curve shows that women at ages thirty and sixty work about the same amount of time. The factors that account for these patterns are quite complex. Women engaged in active child care (for example, nursing) work less than women who are not.[32] This fact probably accounts for female labor time peaking after menopause. Male labor time decreases quite rapidly after age thirty-five, but I am not sure why the rate of decrease is so much greater than for women. There are two interrelated possibilities. Because males have higher rates of mortality than women at all ages, they may also have higher rates of decrepitude than women, that is, their ability to do physically demanding labor may decrease more rapidly. Related to this trend is that as men become older they work more at relatively sedentary tasks, such as manufacturing and the gardening tasks of weeding and harvesting, and work significantly less in hunting and clearing new gardens.

Figure 3
Labor Time of Children

Labor Time of Children

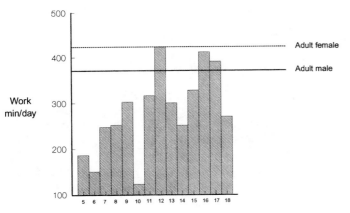

Age

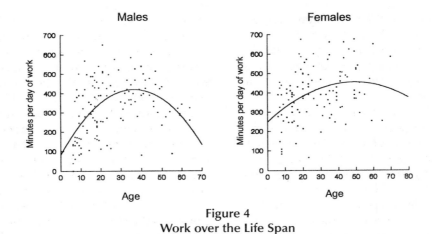

Figure 4
Work over the Life Span

Conclusion

Since 1975, when Allen Johnson reintroduced anthropologists to methods for measuring time allocation,[33] studies of how people use their time have become increasing popular among anthropologists. In this chapter, I have attempted to show some of the uses to which time allocation can be put by showing how it can elucidate fundamental ethnographic problems in intracultural variation. I showed that differences in environment between lowland and highland Yanomamö lead to differences in the allocation of time to basic economic activities. We found that highland groups are much more tied to agricultural pursuits because of a lack of high-quality foraging resources. In the area of the sexual division of labor, we found that men and women work nearly the same amount of time but allocate their efforts much differently. In addition, we found that if child care activities are included in labor time, then women work significantly more than men. Finally, I showed that time allocation patterns show significant patterns associated with age. Both boys and girls are quickly absorbed into the family's labor pool and adult male labor effort peaks earlier and declines more quickly than it does for women.

In closing I should note that time allocation studies are not simply restricted to the documentation of variation in work effort. Researchers now use the method to quantify patterns of social interaction such as how much time husbands and wives spend together, the size and composition of play groups among children, and patterns of cooperation among co-villagers. So long as ethnographers are interested in quantitative measures of variation in social life we can expect that time allocation studies will play a central role.

Notes

1. R. Hames, "The Settlement Pattern of a Yanomamö Population Bloc," in R. Hames and W. Vickers, eds., *Adaptive Responses of Native Amazonians* (New York: Academic Press, 1983), pp. 192–229.

2. N. Chagnon, *Studying the Yanomamö* (New York: Holt, Rinehart & Winston, 1974).

3. N. Chagnon, *Studying the Yanomamö*; R. Hames, "The Settlement Pattern of a Yanomamö Population Bloc."

4. J. Lizot, *Les Yanomami Centrau* (Paris: Editions de L'Ecole des Hautes Etudes en Sciences Sociales, 1984), p. 54, Table 2.

5. W. Smole, *The Yanoama Indians: A Cultural Geography* (Austin: University of Texas Press, 1976).

6. M. Colchester, "Rethinking Stone Age Economics: Some Speculations Concerning the Pre-Columbian Yanoama Economy," *Human Ecology* 12 (1984): 291–314.

7. M. Goulding, *The Fishes and the Forest* (Berkeley: University of California Press, 1980).

8. G. Saffirio and R. Hames, "The Forest and the Highway," in K. Kensinger and J. Clay, eds., *Working Papers on South American Indians #6 and Cultural Survival Occasional Paper #11*, joint publication (Cambridge, MA: Cultural Survival, 1983), pp. 1–52.

9. R. Hames, "Time, Efficiency, and Fitness in the Amazonian Protein Quest," *Research in Economic Anthropology* 11 (1989): 43–85. Anthropologists measure the efficiency of subsistence activities in kilograms of food gained per hour of work, or kilocalories of food gained per kilocalorie of work.

10. W. Smole, pp. 81 and 227.

11. M. Colchester, p. 300, Table 2; Hames, "Time, Efficiency, and Fitness in the Amazonian Protein Quest," p. 64, Table 6.

12. J. Eisenberg, "The Density and Biomass of Tropical Mammals," in M. Soule and B. Wilcox, eds., *Conserva-*

tion Biology: An Evolutionary-Ecological Perspective (Sunderland, MA: Sinauer Associates, 1980), pp. 35–55; J. Eisenberg, M. O'Connell, and V. August, "Density, Productivity, and Distribution of Mammals in the Northern Neotropics," in J. Eisenberg, ed., *Vertebrate Ecology in the Northern Neotropics* (Washington, DC: Smithsonian Institution Press, 1979), pp. 187–207.

13. R. Hames, "Time, Efficiency, and Fitness in the Amazonian Protein Quest."

14. R. Hames, "A Comparison of the Efficiencies of the Shotgun and Bow in Neotropical Forest Hunting," *Human Ecology* 7 (1979): 219–252.

15. Data on Yanomamö garden size is from the following sources: E. Fuentes, "Los Yanomami y las plantas silvestres," *Antropologica* 54 (1980): 3–138; Smole, *The Yanamo Indians*, pp. 36–37; J. Lizot, "Economie Primitive et Subsistence: Essai sur Le Travail et L'alimentation Chez les Yanomami," *Libre* 4 (1980): 69–113; and J. Lizot, "La Agricultural Yanomami," *Antropologica* 53 (1980): 3–93. Information on cultivated bananas and plantains can be found in N. W. Simmonds, *The Evolution of Bananas* (London: Longmans & Green, 1979).

16. M. Colchester, p. 301.

17. N. Chagnon, *Yanomamö: the Fierce People* (New York: Harcourt Brace Jovanovich, 1992).

18. R. Hames, "A Comparison of the Efficiencies of the Shotgun and Bow in Neotropical Forest Hunting."

19. T. Melancon, "Marriage and Reproduction among the Yanomamö of Venezuela" (Ph.D. diss., Pennsylvania State University, 1982). Cross-cousins are offspring of siblings of the opposite sex. For example, your father's sister's children are your cross-cousins and so are your mother's brother's children. Double cross-cousin marriage is set up when two men marry one another's sisters. The Yanomamö prescribe that the offspring of such unions should marry. These people are double cross-cousins because (using the male as an example) a male is marrying a woman who is simultaneously his father's sister's daughter and his mother's brother's daughter.

20. N. Chagnon, *Yanomamö: the Fierce People.*

21. R. Hames, "The Settlement Pattern of a Yanomamö Population Bloc."

22. N. Chagnon, *Yanomamö: The Last Days of Eden* (New York: Harcourt Brace Jovanovich, 1993); N. Chagnon, "Covering Up the Yanomamö Massacre," *New York Times*, October 23, 1993; see also Saffirio and Hames, on the impact of road construction on Yanomamö economy, and N. Chagnon and T. Melancon, "Reproduction, Epidemics, and the Number of Kin in Tribal Populations: A Case Study," in N. Keyfitz, ed., *Population and Biology: a Bridge between Two Disciplines* (Liege: Ordina Editions, 1984), pp. 147–167, on the effects of epidemics spread by whites.

23. R. Hames, "Time, Efficiency, and Fitness in the Amazonian Protein Quest." Adult labor time is the average of male and female labor time.

24. Sources for time allocation data in Table 1 are as follows: Colchester, p. 299; K. Good, "Yanomami Hunting Patterns: Trekking and Garden Relocation as an Adaptation to Game Availability in Amazonia, Venezuela" (Ph.D. diss., University of Florida, 1989); Hames, "Time, Efficiency, and Fitness in the Amazonian Protein Quest"; A. Lhermillier and N. Lhermillier, "Vie Economique et Sociale d'une Unite Familliale Yanomami" (thesis, L'Ecole Pratique des Hautes Etudes, 1974); Lizot, "Economie Primitive et Subsistence."

25. Ibid.

26. J. Brown, "A Note on the Division of Labor," *American Anthropologist* 72 (1970): 1073–1078.

27. G. P. Murdock and C. Provost, "Factors in the Division of Labor by Sex: A Cross-Cultural Analysis," *Ethnology* 12 (1973): 206–212; M. Burton and D. White, "Sexual Division of Labor in Agriculture," *American Anthropologist* 86 (1984): 568–583. In their task linkage model Burton and White show that the sex that begins a task that has a series of steps is more likely to complete the subsequent steps. For example, if women harvest food they are more likely to perform the processing and storage tasks that immediately follow harvesting.

28. R. Hames, "Time, Efficiency, and Fitness in the Amazonian Protein Quest."

29. R. Hames, "Variation in Paternal Care among the Yanomamö," in B. Hewlett, ed., *The Father's Role: Cultural and Evolutionary Perspectives* (Chicago: Aldine de Gruyter, 1992), pp. 85–110.

30. Ibid.

31. The data reported here on the division of labor, male and female labor time, and child labor time are taken from data I collected in the villages of Mishimishimaböwei-teri, Rakoiwä-teri, Bisaasi-teri, and Krihisiwä-teri in 1986 and 1987. The data set consists of seventy-three adult females and seventy-six adult males. Adults are defined as anyone over the age of fifteen years who is married or has been married.

32. Ibid.

33. A. Johnson, "Time Allocation in a Machiguenga Community," *Ethnology* 14 (1975): 301–310. See also the continuing series of studies of time allocation, in various societies, that are published by the Human Relations Area Files.

Suggested Readings

Biocca, E. Yanoama: *The Narrative of a White Girl Kidnapped by Amazonian Indians.* New York: E.P. Dutton, 1970. Helena Valero was captured by Brazilian Yanomamö when she was twelve years old. This book is the exciting account of her capture, problems in adjusting to Yanomamö social life, marriage to several Yanomamö men, and eventual release to missionaries.

Chagnon, N. *Yanomamö: The Fierce People.* 4th ed. New York: Holt, Rinehart & Winston, 1992. This is perhaps the most popular ethnography written in the last several decades. It is an introductory yet detailed ethnography of the Yanomamö with a special focus on kinship, social organization, and politics.

_____. *Yanomamö: The Last Days of Eden.* New York: Harcourt Brace Jovanovich, 1993. A more personal and accessible account of the Yanomamö than Chagnon's standard ethnography listed above. It presents a lucid picture of what it is like to do fieldwork with the Yanomamö and some contemporary problems faced by the Yanomamö.

Early, J., and J. Peters. *The Population Dynamics of the Mujacai Yanomamö.* New York: Academic Press, 1991. This monograph describes Brazilian Yanomamö with a special emphasis on demography in relation to social organization. In addition, it presents a novel explanation of mother-in-law avoidance by the son-in-law, a moderately common cross-cultural phenomenon.

Lizot, J. *Tales of the Yanomami: Daily Life in the Venezuelan Forest.* Cambridge: Cambridge University Press, 1985. Jacques Lizot is a French social anthropologist who has worked with the Yanomamö for nearly two dozen years. He presents vignettes of Yanomamö life in novelistic fashion with stories of romance, vengeance, politics, shamanism, and women's lives.

"Yanomamö: Varying Adaptations of Foraging Horticulturalists"

Raymond B. Hames

1) Who are the Yanomamö and where do they live?

2) Define the Yanomamö in terms of their marriage/kinship patterns, systems of social control, political organization, and other social institutions.

3) Define the differences, in terms of topography, available resources, soil productivity, forest cover, and other factors, between the highland and the lowland environments of the Yanomamö.

4) In general, what are the various components of the Yanomamö economic system, and how does it vary between the lowlands and the highlands?

5) What resources are emphasized in both zones, and what economic, environmental, and human factors affect these differences?

KALAHARI SAN:
SOMETIME HUNTER-GATHERERS

Edwin N. Wilmsen

The San peoples who live in and around the Kalahari Desert in southern Africa speak several languages belonging to a larger linguistic family called Khoisan, all of which have many click sounds among their consonants. The term *Khoisan* is composed of two words, *khoi* and *san*.[1] The first word is derived from khoe, which means simply "people" in one large division of Khoisan languages, while *san* can mean either "aboriginal people" or "people poor in livestock who must forage for food" in those same languages. This distinction came to be solidified in both popular and academic thinking as marking a real difference between "Khoi" peoples (called Hottentot in the past) who were comparatively wealthy herders and "San" peoples (often called Bushmen in the past) who were hunter-gatherers.[2] Thus, San is not like most other ethnographic terms, which are intended to name a particular group that might be thought to have a common ancestry or history. Instead, the peoples ethnographically classified as San speak at least ten mutually unintelligible languages plus a number of distinct dialects today; in addition, several other languages are no longer spoken. Although described as foragers in the ethnographic literature, these peoples have (as we shall see) engaged in a wide range of economic and social practices, the development of which can be traced through the past two thousand years. We will need to look into those years to place these peoples in their social and cultural context.

Some anthropologists paint a very different picture of Kalahari San than I portray here. In order not to be hopelessly confused by this, you need to be aware that a debate about the ethnographic status of these peoples (and, more generally, contemporary hunter-gatherers all over the world) is now going on in anthropology. There are two facets to this debate. One is simply about the history of these peoples and the extent to which they have been engaged with or isolated from other peoples, especially during the last couple of centuries or so. The other facet is connected to a broader concern that is also currently being discussed by anthropologists; this has to do with how we represent other peoples to a Euroamerican audience,

such as students like yourself. In the specific case of the Kalahari San, this second facet includes the question of the extent to which these peoples may be represented as living examples of prehistoric hunter-gatherers on a lower, or more primary, level of cultural evolution than ourselves. Ethnographers who believe the Kalahari San are such examples argue that these peoples had remained, until as late as 1970, relatively isolated from other, non-San peoples—not totally isolated, of course, but enough to avoid outside influences that would change their hunter-gatherer status. In effect, these ethnographers argue that these peoples had little recognizable history and thus feel justified in paying it scant attention. Other anthropologists, of whom I am one, argue to the contrary that far from having been isolated, Kalahari San were actively engaged with their neighbors throughout history and, therefore, this history has a strong bearing on the contemporary appearance of a few of these peoples as hunter-gatherers. We maintain that they are not primal hunter-gatherers at all but are very poor rural people who forage on the fringes of the Kalahari economy because through the unfolding of the social-economic history of the region they are denied access to a more comfortable place in its current social formation.[3]

Before looking at this history, we must consider the distribution and composition of the Khoisan language family and its speakers. There may be one hundred thousand Khoisan-speakers living today; about fifty thousand are ethnographically classified as San. There are three major divisions of this language family—northern (!Kung), central (Khoe), and southern (Twi)—each with a distinct grammatical structure and vocabulary. !Kung has five dialects of which the best known is Zhu|oasi (abbreviated Zhu or Ju),[4] which is also the name of the people made anthropologically famous by the ethnographies of Lorna Marshall[5] and Richard Lee[6] and by John Marshall's film *The Hunters*. Khoe has the greatest number of speakers and the greatest number of currently spoken languages, including Nama—the language of all Khoi herders in Namibia—and Cape Khoi, once spoken by herders over all of western

South Africa but now confined to a few communities near the Orange River; some Khoe languages are not mutually intelligible. Only one Twi language is still spoken, in southern Botswana; those formerly spoken in South Africa have died out.

Peoples who speak these languages are now found only in southern Angola, northern Namibia, and most of Botswana, with a handful in adjacent parts of Zambia and Zimbabwe. While this is a large area (nearly twice the size of Texas), they once occupied a much larger portion of the southern African subcontinent. In the eighteenth century, the first Europeans to enter the region found Khoisan peoples in the entire western half of southern Africa from its tip at the Cape of Good Hope almost to the mouth of the Congo River (an area not quite as large as the continental United States). Archaeological and linguistic evidence shows that about two thousand years ago the ancestors of these peoples lived throughout the entire southern subcontinent below the Zambezi River.

A Short Social History of Southern Africa

An overview of the mosaic of southern African history that brought about these changes will help to locate the San peoples of the Kalahari in their contemporary political and social context. Over two thousand years ago, Khoisan peoples seem to have been the only human inhabitants of this region and had developed a variety of hunting-fishing-gathering economies adapted to its highly diverse local ecologies. Then, about or slightly before two thousand years ago, cattle and sheep were introduced from sources in the north and incorporated into local Khoisan foraging economies. Very little is known about how this took place or who was involved, but we can be confident that Khoe-speakers played an important role because the basic pastoral vocabulary of most southern African herders, including Bantu, is Khoe in origin.

Bantu peoples began moving down from central Africa shortly after this initial introduction of livestock. Small groups of families were the main, if not sole, units of movement. With them, they brought horticulture—sorghum, millet, cowpeas, and melons—and goats, as well as iron and copper metallurgy. Relations between these incoming Bantu and indigenous Khoisan must have involved considerable mutual exchange; Bantu peoples added cattle-keeping to their economies while Khoisan acquired metals, field crops, and goats (all Khoisan languages incorporate Bantu goat terms). But material items

were not the sole elements of exchange. In the eastern half of the subcontinent, the Bantu-Khoisan distinction became increasingly blurred through amalgamation of the peoples themselves. We cannot pinpoint details of the means by which this took place so long ago, but we can be confident that some form of kinship extension associated with marriage between Bantu and Khoisan persons was a key factor. Such marriages, and non-marital matings as well, must have been very common, perhaps preferred, because genetic studies have demonstrated that today people who speak the Bantu languages Kizulu, Isixhosa, and Sindebele[7] have about equal proportions of Khoisan and Bantu ancestry; indeed, this ancestry is praised in the poems that recount the oral histories of these peoples. These languages themselves (and Sesotho to a lesser extent), while Bantu in structure and lexicon, incorporate many click consonants and a large vocabulary (especially in the domain of animal husbandry) from Khoisan sources. The fact that Bantu languages, though radically altered, continued to be spoken while Khoisan was not and Bantu social forms became the norm for all suggests that Bantu-speakers, though increasingly absorbing Khoisan persons and cultural elements into their social formation, were politically hegemonic in the eastern region and Bantu ideology was more highly valued there. Thus, in this eastern region peoples, economies, and languages had long merged to such an extent that when Europeans arrived there were no peoples or languages there that could be called Khoi or San and no economies that could be called hunter-gatherer.

The social history of the western half of the subcontinent is similar in outline, but there are important differences. Bantu peoples arrived at roughly the same time bringing essentially the same economic suite; they encountered Khoisan pastro-foragers who probably spoke !Kung languages in Angola and Khoe languages farther south in the Kalahari of Botswana-Namibia. But here similarities give way to differences, the most salient being that Khoisan-speaking peoples continued to live everywhere in this western region right up to the time Europeans arrived (and, as mentioned above, all peoples who speak Khoisan languages today still live here). Also, with the exception of G|wi and G||ana peoples who live in the central Kalahari, peoples who speak Khoe languages in Angola, Botswana, and Namibia are genetically and physically indistinguishable from their Bantu neighbors and until recently Khoe social forms were predominant in this area. This is strong evidence that, in contrast to the east, during the early centuries of association ideological values and political power were the prerogatives of Khoe peoples and Bantu were drawn into Khoe social networks through marriage and other kinds of mating alliances (these are described in the section on kinship) rather than the reverse. Other than this, the early history of Bantu-Khoisan relations in the west is not so well known. The Bantu language, Shiyei, incorporates a large click inventory of Khoisan origin and, therefore, the Wayei people of the Okavango Delta must have a long history of intimate association with Khoisan peoples. These peoples along with speakers of the western-Bantu Herero group of languages (Otji-herero, Oshivambo, and others)[8] are the only southern African peoples who employ Bantu pastoral terminology, which implies a different economic history in the region for them.

Part of that history seems to be linked to the establishment of Portuguese trading entrepôts on the Atlantic coast between Congo and Luanda in the sixteenth century. These ports vigorously stimulated ancient trade networks stretching into the interior by offering a wide variety of European goods (cloth, clothing, glass beads, guns, pots and pans, tobacco, sugar, coffee, and tea), which rapidly gained the status of necessities in local economies. This set off intensive activity to supply the commodities demanded by the Portuguese in return: ivory, diamonds, hides, cattle, and, later, slaves. In the process, the indigenous social landscape was disrupted and another period of population movements was set in motion; some peoples moved to escape marauders and slavers, some to take advantage of newly opened economic opportunities. Oral histories place the movement of Herero peoples from Angola into Botswana-Namibia during this time and there are suggestions that Zhu then moved down as well (I shall return to this). In the eighteenth and nineteenth centuries, other Europeans—and Americans and Canadians—opened southern routes to trade through South Africa, and in so doing stimulated similar needs and precipitated similar upheavals.

The subsequent colonial history of the region, particularly that of South Africa and Namibia, is filled with bloody atrocities, many involving the massacre of Khoisan peoples—especially those called Bushmen. Because of this, it is often said that these peoples played no further role in the development of southern African history but instead defended an isolated independence from it. Another common belief is that Khoisan peoples were almost entirely exterminated in the colonial encounter; this is true for the mountain and high plains areas of South Africa, but happily not elsewhere. This has led to the romantic notion that, as one writer put it, only in the great wasteland of the Kalahari can a last living remnant of their authentic remains be found; people who think

this way usually are looking for what they believe to be "pure" primitive Bushman hunter-gatherers.[9]

The chronicle of genocide, though grim, is only partly true; large numbers of Khoisan people, perhaps the majority, were incorporated into newly emerging groups. We have already seen that the people who speak Kizulu and Isixhosa as well as some others classified as Bantu have about equal proportions of Khoisan and Bantu ancestry; there are perhaps ten million of these descendants of eastern Khoisan forebears living today. More recently, at the end of the nineteenth century a group of people came to be identified as "Coloured" in South Africa; although they speak Afrikaans[10] rather than a Khoisan language, they are descendants of mainly western Khoisan ancestors who since the seventeenth century had had intimate association with Bantu and Europeans, as well as the Malayans whom the Dutch imported into the Cape as slaves. There are four million of these people today.

The Kalahari in the Nineteenth Century

We now have the necessary historical background to focus more closely on the Kalahari itself. As the nineteenth century began, Khoe-speaking peoples continued to occupy by far the largest part of the Kalahari, as they had done for millennia. But now these Khoe peoples shared most of the region with others who today are collectively known as Bakgalagadi.[11] These peoples had come into the Kalahari at least by 1600 (this date is derived from analysis of oral histories) and most likely much earlier; since then, Khoe and Kgalagadi have maintained close economic and social ties, including a considerable amount of marriage.[12] The economy practiced by all these peoples is called pastro-foraging; in this economic system, hunting and gathering remain important but livestock are also kept, small numbers in poorly watered areas and vast herds on the better ranges. The southern African suite of crops—sorghum, millet, melons, and cowpeas—is grown.[13] In the Okavango Delta-Lake Ngami-Botletli River belt, Khoe and Wayei added intensive fishing and aquatic plant harvesting to this pastro-foraging economy.

Around 1750, Bantu-speaking Tswana peoples began moving up from the south; at that time, these peoples were not very different in most economic and political respects from the Khoe and Kgalagadi peoples they met in the Kalahari. All were organized in small extended family groups under a local leader; groups were composed of thirty to forty households with no more than about three hundred persons in total; associations with other groups were maintained through marriage alliances; identity distinctions of the kind we call "tribal" or "ethnic" were apparently not very important, if they existed at all, judging by the many inter-group marriages recorded in genealogies collected from descendants of the people of this time. A later *kgosi* (chief) of Batswana[14] said of the relations among Bantu and Khoe peoples, "There was in those times no question of overlordship of one people over another. It was simply a mutual understanding; at that time we had no strength by which we could force them to become our servants."[15]

This relative social equality came to an end early in the nineteenth century. European goods were then filtering up in greater quantity to the southern margins of the Kalahari from the South African trading ports, and the Kalahari had become the major source of ivory and ostrich feathers, because the animals that produced these goods had been slaughtered almost to extinction farther south to meet the European demand. This demand accelerated until in the 1860s and 1870s about three thousand elephants were killed every year in the Kalahari. Enormous profits were realized from the ivory produced. Ostrich feathers were even more profitable, selling in London for as much as $1,000 per pound.[16] Batswana, whose lands straddled the area between European traders and Kalahari commodities, were ideally situated to exploit the trade. The Tswana kgosi, Khama III, had an annual income from these sources and his huge cattle herd of £3,000 in the 1870s; this would have made him a millionaire in modern terms. Khama was able to extract this large income because of the enormous growth of the Tswana *merafe* (polities);[17] whereas his grandfather had been leader of about three hundred pastro-foragers who were not very different from peoples classified ethnographically as Bushmen today, Khama was head of a state with more than thirty thousand people and considered himself a king on a par with Queen Victoria.[18] Khama's cousin, Sechele, ruled an equally large Tswana *morafe* and controlled most of the Kalahari.

This is an astonishing social transformation to have taken place in hardly more than half a century; we must look briefly at how it happened. Doing so will help explain how some San peoples were reduced to a state of rural poverty that made them appear to ethnographers in the 1950s and 1960s to be simple hunter-gatherers.

In 1826, Kgari (a kgosi of one of the small Tswana groups described above) strengthened his position by establishing what is called the *kgmelo* (milk-jug) system; in essence, he decreed that half of all products produced by people under his control belonged to the kgosi—half of every jug of milk (hence the

name), one tusk of every elephant, five of every ten feathers, and so on. He also assigned his *dikgosana* (male relatives) the task of overseeing the collection of this tribute and allowed them to keep a part for themselves; it was thus in the interests of dikgosana to collect as much tribute as possible. To do so they recruited hunters from all surrounding groups, Khoe and Kgalagadi as well as Tswana; these hunters produced almost all the ivory and feathers for the trade.

Cattle were important in this system. They were lent out by the dikgosana to the hunters under conditions of patronage called *mafisa*, in which the recipient becomes a client of the cattle owner and assumes not only the responsibility to manage the patron's herd properly but also the obligation to support the patron's wider economic and political interests. Failure on the client's part to perform to the patron's satisfaction results not only in the withdrawal of the mafisa cattle but also the forfeiture of the client's animals. Failure could be simply the production of too little ivory, and as elephants became scarce, this happened frequently. This could, and often did, lead to the client's impoverishment. Batswana elites gained thereby a degree of control over Khoe and Kgalagadi as well as poor Tswana peoples' economic lives.

This economic control was translated into political control as the trade intensified. Dikgosana made sure that they remained the only channel through which commodities could be passed to the kgosi and on to the traders; this meant that Khoe and Kgalagadi hunters had very little direct access to traders and soon were forced to hand over both tusks and all feathers to dikgosana, for they had no other market. But in the 1850s this was not yet the case: in a passage that reveals the nature of earlier indigenous trade, a European trader named Chapman wrote, "My Bushmen begged me to shoot an ostrich, as they were collecting black feathers to adorn the heads of Ndebele warriors"; as Chapman wanted the white feathers popular in Europe, he and his "Bushmen" struck a mutually beneficial deal.[19] Eventually, as kgamelo strengthened elite power, European goods filtered back exclusively through the same dikgosana channels. The kgosi kept the most and best for himself, and dikgosana allowed only a few less valuable items (mainly tobacco and some glass beads) to pass further down the line. This rapidly strengthened the class structure inherent in the social division between chiefly and commoner members of a group (the word kgosi in fact is derived from the same root as the word for wealth), and by mid-nineteenth century a new class, *malata* (serfs), had come into being, composed almost entirely of Khoe and Kgalagadi peoples. However, by no means were all of these latter people reduced to serf status; many had previously become Tswana through marriage, concubinage, and the recruitment of whole groups to meet the growing labor needs of the expanding *merafe*.[20]

Only those whose labor was not needed were not recruited. For the most part, they were in the most desert-like parts of the Kalahari farthest from developing centers. These people were usually dispossessed of cattle, both *mafisa* and their own, and necessarily relied more heavily on foraging than did others. This was the first step to San hunter-gatherer poverty. Until the 1870s, however, even these people retained a significant degree of economic leverage as the primary producers of the wealth that enriched their Tswana masters. Ten years after the ostrich-feather deal, one of Chapman's companions recorded this scene of San bargaining power: "There has been a game of diplomacy between Chapman and the Batswana all the morning, the object of the latter being to persuade the Bushmen to bring the tusks of Chapman's elephants to them, or at least within their power."[21]

The "Bushmen" who were negotiating terms with both Batswana and Europeans in this scene were Khoe peoples living in the Ngamiland district of northwestern Botswana (an area about the size of New Jersey). The great majority of place names in this district as well as in adjacent Namibia are, even today, Khoe. Khoe peoples continue to live in the eastern and southern parts of Ngamiland and farther west in Namibia; but in a narrow strip along the border, most of the San inhabitants today are !Kung-speaking Zhu. A German geographer, Siegfried Passarge, who worked in this area between 1896 and 1898 and wrote the first ethnography of San peoples, thought that this indicated that Zhu were relatively recent immigrants into a country formerly occupied by Khoe;[22] evidence is accumulating which suggests he was right. The move probably has its roots in the upheavals in the sixteenth and seventeenth centuries that followed the establishment of Portuguese trading ports on the Congo-Luanda coast. As I have already said, the indigenous social landscape was severely disrupted by this trade, especially after the demand for slaves became great. In the scramble to supply the trade or to escape slavers, many peoples migrated. The Khoisan peoples of northern Angola, who we may be sure spoke a !Kung language, were displaced 250 miles southward into the middle of the country where they live today. Zhu lived too far south and east to be subject to heavy slaving predation, and as the Portuguese did not reach southern Angola until the late 1840s they were well placed to take advantage of economic opportunities newly opened by the trade.[23] Archaeological evidence shows that glass

beads and implements made from blast-furnace iron (made only in Europe and America at that time) were widespread in Ngamiland and northern Namibia beginning in the seventeenth century; these, along with new introductions of native pottery, mark these emigrants from the north.

Then in 1795, Batswana moved into the area and within fifty years had subjugated the Khoe and Wayei who lived around the Okavango Delta; Batswana generally refer to these peoples as *Makoba* (note the *ma* prefix), which means "menial people." Shortly after 1860, they extended their hunting and herding range westward. A Tswana man described their relations with the Zhu living there: "We just ruled them . . . it was good that they were so afraid of us, because if they had tried to fight, we would have slaughtered them."[24] A Zhu man portrayed the encounter this way: "They put us under the carrying yoke. We had to carry the meat that they shot . . . and a line of porters would carry bales of *biltong* (dried meat strips) back to Tsau."[25] Batswana also brought Zhu persons back to work on their cattle posts, and sent cattle out to the waterholes to be tended by Zhu.

The Atlantic slave trade also came into the area sometime in the early nineteenth century, although by no means as disastrously as farther north. Oral histories describe the social context in which this trade took place:

> They bought Kxoé children with bundles of goods. Sometimes a grandfather-headman sold his nephews to the Mbari, sometimes the son of his older sister, sometimes of his younger sister. Also a father exchanged his son for woven cloth from Mbari men. If he had no slave available he gathered the Kxoé men; they hunted children and women and took them back to their place.[26]

The texts specifically include Zhu among those captured; Zhu in turn captured Kxoé children to sell to the Mbari agents of the Portuguese. We have evidence that substantiates this native oral history. In 1865, a group of European traders organized a posse to avenge the murder of one of their partners by Ovambo; among the avenging party were twenty "Bushmen (almost surely Zhu) willing enough to fight the Ovambos who make slaves of them."[27]

Commodity trade, nevertheless, was far more important. Carl Hugo Hahn, one of the first Europeans in northern Namibia, gives a clear indication of the extent of Khoisan participation in this trade in 1850:

> At the lowest estimate I can make, fifty to sixty tons of copper ore must go yearly to Ondonga. Bushmen are so jealous of this trade, that to this day they have not allowed strangers to see the places where they dig. . . . Other Bushmen

prepare salt from saltpans in the form of sugarloaves and bring them to Ondonga to sell, from where they go on to other tribes.[28]

As in the east, ivory and ostrich feathers were the most valuable items as far as Europeans were concerned and many came to get them; about four hundred of the three thousand elephants killed annually in the Kalahari as a whole during the 1860s and 1870s came from the comparatively small area we are now discussing, most of them killed by Khoe and Zhu. Lee justly remarks that Zhu "recall the period with a great deal of affection as a time of intense social activity and economic prosperity."[29] Although the intensity diminished in the 1880s, a degree of trade continued, almost exclusively in hides and pelts. This caused a German soldier who patrolled the Namibian side of Zhu country in 1912 to remark that on the Botswana side "modern culture is established. Our neighbors [Batswana and British] have ensconced trade relations with the Bushmen."[30] Zhu participated actively in this trade, as they had in previous generations; this gave them a degree of economic security no longer enjoyed by Khoe peoples.

The First Half of the Twentieth Century

Several traumatic changes coincided in the mid-1880s: elephants were wiped out in the Kalahari, so there was no more ivory; ostrich feathers went out of fashion in Europe and ostrich farms were established at the Cape, so Kalahari feathers became worthless. The economic vitality that had attracted hundreds of Euroamerican traders to the Kalahari and engaged almost every one of its inhabitants collapsed. The heyday of hunting had passed; the activity and prosperity of the previous quarter-century was over. Kalahari labor thus lost its value in the Kalahari. As a result, San—Khoe and !Kung alike—lost the little bargaining power they still retained. This was the second step to San hunter-gatherer poverty.

At the same time that hunting collapsed, however, gold and diamonds were discovered in South Africa; a modern capitalist economy was quickly established to exploit these riches and soon dominated the subcontinent. The colonies surrounding South Africa rapidly became what has been called a labor reserve, sending men as needed to work the mines. Kalahari labor found a new market. To meet these capitalist conditions, Khama abolished the kgamelo system and decreed that San were no longer serfs; dikgosi of the other Tswana merafe quickly followed his lead. They did this in order to free San labor from

attachment to any fixed place and to make it more flexibly available to Botswana. This was necessary because Tswana men of all classes were eager to reserve the money wages paid by the mines for themselves. To do so they, of course, had to leave their families and go to the mines; although this brought in money for the family (very little in actual fact), it left a labor vacuum on cattle-posts and farms. This labor was replaced mainly by San (and some Kgalagadi) men who were not allowed to go to the mines until the 1950s. These men and their families were permitted to drink some of the milk of the cattle they tended and eat some of the grains they harvested for their employers, but they were paid very low wages, or none at all. Almost all had to supplement their diet by foraging.

Those who found cattle-post and farm employment were, however, comparatively well off. Relatively few found such employment. The reason is that it takes fewer herders to manage a hundred cattle than it takes hunters to kill one elephant. Furthermore, the tusks of an elephant, when one could be found,[31] were in the 1890s worth only about a third their value of twenty years earlier; in the world economic depression of the 1930s and the 1940s war years, they were worth nothing at all. In addition, a hunter's family contributes nothing to commodity production, while a herder's family—even children as young as five—make substantial contributions to cattle-post production and thus eliminate the need to hire many men. A herd owner had little incentive to accommodate more families than necessary. Most San, many Kgalagadi, and some Tswana families were now without direct means to participate in regional economies. They were relegated to the more difficult ecological zones of the Kalahari where they fell deeper and deeper into subsistence foraging, which had become a condition of poverty in the overall social-economic structure of the subcontinent. This was the final step to San hunter-gatherer poverty. It is a condition from which people constantly aspire to escape.

Social Organization of Kalahari Subsistence Foraging

Land Tenure

Security of land tenure is as important for men who hunt and women who gather as it is for those who herd cattle and grow crops. For this reason, Kalahari San peoples long ago developed ways for assuring that individual persons would acquire such security at birth and retain it throughout life. This is done through rules of kinship inheritance and extensions of these rules through marriage; thus, we will have to look at these rules in order to understand San relations to land. But first I shall outline these relations to land themselves.

All Kalahari San peoples construct very similar land tenure institutions, so all may be considered together. At birth, a San person inherits land rights from both parents; these rights will be those that each parent had in turn inherited at birth. So a San acquires the right to the land of each grandparent; and since every person has four grandparents, every San acquires rights to four areas of land—two from the father's parents and two from the mother's parents. These areas of land are the only ones a San person is entitled to use and to pass on to his/her children. This kind of socially sanctioned security in land is called tenure; the Zhu word for an area of land held in tenure is *n!ore* and the Khoe languages have words derived from the same root (for example, G | wi *n!usa*). A person's primary tenure is the place where he/she was born, usually this will be the place where that person will spend most of his/her life and identify with; for example, a Zhu person born at a waterhole called *CaeCae* will say, "My n!ore is CaeCae." Generational continuity is invoked to validate a claim; a Khoe man asserted, "This is my place—I was born here, and my father and my father's father were born here."[32] Entitlements to other inherited tenures may be retained by visiting relatives in each and exchanging gifts with them; I shall return to this in a moment. Upon marriage, a San person gains rights to use the spouse's tenures, but entitlement to this land is passed to the couple's children only through the spouse.

It should be apparent that a San person gains entitlement to land only through a network of social relations with other persons in the same group. Land, itself, is not inherited, but rights to its use are acquired by being born into a specific social group. What Silberbauer has said of G | wi, "the link between the individual and territory is derived from the bond between community and land,"[33] applies to all Kalahari San in this respect. Membership in that social group carries a set of reciprocal obligations among all the members, including the responsibility for management of the group's land. This means no San "owns" land in the sense of being able to give or sell it to someone else. Rather, the group is the corporate owner of its land; entitlement to use this land is vested in all members of the group. This corporate relation to land is marked in the G | wi girl's puberty ceremony, when the young woman's mother says to her, "this is the country of all of us, and of you; you will always find food here."[34] Among Zhu, members

of such a group are called *n!ore kausi* (owners of a country); these people refer to themselves as "those who have each other" while members of a Khoe group, the Naro, say they are "owned" by their grandparents.[35]

Kinship and Marriage

Unlike land tenure institutions, Khoe and !Kung peoples have different kinship systems; the differences lie mainly in the areas of terminology (what a person calls a specific kind of relative, for example, a cousin) and the way in which kinship is extended to persons who were not born into the same group. But these different terminological systems are employed to achieve very similar sociological results with regard to land and its use. I shall only present the important points here.

All !Kung-speaking peoples separate lineal kin (those descended from the same set of great-grandparents) from collaterals (kin descended from siblings of those great-grandparents). They also use a single term for all cousins of the same sex and another term for cousins of the opposite sex. Thus, a Zhu woman calls all her female cousins *!u!naa* and all her male cousins *txu*, while a man calls his female cousins txu and his male cousins !u!naa. Notice that both use the same terms but apply them reciprocally according to the sex of individuals; because opposite sex cousins are preferred marriage partners, txu can be said to mean "marriageable person." The term !u!naa (literally, "big name") is also applied to the same-sex grandparent (by a woman to her grandmother and by a man to his grandfather); when applied to a grandparent it means "name giver" and when to a cousin "name sharer." This is because a Zhu person receives the name of a same-sex grandparent or someone sociologically equivalent, and the same set of names is passed through many generations of a family line; these are the people who have each other. As Lorna Marshall was told by Zhu at NyaeNyae, "We name our children for our people. Those people [their collaterals] name their children for their own people."[36] Among these people, persons of the opposite sex with the same grandparents (second cousins) or same great-grandparents (third cousins) are preferred marriage partners. We shall see why in a moment.

In contrast, all Khoe peoples use one term for the children of their father's sisters and mother's brothers (cross cousins); they use a different term for the children of their father's brothers and mother's sisters (parallel cousins) and this is the same term they use for their own siblings. No distinction between the sexes is made. In the G | wi case, these terms are $n||odi$ (cross cousin) and *gjibaxu* (parallel cousin/sibling). The latter term has no separate meaning, but Barnard translates $n||odi$-ku as "grandrelatives to each other"; people in this relationship are marriageable.[37]

Both Zhu and G | wi—more broadly, !Kung and Khoe—kinship and marriage practices, while substantially different from each other, produce very similar local descent groups, which are able to perpetuate themselves and their associated claims to land over many generations. Within this incorporative structure of kinship the corporate unity of San land holding is handed down from one generation to the next. In response to the question, "Is it good and just to say that people live in a defined country?", a Zhu elder replied, "If a person stays with his relatives; if a person separates from his relatives it is not right to call that place his."[38]

Property right transfers that occur when people marry are, accordingly, largely matters of reshuffling priorities among latent claims by members of a descent consort. This is because the new married pair will already, as children of their related parents, hold a set of entitlements in common (because they have a grandparental and/or great-grandparental sibling pair in common). Any proper marriage will unite entitlement strands through one parent of the bride and one of the groom; a more desirable marriage will unite strands through each parent of the couple. Marriage strategy is directed toward bringing about this more desirable condition, which strengthens individual security of tenure and consequently local descent group solidarity.

To the extent that the strategy is successfully employed by sibling sets from generation to generation, kinship ties are strengthened for individuals and group solidarity is passed on from grandparental through parental to current sibling sets. San brideservice, in which the man lives with his wife's family and contributes to its economy for a period of years, is crucial to the operation of this system; it can be seen as a form of marriage payment that mediates the conflicts over land which inevitably occur among mutually interdependent groups. Brideservice resolves the question of personal status and locates a marriage union with its offspring within the structure of relations between persons and places through the transferal of property and rights in land that takes place first between the families of bride and groom and later between their parents and their children.

Property and Exchange Networks

The transferal of property begins with negotiations and gift giving between principals to a future marriage, primarily future coparents-in-law. This process may extend over a period of many years and begins to take more concrete form with the establishment of a new household located in association with the woman's parents. The period of brideservice is measured in terms of offspring, its conditions being satisfied when two or more children have been born to the union. Among Zhu, children born during this period in the woman's n!ore will have that locality as their primary country; Khoe follow a similar practice. This confers lifelong mutual obligations between persons in the woman's family and her children, and on the descendants of those children so long as kinship obligations are met.

During the period of service in the Zhu wife's home n!ore, rights in husband's n!ore are kept open by visiting his primary kin who reside there and participating with them in production from their mutually possessed land. This revalidates entitlements through production relations; visitors who stay for longer than a couple of days are expected to contribute to the food supply. After the period of brideservice, if household residence changes to husband's n!ore, rights in wife's n!ore are kept open by visiting her kin who remain there. Such visiting is undertaken not only to enjoy each other's company but to assure n!ore inheritance by children during the lifetime of the parents. Frequent visits are necessary because there are conflicts over rights and without participation in a n!ore threats to withdraw them may become serious. Thus, fights are common during visits; nearly seventy percent of all homicides occur when families are together and a high proportion of the fights and murders occurs between in-laws. These risks are counterbalanced by the need to keep options open through fulfillment of obligations to participate actively in social relations to land.

Exchange networks play important integrative roles in this social-spatial structure, but only Zhu and Naro have developed formal exchange systems, called *haro* and *kamane* respectively. In haro individuals engage in a form of linked-partner exchange; sixty-two percent of haro partners are traceable to same grandparents and eighty-two percent to same great-grandparents.[39] Given the marriage preference, these people will be contiguous, consanguineal relatives among whom are potential as well as actual marriage partners. It is this group of people who form the stable set of descendant tenure holders; they are the *n!ore kausi*, those who have generationally continuous, inherent entitlement of tenure in their land. A high proportion of the exchange they engage in is associated with marriage negotiations designed to insure continuity into the future. *Kamane* works in much the same way and appears to have been adopted by Naro, the only Khoe-speaking people who have such a system, from Zhu, who have been their neighbors and trading partners for several generations.

The Politics of Production

Sharing and Taking

It is in the politics of implementing this strategy that relations of production are created. Negotiations for and legitimation of marriage ties are important in this creative process; they occupy much of the time and energy of descent group elders. Elders are hierarchically dominant—particularly fathers and parents-in-law—and have a defined right to an extra portion of the production of their descent group. Part of that extra portion is the right to arrange marriages, a right that carries with it increased access to material and social resources. This is the reason why Zhu parents strive diligently to reserve for themselves this potentially onerous right, which leads to the fights and homicides just noted. Zhu kinship is thus the product of strategies oriented toward the satisfaction of material and symbolic interests organized by reference to a determinate set of economic and social conditions. It emerges as relationships that can be read in different ways by participants in them. Zhu relations of production are structured in the engagement of this kinship practice with the economic sphere.

No local descent group can independently reproduce itself within the parochial limits of a single n!ore. For this reason a significant number of marriage ties are negotiated with strategically placed collateral in-laws in adjacent and nearby *n!oresi*. Adults with mature children choose to gain strength through intensified haro and other forms of cooperation in specific n!ore areas. While finding spouses in those *n!oresi* for their children, the person with the broadest social influence is likely to be most effective in arranging marriages. To facilitate cooperation and strengthen influence, productive partnerships between first cousins are passed on from parents to children. Such inheritance accounts for forty-five percent of the haro links of Zhu individuals and these links are the most secure and long-lasting of all

partnerships, some of them spanning many generations. Now, first cousins of one's parents are the parents of one's preferred marriage partner; maintaining good relations with them increases the chances of obtaining a desirable marriage partner from them. Haro exchanges between parties to these partnerships begin in childhood. They intensify in the parental generation during the period of marriage negotiations, solidify during the period of brideser-vice, and devolve incrementally upon the next generation. Thus, haro partnerships are inheritances that provide a person with working keys to the future.

Wealth, Status, and Leadership

The impartability of descent group land is assured by the cooperation of homesteads in the negotiation of proper marriages, that is, those marriages that protect the undivided inheritance of that land. Marriage negotiations, therefore, are not the simple prerogatives of single families but involve numbers of senior members of an entire group. Without strong control of marriage the impartability of descent group land inheritance could not be perpetuated. Some kin units are able to retain or expand family land at the expense of politically weaker fractions of the social formation; they are able to do so because a concept of unequal possession is inherent in Zhu ideology. That contrast is expressed in the contrast between "wealthy person" *(xaiha)* and "poor person" *(gaakhòe)*; xaiha is also the term for "chief" or leader of a group. Inequality between the statuses of wealthy and poor persons tends to be enhanced because those who can regularly produce a surplus have a broader sphere of haro.[40] As we have seen, a broader sphere of exchange partners is associated with enhanced political influence, that is, of power.

The basis for wealth resides in n!ore entitlements and the productive benefit that that entails; these entitlements are inherited by all members of a descent group. But it is apparent that leadership positions are passed through a smaller subset of families within the n!ore entitlees. All leaders at CaeCae are descendants of several generations of the same families. Lee describes the basis of power of these leaders: "Because his kin ties to past n!ore owners gave Tsau a strong claim to legitimacy, he did not elicit from his own people the same degree of hostility and criticism that other !Kung leaders suffered when they tried to deal with outsiders."[41] Also clearly, xaihasi are able to mobilize labor and to extract a surplus product. The CaeCae leader and his extended family were the beneficiaries of the ivory and feather trade in the nineteenth century, and it is these families who recall the prosperity of that heyday of the hunters with affection. These same families were able to appropriate for themselves the cattle-post positions that became available after hunting prosperity collapsed. This is visible today in the economy of CaeCae: although they are only forty-five percent of the population, these families own ninety percent of the cattle kept by Zhu in this place; they receive eighty-eight percent of the wages paid there; and they kill and consume sixty percent of the animals hunted in the area. Their success in hunting is due primarily to their ability to invest in horses, which allow them to range widely after the few large animals remaining from nineteenth-century depletion. Poor persons are forced to hunt small animals on foot; and people displaced from other n!orisi have no rights to the land and are not allowed to hunt at all.

This has led to conflicting perceptions among Zhu over what constitutes a "proper" marriage. On the one hand are the wealthy who say that to marry properly is to marry as was proper in the past; these people have secure entitlement in place. Their strategy aims to retain the advantage accruing in entitlement; it results in protection of the undivided inheritance of descent group land. On the other are the poor who insist that one marries anyone other than kin; these people have lost entitlement to any land. Their strategy seeks to gain entrance to entitled entities; these families constantly seek alliances with a large productive group so as to acquire a stronger base for developing reciprocal obligations. These conflicting perceptions are rooted in convergent interests of persons who find themselves in contrasting circumstances and are expressions of strategy options sought to fulfill those interests. These relations have been defined in a particular history of political struggle over access to land resources and their products and to the attendant power conferred by recognized legitimate entitlement to manipulate the disposal of these products. This structure is inherent in Zhu social relations and has not been imposed by external forces in recent decades.

Present conditions of political and economic asymmetry visible at CaeCae are, of course, a result of the colonial era and its aftermath, that is, of the particular modern history of the region. But particular histories engage underlying structures to produce visible results, and these structures—while not deterministic in the sense that the conjunction of certain variable events will have a fixed outcome—do structure the outcome in terms of their own logic. For example, if Zhu ideology were in fact egalitarian, its structural logic would distribute entitlements and leadership positions among individuals on an unbiased, perhaps random, basis. Yet, the evidence demonstrates that quite the opposite is the case. Clearly, *n!orekausi* homesteads reproduce the conditions of their exclusive entitlements, and those families from which the leader is drawn reproduce the conditions of their dominance. These fundamental conditions of class reproduction are endemic in Zhu social relations.

If, nonetheless, to even careful observers, Zhu, along with all Kalahari San, appear superficially classless today, it is because they are incorporated as an underclass in a wider social formation that includes Tswana, Herero, and the other peoples of the region whose coordinated history in the last two millennia we have scanned. A crucial moment in this history occurred in the nineteenth-century colonial encounter when dynamic interaction between the solidarities evoked by kinship and the status in-equalities of political organization facilitated the slipping of collateral branches of descent lines into commoner status and of impoverished individuals and families into servitude. Thus, in the political economy of the Kalahari we cannot speak of social relations particular to San or Tswana or any other separate cultural entity; the peoples' histories are too interlocked for that. It was precisely in the form of the cattle-post system that the chiefs could extract labor from subordinates and initiate the conditions of rural poverty that prevail today.

Current Rural Poverty

These conditions force some people into subsistence foraging. A pattern of San cattle ownership similar to that of rural Botswana as a whole has emerged— fewer than a third of the families in a language group own any cattle at all and, in 1981, cattle-owning San families had on average five head as compared to twenty for all rural Botswana. Typically less than ten percent of these families own more than half of all animals held by their group; among these, a very few have entered the middle-class ranks of rural Botswana. But for the average San, cash income was $10 per adult per year in 1980; those families with a cattlepost wage earner were a bit better off with $25 per adult, which can be translated as $50 per average family of five. When income in kind is added (foraged food, clothing gifts, etc.) an adjusted income of $180 was attained. The poverty level at the time was $250 for such a family, and the average family income for the country as a whole was just over $600. Thus, most San families with wage earners—roughly fourteen percent of all families—fell within the lowest ten percent of income level and did not reach the minimum considered necessary for the bare essentials of life. And this bare existence was available only to those with cattle and/or a wage-paying job. Those without such assets foraged and scavenged and had no disposable income at all. Many of these people have left their home tenures to seek employment on the fringes of towns. Some have been successful. These inequities in the overall political economy are shared by all the rural poor of Botswana regardless of their group identification. They reproduce the structural deprivation of a rural underclass deprived of a market for its labor. These inequities are the modern legacy of the history of progressive deprivation we have witnessed, buttressed by a prejudice that assigns to San an ethnographic bewilderment when confronted by the present. In the 1990s, San peoples have begun to organize to overcome this legacy. A first step toward the realization of their aspirations leads away from a fascination with a fixed forager image, a fascination that sets the present of peoples so labeled out of focus and circumscribes any vision of their future.

Notes

1. The term was coined in 1930 by anthropologist Isaac Schapera, in his book *The Khoisan Peoples of South Africa* (London: Routledge) to distinguish these languages and their speakers from the other broad family of indigenous languages, called Bantu, spoken in southern Africa. Neither Khoisan nor Bantu refer to any specific language or people; rather, they are classifying terms useful for designating sets of languages which may sound quite different when spoken today but which can be shown to have common origins in the distant past—just as the term Indo-European links mutually unintelligible English, German, and Greek (and many more languages) to a common origin different from that of other European languages such as Basque and Finnish.

2. Richard Elphick's *Kraal and Castle: KhoiKhoi and the Founding of White South Africa* (New Haven, CT: Yale University Press, 1977) is the trailblazing work in modern Khoisan studies; Elphick documents the falsity of this distinction.

3. Richard Lee is the most articulate advocate of the relative isolation of Kalahari San; his book *The Dobe !Kung* (New York: Holt, Rinehart & Winston, 1984) is a readable presentation of this point of view. Very good statements of the historical integration position can be found in papers by Carmel Schrire, "Wild Surmises on Savage Thoughts," James Denbow, "Prehistoric Herders and Foragers of the Kalahari: The Evidence for 1500 Years of Interaction," and Robert Gordon, "The !Kung in the Kalahari Exchange: An Ethno-historical Perspective," all in Carmel Schrire, ed., *Past and Present in Hunter Gatherer Studies* (Orlando, FL:

Academic Press, 1984), pp. 1–26, 175–194, 195–224. My book, *Land Filled with Flies: A Political Economy of the Kalahari* (Chicago: University of Chicago Press, 1989) is probably too long and complicated for beginning students, but chapter 3, "The Past Recaptured," and chapter 4, "The Past Entrenched," retell the dynamic history of the region, much of it in the words of the actors themselves.

4. The click consonants are written |, | |, ≠, and !; the sounds these signs represent do not occur in any European language, although many of us use something like them to "talk" to our cats and horses. They are made by clicking the tongue against the teeth and palate.

5. Lorna Marshall, *The !Kung of NyaeNyae* (Cambridge, MA: Harvard University Press, 1976).

6. Richard Lee, *The !Kung San: Men, Women, and Work in a Foraging Society* (Cambridge: Cambridge University Press, 1979).

7. Bantu (also an academically coined term) languages add prefixes to noun roots to modify their meanings; for example, the locative prefix, *bo*, designates "place of" as in Botswana ("place of Tswana people"). Here the prefixes are *ki, isi, sin*, and in the next sentence, *se*; these modify the roots *zulu, xhosa, debele*, and *sotho* (each meaning *people* in some sense) to mean "language of Zulu people" and so forth.

8. The prefixes *shi, otji*, and *oshi* all mean "language of" the people specified by the roots *yei, herero*, and *ambo*; *wa* is the plural applied to people who speak Shiyei.

9. Laurens van der Post, *The Lost World of the Kalahari* (New York: William Morrow, 1958). A similarly idealist notion of people preserving in isolation a remnant of authentic primitive humanity motivated ethnographic research on Kalahari San peoples in the 1950s and 1960s. John Yellen, "The Integration of Herding into Prehistoric Hunting and Gathering Economies," in Martin Hall and Graham Avery, eds., *Frontiers: Southern African Archaeology Today* (Cambridge: Cambridge University Press), p. 54, expresses this motivation well: "This San group has been used as a kind of narrow and opaque window to the Pleistocene." Lee, *The Dobe !Kung*, pp. 1–2, gives it fuller expression: "The !Kung San of the Kalahari Desert, fierce and independent, unknown to the outside world until recently…[were important because] our ancestors had evolved as foragers…thus the study of the surviving foragers—[the San and others]—had much to teach us."

10. Euroamericans think of Afrikaans as the language of South African whites (those who call themselves Afrikaners or Boers). But the language actually evolved as a mixture of Dutch (mainly), French, Portuguese, Malay, and Cape Khoi spoken by many people in Cape Colony; it thus became as much the native language of blacks as of whites.

11. This is also a cover term (plural prefix *ba*, root *kgalagadi*) for a number of peoples who speak a set of closely

related Bantu languages; it means simply "people of the Kalahari."

12. Gary Okihiro, "Hunters, Herders, Cultivators, and Traders: Interaction and Change in the Kgalagadi, Nineteenth-Century" (Ph.D. diss., University of California at Los Angeles, 1976).

13. The most readily available ethnographies of a Khoe people are George Silberbauer's *Hunter and Habitat in the Central Kalahari Desert* (Cambridge: Cambridge University Press, 1981) and Jiro Tanaka's *The San Hunter-Gatherers of the Kalahari: a Study in Ecological Anthropology*, David Hughes, trans. (Tokyo: University of Tokyo Press, 1980). Both focus on G|wi and G||ana peoples who conform most closely to Euroamerican Bushman stereotypes; that is, they are relatively short, have comparatively light-brown skin color, and tend to hunt and gather more than do other Khoe. Alan Barnard, in *Hunters and Herders of Southern Africa: A Comparative Ethnography of the Khoisan Peoples* (Cambridge: Cambridge University Press, 1992), provides a valuable synthesis of much of the literature on all Khoe peoples; this would be an excellent work to consult for ethnographic details.

14. Batswana are the ruling people of Botswana and so will be referred to frequently.

15. This was part of testimony given in the 1930s by Tshekedi Khama to a British commission investigating charges of Tswana enslavement of Khoisan peoples (see Wilmsen, *Land Filled with Flies*, p. 97).

16. The extent to which the "remote" Kalahari was a part of world trade is neatly illustrated here; ivory was wanted to make piano keys and billiard balls. Pianos and billiards were newly fashionable playthings of the European middle class, which was then growing rapidly in numbers and wealth. Ostrich feathers were high-fashion ornaments on women's hats and bustles.

17. The Tswana word *morafe* (plural, *merafe*), is usually translated "tribe" but I prefer "polity" as a translation that avoids a connotation of primitiveness and to stress that these are as fully developed as are any other political organizations.

18. Q. Neil Parsons, "The Economic History of Khama's Country in Botswana, 1844–1930," in Robin Palmer and Q. Neil Parsons, eds., *The Roots of Rural Poverty in Central and Southern Africa* (Berkeley: University of California Press, 1977), pp. 113–143.

19. This passage is from James Chapman's diary, *Travels in the Interior of Africa, 1849–1863*, Edward Tabler, ed. (Cape Town: Balkema, 1971), vol. 1, p. 143, and is quoted in *Land Filled with Flies*, p. 117.

20. It was recruitment of all sorts of peoples, not an impossibly high birth rate, that brought about the rapid expansion of the Tswana merafe.

21. Thomas Baines, *Explorations in South-West Africa* (London: Longman-Green, 1864), p. 409; quoted in *Land Filled with Flies*, p. 118.

22. Siegfried Passarge, *Die Buschmänner der Kalahari* (Berlin: Dietrich Reimer, 1907). I am currently preparing a translation, that will be published by the University of Michigan Press.

23. Zhu have a strong tradition of trading, both to maintain their social networks and for exchanging goods (see Polly Wiessner, "Hxaro: A Regional System of Reciprocity for the Reduction of Risk among the !Kung San" [Ph.D. diss., University of Michigan, 1977]), and their language has a rich vocabulary concerned with trade.

24. Lee, *The !Kung San*, p. 77.

25. Ibid., p. 78. Tsau was the Tswana capitol on the Delta.

26. Oswin Köhler, *Die Welt der Kxoé Buschleute* (Berlin: Dietrich Reimer, 1989), p. 425. A vivid description of the experience of a person captured into slavery is found in Joseph Miller, *Way of Death* (Madison, WI: University of Wisconsin Press, 1988).

27. P. Serton, *The Narrative and Journal of Gerald McKiernan in South West Africa, 1874–1879* (Cape Town: Van Riebeck Society, 1954), p. 167.

28. Carl Hugo Hahn, "Neueste Deutsche Forschungen in Süd-Afrika," *Petermann's geographische Mitteilungen* 8 (1967): 285.

29. Jacqueline Solway and Richard Lee, "Foragers, Genuine or Spurious? Situating the Kalahari San in History," *Current Anthropology* 31 (1990): 116.

30. *Deutsches Kolonialblatt* 23 (1912): 530–541. Ein Erkundungsritt in das Kaukau-Veld, von Hauptmann Müller.

31. It has been estimated that no more than two hundred elephants remained in all Botswana in 1900; remember that during the 1860s and 1870s about three thousand had been killed every year. The latest wildlife census indicates that there are now about sixty-eight thousand in the country.

32. Elizabeth Cashdan, "Property and Social Insurance among the G||ana," paper presented at Second International Conference on Hunting and Gathering Societies, Quebec City, 1980.

33. Silberbauer, *Hunter and Habitat*, p. 99.

34. Ibid., p. 151.

35. See my paper, "Those Who Have Each Other: Land Tenure of San-Speaking Peoples," in Edwin Wilmsen, ed., *We are Here: Politics of Aboriginal Land Tenure* (Berkeley: University of California Press, 1989), pp. 43–67, and Barnard, *Hunters and Herders*, p. 146.

36. Marshall, *The !Kung of NyaeNyae*, p. 340.

37. Barnard, *Hunters and Herders*, p. 111.

38. Wilmsen, *Land Filled with Flies*, p. 180.

39. Wiessner, "Hxaro," p. 119.

40. Ibid., p. 224.

41. Lee, *The !Kung San*, p. 350.

Suggested Readings

Bernard, Alan. *Hunters and Herders of Southern Africa.* Cambridge: Cambridge University Press, 1992. A very good synthesis of ethnographies of all Khoisan groups.

Lee, Richard. *The Dobe !Kung.* New York: Holt, Reinhart & Winston, 1984. The standard classic ethnography of one San group.

Pratt, Mary Louise. "Scratches on the Face of the Earth, or, What Mr. Barrow Saw in the Land of the Bushmen," in Henry Lewis Gates Jr., ed., *Race, Writing, and Difference.* Chicago: University of Chicago Press, 1985, pp. 119–143. An excellent critique of classic San ethnographies.

Schrire, Carmel. "An Enquiry into the Evolutionary Status and Apparent Identity of San Hunter-Gatherers." *Human Ecology* 8 (1980): 9–32. The first use of historical material in San ethnography.

Wilmsen, Edwin. "The Ecology of Illusion: Anthropological Foraging in the Kalahari." *Reviews in Anthropology* 10 (1983): 9–20. A critical review of the four major modern classics of San ethnography.

"KALAHARI SAN: SOMETIME HUNTER-GATHERERS"

Edwin N. Wilmsen

1) What are the two major opposing views regarding the Kalahari San as a viable ethnographic reality?

2) What was the social history of the Khoisan peoples in relationship to the other peoples in southern Africa prior to the arrival of the Europeans?

3) According to Wilmsen, how did the *kgmelo* (milk-jug) economic system contribute to the reduction of some San peoples to a state of rural poverty?

4) How did hunting and changes in fashion trends in Europe contribute to the marginalization of some San in the Kalahari Desert?

5) How did the introduction of a modern capitalistic economic system based on mining and wage labor contribute further to the marginalization of the San?

6) Discuss current San culture in terms of land tenure, kinship/marriage, property/exchange systems, and other social institutions. How close are these to the traditional systems practiced by the San?

TO MARKET

Patricia Shanley

Bacuri are like potato chips: You can't eat just one. When Clemente was a kid, he and his buddies would swipe a canoe from a neighbor, paddle across the river, and scramble up the opposite bank to reach the forest trees that bore this mango-sized fruit, with its sweet white pulp. There they downed bacuri by the dozen and toted even more home. But none of the fruit ever reached market. Located in the Brazilian rainforest on a tributary of the Amazon, Clemente's village was, until recently, accessible only by boat. The nearest town was across the river and severity-five miles away overland; many village folk never set foot there during their lifetimes.

Now a married man with eight children and another one well on the way, Clemente surveys the changes wrought by an influx of loggers and ranchers. The land across the river from the village is burned and badly shaved, and in place of thousands of trees stand a few head of cattle. Beyond the blackened stumps, rough logging trails pierce the remaining forest, winding their way to one of the region's sawmills. Cash poor and under heavy pressure from the loggers, some village leaders have sold off timber from the twelve-square-mile tract the community holds on this side of the river. One man gave up fifty acres of trees for a rustic stove; another traded seven piquiá fruit trees (worth $700 as sawed wood) for one injection for his sick son.

Clemente and his fellow villagers have long harvested and used the vines, medicinal plants, fruit, and game offered by their forest, but because of these desperate deals, the number and the diversity of trees and game animals within their tract is diminishing. Could the sale of forest fruit benefit them more than the sale of trees, providing cash while salvaging the rest, of the forest? The economic potential of such products has been a hot topic among conservationists the world over, who call them non-timber forest products, or NTFPs. Juices, preserves, candies, ice creams, and body oils featuring exotic ingredients have already begun to appear on the shelves of distant shops. Fed up with unfavorable timber deals, the villagers are ready to try something new.

Until now, the villagers' principal marketing experience has been with cassava flour, a staple created from their main agricultural crop through an arduous baking process. They sell more than half of what they produce to a middleman who reaches the village by boat, but their efforts earn them little. As an ethnobotanist and part of a team of ecologists researching ways to slow deforestation, I have been invited to help inventory the resources of the village forest. Among the scores of tree species whose fruit is consumed locally, we identify three—*uxi* as well as bacuri and piquiá—that hold real sales potential. Distant policymakers, however, have failed to reckon with the pitfalls this new enterprise may encounter and to anticipate the practical lessons that must be learned.

The villagers' marketing venture begins as Clemente's nephew hears the sound of a truck across the river and paddles to the ranch upstream to investigate. He comes home with the news that the truck will be going back to town in a few days and that there will be room in it for people and products. We are smack in the middle of Amazonia's rainy winter, the season of forest fruit. The villagers see it as a rare opportunity. But the following morning, as the pink sun rises over the muddy river, Clemente enters my hut to ask, "So where are the fruit trees?"

Most of the large trees that once stood near the village have been destroyed—trucked away or loaded onto barges by logging companies. Others have been cut down to build canoes or to make room for small agricultural fields. Accustomed to gathering fruit only for their own use, local families have been relying on a relatively small number of trees. Today, they need to find more, all with ripe fruit. But forests are not orchards, where trees of the same species grow conveniently in one place. And although some villagers, especially hunters, know where to find the scattered trees, others do not.

Clemente and his friend Branco have to walk two to three miles, past quiltlike patches of overgrown abandoned fields, to find suitable trees. With increasing disappointment, they inspect one piquiá tree after another. The timing and the volume of fruiting varies enormously, both between and within species, and the odds of any one tree producing fruit in a particular year are not good. After two hours, the men have passed twelve enormous piquiá trees, but only three have fruit; the total fruit count is just seven. At a prospective ten cents a piece, this is not a huge haul.

Beneath piquiá number twenty, however, the men spy close to a hundred pieces of fruit. Softball-sized and tan with a greenish tinge, they lie scattered 100 to 130 feet below the massive winding branches from which they have fallen. Clemente opens one that has crashlanded on a log. Its thick rind has been smashed, and the pulp inside is bright yellow. He sniffs it: yes, sweet. He and Branco quickly gather seventy-nine.

This year the piquiá (*Caryocar villosum*) and bacuri (*Platonia insignis*) trees with high fruit yields happen to be growing at the farthest limits of the village tract of forest. Pacas (burrowing rodents), parrots, armadillos, and ants have had first shot at these trees. Fortunately, both bacuri and piquiá, because of their thick skins, survive intact for days on the forest floor. The men also find and collect the egg-shaped fruit of the uxi tree (*Endopleura uchi*). These have a fine skin and require quick pickup. The grainy flesh is a fast food for forest squirrels.

In the shade of the wet forest, with mosquitoes biting their arms and legs, the men gather the fruit and quickly throw it into large, woven plastic sacks. Carried slung over the back, each filled sack weighs about 175 pounds. Finally, Clemente and Branco begin their circuitous three-mile return to the river. The heavy sacks rub against their backs and arms; bruised by pressure, the thick rinds of the piquiá and bacuri begin to ooze, staining clothes and irritating skin. The trails often are flooded or suffocated by vegetation that has sprung up following the heavy rains. The men move with caution; the rains have drawn out a variety of snakes, which inhabit the trails, puddles, and brush.

Reaching the village at last, Clemente and Branco drop the sacks onto the ground outside their homes. They toss some damaged piquiá fruit to a pack of hungry kids, who scoop up the treat and rush off to boil the oily pulp in a pot of river water. The remaining fruit is packed tightly into sacks that are tied closed with vines. Clemente unearths a nub of charcoal from the damp earth and slowly initials each bag.

After three days, some 2,400 pieces of fruit have been collected by Clemente, Branco, Beca, Curumi, and several other village men who have joined the enterprise. Having heard about fruit loss caused by transport in sacks, Clemente and Branco decide to package some of the fruit in boxes. They collect thick slabs of forest trees previously cut for home construction and rig these together using nails they beg from neighbors or scavenge from the soil. With the butt of a machete, Clemente pounds the rusty nails into the hard damp wood. He dumps fruit into the box, conjures a lid out of remaining wood scraps, and seals it

all with thick forest vines. Stars and a cuticle of moon appear, casting pale light. The wooden crates are enormous.

Under the faint moon, a new crisis arises: Clemente's wife begins her labor. The whole scheme is in danger of collapse if someone cannot be found to take his place and accompany Branco and another man, Nego, on the trip to the market. Beca refuses to go, so Clemente decides to awaken Neginho, known for his cooperative nature and his interest in the fruit sale. As his family sleeps in hammocks behind him, Neginho stands silent and immobile, wanting to respond favorably but pondering, troubled. As Clemente walks away, it suddenly occurs to him that Neginho is not good with numbers. In villages along the river, perhaps more than seventy percent of the population have had no schooling. This—together with the villagers' general lack of market experience—cancels out many candidates. Clemente returns to Beca, who has collected the largest share of fruit. Clemente warns Beca that his profits from the sale may be in jeopardy if he does not go with them. Finally Beca consents.

Before dawn, Beca and Clemente, bending beneath loads of fruit, feel their way down a red-ant–infested trail to the riverbank. There they pitch the bags and coffin-like crates into their canoes, which rock under the weight, taking on water. Beca's wife, Lucia, descends the slippery bank, removes a worn slipper, and uses it as a scoop for bailing. The canoes sink deeper in the water as the men clamber in.

The destination is the truck, two and a half miles upstream. Swollen by the rains, the river flows swiftly. But there are no mishaps, and three hours later, with the help of seven men, the truck has been loaded. Clemente watches as his friends depart; seventy-five miles of uncertain logging roads lie ahead. The winter brings not only rain and falling fruit but collapsed bridges, overturned logging trucks, and lost lives.

This day, the journey goes well, and the truck reaches town within four hours. Pulling up to the muddy, rambunctious marketplace, Beca, Nego, and Branco glance about. Milling around are hundreds of poor, hopeful farmers. Some sell cassava flour, some fish, some fruit. By now it is past midday, and the sun is high. Trade began six hours earlier as light first touched the vegetables, the dust, and the dogs. In the cramped marketplace, competition for space is intense. Free to roam twelve square miles of village forest, Beca and his comrades have had little practice brandishing elbows. Their inexperience and heavy loads combine to settle them away from the best locations.

Most families in Clemente's village sell cassava flour, which travels well. Fruit is likely to bruise, break open, or rot. In the commotion surrounding the new undertaking, the quantity of fruit, not the quality, was paramount. The fruit was not washed, dried, selected, or carefully packaged. More than half is spoiled. Meanwhile, freeloaders posing as taste-testing customers visit only to fill their stomachs with fruit samples.

Nonetheless, true customers do appear. A wizened former farmer, accustomed to the taste of uxi on her lips each winter, approaches the stand, happily requesting sixty fruit. Sixty? What can we put them in? While Beca stands guard over their products, Nego and Branco run between makeshift stalls, kicking up dust as they go. With the scant change they carry between them, they purchase twenty-five thin plastic sacks. Christened, they return and await more trade.

At a loss when it comes to prices and numbers, Nego is little help at the booth. He is large, young, and hungry. Beca lets him go. He scouts work and finds some. For eight hours he runs hunched over, carrying 130-pound sacks of flour from truck to market. He spends his earnings on a meal of rice and beans with a sliver of meat and a handful of cassava flour.

At dawn the following day, with nothing to show for his efforts, Nego catches a ride atop a logging truck and heads home, while Beca and Branco linger at the market. When evening comes, the two men drag their unsold fruit to a deposit area. From there, they enter a cement-walled room filled with hammocks. As latecomers the previous night, they had to hang theirs close to the latrine. Mosquitoes orbit their sweaty heads, and the smell of rotting vegetables and urine surrounds them. Exhausted, they fall asleep.

In the morning, Beca and Branco rise early, scramble to the deposit area, and move the remaining fruit to their stand. Lowering the price to liquidate what will soon rot, they sell as much as they can and throw the rest into the gutter. They spend one more night in town and set out for home the next day. What is their net gain? It is hard to know. Meals and several nights of drinking sugar-cane alcohol have eaten into their earnings. By the time Beca and Branco, coated with yellow road dust, have made it back to the village aboard a logging truck, it is a full four days after their departure. Some fruit collectors receive a take of the profits, and others none.

After this first sale, the rural "radio," as swift as any electronic network, spreads word about the earnings to be gained from fruit selling. Jeering or jealous, many villagers remain skeptical and continue working steadily in the cassava fields. But the news inspires some women in a neighboring village. Theodora and her friends are beginning a "mothers' club" to carry out tasks together and better their livelihoods. They hope that with earnings from fruit, they will be able to buy used clothes and also lye, to make soap. They enter the forest together to look for bacuri, piquiá, and uxi.

Three months into the season, trees have already released the bulk of their weighty harvest. The fruit that has not already been eaten by forest creatures is bursting open and rotting on the forest floor. Barefoot, the women carefully pick their way around the red ants and putrescent fruit. Pooling their joint knowledge of the forest, they recall which trees bear late in the season and locate them, rescuing the last of the year's yield. Antoninho, a male relative and a natural entrepreneur, agrees to accompany them to market.

They have learned from the first sale. Fruits are selected, washed, and left to dry. Small boxes of thin wood, with leaves for cushioning, are used for transport. The women leave the village at night, arriving in the city before dawn. They fight their way to the prime sales area. This late in the season, there are no other farmers selling forest fruit, so they now set the price, doubling what the men had asked. Taste testers who have no intention of buying are rebuffed. An ice-cream shop owner purchases all of Theodora's bacuri and promises to buy any others she may bring. The women sell their 2,680 pieces of fruit, go shopping for exactly what they had planned to buy, and return to the community the next day.

One month later, proudly wearing used clothes purchased with fruit money, members of the mothers' club accompany me to another river community to talk about the practical benefits of their forest fruit sale and the findings of my ecological research team. One sack of fruit, we can report, brought ten times the value of a sack of cassava flour for less than a tenth of the time and effort, and the sale of only seven bacuri gave a return equal to what a logger had offered for an entire tree. Fruit that certain village families eat regularly, while not placing money directly in villagers' pockets, amounts to a substantial invisible income. Laughter rings out as Mangueria, a full-bellied fellow, estimates that he and his family have eaten more than 3,000 pieces of forest fruit in one month alone.

Village hunters tell our team that the flowers and fruit of many forest trees "call" wildlife. In one month, for example, three villagers caught 170 pounds of game under fruit trees. Others mentioned the medicinal value of fruit, how it chases away flu and other sicknesses that might otherwise require costly remedies.

By the time Theodora rises to speak, it is dark. A small oil lamp shires light on her blue-and-white lace skirt. Unaccustomed to attention from a crowd, she talks quietly, timidly. She begins by relating what the sale meant to the mothers' club and tells of gathering the fruit, of laughter and singing under the trees. She talks about the lack of any gain from timber sales, of continual impoverishment, of sweating day after day in the production of cassava flour only to sell the product for a pittance. Although their earnings from fruit have been modest, says Theodora, they have not been cheated. This time they did not sweat only to be robbed.

Applause breaks out in the darkness. No, these villagers will not all take fruit to market. They will not all have the time, the transport, the means. They will not all wear "fruit clothes." But they know now that selling off timber is not the only way to earn cash from their trees. And as long as the forest survives, the villagers will all be able to tap trees for medicinal oils, collect vines, hunt game, and eat wild fruit.

Postscript: *After this article was written, men in Clemente's village, desperate for cash during a season of poor crops, sold timber rights to many trees in their village tract. The scant profits bought radios, bicycles, and alcohol but did little to ease hunger. Village matriarch Dona Ana, who was away at the time, was infuriated. She spoke out against any further timber sales. Since then, to help save communities like theirs from a similar calamity, I have worked with women from this village and others in the area who have come together to share their new ecological and economic awareness. Responding to requests, the group, known as the Mulheres do Mata (Women of the Forest), travels by foot and canoe to conduct workshops in eastern Amazonia. Villages that have taken part have improved their forest management through increased use and processing of forest fruits and medicinals, through negotiating more advantageous terms with loggers, and by creating community forest reserves. Research results, songs, and posters presented in the workshops also have been incorporated into illustrated books, useful even for nonliterate audiences. The women's work has garnered attention from organizations elsewhere in Latin America and in Asia and Africa as well.*

"To Market"

Patricia Shanley

1) Contrast the strategies used by both the male and the female fruit sellers. Which were more effective, and why?

2) Why do some villagers sell the fruit of the piquiá tree while others choose to sell off timber rights?

3) What are "mother's clubs" and what are their purposes?

SECTION FIVE

Realities of Gender

New Women of the Ice Age

Heather Pringle

The Black Venus of Dolní Vestonice, a small, splintered figurine sensuously fashioned from clay, is an envoy from a forgotten world. It is all soft curves, with breasts like giant pillows beneath a masked face. At nearly 26,000 years old, it ranks among the oldest known portrayals of women, and to generations of researchers, it has served as a powerful—if enigmatic—clue to the sexual politics of the Ice Age.

Excavators unearthed the Black Venus near the Czech village of Dolní Vestonice in 1924, on a hillside among charred, fractured mammoth bones and stone tools. (Despite its nickname, the Black Venus is actually reddish—it owes its name to the ash that covered it when it was found.) Since the mid-nineteenth century, researchers had discovered more than a dozen similar statuettes in caves and open-air sites from France to Russia. All were cradled in layers of earth littered with stone and bone weaponry, ivory jewelry, and the remains of extinct Ice Age animals. All were depicted naked or nearly so. Collectively, they came to be known as Venus figurines, after another ancient bare-breasted statue, the Venus de Milo. Guided at least in part by prevailing sexual stereotypes, experts interpreted the meaning of the figurines freely. The Ice Age camps that spawned this art, they concluded, were once the domain of hardworking male hunters and secluded, pampered women who spent their days in idleness like the harem slaves so popular in nineteenth-century art.

Over the next six decades, Czech archeologists expanded the excavations at Dolní Vestonice, painstakingly combing the site square meter by square meter. By the 1990s they had unearthed thousands of bone, stone, and clay artifacts and had wrested 19 radiocarbon dates from wood charcoal that sprinkled camp floors. And they had shaded and refined their portrait of Ice Age life. Between 29,000 and 25,000 years ago, they concluded, wandering bands had passed the cold months of the year repeatedly at Dolní Vestonice. Armed with short-range spears, the men appeared to have been specialists in hunting tusk-wielding mammoths and other big game, hauling home great mountains of meat to feed their dependent mates and children. At night men feasted on mammoth steaks, fed their fires with mammoth bone, and fueled their sexual fantasies with tiny figurines of women carved from mammoth ivory and fired from clay. It was the ultimate man's world.

Or was it? Over the past few months, a small team of American archeologists has raised some serious doubts. Amassing critical and previously overlooked evidence from Dolní Vestonice and the neighboring site of Pavlov, Olga Soffer, James Adovasio, and David Hyland now propose that human survival there had little to do with manly men hurling spears at big-game animals. Instead, observes Soffer, one of the world's leading authorities on Ice Age hunters and gatherers and an archeologist at the University of Illinois in Champaign-Urbana, it depended largely on women, plants, and a technique of hunting previously invisible in the archeological evidence—net hunting. "This is not the image we've always had of Upper Paleolithic macho guys out killing animals up close and personal," Soffer explains. "Net hunting is communal, and it involves the labor of children and women. And this has lots of implications."

Many of these implications make her conservative colleagues cringe because they raise serious questions about the focus of previous studies. European archeologists have long concentrated on analyzing broken stone tools and butchered big-game bones, the most plentiful and best preserved relics of the Upper Paleolithic era (which stretched from 40,000 to 12,000 years ago). From these analyses, researchers have developed theories about how these societies once hunted and gathered food. Most researchers ruled out the possibility of women hunters for biological reasons. Adult females, they reasoned, had to devote themselves to breast-feeding and tending infants. "Human babies have always been immature and dependent," says Soffer. "If women are the people who are always involved with biological reproduction and the rearing of the young, then that is going to constrain their behavior. They have to provision that child. For fathers, provisioning is optional."

To test theories about Upper Paleolithic life, researchers looked to ethnography, the scientific description of modern and historical cultural groups. While the lives of modern hunters do not exactly duplicate those of ancient hunters, they supply valuable clues to universal human behavior. "Modern

Reprinted by permission from *Discover*, April 1998. Heather Pringle/© 1998.

ethnography cannot be used to clone the past," says Soffer. "But people have always had to solve problems. Nature and social relationships present problems to people. We use ethnography to look for theoretical insights into human behavior, test them with ethnography, and if they work, assume that they represent a universal feature of human behavior."

But when researchers began turning to ethnographic descriptions of hunting societies, they unknowingly relied on a very incomplete literature. Assuming that women in surviving hunting societies were homebodies who simply tended hearths and suckled children, most early male anthropologists spent their time with male informants. Their published ethnographies brim with descriptions of males making spears and harpoons and heaving these weapons at reindeer, walruses, and whales. Seldom do they mention the activities of women. Ethnography, it seemed, supported theories of ancient male big-game hunters. "When they talked about primitive man, it was always 'he,'" says Soffer. "The 'she' was missing."

Recent anthropological research has revealed just how much Soffer's colleagues overlooked. By observing women in the few remaining hunter-gatherer societies and by combing historical accounts of tribal groups more thoroughly, anthropologists have come to realize how critical the female half of the population has always been to survival. Women and children have set snares, laid spring traps, sighted game, and participated in animal drives and surrounds—forms of hunting that endangered neither young mothers nor their offspring. They dug starchy roots and collected other plant carbohydrates essential to survival. They even hunted, on occasion, with the projectile points traditionally deemed men's weapons. "I found references to Inuit women carrying bows and arrows, especially the blunt arrows that were used for hunting birds," says Linda Owen, an archeologist at the University of Tübingen in Germany.

The revelations triggered a volley of new research. In North America, Soffer and her team have found tantalizing evidence of the hunting gear often favored by women in historical societies. In Europe, archeobotanists are analyzing Upper Paleolithic hearths for evidence of plant remains probably gathered by women and children, while lithics specialists are poring over stone tools to detect new clues to their uses. And the results are gradually reshaping our understanding of Ice Age society. The famous Venus figurines, say archeologists of the new school, were never intended as male pornography: instead they may have played a key part in Upper Paleolithic

rituals that centered on women. And such findings, pointing toward a more important role for Paleolithic women than had previously been assumed, are giving many researchers pause.

Like many of her colleagues, Soffer clearly relishes the emerging picture of Upper Paleolithic life. "I think life back then was a hell of a lot more egalitarian than it was with your later peasant societies," she says. "Of course the Paleolithic women were pulling their own weight." After sifting through Ice Age research for nearly two decades, Soffer brings a new critical approach to the notion—flattering to so many of her male colleagues—of mighty male mammoth hunters. "Very few archeologists are hunters," she notes, so it never occurred to most of them to look into the mechanics of hunting dangerous tusked animals. They just accepted the ideas they'd inherited from past work.

But the details of hunting bothered Soffer. Before the fifth century B.C., no tribal hunters in Asia or Africa had ever dared make their living from slaying elephants; the great beasts were simply too menacing. With the advent of the Iron Age in Africa, the situation changed. New weapons allowed Africans to hunt elephants and trade their ivory with Greeks and Romans. A decade ago, keen to understand how prehistoric bands had slaughtered similar mammoths, Soffer began studying Upper Paleolithic sites on the Russian and Eastern European plains. To her surprise, the famous mammoth bone beds were strewn with cumbersome body parts, such as 220-pound skulls, that sensible hunters would generally abandon. Moreover, the bones exhibited widely differing degrees of weathering, as if they had sat on the ground for varying lengths of time. To Soffer, it looked suspiciously as if Upper Paleolithic hunters had simply camped next to places where the pachyderms had perished naturally—such as water holes or salt licks—and mined the bones for raw materials.

Soffer began analyzing data researchers had gathered describing the sex and age ratios of mammoths excavated from four Upper Paleolithic sites. She found many juveniles, a smaller number of adult females, and hardly any males. The distribution mirrored the death pattern other researchers had observed at African water holes, where the weakest animals perished closest to the water and the strongest farther off. "Imagine the worst time of year in Africa, which is the drought season," explains Soffer. "There is no water, and elephants need an enormous amount. The ones in the worst shape—your weakest, your infirm, your young—are going to be tethered to that water before they die. They are in such horrendous shape, they don't have any extra energy to go anywhere. The ones in better shape would wander off slight distances and then keel over farther away. You've got basket cases and you've got ones that can walk 20 feet."

To Soffer, the implications of this study were clear. Upper Paleolithic bands had pitched their camps next to critical resources such as ancient salt licks or water holes. There the men spent more time scavenging bones and ivory from mammoth carcasses than they did risking life and limb by attacking 6,600-pound pachyderms with short-range spears. "If one of these Upper Paleolithic guys killed a mammoth, and occasionally they did," concedes Soffer dryly, "they probably didn't stop talking about it for ten years."

But if Upper Paleolithic families weren't often tucking into mammoth steaks, what were they hunting and how? Soffer found the first unlikely clue in 1991, while sifting through hundreds of tiny clay fragments recovered from the Upper Paleolithic site of Pavlov, which lies just a short walk from Dolní Vestonice. Under a magnifying lens, Soffer noticed something strange on a few of the fragments: a series of parallel lines impressed on their surfaces. What could have left such a regular pattern? Puzzled, Soffer photographed the pieces, all of which had been unearthed from a zone sprinkled with wood charcoal that was radiocarbon-dated at between 27,000 and 25,000 years ago.

When she returned home, Soffer had the film developed. And one night on an impulse, she put on a slide show for a visiting colleague, Jim Adavasio. "We'd run out of cable films," she jokes. Staring at the images projected on Soffer's refrigerator, Adovasio, an archeologist at Mercyhurst College in Pennsylvania and an expert on ancient fiber technology, immediately recognized the impressions of plant fibers. On a few, he could actually discern a pattern of interlacing fibers—weaving.

Without a doubt, he said, he and Soffer were gazing at textiles or basketry. They were the oldest—by nearly 7,000 years—ever found. Just how these pieces of weaving got impressed in clay, he couldn't say. "It may be that a lot of these [materials] were lying around on clay floors," he notes. "When the houses burned, the walked-in images were subsequently left in the clay floors."

Soffer and Adovasio quickly made arrangements to fly back to the Czech Republic. At the Dolní Vestonice branch of the Institute of Archeology, Soffer sorted through nearly 8,400 fired clay pieces, weeding out the rejects. Adovasio made positive clay casts of 90. Back in Pennsylvania, he and his Mercyhurst colleague David Hyland peered at the casts under a zoom stereomicroscope, measuring warps and wefts. Forty-three revealed impressions of basketry and textiles. Some of the latter were as finely woven as a modern linen tablecloth. But as Hyland stared at four of the samples, he noted something potentially more fascinating: impressions of cordage bearing weaver's knots, a technique that joins two lengths of cord and that is commonly used for making nets of secure mesh. It looked like a tiny shred of a net bag, or perhaps a hunting net. Fascinated, Soffer expanded the study. She spent six weeks at the Moravian Museum in Brno, sifting through the remainder of the collections from Dolní Vestonice. Last fall, Adovasio spied the telltale impressions of Ice Age mesh on one of the new casts.

The mesh, measuring two inches across, is far too delicate for hunting deer or other large prey. But hunters at Dolní Vestonice could have set nets of this size to capture hefty Ice Age hares, each carrying some six pounds of meat, and other furbearers such as arctic fox and red fox. As it turns out, the bones of hares and foxes litter camp floors at Dolní Vestonice and Pavlov. Indeed, this small game accounts for 46 percent of the individual animals recovered at Pavlov. Soffer, moreover, doesn't rule out the possibility of turning up bits of even larger nets. Accomplished weavers in North America once knotted mesh with which they captured 1,000-pound elk and 300-pound bighorn sheep. "In fact, when game officials have to move sheep out west, it's by nets," she adds. "You throw nets on them and they just lie down. It's a very safe way of hunting."

In many historical societies, she observes, women played a key part in net hunting since the technique did not call for brute strength nor did it place young mothers in physical peril. Among Australian aborigines, for example, women as well as men knotted the mesh, laboring for as much as two or three years on a fine net. Among native North American groups, they helped lay out their handiwork on poles across a valley floor. Then the entire camp joined forces as beaters. Fanning out across the valley, men, women, and children alike shouted and screamed, flushing out game and driving it in the direction of the net. "Everybody and their mother could participate," says Soffer. "Some people were beating, others were screaming or holding the net. And once you got the net on these animals, they were immobilized. You didn't need brute force. You could club them, hit them any old way."

People seldom returned home empty-handed. Researchers living among the net-hunting Mbuti in the forests of Congo report that they capture game every time they lay out their woven traps, scooping up fifty percent of the animals encountered. "Nets are a far more valued item in their panoply of food-producing things than bows and arrows are," says Adovasio. So lethal are these traps that the Mbuti generally rack up more meat than they can consume, trading the surplus with neighbors. Other net hunters traditionally smoked or dried their catch and stored it for leaner times. Or they polished it off immediately in large ceremonial feasts. The hunters of Dolní Vestonice and Pavlov, says Soffer, probably feasted during ancient rituals. Archeologists unearthed no evidence of food storage pits at either site. But there is much evidence of ceremony. At Dolní Vestonice, for example, many clay figurines appear to have been ritually destroyed in secluded parts of the site.

Soffer doubts that the inhabitants of Dolní Vestonice and Pavlov were the only net makers in Ice Age Europe. Camps stretching from Germany to Russia are littered with a notable abundance of small-game bones, from hares to birds like ptarmigan. And at least some of their inhabitants whittled bone tools that look much like the awls and net spacers favored by historical net makers. Such findings, agree Soffer and Adovasio, reveal just how shaky the most widely accepted reconstructions of Upper Paleolithic life are. "These terribly stilted interpretations," says Adovasio, "with men hunting big animals all the time and the poor females waiting at home for these guys to bring home the bacon—what crap."

In her home outside Munich, Linda Owen finds other faults with this traditional image. Owen, an American born and raised, specializes in the microscopic analysis of stone tools. In her years of work, she often noticed that many of the tools made by hunters who roamed Europe near the end of the Upper Paleolithic era, some 18,000 to 12,000 years ago, resembled pounding stones and other gear for harvesting and processing plants. Were women and children gathering and storing wild plant foods?

Most of her colleagues saw little value in pursuing the question. Indeed, some German archeologists contended that ninety percent of the human diet during the Upper Paleolithic era came from meat. But as Owen began reading nutritional studies, she saw that heavy meat consumption would spell death. To stoke the body's cellular engines, human beings require energy from protein, fat, or carbohydrates. Of these, protein is the least efficient. To burn it, the body must boost its metabolic rate by ten percent, straining the liver's ability to absorb oxygen. Unlike carnivorous animals, whose digestive and metabolic systems are well adapted to a meat-only diet, humans who consume more than half their calories as lean meat will die from protein poisoning. In Upper Paleolithic times, hunters undoubtedly tried to round out their diets with fat from wild game. But in winter, spring, and early summer, the meat would have been very lean. So how did humans survive?

Owen began sifting for clues through anthropological and historical accounts from subarctic and arctic North America. These environments, she reasoned, are similar to that of Ice Age Europe and pose similar challenges to their inhabitants. Even in the far north, Inuit societies harvested berries for winter storage and gathered other plants for medicines and for fibers. To see if any of the flora that thrived in Upper Paleolithic Europe could be put to similar uses, Owen drew up a list of plants economically important to people living in cold-climate regions of North America and Europe and compared it with a list of species that botanists had identified from pollen trapped in Ice Age sediment cores from southern Germany. Nearly seventy plants were found on both lists. "I came up with just a fantastic list of plants that were available at that time. Among others, there were a number of reeds that are used by the Eskimo and subarctic people in North America for making baskets. There are a lot of plants with edible leaves and stems, and things that were used as drugs and dyes. So the plants were there."

The chief plant collectors in historical societies were undoubtedly women. "It was typically women's work," says Owen. "I did find several comments that the men on hunting expeditions would gather berries or plants for their own meals, but they did not participate in the plant-gathering expeditions. They might go along, but they would be hunting or fishing."

Were Upper Paleolithic women gathering plants? The archeological literature was mostly silent on the subject. Few archeobotanists, Owen found, had ever looked for plant seeds and shreds in Upper Paleolithic camps. Most were convinced such efforts would be futile in sites so ancient. At University College London, however, Owen reached a determined young archeobotanist, Sarah Mason, who had analyzed a small sample of charcoal-like remains from a 26,390-year-old hearth at Dolní Vestonice.

The sample held more than charcoal. Examining it with a scanning electron microscope. Mason and her colleagues found fragments of fleshy plant taproots with distinctive secretory cavities—trademarks of the daisy and aster family, which boasts several species with edible roots. In all likelihood, women at Dolní Vestonice had dug the roots and cooked them into starchy meals. And they had very likely simmered other plant foods too. Mason and her colleagues detected a strange pulverized substance in the charred sample. It looked as if the women had either ground plants into flour and then boiled the results to make gruel or pounded vegetable material into a mush for their babies. Either way, says Soffer, the results are telling. "They're stuffing carbo hydrates."

Owen is pursuing the research further. "If you do look," she says, "you can find things." At her urging, colleagues at the University of Tübingen are now analyzing Paleolithic hearths for botanical remains as they unearth them. Already they have turned up more plants, including berries, all clearly preserved after thousands of years. In light of these findings, Owen suggests that it was women, not men, who brought home most of the calories to Upper Paleolithic families. Indeed, she estimates that if Ice Age females collected plants, bird eggs, shellfish, and edible insects, and if they hunted or trapped small game and participated in the hunting of large game—as northern women did in historical times—they most likely contributed seventy percent of the consumed calories.

Moreover, some women may have enjoyed even greater power, judging from the most contentious relics of Ice Age life: the famous Venus figurines. Excavators have recovered more than 100 of the small statuettes, which are crafted between 29,000 and 23,000 years ago from such enduring materials as bone, stone, antler, ivory, and fired clay. The figurines share a strange blend of abstraction and realism. They bare prominent breasts, for example, but lack nipples. Their bodies are often minutely detailed down to the swaying lines of their backbones and the tiny rolls of flesh—fat folds—beneath their shoulder blades, but they often lack eyes, mouths, and any facial expression. For years researchers viewed them as a male art form. Early anthropologists, after all, had observed only male hunters carving stone, ivory, and other hard materials. Females were thought to lack the necessary strength. Moreover, reasoned experts, only men would take such loving interest in a woman's body. Struck by the voluptuousness of the small stone, ivory, and clay bodies, some researchers suggested they were Ice Age erotica, intended to be touched and fondled by their male makers. The idea still lingers. In the 1980s, for example, the well-known American paleontologist Dale Guthrie wrote a scholarly article comparing the postures of the figurines with the provocative poses of *Playboy* centerfolds.

But most experts now dismiss such contentions. Owen's careful scouring of ethnographic sources, for example, revealed that women in arctic and subarctic societies did indeed work stone and ivory on occasion. And there is little reason to suggest the figurines figured as male erotica. The Black Venus, for example, seems to have belonged to a secret world of ceremony and ritual far removed from everyday sexual life.

The evidence, says Soffer, lies in the raw material from which the Black Venus is made. Clay objects sometimes break or explode when fired, a process called thermal-shock fracturing. Studies conducted by Pamela Vandiver of the Smithsonian Institution have demonstrated that the Black Venus and other human and animal figurines recovered from Dolní Vestonice—as well as nearly 2,000 fired ceramic pellets that litter the site—were made from a local clay that is resistant to thermal-shock fracturing. But many of the figurines, including the celebrated Black Venus, bear the distinctive jagged branching splinters created by thermal shock. Intriguingly, the fired clay pellets do not.

Curious, Vandiver decided to replicate the ancient firing process. Her analysis of the small Dolní Vestonice kilns revealed that they had been fired to temperatures around 1450 degrees Fahrenheit—similar to those of an ordinary hearth. So Vandiver set about making figurines of local soil and firing them in a similar earthen kiln, which a local archeological crew had built nearby. To produce thermal shock, she had to place objects larger than half an inch on the hottest part of the fire; moreover, the pieces had to be so wet they barely held their shape.

To Vandiver and Soffer, the experiment—which was repeated several times back at the Smithsonian Institution—suggests that thermal shock was no accident. "Stuff can explode naturally in the kiln," says Soffer, "or you can make it explode. Which was going on at Dolní Vestonice? We toyed with both ideas. Either we're dealing with the most inept potters, people with two left hands, or they are doing it on purpose. And we reject the idea that they were totally inept, because other materials didn't explode. So what are the odds that this would happen only with a very particular category of objects?"

These exploding figurines could well have played a role in rituals, an idea supported by the location of the kilns. They are situated far away from the dwellings, as ritual buildings often are. Although the nature of the ceremonies is not clear, Soffer speculates that they might have served as divination rites for discerning what the future held. "Some stuff is going to explode. Some stuff is not going to explode. It's evocative, like picking petals off a daisy. She loves me, she loves me not."

Moreover, ritualists at Dolní Vestonice could have read significance into the fracturing patterns of the figurines. Many historical cultures, for example, attempted to read the future by a related method called scapulimancy. In North America, Cree ceremonialists often placed the shoulder blade, or scapula, of a desired animal in the center of a lodge. During the ceremonies, cracks began splintering the bone: a few of these fractures leaked droplets of fat. To Cree hunters, this was a sign that they would find game if they journeyed in the directions indicated by the cracks.

Venus figurines from other sites also seem to have been cloaked in ceremony. "They were not just something made to look pretty," says Margherita Mussi, an archeologist at the University of Rome–La Sapienza who studies Upper Paleolithic figurines. Mussi notes that several small statuettes from the Grimaldi Cave carvings of southern Italy, one of the largest troves of Ice Age figurines ever found in Western Europe, were carved from rare materials, which the artists obtained with great difficulty, sometimes through trade or distant travel. The statuettes were laboriously whittled and polished, then rubbed with ocher, a pigment that appears to have had ceremonial significance, suggesting that they could have been reserved for special events like rituals.

The nature of these rites is still unclear. But Mussi is convinced that women took part, and some archeologists believe they stood at the center. One of the clearest clues, says Mussi, lies in a recently rediscovered Grimaldi figurine known as **Beauty and the Beast**. This greenish yellow serpentine sculpture portrays two arched bodies facing away from each other and joined at the head, shoulders, and lower extremities. One body is that of a Venus figurine. The other is a strange creature that combines the triangular head of a reptile, the pinched waist of a wasp, tiny arms, and horns. "It is clearly not a creature of this world," says Mussi.

The pairing of woman and supernatural beast, adds Mussi, is highly significant. "I believe that these women were related to the capacity of communicating with a different world," she says. "I think they were believed to be the gateway to a different dimension." Possessing powers that far surpassed others in their communities, such women may have formed part of a spiritual elite, rather like the shamans of ancient Siberia. As intermediaries between the real and spirit worlds, Siberian shamans were said to be able to cure illnesses and intercede on behalf of others for hunting success. It is possible that Upper Paleolithic women performed similar services for their followers.

Although the full range of their activities is unlikely ever to be known for certain, there is good reason to believe that Ice Age women played a host of powerful roles—from plant collectors and weavers to hunters and spiritual leaders. And the research that suggests those roles is rapidly changing our mental images of the past. For Soffer and others, these are exciting times. "The data do speak for themselves," she says finally. "They answer the questions we have. But if we don't envision the questions, we're not going to see the data."

"New Women of the Ice Age"

Heather Pringle

1) What are Venus figurines, and what is the traditional interpretation of their use and meaning in prehistoric societies?

2) How did incomplete or inaccurate ethnographic data on historic and modern hunter-gatherer groups contribute to the traditional reconstruction of the sociopolitical and economic organization of prehistoric hunter-gatherer groups?

3) How has recent ethnographic research contributed to a new understanding of the roles of women in prehistory?

4) How has recent archaeological research contributed to a different understanding of the role of hunting in paleolithic societies?

5) Referring back to the Durrenberger article ("Are Ethnographies 'Just-So' Stories?"), have cultural mores and ideas within western culture in the last seven decades influenced how the archaeological record has been interpreted in regard to prehistoric gender roles? Why or why not?

6) What lines of evidence have been employed to construct new theories regarding the use and meaning of Venus figurines in Paleolithic societies?

THE WAR BETWEEN MEN AND WOMEN

Robert Sapolsky

As most newlyweds quickly learn, intimate relationships, even the most blissful, can buzz with tension. Couples typically find themselves struggling over money, in-laws, ex-lovers, and how much the woman's placenta should grow when she gets pregnant. That last one is a killer. The guy wants his woman to have a fast-growing placenta, while the woman does all she can to keep it down to a reasonable size.

Of course, the fight over the placenta doesn't exactly take place out in the open. The average man, if asked what he thinks of his wife's placenta, would probably say he hasn't given it a thought. Instead the placenta conflict gets played out, unbeknownst to either person, inside the woman's body. A strange genetic process called *genomic imprinting* is responsible. And its existence is only one small example of how males and females have conflicting evolutionary goals. Understanding that the struggle takes place can explain a lot of strange behavior and physiology. And it can even explain how we came to be susceptible to certain horrific diseases.

At first, it might seem unlikely that men and women do have conflicting evolutionary goals. The point of life, according to evolutionary theorists, is for organisms to pass on copies of their genes to succeeding generations. Some organisms, such as cockroaches, do this by producing as many offspring as possible, hoping some will survive. Others, such as elephants and humans, have many fewer young but shower them with care.

So yes, both mom and dad want their kid to survive. And in monogamous species, when the father can be pretty sure it really is his kid, he may well cooperate with the mother. But that's not quite the way it is in more polygamous animal species, such as orangutans, nor was it that way, say many evolutionary biologists, among our own ancestors. Those males want their offspring to survive at any cost—even at the cost of the female's health and future fertility with other males. For example, if the male can figure out a way to make the female spend most of her food energy making the offspring grow big and strong, that's okay, even if she starves. That's where the struggle over the placenta comes in: Men and other male mammals pass on genes to their unborn children that encourage the mother's placenta to grow big, nourishing the fetus at the mother's expense and at the expense of her future kids with other guys.

Females want their offspring to survive too, but not at the risk of their future fertility. For example, in mammals, nursing inhibits ovulation. So a mammal mom wouldn't nurse her young for the rest of her life, even if doing so greatly increased its chances of survival. Otherwise, she might never again ovulate, become pregnant, and bear more young.

This conflict is played out viciously among fruit flies. Rather than growing old in each other's arms, *drosophila* mate with multiple partners, none of whom stick around for a second date. And look at what

Stay-at-Home Dads

Conflict between males and females takes a complicated turn in the rare species with high "male parental investment." In such species, a male instinctually takes care of youngsters he thinks are his own. He mates with someone, and babies appear an appropriate length of time later, so he protects them from predators and takes them to ice-skating lessons. A lot of bird species fit this profile. Sometimes the male does more parenting than the female. At the moment the egg hatches, she has invested far more energy in the gestation than he has, but afterward the tide gradually turns. In those cases, what should a heartlessly practical female do if she wants to maximize her reproductive success? She should figure out the exact moment when he's spent more cumulative energy than she has on passing on copies of his genes via these offspring. When that moment arrives, she should abandon the youngsters. He likely will continue taking care of them, guaranteeing her reproductive success, and leaving her free to start a new round of reproduction with someone else.

Reprinted by permission from *Discover*, May 1999. Robert Sapolsky/© 1999.

they've come up with: Male semen contains toxins that kill the sperm of other males. When a male fly mates with a female who has recently had sex with someone else, his spermicide goes to work, killing the competitors' sperm. That's a great adaptation, but unfortunately the stuff is toxic to the female and gradually harms her health. This doesn't bother the male at all. It increases his evolutionary fitness, and he's never going to see her again.

William Rice, an evolutionary geneticist then at the University of California at Santa Cruz, did a wonderfully slick experiment in which he kept female fruit flies from evolving while letting the males compete against each other. After forty generations, the evolutionary winners were males with the strongest toxic punch in their semen. Females who mated with them had a shorter life expectancy.

The same sort of coevolutionary arms race happens in humans and other mammals. As a result, we have developed a bizarre set of genes called *imprinted genes* that seem to violate the basic tenets of genetics.

Think back to Gregor Mendel, high school biology, and dominant and recessive traits. That most monkish of monks taught that genetic traits are coded for by pairs of genes, one from each parent. He figured out how the pairs of genes interact to influence the organism, depending on whether the pair have identical or differing messages. According to Mendel, it doesn't matter which parent contributed which genetic message. Whether the offspring gets the vanilla version of a gene from the mother and the chocolate version from the father or the other way around, the trait coded for by the pair of genes looks the same.

Imprinted genes violate Mendel's rules. With these genes, only the gene from one parent has input—the matching gene from the other parent is silenced, losing its influence over the trait expressed. Most experts in this new field believe that there are only a couple hundred of these genes in humans, but they can be quite influential.

About half the genes in question have something to do with growth—of the placenta, the fetus, or the newborn. And the genes derived from the father favor greater, faster, more expensive growth, whereas the maternally derived genes counter that exuberance. As the evolutionist David Haig of Harvard first suggested in 1989, imprinted genes—including these genes in humans—are a case of intersexual competition, fruit fly sperm wars redux.

The first battleground is the placenta, a tissue that can seem more than a little creepy. It's only partially related to the female, but it invades (a term used in obstetrics) her body, sending tentacles toward her blood vessels to divert nutrients for the benefit of a growing fetus. The placenta is also the scene of a pitched battle, with paternally derived genes pushing it to invade more aggressively while maternally derived genes try to hold it back. How do we know? In rare diseases, maternal or paternal genes related to placental growth are knocked out of action. Lose the paternal input and the antigrowth maternal component is left unopposed—the placenta never invades the mother's endometrium, so the fetus has no chance to grow. In contrast, remove the maternal input, leaving those paternal genes unopposed, and the placenta grows into a stupendously aggressive cancer called choriocarcinoma.

The imprinting struggle continues during fetal development. One gene, which codes for a powerful growth-stimulating hormone in mice and humans, is expressed only by paternally derived genes. This is a classic case of dad pushing for maximal fetal development. In mice (though not in people), the mother counteracts the pro-growth tumult by expressing a gene for a cellular receptor that regulates the growth hormone's effectiveness. Thrust and parry.

When a baby is born, imprinted genes take a particularly impressive turn. Certain paternally expressed genes help make kids active nursers. On the surface, this looks like another example of the usual picture: faster development at the cost of mom's lactational calories. But now we're talking about imprinted genes that influence behavior. Other genes influence brain development in even stranger ways (see Brain Genes, below).

The discovery of imprinted genes may pave the way for curing a number of unpleasant diseases involving tumors, infertility, and fetal overgrowth or underdevelopment. But philosophically, the findings are disturbing. They appear to have some deflating implications about human nature. Among fruit flies, sperm-war genes show that males care little about the females' future. What about us? "In sickness and in health," we promise, "until death do us part." We're the species that came up with Paul Newman and Joanne Woodward. For monogamous animals, the future health and fertility of the female is as much in the male's interest as hers. So what are these imprinted genes doing in a human couple pondering which appetizers to serve at their golden wedding anniversary?

The answer is that reports of our monogamy are greatly exaggerated. Features of human anatomy and physiology argue against it. Most human cultures allow polygamy. And most studies, ranging from genetic paternity tests to *Cosmo* questionnaires, suggest that there's a lot of action going on outside the pair-bond, even in monogamous societies. We have more in common with fruit flies than commonly believed.

Brain Genes

Mom wants you to be clever, but dad cares more about your metabolism. At least, that's the way the evidence of genomic imprinting points. Experiments with mice show that some maternally expressed genes favor a bigger cortex, the intellectual part of the brain. Mutations that knock out those genes cause retardation. In contrast, some paternally expressed genes favor growth of the hypothalamus, which controls many unconscious body functions.

How do these imprinted genes related to brain function fit into the scheme of intersexual warfare? Instead of the usual scenario, in which dad wants more growth while mom wants less, each parent's genes favor a different kind of growth. Does a female enhance her future health and fertility by supplying her young with a thick cortex and super SAT scores? Does a bigger hypothalamus produce a kid who is able to sap more of mom's resources? No one knows, but Eric B. Keverne of the University of Cambridge, England, who has done much of the work on brain-related imprinted genes, continues to wrestle with these intriguing findings, trying to fit them into the framework of intersexual warfare. Meanwhile, some evolutionary biologists speculate that the traits might have evolved for entirely different reasons.

(Mind you, we're not one of the more polygamous species around. Even the busiest patriarchs weigh in with only a few hundred kids.)

Does nature have to be so bloody in tooth and claw and gene? Must everything be based on competition? Why can't we all just get along? Here's where the evolutionary biologists, with Bogartesque weariness, pull out the great clichés of their field. Biology isn't about what should be, they explain, but what is. It's a tough evolutionary world out there. It's dog outreproduce dog. But a recent experiment by Rice and evolutionary behaviorist Brett Holland hints that intersexual competition needn't be inevitable. With careful manipulation, it can be derailed. The researchers isolated pairs of mating flies, forcing them to be monogamous. They then bred the offspring with the offspring of other such enforced monogamous pairs, continuing to maintain the monogamy. And after only forty generations, the monogamous descendants produced less harmful seminal fluid.

They also treated their mates with unusual courtesy —normal fruit-fly courtship looks like sexual harass-ment. When competition between males was no longer a selective force, producing toxic chemicals apparently became a maladaptive waste of energy. Freed of the cost of intersexual warfare, these monogamous flies actually outbred the usual competitive flies.

Just imagine carrying out the same experiment in people. Isolate some humans and force them and their descendants into monogamy for a millennium, and we would probably begin to disarm our mammalian weapons of intersexual warfare, namely imprinted genes. They are an evolutionary burden, making possible some truly horrendous cancers. Remove their advantages by eliminating polygamy, and natural selection should edit them out.

Having arrived at what sounds like a surreal moral—an exhortation to remember the Sixth Commandment as part of the Let's Whip Choriocarcinoma by the Year 3000" campaign—it's time to take a step back. Understanding how intersexual competition started with flies is relatively easy. Thanks to random genetic variability, some male flies stumbled into ever so slightly toxic sperm, which the females

Self-Conscious Scrub Jays

When biologists talk about male orangutans "realizing" that they have less to lose in mating than females, or female scrub jays "calculating" exactly when to abandon their young to a caring father, they're speaking metaphorically. Except for the most cognitively sophisticated primates, animals don't sit there with an evolution textbook and a calculator, strategizing consciously. Instead phrases like "the scrub jay wants to do this, decides that this is the right time," and so on are shorthand for the more correct but cumbersome, "Over the course of evolution, scrub jays who, at least in part through genetically influenced mechanisms, are better able to optimize the timing of their behavior leave more copies of their genes, thus making this attribute more prevalent in the population." Personifying the animals is just an expository device agreed upon to keep from falling asleep during conferences.

had to detoxify or die. And from there, the competition spiraled upward. The story of imprinted genes is a bit more complicated, but when paternally derived genes began pushing for the-hell-with-the-mom growth, the battle inevitably escalated. If the tribe next door shows up at the Paleolithic watering hole with clubs that seem just a wee bit on the big side for the purpose of bonking prey animals over the head, the home team naturally responds by getting even bigger clubs, just in case. And soon we have a world with choriocarcinoma, toxic fruit-fly semen, and umpteen times the education budget buying $600 toilet seats for the military. As in so many other arenas of conflict, it's easier to ratchet up than down.

"THE WAR BETWEEN MEN AND WOMEN"

Robert Sapolsky

1) What are the conflicting evolutionary aims of males and females, according to the article?

2) What are "imprinted genes," and what purpose do they serve?

3) What evolutionary tactics have fruit flies developed to maximize mating success? How does the article relate this to human sexual strategies?

4) What are the potential benefits and drawbacks of both monogamy (one mate) and polygamy (many mates)?

Rituals of Manhood: Male Initiation in Papua New Guinea

Gilbert H. Herdt

Sambia are a mountain-dwelling hunting and horti-cultural people who number some 2,000 persons and inhabit one of New Guinea's most rugged terrains. The population is dispersed through narrow river valleys over a widespread, thinly populated rain forest; rainfall is heavy; and even today the surrounding mountain ranges keep the area isolated. Sambia live on the fringes of the Highlands, but they trace their origins to the Papua hinterlands; their culture and economy thus reflect a mixture of influences from both of those areas. Hunting still predominates as a masculine activity through which most meat protein is acquired. As in the Highlands, though, sweet potatoes and taro are the staple crops, and their cultivation is for the most part women's work. Pigs are few, and they have no ceremonial or exchange significance; indigenous marsupials, such as possum and tree kangaroo, provide necessary meat prestations for all initiations and ceremonial feasts (cf. Meigs 1976).

Sambia settlements are small, well-defended, mountain clan hamlets. These communities comprise locally based descent groups organized through a strong agnatic idiom. Residence is patrivirilocal, and most men actually reside in their father's hamlets. Clans are exogamous, and one or more of them together constitute a hamlet's landowning corporate agnatic body. These men also form a localized warriorhood that is sometimes allied with other hamlets in matters of fighting, marriage, and ritual. Each hamlet contains one or two men's clubhouses, in addition to women's houses, and the men's ritual life centers on their clubhouse. Marriage is usually by sister exchange or infant betrothal, although the latter form of prearranged marriage is culturally preferred. Intrahamlet marriage is occasionally more frequent (up to fifty percent of all marriages in my own hamlet field site) than one would expect in such small segmentary groupings, an involutional pattern weakened since pacification.

Sambia male and female residential patterns differ somewhat from those of other Highlands peoples. The nuclear family is an important subunit of the hamlet-based extended family of interrelated clans.

A man, his wife, and their children usually cohabit within a single, small, round hut. Children are thus reared together by their parents during the early years of life, so the nuclear family is a residential unit, an institution virtually unknown to the Highlands (Meggit 1964; Read 1954). Sometimes this unit is expanded through polygyny, in which case a man, his co-wives, and their children may occupy the single dwelling. Girls continue to reside with their parents until marriage (usually near the menarche, around fifteen to seventeen years of age). Boys, however, are removed to the men's clubhouse at seven to ten years of age, following their first-stage initiation. There they reside exclusively until marriage and cohabitation years later. Despite familial cohabitation in early childhood, strict taboos based on beliefs about menstrual pollution still separate men and women in their sleeping and eating arrangements.

Warfare used to be constant and nagging among Sambia, and it conditioned the values and masculine stereotypes surrounding the male initiatory cult. Ritualized bow fights occurred among neighboring hamlets, whose members still intermarried and usually initiated their sons together. At the same time, though, hamlets also united against enemy tribes and in staging war parties against them. Hence, warfare, marriage, and initiation were interlocking institutions; the effect of this political instability was to reinforce tough, strident masculine performance in most arenas of social life. "Strength" (jerundu) was—and is—a pivotal idea in this male ethos. Indeed, strength, which has both ethnobiological and behavioral aspects, could be aptly translated as "maleness" and "manliness." Strength has come to be virtually synonymous with idealized conformity to male ritual routine. Before conquest and pacification by the Australians, though, strength had its chief performative significance in one's conduct on the battlefield. Even today bitter reminders of war linger on among the Sambia; and we should not forget that it is against the harsh background of the warrior's existence that Sambia initiate their boys, whose only perceived protection against the inconstant world is their own unbending masculinity.

Initiation rests solely in the hands of the men's secret society. It is this organization that brings the collective initiatory cycle into being as jointly performed by neighboring hamlets (and as constrained by their own chronic bow fighting). The necessary feastcrop gardens, ritual leadership, and knowledge, dictate that a handful of elders, war leaders, and ritual experts be in full command of the actual staging of the event. Everyone and all else are secondary.

There are six intermittent initiations from the ages of seven to ten and onward. They are, however, constituted and conceptualized as two distinct cultural systems within the male life cycle. First-stage (*moku*, at seven to ten years of age), second-stage (*imbutu*, at ten to thirteen years), and third-stage (*ipmangwi*, at thirteen to sixteen years) initiations—bachelorhood rites—are collectively performed for regional groups of boys as age-mates. The initiations are held in sequence, as age-graded advancements; the entire sequel takes months to perform. The focus of all these initiations is the construction and habitation of a great cult house (*moo-angu*) on a traditional dance ground; its ceremonialized building inaugurates the whole cycle. Fourth-stage (*nuposha*: sixteen years and onward), fifth-stage (*taiketnyi*), and sixth-stage (*moondangu*) initiations are, conversely, individually centered events not associated with the confederacy of interrelated hamlets, cult house, or dance ground. Each of these initiations, like the preceding ones, does have its own ritual status, social role, and title, as noted. The triggering event for the latter three initiations, unlike that for the bachelorhood rites, is not the building of a cult house or a political agreement of hamlets to act collectively, but is rather the maturing femininity and life-crisis events of the women assigned in marriage to youths (who become the initiated novices). Therefore, fourth-stage initiation is only a semipublic activity organized by the youths' clansmen (and some male affines). Its secret purificatory and other rites are followed by the formal marriage ceremony in the hamlet. Fifth-stage initiation comes at a woman's menarche, when her husband is secretly introduced to additional purification and sexual techniques. Sixth-stage initiation issues from the birth of a man's wife's first child. This event is, de jure, the attainment of manhood. (The first birth is elaborately ritualized and celebrated; the next three births are also celebrated, but in more truncated fashion.) Two children bring full adulthood (*aatmwunu*) for husband and wife alike. Birth ceremonies are suspended after the fourth birth, since there is no reason to belabor what is by now obvious: a man has proved himself competent in reproduction. This sequence of male initiations forms the basis for

male development, and it underlies the antagonistic tenor of relationships between the sexes.

It needs stating only once that men's secular rhetoric and ritual practices depict women as dangerous and polluting inferiors whom men are to distrust throughout their lives. In this regard, Sambia values and relationships pit men against women even more markedly, I think, than occurs in other Highlands communities (cf. Brown and Buchbinder 1976; Meggitt 1964; Read 1954). Men hold themselves as the superiors of women in physique, personality, and social position. And this dogma of male supremacy permeates all social relationships and institutions, likewise coloring domestic behavior among the sexes (cf. Tuzin 1980 for an important contrast). Men fear not only pollution from contact with women's vaginal fluids and menstrual blood but also the depletion of their semen, the vital spark of maleness, which women (and boys, too) inevitably extract, sapping a man's substance. These are among the main themes of male belief underlying initiation.

The ritualized simulation of maleness is the result of initiation, and men believe the process to be vital for the nature and nurture of manly growth and well-being. First-stage initiation begins the process in small boys. Over the ensuing ten to fifteen years, until marriage, cumulative initiations and residence in the men's house are said to promote biological changes that firmly cement the growth from childhood to manhood. Nature provides male genitals, it is true; but nature alone does not bestow the vital spark biologically necessary for stimulating masculine growth or demonstrating cold-blooded self-preservation.

New Guinea specialists will recognize in the Sambia belief system a theme that links it to the comparative ethnography of male initiation and masculine development: the use of ritual procedures for sparking, fostering, and maintaining manliness in males (see Berndt 1962; Meigs 1976; Newman 1964, 1965; Poole 1981; Read 1965; Salisbury 1965; Strathern 1969, 1970). Sambia themselves refer to the results of first-stage collective initiation—our main interest—as a means of "growing a boy"; and this trend of ritual belief is particularly emphatic.

Unlike ourselves, Sambia perceive no imminent, naturally driven fit between one's birthright sex and one's gender identity or role.[1] Indeed, the problem (and it is approached as a situation wanting a solution) is implicitly and explicitly understood in quite different terms. The solution is also different for the two sexes: men believe that a girl is born with all of the vital organs and fluids necessary for her to attain reproductive competence through "natural" maturation. This conviction is embodied in cultural perceptions of the girl's development beginning with the sex assignment at birth. What distinguishes a girl *(tai)* from a boy *(kwulai'u)* is obvious: "A boy has a penis, and a girl does not," men say. Underlying men's communications is a conviction that maleness, unlike femaleness, is not a biological given. It must be artificially induced through secret ritual; and that is a personal achievement.

The visible manifestations of girls' fast-growing reproductive competence, noticed first in early motor coordination and speech and then later in the rapid attainment of height and secondary sex traits (e.g., breast development), are attributed to inner biological properties. Girls possess a menstrual-blood organ, or *tingu,* said to precipitate all those events and the menarche. Boys, on the other hand, are thought to possess an inactive tingu. They do possess, however, another organ—the *kere-ku-kereku,* or semen organ—that is thought to be the repository of semen, the very essence of maleness and masculinity; but this organ is not functional at birth, since it contains no semen naturally and can only store, never produce, any. Only oral insemination, men believe, can activate the boy's semen organ, thereby precipitating his push into adult reproductive competence. In short, femininity unfolds naturally, whereas masculinity must be achieved; and here is where the male ritual cult steps in.

Men also perceive the early socialization risks of boys and girls in quite different terms. All infants are closely bonded to their mothers. Out of a woman's contaminating, life-giving womb pours the baby, who thereafter remains tied to the woman's body, breast milk, and many ministrations. This latter contact only reinforces the femininity and female contamination in which birth involves the infant. Then, too, the father, both because of postpartum taboos and by personal choice, tends to avoid being present at the breast-feedings. Mother thus becomes the unalterable primary influence; father is a weak second. Sambia say this does not place girls at a "risk"—they simply succumb to the drives of their "natural" biology. This maternal attachment and paternal distance clearly jeopardize the boys' growth, however, since nothing innate within male maturation seems to resist the inhibiting effects of mothers' femininity. Hence boys must be traumatically separated—wiped clean of their female contaminants—so that their masculinity may develop.

Homosexual fellatio inseminations can follow this separation but cannot precede it, for otherwise they would go for naught. The accumulating semen, injected time and again for years, is believed crucial

for the formation of biological maleness and masculine comportment. This native perspective is sufficiently novel to justify our using a special concept for aiding description and analysis of the data: masculinization (Herdt 1981:205 ff). Hence I shall refer to the overall process that involves separating a boy from his mother, initiating him, ritually treating his body, administering homosexual inseminations, his biological attainment of puberty, and his eventual reproductive competence as masculinization. (Precisely what role personal and cultural fantasy plays in the negotiation of this ritual process I have considered elsewhere: see Herdt 1981: chaps. 6, 7, and 8.)

A boy has female contaminants inside of him which not only retard physical development but, if not removed, debilitate him and eventually bring death. His body is male: his tingu contains no blood and will not activate. The achievement of puberty for boys requires semen. Breast milk "nurtures the boy," and sweet potatoes or other "female" foods provide "stomach nourishment," but these substances become only feces, not semen. Women's own bodies internally produce the menarche, the hallmark of reproductive maturity. There is no comparable mechanism active in a boy, nothing that can stimulate his secondary sex traits. Only semen can do that; only men have semen; boys have none. What is left to do, then, except initiate and masculinize boys into adulthood?

Note

1. I follow Stroller (1968) in adhering to the following distinctions: the term *sex traits* refers to purely biological phenomena (anatomy, hormones, genetic structure, etc.), whereas *gender* refers to those psychological and cultural attributes that compel a person (consciously or unconsciously) to sense him- or herself, and other persons, as belonging to either the male or female sex. It follows that the term *gender role* (Sears 1965), rather than the imprecise term *sex role,* refers to the normative set of expectations associated with masculine and feminine social positions.

References

Berndt, R. M. 1962. *Excess and Restraint: Social Control among a New Guinea Mountain People.* Chicago: University of Chicago Press.

Brown, P., and G. Buchbinder (eds.). 1976. *Man and Woman in the New Guinea Highlands.* Washington, DC: American Anthropological Association.

Herdt, G. H. 1981. *Guardians of the Flutes: Idioms of Masculinity.* New York: McGraw-Hill.

Meggitt, M. J. 1964. Male-Female Relationships in the Highlands of Australian New Guinea. In *New Guinea: The Central Highlands,* ed. J. B. Watson, *American Anthropologist,* 66, pt. 2 (4):204–224.

Meigs, A. S. 1976. Male pregnancy and the reduction of sexual opposition in a New Guinea Highlands society. *Ethnology* 15 (4):393–407.

Newman, P. L. 1964. Religious belief and ritual in a New Guinea society. In *New Guinea: The Central Highlands,* ed. J. B. Watson, *American Anthropologist* 66, pt. 2 (4):257–272.

_____. 1965. *Knowing the Gururumba.* New York: Holt, Rinehart and Winston.

Poole, F. J. P. 1981. Transforming "natural" woman: female ritual leaders and gender ideology among Bimin-Kuskumin. In *Sexual Meanings,* ed. S. B. Ortner and H. Whitehead. New York: Cambridge University Press.

Read, K. E. 1954. Cultures of the Central Highlands, New Guinea. *Southwestern Journal of Anthropology* 10 (1):1–43.

_____. 1965. *The High Valley.* London: George Allen and Unwin.

Salisbury, R. F. 1965. The Siane of the Eastern Highlands. In *Gods, Ghosts, and Men in Melanesia,* P. Lawrence and M. J. Meggitt, pp. 50–77, Melbourne: Melbourne University Press.

Sears, R. R. 1965. Development of gender role. In *Sex and Behavior,* ed. F. A. Beach, pp. 133–163. New York: John Wiley and Sons.

Stoller, R. J. 1968. *Sex and Gender.* New York: Science House.

Strathern, A. J. 1969. Descent and alliance in the New Guinea Highlands: some problems of comparison. Royal Anthropological Institute, *Proceedings,* pp. 37–52.

_____. 1970. Male initiation in the New Guinea Highlands societies. *Ethnology* 9 (4):373–379.

Tuzin, D. F. 1980. *The Voice of the Tambaran: Truth and Illusion in Ilahita Arapesh Religion.* Berkeley, Los Angeles, and London: University of California Press.

"Rituals of Manhood: Male Initiation in Papua New Guinea"

Gilbert H. Herdt

1) Outline Sambia culture based on information from the article: economics, social and political organization, and other facets of life.

2) How do warfare, marriage, and male initiation rites operate as interlocking institutions in Sambia culture?

3) What is the purpose of male initiation rites? How many stages do the Sambia employ in the rite to reach their goal of adult male status for the boys?

4) How do Sambia men's attitudes towards women and sex contribute to the operation and cultural understanding of the purpose of the initiation rites?

5) How do the Sambia explain their understanding of the biological basis of maleness and femaleness, and how does it affect their behavior?

THE BRUTALIZING OF WOMEN

Jan Goodwin

Even though women in the United States have yet to achieve parity with men when it comes to paychecks or power, our circumstances are ideal when compared with women around the world. And increasingly, we do compare—as news comes into our living rooms from the most far-flung corners of the globe. Unfortunately, much of that news has made us familiar with cultures and governments that are oppressive and even brutal to women.

The often terrible lot faced by many women abroad literally hits home when families immigrate to the United States and bring their customs with them. Nine years ago, in New York City, a Chinese immigrant killed his wife for being unfaithful; after he argued that in his culture the act would have been justified because his shame was so great, he was given only probation. Last November, in Lincoln, NE, a father arranged a double wedding for his two daughters, respectively 13 and 14 years old, to two men, 28 and 34 years old. All the men were recent emigrants from Iraq, where such child marriages are not uncommon among Muslims. When authorities found out, they arrested the father and charged him with child abuse; the grooms were charged with sexual assault of a minor.

Another case that horrified many is that of Fauziya Kasinga, who fled to the United States three years ago at age 17 to escape the ritual of female genital mutilation (FGM), which is still practiced in her homeland of Togo. The ritual involves cutting off a girl's clitoris, and sometimes also the labia minora and majora; in extreme cases the sides are then stitched together, leaving only a tiny opening. One hundred and thirty million girls and women worldwide have undergone this agonizing procedure (often without anesthesia and under unsanitary conditions); some will die from complications. Survivors suffer chronic infection and pain.

Twenty-eight African nations and some minority groups in the Middle East and Asia still practice FGM, believing that it prevents promiscuity among women. A woman's chance of marrying, which in many countries is still her only route to economic survival, depends on whether she has undergone FGM. In a number of places, the price a girl fetches as a bride is higher the smaller her vaginal opening has been made.

A Philadelphia judge initially rejected Kasinga's bid for political asylum. She was jailed for 16 months, during which time women's rights activists launched a highly publicized campaign for her freedom. She was released and finally granted asylum last June, and her case established a legal precedent for FGM as grounds for political asylum.

What follows are examples of barbarism from three other countries. More voices need to be raised against these practices, so that one day they can be stopped.

— Nepal —
Sentenced For Having A Stillbirth

Twenty-nine-year-old Thirtha Maya Baral has been in Central Jail in Nepal's capital, Katmandu, for three years and still has another seven to serve. Her crime: giving birth to a stillborn baby. "It was my third baby," she says through tears. "I was alone when I went into labor. My husband was working abroad. The delivery was long and hard. No one came to assist me. When the baby was finally born, it was very small, and dead."

Four days later, police, tipped off by neighbors who'd known she was pregnant, came and arrested her. No medical opinion was sought, and the only evidence against her was the accusation of the neighboring family, who did not tell the police they were involved in an angry land dispute with Thirtha's husband. She had no lawyer and was quickly found guilty.

Since being jailed, she has not seen her 12-year-old son and 10-year-old daughter, who have been left to survive on the streets alone. Had they been with her at the time of her arrest, they would have been taken with her, but now she does not even have the bus fare it would take to bring them to her cell. "This is the worst," she says, "not knowing how my children are doing."

Nepal has some of the most spectacular scenery on Earth, including Mount Everest, but it also has the most severe prohibitions against abortion on the planet, forbidding it even in cases of rape, incest, or when a woman's life is medically endangered. *Garbhabat*, or destruction of life, is the official abortion charge, but the law also covers infanticide and child abandonment.

Tragically, it is also used against women whose babies are stillborn or who have miscarriages. Women found guilty of garbhabat often have their property confiscated, making them vulnerable to accusations from vengeful or greedy relatives or neighbors who use the law to effect a property or land grab. Police and prosecutors are also known to be bribed into bringing such charges, and in other cases, women are beaten into confessions. But this is rarely necessary in a land where rural women can't afford doctors or lawyers, and where the word of an influential accuser is usually taken on faith.

Jyoti (name changed), 41, has already spent more than a quarter of her life in jail. Widowed two decades ago, she was unable to remarry since Nepalese law requires her to remain faithful to her husband, even after his death. She followed custom and lived with her in-laws. Forced to become her father-in-law's concubine, she became pregnant, and was made to have an abortion. Word leaked—possibly the abortionist talked—and Jyoti was arrested.

"Her father-in-law was among her public accusers, although in private he told her to accept the blame and he would get her out of jail within a month or two," says women's health and welfare activist Roshan Karki. "But eleven years have passed, and she hasn't heard from her in-laws."

Neither Thirtha nor Jyoti's children are with them in jail, but many women's children are. When women are imprisoned, families encourage husbands to divorce and remarry, and traditionally, those children are not accepted by a new spouse. In Central Jail last year, there were 15 children, ranging in age from 2 to 15, effectively "serving" lengthy sentences with their mothers. There are 73 prisons in the country, all of which usually have children living in them under horrendous conditions: crumbling, flea- and rat-infested cells, inadequate food, bedding, and clothing, and no basic health care and schooling.

Anti-garbhabat activists say the situation is made graver by Nepal's extreme poverty and high birth rate—the government's birth control program reaches only 21 percent of women, in part because of limited funding. "Eighty percent of women of reproductive age are severely anemic because of poor diet and simply aren't able to carry their babies to term," says Aruna Upreti, M.D., a maternal and child-care specialist in Katmandu. "Compounding this is the lack of physicians in much of the country, and the practice of women giving birth unaided. Under conditions like these, is it any wonder that babies are frequently born dead, and women too easily accused of garbhabat?"

— *Pakistan* —
Arrested For Being Raped

In rape cases in the United States, only recently have courts stopped blaming the victim, or believing "she must have asked for it." But in Pakistan, not only is a rape victim rarely believed, frequently she is also arrested and jailed, even if she is a child.

Majidah Abdullah was 11 years old when she was abducted and repeatedly raped by her father's employers. He owed money he was unable to repay, so he was punished by having his daughter abused. When the family tried to bring rape charges, the girl was thrown in jail.

In Pakistan, *zina*, or sex outside of wedlock—which includes rape as well as adultery—is a crime. For married women, the maximum sentence is death by stoning. For single women, the punishment is up to 100 lashes and up to ten years' imprisonment. Technically, men can also be charged with zina, but with a simple denial, they can go free.

In Pakistani courts under Islamic law, the judge has the discretion to reject the victim's account and that of any female witness; in such cases, there must be four adult males, "Muslims of good repute," who are witnesses—an unfair standard since few men of good repute would stand by and watch a rape take place. Then the tables are cruelly turned: A woman's complaint of rape is considered a confession of illicit sexual intercourse; a subsequent pregnancy is also evidence against her. Although common law, whose standards of evidence are less stringent, can also be applied, activists say that in practice few cases go that route.

Such was the case of Safia Bibi. She was 16 when she was raped by her employer and his son, and she became pregnant. Her father reported the assaults, but a judge acquitted both men since Safia's family could not produce four male witnesses. Yet Safia's pregnancy was deemed proof of fornication.

Her harsh sentence—a three-year jail term, a public flogging, and a fine—struck a chord with Pakistan's women's rights activists, particularly in view of the fact that she has a disability: She is nearly blind. When their campaign on her behalf was reported by foreign media, the teenager was freed.

Eleven-year-old Majidah was less fortunate. While her attackers went free, she spent several years in jail without a court hearing until her plight was discovered by Asma Jahangir, a human rights activist. Jahangir was able to get Majidah released on bail, but the girl says her life is over. Since it's well known that she's no longer a virgin, her chances of marriage are virtually nil, which means that she becomes a social outcast.

According to Jahangir, some sixty percent of women in Pakistan's jails are there on charges of zina, many after being raped. Once in custody, about seventy percent are physically and/or sexually abused again by the police or prison guards, according to War Against Rape, a Pakistani human rights organization.

It appalls activists that this law exists in a country that has twice elected Benazir Bhutto its prime minister. Educated at Radcliffe and Oxford, Bhutto had promised to reform the law. But needing the backing of religious leaders who support such anti-woman laws, she never followed through. Her government was recently overthrown.

"For Bhutto, this was clearly not a priority, and there is not enough of a will in the country," says Surita Sandosham, head of Equality Now, a New York City-based human rights organization. "Nothing will change," she says, "without international pressure."

— *Thailand* —
Sold Into Sexual Slavery

The California travel agency brochure could not be more explicit: SEX TOURS TO THAILAND, REAL GIRLS, REAL SEX, REAL CHEAP. THESE WOMEN ARE THE MOST SEXUALLY AVAILABLE IN THE WORLD. DID YOU KNOW YOU CAN ACTUALLY BUY A VIRGIN GIRL FOR AS LITTLE AS $200?

What the ad copy doesn't say is that these "virgin girls" are children who have been kidnapped or sold into Thai brothels. They average fifteen customers a day, and are beaten if they don't cooperate. On Phuket Island in 1984, a popular resort for foreigners in southern Thailand, five prostitutes burned to death when a fire broke out in a brothel; they had been chained to their beds to prevent their escape.

Because Thailand has one of the highest AIDS rates in the world, virgins net a higher price for sex traffickers; but given that men can refuse to wear condoms, and the girls' immature bodies make them more vulnerable to tissue tears, HIV infection in brothels is rampant.

Lin-Lin was just 13 when a visitor to her village in Burma told her father he could find the girl work as a domestic. Her impoverished family accepted the offer. But the man was in fact a sex-trade agent, and Lin-Lin was taken to a brothel and sold. (In other cases, the families know the fate their daughters face, but are too poor and without options to refuse.) Two years later, Lin-Lin is HIV-positive—though the brothel does not reveal this to customers.

Brothels are illegal in Thailand, but owners have little fear of arrest. The industry generates $3 billion annually in tourism, and therefore the sex trade, says Human Rights Watch, is protected by graft-taking police and a government that looks the other way.

A 1993 Human Rights Watch report points out that the United States gives Thailand $4 million a year to control the traffic in narcotics but nothing to stop sex trafficking. "The United Nations needs to be very aggressive in fighting this modern form of slavery," says Dorothy Thomas, director of the women's rights project at Human Rights Watch in New York City.

Only recently did it become a felony in the United States for Americans to engage in sex with minors on tours abroad, or for American tour operators to promote such trips. But because of lax enforcement, experts say that American men continue to go abroad and sexually prey on children.

"THE BRUTALIZING OF WOMEN"

Jan Goodwin

1) Compare and contrast problems faced by women in the United States with women in other countries. How do they compare on an ideological, economic, and legal basis?

2) Why is rape seen as a crime *of* women, rather than a crime *against* women, under Islamic law in Pakistan?

3) How does western tourism contribute to the problems of female exploitation, prostitution, and the spread of disease in Thailand and Southeast Asia?

Life Under Cover

Vivienne Walt

Nadia, a 43-year-old doctor with a quiet smile, is wearing a lavender pantsuit and low pumps on this clear, California morning. Light makeup softens her face. Her short-cropped brown hair frames large, square eyeglasses, as she drinks from a bottle of Evian. Little about her suggests her life is any different from that of physicians in the U.S. But Nadia's world is a jolting reality away.

Her very appearance today would put Nadia at substantial risk in her native country, Afghanistan. There, the extremist Taliban government has implemented some of the world's most perverse dictates against women and punishes those who violate them with verbal abuse, physical attack, or even death. No heels: Their click-clack sound stirs men's passion. No short hair: It's a sign of corrupt Westerners. And no outfits in public other than the burqa, a shapeless shroud of heavy cloth that has only a small mesh panel through which to view the world.

Even more devastating are the Taliban decrees forbidding women to attend school or work outside the home except in rare cases of urgent need. The impact of these laws has led to, among other problems, a crisis in women's health—male doctors cannot examine women, and female physicians' freedom to practice is severely restricted. Nadia, though, has kept her work going, risking her life by defying the Taliban and operating a network of schools and health clinics for women in some of Afghanistan's most destitute regions.

A few times a year, she takes her burqa out of the closet and slips over the Pakistani border, clandestinely shuttling medical supplies into Afghanistan. It's a dangerous occupation but one Nadia is convinced saves hundreds of lives.

She opened her first clinic in Pakistan, where refugees from conflict-ravaged Afghanistan have settled along the two countries' border for more than 20 years. From the moment its doors opened in 1988, women mobbed the clinic. "We had 300 patients and only 17 beds," Nadia says. When a visiting European politician asked what her country could do to help, Nadia requested money to open a clinic inside Afghanistan, where health services were scarce. Because the Taliban rules in disparate groups, some areas are more leniently governed than others, which gave Nadia an opening

for building her network. Today, she operates forty schools with 17,000 children and twelve clinics throughout the country. "[Nadia's] contribution is truly significant," says one United Nations official familiar with her work. "She is highly respected among the community and has been committed to maintaining her program—under all conditions."

As she sits on a couch in Los Angeles, the sun glinting through the shades, I find it hard to accept that Nadia would think about returning to her dangerous world. Yet she refuses to consider permanent exile, traveling to the U.S. only to visit her son, a computer programmer in Dallas, and to raise money for her schools and clinics. Nadia's projects receive funds from several agencies under the United Nations' umbrella, as well as from the Norwegian, German, and Canadian governments.

She had agreed in advance to sit for a photographer, but by the time we meet, Taliban supporters in the U.S. have made threatening calls to her hosts, who feel it is now too dangerous to publish her name, let alone her picture. Nadia, she says, is a common enough name to shelter her. (Other biographical details in this story also have been changed to protect her safety.) Nadia herself is not as rattled by the Taliban. "I was always very outspoken," she says, in a tone so even and soft that, for a moment, it is hard to fathom her years of battle. The threats to her life and the continual risk brought by flouting the Taliban edicts, she says, are part of her work. "My friends think I'm crazy," she adds.

Yet as Nadia tells the stories of the women she treats, the world in which she works seems far crazier and her motivations clearer. For example: "One woman was raped by her brother-in-law and became pregnant. But her mother-in-law would have killed her if she knew," Nadia says. "We kept telling the mother-in-law that she had a tumor, that she had to come to the clinic once a month." Unable to keep the woman's pregnancy hidden much longer, Nadia finally performed a cesarean with basic implements and gave the infant to an infertile couple. She presented the in-laws with proof of the woman's "illness"—an ovarian cyst, retrieved from a supply Nadia has removed from other women and preserved for occasions such as these.

As this millennium draws to a close, Afghanistan finds itself catapulted back to near-medieval conditions. The Taliban has risen from an obscure band of extremists to one controlling nearly ninety-five percent of this dirt-poor country. By the time the group seized the capital, Kabul, in September 1996, Afghanistan had already been shattered by two decades of war, including the Soviet Union's long military occupation and grinding battle by U.S.-backed Mujahideen fighters. Millions of land mines covered the mountain passes, and close to six million Afghanis had fled into exile. For a while, it seemed that any order would be a relief, even the Taliban and its promise to create the world's purest Islamic state, based on Koranic interpretations far more conservative than those of any other Muslim state. (Worldwide, most observers of the religion do not condone the Taliban's strict teachings.)

For women, the Taliban takeover has been especially brutal. Until 1996, most teachers in the capital—as well as many civil servants and doctors— were female. Today, while Kabul's buildings lie in ruin, the city's moral police, a special unit that enforces Islamic laws, pace the streets, punishing women who violate their orders. All houses in which women live, as well as the buses in which only women and children ride, must have painted or curtained windows. Music, photographs, and any human images are strictly forbidden. Television sets and radios have been smashed in public squares, audiotape and film burned in open bonfires.

The capital is a place of bundled, frightened women—"a city with no identity of its people," says Zohra Rasekh, an Afghani-born researcher for the Boston-based Physicians for Human Rights. Rasekh snuck into Afghanistan last year to interview women. Her findings make for gruesome reading. One child in the hospital died of measles because the male doctor could not visit the children's ward, housed within the women's wing. A woman died at home because she was too poor to buy the burqa she would have needed to journey to a doctor.

During the past year, the U.S. senate passed a resolution condemning the Taliban's human rights violations against women, and a similar measure in the House of Representatives is awaiting a vote. Neither the United States nor the United Nations has yet to recognize the current Afghani government, and the U.S. State Department has advised Americans not to travel to the country.

The Taliban has finally captured the attention of Hollywood, too. Last March, the Feminist Majority Foundation kicked off a national anti-Taliban campaign at the headquarters of the Directors Guild of America in Los Angeles. The event, chaired by Mavis Leno, wife of "Tonight Show" host Jay Leno, was a glittering affair, featuring numerous celebrities and a videotaped statement from President Clinton. Guests pinned swatches of blue mesh—a symbol of the burqa—to their clothes. (Though she was in California at the time, Nadia did not attend because her sponsors feared for her safety.)

Outside on Sunset Boulevard, sixty or so supporters of the Taliban, many of them women, shouted rebukes. One banner read: "Afghani women are capable of determining their own destiny." Inside, Mavis Leno countered, "Those women were free to come down here and demonstrate without any fear of reprisal. When the women in Afghanistan can do the same, our work will be done."

Yet almost as soon as the empty merlot bottles were cleared from the lobby, e-mails poured in to this reporter from aid officials in Afghanistan, questioning the wisdom of the campaign. Like most political conflicts, this one is less clear-cut on the ground. Nancy Hatch Dupree, an American historian and expert on Afghanistan, admits that "lots of problems exist" for Afghani women. "These need to be challenged, but the Hollywood campaign is not the way to right the wrongs," she wrote from her home in Peshawar, Pakistan, on the Afghani border.

By blaming Afghanistan's ills on the Taliban, foreign aid workers say, Americans risk ruining the workers' delicate, daily massaging of the rules. That painstaking work, they say, has brought the first tentative cracks in the edicts against women, including recent agreements by the Taliban to allow some education for girls.

Judy Benjamin, a researcher on Afghanistan at the International Rescue Committee in New York, says that while she believes the Taliban is "terrible" and has done great harm to women, too few people understand the context of its actions. "So many of Afghanistan's problems have to do with the fact that they've been at war for 20 years," she says. "They have no infrastructure, no economy; there's literally nothing there. To demonize the Taliban and make it totally responsible for everything means that you have not read the history."

Indeed, she says, even before Taliban militia seized power four years ago, it was rare to find women working in many rural parts of Afghanistan. Female poverty and poor health care are old problems, and, in some places, many women have been shrouded for years. "The burqa is even a status symbol in some rural areas," Benjamin adds, a sign that a woman can afford the expensive garment.

Still, Leno's campaign, which she took to New York for a similar event in October, might achieve what others have failed to do: raise awareness among Americans of the plight of Afghani women and bring in more money for the cause. Next to me at the Hollywood event sat an Afghani woman in a trim woolen suit and gold necklaces who had fled to Orange County, California, when war erupted in Kabul in the 1970s. When Clinton's address flashed on the screen on stage, she gripped my hand and whispered, "This is incredible. Now people will know."

For Nadia, each day brings new successes and new dangers. At press time, Taliban authorities in one area granted official permission for girls to attend school, while others raided one of her clinics elsewhere and appear to have taken an administrator; he has not been heard from since.

"LIFE UNDER COVER"

Vivienne Walt

---

1) Discuss the restrictions the Taliban has placed on the women of Afghanistan.

2) What efforts are being made by women like Nadia to circumvent Taliban rules and to assist the women of Afghanistan?

3) Why do some experts and foreign aid workers feel a publicity campaign to pressure and discredit the Taliban is potentially counterproductive and shortsighted?

4) Compare the problems of women in the United States to those in Afghanistan. Taking into consideration cultural context and differences, whose problems would you consider to be worse, and why?

SECTION SIX

Religion and Religious Specialists

THE ABOMINATIONS OF LEVITICUS

Mary Douglas

Defilement is never an isolated event. It cannot occur except in view of a systematic ordering of ideas. Hence any piecemeal interpretation of the pollution rules of another culture is bound to fail. For the only way in which pollution ideas make sense is in reference to the total structure of thought whose keystone, boundaries, margins and internal lines are held in relation by rituals of separation.

To illustrate this I take a hoary old puzzle from biblical scholarship, the abominations of Leviticus, and particularly the dietary rules. Why should the camel, the hare and the rock badger be unclean? Why should some locusts, but not all, be unclean? Why should the frog be clean and the mouse and the hippopotamus unclean? What have chameleons, moles and crocodiles got in common that they should be listed together?

[To help follow the argument the reader is referred to Deuteronomy XIV and Leviticus XI using the text of the New Revised Standard Translation.]

• • •

All the interpretations given so far fall into one of two groups: either the rules are meaningless, arbitrary because their intent is disciplinary and not doctrinal, or they are allegories of virtues and vices. Adopting the view that religious prescriptions are largely devoid of symbolism, Maimonides said:

> The Law that sacrifices should be brought is evidently of great use . . . but we cannot say why one offering should be a lamb whilst another is a ram, and why a fixed number of these should be brought. Those who trouble themselves to find a cause for any of these detailed rules are in my eyes devoid of sense. . . .

• • •

Any interpretations will fail which take the Do-nots of the Old Testament in piecemeal fashion. The only sound approach is to forget hygiene, aesthetics, morals and instinctive revulsion, even to forget the Canaanites and the Zoroastrian Magi, and start with the texts. Since each of the injunctions is prefaced by the command to be holy, so they must be explained by that command. There must be contrariness between holiness and abomination which will make overall sense of all the particular restrictions.

Holiness is the attribute of Godhead. Its root means "set apart." What else does it mean? We should start any cosmological enquiry by seeking the principles of power and danger. In the Old Testament we find blessing as the source of all good things, and the withdrawal of blessing as the source of all dangers. The blessing of God makes the land possible for men to live in.

God's work through the blessing is essentially to create order, through which men's affairs prosper. Fertility of women, livestock and fields is promised as a result of the blessing and this is to be obtained by keeping covenant with God and observing all His precepts and ceremonies (Deut. XXVIII, 1–14). Where the blessing is withdrawn and the power of the curse unleashed, there is barrenness, pestilence, confusion. For Moses said:

> But if you will not obey the voice of the Lord your God or be careful to do all his commandments and his statutes which I command you to this day, then all these curses shall come upon you and overtake you. . . .
> (Deut. XXVIII, 15–24)

From this it is clear that the positive and negative precepts are held to be efficacious and not merely expressive: observing them draws down prosperity, infringing them brings danger. We are thus entitled to treat them in the same way as we treat primitive ritual avoidances whose breach unleashes danger to men. The precepts and ceremonies alike are focussed on the idea of the holiness of God which men must create in their own lives. So this is a universe in which men prosper by conforming to holiness and perish when they deviate from it. If there were no other clues we should be able to find out the Hebrew idea of the holy by examining the precepts by which men conform to it. It is evidently not goodness in the sense of an all-embracing humane kindness. Justice and moral goodness may well illustrate holiness and form part of it, but holiness embraces other ideas as well.

Granted that its root means separateness, the next idea that emerges is of the Holy as wholeness and completeness. Much of Leviticus is taken up with stating the physical perfection that is required of things presented in the temple and of persons approaching it. The animals offered in sacrifice must be without blemish, women must be purified after childbirth, lepers should be separated and ritually cleansed before being allowed to approach it once they are cured. All bodily discharges are defiling and disqualify from approach to the temple. Priests may only come into contact with death when their own close kin die. But the high priest must never have contact with death.

• • •

He must be perfect as a man, if he is to be a priest.

This much-reiterated idea of physical completeness is also worked out in the social sphere and particularly in the warriors' camp. The culture of the Israelites was brought to the pitch of greatest intensity when they prayed and when they fought. The army could not win without the blessing and to keep the blessing in the camp they had to be specially holy. So the camp was to be preserved from defilement like the Temple. Here again all bodily discharges disqualified a man from entering the camp as they would disqualify a worshipper from approaching the altar. A warrior who had had an issue of the body in the night should keep outside the camp all day and only return after sunset, having washed. Natural functions producing bodily waste were to be performed outside the camp (Deut. XXIII, 10–15). In short the idea of holiness was given an external, physical expression in the wholeness of the body seen as a perfect container.

• • •

Other precepts develop the idea of wholeness in another direction. The metaphors of the physical body and of the new undertaking relate to the perfection and completeness of the individual and his work. Other precepts extend holiness to species and categories. Hybrids and other confusions are abominated.

Lev. XVIII
23. *And you shall not lie with any beast and defile yourself with it, neither shall any woman give herself to a beast to lie with it: it is perversion, . . .*

The word "perversion" is a significant mistranslation of the rare Hebrew word *tebhel*, which has as its meaning mixing or confusion. The same theme is taken up in Leviticus XIX, 19.

You shall keep my statutes. You shall not let your cattle breed with a different kind; you shall not sow your field with two kinds of seed; nor shall there come upon you a garment of cloth made of two kinds of stuff.

All these injunctions are prefaced by the general command:

Be holy, for I am holy.

We can conclude that holiness is exemplified by completeness. Holiness requires that individuals shall conform to the class to which they belong. And holiness requires that different classes of things shall not be confused.

Another set of precepts refines on this last point. Holiness means keeping distinct the categories of creation. It therefore involves correct definition, discrimination, and order. Under this head all the rules of sexual morality exemplify the holy. Incest and adultery (Lev. XVIII, 6–20) are against holiness, in the simple sense of right order. Morality does not conflict with holiness, but holiness is more a matter of separating that which should be separated than of protecting the rights of husbands and brothers.

Then follows in Chapter XIX another list of actions which are contrary to holiness. Developing the idea of holiness as order, not confusion, this list upholds rectitude and straight-dealing as holy, and contradiction and double-dealing as against holiness. Theft, lying, false witness, cheating in weights and measures, all kinds of dissembling such as speaking ill of the deaf (and presumably smiling to their face), hating your brother in your heart (while presumably speaking kindly to him), these are clearly contradictions between what seems and what is. This chapter also says much about generosity and love, but these are positive commands, while I am concerned with negative rules.

We have now laid a good basis for approaching the laws about clean and unclean meats. To be holy is to be whole, to be one; holiness is unity, integrity, perfection of the individual and of the kind. The dietary rules merely develop the metaphor of holiness on the same lines.

First we should start with livestock, the herds of cattle, camels, sheep, and goats which were the livelihood of the Israelites. These animals were clean inasmuch as contact with them did not require purification before approaching the Temple. Livestock, like the inhabited land, received the blessing of God. Both land and livestock were fertile by the blessing, both were drawn into the divine order. The farmer's duty was to preserve the blessing. For one thing, he had to preserve the order of creation. So no hybrids, as we have seen, either in the fields or in the herds or in the clothes made from wool or flax. To some extent men covenanted with their land and cattle in the same way as God covenanted with them. Men respected the first born of their cattle, obliged them to keep the Sabbath. Cattle were literally domesticated as slaves. They had to be brought into the special order in order to enjoy the blessing. The differences between cattle and the wild beasts is that the wild beasts have no covenant to protect them. It is possible that the Israelites were like other pastoralists who do not relish wild game. The Nuer of the South Sudan, for instance, apply a sanction of disapproval of a man who lives by hunting. To be driven to eating wild meat is the sign of a poor herdsman. So it would be probably wrong to think of the Israelites as longing for forbidden meats and finding the restrictions irksome. Driver is surely right in taking the rules as an a posteriori generalization of their habits. Cloven-hoofed, cud-chewing ungulates are the model of the proper kind of food for a pastoralist. If they must eat wild game, they can eat wild game that shares these distinctive characters and is therefore of the same general species. This is a kind of casuistry which permits scope for hunting antelope and wild goats and wild sheep. Everything would be quite straightforward were it not that the legal mind has seen fit to give ruling on some borderline cases. Some animals seem to be ruminant, such as the hare and the hyrax (or rock badger), whose constant grinding of their teeth was held to be cud chewing. But they are definitely not cloven-hoofed and so are excluded by name. Similarly, animals that are cloven-hoofed but are not ruminant, the pig and the camel, are also excluded. Note that this failure to conform to the two necessary criteria for defining cattle is the only reason given in the Old Testament for avoiding the pig; nothing whatever is said about its dirty scavenging habits. As the pig does not yield milk, hide, or wool, there is no other reason for keeping it except for its flesh. And if the Israelites did not keep pig, they would not be familiar with its habits. I suggest that originally the sole reason for its being counted as unclean is its failure as a wild boar to get into the antelope class, and that in this it is on the same footing as the camel and the hyrax, exactly as is stated in the book.

After these borderline cases have been dismissed, the law goes on to deal with creatures according to how they live in the three elements, the water, the air, and the earth. The principles here applied are rather different from those covering the camel, the pig, the hare, and the hyrax. For the latter are excepted from clean food in having one but not both of the defining characters of livestock. Birds I can say nothing about, because, as I have said, they are named and not described and the translation of the name is open to doubt. But in general the underlying principle of cleanness in animals is that they shall conform fully to their class. Those species are unclean which are imperfect members of their class, or whose class itself confounds the general scheme of the world.

To grasp this scheme we need to go back to Genesis and the creation. Here a three-fold classification unfolds, divided between the earth, the waters and the firmament. Leviticus takes up this scheme and allots to each element its proper kind of animal life. In the firmament two-legged fowls fly with wings. In the water scaly fish swim with fins. On the earth four-legged animals hop, jump, or walk. Any class of creatures which is not equipped for the right kind of locomotion in its element is contrary to holiness. Contact with it disqualifies a person from approaching the Temple. Thus anything in the water which has not fins and scales is unclean (XI, 10–12). Nothing is said about predatory habits or of scavenging. The only sure test for cleanness in a fish is its scales and its propulsion by means of fins.

Four-footed creatures which fly (XI, 20–26) are unclean. Any creature which has two legs and two hands and which goes on all fours like a quadruped is unclean (XI, 27). Then follows (v. 29) a much disputed list. In some translations, it would appear to consist precisely of creatures endowed with hands instead of front feet, which perversely use their hands for walking: the weasel, the mouse, the crocodile, the shrew, various kinds of lizards, the chameleon and mole, whose forefeet are uncannily hand-like. This feature of this list is lost in the New Revised Standard Translation which used the word "paws" instead of hands.

The last kind of unclean animal is that which creeps, crawls or swarms upon the earth. This form of movement is explicitly contrary to holiness (Lev. XI, 41–44). Driver and White use "swarming" to translate the Hebrew *shérec*, which is applied to both those which teem in the waters and those which swarm on the ground. Whether we call it teeming, trailing, creeping, crawling or swarming, it is an indeterminate form of movement. Since the main animal categories are defined by their typical movement, "swarming," which is not a mode of propulsion proper to any particular element, cuts across the basic classification. Swarming things are neither fish, flesh, nor fowl. Eels and worms inhabit water, though not as fish; reptiles go on dry land, though not as quadrupeds; some insects fly, though not as birds. There is no order in them. Recall what the Prophecy of Habacuc says about this form of life:

> For thou makest men like the fish of the sea, like crawling things that have no ruler. (I. v. 14)

The prototype and model of the swarming things is the worm. As fish belong in the sea so worms belong in the realm of the grave, with death and chaos.

The case of the locusts is interesting and consistent. The test of whether it is a clean and therefore edible kind is how it moves on the earth. If it crawls it is unclean. If it hops it is clean (XI, v. 21). In the Mishnah it is noted that a frog is not listed with creeping things and conveys no uncleanness. I suggest that the frog's hop accounts for it not being listed. If penguins lived in the Near East I would expect them to be ruled unclean as wingless birds. If the list of unclean birds could be retranslated from this point of view, it might well turn out that they are anomalous because they swim and dive as well as they fly, or in some other way they are not fully bird-like.

Surely now it would be difficult to maintain that "Be ye Holy" means no more than "Be ye separate." Moses wanted the children of Israel to keep the commands of God constantly before their minds:

> Deut. XI
>
> *18. You shall therefore lay up these words of mine in your heart and in your soul; and you shall bind them as a sign upon your hand, and they shall be as frontlets between your eyes.*
>
> *19. And you shall teach them to your children, talking of them when you are sitting in your house, and when you are walking by the way, and when you lie down and when you rise.*
>
> *20. And you shall write them upon the doorposts of your house and upon your gates.*

If the proposed interpretation of the forbidden animals is correct, the dietary laws would have been like signs which at every turn inspired meditation on the oneness, purity, and completeness of God. By rules of avoidance holiness was given a physical expression in every encounter with the animal kingdom and at every meal. Observance of the dietary rules would thus have been a meaningful part of the great liturgical act of recognition and worship which culminated in the sacrifice in the Temple.

"THE ABOMINATIONS OF LEVITICUS"

Mary Douglas

1) What does Douglas suggest is necessary for the concept of defilement to occur in any religious system?

2) Holiness (*kadosh* in Hebrew) literally means "set apart." How does Douglas explain how the Jewish to dietary laws served to set the ancient Hebrew people apart from other peoples and from nature?

3) How do the dietary laws supposedly contribute to the ancient Hebrew view of the world as being ordered and complete?

4) What other possible explanations could there be to explain the Jewish dietary laws?

5) What animal prohibitions do we have in American society, and how do they reflect our particular view of the relationship of man to the world?

WORLDS OF THE SHAMAN

WHAT IS A SHAMAN?

Piers Vitebsky

Flying above the earth to the spirit world or descending into the underworld; being stripped to a skeleton, reassembled, and reborn; fighting evil spirits and sorcerers; and protecting their people from famine and disease—these are powers commonly claimed by shamans throughout the world. The word *shaman*, sometimes erroneously used interchangeably with sorcerer or medicine man, comes from the language of the Evenk, a small group of Tungus-speaking hunters and reindeer herders in Siberia. In the strictest sense, it refers to a practitioner who can will his or her spirit to leave the body and journey to upper or lower worlds.

Shamanic beliefs do not constitute a single religion or doctrinal system, although worldwide shamanic traditions approach reality and human experience in similar ways. In shamanic thinking, every element of the world around us, whether human, animal, tree, or rock, is imbued with spirits. Spirits are conscious, often anthropomorphic, and can also be interpreted as representing the essences that underlie surface appearances.

Events in the spirit world are believed to be intimately connected to everyday occurrences, particularly in the realm of human health and fertility. By entering a trance state and allowing his or her soul to venture into other worlds, the shaman can seek out the underlying causes of mundane events, and then fight, beg, or cajole the spirits to intervene in the affairs of the living.

A shaman's soul-journeys are thought to take place within a layered cosmology, with the earth at the center of various upper and lower worlds. Illness is often ascribed to the kidnapping of a patient's soul by spirits. When a fisherman in the Peruvian Amazon is seduced by a freshwater mermaid, his soul must be rescued by a mestizo shaman whose soul travels along the river bottom. In Sulawesi, Indonesia, when a patient's soul wanders off into the sky, the Wana shaman pursues it in a spirit canoe that can traverse the heavens. Many traditional Inuit communities believed that the supply of marine mammals was controlled by a female water spirit who

punished people for moral lapses by withholding the animals. One of the most daunting tests of a great shaman was to travel down to the sea floor to persuade the spirit to release the seals and whales into the hunters' path again.

Shamanic power is usually acquired through difficult initiations, ordeals believed to be imposed by the spirits. The accomplished shaman generally acquires "spirit helpers," with whom he is thought to associate. These may be gods or ancestors but are commonly the spirits of powerful, agile, or cunning animals. Often they enable the shaman to turn into one of these creatures or take on its attributes—flying into the sky in the form of a hawk or diving into the water as a fish. Such powers remain elusive and—as the need for spirit helpers suggests—always partly outside the range of the shaman's unaided abilities. Acquired with difficulty, shamanic powers can be lost again in battles with spirit enemies or through failure to perform the rituals properly.

Shamanic religion may date from the time of the earliest known Paleolithic drawings, which were made some 30,000 years ago by our hunting ancestors. Although many of these cave and rock paintings are of animals, some show humans wearing animal masks and other motifs suggestive of shamanic practices. Even today, belief in shamans seems strongest in societies that rely on hunting and gathering. In the absence of a priestly class, individuals believe they can communicate directly with gods and spirits. Agricultural societies seem somewhat inimical to shamans because of their more institutionalized forms of religion. In our own times, shamans have been widely persecuted and their activities suppressed by secular governments and by the major established religions. Yet, because shamanic thinking is flexible and adaptable, it often persists even in complex urban societies.

Although outside observers have called them madmen or charlatans, within their own cultures shamans are viewed as a combination of priest, doctor, social worker, and mystic. Eighteenth-century anthropologists and travelers encountered shamans in the Arctic and subarctic; throughout Siberia, Lapland, Tibet, and Mongolia; and among the Inuit of North America. Shamanic cultures are also widespread among rain forest tribes of South America, particularly in Amazonia, and throughout Southeast Asia.

Because he or she must often deal with illness, malevolence, and death, the shaman is often concerned with matters that are dark and dangerous. A youngster may dread being called by the spirits to follow the shamanic path, and some strenuously resist at first. Rather than seeing them as mad, their clients believe that shamans have extraordinary insight into the cosmic processes governing health, food supply, and fertility. After painful initiations, a shaman is entrusted with looking over the edge of the abyss without falling in, and returning with help for the people of this world.

DIALOGUES WITH THE DEAD

Piers Vitebsky

Almost every day among the Sora, a jungle tribe in eastern India, the living conduct dialogues with the dead. A shaman, usually a woman, serves as an intermediary between the two worlds. During a trance, her soul is said to climb down terrifying precipices to the underworld, leaving her body for the dead to use as their vehicle for communication. One by one the spirits speak through her mouth. Mourners crowd around the shaman, arguing vehemently with the dead, laughing at their jokes, or weeping at their accusations.

To prepare her for the important position of intermediary, a future shaman is visited in childhood dreams by helper spirits, who are said to turn her soul into a monkey to enable her to clamber down to the underworld. Later, the Sora believe, she learns to make this journey at will during a trance. She marries a helper spirit, bears spirit children, and makes a second home in the underworld, which she visits every time she dreams or goes into a trance.

According to Sora thinking, death is not the end of existence, but merely another phase. After death one becomes a powerful spirit with contradictory motives. On the one hand, the dead nourish their living descendants by infusing their growing crops with their own "soul force." In aggressive moods, however, they may "eat" their relatives' souls and cause in them the same illness to which the deceased succumbed.

At funerals and in divinations to diagnose the cause of illness, people stage dialogues to interrogate the dead about where they are—the landscape, the sky, or the underworld. A spirit that is trying to harm the living is presumed to be in a bad place. The relatives will then try to persuade it to move or offer a sacrificial animal as a substitute for the sick person under attack.

My research has revealed several stages of emotional involvement between living Sora and their dead. Those who died recently are considered the most dangerous because they still retain an intense attachment—often expressed as hostility—to the living. When speaking with the recently dead, people can become extremely distressed, as pity for the dead is mixed with fear for their own safety. Someone who has been dead for some time—a second stage of detachment—is no longer so threatening or aggressive. People who have been dead for many years arouse no strong feelings and (speaking through a shaman) bestow their names on their descendants' children.

Finally, the deceased dies a second death in the underworld and becomes a butterfly, bereft of human memories. As the dead drift inexorably away from the living toward butterflyhood, they become increasingly inaccessible and unknowable. In that form, souls are believed to become characterless and beyond the reach of dialogue.

Sora shamans appear to heal physical illness by helping the bereaved to manage painful and guilty memories about the dead. Healing is thought to occur only through dialogue, not merely from the passage of time. While the shaman goes on her soul journey to the underworld, the bereaved or ailing client also makes an inner journey of discovery. The mourners heal themselves by exploring and modifying the deceased's pain and hostility.

Emphasis on a "talking cure" seems similar to many Western therapies, but with a crucial difference. We may speak to our dead in one-sided conversations, but the Sora expect responses. Without the shaman's intervention, there could be no dialogue and thus no healing. Both systems, I believe, are based on the same insight: that intense emotional attachment gives rise to memories that have the power to cause illness. In Western therapies, however, the memories of a grieving patient are considered isolated and subjective, while Sora memories of the dead are made "objective" by social dialogue. The whole Sora community moves toward a consensus as it traces the dead person's shifting states of mind on a shared psychic landscape.

While the traditional Sora religion met certain psychological and social needs very well, it is proving inadequate for a younger generation that is being exposed to rapid social change. Many of today's youngsters—the first generation to attend school—have joined the Baptist church, believing that the affiliation will help them gain access to mainstream society.

The older Sora know that after they die, their Baptist children will not talk to them or feed them with sacrifices. While some young Baptists extol the benefits of their new religion, others confess to a gnawing uncertainty. "Maybe my father is with Jesus, or maybe he's in the underworld," said one, "but we can't know because we don't speak with him anymore."

SOVIET SUPERPOWERS

Marjorie Mandelstam Balzer

In the Siberian Far East, a story told by the Sakha (Yakut) people recounts how some of their shamans escaped Soviet jails: they simply turned into birds and flew away. The Sakha elder Somogotto recalled that one revered curer, Nikon, was arrested as part of the Soviet persecution of shamanic practitioners. Handcuffed to a policeman, the unprotesting shaman was led to the courthouse. But when they got there, instead of an old shaman, there was just a piece of tree branch handcuffed to the policeman, whom the magistrate accused of being drunk.

For the past ten years, I have collected many such tales of the powers of shamans, their prowess as curers and wiliness in the face of state-led persecution. These tales have not only helped to keep shamanic traditions alive in the Sakha Republic (Yakutia), they have also become a vital source of ethnic identity and resistance to absorption by the dominant Russian culture. Despite centuries of suppression and ridicule by church and state, some ancient worldviews are being reintegrated into the chaotic post-Soviet debates.

The shaman Konstantin of the Abyi region and two others captured by local officials reportedly were released after they made an entire roomful of Party functionaries believe they saw wild bears and snow inside a Young Communist League hall.

The legendary woman shaman Alykhardaakh is said to have bested Sakha Soviet authorities, whom she invited to her cabin for a seance. After dancing and drumming herself into a trance, she called forth water, and the men's ankles were submerged. Then she called forth a large fish, which she caught in her hands. Finally, she asked the officials to remove their pants and hold their male organs. The men, caught in this embarrassing position when she emerged from her trance, vowed never to bother her again.

The thrust of many of these popular stories is that even when shamans were jailed, at least some of them were spiritually more powerful than their captors and could transcend victimization. Such exuberant tales can lead a listener to romanticize the Soviet period, but the reality of ideology-driven repression was bleak. By the 1930s, most shamans were barely able to function. Soviet propaganda against "kulak-shamans" played to villagers' mixture of fear, distrust, and admiration of shamans. Practitioners were accused of political subversion and of being frauds who conned people out of goods, savings, animals, and even their daughters. Villagers who were converts to Communism collected shamans' drums for public burning, and shamans were pressed to donate their cloaks and paraphernalia to museums. One gray-bearded villager told me that when he was a boy, a local Communist activist invited the school-children to help him burn nine drums he had seized. The large, white drum of Tokoyeu, the most powerful local shaman, "jumped out of the fire three times" and had to be replaced each time. The drum burner died a horrible death soon after—but not before begging Tokoyeu for help and forgiveness.

Going into trance without a drum was difficult, but not impossible, for the few shamans who continued to practice. The elderly Marfa Zamorshikova recalled a desperate situation from her childhood, when her younger brother was ill and screaming in pain. Her mother summoned Matrena, an old woman "known for doing things that the shamans had done." To make a proper diagnosis, Matrena took up a frying pan in lieu of a drum and beat it with a wooden spoon. While in a trance, she announced that someone in the family had killed a big animal, whose spirit had entered the sick child. Four days later, after the boy had died, his father returned from a successful hunt. The family accepted the spirit possession interpretation of the child's illness and were resigned to his fate (*d'ylkha*), which derived from forces larger than themselves.

Like Matrena, some women in remote villages were able to cure in secret, while men with high-profile reputations went to jail. Authorities sometimes resorted to various pretexts for arrest, when a curer's true "crime" was shamanic practice. Still more insidious was the post-World War II Soviet policy of having shamans diagnosed as insane. Labeled as "schizophrenics," they were institutionalized and kept in a twilight of sedation. Fear of such treatment, perhaps even more than of jail, kept some from practicing. One black-leather-jacketed, motorcycle-driving young man, grandson of Tokoyeu, tearfully told me of the drugs he was given to silence the spirit voices he had heard from childhood. Recently, he has turned to traditional curers who may help him heed those voices and become a shaman himself.

Many Sakhas perceive modern medicine as being cold and bureaucratic, while shamans practice in a setting of intense, personal concern for the individual patient. Shamanic cures of cancer, gallstones, diabetes, infertility, and other common ailments are widely accepted. One popular story making the rounds is that of a young male shaman from the Viliuisk region, a protégé of Nikon, who cured a Soviet-trained Russian woman doctor of cancer. With a distrust of Soviet hospitals born of first-hand experience, the woman is said to have commissioned secret seances and postponed a risky operation. Later she was gratified to learn her tumor had disappeared.

A successful symbol of a revitalized merging of the old and new is a Moscow-trained surgeon, Aleksandra Chirkova, daughter of the shaman Konstantin. As head doctor of the huge Abyi region, she has incorporated aspects of shamanic seances, human X-ray vision, dream analysis, individual therapy, and herbal medicine into her hospital programs.

Some Sakha intellectuals are wary of the current swing toward folk medicine, fearful of a new wave of charlatanry among those who call themselves "extrasenses," mixing Russian and Sakha curing traditions. Most Sakhas consider only five shamans, from different indigenous groups, to be genuine, and even their authenticity is hotly debated. Few patients have completely forsaken modern medicine. But many Sakhas are finding a new cultural pride and confidence in the emergence of shamans from the underground.

Shamanic functions have been reinforced and reinterpreted in new contexts. One female shaman reputedly used spirit power to fix a broken bus on the way to a meeting with Native American visitors. Another has built a reputation for finding stolen cars, and others have helped police find missing persons. One environmental activist is also a healer, building on a shamanic theme of harmony with nature gained through telepathy, meditation, and spirit propitiation.

A Sakha cultural revival movement called Kut-Sur (Heart-Soul-Mind-Reason) has drawn upon ancient shamanic concepts and rites. Kut-Sur members rejoiced in 1990 when, at their urging, the major Sakha midsummer shamanic celebration of renewal and fertility, *yhyakh*, became a republic holiday. Members stress a renewed respect for the power of spirits, the power of certain words, and the curative benefits of prayer.

Some healers have joined in private practices or in an Association of Folk Medicine, founded in 1990 and headed by the shaman-historian-extrasense Vladimir Kondakov. Although past Sakha shamans rarely worked together, his teams of curers are welcomed in many villages. Kondakov exhorts spiritual seekers and patients to climb a hill at sunrise and "let the first rays of the sun and the first songs of birds give you strength and energy. . . . As the sun rises, so shall you fly higher."

Another team of folk healers, led by Klavdia Maksimova and Petr Sleptsov, has organized group seances, using drumming and a jaw harp (*khomus*) to produce cures, stimulate artistic creativity, and open the "shamanic third eye" of intuition and spirit power. In 1995, I watched twenty patients as they danced and went into trances in a field to the resonating twang of the *khomus*. Some of the participants, who had appeared incapacitated during earlier sessions, now moved joyously, with animal and bird movements. A few rolled on the ground. They laughed and feasted and prayed to the fire spirit, closing with the drawing of solar energies toward their chests. "I am well," they chanted, "I am Sakha. I am here, in and with this land."

THE SHAMAN'S APPRENTICE

Laurel Kendall

Uijongbu, Republic of Korea, September 1989: Chini's dank little rented room and her pale, emaciated figure reflect the hardship suffered by someone who is destined to serve the spirits. The gods and ancestors will torment Chini until she becomes a shaman. Today, experienced shamans will dress her in the costumes of various spirits and coach her until she bursts into inspired words and actions. When Chini's "gates of speech" are finally opened, when she can give divinations in the spirits' own words, clients will seek her out and she will be able to earn a living as a shaman.

Although held in low esteem, the work of a shaman may offer the only hope for thirty-two-year-old Chini, who has so far failed at everything she has tried. Raised in poverty and married to an abusive drunk, she fled her marriage and was forced to leave her two small children behind. Drifting from one menial job to another, she began to hear the spirits' voices, urging her to leave her tasks and run outdoors. "But of course, once I got outside, there wasn't anyone there," she says with a faint smile. Her bizarre behavior earned her two visits to a mental hospital.

Whenever Chini had her fortune told, the shamans insisted that she was destined to be a shaman, that she must accept her fate and be initiated into the profession. Chini's mother and sister were appalled at first, but eventually they supported Chini's apprenticeship and went deep into debt to pay for her initiation *kut*.

A *kut* is a ceremony in which shamans—clothed as gods and ancestors and inspired by dancing to loud, percussive music—become hosts to the spirits. In an initiation *kut*, the apprentice shaman does this for the first time. Early in her ceremony, Chini must balance on an earthen water jar and deliver an oracle. Speaking through Chini, the god known as the Buddhist Sage announces that an intrusive spirit is blocking the way. Then Chini says no more.

The shamans first cajole the spirits, then coach and finally scold their apprentice, berating her for letting her thoughts wander. In mounting desperation, they tell her that the spirits will not move her tongue for her, that performing inspired speech, "whether or not the spirits have made you into a shaman," is more constructive than her stage fright and stony silence.

As the shamans see it, Chini's gates of inspired speech are blocked by an obstinate spirit, but at another level they recognize that Chini is blocked because she cannot clear her mind, opening herself to feelings and losing herself in performance. She does not heed the impulse to clothe herself in a particular spirit's costume, a vehicle of that spirit's presence and power. She does not weep or shout insults, but resists the emotional release and surrender that would bring on the force of the spirits.

Kim Pongsun, the "spirit mother" in charge of Chini's initiation, tries to identify the troublesome spirit. She divines that the culprit is Chini's dead sister, a pockmarked maiden who took her own life at age nineteen. Kim Pongsun now claims that the dead sister was herself a destined shaman. Once installed in Chini's shrine as Princess Hogu, the sister will assist Chini as a potent guardian spirit.

But even when she is clothed in the robes of this new spirit, Chini can't find inspiration. As a last resort, the shamans dress Chini in the gold satin robe of the Heavenly King, since no intrusive spirit would dare to block the high king's path. Swaying on her feet, eyes vacant, a smile on her lips, Chini proclaims the presence of the Heavenly King, then lapses again into silence.

Kim Pongsun castigates the spirits whose painted images hang above Chini's altar, calling them heartless for insisting on a *kut* and then failing to uphold their part of the bargain. She threatens to tear them off the wall and burn them up.

At last, the apprentice seems ready to speak for Princess Hogu. Kim Pongsun urges Chini on, using a now-familiar formula: "If there's a costume the spirit wants to wear, then put it on! Jump and keep shouting out the spirit's commands. That's what we mean by the true words of the spirits—shout out what the spirits have to tell us. That's what it's all about." The shamans pound cymbals, drum, and gong as Chini reaches for Princess Hogu's robe. Kim Pongsun shouts, "You must cry your heart out. Then everything will burst out!"

Sobbing convulsively, Chini covers her tear-streaked face with Princess Hogu's fan and—in the person of the dead sister—laments her pitiful situation, forced to become a shaman. The dead girl calls for her mother and pours out wrenching words that could be Chini's own:

Mother! Mother! I wanted so much to be beautiful,
Mother . . . I'll help my little sister as a shaman.
Mother, I want your blessing, but you don't respond.
Mother, how many times I've called you! . . .
When my mother raised me she wasn't able to give

us decent food. I'm full of pity for Chini.
How can it be helped,
Mother? . . . That's why I've come.

Tears trickle down the mother's wrinkled face. Chini's sister and sister-in-law are weeping in the corner. The shamans wipe away their own tears. Chini gives a round of divinations, staggers drunkenly through her performance of Princess Hogu's praise song, and collapses in a bow in front of her altar.

Although the apprentice has made progress, the outcome of the *kut* is still uncertain. But for the brief, cathartic encounter with her dead sister, Chini's performance has been limited, her divinations commonplace and unremarkable.

The next day—after much coaxing, encouragement, and scolding—Chini undertakes the most difficult ordeal of her *kut*. She climbs six feet to the top of a makeshift edifice and balances on the blades of a fodder-chopper. There she proclaims the presence of the Knife-Riding General, who is one of the most powerful spirits in her pantheon. But she gives no divinations, and when she descends from the blades, she speaks no more.

Chini ends her *kut* deep in debt and not yet empowered to work as a shaman. She has failed, the shamans acknowledge, because she is too self-conscious and inhibited.

Discouraged, Chini breaks off the apprenticeship with her spirit mother and disappears. Her unsuccessful initiation and failed apprenticeship are common in the world of Korean shamans. Although disappointed by Chini's defection, Kim Pongsun is philosophical:

> *Look at it this way. It isn't as if anyone can become a successful shaman right when they get the calling. They must make a great effort and change completely. If it happened automatically, then wouldn't everyone be making their living as a shaman? Everyone has their moment, and all things happen in their season. If this time the spirits vacillated, then by and by the time can come when they will make her into a successful shaman.*

OBJECTS OF POWER

Allen Wardwell

Beset by European-American culture and law, the Northwest Coast tradition of shamanism died out early this century, but not before being recorded by such linguists, anthropologists, and collectors as Franz Boas, John Swanton, George Hunt, and George T. Emmons. Among the Tlingit, Tsimshian, Haida, and other peoples, shamans could be men or women.

They often lived the life of ascetics, away from villages and everyday affairs, and their hair was long and uncut. Accompanied by tales of encounters with helpful and malevolent spirits, journeys to the land of the dead, acquisition of animal languages, and flights to the moon and stars, shamans were fantastic figures. But they were also remembered as human beings, and the masks, rattles, and other objects they used are a reminder of the vital ritual role they played in the life of their people.

Death of a Shaman

In about 1890, the Tlingit shaman Tek-'ic felt it was time to die. His brother had recently passed away, and Tek-'ic realized no one would succeed him as shaman or care for his remains. According to his niece's account, Tek-'ic decided to have himself photographed on the steps of his house in Yakutat Bay. He then called in the members of his clan, who sang spirit songs. Afterward they took him out to the clean sand beach to cut his long hair. He died that same day, and following the custom for shamans, his remains were placed in a grave house above ground. About ten years later, the desiccated body was buried in the ground by a Tlingit convert to Christianity who did not want its spirit powers to cause someone else to become a shaman.

AMAZON GRACE

Kenneth Good

Among the Yanomami of the Amazon forest of Venezuela and Brazil, the normal chatter in the communal house is pierced almost every afternoon by the bellows of the village shaman beginning his chant. It is an all-in-one sermon about the world, a lecture on life's meaning, an explanation of cultural and social origins. As small children dart playfully between the support posts, and men and women roast plantains, weave cotton, repair arrows, or lie back in their hammocks talking, the melodious chanting of the man who is a leader, curer, and defender against evil spirits is a reassuring sound. It engenders a feeling that all is well, that this most important man is in good humor and in control of the all-pervading spirits.

At other times, the sound of the shaman brings village life almost to a standstill. This is when he chants to cure the sick or dying, to make whole a child whose soul has escaped the body and left him or her vulnerable to dangerous forces. Then women weep or sometimes wail, and everyone feels a combination of anger and sorrow.

As an adolescent, Rinawe spent innumerable afternoons sitting in the semicircle of Yanomami elders, participating in shamanic sessions. To experience the supernatural world, he took *ebene*, hallucinogenic snuff made from psychoactive plants and blown through three-foot-long bamboo tubes into each nostril. When he was no more than fifteen, he felt the calling to become a shaman himself and began to practice chants, rhythms, and struts, at first on his own and later with a few other young men as an audience. Eventually, he was taken seriously by the senior shamans, who guided his chanting.

Now the crucial time has come for Rinawe to be initiated. For this he must present himself as a worthy host to the spirits. Day after day he sits on the ground in the communal house, his legs extended in front of the headman's section, taking large doses of *ebene* and repeating the phrases chanted by the master shaman. As the spirits, summoned and encouraged by the master, approach Rinawe, the youth is overcome and falls prostrate on his back. A village mate props him up and holds him steady as the shaman blows more drugs into him and continues with his instruction.

After five days of taking *ebene*, and almost no food or water, Rinawe is emaciated and covered with dried mucus, *ebene*, and soil. He is so weak that he appears barely conscious, and his repetitions of the shaman's phrases are almost inaudible. Will the spirits come? Will they accept him? Or will they flee, depriving him of his hopes of becoming a shaman? Some women begin to cry in fear for Rinawe's life and from compassion for his ordeal. Even one of the men sitting close to the participants begins to sob.

Rinawe survives the ordeal, and on the seventh morning the shamans decide the time has come for the crucial rite. They leave for the forest, where they cut a young tree to make a seven-foot ceremonial pole. Decorated along its length with feathers, the pole is called the rock, or rock outcrop; it is the place where the spirits live. The spirits that swarm around it must be guided to the new shaman.

With great ceremony and thunderous shouts, two shamans decorated with feathers carry the pole into the village clearing. As the entire community watches, they move toward the initiate, crouching and swinging their arms to drive off the malevolent spirits that seek to interfere. Finally they plant the pole in the ground between Rinawe's legs. *Pei!*—"It is done!" The master shaman grasps Rinawe's head and tilts it forward to touch the ceremonial mast, the rock, the dwelling of the spirits; and thus Rinawe enters the venerable realm of the shaman.

NEW SPIRITS FOR OLD

Shoefoot (Bautista Cajicuwa), as told to Kenneth Good and Mark Ritchie

Until their first contact with outsiders, about fifty years ago, the Yanomami Indians of Venezuela led an isolated existence in the Amazon rain forest. Once these Indians became known to the outside world, anthropologists wanted to study them, and missionaries sought to win their minds and souls. Within a few decades, the Yanomami have been exposed not only to new technologies but also to new "spirits."

Although communal life in the jungle can be pleasant—replete with laughter, friendship, and family—there is also a full measure of paranoia, sickness, and violence. Malaria remains rampant, food is often scarce, and vengeance raids are a fact of life. Shamans often tell their people that the cause of a relative's illness or death is a malevolent spirit sent by someone in a neighboring village. Wars of retaliation are commonly carried out with clubs and bows and arrows. During such tension-filled times, people are afraid to venture out of their villages alone, even to hunt or draw water from the river.

In the early 1960s, a Yanomami shaman and village leader known as Shoefoot, tired of living in fear and seeing people killed, felt betrayed by his spirits. Then he met Joe Dawson and his family, independent Evangelical missionaries from the United States, who convinced him to follow a foreign spirit that would help him find peace. In September 1996, Shoefoot, then sixty-five years old, visited the American Museum of Natural History, along with Joe Dawson's son Gary (Keleewa) and writer Mark Ritchie, who had told Shoefoot's story in his book Spirit of the Rain Forest. *Kenneth Good, an anthropologist who speaks fluent Yanomami, attended as an independent observer for this magazine. During the interview, Good was convinced of the sincerity of Shoefoot's conversion, although it is unique in his twelve years' experience of living with the Yanomami. The following is Shoefoot's statement:*

When I was a little boy, I used to sit in my hammock across from the communal dwelling and listen to the village shamans chant, calling out to the spirits. Everyone held these men in awe: they guided the community, controlled the spirits, and understood all things in life. I watched them blow *ebene* powder into each other's nostrils through long, hollow reeds. This potent drug is made from several jungle plants; it makes strong men's heads snap backward, but then it helps them talk to spirits. One day, I thought, I will become one of the village shamans, as the *hekura* (forest spirits) were already speaking to me.

When I was about fifteen, my father, a shaman himself, called on me to carry on this solemn service to the community. He said the village needed more

powerful shamans, because it had so many enemies. Following him and his older brothers, I began to inhale *ebene* and chant. After several years of training, I was publicly initiated into the world of the *hekura*. Various spirits came to make a home within my chest.

Many sick and dying people were brought to my hearth to be healed. I inhaled the drug, called up the spirits, and tried to drive away those who came to do harm. Some of the sick recovered, but many died, because the spirits of the forest are powerful. When someone died, their relatives would cremate the body and drink the ashes. And they would ask me who was the evil shaman from another village who had caused their misfortune. Sometimes I would understand who it was who had done this, so I would call the men to take up clubs and arrows and raid the village where the evil shaman lived. We would kill as many men as we could, rape the women, and take some back to our village. Then we knew we might be raided ourselves, so I would advise everyone to move out into the forest on a trek of many days to escape the dangers. When a soul was stolen, I would try to send my spirits to retrieve it, but usually without success. I took great amounts of *ebene* so I could see the spirits and magically travel to far places and find them.

When I began my own family, I planted a garden and hunted to feed my children. Many times others would bring sick children, and I would take my drug and chant to cure them. At some times, very many got sick at once, and I was chanting and taking the drug all day and night. But young and old died anyway, and I doubled my efforts to heal until I was exhausted. When food was scarce in the village, I led trekking parties into the forest in search of fruits and berries. I was strong and respected as one who guided his community, and I received the largest portions of meat after a hunt.

As the years went on, the responsibilities of a shaman weighed heavier and heavier upon me. I was tired. So many sick and dying. I could not cure them, no matter how hard I tried. So many threats to my village. People were raiding and killing one another. I could not protect them. Often there were food crises. I took more and more *ebene* to get assistance from the spirits, but my mind began to play tricks. Instead of help, my spirits left me with nothing but worry and fear. Sometimes I was so confused I wanted to escape into the forest, but I never ran off. Some men got lost in the spirit world when they took the drug; many ran into the jungle and were never heard from again. Now and then, one of them was found dead. I was strong, but I was thinking I wasn't strong enough to go on like this.

A visitor from another village told me about foreign people, *nabas*, who had come to live on the river.

One older couple had a son called Keleewa, who talks and hunts just like us, because he grew up in a Yanomami village. We call him "the white Yanomami." Keleewa and his father told me of a big spirit that could help us, one that was friendly and not desiring death and destruction. I began to think about this peaceful new spirit, and pretty soon after, my spirits got jealous and gave me bad dreams. They said they were afraid I would abandon them and that they would kill me if I tried. When I stopped taking *ebene* and turned to the spirit of the *nabas*, I was happy to see that it was stronger than my forest spirits. They became afraid and went away. They didn't tell me to kill people or lead raids anymore. Instead, the new spirit told me to stop fights whenever I could.

I became calm in my mind and my fear went away. I no longer hated anyone or wanted to cause their death. My old spirits were happy whenever someone died, and they kept telling the shamans to stir up more violence. We thought we had power over these spirits, but they really had the power over us—causing our own people to die. Even when we shamans were chanting and taking *ebene* and looking content, there was turmoil inside, for our spirits kept telling us to kill. Some men lost all control when they took the drug, sometimes even killing their own wives and children.

Today I no longer live in fear and I'm a friend to everyone. We have ended our feuds and stopped the killing. Now that we are living in a bigger, more secure village, we are able to devote ourselves to growing more food; we have some cattle, and we have better homes to protect ourselves from the mosquitoes. The *nabas* told us that malaria comes from mosquitoes, not from evil shamans, and we have changed our belief. Some of us have learned to look at blood slides under Keleewa's microscope and tell what kind of malaria someone has. Our population at Honey Village is growing, while many others are decreasing. The new spirit freed me from the fear I had all the time. Today my people are better off and at peace.

ON THE PEYOTE ROAD

Mike Kiyaani, as told to Thomas J. Csordas

Most Americans know peyote only as a cactus containing an illegal psychotropic substance, but to some 250,000 American Indian adherents of the peyote religion, it is a sacrament and a spirit. To live according to its inspiration is to follow the peyote road of personal dignity and respect for nature and for other people. Those recognized as having the ability to lead others along this path are known as "road men." Mike Kiyaani, who underwent his own long

apprenticeship, is such a road man. Now seventy-seven, Kiyaani is a Navajo who first used peyote in the late 1940s, after returning to his native Arizona as an honored veteran of military service. He had served in an elite Marine unit, along with other Navajos who used their complex native language to communicate sensitive information—a code that defied penetration.

The peyote religion, formally institutionalized as the Native American Church, was introduced to the Navajos in the 1930s by members of several Plains Indian tribes. Its practices and spirituality differ from those of the traditional Navajo religion, although both are fundamentally concerned with healing. Traditional Navajo medicine men—Kiyaani's own father was one—lead ceremonies known as chants. Lasting as long as nine consecutive nights, chants involve prayers in the form of songs, specific acts by the healer and patient, and the creation of potent visual symbols, such as sand paintings. A peyote ceremony, in contrast, is a prayer meeting during which peyote is eaten by participants under the leadership of a road man. Combining singing, drumming, and prayers, the ceremony typically lasts one night, from dusk to dawn.

Assembled in a tepee or hogan, the participants focus their prayers on an altar or a fireplace. In the style learned by Mike Kiyaani, the centerpiece of the fireplace is a crescent of heaped-up earth on which rests a special cactus button known as the chief peyote. The road man cherishes his chief peyote and may pass it down through several generations. Kiyaani concentrates on his chief peyote and the fire place to facilitate his dialogue with nature. He says that whereas white people talk directly to God, the humble prefer going through the intermediary of nature—the air and the sunshine, which are God's creations. Kiyaani is not a shaman who takes spirit flights to other worlds but a healer who prays through the elements of nature in which, for him, God already resides.

Mike Kiyaani's mentor was Truman Dailey, an Oto Indian who instructed him not to imitate Plains Indian ways but to take the medicine home and adapt its use to the Navajo culture and way of life. For Dailey, the elements of the altar represent parts of the eagle, which is sacred to his clan. Kiyaani stresses the Navajo understanding of corn as a symbol of growth and life. He performs the traditional corn pollen blessing, sprinkling some grains to make a path that corresponds to the peyote road. He also uses a song learned from his father that metaphorically connects the prayer meeting to the growth of the life-giving corn plant.

Navajo adherents of the peyote religion once faced opposition from their own tribal government, which decreed the religion illegal in 1940 and did not move for tolerance until 1966. Only in 1994 did the federal government adopt a law that guarantees the right of American Indians to practice the peyote religion. Mike Kiyaani remains deeply concerned that, against the background of a long struggle for freedom of religion, the use of peyote be protected for its importance in healing, spirituality, and identity. He has traveled widely to describe his work to audiences of health care professionals, and on the reservation his reputation as a road man keeps him in great demand by Navajos who travel considerable distances to seek his assistance.—T. J. C.

I'm a Navajo veteran—World War II, Navajo Code Talker, wounded in action. My clan is Salt Clan. I got my name from Kiyaani; that's my grandfather's clan. When I came back from the war, I was a sick man. There was something wrong with my mind, something wrong all over my body. No pain, but I felt kind of lousy. My father had died in 1944, and I guess that's what got into me. One man I got acquainted with took me to Oklahoma. I met this man Truman Dailey there, and he noticed my condition. He said, "You take this peyote," and gave me a 25-pound flour sack filled with Mexican dry peyote. I took that back home.

During that time, I was way up there where nobody lives, herding sheep, and I used peyote. Just a little bit during the day, every day. It seemed like it went all through my system. Then one particular day I felt like eating, and I had fifty buttons. In about another hour and a half, I ate another fifty buttons—maybe four times, fifty buttons. At midnight, everything started coming. My life seemed to be coming to an end. That's the way the medicine showed me, but I still kept on eating until morning. Everything began coming out different. There was a lot of sagebrush out there, and everything was too beautiful. But every time I looked to the peyote, it wasn't pleasant to look at.

Then toward noon I looked for that peyote, and now I saw it was real pure, real white. It kind of talked to me, "Your body is like that, your body is pure. Now you don't need treatment, you're a well man. You wanted to get well, now you're well." I understood it to be that way. At that time I sure cried. I was all right then. After that I was pretty much on the go most of the time performing ceremonies for sick people. I kind of experimented with the peyote eating, how it works, how it can heal.

At the start of the ceremony, I don't know what's ailing the patient, but when you take some peyote into your system, the peyote affects you, and then you kind of know. A lot of people just say, "I'm sick," that's all. They don't know exactly what's bothering them. But peyote does wonderful things. My patient eats peyote. He has peyote in his system. Peyote is in my system, too. He's talking; then I kind of know. I kind of see things, what's wrong in that way. It's the peyote that shows me things. It's my patient talking his mind—the way he talks, the way he expresses

himself. It might be his action in there that's kind of unusual; that tells me. But I don't watch him directly, I keep my eyes on the fire all the time.

I say, "You come to me, and I want you to help yourself; whatever it is that's bothering your mind, whatever it is you think that's bothering your health, get your mind off of it. You get on to this medicine, this fire place, this singing that you hear, the prayers that you are hearing in here, which are all for you. The people sitting here, they're talking for you. They're singing for you. Everybody wants you to get well. Whatever's bothering you—maybe it's an evil, maybe it's that lightning struck near you, maybe something else. Get your mind off of it." He might have a hard time [from nausea] through the peyote effect, but that's going to help him. That's the time he's going to figure out what's wrong, why he's sick.

I go outside for a special ceremony at midnight. I get my bone whistle out. Some medicine men take their flashlight out there or maybe take somebody with them out there. I don't do those things. I'd rather be in the dark, praying by myself. A lot of Navajos, while they're out there, they see something, visualize something. I don't look for those things. But I might be hearing that the patient's mind is bothered by witchcraft or maybe some lightning struck that might be affecting his body, his mind.

Peyote. You eat it and it goes through your body, your blood veins, your flesh, your bone, your brain, and we talk to this peyote. And this peyote goes through all the patient's blood veins, goes to his brain, brain vessel; it seems like we talk to the peyote like that. Talking with nature; that's all it is. Whatever you do, peyote knows it, nature knows it. Whatever is wrong inside here, nature knows it. The Almighty knows it, so there's no way you can get away from this peyote, from this Almighty, from nature. If at some place you get off the road, then you notice it. Then you come back and pray. You go back to the Almighty, back to peyote. You get back on the road.

The spirit peyote came up among the Navajo people on a very hard road. But peyote found its way here, and so you see it has some kind of power. It found its way into the Navajo people, into the Navajo hogan, into the heart. Where the heart is, this peyote goes in there. So I want this thing to go on, this peyote religion, peyote worship. It's something for Indians who are humble. Just like in the Bible—it says the meek shall inherit the earth.

Now I'm worried the white man is going to go for it. That's what they usually do. That's what we don't want to happen. I don't think it's for the white people. This natural herb peyote is used by Native Americans with more sincerity. Indian people are more serious in their mind, in their heart, in the way they worship. Just let the Indians have it, let the

Indians use it the way they want it, just natural. Our identity is there.

A DIFFERENT DRUMMER

Michael Harner

While on an anthropological expedition to the Peruvian Amazon for the American Museum of Natural History in 1960–1961, I lived for the better part of a year in a village of Conibo Indians on a remote lake near the lower Río Tamaya. After I had spent months in a relatively futile effort to learn about their spiritual beliefs, the Conibo finally advised me that there was only one way to learn, and that was to take *ayahuasca*, the consciousness-changing brew their shamans used to reach the hidden worlds of the spirits. *Ayahuasca* is a boiled mixture that contains a particular species of *Banisteriopsis* vine, along with one or more other components, such as *Psychotria* leaves or the leaves of another species of *Banisteriopsis*.

At the time I first took the brew, I was unacquainted with psychedelics. Timothy Leary was only just having his first psychedelic experience, and knowledge of LSD was not yet a part of American culture. I also believed myself to be an atheist. I was simply taking the *ayahuasca* potion in the interests of anthropology because participant observation is one of the cornerstones of serious research.

The Conibo were right, for when I finally drank the potion one night, the results astonished me. Not only did I enter amazingly real, unknown worlds, but in later describing them to a Conibo shaman, I discovered he was already familiar with them, even volunteering details I had not yet had a chance to tell him. I realized anthropology had underestimated the seriousness of shamanic knowledge and that I had entered a reality far deeper than human culture.

The same shaman encouraged me to continue to work with *ayahuasca* so that I could become initiated into full-fledged shamanic practice. As we worked night after night in an altered state of consciousness, I learned much more about the nonordinary worlds of the shaman, especially that in them one can find and merge with compassionate spiritual powers to help heal the sick and suffering of our ordinary world. I also learned techniques of shamanic divination, methods of obtaining spiritual anwers to difficult questions.

Following this experience, I received similar initiations into Amazonian shamanism from the Untsuri Shuar (Jívaro) people of eastern Ecuador, with whom I had previously lived for a year as an ethnographer. I also started to search the cross-cultural literature, expecting to find evidence of the use of indigenous psychedelics in shamanism worldwide. I eventually concluded, however, that the Amazonians' use of psychedelics was a minority practice. The much more common method to enter the shaman's altered state of consciousness was monotonous percussive sound, achieved especially through drumming.

With experimentation, I learned what the shamans already knew; monotonous drumming, in a frequency of four to seven beats per second, was another valid doorway to the other reality. This "sonic driving" is in approximately the same frequency range as the brain's own theta waves, and its effectiveness is probably partly due to its stimulation of the brain in that range. Compared with drugs, such drumming was also safe, and its effects were short term.

My research among the Inuit of the Canadian Arctic and the peoples of the Northwest Coast of North America reinforced my conclusion that most of the world's shamans use drums or other percussion instruments as "horses" or "canoes" that transport them into the hidden reality of the spirits. Among the Sami (Lapps) of northern Scandinavia, who retained shamanism longer than any other culture in Europe, a few households still have what they call the magic drum. Doing research in the Soviet Union, I learned that the truly professional Siberian shamans generally employed only the drum, even when the psychedelic mushroom *Amanita muscaria* was locally available and was being used by others.

With the shaman's drum, I was able to continue my practice of shamanism in the United States. I lectured on the subject, in and outside of my university teaching, and inevitably, others asked me to introduce them to the practice of shamanism. Thus I began to teach shamanic healing and divination work, first to one or two people at a time, and then, by the mid-1970s, in workshops for groups of students at New Age learning centers such as California's Esalen Institute.

Continuing cross-cultural research, fieldwork, and personal experimentation led me to the fundamental principles of shamanic practice, which I found to be basically the same among indigenous peoples, whether in Siberia, Australia, southern Africa, or North and South America. This "core shamanism," as I call it, is what I taught. Instead of imitating the practices of some ethnic group, my students were able to build on these bare bones of practical shamanic knowledge to fit their own culture. With this basis, the spirits became their teachers—the classic way for shamans to acquire most of their knowledge.

Shamans probably played an important role in European societies from at least the Upper Paleolithic, but this heritage was virtually destroyed in the Middle Ages and early Renaissance by the Church and the Inquisition. Such persecution was common in most of the major civilizations, East and West, because the shamans' ongoing journeys to the gods tended to undermine the authority of state religions. With this in mind, I gave up my university career in 1987 and founded the Foundation for Shamanic Studies, whose purpose is to help Westerners recover this lost shamanic heritage and to help indigenous peoples revive and preserve their own shamanic practices.

Recently, for example, a team from the foundation traveled to the central Asian republic of Tuva (part of the Russian Federation) at the invitation of its president, to help revive shamanism, which had been outlawed there—with the death penalty for practitioners—during the period of Communist domination. In cooperation with the remaining Tuvan shamans, the team performed numerous public healings, demonstrating that shamanism and shamanic healing were valued in America and compatible with modern life. At the conclusion of our visit, the president announced that thereafter shamanism would be respected on a par with Buddhism and Christianity.

In the United States, Europe, and elsewhere, more and more people are learning the practice of shamanism, including health care professionals seeking a more holistic approach. Shamanism has always been done in conjunction with the application of plant remedies, bone setting, and other healing practices. It is not an "alternative" method but a complementary one that looks after the spiritual side of healing.

Much has happened since the shamans introduced me to hidden spirit worlds thirty-six years ago. For me, entering these worlds has transformed my understanding of reality and added great meaning to existence. To the question you often hear today, "Is this all there is?" I can answer with assurance, "No, there is far more than one can even imagine."

DESPERATELY SEEKING REDEMPTION

Diane Bell

Writing for the *Lakota Times* in 1991, Avis Little Eagle summed up the growing anger of many indigenous peoples concerning the practices of self-styled New Age shamans. Throughout the 1980s, the American Indian Movement had protested, picketed, and passed resolutions condemning those individuals and institutions that packaged Indian sweat lodges, vision quests, shamanic healing, and sun dances for the spiritually hungry. Two years later, at the Parlia-

ment of the World's Religions in Chicago, the Dakota, Lakota, and Nakota Nations issued a Declaration of War Against Exploiters of Lakota Spirituality.

This theme has been developed by a number of Native American writers and activists. Ward Churchill, in *Fantasies of the Master Race* (1992), calls the exploiters "plastic medicine men" and cites them as evidence of the continuing genocidal colonization of Native Americans. Poet-anthropologist Wendy Rose writes of "white shamanism" as a form of cultural imperialism, and feminist Andrea Smith, in her article "For All Those Who Were Indian in a Former Life," calls these "wannabes" to account. Echoing the defiant stand taken in the nineteenth century by the Lakota and Cheyenne over the Black Hills, these activists insist that their "spirituality is not for sale."

Lynn V. Andrews, the Los Angeles–based author of the highly successful *Medicine Woman* trilogy says, "I write of my own experience. I am not an anthropologist." The books, workshops, and promotional tours of this self-proclaimed shaman, however, have been cited as a prime example of the appropriation and commercialization of indigenous peoples' spirituality. According to Andrews, the teachings of her Canadian spiritual guide, a "Native American medicine woman" named Agnes Whistling Elk, include Lakota, Cree, and Hopi terms and concepts. Such eclecticism deeply troubles many Native Americans, who see the mixing and matching of different traditions from different tribes as an assault on the integrity of the extremely personal and specific ties of kin and country that underpin their beliefs and practices. In addition, Andrews writes of being introduced into the Sisterhood of the Shields, a secret organization of forty-four women from different Native American tribes. Andrews's loyal readers, however, are not deterred. Over and over, as I research the appeal of these texts, I hear, "I don't care if it's not true; it speaks to me."

In *Mutant Message Down Under*, Marlo Morgan—a self-described alternative health care provider from Kansas City—describes her 2,000-mile trek across the burning deserts of Australia with a hitherto unknown tribe of Aborigines she calls the Real People. She claims she must keep the location of their "opal cave" secret for fear that the government might imprison them or blow up their sacred site. Australian Aborigines have protested that her book is, at best, nonsense and, at worst, a violation of their law. HarperCollins lists her book as fiction, but Morgan continues to lecture on the Real People as though they were real. Although exposés have appeared in the American and Australian media, this best-seller has reached millions of readers, many of whom report, "It changed my life."

In both Morgan's book and Andrews's *Crystal Woman*, Aboriginal life is simple. Neither author (unlike ethnographers whose careful work rarely reaches a general audience) finds the need to grapple with the intricacies of kinship and land-based relations among Aboriginal groups. Both authors avoid the complexities of local languages, and the books' spiritual folks frequently communicate by telepathy or by giggling and winking their way through the stories. Andrews's meeting with the Sisterhood of the Shields takes place in a native "village" near a brook in the middle of the arid Australian desert. At this unlikely site, she meets with her Native American Sisters, as well as with female Aborigines. In reality, no group of people could travel for a thousand miles through Australia without having to negotiate access through the territories of many other groups. (But how convenient for government authorities if this were true! Relocation policies would be perfectly acceptable because one piece of land would be as good as the next to the Aborigines.)

Enraged that a gullible public was consuming these misrepresentations—and that yet again exotic stereotypes of Aborigines were obscuring the gritty realities of the lives of many of these peoples—Robert Eggington, coordinator of the Dumbartung Aboriginal Corporation (Western Australia), led a group of Aboriginal elders to Los Angeles in January 1996 to protest Morgan's book and a planned film. Morgan responded to the protest in a radio interview reported in the *Weekend Australian*. "I'm terribly sorry," she said, "and my sincere apologies to any Australian Aboriginal person if I have offended them in any way . . . please read this book . . . with an open mind and see if there is anything, anything at all that is derogatory."

Morgan's and Andrews's readers often tell me that these books offer a vision of a world in which all life forms coexist in physical and spiritual harmony; where one person's journey can undo centuries of abuse; where women are wise; where, despite differences in language, history, geography, economic status, and personal skills, we are all one. Here is community, meaning, belonging—all the connectedness for which the self-absorbed, postindustrial, fragmented individual yearns. I certainly agree that we should be open to wisdom from a range of sources, but must we suspend all critical faculties in the process? It matters that the beliefs and practices of Native Americans and Australian Aborigines have been put through a cultural blender. It matters that the stories of those engaged in ongoing struggles for their very lives are marginalized, and that these representations of indigenous peoples are romantic and ahistorical. Morgan and Andrews shroud their "native teachers" in mystery while telling us that they hold the keys to true and authentic ways of knowing.

Marketers of neo-shamanic books and workshops claim that indigenous wisdom is part of our common human heritage. By sharing such knowledge, the argument goes, together we can save the planet. But is this sharing or a further appropriation? There is a bitter irony in turning to indigenous peoples to solve problems of affluent urbanites. In the midst of the wealth of first-world nations, most native peoples endure appalling health problems, underemployment, and grinding poverty. A philosophy of reverence for the earth rings hollow in the reality of toxic waste dumps and nuclear testing on native lands. As Inès Talamantez, of the University of California, Santa Barbara, says: "If the impulse is for respect and sharing, then come stand with us in our struggles for religious freedoms and the return of skeletal remains and against hydroelectric dams and logging roads."

We anthropologists, too, have been part of the problem. Too often our power to define "the other" has displaced and silenced indigenous voices. Here, I am not speaking *for* indigenous peoples; rather I am turning the anthropological gaze on Western cultures so that we may understand why so many individuals seek healing, meaning, and spiritual answers in the lives of peoples whose lands and lives have been so devastated by Western colonialism.

"WORLDS OF THE SHAMAN"

1) What *is* a shaman?

2) Define the necessary qualities one must have to be a shaman.

3) What various paths can one take to achieve the position and status of a shaman?

4) What role(s) or job(s) does a shaman generally undertake in his/her society?

5) How have state-level societies, particularly the USSR, viewed shamans and shamanistic belief systems?

6) What trends in American society, both religious and secular, have contributed to the trend of Americans turning to "traditional" shamanistic systems of belief for answers to their spiritual problems?

7) How do individuals in "traditional" societies view this shamanistic trend in American culture?

POSSESSION STATES ACROSS THE WORLD: AN ANTHROPOLOGICAL APPROACH

Kevin Rafferty

Religion has always been a subject of keen interest to anthropologists, particularly those of traditional peoples. A large percentage of research has been concerned with the phenomenon of trances and possession states, no more so than in the last three decades of the twentieth century. Popular culture has dealt with the issue for years, with movies such as *The Exorcist*, and the rash of imitators such as *The Omen*, *The Night Child*, *The Devil In Miss Jones* (an X-rated film), and others dealing with the phenomenon from a spectacular, entertaining point of view. However, a spate of books by anthropologists, theologians, and layman have appeared, discussing possession from a biological, psychological, cultural, and theological/spiritual perspective. This literature appears to be divided between two main schools. On the one hand, there is the school composed of theologians and educated laymen interested in possession from a perspective of the western cultural tradition. They delve into the history of possession in the western tradition, and how this state is seen and occurs in the present day.

On the other hand, there are anthropologists who tend to study the subject matter mainly in its non-western setting. They examine and explain the utility of possession and possession cults from a utilitarian perspective—that is, the function of such cults, how possession states are induced, and other facets of the subject as applied to traditional peoples. Many seem reluctant to apply similar techniques and approaches to our western tradition, acting almost as if this type of belief system was an embarrassment, a holdover from medieval times that is an interesting historical sidelight but with little utility to present-day western concerns. The one significant exception to this rule would be Michael Harner, who has emphasized that the existence of spirits had not been conclusively disproven by science and thus should not be ignored because he suggests that scientists would be basing their dismissal on "faith," a decidedly unscientific attitude (Hriskos 1999).

The fact remains that possession states and the correlating rites of exorcism exist today in the "modern" world. The major and minor sects of Christianity retain this belief as a viable tenet of belief, with well-defined concepts about possession states and the rituals whose function it is to treat such states. Modern science and anthropological reasoning has not driven the idea from the corpus of western cosmology and thought. We would do well to heed Lewis's (1971: 28) advice in this matter: "the anthropologist's task is to discover what people believe in and relate their beliefs operationally to other aspects of their culture and society." He has neither the skills nor authority to pronounce upon the absolute 'truth' about ecstatic manifestations in different cultures. That this is true is evidenced by a number of reports regarding possession and exorcism in North America and elsewhere in the western world in the last few years:

—"Woman Admits Guilt in Exorcism Death"
(The Globe and Mail, 6/22/95)
—"French Villagers Summon Exorcist" (CNN, 10/22/98)
—"Vatican Issues First New Exorcism Ritual Since 1614" (CNN, 1/26/99)

Other examples are recounted (Ebon 1974, Martin 1976) mostly by clergy and laymen. Only a few anthropologists have discussed possession in western civilization, foremost of which are Bourguignon (1976) and Zaretsky and Leone (1974). This short essay will correlate ideas, concepts, and information from the anthropological and non-anthropological perspectives in a non-exhaustive cross-cultural comparison of these states around the world.

Definitions

Numerous definitions of possession/trance states are available. Winick (1970: 43) described possession as "an extranatural force that enters a worshiper of a deity so that he temporarily is the deity. It is the ultimate religious experience." He further defines possession in light of voluntary categories, institutionalized or semi-institutionalized forms in traditional societies where possession is seen as a desirable and even necessary adjunct to the worship of a deity.

Wallace (1959) and Walker (1972) stress the differences between possession and trance states from the perspective of individual cultures in which such phenomena occur. Wallace (1959: 59) defines trance and possession as "any native theory which explains any event of human behavior as being the result of the physical presence in the human body of an alien spirit which takes control of the hosts' executive functions, most frequently speech and control of the skeletal musculature." Refining Wallace, Walker (1972: 3) describes trance as "the scientific description of a psychological state in western terminology, whereas possession is the folk explanation, in more philosophical terms, for the same type of state." These will the operative definitions throughout this article.

The important point is that such states occur only where native folk theory recognizes these states as a viable category of reality, that has meaning and relevance in the lives of the bearers of the culture, and not where the category is imposed on the data by outside observers (Walker 1972: 3). Douglas's (1966) discussion about purity rules has general relevance here, in that possession and trance states (like defilement) are not isolated events but occur only within the context of a systematic ordering of ideas about the world and the universe. This holds true whether one is discussing these states in a traditional society or within the western cultural tradition.

In addition to a working definition, it must be realized that possession and trance states cover a variety of phenomena. In western terms, possession is a serious psychological state, an "altered state of consciousness" that causes an individual to lose touch with everyday cultural reality and enter a culturally defined religious plane of existence. These "realities" serve as ideas, beliefs, and concepts that serve to define and interpret behavior (Bourguignon 1976: 7). A person's patterns of thought, speech, and behavior may undergo such marked changes that these changes are interpreted as the presence of a second personality inhabiting the body of the possessed. As a corollary, where similar behavior is interpreted as being the result of a psychosis or mental aberration, then it must be treated as such by the anthropologist.

Such belief systems and states have been studied by anthropologists in numerous traditional cultures, and this article discusses a number of cases (see Lewis 1971 for a general overview). Almost all Christian denominations have a belief in demonic possession and exorcism. The Roman Catholic Church has a well defined belief system in possession (Roman Catholic Church 1994: 416–417, Sec. 1673) and a distinctive ritual, the *Rituale Romanum,* to drive out Satan and his demons. The Church of England has issued commission reports on the subject (Petitpierre 1972). The Greek Orthodox Church has a well defined belief in this area (Mastrantonis 1990–1996), and most Protestant denominations also follow suit (Cogan n.d.).

In a discussion regarding the psychological aspects of possession, Wallace (1959) suggests that such beliefs are the folk explanations for three types of psychosomatic behavior:

1) Obsessive ideation and compulsive action.

2) Hysterical disassociation, including multiple personalities, somnambulism, and conversion hysteria.

3) Hallucinations, defined as pseudo perception without relevant stimulation of external or internal sensory perceptors, but with such subjective vividness equal to or greater than that aroused by such stimulation.

Bourguignon refers to these states as "altered states of consciousness" that share general characteristics that can be observed and studied. These characteristics include alterations in thinking, a disturbed time sense, loss of control, a change in body image, a change in emotional expression, changes in the meaning or significance of everyday events, a sense of the ineffable, feelings of rejuvenation, and hyper suggestibility (1973: 3). In most traditional societies, these states become institutionalized religious experiences and can be seen as a means of worship or contact with the supernatural world.

In regards to the Christian world view, these same concepts can be applied. Possession by an evil spirit involves an "altered state of consciousness," alterations of personality and thought patterns, loss of control, changes in emotional expression and body image, and other accompanying symptoms (Martin 1976). Possession states are explicable cultural phenomena, even in the western context, as are the culturally acceptable rituals used to end such states of being.

Archaeological and Historical Background

There are numerous examples of archaeological, historical, and early anthropological ruminations on the subject of possession. The earliest written records, dating from approximately 6000 B.C. in Mesopotamia, already reveal a well-developed structure of thought regarding possession. This suggests that such beliefs must have existed for a significant length of time prior to the advent of writing. Surviving cuneiform tablets found in Mesopotamian cities describe a multitude of spirits waiting to attack unsuspecting humans to cause many types of illnesses through possession. There are numerous formulae of conjurations and exorcisms that were available (Oesterreich 1930: 147–148).

Egypt, Rome, and the Greek city-states left records concerning the belief in the reality of possession. Many records deal with involuntary possession states where the individual was inhabited by a spirit without the host's consent (Dodds 1951). Also recognized were voluntary possession states employed by ecclesiastical religions used in ceremonies for divining the future. This form of possession was encouraged and controlled by priests or mediums whom the gods entered. The most famous example of this was the Oracle of Apollo at Delphi, Greece, where a medium would attempt to induce possession by Apollo to acquire knowledge about the future or the hidden present (Dodds 1951: 69–70).

The ancient Hebrews also had a belief in the possibility of spirit possession, which helped form the later Christian concepts about this subject. The only detailed discussion of such states in the Tanakh (Old Testament) is found in the Book of Samuel, where God sent an evil spirit to possess and plague King Saul (I Samuel 14:14). In the New Testament, later Jewish beliefs about such states become apparent. The Apostles who recorded the Gospels noted a number of incidents where Jesus of Nazareth acted as an exorcist to cure cases of possession. Such states could only have been recognized as such if this category of cultural reality was prevalent among the Jewish populations of first century A.D. Israel. The most famous exorcism performed by Jesus occurred at Cepharnum (Mark 1: 23–27). It should be noted that most of the biblical possessions seem to have been of the involuntary demonic sort where individuals were seized by spirits against their will requiring exorcisms to free the possessed. The exceptions happen when Jesus' followers were "filled" with the Holy Spirit as part of religious devotions and as a gift from Jesus.

The early and medieval Christian Church elaborated on these early ideas. One of the four minor orders of early clergy was that of the exorcist, a function gradually absorbed by regular clergy in the Middle Ages. The medieval mind saw the world as a battleground between God and Satan, Good and Evil, and possession was one of many weapons employed by Satan (Naumann 1974: 74–76). The Middle Ages saw many recorded cases of possession outbreaks, some involving a single person, but many others involving mass outbreaks of possession in convents (Lyons 1970: 96). Priests sent to deal with such incidents often became possession victims themselves (Oesterreich 1930), probably due to autosuggestion from a combination of contact with victims and the strength of the priest's own belief in demonic possession.

During the period of European expansion, evidence was uncovered regarding possession beliefs from all parts of the globe. The Chinese had well-developed tenets about possession and exorcism, and these can possibly be traced back in history nearly 2,700 years before the Christian era (Ebon 1974: 41–42). Similar reports cropped up regarding such beliefs among peoples under the control of the various European colonial empires, stirring an interest in such phenomena among early anthropologists.

One such anthropologist, E. B. Tylor, synthesized many such reports in his book *Primitive Culture* (1958). Employing ethnographic examples from around the world, he discussed the allied concepts of possession and exorcism as being logical adaptations of "primitive" man's animistic beliefs. He wrote of the ideas that many peoples had regarding a second personality inhabiting a person (1958: 219). There are numerous other early anthropological examples, many of which can be found in Zaretsky (1966).

Much of the early discussion on possession presented the state within the context of the larger cultural institutions of a specific culture an anthropologist was examining. The most recent research on the subject attempts to deal with possession as a multi-componential phenomenon that has cross-cultural similarities. This work tends to treat possession as a subject whose causes are many and varied, taking into consideration human experiences in the biological, psychological, and cultural realms. In addition, none of this work deals with the questions as to whether there is a spiritual reality to possession, whether spirits are "real" or not. They treat with visible behaviors that can be observed and measured, leaving the "reality problem" to theologians.

The Atmosphere of Belief and "Native" Theories of Possession

In general, possession may consist of either voluntary or involuntary states. Voluntary possession is when a potential human host actively seeks possession by a god or a spirit to act as a medium or as an act of worship. Involuntary possession occurs spontaneously, without the willing consent or active participation of the afflicted individual. Both states have many of the same social, cultural, and psycho biological triggers, but the relative importance of these triggers vary between cultures and even between individuals of the same culture. Most of these factors play a role in possession states in both traditional and western society.

Walker (1972) has undertaken a detailed discussion of these trigger factors. The first and primary factor is the necessity of a prevailing "atmosphere (or environment) of belief" surrounding the event, a well-developed belief that possession can truly occur. Possession must be a strongly accepted societal reality and be widespread in its belief (Walker 1972; Bourguignon 1976: 16–18). Without this belief, such psychosomatic activities as described by Wallace (1959: 59–60) are dismissed as mental aberrations or as the result of disease as defined by western medicine.

Haiti is a fine example of this, where the peasants believe not only in God but in a host of lesser spirits called *loa*. It is "known" that during religious celebrations loa can enter individuals and "ride them like horses," using the host to speak and dispense advice to believers (Metraux 1972: 120). Children regularly witness such ceremonies and are filled with such stories outside of the ceremonies and thus are steeped in the "atmosphere of belief necessary for a belief in the reality of possession. They expect that some day such states may occur to them, laying the groundwork for the entry into possession states later in their lives" (Bourguignon 1965; 1976: 16–18).

Christian sects also create similar atmospheres, due to the fact that there is a long tradition of belief in the possibility that spirits exist, both good and evil, that can possess an individual. Among Pentecostal or extreme fundamentalist groups that interpret the Bible literally, and among charismatic Catholics, there is a phenomenon known as *glossolalia* or "speaking in tongues" where the Holy Spirit enters an individual and endows that person to speak and interpret totally unknown languages. Without such an unshakeable faith in the power of God through the Holy Spirit, there can be no *glossolalia* (Kildahl 1972: 60; Bourguignon 1976: 55–57).

Even demonic possession, seizure by spirits of evil, requires an intense belief system. Satan has been a prominent figure in Christian belief for centuries, becoming especially important in the late Middle Ages as a figure of ungovernable evil (Cohn 1970; Armstrong 1994). Many fundamentalist sects steep their believers in a "fire and brimstone" atmosphere about evil, and the Roman Catholic Church also expounds on the reality of Satan and his demonic minions (1994: 4–6–417, Sec. 1673). This leads to incidents such as that reported in Yakima, Washington, in 1976:

> The decomposed body of a 3 year old boy, David Weilbacher, was found in a fly infested room sealed with tape, a Yakima County Superior Court jury was told yesterday in the trial of his mother and four other adults charged with beating the boy to death because they believed he was possessed by the Devil ...David was beaten by adults for four months prior to his death because they believed he was inhabited by the Devil (*Newsday* November 12, 1976).

In Germany in 1976 two Catholic exorcists were investigated for their role in the death of a girl during an exorcism. The girl had built her life around extreme religious devotion, covering the walls of her room with pictures of the saints and saying daily rosaries. The faith included a firm belief in Satan and the reality of his powers (*Time* September 6, 1976), creating the necessary "atmosphere of belief" within which possession states can be expressed. This belief was probably reinforced by the exorcists' belief in the reality of the situation they viewed unfolding before them.

When the proper environment has been established, a number of different factors must be in place to trigger a possession state, and symptoms may vary from culture to culture. In many cases, the first possession may occur spontaneously without the human host seeking out the privilege. This is often heralded by a sickness that lingers or recurs. In many traditional societies, this is a sign that the afflicted individual is being selected by the spirit world to serve as a host or a medium. Eventually, with proper training, the selected can learn to control the onset of such states under specified conditions, such as in religious ceremonies or rituals (Lewis 1971).

The "call" varies from culture to culture. Shamans in Siberia and Alaska, who have the ability to be possessed voluntarily, often exhibit their select status from an early age. Among the Vogul a future shaman usually exhibit a generally nervous condition or personality and is often seized by epileptic fits that are interpreted as meetings with a god or a spirit choosing the shaman as a vessel (Eliade 1964: 15). Among the Korekore of eastern Africa, future mediums are called via a series of extended illnesses that curing rituals do not alleviate. The ailing person is sent to a medium for extended observation and, if it persists, is determined that a spirit guardian is calling the afflicted to be its spokesman (Garbett 1969: 115).

In Christianity, the only certain determinant of possession, usually demonic in nature, is the expression of a full-blown possession state, with the accompanying physical, mental, and moral manifestations created by the possessing demon. Most theologians agree that by the time the victim (or anyone else) realizes what is happening, the possession is *well* underway and has actually commenced some years prior to its manifestation. Symptoms such as convulsions and shaking, multiple personalities, and psychokinetic phenomena are normal, but one Christian denomination, the Roman Catholic Church, insists that the victim undergo a battery of physical and psychological tests to rule out disease or mental illness as the cause of the symptoms. The life history of the patient also is investigated to see if incidents in the sufferers past, suppressed by his or her mind, are responsible for the behavior (Nicola 1974: 29–32; Martin 1976: 11).

If these tests are negative, then spiritual criteria are applied as a final determinant. Most authorities agree that the following symptoms help define a true case of possession: revulsions to symbols and truths about religion; an inexplicable stench emanating from the possessed; freezing temperatures in the possessed's room; telepathic powers about purely religious and moral matters; a peculiarly unlined, completely smooth or stretched skin or an unusual distortion of the face; "possessed gravity" where the victim becomes physically immovable or those about him become weighted down by a suffocating pressure; levitation of the possessed with no visible means of support; violent smashing of furniture, opening and slamming of doors and windows untouched by human hands; superhuman strength; the eating of offal or other disgusting aberrations of normal human activities and bodily functions (Lewis 1971: 98–99; Ebon 1974: 94; Leek 1975: 90–92; Martin 1976: 13).

In both traditional societies and Christian sects, there are general culturally accepted patterns of events that occur during possession states. In traditional societies that practice shamanism, such states often begin with illnesses that linger and cannot be cured, leading to observation of the victim by a professional curer or medium. The afflicted is then taught the esoteric knowledge he/she requires to control such states and they are initiated into a possession cult. After this, the shaman or medium can bring on voluntary states of possession on demand or request. In cases of demonic possession in such societies, the seizure of the individual usually occurs quickly with the onset of a serious illness and then a full-blown possession experience. This is then followed by an exorcistic ritual to drive out the offending spirit.

In Christian sects, in cases of *glossolalia* or possession by the Holy Spirit, some patterns also occur. Such states usually occur within the throes of religious ritual and expectation, but no particular pattern of events seem to occur before or during such states. No particular sequence of thoughts needs to be followed, although there is an intense atmosphere of belief that exists, and there are no special bodily movements that are attached to the experience (Kildahl 1972: 5–6).

In cases of demonic possession, there appears to be a specific sequence of events, at least from the Roman Catholic perspective. Step one is the *Entry Point,* where the demon enters the victim upon their decision, however tenuous, to allow the demon to enter the body. Next comes a series of *Erroneous Judgements* in matters of faith and morality, influenced by the demon. This sets the stage for the *Voluntary Yielding of Control* to the demon because temporary advantages accrue to the possessed as a result of this yielding. Finally, there occurs the *State of Perfect Possession* where the demon is in total control of the individual's will so that free will no longer exists (Martin 1976: 435–436).

The most important difference between possession states in traditional societies and Christian sects, especially Roman Catholicism, is the idea of choice of free will. In many traditional societies, the initial onset of possession states seems to be totally involuntary, even in individuals who later become practitioners of voluntary possession states. Among Siberian groups such as the Buryat and Altai, potential shamans have an obligation to accept initial possession and accept their calling as shamans. The spirit world will not allow them to refuse but persistently return until the future shaman submits (Eliade 1964: 18). Among the Sidamo of Ethiopia, a spirit induced illness can be cured only if the victim agrees to feed the spirit and accept it as his/her guardian spirit (Hamer and Hamer 1966: 397). In Suriname, a person's soul may resist possession and keep out an intrusive spirit, but the rebuffed spirit returns and creates serious illness until the unfortunate individual submits to the spirit (Herskovits 1966: 266).

Modern Christian theology holds that in demonic possession a demon can never force its way inside a person; some form of consent, conscious or subconscious, must be granted, and various temptations are used by the demon to achieve this goal. These temptations are adapted to the temper and circumstances of the victim and are unleashed at the extremes of the physical and emotional extremes of the human experience, such as extremes of poverty or prosperity, the pinnacle of joy or depths of despair, or other similar circumstances. It is here that the potential victim is most off-guard and vulnerable to attack. Once inside, the demon cannot force an individual to act in a certain way. It can only cajole, convince, frighten, bully, or lie to an individual into making a series of bad choices regarding faith and morality. This prepares the person to yield control and accept demonic possession (Buck 1974: 24–25).

In a traditional setting, the situation often affects the nature of the spirit entering an individual. In

Haitian vodoun, only good spirits, the *loa*, may possess an individual. These spirits concern themselves with how people live their lives and dispense advice to believers through the medium to other believers. In other circumstances, such as possession of sick individuals by spirits of the dead, this state is feared and exorcistic rituals are required to save the person's life (Bourguignon 1976: 27).

Sometimes the spirits have a sexual identity as either male or female. In some societies, the victims are usually female and are possessed by female spirits, and victims are organized into cults to cure periodic attacks of possession. This usually happens in heavily male-dominated societies (Lewis 1971). Among the Gurage of Ethiopia, poor males regularly are afflicted by spirits that can be placated only by ceremonies where the victims are allowed to gorge themselves on food until the offending spirit is full and satisfied (Shack 1971).

Possession within Christian sects is also somewhat situationally dependent. The glossolaliast form is actively sought and usually occurs in the context of group prayer or ritual where the Holy Spirit descends on a believer with the assistance of a cult leader. The spirit has no real gender identity although it usually is symbolized as a dove. In cases of demonic possession, there appears to be no particular context that triggers such states, which usually occur over a long period of time. Demons are also usually sexless because although Satan often is depicted as a male, in reality it was originally an angel serving God, which is genderless. Also, it seems that diabolical possession is more prevalent in the west than the glossolaliast type, or at least it gets the most publicity and can strike both genders equally (Martin 1976; Ebon 1974).

An additional difference between traditional and western concepts concerns the number of spiritual entities that can enter an individual. Most traditional societies believe that a large number of entities, both good and evil, can possess an individual. Christians usually only have a "choice" between the Holy Spirit and the Devil and its associated minions, which can be quite numerous (Ebon 1974: 133). In the earthly realm, the Devil's agents are numerous and theology asserts that God allows such entities to exist as tests of the believer's love in and trust of God. This moral dimension is a concept that appears to be missing in traditional cosmologies.

Non-religious Explanations of Possession States

In the west, a number of alternative explanations serve to deal with such possession states. Western medical culture suggests a number of biological and psychological triggers that can be used to explain seeming states of possession. As previously noted, an individual entering into or within a possession state exhibits markedly abnormal patterns of motor and mental activity. An excess of sensory stimulation is aimed at an individual within a religious context where glossolalial possession is the goal. Such sensory stimulation also can be created in situations where an individual's mental faculties are overwhelmed by psychological harassment, indoctrination similar to brain washing, or physical deprivation, often all at the same time (Walker 1972).

Some specific factors that can create sensory overload and hyper-stimulation include rhythmic drumming, dancing, and singing. Often public religious ceremonies such as those held in Haiti involve an intense mental involvement in the activities and emotional atmosphere of the occasion. Both participants in ceremonies and the onlooking crowds create an atmosphere of religious fervor and expectation that the arrival of the *loa* is imminent. Drums beating out several monotonous repetitive rhythms, strenuous dancing, and loud fervent singing leads to sensory overload within the potential spirit host, heightening the possibility that he or she will soon enter a possession trance and be the *cheval* (horse) of a *loa*. (Metraux 1972; Walker 1972; Bourguignon 1976).

As far as can be determined, modern cases of demonic possession in the West lack such a context. There are no drums and no rhythmic dancing or singing, although in some cases an atmosphere of expectation and heightened emotion can be created under certain conditions. Ebon (1974) reported a case in Europe where a young girl fell under the mental and religious domination of two people who claimed to be her "holy parents." This couple led a strict apocalyptic cult that expected a momentary end of the world and they brought this girl, her sisters, and her parents under their control. The girls were indoctrinated in the "divine education" of the cult, continually harangued about sin and Satan in brainwashing sessions that often lasted all day and night. The leaders became convinced that one of the girls, Bernadette, had made a pact with the Devil and was possessed by him. The fanatic attempts by the cult to exorcize Satan and the "evil within her" led ultimately to her death and the prosecution of cult members for murder (Ebon 1974: 168–176).

In this case, the constant haranguing and questioning, the lack of sleep from all night sessions leading to sensory deprivation and overstimulation, and a heightened mental state maintained by the cult probably led to the girls' "state of possession." The proper environment was created by the religious fervor of the "holy parents" and the cult members who created the atmosphere of belief for possession. Eventually, the girl succumbed to the pressure and admitted to being possessed.

In circumstances of glossolalia, people often participate in ecstatic ceremonies involving dramatic religious conversions, spiritual healing, group participation in ritual, singing and music, and often dancing creates hyper stimulation of believers. There is a group feeling of religious emotion and fervor, leading to heightened expectations of the Holy Spirit entering true believers (Kildahl 1972: 70; Bourguignon 1976: 55–56). This is similar to practices found in many traditional cultures.

Hypnosis and autosuggestion also usually play a role in these "altered states of consciousness." Hypnosis and hypnotic states can be triggered by a variety of external stimuli. In hypnosis, the first step is to detach the subject from his or her external and internal realities to create a new set of realities. In traditional societies, rhythmic drumming, dancing, singing, and other stimuli affect the neurological and physiological functions of the body to create a detachment from reality. Then an object of transference, often a spirit or deity, is used to create a new reality for the believer. In the West, a priest or a religious leader may act as this object of transference during a religious ceremony, such as a charismatic prayer meeting or an exorcism. The victim is on the verge of a possession state and the priest/ practitioner may then devote all of his attention to the believer, staring intently into his eyes and talking in an incessant, insistent monotone while demanding the entity to manifest itself. Crowds witnessing such ceremonies also can act as such objects of transference by their unspoken yet fervent belief in the reality of the possibility of possession. This all works to detach a potential host's mind from the present reality and create a new reality where possession may occur (Walker 1972: 27–28).

In glossolalia, the group leader may act as the hypnotist or transference object for his followers. He directs activities and rituals, leads the singing and prayers, and plants the suggestion among the faithful that the Holy Spirit is on the verge of entering the group. Research suggests that glossolaliasts are more submissive, dependent, and suggestible in the presence of authority figures who assist in the triggering of such states. The glossolaliast submits to the person who first introduced him or her to this realm of belief and who then acts as the object of transference to trigger the possession event (Kildahl 1972: 40, 50).

In more formal Christian cults, such as Catholicism, Anglicanism, and others, the priest-exorcist may unwittingly give the victim of diabolical possession the appropriate hypnotic suggestions that push the afflicted into their altered state of consciousness. To be effective, the exorcist must firmly believe that there is a Devil who can possess individuals and that this evil entity is within the person confronting the priest. This attitude can serve as a form of hypnotic suggestion to a person on the verge of an altered state of consciousness, locking the belief in the reality of his/her possession firmly within the mind of the believer. He serves as the necessary object of transference that completes the person's entry into the possession state (Ebon 1974: 22–23). The priest thus has unwittingly helped to make the enemy he fears most, Satan, a reality that he must then confront until one of them is defeated.

Such factors must also enter into such cases of demonic possession that occur within fundamentalist cults, such as the one that killed Bernadette. After "brainwashing" and the entry into the altered state of consciousness, the cult leader serves as an appropriate object of transference by the strength of the belief of the leader in Satan and in his insistence that the person he is haranguing is truly possessed by the Devil.

A number of social and cultural factors must also be considered as causes in the onset of "possession states." The socialization process that creates the necessary atmosphere of belief is a necessary cause. In traditional societies where possession states are commonplace occurrences, children are raised to view this phenomenon as a normal factor in religious belief and are led to believe that such events can occur to them. The same may be said about Christian sects who have a strong belief in the reality of demonic possession and Satan's power. This lays the groundwork for future states of possession. If one is suddenly immersed in such an atmosphere of belief and is "brainwashed" into believing in this reality, as Bernadette was, this enhances the possession possibilities.

In Bali, socialization of children occurs in such a way as to encourage future states of possession. Walker (1972) suggests that Balinese culture fosters a personality structure that is susceptible to hypnotic suggestion or trance states. Children are taught nearly everything via the manipulation of their limbs by parents or teachers, not by verbal communication. The child must be "waxy limp" in the hands of an adult, with his consciousness almost in reserve. Walker suggests that this leads to a loose ego boundary, one that is fluid enough to be extended to include anything in the child's external environment, for early in life the child and teacher become extensions of one another's ego boundaries. These loose ego boundaries are a factor in inducing autohypnosis and possession states (Walker 1972: 61–63).

In many societies, certain social institutions may actually encourage and bring on possession states, either overtly in the case of possession cults, or covertly in that these institutions aim not to purposely bring on states of possession. In the latter case, possession serves as a means of aiding an individual to bypass or cope with societal pressures and demands.

In many traditional societies, possession cults play a major role in the life of the common people. These cults establish a dogma or doctrine that places spirit possession in a central role, and initiates true believers by training them in the proper manner of propitiating and controlling the spirit(s) that will occupy their bodies on occasion. In Haiti, a person experiences his first involuntary possession upon entering adolescence. Priests are consulted to identify the possessing spirit and then conduct rites of initiation into the cult associated with that spirit. This is a learning experience where the neophyte is taught the appropriate behavior to engage in when participating in the periodic rituals that bring on possession states as part of religious worship (Bourguignon 1976: 17). Similar cults exist in Bahia (Verger 1954), parts of Africa (Beattie and Middleton 1969), and on the Indian subcontinent (Jones 1976).

In some traditional societies, the social institutions and behaviors bring on possession states rather than specific cults oriented towards that end. These institutions and their association belief structure may invite the state as a means of responding to the everyday pressures of social life. The custom of men among the Ethiopian Gurage is to restrict public food consumption to an absolute minimum, despite yearly crop yields that are plentiful. At night, though, wealthier males gorge themselves on hoarded food, thus avoiding sharing food with their kin and neighbors, which is considered a cultural obligation. The wealthy also conduct monthly ritual feasts that are socially acceptable outlets for hunger gratification (Shack 1971: 32–33).

Poor males have no such outlets because they lack food to both hoard and participate in the public feasts of the wealthy. Possession appears to be the socially acceptable manner to satisfy their hunger. A possessed male has curing rituals run for him, and if those fail, the "wizard" orders that an exorcistic ritual be run. A portion of the ritual requires the victim to eat until he is satiated, thereby satiating the occupying spirit. Such states can reoccur and necessitate the repetition of the exorcistic ritual (Shack 1971: 34–37). Thus two

societal institutions, food deprivation and possession trances, interact so one alleviates the other.

Institutionalized male superiority also can be a trigger mechanism for possession or trance states among women as oblique "strategies of aggression" to be used against men. I discuss such events and their onset when I discuss the social value of possession states.

In the west, Pentecostal groups that encourage possession by the Holy Spirit are societal institutions that allow believers to cope with the everyday pressures of life. Personal pressures create a turn to glossolalia states: anxiety over a life crisis; feelings of worthlessness; a desire to regress to childhood and place yourself in the stronger, surer hands of group leaders or of the Holy Spirit; and a general low level of emotional stability (Kildahl 1972: 57–63). Groups such as Pentacostalists provide a reasonably complex integrated pattern of behavior to meet basic social needs and desires and to exert social control over their followers, including a ritual designed to deal with the pressures of everyday life (possession by the Holy Spirit) (Winick 1970: 287–288).

In the belief in Satan and his powers, other Christian denominations become institutions that can encourage the onset of possession, both glossolalial and demonic, that are most visibly manifest in possession states and exorcism rituals. The sincere belief in the Devil and his powers can goad individuals desirous of attention, such as the poor, women who feel victimized or oppressed (such as nuns in medieval times), those suffering from real or imagined social injustices, and the socially unimportant to become "possessed" and to undergo exorcisms in search of the attention and social affect they crave and need. The Roman Catholic Church may have been the unwitting creator of the epidemic of possession that swept Europe from the Dark Ages to the middle of the Renaissance that affected thousands, especially nuns in convents under strict male control and domination (Nicola 1974: 141–143).

In modern times, fundamentalist groups like those led by the previously mentioned "holy parents" have an extreme emphasis on strict biblical interpretation, the reality of Satan and demonic possession, a "fire and brimstone" approach to ideas of good and evil, and thus encourage, explicitly or tacitly, possession states. These institutions, though not formally structured and often of short duration, organize and control the lives and worlds of their followers and thus regulate their followers' lives and fulfill their need for structure and social affect. They help create a community that creates a social reality that includes rejection of the world as the "realm of Satan." They see themselves under siege by Satan and his minions and regard demonic possession states as attempts by the Devil to destroy the community of "true believers." The belief in an essentially evil world may actually encourage possession states as symbols of the reality of the "truth" of the belief system of the group.

Possession and the Individual

Although patently obvious, the social circumstances and individual personality of the possessed are primary factors in the onset of possession states. The individual is at least partly responsible for the onset of such states due to his/her reactions to societal pressures and the strains of everyday life. In many traditional societies, the history and the institutions of possession cults can combine with the life circumstances of an individual to bring on altered states of consciousness. First occurrences of possession in Haiti are often the result of life circumstances that cause tension and stress to build up, such as a change in social status or responsibilities, or the death of a family member (Walker 1972: 81). Among Somali women, possession appears to be closely correlated with societal situations that create conflict, competition, rivalry, or tension within the family, especially in regard to members of their own gender. Somali are polygynous, allowing men to have more than one wife at a time, and often the first wife of a man feels that her status and competence as a wife is being threatened by her husband's desire to take a second wife. It may be that an attack of spirit possession is the senior wife's way of reaffirming her status and prestige: the cure for such attacks requires luxurious feminine gifts be presented to the victim to obviate the condition (Wilson 1967: 366, 370). Although not specifically studied, an assumption can be made that in monogamous marriages or marriages where the senior wife feels secure in her status that there are few or no cases of possession.

In Christian denominations, personal life crises or changes in social status may trigger possession states. Such circumstances among glossolaliasts have been recounted above. Freud (1959; original 1923) analyzed a case of diabolical possession in the seventeenth century and what he concluded in this case is still pertinent in examining current occurrences of demonic possession and their onset. In 1677, a painter named Christoph Haitzmann came to a priest for help in being released from a pact with the Devil he had made many years ago. He said that he bound himself to the Devil as a son for nine years, and promised

himself totally to the Devil after his death. This "pact" was entered into shortly following the death of Haitzmann's father, a period in which he sank into a deep melancholia and could not work. Freud suggested that "the train of thought motivating this pact seems to be as follows: owing to my father's death I am despondent and can no longer work; if I can but get a father substitute I shall be able to regain all that I have lost" (1959: 446). Freud concludes that the individual circumstances of Haitzmann and his reaction to them are what brought on the supposed pact with and possession by the Devil. Freud was analyzing this case from the twentieth century psychoanalytical perspective, but did not necessarily take into careful consideration the atmosphere of belief within the culture that could have influenced Haitzmann in his belief in the reality of this satanic pact he had entered into. However, this sort of analysis can very likely be fruitfully applied to most cases of possession in both the western world and traditional societies of the present time.

The individual is also quite important in determining how the possessing spirit will act and what sort of personality it will evidence. In most traditional societies, each spirit or deity has unique personality and behavioral characteristics that they exhibit. As with most social constructs, these characteristics are sufficiently flexible enough to permit variations according to the personality of the host body. The personality of the host appears to help determine the traits and speech patterns of the spirit, giving the afflicted flexibility to express their hidden desires, tensions, or hatreds in a socially acceptable manner. Belo (1960: 1) suggests that the possession trance sets into action "behavior springing from a deeper level of the personality." Yap (1960) argues that possession or trance states are problem solving processes that result in the dramatization of a certain part of the ego or self, "that part being constituted by forced and urgent identification with another personality believed to be transcendent in nature. The nature of the possessing personality can be psychologically understood in the light of the subject's own personality needs; his life situation, the personality characteristics . . . of the possessing agent; and the subject's cultural background. . . ."(Yap 1960: 125).

It seems to be more difficult to apply this generalization to practitioners of glossolalia or possession by the Holy Spirit. They believe in possession by one transcendent being who is part of a triune god, and not in possession by a myriad of individual spiritual entities or personalities. These people may develop more or less individualized patterns of glossolalia or motor responses, but little else to mark off their uniqueness. They act within a group setting where a group leader is there to conduct prayers and to usher in the possession state, but there is little variation, it appears, in personality manifestations (Bourguignon 1976: 57).

In demonic possession in the west there appears to be an overall generalized behavioral pattern but in terms of personality there are any number of personalities and identities that can be expressed. Repressed fears and desires, resentments and frustrations can cause an individual to manifest all of their culture's outward symptoms of possession in order to draw attention to themselves and their life circumstances. Lyons talks about just such circumstances when discussing the psychological causes of satanic possession in the Salem colony and elsewhere in America:

> The psychological affliction remained the same. Firstly it provided a means of throwing off authority for, once possessed, a man is no longer responsible for his actions, all of his actions being perpetrated by the demonic invader. Secondly it provided a method of projecting any doubts or guilt feelings held by the tormented person to the outside. Like schizophrenia, it enabled a man to split his own personality, attributing those elements of his personality which he found undesirable or of which he was ashamed to someone on the outside; that part of himself is externalized and takes the shape of the tormentor, the demon. Taking these facts into consideration, it is possible to conclude that possession would be most likely to occur in those areas where authority, manifested in overpowering social structure or system of values, was the greatest and the emotional safety valves the least (1970: 96).

This is especially true of fundamentalist Christian sects that can create such an overpowering system of values and controls with few safety valves save that of possession.

Bourguignon (1976: 53) attributes such attacks as being partially due to disassociated or split off parts of the personality that the conscious mind represses or disowns. Ebon (1974: 220) calls possession "a cry for help; call it a ritualized tantrum if you like. At any rate the patient calls attention to himself for a variety of social, emotional, or even economic reasons. He, or more frequently she, dramatizes a cry for help. . ." The importance of the individual in possession manifestations cannot be overemphasized, for it is he or she who internalizes the cultural beliefs and expectations regarding this phenomenon, helps create or participates in the external conditioning necessary to trigger the onset of such states, and then displays the manifestations of this cultural belief and behavioral system within an appropriate context. Many of the reasons for these states are found deep within the individual mind, as conditioned and influenced by cultural belief systems.

The Social Value of Possession

Such states of being provide a number of benefits to the society within which possession beliefs and possession states are found. One of the more mundane factors in traditional society is the entertainment factor derived from public displays of possession and exorcism rituals. Public ceremonialism relieves the day to day routine of life, which often is oppressively monotonous, often within the midst of grinding poverty. Possessed individuals and the public ceremonies performed to cure them provide a break from this routine and give people a chance to participate in a dramatic, uplifting, religious activity and have fun at the same time. Spectators are entertained by the activities of the possessed individual, the priests or exorcists, and by the rituals used to bring such states of being to an end (Walker 1972: 97).

In the Middle Ages in Europe, exorcisms were often conducted in public, with crowds surrounding the principal actors in the drama, the priest-exorcist and the victim. The public spectacle concerning the struggle between good and evil, presented in such a concrete fashion, must have been of great interest to the local populace. Even today, in modified form, possession supplies public entertainment, albeit on the silver screen or the television screen. People still love to be frightened in a controlled safe setting, despite the general drop-off in belief in the reality of possession, as the success of such movies as *The Exorcist* and others of the genre can testify to.

Possession and possession cults also contribute to social solidarity and stability by focusing on areas of stress and strain in societal structure that threatens the status quo (Walker 1972: 101; see also Shapiro 1998 for Brazilian possession cults; Lewis 1986). Among the Watarto of Kenya, married women are often struck by possession states, called *saka*, which are characterized by compulsive body movements. This society is heavily male dominated, women have little structural power, and are almost totally dependent on men, first their fathers and later their husbands. They are barred from sharing in their father's estates, they cannot participate in trade or wage labor, and they have little effective say in how their lives are to be handled. This is particularly true when family funds are allocated for items considered to be prestigious or important (Harris

1971: 1050–1052). Women afflicted with *saka* exhibit an inordinate desire for material goods or experiences normally within the male domain; owning cattle, participating in wage labor, and other male activities. The cure for *saka* is to give women the goods they desire and/or to have them participate in a public curing dance. Harris suggests that this dance is a symbolic public presentation of societal conflicts between men and women. He states, "In this way, participating in ritual indicates agreement on the forms of social relationships . . . the *saka* attack allows a roundabout acknowledgment of conflict, but in the saka dance the theme is peace, dignity, and festivity" (Harris 1971: 1064). The saka attacks and the public dance appear to reaffirm the status quo while allowing women the opportunity to publicly express their desires and frustrations.

In a smaller way, possession cults in the west perform similar duties, but not in a societal wide manner. They may serve to express frustration with society for a small segment of the population, the true believer, but mass movements seem to have usurped this function for most individuals in the west, particularly in the United States. Political parties, special interest groups, and single-cause groups serve the function of protesting the status quo in a public forum, allowing the disaffected a voice in the larger society.

Possession cults and their rituals focus on the group and its needs, define reality for the group, and provide the means by which this reality is to be dealt with (Walker 1972: 98). The cult enlists the aid of the supernatural world in solving group problems and meeting group needs. The gods or spirits can give advice on matters of importance and can give the group confidence that, in serious crises, the group has avenues and definite courses of action it can pursue to influence the outcome of events, mainly by turning to the supernatural for assistance. They are not helpless in the face of turbulent times and therefore can deal successfully with the world.

Some cults use possession states as a way to define the reality of their belief systems. By publicly displaying the presence of the possessed and the ability of the cult to assist the afflicted, such cults "prove" the reality of their cosmology by means not normally available. The Roman Catholic Church (1994) requires the afflicted individual to undergo a battery of physical and psychological tests to rule out medical causes to the behavior and activity of the victim of demonic possession. It then applies spiritual criteria as a final form or proof of the "reality" of the possession state. Then the efficacy of the *Rituale Romanum* in driving out the possessing entities corroborates the existence of God as defined by the Roman Catholic Church

specifically, and Christianity in general. In this manner, the Roman Catholic Church "proves" the reality of its cosmological and theological structure of reality by employing both modern science and age old spiritual practices. The possession state and the exorcism demonstrates that where medical science has failed to alleviate the condition, the power of Jesus Christ has provided the victim with relief and succor from the forces of evil. Such proof allows the church to be forward looking while still confirming the ancient truths taught for two millennia.

Glossolaliast cults also employ possession states in a similar manner. They become a group set apart from the everyday world and united by commonly experienced phenomenon. They generally suffer rejection, or at least suspicion, from larger mainstream Christian sects and society at large. This aids in increasing the cohesiveness of the association of these individuals (Kildahl 1972: 70). The existence of possession by the Holy Spirit supports the theological beliefs of the followers and leaders of such groups.

Such an occurrence must also buttress the solidarity of fundamentalist and/or millenarian groups with a belief in demonic possession. In the case of the unfortunate Bernadette recounted earlier, the "holy parents" of the "family" to which Bernadette belonged were convinced of the reality of her demonic possession and convinced Bernadette of this reality sufficiently enough to extract a "confession" from her. This must have enhanced the stature of the leaders and increased the faith of the followers, for ferreting out the Devil's handiwork would have been seen as proof of the special status of the leaders. This belief must have been so strong that the followers obeyed the orders of the leaders without hesitation or questioning, for it resulted in the death of the unfortunate Bernadette. I suspect that even the death may have seemed proper to the followers, as a confirmation of the terrible strength of the evil inhabiting the girl. The solidarity of the group was probably enhanced, at least temporarily, but at a terrible price.

Conclusion

When a cultural phenomenon of this magnitude, cross-cultural extent, and time depth is being examined, firm conclusions are difficult to come by. The subject of possession and exorcism is a vast and difficult one, bringing into play psychological, biological, cultural, and theological viewpoints in an attempt to understand the whys and wherefores of this behavior.

There are both differences and similarities in the way possession states are viewed by different societies, and the various factors that trigger such states vary from culture to culture and person to person. One final point to be considered is this: Why has there been a marked reduction in incidents of possession in western culture since their heyday in the Middle Ages? One answer is found in the nature of western epistemological thinking. The culture of the west has become much more secularized and scientifically oriented in the last 300 to 400 years. We can concoct and examine numerous scientific explanations of phenomena that could once be explained only in terms of the cosmology of good and evil within the western Judeo-Christian context. Religion, particularly the various denominations of Christianity, no longer dominates the thinking of the majority of people in the west in the same manner as it once did. Even the veracity of the basic tenets of Christianity are under attack by critics and researchers dealing with the origins and basic belief systems of this world religion. It is hard for many to believe that, in this "scientific" day and age, that belief in the Devil and demonic possession still exists in our world.

Possession states are rare in the western context because more adequate paradigms and explanations have been developed that explain the onset of possession states more completely and accurately than did previous "native" explanations about it. Seizures that were once the hallmark of this state can now be explained as epileptic fits or the results of Tourette's Syndrome or Parkinson's Disease. Manifestations of other personalities can be explained by resorting to a diagnosis of schizophrenia or other psychological causes (Allison 1998, n.d.). Even mainstream denominations such as the Catholic Church insist that medical or psychological causes be ruled out prior to even considering the alternative explanation of demonic possession (Mahoney n.d.).

Perhaps more importantly, Ebon (1974) has suggested that western culture has developed its own, more subtle form of possession that has in part replaced the traditional form. They may not be as dramatic but are just as effective. He suggests that the potential of "mass man" to be possessed by an idea, to be a "true believer" in a cause and get caught up in a "we versus they" syndrome is perhaps the most pervasive form of possession active in today's world. It is certainly the form most acceptable to modern societies, and is even considered highly valuable and extremely desirable by those holding the reins of power (Ebon 1974: 233). Anyone who was present during the Cuban Missile Crisis of the 1960s, or lived through the "Cold War" until its demise in 1989 could testify to the existence of this phenomenon. The same could be suggested as partial explanations for the Gulf War, the "ethnic cleansing" in Bosnia and Kosovo, the gulags of the Soviet Union, or the Holocaust. Caught up in such situations, individuals do not have to take responsibility for their actions, only believe what the leaders tell them and follow orders, and all personal ethical and moral responsibility falls by the wayside. This is similar in a mass way to the abdication of personal responsibility within individual possession states, whether found in traditional societies or pockets of western culture. In fact, suggests Ebon, if Satan does exist "a good case can be made that he hasn't really bothered possessing individuals for some time, finding a much more receptive vessel in mass man, whether in a lynch mob, a military or civilian crowd set upon massacre, the rioters, the self-degraders who by means of word, drug, or drum, turns into a thousand-footed super animal" (Ebon 1974: 233).

The discomforting question we must ask ourselves in the west is this: Are we that much different from our brethren in traditional societies? Have we traded individual possession states and personal encounters with the spirit world, particularly with evil entities, for mass possession and evil on an industrialized scale and in an impersonal form? And if the answer is yes, does this make us different only in form and not functioning of these states of being? If anthropology truly studies man in all times and in all places then these are questions we must face in order to do our jobs as students of humanity correctly.

References

———. 1949. *The Holy Bible.* Cleveland: World Publishing Company.

———. 1976. A Phenomenon of Fear. *Time,* Vol. 109, No. 34. September 6.

———. 1976. Exorcists on Trial in Death. Newsday, Vol. 37, No. 60.

———. 1995. Woman Admits Guilt in Exorcism Death. *The Globe and Mail,* June 22. http://wchat.on.ca/humanist/rlv03.htm

Allison, Ralph B.N.d. "If in Doubt, Cast It Out? The Evolution of a Belief System Regarding Possession and Exorcism." www.disassociation.com/index/unpublished/CastItOut.txt.

———. 1998. Multiple Personality Disorder, Disassociative Identity Disorder, and Internalized Imaginary Companions. *Hypnos* 25: 125–133.

Armstrong, Karen. 1994. *A History of God.* New York: Alfred A. Knopf

Beattie, John, and John Middleton. 1969. *Spirit Mediumship and Society in Africa*. New York: Africana Publishing Company.

Belo, Jane. 1960. *Trance in Bali*. New York: Columbia University Press.

Bourguignon, Erika. 1965. "The Self, the Behavioral Environment, and the Theory of Spirit Possession." In *Context and Meaning in Cultural Anthropology*, edited by Melford E. Spiro, pp. 39–60. New York: The Free Press.

———. 1973. "A Framework for the Comparative Study of Altered States of Consciousness." In: *Religion, Altered States of Consciousness, and Social Change*, Erika Bourguignon, ed. pp. 1–30. Columbus: Ohio State University Press.

———. 1976. *Possession*. San Francisco: Chandler and Sharp Publishers, Incorporated.

Buck, Charles. 1974. "Exorcism and the Bible." In: *Exorcism through the Ages*, St. Elmo Naumann, Jr., ed. pp. 21–30. New York: Philosophical Library.

Cohn, Norman. 1970. *The Pursuit of the Millennium*. New York: Oxford University Press.

CNN. 1998. French Villagers Summon Exorcist. CNN.com, October 22, 1998. WWW.CNN.Com/WORLD/europe/9810/22.france.devil.church/

———. 1999. *Vatican Issues First New Exorcism Ritual Since 1614*. CNN.Com, January 26, 1999.WWW.CNN.com/WORLD/europe/9901/26/exorcism/

Cogan, J. F.N.d. *Handbook about Demonic Possession for Human Service Workers*. WWW.gelservices.com/hs.html.

Dodds, E. R. 1951. *The Greeks and the Irrational*. Berkeley: The University of California Press.

Douglas, Mary. 1966. *Purity and Danger: An Analysis of Concepts of Pollution and Taboo*. Harmondsworth: Penguin Books.

Ebon, Martin. 1974. *The Devil's Bride*. New York: Harper and Rowe Publishers.

Eliade, Mercea. 1964. *Shamanism: Archaic Techniques of Ecstasy*. New York: Pantheon Books.

Freud, Sigmund. 1959. "A Neurosis of Demoniacal Possession in the Seventeenth Century." In: *Sigmund Freud: Collected Papers*, Vol. 4: 436–472. Edited by Ernest Jones. New York: Basic Books.

Garbett, G. Kingsly. 1969. "Spirit Mediums as Mediators in Valley Korekore Society." In: *Spirit Mediumship in Africa*, John Beattie and John Middleton, eds. pp. 104–127. New York: Africana Publishing Company.

Hamer, John, and Irene Hamer. 1966. "Spirit Possession and its Socio-Psychological Implications among the Sidamo of Southwest Ethiopia." *Ethnology* 5: 392–407.

Herskovits, Melville. 1966. *The New World Negro*. Bloomington: Indiana University Press.

Hriskos, C. 1999. "Review of Spirit Hypothesis Panel in the Society for the Anthropology of Consciousness Section." *Anthropology Newsletter* 40: 52.

Jones, Rex. 1976. "Spirit Possession and Society in Nepal." In: *Spirit Possession in the Nepal Himalayas*, John T. Hitchcock and Rex Jones, eds. pp. 1–11. Warminster: Axis and Philps Limited.

Kildahl, John P. 1972. *The Psychology of Speaking in Tongues*. New York: Harper and Rowe Publishers.

Leek, Sybil. 1975. *Driving Out Devils: An Exorcist's Handbook*. New York: G.P. Putnam's Sons.

Lewis, I. M. 1971. *Ecstatic Religions*. Baltimore: Penguin Books Incorporated.

———. 1986. "Religion." In: *Context: Cults and Charisma*. Cambridge: Cambridge University Press.

Lyons, Arthur. 1970. *The Second Coming: Satanism in America*. New York: Dodd, Mead, and Company.

Martin, Malachi. 1976. *Hostage to the Devil*. New York: Thomas Y. Crowell Company.

Mastrantonis, Reverend George. 1990–1996. "Exorcism. Greek Orthodox Diocese of America." www.goarch.org/access/orthodox faithexorcism.html.

Metraux, Alfred. 1972. *Voodoo in Haiti*, translated by Hugo Charteris. New York: Schocken Books.

Naumann Jr., St. Elmo. 1974. "Exorcism and Satanism in Medieval Germany." In: *Exorcism Through the Ages*, St. Elmo Naumann, Jr., ed. pp. 73–86. New York: Philosophical Library.

Nicola, Reverend John T. 1974. *Diabolical Possession and Exorcism*. Rockford: Tam Books and Publishers, Incorporated.

Oesterreich, T. K. 1930. *Possession, Demoniacal and Other, among Primitive Races, in Antiquity, The Middle Ages, and Modern Times*. New York: Richard R. Smith, Incorporated.

Petitpierre, Father Robert. 1972. *Exorcism: The Report of a Commission Convened by the Bishop of Exeter*. New York: Popular Library.

Roman Catholic Church. 1994. *Catechism of the Catholic Church*. Liguori: Liguori Publications.

Shack, William A. 1971. "Hunger, Anxiety, and Ritual: Deprivation and Spirit Possession among the Gurage of Ethiopia." *Man* 6: 30–43.

Shapiro, Dolores J. 1998. "Blood, Oil, Honey, and Water: Symbolism in Spirit Possession Sects in Northeastern Brazil." In: *Religion In Culture and Society*, John R. Bowen, ed. pp. 94–116. Needham Heights: Allyn & Bacon.

Tylor, E. B. 1958. *Religion in Primitive Culture: Part II of Primitive Culture*. New York: Harper and Brothers Publishers.

Verger, Pierre. 1954. Role Joue Par L'Etat d'Hebetude aux Cours de L'Initiation des Novices aux Cultes des Orisha et Vodun. *Bulletin de L'Institute Fondamental d'Afrique Noire*. Serie B, No. 16: 322–340.

Walker, Sheila. 1972. *Ceremonial Spirit Possession in Africa and Afro-America*. Leiden: E. J. Drill.

Wallace, A.F.C. 1959. "Cultural Determinants of Responses to Hallucinatory Experiences." *AMA Archives of General Psychiatry*, No. 1.

Wilson, Peter J. 1967. "Status Ambiguity and Spirit Possession." *Man* 2: 366–378.

Winick, Charles. 1970. *Dictionary of Anthropology*. New York: Philosophical Library.

Yap, P. M. 1960. "The Possession Syndrome: A Comparison of Hong Kong and French Findings." *Journal of Mental Science* 106 (44): 114–137.

Zaretsky, Irvin I. 1966. *Bibliography of Spirit Possession and Spirit Mediumship*. Evanston: Northwestern University Press.

Zaretsky, Irvin I. and Mark P. Leone. 1974. *Religious Movements in Contemporary America*. Princeton: Princeton University Press.

"Possession States Across the World: An Anthropological Approach"

Kevin Rafferty

1) What are the differences between "native" theories of possession and western explanations for the same phenomenon?

2) What is an "altered state of consciousness" from a western perspective, and what conditions can trigger one?

3) How can possession beliefs be used to enhance social solidarity and group cohesion?

4) What is the role of the individual and his/her enculturation within a society in the onset of possession states?

5) What would the Christian "native explanation" for possession states be, and what forms do such states take?

6) Give an example of a traditional possession cult from the article—where is it located, what can trigger possession in the believer in the cult, and what social and cultural purpose does that cult serve within that society?

THE PLACE WHERE VODUN WAS BORN

Suzanne Preston Blier

In Benin, West Africa, Vodun permeates life. People come into the world through the auspices of a deity and live out their lives in a world filled with deities who connect the natural and material worlds to the worlds of the living and the dead. They inhabit the trees, the earth, the stones. Ask and you'll be told that not everything has a god, but listen long enough and you'll realize that the gods are everywhere. You couldn't begin to count the Vodun gods. There may be 2,000, there may be 200,000. Gu, the god of iron, serves as the god of cars. But the Gu dwelling in your car would be different from the one dwelling in mine.

The gods are involved in everyday life: They settle arguments and take offerings to allay illness, relieve curses, or bring luck. Legba, the messenger god, is enshrined in front of every house. The various offerings to the gods must be mediated through this youngest of them. Take a look at a representation of Legba in a diviner's home; the god may be wearing sunglasses, an appropriate accessory because Legba is the trickster god, always inscrutable. He may deliver the message; he may not.

Vodun recognizes the complex layering of phenomena. A characteristic of every shrine—anything from a refined piece of sculpture to a simple earthern mound—is that the material of its construction becomes a metaphor for the connectedness of things. Wet earth is mixed with plant leaves, with colored beads, with bits of metal, with patches of cloth, with the blood of animals; all the components are pulverized so that they are enmeshed within the whole to become a symbol of the deity's identity and character.

Rooted in ancient beliefs, Vodun (or Voudou, as it is known in the Americas) was born in what is now southern Benin and nearby Togo, on the Gulf of Guinea. Lying on the coastal route between rain forest and savanna, the region has been a crossroads of the Fon, Ewe, and Gun cultures, among others. Beginning in the fifteenth century, the variegated nature of Vodun was further intensified as a result of the European slave trade, when captives from many West African cultures passed through the region on their way to the slave ships.

This part of West Africa was ruled by successive kingdoms, including Allada and, beginning in about 1700, Dahomey. The Dahomey king, Guezo, who reigned from 1818 to 1858, demonstrated the inclusiveness of Dahomey culture when he ordered a shipment of Vodun sculptures from Europe. What he acquired were actually representations of Roman Catholic saints—Saint Roche, Saint Laurent, and others. These ultimately served as models for some of the most visually powerful royal Vodun sculptures. Another example of Vodun's adaptable iconography is the cult of Mami-Wata, familiar to people all along the coast of West Africa. The cult had its origins in a poster portraying a touring circus performer from Hamburg who advertised herself as an Indian snake dancer. The poster appeared all over West Africa, and her image became a prominent and powerful symbol for women, representing a "mother of the waters," who could summon health and well-being.

The term *vodun* first appeared in print in 1658 in the *Doctrina Christiana,* a work by the ambassador of the king of Allada to the court of Spain. In this work, *vodun* generally is translated as "god" or "sacred." Although the puzzle over the word's etymology remains unresolved, two diviners I met during my time in Benin both told me that *vo* means "to rest" and *dun,* "to draw water." They explained that "in this life, there is a pool that is below, and one draws from it," but "one should rest before drawing." For devotees, the essence of Vodun resides in ideas of calmness and composure. When women go to the spring or river to draw the daily water, they rest for a moment on the bank before filling their containers.

Vodun teaches that one must take time to sit quietly rather than rush through life. One should accept the flow of events. Even at funerals, relatives are chastised if they cry: Outward signs of emotion are taken to be evidence of frailty and loss of control. Only during religious possession and war is it considered appropriate to display emotion.

The rites of Vodun I observed were emotional experiences designed to provoke responses from the gods. Just as an amalgam of materials is used to represent the external world in a Vodun sculpture, so in religious practice the natural world of things—herbs, wine, perfumes, decoctions of leaves or bark, pastes of blood and ashes, each thing a dwelling place of gods—is brought to bear upon the spiritual realm.

The resultant ritual can be as mundane as dropping a bit of food on the ground before one eats as an offering to the ancestors, or it can be as elaborate as coating the body with pastes designed to turn the worshiper into a living Vodun sculpture. It can be as heated and intense as dancing to the driving beat of a drum in order to induce a hypnotic trance.

In one ritual I observed outside a temple of Sagbata—the god of the earth, whirlwinds, and disease—a devotee in a trance spun around and around, his acrobatic wheeling as beautiful to watch as it was difficult to perform. Another exuberant dancer balanced two straight-backed chairs precariously on his arms while moving his body into a series of angled positions. More dancers followed, in round-robin fashion, each devotee displaying the special acrobatic talent that the god Sagbata had accorded him. The emotionless faces and fixed, seemingly unseeing eyes of the trance dancers contrasted with their taut-muscled backs and limbs, glistening with sweat.

The dances both honored the gods and were believed to be brought on by them. Because this was a sacred event, the audience of family members, together with other villagers and cult members, watched spellbound, in complete silence, neither clapping nor offering verbal encouragement or praise.

After an hour, when each dancer had appeared several times, the drum beats ceased and the devotees of Sagbata went back inside the temple. With the departure of the dancers, the other villagers returned to their daily activities, knowing that they had once more been blessed by an appearance of the gods.

"THE PLACE WHERE VODUN WAS BORN"

Suzanne Preston Blier

1) Why does the author suggest that Vodun originated in western Africa? What evidence does she give?

2) Discuss the number and the variety of Vodun gods and spirits.

3) Why does Blier say that Vodun's iconography is extremely adaptable?

4) What does the article say about the general teachings of Vodun?

SECTION SEVEN

Symbolic Expression

THE CREATION OF THE UNIVERSE

Steven H. Gale

For centuries, Ife was the principal city of the Yoruba people. Located in the southwest corner of Nigeria, it was also a sacred city. "The Creation of the Universe" describes how the universe, life, and human beings were created.

At the beginning of time, the universe consisted only of the sky, the water, and marshland. Olorun, the most powerful and wisest of the gods, was the creator of the sun and the ruler of the sky. Olokun was the ruler of the waters and the marshes. Even though her kingdom contained no plants, animals, or human beings, Olokun was happy with it. Unfortunately, Obatala, one of Olorun's favorites, was not pleased.

"The world would certainly be more interesting if living things inhabited it," he said to Olorun. "What can we do so that Olokun's kingdom can be inhabited? What she needs is mountains, forests, and fields."

"Well," Olorun answered, "I agree that mountains, forests, and fields would be better than water alone, but how would it be created?"

"With your permission, I will create the solid land."

Olorun gladly gave Obatala permission to create the solid land. Obatala immediately went to see Orunmila, Olorun's oldest son, a god with the gift of being able to foresee the future.

"Olorun has given me permission to create solid land where now only water and marshland exist," he said to Orunmila. "Will you teach me how to do this so that I can then populate the world with living things?"

"I will be happy to, Obatala. You must first obtain a golden chain that is long enough to reach from the sky to the water. You must then take a snail's shell and fill it with sand. Next you must place the snail's shell, a white hen, a black cat, and a palm nut in a bag. When you have done this, you must carry them down to the marshland by way of the chain."

Obatala immediately went to find the goldsmith. The goldsmith agreed to make such a chain, but he did not have enough gold on hand to complete the task. So, Obatala went to all of the gods and asked them for the gold that they possessed so that the chain could be made. Because the gods agreed that Obatala's project was a worthy one, they gave him their golden necklaces, bracelets, and rings. Still, according to the goldsmith, Obatala had not collected enough gold to make a chain of sufficient length to reach from the sky to the water. He returned to the goldsmith anyway, and he asked the smith to fashion a chain as long as possible with what gold they had and to put a hook at the end of it.

When the chain was readied, Obatala and Orunmila hooked one end of it to the edge of the sky, and Orunmila gave Obatala the sand-filled snail shell, the white hen, the black cat, and the palm nut to put into a bag, which he slung over his shoulder. Obatala then began to climb down the golden chain.

When he had climbed down about half the length of the chain, Obatala realized that he was leaving the world of light and entering the world of twilight. Still he continued to climb down. When he reached the end of the chain, he was still far above the ocean, much too high to jump safely.

As he was wondering what to do, he heard Orunmila's voice call out from above. "Obatala," he said, "use the sand in your snail shell."

Obatala did as Orunmila dictated. He pulled the snail shell out of his bag and poured the sand into the water.

"Now free the white hen."

Obatala again obeyed Orunmila's command. The white hen fluttered down to land upon the sandy waters. She immediately began to scratch at the sand, scattering it far and wide. Wherever the grains of sand landed, dry land was created, the largest piles becoming hills.

Seeing the dry land grow high beneath him, Obatala let go of the golden chain and fell the short distance to the earth. The place where he landed he named Ife. He looked around and saw that the ground stretched as far as the horizon in every direction that he could see, but it was still barren.

Now Obatala dug a hole in the ground and buried the palm nut. He had barely shoveled the last handful of dirt over the nut when a palm tree began growing out of the buried nut. The tree quickly reached its full height and grew more palm nuts, which dropped upon the land and grew into mature trees before his eyes. Obatala took the bark from the trees and built a house. He gathered palm leaves and made a thatched roof for the house. When he went inside his new house, Obatala took the black cat out of the bag, and he settled down with the cat as his companion.

After some time, Olorun wondered how Obatala was doing, so he asked one of his servants, Chameleon, to go down the golden chain to visit Obatala. When the Chameleon saw Obatala, he said, "Olorun, the ruler of the sky, has asked me to find out how you are doing."

"Tell Olorun that the land and vegetation that I created are quite nice, but it is always twilight here and I miss the brightness of the sky world."

The Chameleon returned to Olorun and told him what Obatala had said. Olorun was so pleased with Obatala's effort that he said, "I will create the sun." He then did just that, and every day the sun's light and warmth poured down upon Obatala and his creations.

A great deal more time passed, and Obatala found that he was still not satisfied. "As much as I love my black cat," he said, "I think that I need another kind of companionship. Perhaps it will be good for me to populate this world with creatures more like myself."

Obatala set about to accomplish this task. He began digging in the soil, and he gathered together bits and pieces of clay that stuck together. Taking this clay, Obatala created small figures shaped like himself. This endeavor proved to be very tiring, and soon Obatala decided to take the juice from the palm trees to make palm wine. As tired as he was, he drank more of the wine than he realized, and soon he was drunk.

When Obatala began making the clay figures again, the effects of the wine made him a little clumsy. As a result, the figures that he created were not as well made as those that he had fashioned earlier. Some of the new figures had arms that were too short or legs of uneven length or a curved back, although Obatala's senses were so dulled from the drink that he did not notice that these figures were not perfect.

After he had created a large number of clay figures, Obatala called up to Olorun: "Olorun, I have created clay figures to populate my world and be companions to me, but they are devoid of life. Of all of the gods, you are the only one who can bestow life. I ask that you do this so that I may spend the rest of my life with companions who are like me."

Once more Olorun was pleased to do what Obatala asked. The sky god breathed life into the clay figures, which became living human beings. As soon as the figures were endowed with life, they saw Obatala's hut, and they began to build homes for themselves all around it. Thus was the first Yoruba village created. That village was called Ife, and it still exists today.

Obatala was very pleased with his work. Then, as the effects of the palm wine wore off, he saw that some of the people whom he had created were not perfect, and he promised that he would never drink palm wine again and that he would devote himself to protecting those who suffered because of his drunkenness. This is how Obatala became the protector of those who are born deformed.

The people whom Obatala had created needed food, so they began to work the earth. Since iron did not yet exist, Obatala presented his people with a copper knife and a wooden hoe, which they used to raise grain and yams. Ife slowly turned from a village into a city as the people prospered.

Seeing that his work on earth was done and having grown tired of being the ruler of Ife, Obatala climbed back up the golden chain to the sky. From that time afterward, he spent half of his time in the sky and half of his time in Ife.

When he was living in his home in the sky, Obatala told all of the other gods about the things that he had created on earth. Many of the gods were excited by his tales, and they decided to travel to the earth to live among the clay figures called human beings that Obatala had created. Before they left the sky, however, Olorun called them together and said, "Because you are gods, you must remember that you have certain obligations to the human beings. Among other things, you must listen to their prayers and help them when they need help." To each of the gods Olorun assigned a specific task that he or she would be responsible to fulfill on the earth.

Unfortunately, when he created the Yoruba world, Obatala had not consulted with Olokun, the ruler of the sea, and she became quite angry. She felt that he, a sky god, had usurped her power by changing a large portion of her domain and by assuming rulership over that kingdom. She thought long and hard, and finally she decided upon a plan that she felt would bring her revenge for Obatala's insulting actions.

One day, after Obatala had returned to the sky, Olokun brought together the great waves of her ocean world and flung them one after another across the land that Obatala had created. Before long the land was completely flooded and only marshland remained. The palm trees that Obatala had grown, the yams that the people had planted, and even most of the people themselves were washed away from the soil and drowned. The people who still lived called out to Obatala for help, but the noise of the waves was so great that he could not hear them.

The people found Eshu, the messenger god who had come to live among them, and asked him to carry their plea for help to Obatala and Olorun. Eshu told them to prepare a sacrifice to go along with their message in order to make sure that the great sky gods would listen to their plea, and he asked for a sacrifice for himself in return for his service. The people sacrificed a goat to Obatala and a white chicken to Eshu, and Eshu climbed back up the golden chain to tell Obatala about the flood.

Obatala was overwhelmed when he heard about the floods. He did not know how to deal with Olokun. Orunmila, after hearing about the destruction that the waves had brought to the land that Obatala had created said that he would make the water withdraw. Orunmila climbed down the golden chain and used his vast power to make the waves return to the water. The marshland dried and the people pled with Orunmila to stay with them and protect them from Olokun. While Orunmila had no desire to remain in the Yoruba world, he agreed to teach both the gods and the humans who lived there how to foretell the future and how to control the forces that they could not see. Then he climbed back up to his home in the sky, though like Obatala before him, he felt a kinship with the Yoruba people and he often returns to their world to see how they are doing.

Olokun was not defeated yet, however. She decided to make another attempt to show that she was the equal of the ruler of the sky. A skilled weaver and dyer of cloth, Olokun challenged Olorun to a weaving contest.

Olorun knew that Olokun was the best weaver ever, yet he knew that he could not avoid her challenge, so he determined to accept it without actually undergoing the test. He called Chameleon and ordered him to go to Olokun with his reply: "Olorun, the ruler of the sky, greets Olokun, the ruler of the sea. Olorun asks that Olokun show his messenger, Chameleon, samples of the cloth that she has woven so that Chameleon can judge her skill. If Chameleon determines that the cloth that Olokun has woven is as beautiful as she claims, then Olorun will gladly engage in the contest."

Chameleon traveled down the golden chain to Olokun's abode, where he delivered Olorun's message. Olokun was pleased by Olorun's reply, and she put on a bright green skirt made from material that she had woven and dyed; amazingly, Chameleon turned the same color as the skirt. Olokun then put on a bright orange skirt; amazingly, again, Chameleon changed to the color of the garment. Next Olokun put on a bright red skirt; once more, Chameleon became the color of the skirt. For the rest of the day, Olokun put on the brightly colored skirts that she had woven. Each time Chameleon turned into the exact color of the skirt that she was wearing. By the end of the day, Olokun was ready to give up. She thought to herself that if even Olorun's messenger could duplicate the bright colors of her finest fabrics, surely the greatest of the gods could easily beat her in the contest. Therefore, she told Chameleon, "Tell Olorun, your master and the ruler of the sky, that Olokun, the ruler of the sea, sends her greetings. Tell him that I acknowledge his superiority in all things, including weaving." Thus it was that peace was restored between Olorun, the ruler of the sky, and Olokun, the ruler of the sea, and that order again returned to the universe.

"THE CREATION OF THE UNIVERSE"

Steven H. Gale

1) Discuss examples of ways in which the ordering and organization of the universe portray gender divisions among the Yoruba.

2) How is the contest between Olorun, the ruler of the sky, and Olokun, the ruler of the waters and the marshes, a metaphor for gender relations?

3) What implications for male dominance and female subordination can be deduced from the story?

IN THE FIELD: MANDE BLACKSMITHS

Patrick R. McNaughton

Blacksmiths in sub-Saharan Africa occupy confusing social spaces, as if they lived in two conflicting dimensions. They are at once glorified and shunned, feared and despised, afforded special privileges and bounded by special interdictions. To western observers, the status of smiths in African societies seems enigmatic, and most authors, from the earliest colonial officers and missionaries to contemporary scholars, have felt hard pressed to make sense of it. A statement of the dilemma is provided by anthropologist Laura Makarius:

> The status of the blacksmith in tribal societies poses one of the most puzzling problems of anthropology. By a strange paradox, this noted craftsman, whose bold and meritorious services are indispensable to his community, has been relegated to a position outside the place of society, almost as an "untouchable." Regarded as the possessor of great magical powers, held at the same time in veneration and contempt, entrusted with duties unrelated to his craft or to his inferior social status, that make of him performer of circumcision rites, healer, exorcist, peace-maker, arbiter, counselor, or head of a cult, his figure in what may be called the "blacksmith complex," presents a mass of contradictions.[1]

In the vast savanna lands of the Western Sudan among the large group of societies that speak Mande languages, there is a third dimension to this problem: here, the Mande blacksmiths are also important artists, making most of their culture's wood and iron sculpture. This art, along with the other things they do, gives smiths important roles in everyone else's professional, social, and spiritual lives, thereby putting them in a surprisingly prominent position, given their enigmatic status.

How can artists fill so many other roles, and how do these other roles influence their art? This article seeks a preliminary answer to these questions. Exploring the principal roles of the Mande smiths, it shows that their work as artists is enhanced, in a sense even made possible, by their activities as technicians, healers, sorcerers, and mediators. At the same time it demonstrates that all the work they do is aimed at shaping the environments and the individuals around them, while their social status both enhances their work and is the result of it.

Officers and missionaries of the colonial era were the first to write at length about Mande culture. Early in this century, Father Joseph Henry described the sculpture types. Over the next few decades, Maurice Delafosse, Louis Tauxier, Charles Monteil, and Henri Labouret provided useful materials on the culture. Around mid-century the French anthropologists Marcel Griaule, Germaine Dieterlen, Salonge de Ganay, Viviana Pâques, and Zacharie Ligers examined various aspects of the culture and cosmology, while Carl Kjersmeier and F. H. Lem assembled fine collections of sculpture. More recently, Mary Jo Arnoldi, Charles Bird, Sarah Brett-Smith, James T. Brink, George E. Brooks, Gerald Anthony Cashion, Kate Ezra, Barbara E. Frank, Bernhard Gardi, Kathryn L. Green, Pascal James Imperato, John William Johnson, Martha B. Kendall, Peter Weil, and Dominique Zahan have made valuable contributions to the literature. Since the early decades of this century, West African scholars, including Youssouf Cissé, Bokar N'Diaye, Massa Makan Diabaté, Mamby Sidibé, and Moussa Travélé, have also published materials that greatly enrich our understanding of Mande culture. Still, the corpus of Mande sculpture is large, and its contexts are complex. It will take many more scholars and many more studies before we may claim a systematic understanding of the culture.

I went to the Republic of Mali as a Ford Foreign Area Research Fellow in 1972–1973 and returned for the summer of 1978, with hopes of learning about traditional blacksmiths. I knew what the literature told us: that the Mande smiths were also sculptors and that they possessed much notoriety as sorcerers. I had also read that they were casted and in some measure looked down upon. In actual fact, I knew little about these artists and their roles in society, because only a small percentage of the scholarly literature addressed them directly. By extension, then, I realized that I also knew little about the motivations and intentions of their art.

The majority of my time that first year was spent in small towns between Bamako and Bougouni, just east of the Niger River. I also made some brief excursions: north to the area around the town of Banamba; east to the areas around Ségou, Markala, and San; south through Sikasso; and west on the roads to Sibi and Kita. In 1978 I visited San, but spent most of my time in the Mande Plateau near Bamako.

In the early months, I traveled from one town to another, asking youngsters and elders where I might find blacksmiths. In every town I was introduced to at least one and sometimes several. I watched them work and asked them questions. I saw many of them on a regular basis, and some, including Dramane Dunbiya, Magan Fane, and Sedu Traore, I visited quite often. I also saw a good deal of Seydou Camara. He was born a smith and maintained a forge in his hometown in the Wasoulou region of southern Mali, but he had found that he loved music and so gave up smithing to become one of Mali's most renowned hunters' bards. He was extremely knowledgeable about the institution of smithing, and he provided me with a great deal of information. His nephew, Bourama Soumaoro, was also very knowledgeable, and, though I saw less of him, he too helped me greatly.

Ultimately, I found myself in a causal way apprenticed to the blacksmith Sedu Traore, and, while maintaining my contacts with the others, I worked with Sedu constantly. Sedu was from the southernmost region of the Bèlèdougou area north of Bamako. His father, in later life, had built a small blacksmiths' hamlet at the top of the Mande Plateau, which afforded a magnificent view of the great plains astride the Niger River. But I met Sedu in a town south of Bamako, where we spent most of our time together. I began to work intensely with him just before he became busy in the planting season with tool making and repairing, and, since his sons were all grown up and on their own, he let me spend many hours developing my technique on the bellows. Occasionally, Sedu had me try my hand at wood carving. More occasionally, I sat behind his anvil with a hammer in my hand, trying to make red-hot iron move the way Sedu did. The results of these enterprises were dismal but instructive; they made clear the depth of skill and acumen good sculpting requires of its practitioners.

Clients often came to Sedu, to have old tools repaired or new tools made. But they also came with requests for soothsaying, amulet-making, medical diagnoses and treatment, and general advice on all kinds of problems. I watched and listened and learned a great deal. When we were alone, working wood or iron, we talked for hours about every aspect of blacksmithing, from sculpting to sorcery. Sedu explained the importance of knowledge to every aspect of his trade. He related to me the experiences of his youth and what they had meant to his development as a smith. He discussed the usefulness of travel for the acquisition of wisdom, the importance of attaining genuine expertise, and the equal importance of maintaining a good name. He often discussed the rudiments of herbal and occult lore and the ethics that smiths should apply in their manipulation. He explained the tensions that develop regularly in communities as individuals negotiate their lives, families negotiate their community positions, and communities address an array of problems from the socialization of their youth to the inhibition of antisocial forces in the human and spiritual environments. He made the role of smiths in all these problems quite clear to me, and other smiths I talked to corroborated his account.

Sedu generally was fond of company, and so we visited a lot and were visited in turn. Dramane Dunbiya, the senior smith in Sedu's town, was a frequent companion with a wealth of information. So were several other community smiths with whom Sedu associated. A commonality of interests binds smiths together, and they tend to maintain extensive networks of friendship and communication. Therefore, Sedu and I traveled often and rather widely. I had a car, and we took full advantage of it to visit his fellow smiths in distant towns as well as his clients, his hunting companions, and other friends. He knew people everywhere, and I was pleased to be his chauffeur, because in these gregarious contexts I learned a great deal about smiths, their clients, and their cosmos.

When my informal apprenticeship began, Sedu marked me with a small white bead he hung around my neck. He passed a piece of string through it, which he knotted as he chanted. The bead was a special blacksmiths' device, used to announce membership in the profession and to protect the wearer from the unpleasant occult activities of others. For me it became a passport and an agent of transformation. Everywhere I went, both with and without Sedu Traore, people knew its meaning and accepted me on different terms from those they had applied before. Just once I used the bead avariciously. Back in Bamako at the main cloth market I had long been negotiating with a recalcitrant vendor over the price of a fine piece of cloth. He wanted to charge me the tourist price and I would not pay it. Finally one day I noticed a middle-aged woman watching us from an adjacent table, and I concluded that she was my vendor's boss. I marched straight over to her and, pointing to my bead, indicated that I was not a tourist. The fine piece of cloth instantly became mine.

The bead initiated a fundamental change in what people perceived me to be. Mande smithing is steeped in beliefs about the manipulation of nature's most powerful forces. The act of working iron and the myriad other acts that blacksmiths undertake embed them in a dangerous atmosphere of energies that we would define as occult or supernatural. My bead became the first link in a chain of protection from these forces. Gradually, Sedu gave me more amulets and some of his own tools; through these devices, Sedu and his colleagues believed, I gradually acquired the energies needed by someone who expected to spend much time in the intimate company of blacksmiths and their forges. I was not born a smith. But they made me resemble one closely enough to do my work.

The dimension of power that blacksmiths inhabit is matched by an equally important dimension of secrecy. The profession floats on a sea of secret expertise that outsiders have no right to learn about. My developing status as an informal apprentice began to make up in large measure for my foreign nature. Yet, I made plain from the start that I was doing research, with the goal of writing up whatever they would permit me to share with Westerners wanting to learn about Mande smiths. It was made equally plain to me that I would learn only what I was worthy of and only what they believed would do no harm. In fact, I learned what any beginning Mande apprentice might learn: the Mande principles of secrecy but not the secrets. Sedu, the other smiths of his community, and the elders who governed it were extremely careful about what I could be told, but they told enough for me to build a sound picture of their world.

I also made a point of interviewing Mande citizens who were not blacksmiths, both before and after I wore the bead that Sedu gave me. As a result, I acquired an idea of how the general Mande populace perceives the smiths. Nevertheless, my perceptions, as presented in this book, are aligned more closely with those of the blacksmiths than with those of the general population.

Most of my research assistants and colleagues were not smiths, and I enjoyed many hours of talk with them. They were quite different from one another, and quite different from the smiths. Chiekna Sangare was a teacher in Mali's public school system. Possessed of an open mind and a great curiosity, he had nevertheless known very little about blacksmiths until he began spending time in their forges with me. Abdulaye Sylla worked with the Ministry of Education as a curator at the National Museum in Bamako. He was quite knowledgeable about art and took a great interest in efforts to preserve and explain it. Dugutigi Traore was a farmer who came to Bamako with the hope of discovering another line of work. I met him through my friend Adbulaye Sissoko and decided it might be helpful to work with him for a while and watch his responses

to smiths. Sissoko was himself born a smith, but he made a living welding and repairing all types of vehicles. He also owned several trucks that carried trade goods to Mauritania and elsewhere. He was an amateur inventor, and at one point he built and ran a restaurant-nightclub on the banks of the Niger River. Although I never really worked with him, we spent much time together and he provided me with many insights. Sekuba Camara was also born a smith; he was the son of the hunters' bard Seydou. Rather than practice smithing, however, or taking up the hunters' harp like his father, Sekuba was a student aspiring to teach or to work for the Ministry of Education. Having been raised in the Wasoulou as a smith, he knew a great deal about the many enterprises of smiths. In the summer of 1978, when I returned to Mali for a second visit, I spent much of the time with Sekuba, transcribing, translating, and interpreting blacksmith songs sung by his father.

Finally, there was Kalilou Tera, who was finishing his degree at Mali's École normale supérieure when I encountered him working with Charles Bird at Indiana University in the summer of 1977. We had many discussions that summer and then worked together in Mali during the summer of 1978. I found his depth and clarity of understanding to be invaluable. He was the son of a well-known ascetic Muslim and the grandson of an equally well-known marabout. But he believed in the value of Mande traditional religion and wanted to know as much as possible about Mande beliefs and practices. All his life he had talked with elders. He had acquired as a result a sense of Mande civilization as supple and complex as the culture itself.

Note

1. Makarius 1968:25. Cline 1937: 114–139 and Barnes 1980: 8–13 summarize much of the literature on the status of smiths in African cultures.

References

Barnes, Sandra T. 1980 *Ogun: An Old God for a New Age. Occasional Papers in Social Change,* 3. Philadelphia: Institute for the Study of Human Issues.

Cline, Walter Buchanan 1937 *Mining and Metallurgy in Negro Africa.* Menasha, Wisconsin: George Banta Publishing.

Makarius, Laura 1968 *The Blacksmith's Taboos: From the Man of Iron to the Man of Blood.* Diogenes 62 (Summer): 25–48.

"In The Field: Mande Blacksmiths"

Patrick R. McNaughton

1) Discuss the contradictory roles of the Mande blacksmith.

2) How is social status linked to the role of the blacksmith in Mande society?

3) Discuss the role of supernatural forces in Mande blacksmithing.

RADIANCE FROM THE WATERS: MENDE FEMININE BEAUTY

Sylvia Ardyn Boone

Beauty and Goodness

Mende expect women to be beautiful, graceful, delicate, curvaceous, pretty, clean, fresh, perfumed, groomed, adorned. And Mende expect women to be good, kind, sweet, patient, gentle, modest, loving, helpful, cheerful, honest, understanding. A beautiful girl must be a good girl, and goodness alone can make a girl beautiful. The Mende word *nyande* means both to be good and to be beautiful, to be nice—character, looks, and comportment refracting and overlapping. In any discussion of the physical aspects of beauty, before very long somebody would say: "but no one can be beautiful if she doesn't have a fine character." If I could make any distinction in the answers it would be that older men were the most precise and detailed in their descriptions of the physical, while older women held that comportment and character are more important. And so the Mende community, like all human societies, struggles to harmonize the short-term physical desires of the men for sexual contact with the longer-range goals of the women for family life, and with the sustained goals of the community for progeny and prosperity.

Toward these wider ends, older women train young girls in good behavior, discipline young women to their serious responsibilities, and themselves serve as examples of high morals and ethical behavior. In the larger sense, the mind of the Mende is concerned with questions of ethics and morality; the guiding ideology is moral rather than religious or scientific. The *hale* (men's and women's societies) formed by the Mende all have in part or full the intention of upholding the moral standards of the community. Considering this overwhelmingly moralistic cast to Mende thought, it is no surprise that beauty, too, is judged for its goodness.

The dangers of beauty are an outcome of its extraordinary impact and power—a beautiful girl can become arrogant, her pride turn to narcissism. One oft-told tale on the subject of beauty concerns a chief's daughter who is the most beautiful girl in the land.[1] When it comes time for her to marry, she declares she will marry only the most handsome man, one as good-looking as herself. Her father brings her proposals from wealthy, important men of the area, but she refuses them all. Then a most handsome man, resplendently dressed, presents himself at the chief's court. After inspection he is found to be perfect in every detail, without scar or flaw. The girl welcomes him as her husband, only to discover in the marriage chamber that he has removed his disguise of physical perfection and has resumed his true form of an *ndili*-python.[2] She cries out for help but is ignored, as the serpent swallows her whole. Here, the perils of youthful willfulness and the misuse of attractiveness conferred by beauty connect with implications of non-productive autoeroticism.[3] The punishment for such social crimes is violent death, the python doing the job of removing the offender from the community.

Beauty is closely inspected all the time to make sure it is good. Mende fear that beauty will blind the eye to some evil that hides within. Many beautiful women resent the fuss made about them and feel they are unjustly harassed and harshly treated. Their beauty serves to draw attention to them and excite added criticism from their superiors. People seem to expect the best but fear the worst. Lovers may be tough with her, declaring that the girl may have used her looks to impress other men, but that *he* is not going to be taken in. Others feel bothered for minor infractions interpreted by their families as signs that they may become lazy or irresponsible and try to slide by on looks alone. One woman expressed bitterness about all this. She was nagged and punished all her life, she complained. Though she lived in town and was a bright pupil interested in a career in nursing, missionary teachers made her marry very young for fear that she could not resist urban pressures and would become a concubine or a prostitute. "This beauty, this beauty, what did all this beauty ever get me!"

A more positive illustration of Mende reflections on beauty lies in their interest in transcendence of the physical to an even greater *nyande* (i.e. beauty) through art. Mende declare that any girl with a beautiful voice is a beautiful girl: She may be quite ordinary to look at, but if she can sing well she will be considered lovely by any man in town. As we have already observed, "Beauty as a quality seems to emerge from a certain quantitative threshold" (Memel-Fotê 1968: 52). We have seen how it works in physiological terms, but it also seems to apply to what Mende call delicate, *yěngělě*, performances: artistic activities depending on wit, skill, talent, dedication, practice. Everybody in a Mende community is taught the rudiments of musical performance, singing, dancing, playing an instrument. But when a woman goes beyond the ordinary to become the soloist, not the chorus, this transcendence of the ordinary is called Beauty, and transfigures its owner into an Object of Beauty, a beauty that has all the allure and impact of physical beauty, and is even on a higher plane because it is derived from the "goodness"—pleasure-giving, group-forming—of fine performance.

Mende assume that a beautiful exterior enshrines the most useful something. It is a big disappointment for something to be beautiful to look at but not good, not useful, not fine. A "good thing" must be efficacious, do its job well. Part of the goodness can only be judged in its performance of the task for which it was created or fashioned. A good thing is utilitarian and is well-suited to fulfilling a useful purpose. In almost every discussion of beauty, someone would say how awful it is if a pretty girl is lazy or does not have a fine character. Mende call this *nyande gbama*, empty beauty, *gbama* meaning "for nothing, in vain" (Innes 1969: 17). *Nyande gbama* refers to many of the functional and moral issues. It is *gbama* for a good-looking girl to be rude, insolent, disrespectful. It is *gbama* for her to be nonfunctional in the community: "She can't work, can't cook, can't dance, can't sing—of what use is she?" It is *gbama* to be poor, low status, living in coarse company although because of your looks you would be welcomed among those of refinement and prestige. It is beauty wasted. Beauty without a dimension of goodness is hollow, without substance, a deception.

Certainly the most serious *gbama* is barrenness. There can be no more horrible deception than that the beautiful girl—so sought after since childhood, so fought over by relatives, Sande, (i.e. women's society) and suitors—should, finally married, prove incapable of having children. It is a blow to the community, a vile mockery of all that they hold sacred. Beauty, in Mende thought, "is required to aid, it is called upon to participate and is a participant in the efficacy of the object. . . . The more beautiful the object, the better it accomplishes its affectively desired, imaginatively dreamed, technically hoped-for effect" (Memel-Fotê 1968: 57). The irreducible, primary function of a woman is to bear children. For beauty to be associated with sterility brings sad musings of "how can beautiful people not be good."[4]

If we look closely at the Mende words for beauty and goodness, we will see them overlapping, intersecting, and blending into a Möbius strip of meanings. *Nyande* is the word for beauty and *kpekpe* is the word for goodness.[5] *Nyande* can go off in the direction of describing the physical, the external, so it relates to prettiness, desirable body shape, admirable skin, hair, or eyes, and other physical attributes. In speaking of any one of these features for each of which there is a definite canon of beauty, *nyande* stands for the fulfillment of that canon. Thus *nyande yama*, "beautiful eyes," means the eyes are big, round, prominent, bright, and expressive. *Nyande nyini*, "beautiful breasts," means the breasts are low, firm, thick, covering the entire chest area; and so on.

Kpekpe relates to worth in the utility of objects and the behavior of human beings. For instance, *kpatoi kpekpe-ngò*, "the cutlass is good," means that it is comfortable to hold, useful to work with, performs well the job for which a cutlass is designed. Also, though, it is nothing else but a cutlass, doing the cutlass job.[6] When referring to people, the goodness of *kpekpe* means a person is kind-hearted, helps you, gives you gifts. As with objects, this is an appreciation based on the disposal of the object or the person to offer its services for your benefit.

In talking of objects, *nyande* can also express utility. However ugly-looking a cutlass may be, Mende can also say, "*Kpatoi nande-ngò*," meaning that the cutlass is beautiful because it is indeed a cutlass, a functional object, and not just a piece of useless, worthless junk. In a way, the two words are interchangeable; however, *nyande-ngò* is a more gentle use of the language. *Nyande* is broader, implying that the thing in question is comprehensively good, and includes a positive evaluation of both its looks and its usefulness.

When describing human beings, at a more abstract level, the two words converge at a point—the point of kindness and generosity. *Ngi kpekpe-ugò*—"He is good, he is *kind*, he is *generous*." *Ngi hinda nyande-ngò*—"His ways are fine, he is *kind*, he is *generous*." At the highest level of Mende conceptualization, beauty and goodness meet to express a sympathetic interest in the welfare of others and a warm-hearted readiness to give.[7]

Beauty as a Historical Fact

As beauty is physical and metaphysical, it is also "an historical fact."[8] By interviewing some thirty persons over the age of sixty-five, each of whom had been trained by an old grandmother or aunt, I was able to obtain information about beauty in a time span of about one hundred and twenty-five years. It was quickly evident that a young girl in 1885 was judged by the same standards as her counterpart in 1985! If Mende canons appear to have been so static for such a long time, I do not believe it is due to isolation or xenophobia. Although Mende culture has matured in small rural farming communities, like all West African peoples, Mende have extensive contact with neighboring groups. Since the people with whom Mende have mingled hold to similar views, ethnic interaction has probably served only to reinforce the existing Mende standards.[9] And, since beauty is body-based, and since all bodies resemble each other and the same features constantly recur over time, they are seen to have the permanence of nature itself as a manifestation of God.

Properly speaking, Mende people were never colonized (they were governed by the British as a protectorate), and they do not feel themselves the victims of cultural rape. The British colonial presence and its exploitation of mineral and farming resources served in part to introduce a number of innovations into Mende life that offered a new set of opportunities and challenges. Through it all, beauty, as an aspect of the "absorptive" Mende culture, managed to pick out what it needed and thus enhance the aesthetic qualities that are valued. So now for the first time beauty can be faked by makeup or flattering clothes. Short, thin hair can be augmented by hairpieces and covered by wigs, a flat chest enlarged by falsies, a fallen bust line uplifted by a brassiere, brows thickened with a pencil, and a healthy glow applied with makeup. Islamic styles for women made popular by *haja* have meant a beauty of clothing and adornment rather than of face and body; these voluminous robes, veils, and jewelry give older women more opportunity for glamor and elegance.

When Mende say that "before" beauty was "natural," they are saying several things. The remark goes back to a time when a virgin stood naked before the criticisms of the community, then the sole arbiter of taste but now only one of several. The release of many girls from this evaluation marks the outside influences that have brought upset to all sectors of Mende life. The vast majority of Mende girls who live in the villages still maintain the same lifestyles, but town girls, schoolgirls, and the chiefs' daughters are freer, less subject to the decisions of elders. Among the elders themselves, before, a woman in her fifties or sixties was sought after as a love-partner only if she had the prestige of being an artist or a Sowei. Now another group of mature women have attained social prominence and sexual

desirability: the rich wives and mothers of the new political and governmental elite, whose prestige is based on money rather than, as it had been for women before, on service to the community. In Mendeland, as elsewhere in the world, "beauty changes."

Notes

1. I term "oft-told-tales" those stories I was told repeatedly by Mende who liked me and wanted to help me understand Mende ways. They are all tales of supernatural, mysterious happenings that are said to happen in different places at different times. Among them: (1) The Sande initiates turned to stone; (2) The relative who visits from afar and then you hear the next day that he died last week; (3) The orphan girl whose Sande tuition is mysteriously paid and she graduates and marries the president; (4) The beautiful girl who is a bed-wetter; (5) The pond you drink from which makes you return to that spot; (6) The *Tingoi* who brings a particular man great riches. These stories never appear in collections of folktales, and they do not seem to fit into any standard form. "Mende literature comprises many forms including prayers to the dead (*ngo gbia*), ritual slogans addressed to dancing spirits, dream (*kibalo*) narrations, fictitious tales (*dòmè njele*), myths and legends (*njia wova; njepe wowa*), place puzzles (*hoboi*), proverbs and riddles (*sale*), and songs (*ngule*)." They are perhaps closest to *njia wova*, since such a narrative "recounts actual events, . . . may be told to an individual" (Kilson 1976: 17). The question is whether or not they "recount actual events." Under the guidance of my preceptors I have come to see that they encapsulate Mende thought and, like moral tales, "are used for the socialization of the young, and therefore embody the mores of the society (Innes 1964: 15). Mende kindly saw me as a "child Mende" who needed to be socialized. The lessons these "oft-told tales" teach and the way they function in the life of the community would be the topic of an interesting paper.

2. This is not the natural python so revered by Mende cultists, but the vampire *ndili*, "a mythical creature in the shape of a python that is believed to attack children at night" (Innes 1969: 95). The *ndili* is a complicated notion of evil; discussed by Harris and Sawyerr 1968: 77–79, 118, 122; and by Little 1967: 231.

3. The very perfection of her suitor should have warned the girl that he was not a normal human being, but a monster. This tale is an admonition to be suspicious of perfect beauty; Mende are sure that the very loveliest girls, for example, have serious, secret physical flaws. There is a prevalent notion that what can be seen may be fine, but what is completely hidden, the genitals, may be amiss in some way. Or a girl may have scars from infections that are covered by the long lappa. Three different men told me of encountering girls whose public and private parts were all exquisite, only to find that they were bed-wetters.

4. This is real dilemma to Mende, rather like a Western Christian brought up with a sense of guilt and retribution who questions "why innocent babies die." Both sets of speculations are unanswerable and express the layman's confusion about the ethical bases of the world he lives in.

5. In Innes: "*Kpekpe*—goodness, generosity; be good, be generous" (1969: 57). "*Nyande*—be nice, be good looking, good, beauty, good looks . . . *Ngi wie hinda nyandengó*—he is good, kind" (p. 118).

6. "No matter how important its artistic content may be, the making of a garment, a uniform, an ornament, a piece of jewelry, or a tool is subordinated to its function, its efficacy. Any adjunctions whose only purpose would be beauty [ornament] are excluded insofar as it would overburden or hamper proper utilization of the object" (Memel-Fotê 1968: 57).

7. I am grateful especially to the Bo preceptor and to the Mme. K. compound for their patient and lucid explanations of Mende aesthetic and moral concepts.

8. Susan Sontag, "Beauty, How Will It Change Next?" *Beauty in Vogue* (London), Autumn/Winter 1975, p. 86.

9. The comparisons Memel-Fotê has made of fourteen different cultures indicates their considerable agreement in aesthetic matters (1968: 47–56).

References

Harris, W. T., and Harry R. Sawyer. 1968. *The Springs of Mende Relief and Conduct.* Freetown: Sierra Leone University Press.

Innes, Gordon. 1964. *Some Features of Theme and Style of Mende Folktales.* Sierra Leone Language Review, no. 3.

_____. 1969. *A Mende-English Dictionary.* Cambridge: Cambridge University Press.

Kilson, Marion De B. 1976. *Royal Antelope and Spider: West African Mende Tales.* Cambridge, Massachusetts: The Press of the Langdon Associates.

Little, Kenneth. 1967. *The Mende Chiefdoms of Sierra Leone.* In P. M. Kaberry and C. D. Forde, eds., *West African Kingdoms in the Nineteenth Century.* London: Oxford University Press.

Memel-Fotê, Harris. 1968. *The Perception of Beauty in Negro African Culture. In Colloquium on Negro Art, Dakar, First World Festival of Negro Arts.* Paris: Présence Africaine.

Sontag, Susan. 1975. *Beauty, How Will It Change Next? Beauty in Vogue.* London. Autumn/Winter.

"Radiance from the Waters: Mende Feminine Beauty"

Sylvia Ardyn Boone

1) Discuss the symbolic significance of beauty among the Mende.

2) Discuss the similarities and differences between physical beauty and inner beauty as perceived by the Mende.

CALENDAR

David Ewing Duncan

He was a tiny man, the fellow responsible for the year 2000—and by extension for millennial cruises to the Pyramids, talk of millennial apocalypse, and millennial fetes from Times Square to Timbuktu. The Romans literally called him Dennis the Little—Dionysius Exiguus. His stature, however, had nothing to do with his out-size ambition: to transmute time itself.

Dennis the Little was an abbot and a mathematician. He lived in Rome in the sixth century, a century that today, thanks to him, we designate as A.D. Romulus Augustulus, the last boy-emperor, had been ousted, and the eternal city, its walls breached, was a shattered husk. The only district with a pulse still beating lay outside the city, across the Tiber at St. Peter's, in what we now call the Vatican. Dennis spent his career there, organizing church writings and tinkering with time. His contemporaries considered him brilliant, but he was also a bit humorless and stodgy, to judge by the letters he wrote.

In 525, Pope John I asked Dennis to calculate dates on which all future Easters should be celebrated. Then as now this was a complicated task, given the formula adopted by the church just two centuries before—that Easter shall fall on the first Sunday after the first full moon after the spring equinox. But Dennis dutifully studied the positions of the moon and the sun, and created a chart of upcoming Easters, beginning in 532. Except that in the Rome of Dennis' day, nobody designated the year as "532." For Roman citizens, it was either the year 1285, dated from the founding of Rome, or the year 248, based on a calendar that started with the first year of the reign of Emperor Diocletian.

It was that fact that gave Dennis his great inspiration. Instead of using a time line glorifying Diocletian, a notorious persecutor of Christians, Dennis calculated his dates based on the birthdate of Christ. As he put it, he "preferred to count and denote the years from the incarnation of our Lord, in order to make the foundation of our hope better known. . . . " The good abbot's preference appeared on his new Easter charts, which began with *anno Domini nostri Jesu Christi* DXXXII—the year of our Lord Jesus Christ 532, or A.D. 532 for short.

Using much the same logic, if a different worldview, some today prefer to call the calendar years C.E. or B.C.E.—for "common era" and "before common era" rather than A.D. or B.C. But the crucial date remains the same, the one that Dennis the Little thought he'd pinned down, the date of Christ's birth. In fact, Dennis got it slightly wrong. As modern biblical historians know, Jesus of Nazareth was most likely not born in what Dennis called A.D. 1. Modern scholars lean toward 5 or 6 B.C.

Dennis' effort is just one of many failed attempts to create an accurate calendar. That may seem ridiculous to people living in a time when calendars dangle from a billion walls and timepieces festoon dashboards, nightstands and office cubicles: squawking, beeping, purring; waking us up and putting us to sleep. We live and breathe time with the faith of monks, believing that our division of time into months, weeks, days, hours, minutes, and seconds is as solid as granite. But with the exception of the day, which is a natural phenomenon that would occur with or without Swatches and Rolexes, these units of time were all made up. As arbitrary as driving on the right-hand side of the road in America, they are simply traditions that everyone at some point agreed upon, though no one can quite remember when or why.

The calendar now used by some six billion people did not even become the world's common calendar until the year 1949, when Mao Tse-tung seized power. Cheered by his People's Army as he stood atop the Gates of Heavenly Peace, Mao announced the formation of the People's Republic. The Communist flag would thenceforth be China's official flag; Peking would be the capital of the new republic; and the Chinese would, once and for all, use the Gregorian calendar that had been officially, but ineffectively, adopted by China in 1912. This completed the world conquest of a version of the calendar named after an otherwise lackluster sixteenth-century pope, Gregory XIII. He earned this timeless epitaph by revising the calendar already modified by Dennis the Little and first launched some sixteen centuries before Gregory by Julius Caesar, who in turn had borrowed it from Egypt. The people of the Nile had invented the basis of their version 4,000 years earlier. On the way, smatterings of other time-measuring schemes were incorporated—calendric fragments from India, Sumer, Babylon, Palestine, Arabia, and pagan Europe.

It was an effort as monumental as raising the Pyramids and landing men on the moon—except that nearly every calendar in history has been inaccurate. One reason is that the tropical, or solar, year—the precise measure of time between recurring seasons—runs an awkward 365.242199 days, a tough number to calculate without modern instruments. A further complication is the tendency of our asymmetrical little planet to wobble and wiggle ever so slightly, yanked this way and that by the moon's elliptical orbit, and the gravitational tug of the sun, as well. Result: Each year varies by a few seconds, making the exact length of The Year almost as unpredictable as where lightning will strike next. If this sounds like hairsplitting, it is. Yet it also points out some of the conundrums faced by ancient astronomers, kings, priests, and calendar-makers—driven by the need to know when to plant crops, collect taxes, and offer sacrifices to appease their gods—in trying to conjure accurate calendars.

Which they all failed to do. The first efforts to keep a record of time may have come as early as 30,000 years ago, when Cro-Magnons in Europe and Africa peered upward at the moon, apparently noticing that Luna's phases are not only diverting, but steady and predictable. Then, it seems, they did something remarkable. They scratched what they saw into rocks and bones, creating what may indeed have been the world's first calendars. One Paleolithic artisan, working 13,000 years ago at Le Placard on the Dordogne River in France, carved a sequence of notches into an eagle bone, daily symbols that seem to keep track of the phases of the moon. Heady stuff for fur-clad hominids living at the end of the last ice age. Such notches may have allowed moon-gazers to predict a full moon for hunting or raiding a rival clan, or to count how many moons would pass until winter ended and spring returned. At some point in history, ancient astronomers also realized that 12 lunar cycles come very close to equaling a "year" of seasons.

The moon was not the only natural clock used by the ancients. Living in intimate contact with nature, early calendar-makers also noticed that when certain birds flew south, winter was on its way, and that the appearance of certain stars in the sky signaled spring. In the eighth century B.C., the poet Hesiod wrote his epic *Works and Days*, much of which is essentially a calendar in verse—a record of Greek oral lore about time and nature. He advises waiting until the month when the cuckoo sings before harvesting cereals, and warns that men's sex drive diminishes in the late summer, when "goats are at their fattest" and "the wine tastes best." More recently, the Natchez of the Mississippi River Valley used seasonal cues to name their months, which included Deer month, Strawberries month, and Little-Corn month. So did the Malagasy people of Madagascar. Their list of months include a Tamarinds-and-Beans-Are-Ripe month and a Rains-Rot-the-Ropes month.

But nothing intrigued the ancients more than the moon. Mystical and alluring, it became not only a celestial clock but a goddess as well. She was Khonsu to the Egyptians, Nanna to the Sumerians, and three different names to the Greeks and Romans: Hecate when the moon was dark, Artemis (Diana) when it waxed, and Selene (Luna) when it was full.

But alas, twelve lunar months (at about 29.5 days each) equal only 354 days—11 days and several hours short of a solar year. Such a temporal discrepancy quickly throws lunar calendars out of alignment with the seasons, flip-flopping the summer and winter solstices in just a little more than sixteen years. In order to compensate, devotees of Luna resorted to various schemes.

In the twenty-first century B.C., the Sumerians found that their various lunar calendars—including one with twelve months of 30 days, totaling 360 days in a year—were still many days off, requiring the insertion of additional months every few years. As early as 2357 B.C., legendary Chinese emperor Yao put sun and moon in sync with a calendar that intercalated two extra months every five years. That was later revised to allow for seven extra months every nineteen years, which more or less averaged to 365-day years. By the end of the fifth century B.C. others, including the Babylonians and the Greeks, had come up with essentially the same system, called "Metonic" after the Greek astronomer Meton.

Though cumbersome, the system of adding seven months over nineteen years—with other minor adjustments—proved lasting. The Jewish calendar, which adopted this and other elements of the Babylonian, is still in use today. But it's a rare holdout. In ancient times, since there were few—if any—accurate measurements of a year or a lunar month, these stratagems always fell short (or long). They also proved too complicated: People forgot to add days and months on schedule; years ebbed and flowed more with the whims of priests and kings than according to science.

Not all early civilizations were seduced by the moon, though. In the Americas, both the Maya (who developed an elaborate system of recording dates) and the Aztecs created distinct 365-day years, coming very close to a solar year, as well as separate lunar years. And some 4,000 years ago on Salisbury Plain in England, the enigmatic builders of

Stonehenge arranged great slabs of bluestone to capture the exact moment of the summer solstice. This provided them with a calendar capable of determining a year of 365 days and several hours.

But the first people of the sun were the Egyptians. As early as the fifth millennium B.C. they figured out a 365-day year, apparently when someone along the Nile got the idea of planting a stick on its shoreline to measure the high point of the river's annual flood, which falls at the same time each year. What these anonymous calendar-makers discovered was yet another giant clock: 4,000 miles of rushing water driven by the seasonal movements of the earth and the rains in Central Africa. This allowed them to create a solar calendar before they had raised the great pyramids, establishing a system of twelve months of thirty days, with five days tacked on as holidays to celebrate the birthdays of Osiris, Isis, Horus, Nephthys, and Set.

The Egyptians made another timely discovery: Sirius, the Dog Star, arises in the dawn sky once a year in a direct line with the rising sun, and at a time coinciding with the flooding of the Nile. By mounting special brass rings on the tops of obelisks, Egyptian astronomers were able to record with great precision the exact moment when Sirius crossed through the ring, as observed from a fixed point on the ground. They began to notice that this event was lapsing by about six hours each year, leading them to conclude that the year is longer than 365 days by about a quarter of a day. This revelation brought them within about eleven minutes of the rue year, though for centuries Egypt's tradition-obsessed priests refused to adjust their 365-day calendar. They let it drift some six hours a year, dropping a day every four years.

Almost everywhere else, Luna reigned supreme—including in what was then a small, backwater enclave perched above the Tiber River, and that would one day subsume not only Egypt but its calendar. According to legend, Rome's original calendar was invented by the city's first king, the mythical Romulus, who is said to have founded Rome in 753 B.C. He created a calendar with only ten lunar months—possibly, says the Roman poet Ovid, "because that is the number of fingers by which we are wont to count." Whatever the reason, his calendar was off by 61 days, but it gave us the names of all but two of our months. Romulus gave the first four months descriptive names—Martius, for Mars, the god of war; Aprilis, which seems to have referred to either the goddess of love or the raising of hogs; Maius, for Maia, mother of Mercury; and Junius, for Juno, the queen of the Roman gods. Then he fell back on ordinal numbers, starting with "fifth": Quintilis, Sextilis, September, October, November, and December.

Around 700 B.C., Numa Pompilius—Romulus' supposed successor—is said to have added Januarius, named for the two-faced Janus, god of looking forward and backward; and Februarius, named for a Roman festival of purification. This left the Roman calendar as accurate—and as flawed—as every other 354-day year, though the Romans got a bit closer by adding a day to make it 355 (they had a superstition about even numbers).

All this changed one October day in 48 B.C. when a Roman warship arrived off the coast of Egypt. On board was Julius Caesar, in hot pursuit of Pompey, his rival in Rome's civil war. This was a critical moment in calendric history. In Alexandria, Caesar met the woman who became his most famous mistress; their love affair gave the world its present calendar.

A dazzling intellect and exotic beauty, 21-year-old Cleopatra (*Smithsonian*, February 1997) was then embroiled in civil war against her teenage brother, Ptolomy XIII. The 52-year-old Caesar helped her win it, but only after several busy months of battles, feasts, and trysts. One wonders how they found time to talk calendrics. But Alexandria, the site of the world's greatest library, had long been a magnet for scholars and artists from far and near. Astronomers came, too—some of the greatest in the ancient world. They had pondered the length of the year, calculating it to within six minutes of its true duration.

Caesar was attending a lavish feast when Cleopatra's court scholars first told him about the Egyptian calendar. According to the Roman poet Lucan, the queen was decked out that night in a wreath of roses for her hair and a diaphanous gown that revealed "her white breasts," an outfit that Caesar overlooked long enough to discuss with assorted scholars the fine points of the star Sirius and the flooding of the Nile.

In 47 B.C., with Cleopatra pregnant with Julius Jr., Caesar returned to Rome as dictator, and grafted Egypt's calendar onto Rome's. By then, the empire's calendar was running a full 90 days slow against the true year. To repair it, Caesar fixed the Roman year at 365 days, borrowing the leap-year system invented (and then abandoned) by the Egyptians, which added an extra day every fourth year to compensate for the additional quarter-day.

Roman months would no longer be in thrall to the moon. Instead, he decreed that they would alternate in length between 30 and 31 days, with the exception of February, set at 29 days—30 in a leap year. That still left Rome's calendar in error by some eleven minutes a year.

To bring the calendar back in alignment, Caesar also ordered one of the more radical time alterations in history, lengthening the year 46 B.C. by ninety days. This created a year that stretched on for a time-numbing 445 days. Optimistically, Caesar called it the *ultimus annus confusionis,* the "last year of confusion." The extra days caused disruptions throughout the empire in everything from contracts to shipping schedules, so everyone else simply called it the Year of Confusion. But when January 1, 45 B.C., finally rolled around, most Romans were happy to have the stable, uncomplicated Julian calendar.

Or so it seemed. But Rome's priests managed to foul up even this simple calendar, counting leap years every three years instead of four. This threw the calendar out of whack once again. Confusing corrections followed for decades until Caesar's convenient system of alternating 30- and 31-day months was dropped, leaving us with the basis for that annoying Old English ditty that starts with "Thirty days hath September. . . "

Three centuries later, time took another turn in Rome because Emperor Constantine had embraced a new religion, Christianity. As part of his conversion, he added a new slate of holidays and festivals, adopted the Jewish seven-day week and designated Sunday, rather than the Jewish Sabbath or the Roman Saturn's Day, as a day of worship. This officially established the seven-day week for the Roman Empire—and eventually for the world.

Constantine also set in motion a profound shift from Caesar's science-based approach, to a calendar that gradually was usurped by religion. This process accelerated as the political and economic might of Rome collapsed, leaving behind only one intact imperial institution: the Catholic Church. The imperial calendar became the sacred calendar of the church, a system of dates no one dared to challenge—because it was believed ordained by God—even though it was still faulty by eleven minutes and fourteen seconds a year.

Easter complicated matters further, because the early church decided not to celebrate it on the same calendar day each year, but according to a system that attempted to date Christ's resurrection according to the Jewish lunar calendar. This was because eyewitness accounts in the Gospels fail to name a specific date for the Resurrection beyond noting that it occurred on a Sunday during the Jewish Passover. Breaking from any association with Jewish timekeeping, Christians began to use a complicated formula that places Easter on the first Sunday after the first full moon after the spring equinox, a method established by a great council of bishops convened by Constantine in 325 at Nicaea. For centuries, the Easter rule condemned monks to pore over endless calculations in a mostly futile attempt to determine the exact date of upcoming Easters.

Still, it was that concern about Easter that gave the world Dennis the Little and its current common calendar. His error about the exact date of Christ's birth is hardly surprising, given the intellectual chaos engulfing Europe in what used to be called the Dark Ages. The epicenter of learning was shifting east to the domains of Islam.

Spurred on by their potent new religion, the armies of Islam had stormed out of the Arabian Desert in 632 to seize a vast swath of territory, stretching from the Indus River and the steppes of east-central Asia across North Africa to the Pyrenees. One Arab scholar, Abu Abdallah Mohammed Ibn Jabir al-Battani, came within 22 seconds of the true year in the ninth century. Two hundred years later, the Persian poet and scientist Omar Khayyam came even closer. Despite these remarkable accomplishments in the realms of astronomy and mathematics, the Islamic calendar remained—as it does today—strictly a lunar affair, drifting behind the seasons by ten or eleven days a year.

Slumbering cerebrally through this period, Europe did not seriously begin to stir until the eleventh and twelfth centuries, when Arab learning and the long forgotten texts of ancient Greeks and Romans began to permeate the gloom. Eventually, European scholars, using Greek and Arab science to prove their findings, confirmed that the standard calendar was flawed. Yet not many were bold enough to challenge the church on a matter so fundamental as measuring time.

Then came a remarkable English friar named Roger Bacon, a true original. "The calendar," he wrote in 1267, "is intolerable to all wisdom, the horror of all astronomy, and a laughing-stock from the computors [mathematician's] point of view." Bacon was ahead of his time. His ruminations dazzled his contemporaries, but also frightened them. What were they to think of a man who pondered what causes a rainbow, invented a formula for gunpowder, designed a telescope, and predicted such things as the invention of eyeglasses, airplanes, and high-speed engines?

In 1265, Pope Clement invited Bacon to write down his thoughts. He worked furiously to prepare a series of treatises that were highly critical of the church, but had the bad luck to finish them only just before Clement died. Roger Bacon's own religious order, the Franciscans, eventually imprisoned him for his heretical tendencies.

It took the church 300 years more to admit that its calendar was defective. By then, Caesar's 11-minute gap had accrued to about ten days, pushing the true spring equinox, for instance, back from its calendar date of March 21 to March 11. More horrific for devout Christians was the realization that every holy day, including Easter, was being celebrated at the wrong time.

Change did not come until February 24, 1582, when 80-year-old Pope Gregory XIII signed an edict restoring Europe's calendar to a proper alignment with the sun. The core of Gregory's reform was something called the leap-century rule, which cancels out three out of four leap years falling at the turn of each century, shortening Caesar's average year to compensate for the 11-minute drift. Under this rule, the year 2000 would be a leap year, but 1700, 1800, and 1900 would not. To repair the ten-day rift, Gregory ordered his own version of Caesar's Year of Confusion, simply striking ten days out of the year 1582. The cut occurred in October. People in the affected countries went to bed on Thursday the 4th and woke up not on Friday the 5th, but on Friday the 15th.

In Frankfurt, angry mobs rioted, convinced the pope had stolen ten days out of their lives. Bankers wondered how to calculate interest in a month only twenty-one days long. Sailors, smiths, weavers, and muleteers fussed over wages missed, and kings and accountants fretted over taxes not collected. Enraged Protestants, already in a fever pitch of anti-Catholic hysteria—this was the century of Luther and Calvin—railed against the cut as work of the devil. "We do not recognize this Lycurgus (or rather Draco, whose laws were said to be written in blood) this calendar-maker," fumed a fiery German theologian named James Heerbrand, "just as we do not hear the shepherd of the flock of the Lord, but a howling wolf."

But the astronomy behind the new calendar was unshakable. It was based on the new observations (if not the controversial theories of Nicolaus Copernicus, among others, and the painstaking calculations of Aloysius Lilius, a little-known physician-astronomer. Lilius is the unsung hero of our calendar, the man who crafted the complex equations that proved the leap-century rule was simpler and neater than dozens of rival solutions.

The papal mandate was not accepted everywhere in 1582. Only Italy, Spain, Portugal, and Poland complied right away. France waited until December. Belgium and the Catholic states of the Netherlands dropped the ten days after December 21, which meant skipping right over Christmas and New Year's Eve. By 1584, most other Catholic states had gone along. Protestants continued to resist, however, leaving Europe a patchwork of dates as people coped with having two calendars—the "Old Style" and "New Style," or O.S. and N.S. for short. This meant

that if you departed from, say, Catholic Regensburg in Germany on January 1, you would arrive 60 miles away in Lutheran Nuremberg on December 22 or 23 of the previous year. Protestant Germany finally accepted the new calendar in 1700.

The last major holdout for the Old Style in the west was Britain. Englishmen waited 170 years, until 1752, in fact, to make the transition. It was finally done because author and politician Philip Dormer Stanhope, Earl of Chesterfield—famous for his letters to his son—became so outraged by the situation that he took on calendar reform as a personal crusade. Chesterfield finally convinced Parliament to act in a unanimous vote in 1751. In one of his letters to his son, he wrote: "It was notorious, that the Julian calendar was erroneous, and had overcharged the solar year with eleven days" (eleven because, since Gregory's reform, the Old Style had slipped by yet another day). The days dropped by the British parliament fell between Wednesday, September 2, and what would become Thursday, September 14. To ease the bedlam that might have resulted in a society far more complex than Europe in 1582, Stanhope penned a long list of practical rules governing the changeover in such matters as contracts, court dates, elections, and even staggered release dates for prisoners.

Still, mobs apparently gathered in London and elsewhere to shout, "Give us back our eleven days." In Bristol, riots reportedly left several people dead. London bankers refused to figure taxes on the usual date of March 25, 1753. They waited eleven days, until April 5—which is still the end of the tax year in Britain. In Philadelphia, Benjamin Franklin greeted the change with aplomb. "And what an indulgence is here," he wrote in *Poor Richard's Almanack*, "for those who love their pillow to lie down in peace on the second of this month and not perhaps awake till the morning of the fourteenth."

During the next 200 years, other unreformed countries in Europe converted, but not without resistance. The new republic formed by the French Revolution cast off all links to its timekeeping past, creating a calendar of 30-day months and 10-day weeks (with 5 days thrown in for good measure). Russia did not first adopt the Gregorian calendar until 1918, after the Bolsheviks seized power (by which time they had to drop 13 days—February 1–13—to get even).

The world's agreed-upon calendar is not perfect to be sure. Utopian calendar reformists, insisting that months should have a more consistent number of days or that dates should fall on the same day of the week each year, demand that the whole thing be revamped.

But by and large, we muddle along with the Gregorian calendar with few complaints, despite modern atomic clocks that now keep time accurately to within a billionth of a second. Ironically, given all the effort over the millennia to calculate an exact year, this hyperprecision has overshot the mark, since the Earth wiggles and wobbles in space, causing fluctuations of a few seconds each year—which means the atomic clocks must be adjusted to keep in sync with it. The Gregorian calendar is also running slow by about twenty-six seconds per annum. It's already put us back three hours; eventually, we will be behind by an entire day. But not to worry. It won't happen until 4909, in the last century of the fifth millennium.

And by then, who knows what clocks, calendars—or civilization itself—will look like?

"CALENDAR"

David Ewing Duncan

---

1) Who was Dionysius Exiguus, and what cultural innovation is he responsible for?

2) Why does the author say units of timekeeping are arbitrary?

3) Why does the author say that all attempts at calendrical timekeeping have been inaccurate?

4) Discuss, in outline form, the history of Roman timekeeping as detailed in the article.

5) What problems occurred in the change to the Gregorian calendar during the switchover days?

6) Why does timekeeping have symbolic significance for humans? (Hint—Examine the calendrical changeover problems discussed in the article.)

THE SOUND OF MUSIC:
SUYÁ SONG STRUCTURE AND EXPERIENCE

Anthony Seeger

Is there anything about the *sounds* of a particular community's music that lends its performance a particular significance? Does it matter what kind of music people perform, as long as they perform something? Although the obvious answer might be "of course it matters," the evidence isn't plentiful. I argue below that the structure of Suyá musical performance has deep cosmological significance; I shall show how the sound quality of a persona's performance expresses his or her life experiences and current attitudes; and I shall argue that the feeling of "euphoria" that is supposed to characterize all ceremonies is derived partly from the experience of singing and dancing for long periods of time. Suyá singing (re)creates society, repositions the individuals within it, and (re)structures their cosmos in specific and significant ways. The purpose of the discussion is to focus attention on the *sounds* of music as well as on context.

Anthropologists since Emile Durkheim have written at length about how ceremonies strengthen social ties and increase social solidarity. But few anthropologists have paid much attention to musical sounds. They have tended to focus on economics, religion, kinship, and other facets of musical performances. The Suyá certainly support the anthropological argument that rituals have important non-musical components. "When we sing, we eat," an older Suyá man once exclaimed with enthusiasm, gleefully anticipating the way in which organized community labor would result in large village-wide feasts during the weeks of ceremony. "When we sing we are rough," stated a young bachelor, anticipating how the days of hard work and long hours at strenuous singing would make him stronger. A married man with young children remarked, "When we sing, we are euphoric," highlighting the intense feeling of happiness and euphoria that are supposed to be felt by all participants when a ceremony is well performed. "When everyone sings, it is beautiful; when just a few people sing, it is bad," explained a political leader; always concerned that factional disputes might erupt during the ceremony and prevent the satisfying euphoria from being felt by all. "When we stop singing, we will be finished," said a man whose knowledge of Brazilian society was probably the best in the community, giving expression to the Suyá belief that community rituals are one of the defining features of the Suyá as a people.

To eat, grow strong, feel intense emotions, act together, and preserve a cultural identity, people need not sing at all. There are other ways these can be accomplished—even in silence. Yet the Suyá sing and dance (a single verb covers both) from the rise of the morning star to the first hint of daybreak; they sing in the evening; soloists sing during the daylight or night hours; the whole community sometimes sings through the entire night. They talk about songs and evaluate one another as singers; they admire those among them who can introduce new songs to the existing repertory. They claim that a defining feature of Suyá culture compared to their neighbors is the *akia* shout song.

The Suyá Indians of Brazil

The Suyá Indians belong to the northern branch of the Gê language family. They live in the Parque Indigena do Xingu, on the Suiá-missu River, near where it flows into the Xingu River, which is an affluent of the Amazon River. I have been researching and collaborating with the Suyá over a period of twenty-five years, since I was a graduate student at the University of Chicago. During this time, I have watched them change from a small, virtually monolingual community at the very edge of the frontier, to becoming a larger village living near Brazilian settlers, whose clear-cut ranches lie only minutes away by motorboat.

The Suyá, like other Gê-speaking peoples such as the Gavião, Kayapo, and Xavante, are able to mobilize their entire community and act together to protect their land. One of the ways they create consensus, and one of the ways they express their collective strength, is through singing and dancing. Both before and after decisive actions, such as retaking their traditional lands from neighboring ranches, the Suyá paint themselves, sing, and (re)create themselves as a powerful and united force. Musical performance—an important part of ritual life—is a key to their ability to act and to survive as a community.

The Dual Structure of Songs

All Suyá music is vocal, and the only musical instruments commonly used are rattles that accompany singing. They perform two principal types of songs: individual songs (*akia*) that are sung solo or in groups where each individual sings a different song to the same beat set by rattles and stamping feet; and unison group songs (*ngere*). Although these song types are quite different in a number of respects, they share a similar overall structure.

Both akia and ngere are based on a melody, comprised of between three and six phrases, that is repeated a minimum of four times, and usually many more times. The melody is repeated until either the individual or the group's song leader wants to change to another section of the song or begin another song altogether. Sometimes the melody is repeated until a certain ceremonial action is completed, and then it is changed. Although the melody is repeated virtually identically throughout the song, both pitch and tempo may be altered during the performance. The text that accompanies the melody, however, usually changes in predictable ways, following the Suyá idea of song structure.

Virtually all songs have two halves, *kradi* and *sindaw*, which could be translated as "the first half" and "the second half" or "the beginning" and "the end." Each half is structured in a similar way. Most halves begin with a section that is "empty" or comprised of song syllables that do not refer to anything outside the song itself (what the Suyá called "song-speech"). In an akia, these syllables are "te-te-te-te" with one "te" to every note of the melody. At the start of a repetition of the melody, an incomplete presentation of the text is added using everyday Suyá language. This describes an action without referring to the animal that did it—after the words describing the action. For example, the text might be, "I paint my cape and leap and sing, I paint my cape and leap and sing." Later, the text is amplified to include the name of an animal species, which completes the text and is the full text of that half. In an akia, that might be, "Black forest deer, I paint my cape and leap and sing." After singing that one or more times, a short coda ends the section. After the first half, the singer or the singers begin the second half and proceed in the same way. Figure 1 presents a single akia and shows how the text is sung in the eight text lines below the melody.

The reason Suyá song structure is significant is that the two-part song structure is an example of a dualism that appears over and over again in the Suyá belief system and social institutions. A Suyá once told me that "Everything comes in twos: if you see one, you look around and say 'Where is the other one like this one?'" Time, space, and social groups are just three of the important domains that the Suyá structure in a dual way. They name two directions, east (*kaikwa kradi* or the beginning of the sky) and west (*kaikwa indaw* or the end of the sky). They divide the year into two large seasons, the rainy season (*nda*) and the dry season (*ambedi*). All Suyá men also divide themselves into two ceremonial groups or *moieties*, the piranhas (*amban*-yi) and the parakeets (*kren-yi*), which are associated, respectively, with the east and west sides of the village plaza. There is an association between the piranhas and the east and the beginning or first half, and between the parakeets and the west and the end. At a certain moment in some ceremonies, all singers sing the first half of their song in front of the half of the men's house belonging to the piranhas and located in the east, and then circle the plaza and go sing the second half of their song in front of the parakeet part of the men's house. In log races, the piranhas always carry the lower or kradi side of the racing logs, and the parakeets always carry the top or sindaw. The superimposition of dual divisions (in space, in objects, and in sound) is an important part of ritual performance, where season of performance, movement in dance through space, and sounds each replicate the same patterns.

The division of music into two parts pervades all levels, from the verse level (meaningful words versus song-syllables) from the level of the song itself (the two halves of the song) to the genre level (one genre is only sung in the rainy season, another only in the dry season). Singing a song, in a very elementary way, replicates and reiterates the structure of the universe—it is an aural/oral representation of the structure of the entire cosmos—space, time, human society, and sound all expressed through sound.

Why sing dualism when it is so repeatedly expressed visually, temporally, and cosmically? The dualism of Suyá song structure makes the performance of a song the presentation (or re-creation) of an important cosmological structure. Singing the structured songs, Suyá create and express the dual organization of the universe and of their own ritual groups. But there is more to singing than just dividing a song in half. Singing style also can express individual perspectives and experiences, and music also can create significant feelings and motivations.

Singing Who You Are with Happiness

If the *structure* of all songs is generally similar, the *way they are sung* varies according to the specific characteristics of the group or individual who is singing them. By "way they are sung," I mean the

Figure 1 . Song text of an individual akia shout song

Here is the way the text develops in a shout song, moving from A1 (the empty start) to B4 (the coda of the second half).

A1: te-te-te-te-te-te-te-te, te-te-te-te-te, te-te-te-te-te-te-te-te, te-te-te-te-te-te

Kradi 1. "Empty, having nothing" (kaikaw). A "te" sung on each syllable, in an akia and typical song texts are sung in ngere (varying according to the ceremony). The Suyá say the opening verse is "empty." The melody is sung with only syllables that don't have any reference to anything besides the type of song. In this akia, the syllables are te-te-te-te-te-te, for each note.

A2: I-moi-po-ku-naw, I-moi-po-ku-naw, I-moi-po-ku-naw wa ia-rin-ne, te-te-te-te-te-te, te-te-te

Kradi 2. "Going toward the name/looking for the name" (sinti sulu). Here the melody is divided into two parts, the part with the text that says "paint my dance cape, paint my dance cape, paint my dance cape and leap and sing," which is followed by two phrases of just song syllables, te-te-te-te.

A3: Am-a-to-ti, I-moi-po-ku-naw, I-moi-ku-naw wa I-rin-ne, te-te-te-te-te, te-te-te-te-te . . .

Kradi 3. "Telling the name" (sinti iaren). In this section, the name of an animal is inserted before the action, and the text is complete: "Big forest rat, paint my dance cape, paint my dance ornament and leap and sing. " When the Suyá talk about song texts, they usually name the animal first (as in "the first half is a forest rat, the second half is a red mouse"), then may mention the action. As far as I know, they have no classification of melody types, but just say "it goes like this. . . . "

A4. [phrases with words omitted]   te-te-te-te-te-te-te-te-te . . .

Kradi 4. "The end" (kure). To end this part, the singer repeats the te-te-te-te part of the verse again. Different unison song genres have different formal endings—sometimes the tempo slows dramatically, sometimes a short end and an animal cry may end the section.

BI: te-te-te-te-te-te-te-te, te-te-te-te-te, te-te-te-te-te-te-te-te, te-te-te-te-te-te

Sindaw 1. This section is identical in sound to Kradi 1.

B2: I-moi-po-ia-kaw, I-moi-po-ia-kaw, Imoi-po-ia-kaw wa ia-rin-ne, te-te, te-te, te-te-te-te-te . . .

Sindaw 2. The action is different in the "second half. " Here the translation would be "cut my dance ornament, cut my dance ornament, cut my dance ornament and leap and sing, te-te-te-te . . . . "

B3: am-to-kam-brik-ti, I-moi-po-ia-kaw, I-moi-po-ia-kaw wa ia-rin-ne, te-te, te-te, te-te-te-te-te . . .

Sindaw 3. The animal is also different in the second half. "Red mouse, cut my dance ornament, cut my dance ornament and leap and sing, te-te-te-te-te . . . . "

B4: [phrases with words omitted]   te-te-te-te-te-te-te-te-te . . .

Sindaw 4. The ending section is identical to A-4 in the case of the shout song. In some unison song genres, the ending of the "second half" is more elaborate than that of the "first half."

timbre, the attacks and decays of notes, and the loudness or softness of the singers.

Men and women sing differently and often sing separately, each gender with its own ceremonies. Sometimes they sing together, but form two separate lines of dancers. In general, men sing more frequently than women, who make other contributions to ceremonies through food preparation and gift giving.

Within a given gender, unison songs generally are sung the same way each time, with a great effort made by the singers to blend their voices. This is because the groups that sing together are enduring ceremonial groups—as some members age and die, they are replaced by younger members who have the same ceremonial identity. The men of the eastern moiety (piranhas) are said to sing songs slower and to sing songs about "beautiful" animals, while the western moiety (parakeets) sing faster, and name different animals. They are said to have maintained these differences for generations.

Individual shout songs, however, are performed differently by males of different ages, and performance varies also according to the mood of the singer. The singers stamp and sing separate songs. They maintain a unified rhythm by stamping in unison, but they make no attempt to blend their voices. On the contrary, the differences in their voices express differences in their age and social position. To a certain extent, the development is cyclical—young boys sing "funny" shout songs with only one half while very old men (grandfathers with several grandchildren) also sing "funny" shout songs, or don't sing them at all. Figure 2 illustrates how different ages sing individual shout songs.

Figure 2. Age and akia shout song style

Boys (4–10 years) *perform shout songs with short phrases and only one "half" (name only one thing). The songs name an "odd" or funny animal/item/substance.*

Young adolescents (10–15 years) *perform shout songs that have longer phrases, two halves, and a full structure, but use fairly simple melodies.*

Older adolescents (15–25 years/through birth of second child) *are given particularly challenging songs to learn. These have full-length phrases, complex melodies, and fully adult structure. Young men of this age should sing as high as possible—a kind of forcing of the upper limits of each person's voice. They also are supposed to sing loudly.*

Married men with a few children *are expected to continue to sing shout songs, but may sing them at a slightly lower pitch—forcing their voices less.*

Grandfathers with several grandchildren *enter a new age grade. Instead of singing akia, they give a falsetto shout, characteristic of old people. They also may sing obscene and funny shout songs, a prerogative of "old clowns. "*

A man receives his shout song from a specialist who introduces new songs into the community. Because he does not make up his own, the length of the phrases and the structure are determined by a prestigious adult. He does, however, have considerable attitude about how he sings it.

When a man begins a ceremony, he has a fair amount of latitude with regard to how he sings his shout song. He may sing like an adolescent to stress his enduring youth and strength, or he may begin to sing like an elder to indicate his affiliation with the elders. Every time he sings, he re-states his social position—he expresses through his voice his perception of his position in the community.

In addition to expressing social position, a man can express his own personal feelings through the way he sings shout songs. Women may also express similar things through their participation (or not) in unison singing. (I use a male example here because the shout song is a male genre.) A man can communicate certain emotions that are rarely spoken, but may be expressed through song. The emotions he may express are sadness (as in sadness over the death of a relative), anger (as in anger about the distribution of food during the ceremony), or enthusiasm and euphoric happiness (the appropriate emotion for a singer). His options range from refusing to sing (and therefore publicly indicating that he is sad or angry about something) to singing with an exaggerated forcefulness that communicates his euphoria and complete immersion in the performance. When a man is very angry he remains quiet, an action that is interpreted as a very direct criticism of the event. When he is somewhat unhappy but not actually angry, he may sing an old song rather than learn a new one, or sing without energy and for a short time compared to "euphoric" participants. When he wishes to indicate his happiness and full involvement, his stamping will be exaggerated, his singing loud, and he will perform for hours without resting. When Suyá listen to a group of men singing individual shout songs, what they listen for are the individual melodies and songs, and the individual expressions of position and emotion.

Completely Involved Happiness

Euphoria is an essential component of Suyá music and dance, just as it is for a great deal of music around the world. According to the Suyá, participants in song and dance experience a physiological thrill, a special "flow," a particular satisfaction from singing and dancing strenuously for hours on end. To a certain extent, this may be the result of an altered state of consciousness brought on by strenuous rhythmic singing and dancing for long periods of time. Unlike many other Amazonian communities, the Suyá rarely use home-made alcoholic beverages and never use hallucinogens as part of their ritual activities. The Suyá have said over and over again, "When we sing, we are happy; when we are happy, we sing." This circularity may explain the importance of singing to the cosmological structure and not just talking about it, and of singing in rituals and not just walking through the events. They say there is a unique and enjoyable feeling derived from this physical and cosmological activity.

Conclusion

There are many other significant parts of Suyá musical performance that space does not allow me to describe—including body ornamentation, dance, the origin of songs and the way new songs are introduced—but these are discussed in a book (Seeger 1987). I have demonstrated, however, some of the ways in which the cosmos, the life cycle, and deep personal experiences are expressed through song.

Although it has often been argued that singing and dancing can reinforce cultural identity by unifying participants around an event, scholars have rarely recognized that the sounds of the music are a part of the process. For the Suyá, however, the sound and the structure of musical performances are clearly a means of experiencing the cosmos and expressing individual attitudes. The act of singing in itself creates the structures and creates feelings that are important to the Suyá. It is no wonder they sing before embarking on collective activities, and it is perhaps prescient of the Suyá elders to say, "When we stop singing, we will be finished."

References

Seeger, Anthony. 1981. *Nature and Society in Central Brazil, the Suyá Indians of Mato Grosso Brazil.* Cambridge: Harvard University Press.

————. 1987. *Why Suyá Sing, A Musical Anthropology of an Amazonian People.* Cambridge: Cambridge University Press.

Audio tape that accompanies the book *Why Suyá Sing.* 1987. Cambridge: Cambridge University Press, 1987. This is currently out of print. A video tape is in preparation.

THE SOUND OF MUSIC:
SUYÁ SONG STRUCTURE AND EXPERIENCE

Anthony Seeger

1) According to the article, what is the purpose of Suyá singing?

2) What do the Suyá themselves say about their singing during ceremonies?

3) Describe the structure of Suyá songs. How do they relate to other concepts in Suyá culture?

4) What are the gender differences in Suyá singing, and how does singing differ from person to person?

5) Why is euphoria an essential component of Suyá singing?

SECTION EIGHT

Politics: Who Gets What, When, and How

FROM EGALITARIANISM TO KLEPTOCRACY

Jared Diamond

In 1979, while I was flying with missionary friends over a remote swamp-filled basin of New Guinea, I noticed a few huts many miles apart. The pilot explained to me that, somewhere in that muddy expanse below us, a group of Indonesian crocodile hunters had recently come across a group of New Guinea nomads. Both groups had panicked, and the encounter had ended with the Indonesians shooting several of the nomads.

My missionary friends guessed that the nomads belonged to an uncontacted group called the Fayu, known to the outside world only through accounts by their terrified neighbors, a missionized group of erstwhile nomads called the Kirikiri. First contacts between outsiders and New Guinea groups are always potentially dangerous, but this beginning was especially inauspicious. Nevertheless, my friend Doug flew in by helicopter to try to establish friendly relations with the Fayu. He returned, alive but shaken, to tell a remarkable story.

It turned out that the Fayu normally lived as single families, scattered through the swamp and coming together once or twice each year to negotiate exchanges of brides. Doug's visit coincided with such a gathering, of a few dozen Fayu. To us, a few dozen people constitute a small, ordinary gathering, but to the Fayu it was a rare, frightening event. Murderers suddenly found themselves face-to-face with their victim's relatives. For example, one Fayu man spotted the man who had killed his father. The son raised his ax and rushed at the murderer but was wrestled to the ground by friends; then the murderer came at the prostrate son with an ax and was also wrestled down. Both men were held, screaming in rage, until they seemed sufficiently exhausted to be released. Other men periodically shouted insults at each other, shook with anger and frustration, and pounded the ground with their axes. That tension continued for the several days of the gathering, while Doug prayed that the visit would not end in violence.

The Fayu consist of about 400 hunter-gatherers, divided into four clans and wandering over a few hundred square miles. According to their own account, they had formerly numbered about 2,000, but their population had been greatly reduced as a result of Fayu killing Fayu. They lacked political and social mechanisms, which we take for granted, to achieve peaceful resolution of serious disputes. Eventually, as a result of Doug's visit, one group of Fayu invited a courageous husband-and-wife missionary couple to live with them. The couple has now resided there for a dozen years and gradually persuaded the Fayu to renounce violence. The Fayu are thereby being brought into the modern world, where they face an uncertain future.

Many other previously uncontacted groups of New Guineans and Amazonian Indians have similarly owed to missionaries their incorporation into modern society. After the missionaries come teachers and doctors, bureaucrats and soldiers. The spreads of government and of religion have thus been linked to each other throughout recorded history, whether the spread has been peaceful (as eventually with the Fayu) or by force. In the latter case, it is often government that organizes the conquest, and religion that justifies it. Although nomads and tribespeople occasionally defeat organized governments and religions, the trend over the past 13,000 years has been for the nomads and tribespeople to lose.

At the end of the last Ice Age, much of the world's population lived in societies similar to that of the Fayu today, and no people then lived in a much more complex society. As recently as A.D. 1500, less than 20 percent of the world's land area was marked off by boundaries into states run by bureaucrats and governed by laws. Today, all land except Antarctica's is so divided. Descendants of those societies that achieved centralized government and organized religion earliest ended up dominating the modern world. The combination of government and religion has thus functioned, together with germs, writing, and technology, as one of the four main sets of proximate agents leading to history's broadest pattern. How did government and religion arise?

Fayu bands and modern states represent opposite extremes along the spectrum of human societies. Modern American society and the Fayu differ in the presence or absence of a professional police force, cities, money, distinctions between rich and poor, and many other political, economic, and social institutions. Did all of those institutions arise together, or did some arise before others? We can infer the answer to this question by comparing modern societies at different levels of organization, by examining written accounts or archaeological evidence about past societies, and by observing how a society's institutions change over time.

Cultural anthropologists attempting to describe the diversity of human societies often divide them into as many as half a dozen categories. Any such attempt to define stages of any evolutionary or developmental continuum—whether of musical styles, human life stages, or human societies—is doubly doomed to imperfection. First, because each stage grows out of some previous stage, the lines of demarcation are inevitably arbitrary. (For example, is a 19-year-old person an adolescent or a young adult?) Second, developmental sequences are not invariant, so examples pigeonholed under the same stage are inevitably heterogeneous. (Brahms and Liszt would turn in their graves to know that they are now grouped together as composers of the romantic period.) Nevertheless, arbitrarily delineated stages provide a useful shorthand for discussing the diversity of music and of human societies, provided one bears in mind the above caveats. In that spirit, we shall use a simple classification based on just four categories—band, tribe, chiefdom, and state—to understand societies.

Bands are the tiniest societies, consisting typically of 5 to 80 people, most or all of them close relatives by birth or by marriage. In effect, a band is an extended family or several related extended families. Today, bands still living autonomously are almost confined to the most remote parts of New Guinea and Amazonia, but within modern times there were many others that have only recently fallen under state control or been assimilated or exterminated. They include many or most African Pygmies, southern African San hunter-gatherers (so-called Bushmen), Aboriginal Australians, Eskimos (Inuit), and Indians of some resource-poor areas of the Americas such as Tierra del Fuego and the northern boreal forests. All those modern bands are or were nomadic hunter-gatherers rather than settled food producers. Probably all humans lived in bands until at least 40,000 years ago, and most still did as recently as 11,000 years ago.

Bands lack many institutions that we take for granted in our own society. They have no permanent single base of residence. The band's land is used jointly by the whole group, instead of being partitioned among subgroups or individuals. There is no regular economic specialization, except by age and sex: all able-bodied individuals forage for food. There are no formal institutions, such as laws, police, and treaties, to resolve conflicts within and between bands. Band organization is often described as "egalitarian": there is no formalized social stratification into upper and lower classes, no formalized or hereditary leadership, and no formalized monopolies of information and decision making. However, the term "egalitarian" should not be taken to mean that all band members are equal in prestige and contribute equally to decisions. Rather, the term merely means that any band "leadership" is informal and acquired through qualities such as personality, strength, intelligence, and fighting skills.

My own experience with bands comes from the swampy lowland area of New Guinea where the Fayu live, a region known as the Lakes Plains. There, I still encounter extended families of a few adults with their dependent children and elderly, living in crude temporary shelters along streams and traveling by canoe and on foot. Why do peoples of the Lakes Plains continue to live as nomadic bands, when most other New Guinea peoples, and almost all other peoples elsewhere in the world, now live in settled larger groups? The explanation is that the region lacks dense local concentrations of resources that would permit many people to live together, and that (until the arrival of missionaries bringing crop plants) it also lacked native plants that could have permitted productive farming. The bands' food staple is the sago palm tree, whose core yields a starchy pith when the palm reaches maturity. The bands are nomadic, because they must move when they have cut the mature sago trees in an area. Band numbers are kept low by diseases (especially malaria), by the lack of raw materials in the swamp (even stone for tools must be obtained by trade), and by the limited amount of food that the swamp yields for humans. Similar limitations on the resources accessible to existing human technology prevail in the regions of the world recently occupied by other bands.

Our closest animal relatives, the gorillas and chimpanzees and bonobos of Africa, also live in bands. All humans presumably did so too, until improved technology for extracting food allowed some hunter-gatherers to settle in permanent dwellings in some resource-rich areas. The band is the political, economic, and social organization that we inherited from our millions of years of evolutionary history. Our developments beyond it all took place within the last few tens of thousands of years.

The first of those stages beyond the band is termed the tribe, which differs in being larger (typically comprising hundreds rather than dozens of people) and usually having fixed settlements. However, some tribes and even chiefdoms consist of herders who move seasonally.

Tribal organization is exemplified by New Guinea highlanders, whose political unit before the arrival of colonial government was a village or else a close-knit cluster of villages. This political definition of "tribe" is thus often much smaller than what linguists and cultural anthropologists would define as a tribe—namely, a group that shares language and culture. For example, in 1964 I began to work among a group of highlanders known as the Foré. By linguistic and cultural standards, there were then 12,000 Foré, speaking two mutually intelligible dialects and living in 65 villages of several hundred people each. But there was no political unity whatsoever among villages of the Foré language group. Each hamlet was involved in a kaleidoscopically changing pattern of war and shifting alliances with all neighboring hamlets, regardless of whether the neighbors were Foré or speakers of a different language.

Tribes, recently independent and now variously subordinated to national states, still occupy much of New Guinea, Melanesia, and Amazonia. Similar tribal organization in the past is inferred from archaeological evidence of settlements that were substantial but lacked the archaeological hallmarks of chiefdoms that I shall explain below. That evidence suggests that tribal organization began to emerge around 13,000 years ago in the Fertile Crescent and later in some other areas. A prerequisite for living in settlements is either food production or else a productive environment with especially concentrated resources that can be hunted and gathered within a small area. That's why settlements, and by inference tribes, began to proliferate in the Fertile Crescent at that time, when climate changes and improved technology combined to permit abundant harvests of wild cereals.

Besides differing from a band by virtue of its settled residence and its larger numbers, a tribe also differs in that it consists of more than one formally recognized kinship group, termed clans, which exchange marriage partners. Land belongs to a particular clan, not to the whole tribe. However, the number of people in a tribe is still low enough that everyone knows everyone else by name and relationships.

For other types of human groups as well, "a few hundred" seems to be an upper limit for group size compatible with everyone's knowing everybody. In our state society, for instance, school principals are likely to know all their students by name if the school contains a few hundred children, but not if it contains a few thousand children. One reason why the organization of human government tends to change from that of a tribe to that of a chiefdom in societies with more than a few hundred members is that the difficult issue of conflict resolution between strangers becomes increasingly acute in larger groups. A fact further diffusing potential problems of conflict resolution in tribes is that almost everyone is related to everyone else, by blood or marriage or both. Those ties of relationships binding all tribal members make police, laws, and other conflict-resolving institutions of larger societies unnecessary, since any two villagers getting into an argument will share many kin, who apply pressure on them to keep it from becoming violent. In traditional New Guinea society, if a New Guinean happened to encounter an unfamiliar New Guinean while both were away from their respective villages, the two engaged in a long discussion of their relatives, in an attempt to establish some relationship and hence some reason why the two should not attempt to kill each other.

Despite all of these differences between bands and tribes, many similarities remain. Tribes still have an informal, "egalitarian" system of government. Information and decision making are both communal. In the New Guinea highlands, I have watched village meetings where all adults in the village were present, sitting on the ground, and individuals made speeches, without any appearance of one person's "chairing" the discussion. Many highland villages do have someone known as the "big-man," the most influential man of the village. But that position is not a formal office to be filled and carries only limited power. The big-man has no independent decision-making authority, knows no diplomatic secrets, and can do no more than attempt to sway communal decisions. Big-men achieve that status by their own attributes; the position is not inherited.

Tribes also share with bands an "egalitarian" social system, without ranked lineages or classes. Not only is status not inherited; no member of a traditional tribe or band can become disproportionately wealthy by his or her own efforts, because each individual has debts and obligations to many others. It is therefore impossible for an outsider to guess, from appearances, which of all the adult men in a village is the big-man: he lives in the same type of hut, wears the same clothes or ornaments, or is as naked, as everyone else.

Like bands, tribes lack a bureaucracy, police force, and taxes. Their economy is based on reciprocal exchanges between individuals or families, rather than on a redistribution of tribute paid to some central authority. Economic specialization is slight: full-time crafts specialists are lacking, and every able-bodied adult (including the big-man) participates in growing, gathering, or hunting food. I recall one occasion when I was walking past a garden in the Solomon Islands, saw a man digging and waving at me in the distance, and realized to my astonishment that it was a friend of mine named Faletau. He was the most famous wood carver of the Solomons, an artist of great originality—but that did not free him of the necessity to grow his own sweet potatoes. Since tribes thus lack economic specialists, they also lack slaves, because there are no specialized menial jobs for a slave to perform.

Just as musical composers of the classical period range from C. P. E. Bach to Schubert and thereby cover the whole spectrum from baroque composers to romantic composers, tribes also shade into bands at one extreme and into chiefdoms at the opposite extreme. In particular, a tribal big-man's role in dividing the meat of pigs slaughtered for feasts points to the role of chiefs in collecting and redistributing food and goods—now reconstrued as tribute—in chiefdoms. Similarly, presence or absence of public architecture is supposedly one of the distinctions between tribes and chiefdoms, but large New Guinea villages often have cult houses (known as *haus tamburan*, on the Sepik River) that presage the temples of chiefdoms.

Although a few bands and tribes survive today on remote and ecologically marginal lands outside state control, fully independent chiefdoms had disappeared by the early twentieth century, because they tended to occupy prime land coveted by states. However, as of A.D. 1492, chiefdoms were still widespread over much of the eastern United States, in productive areas of South and Central America and sub-Saharan Africa that had not yet been subsumed under native states, and in all of Polynesia. The archaeological evidence discussed below suggests that chiefdoms arose by around 5500 B.C. in the Fertile Crescent and by around 1000 B.C. in Mesoamerica and the Andes. Let us consider the distinctive features of chiefdoms, very different from modern European and American states and, at the same time, from bands and simple tribal societies.

As regards population size, chiefdoms were considerably larger than tribes, ranging from several thousand to several tens of thousands of people. That size created serious potential for internal conflict because, for any person living in a chiefdom, the vast majority of other people in the chiefdom were neither closely related by blood or marriage nor known by name. With the rise of chiefdoms around 7,500 years ago, people had to learn, for the first time in history, how to encounter strangers regularly without attempting to kill them.

Part of the solution to that problem was for one person, the chief, to exercise a monopoly on the right to use force. In contrast to a tribe's big-man, a chief held a recognized office, filled by hereditary right. Instead of the decentralized anarchy of a village meeting, the chief was a permanent centralized authority, made all significant decisions, and had a monopoly on critical information (such as what a neighboring chief was privately threatening, or what harvest the gods had supposedly promised). Unlike big-men, chiefs could be recognized from afar by visible distinguishing features, such as a large fan worn over the back on Rennell Island in the Southwest Pacific. A commoner encountering a chief was obliged to perform ritual marks of respect, such as (on Hawaii) prostrating oneself. The chief's orders might be transmitted through one or two levels of bureaucrats, many of whom were themselves low-ranked chiefs. However, in contrast to state bureaucrats, chiefdom bureaucrats had generalized rather than specialized roles. In Polynesian Hawaii the same bureaucrats (termed konohiki) extracted tribute *and* oversaw irrigation *and* organized labor corvées for the chief, whereas state societies have separate tax collectors, water district managers, and draft boards.

A chiefdom's large population in a small area required plenty of food, obtained by food production in most cases, by hunting-gathering in a few especially rich areas. For example, American Indians of the Pacific Northwest coast, such as the Kwakiutl, Nootka, and Tlingit Indians, lived under chiefs in villages without any agriculture or domestic animals, because the rivers and sea were so rich in salmon and halibut. The food surpluses generated by some people, relegated to the rank of commoners, went to feed the chiefs, their families, bureaucrats, and crafts specialists, who variously made canoes, adzes, or spittoons or worked as bird catchers or tattooers.

Luxury goods, consisting of those specialized crafts products or else rare objects obtained by long-distance trade, were reserved for chiefs. For example, Hawaiian chiefs had feather cloaks, some of them consisting of tens of thousands of feathers and requiring many human generations for their manufacture (by commoner cloak makers, of course). That concentration of luxury goods often makes it possible to recognize chiefdoms archaeologically, by the fact that some graves (those of chiefs) contain much richer goods than other graves (those of commoners), in contrast to the egalitarian burials of earlier human history. Some ancient complex chiefdoms can also be distinguished from tribal villages by the remains of elaborate public architecture (such as temples) and by a regional hierarchy of settlements, with one site (the site of the paramount chief) being obviously larger and having more administrative buildings and artifacts than other sites.

Like tribes, chiefdoms consisted of multiple hereditary lineages living at one site. However, whereas the lineages of tribal villages are equal-ranked clans, in a chiefdom all members of the chief's lineage had hereditary perquisites. In effect, the society was divided into hereditary chief and commoner classes, with Hawaiian chiefs themselves subdivided into eight hierarchically ranked lineages, each concentrating its marriages within its own lineage. Furthermore, since chiefs required menial servants as well as specialized craftspeople, chiefdoms differed from tribes in having many jobs that could be filled by slaves, typically obtained by capture in raids.

The most distinctive economic feature of chiefdoms was their shift from reliance solely on the reciprocal exchanges characteristic of bands and tribes, by which A gives B a gift while expecting that B at some unspecified future time will give a gift of comparable value to A. We modern state dwellers indulge in such behavior on birthdays and holidays, but most of our flow of goods is achieved instead by buying and selling for money according to the law of supply and demand. While continuing reciprocal exchanges and without marketing or money, chiefdoms developed an additional new system termed a redistributive economy. A simple example would involve a chief receiving wheat at harvest time from every farmer in the chiefdom, then throwing a feast for everybody and serving bread or else storing the wheat and gradually giving it out again in the months between harvests. When a large portion of the goods received from commoners was not redistributed to them but was retained and consumed by the chiefly lineages and craftspeople, the redistribution became tribute, a precursor of taxes that made its first appearance in chiefdoms. From the commoners the chiefs claimed not only goods but also labor for construction of public works, which again might return to benefit the commoners (for example, irrigation systems to help feed everybody) or instead benefited mainly the chiefs (for instance, lavish tombs).

We have been talking about chiefdoms generically, as if they were all the same. In fact, chiefdoms varied considerably. Larger ones tended to have more powerful chiefs, more ranks of chiefly lineages, greater distinctions between chiefs and commoners, more retention of tribute by the chiefs, more layers of bureaucrats, and grander public architecture. For instance, societies on small Polynesian islands were effectively rather similar to tribal societies with a big-man, except that the position of chief was hereditary. The chief's hut looked like any other hut, there were no bureaucrats or public works, the chief redistributed

most goods he received back to the commoners, and land was controlled by the community. But on the largest Polynesian islands, such as Hawaii, Tahiti, and Tonga, chiefs were recognizable at a glance by their ornaments, public works were erected by large labor forces, most tribute was retained by the chiefs, and all land was controlled by them. A further gradation among societies with ranked lineages was from those where the political unit was a single autonomous village, to those consisting of a regional assemblage of villages in which the largest village with a paramount chief controlled the smaller villages with lesser chiefs.

By now, it should be obvious that chiefdoms introduced the dilemma fundamental to all centrally governed, nonegalitarian societies. At best, they do good by providing expensive services impossible to contract for on an individual basis. At worst, they function unabashedly as kleptocracies, transferring net wealth from commoners to upper classes. These noble and selfish functions are inextricably linked, although some governments emphasize much more of one function than of the other. The difference between a kleptocrat and a wise statesman, between a robber baron and a public benefactor, is merely one of degree: a matter of just how large a percentage of the tribute extracted from producers is retained by the elite, and how much the commoners like the public uses to which the redistributed tribute is put. We consider President Mobutu of Zaire a kleptocrat because he keeps too much tribute (the equivalent of billions of dollars) and redistributes too little tribute (no functioning telephone system in Zaire). We consider George Washington a statesman because he spent tax money on widely admired programs and did not enrich himself as president. Nevertheless, George Washington was born into wealth, which is much more unequally distributed in the United States than in New Guinea villages.

For any ranked society, whether a chiefdom or a state, one thus has to ask: why do the commoners tolerate the transfer of the fruits of their hard labor to kleptocrats? This question, raised by political theorists from Plato to Marx, is raised anew by voters in every modern election. Kleptocracies with little public support run the risk of being overthrown, either by downtrodden commoners or by upstart would-be replacement kleptocrats seeking public support by promising a higher ratio of services rendered to fruits stolen. For example, Hawaiian history was repeatedly punctuated by revolts against repressive chiefs, usually led by younger brothers promising less oppression. This may sound funny to us in the context of old Hawaii, until we reflect on all the misery still being caused by such struggles in the modern world.

What should an elite do to gain popular support while still maintaining a more comfortable lifestyle than commoners? Kleptocrats throughout the ages have resorted to a mixture of four solutions:

1. Disarm the populace, and arm the elite. That's much easier in these days of high-tech weaponry, produced only in industrial plants and easily monopolized by an elite, than in ancient times of spears and clubs easily made at home.

2. Make the masses happy by redistributing much of the tribute received, in popular ways. This principle was as valid for Hawaiian chiefs as it is for American politicians today.

3. Use the monopoly of force to promote happiness, by maintaining public order and curbing violence. This is potentially a big and underappreciated advantage of centralized societies over noncentralized ones. Anthropologists formerly idealized band and tribal societies as gentle and nonviolent, because visiting anthropologists observed no murder in a band of 25 people in the course of a three-year study. Of course they didn't: it's easy to calculate that a band of a dozen adults and a dozen children, subject to the inevitable deaths occurring anyway for the usual reasons other than murder, could not perpetuate itself if in addition one of its dozen adults murdered another adult every three years. Much more extensive long-term information about band and tribal societies reveals that murder is a leading cause of death. For example, I happened to be visiting New Guinea's Iyau people at a time when a woman anthropologist was interviewing Iyau women about their life histories. Woman after woman, when asked to name her husband, named several sequential husbands who had died violent deaths. A typical answer went like this: "My first husband was killed by Elopi raiders. My second husband was killed by a man who wanted me, and who became my third husband. That husband was killed by the brother of my second husband, seeking to avenge his murder." Such biographies prove common for so-called gentle tribespeople and contributed to the acceptance of centralized authority as tribal societies grew larger.

4. The remaining way for kleptocrats to gain public support is to construct an ideology or religion justifying kleptocracy. Bands and tribes already had supernatural beliefs, just as do modern established religions. But the supernatural beliefs of bands and tribes did not serve to justify central authority, justify transfer of wealth, or maintain peace between unrelated individuals. When supernatural beliefs gained those functions and became institutionalized, they were thereby transformed into what we term a religion. Hawaiian chiefs were typical of chiefs elsewhere, in asserting divinity, divine descent, or at least a hotline to the gods. The chief claimed to serve the people by interceding for them with the gods and reciting the ritual formulas required to obtain rain, good harvests, and success in fishing.

Chiefdoms characteristically have an ideology, precursor to an institutionalized religion, that buttresses the chief's authority. The chief may either combine the offices of political leader and priest in a single person, or may support a separate group of kleptocrats (that is, priests) whose function is to provide ideological justification for the chiefs. That is why chiefdoms devote so much collected tribute to constructing temples and other public works, which serve as centers of the official religion and visible signs of the chief's power.

Besides justifying the transfer of wealth to kleptocrats, institutionalized religion brings two other important benefits to centralized societies. First, shared ideology or religion helps solve the problem of how unrelated individuals are to live together without killing each other—by providing them with a bond not based on kinship. Second, it gives people a motive, other than genetic self-interest, for sacrificing their lives on behalf of others. At the cost of a few society members who die in battle as soldiers, the whole society becomes much more effective at conquering other societies or resisting attacks.

The political, economic, and social institutions most familiar to us today are those of states, which now rule all of the world's land area except for Antarctica. Many early states and all modern ones have had literate elites, and many modern states have literate masses as well. Vanished states tended to leave visible archaeological hallmarks, such as ruins of temples with standardized designs, at least four levels of settlement sizes, and pottery styles covering tens of thousands of square miles. We thereby know that states arose around 3700 B.C. in Mesopotamia and around 300 B.C. in Mesoamerica, more than 2,000 years ago in the Andes, China, and Southeast Asia, and more than 1,000 years ago in West Africa. In modern times the formation of states out of chiefdoms has been observed repeatedly. Thus, we possess much more information about past states and their formation than about past chiefdoms, tribes, and bands.

Protostates extend many features of large paramount (multivillage) chiefdoms. They continue the increase in size from bands to tribes to chiefdoms. Whereas chiefdoms' populations range from a few thousand to a few tens of thousands, the populations of most modern states exceed one million, and China's exceeds one billion. The paramount chief's location may become the state's capital city. Other population centers of states outside the capital may also qualify as true cities, which are lacking in chiefdoms. Cities differ from villages in their monumental public works, palaces of rulers, accumulation of capital from tribute or taxes, and concentration of people other than food producers.

Early states had a hereditary leader with a title equivalent to king, like a super paramount chief and exercising an even greater monopoly of information, decision making, and power. Even in democracies today, crucial knowledge is available to only a few individuals, who control the flow of information to the rest of the government and consequently control decisions. For instance, in the Cuban Missile Crisis of 1963, information and discussions that determined whether nuclear war would engulf half a billion people were initially confined by President Kennedy to a ten-member executive committee of the National Security Council that he himself appointed; then he limited final decisions to a four-member group consisting of himself and three of his cabinet ministers.

Central control is more far-reaching, and economic redistribution in the form of tribute (renamed taxes) more extensive, in states than in chiefdoms. Economic specialization is more extreme, to the point where today not even farmers remain self-sufficient. Hence the effect on society is catastrophic when state government collapses, as happened in Britain upon the removal of Roman troops, administrators, and coinage between A.D. 407 and 411. Even the earliest Mesopotamian states exercised centralized control of their economies. Their food was produced by four specialist groups (cereal farmers, herders, fishermen, and orchard and garden growers), from each of which the state took the produce and to each of which it gave out the necessary supplies, tools, and foods other than the type of food that this group produced. The state supplied seeds and plow animals to the cereal farmers, took wool from the herders, exchanged the wool by long-distance trade for metal and other essential raw materials, and paid out food rations to the laborers who maintained the irrigation systems on which the farmers depended.

Many, perhaps most, early states adopted slavery on a much larger scale than did chiefdoms. That was not because chiefdoms were more kindly disposed toward defeated enemies but because the greater economic specialization of states, with more mass production and more public works, provided more uses for slave labor. In addition, the larger scale of state warfare made more captives available.

A chiefdom's one or two levels of administration are greatly multiplied in states, as anyone who has seen an organization chart of any government knows. Along with the proliferation of vertical levels of bureaucrats, there is also horizontal specialization. Instead of konohiki carrying out every aspect of administration for a Hawaiian district, state goverments have several separate departments, each with its own hierarchy, to handle water management, taxes, military draft, and so on. Even small states have more complex bureaucracies than large chiefdoms. For instance, the West African state of Maradi had a central administration with over 130 titled offices.

Internal conflict resolution within states has become increasingly formalized by laws, a judiciary, and police. The laws are often written, because many states (with conspicuous exceptions, such as that of the Incas) have had literate elites, writing having been developed around the same time as the formation of the earliest states in both Mesopotamia and Mesoamerica. In contrast, no early chiefdom not on the verge of statehood developed writing.

Early states had state religions and standardized temples. Many early kings were considered divine and were accorded special treatment in innumerable respects. For example, the Aztec and Inca emperors were carried about in litters; servants went ahead of the Inca emperor's litter and swept the ground clear; and the Japanese language includes special forms of the pronoun "you" for use only in addressing the emperor. Early kings were themselves the head of the state religion or else had separate high priests. The Mesopotamian temple was the center not only of religion but also of economic redistribution, writing, and crafts technology.

All these features of states carry to an extreme the developments that led from tribes to chiefdoms. In addition, though, states have diverged from chiefdoms in several new directions. The most fundamental such distinction is that states are organized on political and territorial lines, not on the kinship lines that defined bands, tribes, and simple chiefdoms. Furthermore, bands and tribes always, and chiefdoms usually, consist of a single ethnic and linguistic group. States, though—especially so-called empires formed by amalgamation or conquest of states—are regularly multiethnic and multilingual. State bureaucrats are not selected mainly on the basis of kinship, as in chiefdoms, but are professionals selected at least partly on the basis of training and ability. In later states, including most today, the leadership often became nonhereditary, and many states abandoned the entire system of formal hereditary classes carried over from chiefdoms.

Over the past 13,000 years, the predominant trend in human society has been the replacement of smaller, less complex units by larger, more complex ones. Obviously, that is no more than an average long-term trend, with innumerable shifts in either direction: 1,000 amalgamations for 999 reversals. We know from our daily newspaper that large units (for instance, the former USSR, Yugoslavia, and Czechoslavakia) can disintegrate into smaller units, as did Alexander of Macedon's empire over 2,000 years ago. More complex units don't always conquer less complex ones but may succumb to them, as when the Roman and Chinese Empires were overrun by "barbarian" and Mongol chiefdoms, respectively. But the long-term trend has still been toward large, complex societies, culminating in states.

Obviously, too, part of the reason for states' triumphs over simpler entities when the two collide is that states usually enjoy an advantage of weaponry and other technology, and a large numerical advantage in population. But there are also two other potential advantages inherent in chiefdoms and states. First, a centralized decision maker has the advantage at concentrating troops and resources. Second, the official religions and patriotic fervor of many states make their troops willing to fight suicidally.

The latter willingness is one so strongly programmed into us citizens of modern states, by our schools and churches and governments, that we forget what a radical break it marks with previous human history. Every state has its slogan urging its citizens to be prepared to die if necessary for the state: Britain's "For King and Country," Spain's "Por Dios y España," and so on. Similar sentiments motivated 16th-century Aztec warriors: "There is nothing like death in war, nothing like the flowery death so precious to Him [the Aztec national god Huitzilopochtli] who gives life: far off I see it, my heart yearns for it!"

Such sentiments are unthinkable in bands and tribes. In all the accounts that my New Guinea friends have given me of their former tribal wars, there has been not a single hint of tribal patriotism, of a suicidal charge, or of any other military conduct carrying an accepted risk of being killed. Instead, raids are initiated by ambush or by superior force, so as to minimize at all costs the risk that one might die for one's village. But that attitude severely limits the military options of tribes, compared with state societies. Naturally, what makes patriotic and religious fanatics such dangerous opponents is not the deaths of the fanatics themselves, but their willingness to accept the deaths of a fraction of their number in order to annihilate or crush their infidel enemy. Fanaticism in war, of the type that drove recorded Christian and Islamic conquests, was probably unknown on Earth until chiefdoms and especially states emerged within the last 6,000 years.

How did small, noncentralized, kin-based societies evolve into large centralized ones in which most members are not closely related to each other? Having reviewed the stages in this transformation from bands to states, we now ask what impelled societies thus to transform themselves.

At many moments in history, states have arisen independently—or, as cultural anthropologists say, "pristinely," that is, in the absence of any preexisting surrounding states. Pristine state origins took place at least once, possibly many times, on each of the continents except Australia and North America. Prehistoric states included those of Mesopotamia, North China, the Nile and Indus Valleys, Mesoamerica, the Andes, and West Africa. Native states in contact with European states have arisen from chiefdoms repeatedly in the last three centuries in Madagascar, Hawaii, Tahiti, and many parts of Africa. Chiefdoms have arisen pristinely even more often, in all of the same regions and in North America's Southeast and Pacific Northwest, the Amazon, Polynesia, and sub-Saharan Africa. All these origins of complex societies give us a rich database for understanding their development.

Of the many theories addressing the problem of state origins, the simplest denies that there is any problem to solve. Aristotle considered states the natural condition of human society, requiring no explanation. His error was understandable, because all the societies with which he would have been acquainted—Greek societies of the fourth century B.C.—were states. However, we now know that, as of A.D. 1492, much of the world was instead organized into chiefdoms, tribes, or bands. State formation does demand an explanation.

The next theory is the most familiar one. The French philosopher Jean-Jacques Rousseau speculated that states are formed by a social contract, a rational decision reached when people calculated their self-interest, came to the agreement that they would be better off in a state than in simpler societies, and voluntarily did away with their simpler societies. But observation and historical records have failed to uncover a single case of a state's being formed in that ethereal atmosphere of dispassionate farsightedness. Smaller units do not voluntarily abandon their sovereignty and merge into larger units. They do so only by conquest, or under external duress.

A third theory, still popular with some historians and economists, sets out from the undoubted fact that, in both Mesopotamia and North China and Mexico, large-scale irrigation systems began to be constructed around the time that states started to emerge. The theory also notes that any big, complex system for irrigation or hydraulic management requires a centralized bureaucracy to construct and maintain it. The theory then turns an observed rough correlation in time into a postulated chain of cause and effect. Supposedly, Mesopotamians and North Chinese and Mexicans foresaw the advantages that a large-scale irrigation system would bring them, even though there was at the time no such system within thousands of miles (or anywhere on Earth) to illustrate for them those advantages. Those farsighted people chose to merge their inefficient little chiefdoms into a larger state capable of blessing them with large-scale irrigation.

However, this "hydraulic theory" of state formation is subject to the same objections leveled against social contract theories in general. More specifically, it addresses only the final stage in the evolution of complex societies. It says nothing about what drove the progression from bands to tribes to chiefdoms during all the millennia before the prospect of large-scale irrigation loomed on the horizon. When historical or archaeological dates are examined in detail, they fail to support the view of irrigation as the driving force for state formation. In Mesopotamia, North China, Mexico, and Madagascar, small-scale irrigation systems already existed before the rise of states. Construction of large-scale irrigation systems did not accompany the emergence of states but came only significantly later in each of those areas. In most of the states formed over the Maya area of Mesoamerica and the Andes, irrigation systems always remained small-scale ones that local communities could build and maintain themselves. Thus, even in those areas where complex systems of hydraulic management did emerge, they were a secondary consequence of states that must have formed for other reasons.

What seems to me to point to a fundamentally correct view of state formation is an undoubted fact of much wider validity than the correlation between irrigation and the formation of some states—namely, that the size of the regional population is the strongest single predictor of societal complexity. As we have seen, bands number a few dozen individuals, tribes a few hundred, chiefdoms a few thousand to a few tens of thousands, and states generally over about 50,000. In addition to that coarse correlation between regional population size and type of society (band, tribe, and so on), there is a finer trend, within each of those categories, between population and societal complexity: for instance, that chiefdoms with large populations prove to be the most centralized, stratified, and complex ones.

These correlations suggest strongly that regional population size or population density or population pressure has *something* to do with the formation of complex societies. But the correlations do not tell us precisely how population variables function in a chain of cause and effect whose outcome is a complex society. To trace out that chain, let us now remind ourselves how large dense populations themselves arise. Then we can examine why a large but simple society could not maintain itself. With that as background, we shall finally return to the question of how a simpler society actually becomes more complex as the regional population increases.

We have seen that large or dense populations arise only under conditions of food production, or at least under exceptionally productive conditions for hunting-gathering. Some productive hunter-gatherer societies reached the organizational level of chiefdoms, but none reached the level of states: all states nourish their citizens by food production. These considerations, along with the just-mentioned correlation between regional population size and societal complexity, have led to a protracted chicken-or-egg debate about the causal relations between food production, population variables, and societal complexity. Is it intensive food production that is the cause, triggering population growth and somehow leading to a complex society? Or are large populations and complex societies instead the cause, somehow leading to intensification of food production?

Posing the question in that either-or form misses the point. Intensified food production and societal complexity stimulate each other, by autocatalysis. That is, population growth leads to societal complexity, by mechanisms that we shall discuss, while societal complexity in turn leads to intensified food production and thereby to population growth.

Complex centralized societies are uniquely capable of organizing public works (including irrigation systems), long-distance trade (including the importation of metals to make better agricultural tools), and activities of different groups of economic specialists (such as feeding herders with farmers' cereal, and transferring the herders' livestock to farmers for use as plow animals). All of these capabilities of centralized societies have fostered intensified food production and hence population growth throughout history.

In addition, food production contributes in at least three ways to specific features of complex societies. First, it involves seasonally pulsed inputs of labor. When the harvest has been stored, the farmers' labor becomes available for a centralized political authority to harness—in order to build public works advertising state power (such as the Egyptian pyramids), or to build public works that could feed more mouths (such as Polynesian Hawaii's irrigation systems or fishponds), or to undertake wars of conquest to form larger political entities.

Second, food production may be organized so as to generate stored food surpluses, which permit economic specialization and social stratification. The surpluses can be used to feed all tiers of a complex society: the chiefs, bureaucrats, and other members of the elite; the scribes, craftspeople, and other non-food-producing specialists; and the farmers themselves, during times that they are drafted to construct public works.

Finally, food production permits or requires people to adopt sedentary living, which is a prerequisite for accumulating substantial possessions, developing elaborate technology and crafts, and constructing public works. The importance of fixed residence to a complex society explains why missionaries and governments, whenever they make first contact with previously uncontacted nomadic tribes or bands in New Guinea or the Amazon, universally have two immediate goals. One goal, of course, is the obvious one of "pacifying" the nomads: that is, dissuading them from killing missionaries, bureaucrats, or each other. The other goal is to induce the nomads to settle in villages, so that the missionaries and bureaucrats can find the nomads, bring them services such as medical care and schools, and proselytize and control them.

Thus, food production, which increases population size, also acts in many ways to make features of complex societies *possible*. But that doesn't prove that food production and large populations make complex societies *inevitable*. How can we account for the empirical observation that band or tribal organization just does not work for societies of hundreds of thousands of people, and that all existing large societies have complex centralized organization? We can cite at least four obvious reasons.

One reason is the problem of conflict between unrelated strangers. That problem grows astronomically as the number of people making up the society increases. Relationships within a band of 20 people involve only 190 two-person interactions (20 people times 19 divided by 2), but a band of 2,000 would have 1,999,000 dyads. Each of those dyads represents a potential time bomb that could explode in a murderous argument. Each murder in band and tribal societies usually leads to an attempted revenge killing, starting one more unending cycle of murder and countermurder that destabilizes the society.

In a band, where everyone is closely related to everyone else, people related simultaneously to both quarreling parties step in to mediate quarrels. In a tribe, where many people are still close relatives and everyone at least knows everybody else by name, mutual relatives and mutual friends mediate the quarrel. But once the threshold of "several hundred," below which everyone can know everyone else, has been crossed, increasing numbers of dyads become pairs of unrelated strangers. When strangers fight, few people present will be friends or relatives of both combatants, with self-interest in stopping the fight. Instead, may onlookers will be friends or relatives of only one combatant and will side with that person, escalating the two-person fight into a general brawl. Hence a large society that continues to leave conflict resolution to all of its members is guaranteed to blow up. That factor alone would explain why societies of thousands can exist only if they develop centralized authority to monopolize force and resolve conflicts.

A second reason is the growing impossibility of communal decision making with increasing population size. Decision making by the entire adult population is still possible in New Guinea villages small enough that news and information quickly spread to everyone, that everyone can hear everyone else in a meeting of the whole village, and that everyone who wants to speak at the meeting has the opportunity to do so. But all those prerequisites for communal decision making become unattainable in much larger communities. Even now, in these days of microphones and loud-speakers, we all know that a group meeting is no way to resolve issues for a group of thousands of people. Hence a large society must be structured and centralized if it is to reach decisions effectively.

A third reason involves economic considerations. Any society requires means to transfer goods between its members. One individual may happen to acquire more of some essential commodity on one day and less on another. Because individuals have different talents, one individual consistently tends to wind up with an excess of some essentials and a deficit of others. In small societies with few pairs of members, the resulting necessary transfers of goods can be arranged directly between pairs of individuals or families, by reciprocal exchanges. But the same mathematics that makes direct pairwise conflict resolution inefficient in large societies makes direct pairwise economic transfers also inefficient. Large societies can function economically only if they have a redistributive economy in addition to a reciprocal economy. Goods in excess of an individual's needs must be transferred from the individual to a centralized authority, which then redistributes the goods to individuals with deficits.

A final consideration mandating complex organization for large societies has to do with population densities. Large societies of food producers have not only more members but also higher population densities than do small bands of hunter-gatherers. Each band of a few dozen hunters occupies a large territory, within which they can acquire most of the resources essential to them. They can obtain their remaining necessities by trading with neighboring bands during intervals between band warfare. As population density increases, the territory of that band-sized population of a few dozen would shrink to a small area, with more and more of life's necessities having to be obtained outside the area. For instance, one couldn't just divide Holland's 16,000 square miles and 16,000,000 people into 800,000 individual territories, each encompassing 13 acres and serving as home to an autonomous band of 20 people who remained self-sufficient confined within their 13 acres, occasionally taking advantage of a temporary truce to come to the borders of their tiny territory in order to exchange some trade items and brides with the next band. Such spatial realities require that densely populated regions support large and complexly organized societies.

Considerations of conflict resolution, decision making, economics, and space thus converge in requiring large societies to be centralized. But centralization of power inevitably opens the door—for those who hold the power, are privy to information, make the decisions, and redistribute the goods—to exploit the resulting opportunities to reward themselves and their relatives. To anyone familiar with any modern grouping of people, that's

obvious. As early societies developed, those acquiring centralized power gradually established themselves as an elite, perhaps originating as one of several formerly equal-ranked village clans that became "more equal" than the others.

Those are the reasons why large societies cannot function with band organization and instead are complex kleptocracies. But we are still left with the question of how small, simple societies actually evolve or amalgamate into large, complex ones. Amalgamation, centralized conflict resolution, decision making, economic redistribution, and kleptocratic religion don't just develop automatically through a Rousseauesque social contract. What drives the amalgamation?

In part, the answer depends upon evolutionary reasoning. I said at the outset of this chapter that societies classified in the same category are not all identical to each other, because humans and human groups are infinitely diverse. For example, among bands and tribes, the big-men of some are inevitably more charismatic, powerful, and skilled in reaching decisions than the big-men of others. Among large tribes, those with stronger big-men and hence greater centralization tend to have an advantage over those with less centralization. Tribes that resolve conflicts as poorly as did the Fayu tend to blow apart again into bands, while ill-governed chiefdoms blow apart into smaller chiefdoms or tribes. Societies with effective conflict resolution, sound decision making, and harmonious economic redistribution can develop better technology, concentrate their military power, seize larger and more productive territories, and crush autonomous smaller societies one by one.

Thus, competition between societies at one level of complexity tends to lead to societies on the next level of complexity *if* conditions permit. Tribes conquer or combine with tribes to reach the size of chiefdoms, which conquer or combine with other chiefdoms to reach the size of states, which conquer or combine with other states to become empires. More generally, large units potentially enjoy an advantage over individual small units *if*—and that's a big "if"—the large units can solve the problems that come with their larger size, such as perennial threats from upstart claimants to leadership, commoner resentment of kleptocracy, and increased problems associated with economic integration.

The amalgamation of smaller units into larger ones has often been documented historically or archaeologically. Contrary to Rousseau, such amalgamations never occur by a process of unthreatened little societies freely deciding to merge, in order to promote the happiness of their citizens. Leaders of little societies, as of big ones, are jealous of their independence and prerogatives. Amalgamation occurs instead in either of two ways: by merger under the threat of external force, or by actual conquest. Innumerable examples are available to illustrate each mode of amalgamation.

Merger under the threat of external force is well illustrated by the formation of the Cherokee Indian confederation in the U.S. Southeast. The Cherokees were originally divided into 30 or 40 independent chiefdoms, each consisting of a village of about 400 people. Increasing white settlement led to conflicts between Cherokees and whites. When individual Cherokees robbed or assaulted white settlers and traders, the whites were unable to discriminate among the different Cherokee chiefdoms and retaliated indiscriminately against any Cherokees, either by military action or by cutting off trade. In response, the Cherokee chiefdoms gradually found themselves compelled to join into a single confederacy in the course of the 18th century. Initially, the larger chiefdoms in 1730 chose an overall leader, a chief named Moytoy, who was succeeded in 1741 by his son. The first task of these leaders was to punish individual Cherokees who attacked whites, and to deal with the white government. Around 1758 the Cherokees regularized their decision making with an annual council modeled on previous village councils and meeting at one village (Echota), which thereby became a de facto "capital." Eventually, the Cherokees became literate and adopted a written constitution.

The Cherokee confederacy was thus formed not by conquest but by the amalgamation of previously jealous smaller entities, which merged only when threatened with destruction by powerful external forces. In much the same way, in an example of state formation described in every American history textbook, the white American colonies themselves, one of which (Georgia) had precipitated the formation of the Cherokee state, were impelled to form a nation of their own when threatened with the powerful external force of the British monarchy. The American colonies were initially as jealous of their autonomy as the Cherokee chiefdoms, and their first attempt at amalgamation under the Articles of Confederation (1781) proved unworkable because it reserved too much autonomy to the ex-colonies. Only further threats, notably Shays's Rebellion of 1786 and the unsolved burden of war debt, overcame the ex-colonies' extreme reluctance to sacrifice autonomy and pushed them into adopting our current strong federal constitution in 1787. The 19th-century unification of Germany's jealous principalities proved

equally difficult. Three early attempts (the Frankfurt Parliament of 1848, the restored German Confederation of 1850, and the North German Confederation of 1866) failed before the external threat of France's declaration of war in 1870 finally led to the princelets' surrendering much of their power to a central imperial German government in 1871.

The other mode of formation of complex societies, besides merger under threat of external force, is merger by conquest. A well-documented example is the origin of the Zulu state, in southeastern Africa. When first observed by white settlers, the Zulus were divided into dozens of little chiefdoms. During the late 1700s, as population pressure rose, fighting between the chiefdoms became increasingly intense. Among all those chiefdoms, the ubiquitous problem of devising centralized power structures was solved most successfully by a chief called Dingiswayo, who gained ascendancy of the Mtetwa chiefdom by killing a rival around 1807. Dingiswayo developed a superior centralized military organization by drafting young men from all villages and grouping them into regiments by age rather than by their village. He also developed superior centralized political organization by abstaining from slaughter as he conquered other chiefdoms, leaving the conquered chief's family intact, and limiting himself to replacing the conquered chief himself with a relative willing to cooperate with Dingiswayo. He developed superior centralized conflict resolution by expanding the adjudication of quarrels. In that way Dingiswayo was able to conquer and begin the integration of 30 other Zulu chiefdoms. His successors strengthened the resulting embryonic Zulu state by expanding its judicial system, policing, and ceremonies.

This Zulu example of a state formed by conquest can be multiplied almost indefinitely. Native states whose formation from chiefdoms happened to be witnessed by Europeans in the 18th and 19th centuries include the Polynesian Hawaiian state, the Polynesian Tahitian state, the Merina state of Madagascar, Lesotho and Swazi and other southern African states besides that of the Zulus, the Ashanti state of West Africa, and the Ankole and Buganda states of Uganda. The Aztec and Inca Empires were formed by 15th-century conquests, before Europeans arrived, but we know much about their formation from Indian oral histories transcribed by early Spanish settlers. The formation of the Roman state and the expansion of the Macedonian Empire under Alexander were described in detail by contemporary classical authors.

All these examples illustrate that wars, or threats of war, have played a key role in most, if not all, amalgamations of societies. But wars, even between mere bands, have been a constant fact of human history. Why is it, then, that they evidently began causing amalgamations of societies only within the past 13,000 years? We had already concluded that the formation of complex societies is somehow linked to population pressure, so we should now seek a link between population pressure and the outcome of war. Why should wars tend to cause amalgamations of societies when populations are dense but not when they are sparse? The answer is that the fate of defeated peoples depends on population density, with three possible outcomes:

Where population densities are very low, as is usual in regions occupied by hunter-gatherer bands, survivors of a defeated group need only move farther away from their enemies. That tends to be the result of wars between nomadic bands in New Guinea and the Amazon.

Where population densities are moderate, as in regions occupied by food-producing tribes, no large vacant areas remain to which survivors of a defeated band can flee. But tribal societies without intensive food production have no employment for slaves and do not produce large enough food surpluses to be able to yield much tribute. Hence the victors have no use for survivors of a defeated tribe, unless to take the women in marriage. The defeated men are killed, and their territory may be occupied by the victors.

Where population densities are high, as in regions occupied by states or chiefdoms, the defeated still have nowhere to flee, but the victors now have two options for exploiting them while leaving them alive. Because chiefdoms and state societies have economic specialization, the defeated can be used as slaves, as commonly happened in biblical times. Alternatively, because many such societies have intensive food production systems capable of yielding large surpluses, the victors can leave the defeated in place but deprive them of political autonomy, make them pay regular tribute in food or goods, and amalgamate their society into the victorious state or chiefdom. This has been the usual outcome of battles associated with the founding of states or empires throughout recorded history. For example, the Spanish conquistadores wished to exact tribute from Mexico's defeated native populations, so they were very interested in the Aztec Empire's tribute lists. It turned out that the tribute received by the Aztecs each year from subject peoples had included 7,000 tons of corn, 4,000 tons of beans, 4,000 tons of grain amaranth, 2,000,000 cotton cloaks, and huge quantities of cacao beans, war costumes, shields, feather headdresses, and amber.

Thus, food production, and competition and diffusion between societies, led as ultimate causes, via chains of causation that differed in detail but that all involved large dense populations and sedentary living, to the proximate agents of conquest: germs, writing, technology, and centralized political organization. Because those ultimate causes developed differently on different continents, so did those agents of conquest. Hence those agents tended to arise in association with each other, but the association was not strict: for example, an empire arose without writing among the Incas, and writing with few epidemic diseases among the Aztecs. Dingiswayo's Zulus illustrate that each of those agents contributed somewhat independently to history's pattern. Among the dozens of Zulu chiefdoms, the Mtetwa chiefdom enjoyed no advantage whatsoever of technology, writing, or germs over the other chiefdoms, which it nevertheless succeeded in defeating. Its advantage lay solely in the spheres of government and ideology. The resulting Zulu state was thereby enabled to conquer a fraction of a continent for nearly a century.

"FROM EGALITARIANISM TO KLEPTOCRACY"

Jared Diamond

1) How do anthropologists define stages of cultural evolutionary development? What are the benefits and pitfalls of such an approach?

2) Define the "band" level of sociopolitical development. How do bands function? Give an example from the reading or from class discussions and material.

3) Define the "tribal" level of sociopolitical development. How do they function? Give an example from the reading or from class discussions and material.

4) Define the "chiefdom" level of sociopolitical development. How do they function? Give an example from the reading or from class discussions and material.

5) Why do chiefdom-level societies no longer exist in the modern world?

6) Define the "kleptocracy"/state level of sociopolitical development. How do such organizations function?

7) What solutions have "kleptocrats" used to gain popular support for their positions? Which solution does Diamond seem to think is the most important?

8) Define and discuss the various theories that have been put forward to explain the evolution of state-level societies, including Diamond's discussion of the interrelationship between dense populations, food production, and warfare.

9) What reasons does Diamond suggest to explain why all large societies have complex centralized organizations? Give examples from the article and other material you have read or discussed.

Haitians: From Political Repression to Chaos

Robert Lawless

Haiti may be regarded as a predatory state run by an elite class that extorts its living from the masses. The institutional structures of government do not operate for the benefit of the people as a whole. Rather, the government largely serves the elite. Directly and indirectly, members of the elite depend on the government to make their living. Thus, in order to earn and increase their incomes, members of the elite have to stay in power. All members of the elite, however, cannot be in control at the same time, and so individuals, families, and groups must make alliances with those who manage the agencies of government.

The political repression seen in the succession of arrests, torture, and gross violations of human rights in Haiti represents the efforts of the elite to maintain itself economically at the direct expense of the poor. Their loss of power would result not only in the loss of control and prestige but also in the loss of income.

It is my view that the long Duvalier reign from 1957 to 1986 destroyed the traditional balance among the competing members of the elite and raised both the degree of violence of the state against the people and the techniques of stealing from the people to their highest levels in Haitian history. For example, although the Central Bank maintained a minimum of integrity and kept the Haitian currency tied to the U.S. dollar, all other state units and agencies were absolutely personal sources of household income for the Duvaliers and their cohorts. After the downfall of the Duvaliers in February 1986 the machinery of political repression had no traditional channels for its expression and devolved into a chaotic situation with no conventional, indigenous solutions currently in sight (as of the time of this writing in Spring 1994).

Laying the basis for such a thesis requires some knowledge of basic information about Haiti and also some knowledge of the history of Haiti.

Introduction

Located in the Caribbean Sea just fifty-four miles (ninety kilometers) southeast of Cuba and part of the Greater Antilles, Haiti shares the island of Hispaniola with the Dominican Republic. Taking up the western third of the island, Haiti contains about 11,100 square miles (27,750 square kilometers)—approximately the size of Maryland. Its topography varies from a few flat, semiarid valleys to some densely forested, deeply dissected mountains and many semidenuded, gently sloping mountains. About one third of Haiti is at an elevation between 660 and 1,650 feet (200 and 500 meters) above sea level and about two thirds is divided into three mountain ranges with the highest elevation, the La Selle Peak, at about 8,840 feet (2,680 meters).

The average annual temperature falls somewhere between 75 and 81 degrees Fahrenheit (24 and 27 Celsius). The major changes in temperature are caused by changes in elevation. Starting at the capital of Port-au-Prince with an altitude of 130 feet (40 meters) and a mean temperature of 79, a perspiring person can walk up to nearby Petionville at an elevation of 1,320 feet (400 meters) and experience a mean temperature of 76, and the same person can continue up the road to an elevation of 4,785 feet (1,450 meters) at the vegetable center of Kenscoff with a quite enjoyable mean annual temperature of 65 degrees Fahrenheit.

Demographic information is difficult to come by, but an educated estimate would put the total population at about 6.5 million. Port-au-Prince has about 1.25 million people, and the second largest city, Cap-Haitien, has maybe 70,000. The important regional cities such as Les Cayes, Gonaives, Port-de- Paix, Jacmel, Jeremie, St. Marc, and Hinche have populations of only ten thousand to fifty thousand at the most. Probably about eighty percent of the Haitian population lives in rural areas and subsists through farming.

Outsiders have traditionally misunderstood the language situation of Haiti. It has often been stated that the elite speaks French, and the masses speak some sort of degraded version of French called *patois* or Creole. Anthropological linguists wring their hands in despair at such notions. All languages that have been in use for more than a couple of generations are structurally and functionally complex enough to handle all the descriptive, emotional, and expressive needs of the people speaking the particular language. The language of Haiti, the language spoken by *all* Haitians, is properly referred to as Haitian Creole. For much of the modern history of Haiti, however, the official language of government, business, and education has been French, even though only about eight percent of the people speak French consistently. The reason for the usage of French is that members of the educated elite have found that they can exclude the masses from competing for scarce jobs by requiring knowledge of the French language for positions in government and business.

The contrast between "Blacks" and "mulattoes" is a salient theme in Haitian history. A nineteenth-century writer, for example, pointed out that color distinctions were extremely important and he included an appendix with charts on color types in the Haitian population.[1] Even Leslie Manigat, a political science professor who was briefly president of Haiti in 1988, spoke in the mid-1960s at North American universities in terms of these color distinctions, saying:

> On the one hand, there has been the light-skinned elite, claiming to be ideologically liberal, in reality, politically autocratic, economically conservative, socially sectarian, and culturally pro-European. When in power, this elite has represented the interests of the urban, moneyed oligarchy. Against its traditional hegemony, on the other hand, there has been a coalition led by the dark-skinned elite. Although socially progressive because of the need to maintain solidarity with the middle classes and masses through the common denominator of color, this coalition was also politically autocratic, ideologically authoritarian, economically quasi-traditional, and culturally nationalistic.[2]

The "color issue" was nonexistent in the election campaigns leading up to the November 1987 aborted elections, in which Manigat was originally a minor candidate. Almost all families in Haiti can claim members whose skin color ranges from light to dark, but the idea of a society divided into a small sophisticated, Westernized mulatto segment and a large dangerous, Africanish Black segment does benefit some groups. In particular, the traditional power elite gains an advantage by presenting this picture of Haiti to the white world, that is, the mulatto elite can claim outside help in its efforts to rule the unruly masses.

Despite its political difficulties Haiti is internationally famous for its art and literature. In the 1940s Haiti burst into the consciousness of the art world with an astonishing display of paintings. Her artists justly deserved the worldwide attention they received for their so-called primitive or naive art.

Haitian writers initially focused on concepts of negritude foreshadowing the black power and anti-colonial post-World War II movements. Haiti's literary production is even more amazing in light of the high rate of illiteracy, probably around eighty-five percent. Fewer than half of the rural children attend school, and only about twenty percent of those complete the primary grades. Most of the literature is strikingly indigenous. Voodoo has been a major theme in many of the novels.

The current chaos, however, has closed down the traditional channels for the production of art and literature. Writers had usually depended on bookstores with small print shops to put out limited editions of their works, which were sold by the bookstores. These book stores and print shops have been virtually put out of business through losing their primary customers (because schools have been closed) and through harassment by army and police personnel, who see any printed work as anti-government. Artists had depended largely on the tourist trade to earn a living. The few hardy tourists who were not turned off by the AIDS scare are now thoroughly repulsed by the continuing chaos and perceived lack of safety in Haiti.

Religion

A cementing element of the Haitian population is religion. Although some of the population is nominally Roman Catholic and although Protestant missionaries have made considerable headway in the poorer rural areas of Haiti, the religion of Haiti is still Voodoo, a religion that focuses on contacting and appeasing immediate relatives, such as dead parents and grandparents, and ancestral spirits, who include distant, stereotyped ancestors.

Voodoo is an egalitarian religion with both men and women serving as priests presiding over ceremonies that include divination rites, which are used to find out the course of the future or the causes of various difficulties. It has healing rites in which a Voodoo priest interacts directly with sick people to cure them, propitiatory rites in which food and drink are offered to specific spirits to get into their good graces, and preventive rites in which ancestors are offered sacrifices to help head off any possible future trouble. Indeed, many Voodoo rituals can be seen as healing rites, since many of the rituals are performed at times of sickness and death. Much of Voodoo, then, can be seen as a folk medical system that attributes illness to the work of angry ancestors and that consists of ceremonies performed to appease those ancestors in order to cure illness.

The influence of Voodoo on politics has always been problematic since Voodoo is practiced largely on a household level and has no regional or national connections. Due to its egalitarian ideology, Voodoo has often been the target of repression by the government. Voodoo may, indeed, be the one aspect of Haitian life surviving quite well through the current period of chaos.

Health

Voodoo healers are a major part of the medical system of Haiti, though Western medicine has been available to the urban elite for several decades and is, indeed, available from a few rural clinics. For the most part, however, health and healing for poorer Haitians is handled by herb medicine, bone setters, injectionists, Voodoo rituals, and by a rich body of folk knowledge. The poorer masses, nevertheless, suffer many health problems of malnutrition and disease. The daily per capita food consumption is estimated at sixteen hundred calories, and measles, diarrhea, and tetanus kill many children before they reach their teens.

Tuberculosis is Haiti's most devastating disease, followed closely by malaria, influenza, dysentery, tetanus, whooping cough, and measles. Eye problems are endemic, with the chief causes of blindness being cataracts, scarring of the cornea, and glaucoma.

A ninety-two–page study released in September 1992 by the Permanent Commission on Emergency Aid, which represents over sixty nongovernmental development and democracy organizations in Haiti, said that the death rate has been rising and the health of the population dropping since the September 1991 military coup that ousted the democratically elected government. It also pointed out that there has been a deterioration in state services amounting to a descent into chaos, with the Departments of Public Health and Water totally mismanaged. The supply of drinkable water, for example, has dropped by fifty percent in the cities and twenty percent in the countryside. According to the report, "The situation is extremely critical and just waiting for cholera to strike."[3] Other problems include an increase in garbage in the streets (with only about twenty-five percent of the country's garbage being collected), a rise in the number of preventable illnesses, and a deterioration in mental health.

History

Haitian history is unique among Caribbean nations and, in fact, unique in the world; Haiti's slave uprising was the only one that grew into a modern nation. How Haitians view themselves and how the world views Haiti must always be filtered through the prism of this momentous historical fact.

Slave Beginnings

Haiti became a slave colony of the French after Europeans, mainly the Spaniards, killed off the pre-Columbian Indian population on the island of Hispaniola through murder, diseases, and slavery. Then the Europeans looked toward Africa for the labor they needed to work the farms that were to become enormous sugarcane plantations. In 1502, just ten years after Columbus landed in Haiti, the Spanish governor brought the first black slaves to Hispaniola, and in 1505 sugar cane was introduced to Hispaniola from the Canary Islands. In 1697, Spain recognized France's claim to the western part of Hispaniola, to be known as the French colony of Saint Domingue.

Independence

The brutality and exploitation of the French resulted in many failed slave uprisings until, in August 1791, the slaves managed a major revolt that the plantation owners could not contain. By 1796 white supremacy was at an end, and Black rule was established under the leadership of Toussaint Louverture, a charismatic ex-slave. In 1800 Napoleon sent twenty-eight thousand troops to retake the colony and re-enslave the Blacks, but by late 1803 the Haitians had defeated the French troops. On January 1, 1804, Jean-Jacques Dessalines, Toussaint's successor, proclaimed the independence of Haiti, an event that shocked the white world to its foundations. Haitians further goaded the white world by proclaiming Haiti as a symbol of redemption for the whole African race. For example, the first Haitian constitution designated Haitians of whatever color as "Black" (including those Germans and Poles who had been given Haitian citizenship), opened Haitian citizenship to all persons everywhere of African or Indian descent, and forbade whites to own land.

At the time of the Haitian Revolution, fully two thirds of the slaves had been born in Africa. By the end of the revolution virtually all the whites had been eliminated, and there were several massacres of the mulattoes. As a consequence, Haiti was ostracized by the white world. It was not until 1862 that Haiti's most important neighbor, the United States, recognized Haitian independence. Great Britain was one of the few nations that did have early diplomatic relations with Haiti, but it was in the writings of the English racists and anti-abolitionists that Haiti began to get its unwarranted bad press,[4] focusing largely on the savagery of these "African" Haitians and the barbaric practices of Voodoo—especially its alleged ritual cannibalism.

In actuality, Haiti represents the only time in history when a slave population on its own suddenly faced the task of organizing a government and an economic system. The press on Haiti, nevertheless, focused almost entirely on the former prosperity of the French system in Saint Domingue in contrast to the poverty, ignorance, and disorder in independent Haiti—just as the press today largely emphasizes the destitution found in Haiti. Such depictions, however, neglect the fact that in colonial Saint Domingue only an extraordinarily small percentage of the population enjoyed the good life—and, indeed, even today only a small percentage of the Haitian population enjoys considerable wealth.

One of the crucial problems facing Haiti immediately after independence concerned access to the land previously owned by the French and how to maintain the agricultural productivity of this land. Initially the Haitian government attempted to reinstate the painful plantation system of colonial Saint Domingue. When these attempts failed because plantations were associated with slavery, land was, for the most part, simply distributed among the ex-slaves. As a result, from sixty to eighty percent of the farmers currently own their own land, though the plots are fragmented and small. The urban-based government has rarely shown a sustained interest in agriculture, and although the state owns land, nobody seems to pay much attention to it and peasants occupy most of it rent-free.

Modern Developments

Except for a brief period between 1915 and 1934 when it was occupied by United States Marines, Haiti has remained self-consciously independent. The twenty-three–year period after the occupation and until the election of François "Papa Doc" Duvalier as president saw increased feelings of nationalism and pride in the African heritage, a growth in trade and political interaction with other Caribbean nations, the development of peasant economic cooperation, the introduction of a progressive income tax, and, especially, the rise of a new Black middle class. In 1957 Duvalier won the presidency with a decisive margin as the self-proclaimed heir to these new developments.

In addition, Haitians have always taken a special interest in the affairs of Blacks throughout the world. In 1859, the Haitian government ordered a special requiem mass for the death of John Brown, the famous American abolitionist. In that same year, the Haitian Secretary of State called for immigration to Haiti by "members of the African race, who groan in the United States" (quoted in DuBois).[5] More than a hundred years later, the Duvalier regime declared several days of national mourning after the assassination of Martin Luther King, Jr. And two major thoroughfares in Port-au-Prince are named after John Brown and Martin Luther King, Jr.

Duvalier the Senior

Widely regarded as a tool of the army by some and as a lackey of the U.S. embassy by others, Duvalier, instead, proved to be an extraordinarily astute politician; initially he gained the trust of the indigenous clergy, the peasants, and the urban proletariat, and then he brought diverse elements into his circle of advisers, including communists, North Americans, Haitian exiles, taxi drivers, Voodoo priests, and Black power intellectuals. To keep the army in control, he cut its funding and created an alterative volunteer militia loyal only to him, the organization that came to be known as the notorious *tonton-makout*—named after a character in Haitian folklore who stalks bad children and carries them off in his basket.

The first few years of Duvalier's rule were marked by several unsuccessful coups and invasions. In 1958 and 1959 invasions by Haitian exiles were thwarted, and in 1963 Clément Barbot, chief of the tonton-makout, attempted a major coup that was accompanied by a small guerrilla war and a number of bombings and shootings in and around Port-au-Prince. Also in 1963 an attempt was made on the life of Duvalier's children Simone and Jean-Claude. In April of the next year Duvalier declared himself president-for-life, and in August yet another invasion failed. In 1968 the National Palace was bombed but an accompanying invasion fizzled out. Duvalier's reprisals were swift, vicious, and widespread. The result of his campaign of oppression against opponents was increased isolation from the international community, which began to attribute all of Haiti's problems to Duvalier.

During the years of Duvalier's rule, thousands of Haitian professionals fled to the United States, Canada, the Bahamas, the Dominican Republic, Venezuela, French Guyana, Africa, and France. During the rule of his son, from 1971 to 1986, thousands more from all classes fled to Florida. The Haitians who left greatly influenced politics back in Haiti. Those who went to the United States tended to have little patience with the traditional French-oriented elite. Haitians of all classes mixed extensively and intensively overseas, and the Duvalier brand of Black national-ism found little support among these upwardly mo-bile, welfare-conscious Haitian exiles.

Duvalier the Junior

In January 1971, Duvalier announced that his son would succeed him as president-for-life, and in April of that year Duvalier died and was, indeed, suc-ceeded by his nineteen-year-old son, Jean-Claude. The junior Duvalier closely tied the fortunes of Haiti to the United States—a relationship featuring private investments from the United States wooed by such incentives as no customs taxes, a minimum wage kept very low, the suppression of labor unions, and the right of U.S. companies to repatriate profits from their off-shore plants. So, with the help of U.S. government agencies Haiti became economically dependent on its powerful North American neighbor. Also, with the aid of the international lending enterprise Haiti joined the ranks of the debtor nations for the first time in its history. And with the Reagan administra-tion giving five times as much military aid to the dic-tatorship as had President Carter, the army in Haiti finally regained the power under the junior Duvalier that it had lost under the senior Duvalier.

In addition to the economic exploitation by the United States, Haiti suffered greatly from the oil cri-ses of 1973–1974 and 1980. In addition, Hurricane Allen in 1980 devastated the coffee trees and ruined the production of coffee, one of Haiti's most signifi-cant exports.

Initially, Jean-Claude did make some progressive changes under pressure from the Carter administra-tion and its emphasis on human rights. By the end of 1979, however, Jean-Claude's administration had slid back toward repression as the Carter administration became occupied with other matters. Correctly read-ing the incoming Reagan administration's lack of interest in human rights, the Haitian government increased its control of political, press, and labor groups. Immediately following Reagan's election in November 1980, several hundred progressive Hai-tians were arrested and many were deported.

According to a study of the North American mass media, "The foreign media seemed confused by the attitude of the American government, and, under-standably, could not present a clear picture of the enigmatic Jean-Claude. Some journalists, especially Americans, who had written about the hopelessness of François Duvalier's Haiti, began writing about the sudden improvement in Haiti after the death of Papa Doc. Others, especially Haitians, claimed that repres-sion was just as bad under Jean-Claude as it had been under François."[6]

Clearly, Jean-Claude was not as politically astute as was his father. Some Haitians have emphasized to me that the beginning of his end was his elaborate wedding in 1980 to Michèle Bennett, the daughter of a mulatto business family. This event alienated many of the Black power followers of his father. At any rate, after fourteen years of rule by a second Duvalier and precious few, if any, economic gains, Haitians reached the end of their patience. In late November 1985, street protests began in towns throughout Haiti, and the violent police responses led to further protests. Despite these attempts at repression, some reshuf-fling at high levels of government, and a farcical "ref-erendum" that gave Jean-Claude "99.98 percent" of the vote, the second of the Duvaliers could not hang onto power. Just a little over a year later, on the morn-ing of February 7, 1986, Jean-Claude Duvalier fled to France. An era had ended. That morning the streets of Port-au-Prince were full of Haitians with tree branches symbolically sweeping away the evil spir-its of the Duvaliers.

Later in the day, it was announced that Haiti would be run by an interim government initially com-posed of a five-member council. Headed by Lt. Gen. Henri Namphy, it was pared down to three mem-bers six weeks later. A few days after the ouster of Jean-Claude the council abolished the widely hated tonton-makout, but the interim government did not pursue supporters of Duvalier except under intense public pressure. Namphy and others still in power obviously did not view the end of Duvalier as a revo-lution signaling the end of authoritarianism in Haiti.

Current Events

For several years, Haiti limped along with various forms of the council, all of them inevitably run in one way or another by the army. With assorted groups jockeying for influence, Haiti attempted to have presi-dential and National Assembly elections in Novem-ber 1987 and presidential and National Assembly (and mayoral) elections in January 1988. Despite the indifference of the council to the public welfare, at-tempts to form a progressive government continued. The 1987 constitution is, in fact, a good example of an indigenous document created by progressive Hai-tians to solve the peculiar political problems that have arisen out of Haitian history. It was, of course, pro-duced in opposition to the wishes of the ruling military-dominated council.

The referendum on the constitution, held in March 1987, represented the highest level of politi-cal participation by the Haitian general public since the elections that led to the installation of the Duvalier dynasty in 1957. Almost all Haitians that I have talked with regard the twenty-day period leading up to the referendum as the freest political period in living memory and the period in which cultural expressions reached their height. The constitution was published both in French and Creole. Several hundred thousand comic books and posters explaining the constitution were distributed throughout Haiti. Radio stations devoted many hours of their air time to the reading and discussion of the constitution.

After the overwhelming approval of the new constitution, various thugs, including those identified as former tonton-makout, began attacking institutions identified with the new democratic processes, such as radio stations and the elections offices. It seems that these attacks occurred because the military and other elite elements saw the involvement of the masses as a threat to their position, and preferred the appearance of chaos in the hope that they would be called back to power to restore order.

In the ensuing descent into disorder, two presidential candidates were killed—one in front of a police station clutching a copy of the constitution. Another candidate refused to campaign because of the lack of police protection. A few days before the elections the polling headquarters was burned down, a popular radio station was set on fire, and arsonists screaming "Long live the army!" destroyed a large open-air market in Port-au-Prince.

On the morning of the November 1987 presidential and National Assembly elections, gunmen roamed the streets of Port-au-Prince firing at those going to vote and invading some voting sites killing several people. Haitians have told me that uniformed soldiers often joined in these attacks. Outside of Port-au-Prince the ballots were rarely delivered because the trucks had been hijacked, usually by soldiers.

At least thirty-four people were killed in these aborted elections, which the council cancelled later in the day. On the very next day a friend in Cap-Haitien wrote to me,

> For many months, November 29, 1987, has stood out in the hearts and minds of Haitians as a day of hope. Yesterday it became a day of deception. Yesterday, we saw, in one day, our hopes and dreams for a democratic and free Haiti crushed. We feel we no longer have a hope that there will be a change in the country.

Another told me in Creole the same day over the telephone, "Kè-m grenn" (My heart is broken).

While the military council tried to control politics, social controls in the streets began breaking down. Starting soon after Duvalier's departure, Haitians spoke to me about the lack of control in Port-au-Prince and Cap-Haitien and complained about the unprecedented frequency of crimes in these two largest Haitian cities. During the first week of October 1986 the opening of schools was delayed in Cap-Haitien because of rioting that included the sacking of the CARE warehouse and the main post office.

Personal violence that had been extremely rare in Haiti began occurring. Haitians were shocked by several rapes in Port-au-Prince in February and March 1987. One Haitian told me, "There were people so frustrated by what they saw as a worsening situation here that rioting and burning barricades was their only means of expression." A returning exile is quoted as saying, "We have no work, nothing to live on; the country is in ruins."[7]

After the 1987 elections were undermined by the army and aborted, the 1988 elections were controlled by the army and widely regarded as illegitimate. Leslie Manigat, the president installed from this 1988 election, attempted to finesse the army and was thrown out by the military after four months.

For a couple of years after 1988 there were a series of military coups, and then a legitimate election was held in December 1990. Scheduled first for November 4 and then postponed to December 16, this election was monitored by more than four hundred international observers, including former U.S. President Carter. Jean-Bertrand Aristide won the presidency in a landslide approaching seventy percent of the estimated seventy-five percent of the two million registered voters who cast ballots, and his election raised expectations both in Haiti and elsewhere in the Caribbean. For example, at Aristide's inauguration Jamaica's prime minister said that he sensed "a very great moment in Caribbean history after all the generations of struggle and tyranny."[8]

Installed in office on February 7, 1991, five years to the day after the end of the Duvalier dictatorship, Aristide was a thirty-seven-year-old charismatic priest who had been active in Haitian human rights movements for many years. At the time of his election he had escaped at least three assassination attempts, one by uniformed soldiers. He has an obvious and perhaps volatile appeal to many segments of the Haitian population, especially the peasantry and the urban poor.

While attempting to reorganize military policy, Aristide was ousted by the army a little over seven months after he took office. The Organization of American States declared the new government to be illegitimate, and in November 1991 the United States imposed an embargo on Haiti demanding that the army allow a democratically elected government to take its place. Aristide has lived since his ouster mostly in the United States negotiating with the United States, the Organization of American States, and various power brokers in Haiti for his return to what can only be some limited form of presidential power.

Part of the current chaos no doubt comes from heightened expectations. After the ouster of the Duvalier regime a very wide variety of urban and rural groups attempted to develop a progressive government. Even peasants in some of the most isolated areas of Haiti came to think of the government not only as the cause of problems (the shortage of drinkable water, for example) but also as the source of possible solutions to such problems.

Haitian Social and Economic Life

Since political repression has traditionally resulted from the elite's exploitation of the rural farmers, an understanding of Haiti must include knowledge about the peasantry. About sixty-five percent of the labor force works in agriculture and only about seven percent in manufacturing (with one percent in construction and twenty-seven percent in other sectors).

The greatest accomplishment of the early Haitian nation was total land reform. Changing the country from a collection of slave-worked plantations to a nation of land-owning Black peasants involved, as I have stated, dividing the land among the former field slaves and their descendants. After these rural farmers received their small subsistence plots they wanted nothing further to do with the government, which they had always seen as being responsive to the slave owners. And, indeed, until very recently—beginning ironically with François Duvalier's efforts to court rural support—they have regarded the government as having little relevance to their lives. Another result of the land reform is that—in striking contrast to the rest of the Caribbean and Latin America—the largely mulatto elite, descended from the former house slaves or freed mulattoes, retreated to the cities and, with no land to its name, made its living from taxing peasant markets and the nation's imports and exports.

Peasant Farmers

In addition to constantly attempting to deflect a parasitical elite, the Haitian farmers face many problems, perhaps the most immediate being how to cope with small, scattered plots that are subdivided each generation. In addition, farmers often denude the land of trees to make charcoal for cooking fuel, lack

capital to buy fertilizer, seeds, pesticides, and farm equipment, and are always dealing with increasing soil erosion. Since 1983 farmers have also had to deal with the loss of their major livestock population due to the total pig eradication project carried out by U.S. and international agencies after the discovery of African Swine Fever.

The peasants, however, do endure. Most of the people of Haiti, in fact, can be found living in scattered huts in villages loosely tied together by well-traveled trade routes. They organize their lives around a cluster of households composed of loosely related residents serving a particular Voodoo spirit under the guidance of the oldest male member. In the past there were also regional centers that had considerable importance culturally and commercially. Since the 1915–1934 U.S. occupation, however, Port-au-Prince has become a more important city that now dominates the country.

In his classic study of the peasant farmers of Mirebalais in central Haiti the anthropologist Melville J. Herskovits described a scene that rings true even today more than half a century after his fieldwork there in 1934:

> The small cultivator holds the center of the economic stage. In the main he works his own land, inherited from his father or acquired through purchase…. The life of the Haitian farmer, though hard, is simple and self-contained. With but few exceptions, he supplies all his necessities. . . . The day's work begins at dawn, the women rising before the men to prepare coffee. . . . When finished with his breakfast, the farmer goes to his field, where, except for the hottest hours, he works until sundown, his own meal being brought to him at about nine or ten o'clock in the morning. His wife meanwhile occupies herself with her household tasks, pounding grain in her mortar or working in her garden. . . . On market days she takes the produce of the family's fields to the town to sell. If she has young children, she cares for them while she does her other work, but when they are old enough, they help her about the house if they are girls, or, if boys, go with their father to the garden. From time to time, when house repairs are needed or there are implements to be mended, the man spends a day at home getting these odd jobs done.[9]

Rural Markets

The involvement of Haitian peasants with the wider world is through marketing. And it is women who usually market and make marketing decisions. As Herskovits wrote,

The woman, who is held to be more thrifty than the man, is thus the banker of the family. Her opinion is prized by her husband, and though a man has the legal right to dispose of a horse or a cow or his own land as he desires, in most households nothing would be done until the wife was consulted.[10]

The anthropologist Sidney Mintz has done the pioneering and still the best studies on Haitian markets, and he has pointed out that market women are "as typically Haitian as voodoo."[11] In fact, the market women and the bustling markets scattered all over the Haitian country are the very heart of the Haitian economy. These rural markets fill the roles of banks and warehouses; they operate as a socioeconomic network that moves the goods, as well as the gossip, that the people need in order to live materially and socially.

Haiti's primary products of coffee, sugar, rice, and cocoa have traditionally moved through these rural markets. Many Haitians also engage in part-time craft work, particularly in the manufacture of wood utensils, tools, and furniture. Haiti was, in fact, well-known for its fine mahogany carvings, and most of the products of the industrial arts were aimed at tourists. Due to the AIDS scare, however, the tourist trade declined drastically beginning in the early 1980s and declined to nearly zero following the sociopolitical instability after Duvalier's 1986 ouster.

Nonrural Markets

In recent history there has been a market for products from light manufacturing in Haiti, which has consisted largely of shoes, soap, flour, cement, and domestic oils. The industries owned by foreign interests produced items such as garments, toys, baseballs, and electronic goods almost exclusively for the U.S. market. This small-scale industrialization has, however, always been a minor part of the Haitian economic scene and has not added much to the national economy since the purpose of it is to supply cheap labor that the U.S. corporations can exploit. In addition, the instability of the government since 1986 has resulted in a number of these foreign-owned industries leaving Haiti. Those that had not left before November 1991 did leave during the imposition of the U.S. embargo during that month.

Family and Household

With the men in the fields and the women in the markets it may be stated—at the risk of oversimplification—that men handle the agricultural production and that women handle the produce of agriculture. The men who do the agriculture, however, usually do it for the women. In other words, the women depend on the men to have a product to sell, and the men depend on the women for domestic labor and marketing. The Haitian family structure, then, contains a great deal of gender complementarianism, as well as generational complementarianism; the children are seen as working for the parents. Growing out of these complementary roles and statuses is a complex system of mating, parenting, and day-to-day subsisting that is maintained through a variety of household arrangements.

Herskovits, in his classic anthropological ethnography, made the important clarification that "the word 'family' as employed in Haiti can be understood only in terms of a broader meaning than is given it in Europe and America...; the Haitian 'family' includes a wide range of relatives...on the sides of both parents."[12] It is, in fact, relatively rare that the small group of people contained in a household acts on its own without consulting with a large number of relatives.

The plantation system and the institution of slavery throughout the eighteenth and nineteenth centuries certainly did not encourage slaves to develop a legally recognized family institution, and the urban orientation of the republic reinforced the tendency of the peasants to avoid legal and church marriages. Consequently a wide variety of households exists, such as long-term co-residing couples, unions without formal sanction, couples who do not live together, fathers who do not participate actively in rearing their children, as well as, of course, conventional church weddings. In addition, the same man may simultaneously marry, maintain a consensual union in a second household of which he is the titular head, and conduct one or more relatively stable extraresidential affairs in which the women head the household. Women also may legitimately enter several different kinds of unions. As it turns out, then, children may be born to a married couple, to a married man with another woman, to a couple in a consensual union, to a mother not in union with any man, and so forth.

Due to the great variety of households, inheritance can be a troublesome problem. In general, all children from all the varieties of marriage have equal rights of inheritance, but, in practice, residence, contacts, and personal feelings play important roles. Since both adults and children change residences frequently, children have a variety of temporary residential rights and come into contact with a relatively large number of adults who may discipline and train them. In general, a great deal of emphasis is placed on respect for adults, who are quick to use corporal punishment in enforcing that respect.

Living in Chaos

Current Reports

In March 1993, a student of mine made a trip from Port-au-Prince to the interior regional center of Hinche. The 750-mile trip used to take about two hours. Due to the deterioration of the roads in Haiti, however, it took him six hours. Coming into Hinche he was stopped at five different military checkpoints, and he, his driver, and his vehicle were searched at each checkpoint. Hinche itself had no electricity and no running water. The people were afraid to use the water from wells and streams because there was no sewage treatment. He was told many stories of arrests, tortures, and the disappearance of numerous townspeople. He also mentioned to me that, as a sport, soldiers often aimed their jeeps at people in the streets and sped toward them, apparently killing one little girl.

A February 1993 report from the Chicago Religious Task Force Delegation to Haiti stated that a Mennonite Central Committee worker was detained because he carried pamphlets about Haiti Solidarity Week, a celebration scheduled for February 7 through February 13, marking the February 7, 1986, fall of the Duvalier regime and the February 7, 1991, inauguration of Aristide. The worker had to stand by helpless as his Haitian guide was beaten.

The same report noted that Gonaives, a city where Dessalines declared Haitian independence and also a city where the first anti-Duvalier protests took place, was heavily patrolled by the army. Arrests, torture, and violence were rampant there.

In January 1993, representatives from over fifteen international organizations concerned with human rights and refugee issues in Haiti met in Port-au-Prince to attend the International Colloquium on Human Rights. Colloquium participants strongly condemned the human rights violations by the Haitian military regime. The colloquium estimated that since the September 1991 military coup approximately three thousand Haitians have been killed, six thousand injured, forty thousand have fled by boat, and up to four hundred thousand have been internally displaced.

Personal Consequences

A newsletter published in Haiti by a coalition of grassroots democratic movements recently detailed a typical story of a delegate who was elected to the National Assembly in December 1990. Samuel Madistin, the twenty-nine-year-old son of a Protestant minister, was to represent about forty thousand citizens in the Artibonite Valley. After only a few months in office, he found the government taken over by the army. He stated, "Today we are witnessing an unimaginable situation. People are arrested, taken to jail, sometimes beaten to death. They are gravely injured, they lose their eyes, they are forced to eat their excrement. These are all things we have been witnessing for the past twelve months."[13]

In March 1992, when the Assembly convened to vote on the "Washington Accord," a compromise agreement between the legitimate government and the de facto military government, Madistin and others who were going to vote in favor of it were taken out of the Assembly room and beaten by soldiers. Since then Madistin has apparently been blacklisted by the military and is in hiding.

Conclusion

The elite of Haiti has always made its living through their control of the state apparatus, a situation that one contemporary Haitian scholar calls "state fetishism."[14] The new Black middle class,—largely a product, ironically, of François Duvalier's efforts to counter the old, mulatto elite—makes its living from mercantile, capitalist, and service enterprises. For the most part, this middle class has been politically neutral and socially silent throughout the recent upheavals.

Indeed, arguments about governance have mostly involved only a small number of members of the elite class. Although their college experiences may differ, members of the elite pretty much attend the same schools in Haiti and accept the same values. What divides them from the rest of the nation is the extremely unequal allocations of resources between rural regions (including the increasingly slum-like urban fringes) and downtown urban (and outer suburban areas); the elite is wealthy and the rest of the people are poor. Keeping the poor from claiming their fair share of the meager resources is what has led to sociopolitical repression. What divides the elite into seemingly arbitrary, and often competing, segments is their noncooperative efforts to gain individual and familial power.

This competition enjoyed a certain balance throughout most of Haitian history, but the supporting structure began, as we have seen, to collapse under Duvalier policies. At least four factors have recently come together that seem to lead to the chaos: (1) The various group and family elites have become increasingly smaller (with many members living abroad); (2) The resources of Haiti are increasingly limited, rural markets exhausted, and foreign aid virtually shut off; (3) The new Black, politically neutral middle class is trying to tap into these same finite resources (and expecting government services); and (4) The military has been left as the only existing instrument of government (and, for the most part, they neither desire nor are capable of governance).

My expectations for the future of Haiti are both optimistic and pessimistic. Haitians have survived incompetence, corruption, ignorance, the military, the greed of powerful neighbors, and even the machinations of their own elite; most of them will probably survive the current chaos. How long, however, will they have to yearn for their freedom?

Notes

1. John R. Beard, *The Life of Toussaint L'Ouverture: The Negro Patriot of Hayti* (1853; reprint Westport, CT: Negro Universities Press, 1970).

2. Leslie F. Manigat, *Haiti of the Sixties: Object of International Concern* (Washington, D.C.: Washington Center of Foreign Policy Research, 1964), p. 33.

3. Staff Report (Port-au-Prince: CPAU, 1992).

4. James Franklin, *The Present State of Hayti (Santo Domingo): With Remarks on Its Agriculture, Commerce, Laws, Religion, Finances, and Population* (1828; reprint London: Cass, 1971); Charles MacKenzie, *Notes on Haiti: Made During a Residence in that Republic*, 2 vols. (1830; reprint London: Cass, 1971); and Spenser St. John, *Hayti: Or the Black Republic* (London: Smith, Elder, 1884).

5. F. E. DuBois, "Call for Immigration," in James Redpath, ed., *A Guide to Hayti* (1861; reprint Westport, CT: Negro Universities Press, 1970), p. 99.

6. Robert Lawless, *Haiti's Bad Press: Origins, Development, and Consequences* (Rochester, VT: Schenkman, 1992), pp. 160–161.

7. Annick Billard, "Haiti: Hope, Return, Disillusion," *Refugees* 39 (1987): 16.

8. Susana Hayward, "Priest Becomes Haiti's First Freely Elected President," *Gainesville Sun*, February 8, 1991, p. 5A.

9. Melville J. Herskovits, *Life in a Haitian Valley* (New York: Knopf, 1937), pp. 67–68.

10. Ibid., p. 125.

11. Sidney W. Mintz, "Markets in Haiti," *New Society* 26 (1963): 18.

12. Herskovits, *Life in a Haitian Valley*, p. 123.

13. Staff, "Profile," *Haiti Info* 1, no. 2 (1992): 2.

14. Michael-Rolph Trouillot, *Haiti: State against Nation: The Origins and Legacy of Duvalierism* (New York: Monthly Review Press, 1990), p. 9.

Suggested Readings

Aristide, Jean-Bertrand. *In the Parish of the Poor: Writings from Haiti*. Maryknoll, NY: Oris, 1990. A revealing book by the charismatic priest who was popularly elected as president of Haiti.

Bellegarde-Smith, Patrick. *Haiti: The Breached Citadel*. Boulder. CO: Westview, 1990. A brilliant account of modern Haiti by a Haitian-American.

Brown, Karen McCarthy. *Mama Lola: A Vodou Priestess in Brooklyn*. Berkeley: University of California Press, 1991. A sympathetic reading of Voodoo.

Laguerre, Michel S. *Urban Life in the Caribbean: A Study of a Haitian Urban Community*. Cambridge, MA: Schenkman, 1982.

Nicholls, David. *From Dessalines to Duvalier: Race, Colour, and National Independence in Haiti*. Cambridge: Cambridge University Press, 1979. A contemporary account of the ideology of the Haitian elite.

Roumain, Jacques. *Masters of the Dew*. New York: Reynal and Hitchcock, 1944. The most famous novel written by a Haitian.

"HAITIANS: FROM POLITICAL REPRESSION TO CHAOS"

Robert Lawless

1) What significance does skin color play in Haiti in terms of political, economic, and social structure and functioning?

2) What is Voodoo, and what purpose does it serve for most Haitians?

3) How has the history of Haiti influenced present-day politics?

4) Who were the Duvaliers and why were they important in Haitian political history?

5) Since the overthrow of the repressive regime, have conditions in Haiti improved?

6) Discuss the role of peasantry in Haitian economic and political life.

THE COLD WAR THROUGH THE LOOKING GLASS

Sergei Kruschev

When the Cold War began, people my age were in school, and when it ended, we were increasingly thinking about our pensions. Our whole lives were spent amid the fear that our great national enemy would strike a fatal blow if we made the slightest false step or showed the least weakness. Who "we" were and who the enemy was depended on which country we considered our own, the Soviet Union or the United States.

Virtually my entire life has been spent in Russia. When, already past maturity, I came to the United States, I was surprised by how much our fears and our determination to defend our ideals and our countries had coincided. For Americans, of course, the Soviet Union was the Evil Empire. Readers will be surprised and even indignant to learn that to us—or at least for most of my compatriots—the United States was the Evil Empire. Each side came very close to seizing the other by the throat in a fit of righteous indignation and, in defense of its ideals, using force to make it admit it was wrong (always a hopeless approach). Thanks to the statesmanlike and human wisdom of the leaders of both countries—and a certain amount of luck—we succeeded in avoiding such a "resolution" of the ideological quarrel. The Cold War expired by itself, and we, having survived, can now look back, evaluate our recent past, and even joke about it.

But at the time of Joseph Stalin's death in 1953, everything seemed to be heading toward a real war, a nuclear war. Today, when many secrets are secrets no longer, we know that at the beginning of the 1950s, Stalin ordered an accelerated buildup not only of the Soviet Union's armed forces but of those of his Warsaw Pact allies as well, in order to be fully mobilized and ready for an armed clash by 1954 or 1955. By March 1953, the number of Soviet military personnel had reached 5,394,038, an insupportable burden for the economy of a country in peacetime. However, this gigantic army could have done little in case of a conflict, because the strategic air force of the United States, whose bases surrounded the Soviet Union, could have destroyed whatever it chose. Stalin did not possess a weapon capable of responding with a comparable retaliatory strike on American territory. He knew this and was deathly afraid of war, but at the same time he considered it inevitable. Motivated by fear, he ordered that ten thousand tactical IL-28 bombers with a range of about fifteen hundred miles be produced and stationed at airfields built on the Arctic Ocean ice, closer to U.S. territory. Soviet generals were fully aware that this was an impractical plan, but they did not dare contradict Stalin. Preparations to implement it ended only with his death.

Another crazy scheme, similarly born out of fear, was actually carried out. An army of one hundred thousand men was stationed in tents on the Chukotsk tundra and charged with resisting an invasion from Alaska. It was assumed that the Americans would cross the Bering Strait on the ice. However, where they could go from there, surrounded by swamps, permafrost, and the taiga, has always remained a mystery to me. From Chukotka, it is a good 8,000 miles to Moscow and at least 2,500 miles to relatively inhabited regions of Siberia.

Anti-aircraft batteries were ranged like a fence around Moscow. Beside them lay open crates of gleaming shells ready to be fired. The sudden German air attack in June 1941 was continuing to dominate the Kremlin's thinking, just as Pearl Harbor lived on in Washington's.

I finished school and began studying at the Electric Power Institute in September 1952. I wanted to become an engineer in the field of automated control. We schoolboys and students were inclined to be militant, even aggressive: "Just let them [whomever you like] poke their noses in here and we'll show them a thing or two." Sitting at our school desks, we, like our leaders in the Kremlin, felt sure that war was not far off. When America elected Gen. Dwight D. Eisenhower, a hero of the Second World War, as President in November 1952, we had no doubt what it meant: "The U.S.A. has decided to fight. Otherwise, why would they need a general as President?"

After living through the horrors of German bombings, we were not frightened by the atomic bomb. We flaunted our courage. During civil defense classes, we were told to cover ourselves with something white, preferably a sheet, in the event of a nuclear blast, to reduce the radiation impact (I don't know how effective that would have been). A joke immediately went the rounds: "If an atomic bomb explodes, cover yourself with a sheet and crawl to the cemetery, but without hurrying. Why without hurrying? So as not to cause panic."

Then Providence intervened. On March 5, 1953, Stalin died. My father, who soon became the head of the new Soviet leadership, knew from personal experience what war was like. He had traveled the country's roads for four years during World War II, retreating from the western borders to Stalingrad and then advancing from Stalingrad to Kiev. From his first months in power, he tried to discover whether the Americans were irrevocably bent on war or whether it was possible to reach agreement with them. Interestingly enough, the White House was thinking along more or less the same lines.

In April 1953, President Eisenhower took the first step, delivering a rather conciliatory speech at the National Press Club, in Washington. The next day, it was published in full in *Pravda,* an unprecedented event in those times. Probably this was the turning point from war to peace, and the beginning of dialogue. But it was only the beginning. Both parties had to learn to understand each other. Living on either side of the iron curtain, we knew nothing about each other. Diplomats and intelligence agents supplied their leaders with information, of course, but that was not enough to gain an understanding of the other side. We had to look into each other's eyes.

The first time that my father and President Eisenhower met (aside from a fleeting encounter in June 1945 atop the Lenin Mausoleum, during the Victory Parade in Moscow) was in Geneva in 1955, at the Four-Power Summit Conference. In preparing for the trip to Geneva, Father tried to anticipate every minor detail in order to prevent any possible sign of disrespect or discrimination against our country. He preferred to demand even more than protocol made his due rather than allow his conference partners to wound our national pride. Still, our pride was damaged from the moment of his arrival on Swiss soil, but not because of any malicious scheme by the West. The Soviet delegation arrived in Switzerland on a small two-engine IL-14, while President Eisenhower landed on a giant four-engine Constellation. That did not escape Father's attention. The next year he took his revenge during a visit to England. A TU-104 passenger jet, which had not yet completed all its test flights, brought his mail from Moscow to London every day. Even the Americans did not yet have such a plane. The British queen, hearing an unusual roar coming from the sky (as she told

Father when they met), went out on the balcony of her palace to gape at the marvel.

But to return to the Four-Power Summit Conference: The most important thing that happened in Geneva was that Khrushchev and Eisenhower got to know each other, made their first contacts, and held their first talks. The first step is the most difficult. The process of getting acquainted was not without its curious moments. During one of the breaks between sessions, Eisenhower introduced Father to his assistant Nelson Rockefeller. Father inquired, "Is he *that* Rockefeller?" As Father told me when he returned to Moscow, his curiosity was very much aroused when he was told that this was indeed that Rockefeller. A multimillionaire, but looking no different from anyone else, not in top hat and tails but modestly dressed, moreover serving in a subordinate position. Continuing his account, Father said that he was dying to touch a real multimillionaire, but he didn't know how that would be taken. He didn't hesitate for long, though, but spread his arms and embraced Rockefeller somewhere around the waist (Rockefeller was a head and a half taller than Father). At first Rockefeller was taken aback, but after a moment he responded in kind. I'm describing this to give the reader a sense of what the atmosphere was like in those years. It is hard for us now to imagine how distant we were from each other and how little we understood each other. Such episodes were more valuable than any routine session of negotiations, which were as yet essentially unproductive.

The first misunderstandings also arose in Geneva, and some of them had far-reaching consequences. Eisenhower presented his Open Skies plan, which would allow each side to fly over the territories of the opposing group of countries in order to prevent a surprise attack. Father rejected such a plan outright. Not that he was against the idea itself. But if the American President feared a Soviet attack, Father was afraid of something quite different: That in the process of flying over our country, the Americans would discover our most important secret—how much weaker we were than they—and that discovery might prompt the United States to carry out a preventive strike. In subsequent years, Father continued to oppose inspections for same reason.

In Geneva, initial judgments and opinions were formed on both sides. Father came to the conclusion that he could do business with Eisenhower, who had also experienced the recent war firsthand and would not seek a new one. But a long and difficult path lay ahead before mutual understanding could be reached, and the time had not yet come for an agreement. To be taken seriously, you had to become powerful, because peace on earth can only be achieved through strength—or from a position of strength, as people put it then.

It sometimes happens that seemingly unimportant events turn out to be of historic significance. I think that an editorial published at about that time in an Iowa newspaper, the Des Moines *Register,* played no less important a role than the Geneva meeting in contributing to mutual understanding between the Soviet Union and the United States. The paper's editor called on Father to compete in agriculture, on farm fields, instead of in the arms race. Let each side show what kind of harvest it could produce. The article concluded with a direct appeal to Father: "Come here and we will share our achievements with you. There are no secrets in agriculture." The author surely did not expect the article to reach Father; he probably just had to fill the editorial page. But Intelligence agencies, the KGB and CIA alike, nourish a particular passion for provincial publications and think they may find in them information that is inaccessible in the center. Embassies try to subscribe to everything they can. A translation of the Des Moines *Register* editorial lay on Father's desk in his Kremlin office the day after it was published. After reading it, Father called U.S.S.R. Minister of Agriculture Vladimir Matskevich and asked him to gather together the best Soviet scientists and send them to the United States, to the state of Iowa, to see what they were growing and what innovations they might have thought up there, across the ocean.

The result of the two-week trip by the delegation headed by Matskevich was a four-hundred-page report containing recommendations for how to catch up with American farmers. Father read the weighty tome from beginning to end and kept it near him. He consulted its pages many times afterward. The report described what would be advantageous to imitate, primarily hybrid corn seeds and seed-grading facilities. Father had a special enthusiasm for corn. He thought it could help supply feed for livestock and thereby raise meat consumption in our country to American levels. It was thought that when this was achieved, true communism would come to the U.S.S.R. Father very much wanted to have a look, however fleeting, at what life would be like under communism—in other words, when Russians lived no worse than Americans, than those Americans who had dreamed of destroying communism.

Father did not doubt the superiority and greater economic efficiency of socialism compared with capitalism, and he believed that sooner or later

capitalism would die out and that he would bury it. But in the meantime, as he said in one of his speeches in the United States, "You Americans work better than we do and produce goods that we can only dream about, so we will learn from you; we will study diligently. And once we've learned, we'll begin working better than you, and you will just have to jump onto the running board of the train of socialism, which is leaving for the future. Otherwise you'll be left far behind, and we will wave good-bye from the rear platform of the last car."

Father believed that the system that gave people the best living standards would win. That was the sole criterion. Nothing would help the losing side— not nuclear bombs, ideological dogmas, or propaganda. He was convinced to the end of his life that socialism would come out on top. He died secure in that belief. His principal goal was never competition in the field of weaponry. He was not captivated by the missile race or even by the space race. No, his slogan became, if I may call it that, the food race. Fences, walls of buildings, and billboards were plastered with signs reading: "Catch up and pass the United States in per capita production of meat, milk, and butter." Jokers, numerous in Russia in any era, sometimes wrote in a slogan from the traffic police: "If you aren't sure, don't pass!" However, we were in no real competition with anyone in this sphere. Our people were emerging painfully from a condition of semistarvation.

In Iowa, the Soviet delegation invited farmers to visit the Soviet Union. Almost no one responded. The Cold War was at it most frigid. But there was one person who dared. His name was Roswell Garst, and he was a rather wealthy farmer and seed manufacturer who had specialized in growing corn to fatten hogs, cows, and other livestock. He had hosted the Soviet delegation and now hoped, during a return visit, to sell seeds and some agricultural equipment to the Soviets. Everyone thought this was a preposterous idea, because trade between our countries was nonexistent at the time; the United States didn't even buy Stolichnaya vodka or caviar from the Soviet Union. Garst received a firm "no" from the State Department in response to his proposal, but he didn't give up. He cited the principle of free trade, explaining that hybrid corn seeds would be impossible to use in military technology, however much one might wish to do so. The State Department finally yielded and gave its permission, with the comment "They won't buy anything from you anyway!"

As soon as he got to Moscow, Garst met with Father. They talked for five hours in the Kremlin, and then left for the dacha to look at Father's crops. Garst made many subsequent visits to Moscow. He and Father became real friends. Their love for the earth brought them together. On one such visit, I think in the spring of 1962, Father asked Garst to travel to the south of Russia and take a professional look at how collective farmers were dealing with corn. There Garst noticed that farmers were sowing corn but that their fertilizers, which should have been added to the soil earlier, were piled up along the roads. They were simply too lazy to spread them on the fields. Moreover, the regional managers, who insisted on strict observance of the sowing schedule, were not terribly interested in fertilizers.

Garst was infuriated by such mismanagement. Tracking down the collective farm's field supervisor, he began driving home the point that this was wrong, that they should spread the fertilizers immediately and only then carry out the sowing. Otherwise, they would have a poor harvest. Looking bored, the field supervisor heard out this tiresome foreigner who had descended on him from God knows where. He finally got tired of listening and rather rudely interrupted Garst, advising him to beat it and not interfere where he didn't belong. Garst flew into a rage and threatened to complain to Khrushchev himself if they didn't follow his recommendations.

The supervisor didn't know whether to believe him, but to be on the safe side he stopped the sowing and ordered the collective farmers to spread the fertilizers. What if this crazy American really did complain to one of the higher-ups? After seeing that everything was being done properly, Garst resumed his travels. When he returned to Moscow, he described everything to Father, who later noted regretfully, "This American capitalist cares more than Soviet collective farmers do about our harvest." However, he didn't elaborate.

It seems to me that in those years, when the turn came from war toward peace or, to be more precise, toward peaceful coexistence between the two systems (as Father put it), the friendship between those two men, Garst and Father, was no less fruitful than many months of negotiations by veteran diplomats. Several years ago, I gave a talk at a university in Iowa and was invited by Roswell Garst's son to visit the family farm and drive along the roads my father had traveled nearly forty years earlier. At the end of my visit to the state, I was received by the governor of Iowa. During our conversation he joked: "During all my years as governor I have visited practically every country in the world, and hardly anyone has heard of Iowa. When I went to Russia, at the first mention of Iowa people exclaimed: 'Iowa! The most famous American state! Nikita Khrushchev brought corn from there to the Soviet Union.'"

After agriculture, Father's main concern was housing construction. By the time he came to power, this problem had become acute. Soviet citizens did not live in their own houses or apartments, as people in the United States and Europe did. In Russia, several generations of a family—grandparents, their children, and grandchildren, ten or more people—might be cooped up in one room of 150 square feet. They slept on the floor. In the morning, long lines formed for the only toilet at the end of a hall with doors to a dozen similarly overpopulated rooms. It is hard to describe in words what it's like to stand in such a line; it has to be experienced.

The housing problem had been growing worse for decades. Housing had been destroyed during war: the First World War, the civil war, and the Second World War, when the Germans set fire to cities and villages right up to the walls of Moscow and Stalingrad. Virtually no new housing units, except for huts on factory grounds, had been built. In the 1930s, all the money was spent on industrialization, and in the 1940s it went into rebuilding factories destroyed by the fascists. There was no time or money for people's needs.

Father was determined to resolve this problem, and he initiated the mass construction of apartment buildings. They were put together from concrete panels manufactured quickly on factory conveyor belts, like cars. Tin houses, like cars, looked exactly alike. Housing construction and agriculture required money, a great deal of money, and we had to economize on everything else.

During those years, Father strictly prohibited the construction of administrative buildings, luxury houses for the leadership, and even theaters. All such money was channeled into building inexpensive housing, which was free for its new occupants. Even the Ministry of Defense had to line up for money. However, only a madman or a traitor could neglect the country's security during the Cold War. Defense demanded its share of government spending. Because resources were inadequate, some way had to be found to manage, and that required major decisions. The most important decision was how to combine strengthening the country's security with reducing military spending.

Military professionals demanded that the Soviet army, air force, and navy be given equipment precisely symmetrical to that of the U.S. military. But that would take all the nation's financial resources, leaving nothing in the budget to build housing and provide people with normal lives. Father chose a different path. He tried to make the admirals and generals understand that the United States was much wealthier than we were and that if we competed with the Americans on that basis, we would spend our resources in vain and bring the country to ruin and even then not reach parity. The military insisted. Father angrily exclaimed, "You'll leave the country stark naked!"

Father finally decided to make use of his power and authority. He made the tough decision to formulate an asymmetrical defense doctrine. He thought that we ourselves could determine the necessary minimum to ensure the country's security and ruthlessly eliminate the rest. Negotiations, he believed, would not be effective at this stage.

He started with the navy. Stalin had planned to build an oceangoing surface fleet capable of competing with America's. The admirals needed about 130 billion rubles ($32.5 billion) in the 1955–65 period to carry out the second stage of Stalin's program. That was an enormous sum at the time, and the only way to get it was to cut funds for essential human needs. Discussion of the program continued for about a year without any apparent result. Finally, Father could not restrain himself and posed a direct question to the navy's commander in chief, Adm. Nikolai Kuznetsov: "If today, and not ten years from now, you had all the ships you're asking for, could you defeat the Americans at sea?" The admiral gave a militarily direct answer: "No." The discussion ended with the decision to stop building a surface fleet and to limit construction to submarines, primarily missile submarines, and antisubmarine and shore-defense forces. To this day, Russian naval officers have never forgiven Father, but he simply would not give them money to waste.

Strategic aviation met a similar fate somewhat later. Its development was held to a minimum, while preference was given to ballistic missiles. From then on air force officers also disliked Father. But there were practically no missiles at the time either. In 1956, only one type of ballistic missile was being built, the R-5M, with a nuclear warhead of seventy kilotons. The U.S.S.R. had a total of 426 nuclear warheads. That year the United States had an overall superiority 10.8 times greater.

To restrain the West from a possible attack on the Soviet Union, Father decided to resort to bluff and intimidation. During his visit to England in April 1956, he casually inquired from time to time—once during an official lunch, once in the course of a five-hour tea at the fireplace of the prime minister's country residence at Chequers—if his hosts knew how many nuclear warheads it would take to wipe their island off the face of the earth. An awkward silence followed. But Father did not drop the subject, and with a broad smile on his face he informed those present that if they didn't know, he could help them, and he mentioned a specific number. Then he added, quite cheerfully, "And we have lots of those nuclear warheads, as well as the missiles to deliver them."

Sir Anthony Eden had occasion to recall those talks by the fireplace when, during the Suez crisis, in the autumn of 1956, Father issued an ultimatum to the Anglo-French-Israeli coalition to stop the war within twenty-four hours (the letter was signed by Nikolai Bulganin, head of the Soviet government at the time, but had been written by Khrushchev). As Father described it, his warning got Eden out of bed and hurrying to a telephone in his pajamas to call the French prime minister, Guy Mollet. How did Father know such intimate details? It's not hard to guess. The Cambridge ring of Soviet intelligence, comprising highly placed English diplomats and intelligence agents, was operating at the time, and they sent their reports first to the Kremlin and only afterward to 10 Downing Street. One way or another, the warning worked, military actions ceased, and the troops of the aggressors left Egyptian territory soon thereafter. From then on Father reacted just as sharply to every crisis in the vicinity of the Soviet Union, whether in the Near East, the Far East, or Europe. By frightening the world with Soviet missile superiority, he tried to have the Soviet Union recognized as equal to the United States.

It was in those years that he used the famous phrase "We are producing missiles like sausages." When I asked him how he could say that, because the Soviet Union had no more than half a dozen intercontinental missiles, Father only laughed: "We're not planning to start a war, so it doesn't matter how many missiles are deployed. The main thing is that Americans think we have enough for a powerful strike in response. So they'll be wary of attacking us."

The history of the so-called global missile was similar. The project called for lifting a nuclear warhead into earth orbit. Upon a command from earth, it would explode over an enemy on a trajectory that couldn't be predicted by an (as yet hypothetical) antimissile defense system. The organization where I worked, which was located in a carefully guarded area, had several even more secret rooms equipped for planning this global missile, and we worked there on this new superweapon. Suddenly, just a few months after we started work, Father joyfully informed journalists at a press conference that the Soviet Union would soon possess a global missile, a weapon against which no defense existed. I was profoundly upset and thought of his loquaciousness as a betrayal of the country's national interests. During a walk that evening, I expressed my complaints to Father.

"Don't tell me you thought the government would actually allow someone to launch a nuclear warhead into orbit," he retorted with amazement. "What if something happened to it in orbit, in space? We would be hostages to our own thoughtlessness. The global missile is a propaganda weapon. Let the Americans rack their brains over what I said."

Such statements by Father were in fact received with enthusiasm on the other side of the ocean; they made it easier for the American military to receive additional funds, and so the missile race was born and gained strength, bringing President John F. Kennedy to the White House. The race, which never existed, or rather in which only America took part, was the United States's internal competition to see who could grab more funds from the budget. Insofar as there was a real race, the United States always led. For example, only beginning in 1967 were large numbers of the UR-100 (SS-11) light ballistic missile deployed in the Soviet Union, five years later than the analogous American Minuteman I. The CIA must have known this, but the myth of Soviet missile superiority was useful, or seemed to be useful, not so much to Father as to the American military industrial complex.

President Eisenhower understood this very well. He and Father held meetings at Camp David in September of 1959. As they were taking a walk one day, Eisenhower brought up the subject of relations with the military and asked Father how he coped with his generals. Father reacted cautiously. He was not prepared to discuss such a subject with the American President.

"Then I'll start," said Eisenhower, smiling. "My military leaders come to me several times a year and ask for additional appropriations for new types of weapons. When I reply that the budget has been approved and printed and there's no place to find the money, they begin frightening me by saying that the Soviet Union is already developing such 'toys' and I'll be responsible if the United States is defeated in a future war. Naturally, I have to give them the money."

Father replied that he was often subjected to such pressure from his own military-industrial complex.

"Maybe we should make a secret agreement between us to curb our military," proposed the President.

"That would be good," responded Father. "But the time has not yet come."

The time for confidential relations between Soviet and American leaders had truly not yet come, but, by 1959, a great deal had changed since 1955. Eisenhower and Father had learned to talk with each other, and the first signs of mutual confidence had appeared. A foundation was built for all of Father's future negotiations with Kennedy, Leonid Brezhnev's with a whole series of American Presidents, and Mikhail Gorbachev's with Ronald Reagan. In 1959, there was no longer talk of an inevitable and imminent war. Leaders of the two countries were working out the conditions for peaceful coexistence on our planet.

But incidents could not be avoided. The flight of the American U-2 spy plane, shot down by a Soviet antiaircraft missile over Sverdlovsk, in the very heart of Russia, blew away everything that Father and Eisenhower had worked for during the previous years. It derailed the Paris Four-Power Conference, resulted in the cancellation of the American President's forthcoming visit to the Soviet Union, which had inspired great hopes, and in my opinion delayed the signing of the Nuclear Test Ban Treaty by three years. Still, the foundation was preserved, and the new American President, John F. Kennedy, did not begin his dialogue with Father on a blank page. Their only meeting, in Vienna in June 1961, was notable for showing a new approach to evaluating the balance of nuclear forces, and not just for the famous fruitless arguments about a new world order—about which agreement was impossible—and not just for disagreements over Berlin or the agreement on Laos. Although the two leaders did not reach an agreement, neither were they busy calculating how much destruction they could wreak on each other. They talked about the price that they were ready to pay for a victory and about how many of their compatriots' lives they were ready to sacrifice for it. As a result, they agreed that nuclear parity existed in the world, even though the U.S.S.R. had deployed only six intercontinental ballistic missiles (naturally, this figure was not officially cited by either party). This was at a time when Americans estimated their superiority in nuclear warheads and missiles to be 20 to 1 (actually it was almost 10 to 1, which is also a lot. The Soviet Union had 2,471 nuclear warheads, the United States 24,173).

Another significant fact: Both sides began to feel the need for direct contact. In other words, they started to trust each other and to believe in the possibility and productivity of a dialogue devoted to preventing a nuclear war. In Vienna, both leaders agreed to establish a direct link between the Kremlin and the White House by means of special couriers.

Kennedy made this initiative. He proposed exchanging confidential letters outside of State Department channels. Father readily agreed. He always favored a direct dialogue, without intermediaries.

This agreement served the parties well during the Cuban Missile Crisis, which broke out soon afterward, in October 1962. How the dramatic events of those years looked from the Soviet side is a separate and very fascinating story. My new book, *The Creation of a Superpower*, investigates that history and provides many other details of Kremlin life. I shall only note here that for the first time in the history of the Cold War a secret personal correspondence between two leaders, and not mutual threats and propaganda escapades, was the main instrument for resolving the Cuban Missile Crisis. This is an extraordinarily important indication that both the President of the United States and the head of the Soviet government understood that although they may have been determined to defend their own principles and values, which were not compatible, it was only through dialogue that they could achieve their common goal of preserving life on earth.

The Cuban Missile Crisis erupted truly out of the blue. When Fidel Castro and his companions-in-arms entered Havana, on January 1, 1959, no one in Moscow took the slightest interest. The Soviet embassy in Cuba had been considered unnecessary and was closed in 1952. Diplomatic relations had continued, but neither an embassy nor a single Soviet representative remained in Cuba.

After reading western agency reports about Castro's triumph, Father became curious about what had happened on that distant island and received the following reply from the intelligence service and the Party Central Committee's International Department: "Castro is the usual Central American dictator, probably closely connected to the CIA, and will dance to the American tune, just like Batista."

Sometime later, when the Cuban leader went to Washington expecting to meet with President Dwight D. Eisenhower, a high-level international specialist from the Party Central Committee said to Father in my presence: "You see, Nikita Sergeyevich, we were right. Castro's hurrying to bow to his master." The fact that Castro intended to conduct an independent policy was apparent only later, and Father himself was the first to realize it. Then he decided that the only way to defend Cuba from the inevitable aggression of the United States was by deploying missiles with nuclear warheads on the island. In so doing, he was warning Washington that military action in that region would automatically lead to a third world war.

In that, the political precepts of the leaders of both superpowers hardly differed, and indeed could not differ. In 1963, President Kennedy behaved like Father when he declared that he considered himself a West Berliner and was ready to defend the city from possible Soviet seizure with all the power America possessed. In economic and other terms, West Berlin was even more useless to Kennedy than Cuba was to Father. But the status of a superpower leaves its special mark on the conduct of world leaders. They have to defend their allies with all the means available to them. If they retreat even an inch, it's farewell to superpower status forever. No one will believe them any more, just as in our time no one believes Boris Yeltsin. Such are the implacable rules of the game in power politics.

People have always loved to retouch history after the fact. The history of the Cuban Missile Crisis is no exception. It has become customary to argue that Father gave in because of America's firm stance, that he yielded and blinked first. In fact, both leaders realized they could have control of the situation only until the first shot was fired, until the first bomb dropped on Cuba. Subsequent events would develop according to other rules, the rules of war, of a third world war. Father loved to say, "Any fool can start a war, but then where are we going to find the wise men to stop it?" Both Father and Kennedy tried to prevent that first shot by every possible means. However, Kennedy was under tremendous pressure. Father knew this, and he took it into account when he decided to withdraw the missiles from Cuba in exchange for the President's promise not to invade the island—a promise that he trusted. That would have been inconceivable in 1952. Trust an American President!

When Father argued at a meeting off the Soviet leadership in favor of withdrawing the missiles, he made this unprecedented statement: "We have to help Kennedy withstand pressure from the hawks. They are demanding am immediate military invasion." A little later, after the withdrawal of the Soviet missiles from Cuba had begun, Kennedy asked journalists to help Khrushchev by not crowing about the American victory. Five years earlier could anyone have imagined hearing such words in the White House?

One other comment. I don't want to talk about winners in this crisis. It's easy to view it superficially as Kennedy's victory; he forced the Soviet Union to withdraw. Father thought that he won by protecting Cuba from possible aggression and by averting a great war. In the political game of brinkmanship, he stuck to his opinion: The one who decides to blink first doesn't possess weaker but greater wisdom.

The real main consequence of the Cuban Missile Crisis was American society's irrevocable perception of parity, of equality between the U.S.S.R. and the United States in nuclear destructive force. And the American media, not Father, were responsible for that. They so frightened their countrymen that after the crisis it made no sense to talk about nuclear superiority in terms of numbers. The nation's subconscious would not absorb them.

The Cuban Missile Crisis ended the cycle of crises and missile—bluff diplomacy. Both sides recognized that they were now capable not only of inflicting a mortal blow on each other but of destroying civilization, of ending life on earth. A great deal changed in the world after the crisis, but even more could have changed. In August 1963, the United States, the U.S.S.R., and Great Britain signed an agreement prohibiting nuclear testing in the atmosphere, underwater, and in outer space. That same August, Kennedy sent Father a proposal about joining Soviet and American forces for a flight to the moon. He had first mentioned the idea in Vienna, in June 1961, but at the time Father hadn't replied. He thought it might enable the United States to obtain intelligence information and to discover that our missile capability was far beneath what we claimed. And that might provoke the Americans to carry out a pre-emptive strike. It was the same fear that had pursued Father in Geneva.

In 1963, several dozen R-16 intercontinental missiles were deployed in the Soviet Union, and Father considered the number sufficient to cool off any hotheads. If the Americans knew about them, that knowledge would benefit everyone. Furthermore, with spy satellites flying around the planet for the second year, secrets were no longer secrets.

After the deployment of nuclear-tipped intercontinental missiles, Father took an even tougher approach to the concept of national security. He thought that deployment of three hundred to five hundred of these missiles would make a war impossible, which in turn made it senseless to maintain a gigantic army. Father did not believe that local wars could be waged without using nuclear weapons. He thought that the U.S.S.R. and the United States would always stand behind their participants and that the losing side could not resist resorting to nuclear weapons. Therefore it made sense to warn governments that they would be used at the very beginning of a conflict, not at the end. Father thought a professional army of half a million would be adequate to defend our strategic nuclear forces. The remaining armed forces should be organized on the basis of a militia, similar to the U.S. National Guard, freeing up young working hands.

He did not think it made sense to continue pouring money into conventional weapons, so he proposed reducing the production of tanks, cannon, and tactical aircraft to a minimum and shifting the freed resources to the production of consumer goods and the construction of housing. Of course, the military opposed this with all its might. I remember how at a Defense Council session in March 1963 the Warsaw Pact commander in chief, Marshal Andrei Grechko, tried to persuade Father to increase the production of tactical nuclear warheads. Father patiently explained to him that the use of this weapon on the battlefield was questionable and would lower the moral threshold, the threshold of fear of using nuclear weapons. Another very important argument for Father was the fact that a ten-kiloton warhead cost as much as a one-megaton warhead. Father preferred a multi-megaton nuclear club to tactical nuclear weapons; it was far more convenient—not to use but to threaten with. But bash everyone indiscriminately over the head from nuclear cannon? You couldn't preserve peace on earth that way.

At the same meeting, Grechko insisted that nuclear cannon should be mass-produced, because the Americans were already making them and we lagged. Father's reaction was typical. He said that Soviet designers had created two such weapons. They were displayed regularly on Red Square in Moscow, on May 1 and on November 7, so everyone, including the Americans, knew we had them. "So two cannon are enough for you, Marshal, and for the Americans," concluded Father. "We won't squander the people's money on more of them."

I don't know how Americans would have reacted to knowledge of the radical reduction in Soviet armed forces that was planned, but I would like to hope that the response would have been proportionate. If so, the Cold War might have ended in 1969, and that year an American astronaut and a Soviet cosmonaut might have stepped onto the moon's surface together. But life turned out differently. In November 1963, John F. Kennedy died, and a year later, in October 1964, my father was removed from power. The leaders who replaced Father hurried to "correct his mistakes" by giving a new impetus to the arms race and producing tens of thousands of tactical nuclear weapons. By 1989, the Soviet army had 7,000 nuclear cannon. The Cold War was prolonged by twenty years and did not end until the start of the 1990s, with the dissolution of the Soviet Union.

Was the fact that the Cold War did not end sooner a wasted opportunity? Or was the world not ready for it to end in the 1960s? We can only guess, and regret that it did not happen.

What was the Cold War? Could it have been avoided? Was it a product of the ill will of politicians or was it historically inevitable? Probably the latter. For thousands of years, peoples have resolved their conflicts by armed clashes. There was good reason for Karl von Clausewitz to write that war is a continuation of politics by other means. With the invention of nuclear weapons, politicians suddenly realized that war would no longer lead to victory, that both sides would lose. But they didn't know how to behave differently. So they behaved the same way, but without going to war. War without war was called "cold war." A very accurate definition. And at the beginning of this process, at the dawn of the Cold War, when a great deal was still unsettled and all the destructive consequences of the use of nuclear weapons were not apparent, it would have been very easy to yield to temptation and drift into a real war. I consider it a great achievement, a heroic deed, if you will, of the world leaders of those years, primarily American Presidents Dwight D. Eisenhower and John F. Kennedy and my father, the chairman of the U.S.S.R. Council of Ministers, Nikita Khrushchev, that they showed the wisdom to pass safely over the reefs of a hot war and preserve the life of humankind. Thus the Cold War was a kind of transitional period from a disconnected world that used weapons as its main instrument for resolving world conflicts to some kind of different state of being—to a new world order, if you like.

The Cold War has now passed into history. But the transition is far from complete. We stand at the beginning of a new phase of the transitional period and again face a real danger of new (so far limited, nonnuclear) armed conflicts. And God forbid that my Father's prophecy—that as soon as a nonnuclear war seriously affects the interests of the world's great powers, it will inevitably grow into a nuclear conflict—should come to pass. Again, just as forty years ago, our fate, the fate of the world, and of humankind, depends on the wisdom of the political leaders in power.

The next historical fork in the road is now visible. We can choose the path that now appears to the strong (we don't know who will be strong tomorrow) to be the simple and easy one: that of imposing order by fire and the sword. But this path is easy only at first; the mindless use of force will provoke the rest of the world to increase its military and nuclear might, and the result will at best be a new spiral in something similar to the Cold War, but with new participants. At worst. . . . One doesn't even want to imagine.

Or we can choose another path, the complicated, long, and tedious one of introducing a new world order by strengthening world institutions, primarily the United Nations. That holds no appeal for political cowboys, but the UN's seemingly excessive bureaucratization, its habit of following every conceivable and inconceivable bureaucratic procedure, suppresses inflamed emotions and allows for consideration of the contradictory diversity of positions held by dissenting countries. Here is where we can detect the wisdom of the founding fathers of the United Nations. I think it would be just as counterproductive to neglect their counsel as to rewrite the American Constitution. UN procedures irritate the world's politicians, just as they irritated my father in the 1960s, but that only confirms that those who devised this balanced system knew what they were doing. We can make progress only along this path. All other will lead the world into a vicious circle from which it will always be difficult to break loose.

"THE COLD WAR THROUGH THE LOOKING GLASS"

Sergei Kruschev

1) How did the perspectives of the United States and the Soviet Union come to coincide during the Cold War?

2) What attitudes and judgments, both good and bad, came out of the first Geneva Summit between Eisenhower and Krushchev?

3) What did Nikita Krushchev believe would ultimately win the Cold War for the Soviet Union?

4) What problems faced the Soviet Union during the Cold War? How did Krushchev go about trying to solve them?

5) What tensions existed between the Soviet Union's desire for military security and its need to develop economically, according to the article?

6) How did the dialogue between Eisenhower and Krushchev pave the way for closer dialogue between the U.S. and the U.S.S.R. in the 1960s? How did this help to alleviate the Cuban Missile Crisis?

7) Why would the Soviet Union consider the United States to be the "Evil Empire"?

SECTION NINE

Family, Marriage, and Kinship

THE DISAPPEARANCE OF THE INCEST TABOO

Yéhudi Cohen

Several years ago a minor Swedish bureaucrat, apparently with nothing better to do, was leafing through birth and marriage records, matching people with their natural parents. To his amazement he found a full brother and sister who were married and had several children. The couple were arrested and brought to trial. It emerged that they had been brought up by separate sets of foster parents and never knew of each other's existence. By a coincidence reminiscent of a Greek tragedy, they met as adults, fell in love, and married, learning of their biological tie only after their arrest. The local court declared their marriage illegal and void.

The couple appealed the decision to Sweden's Supreme Court. After lengthy testimony on both sides of the issue, the court overturned the decision on the grounds that the pair had not been reared together. The marriage was declared legal and valid. In the wake of the decision, a committee appointed by Sweden's Minister of Justice to examine the question has proposed that criminal sanctions against incest be repealed. The committee's members were apparently swayed by Carl-Henry Alstrom, a professor of psychiatry. Alstrom argued that psychological deterrents to incest are stronger than legal prohibitions. The question will soon go to Sweden's Parliament, which seems prepared to follow the committee's recommendation.

Aside from illustrating the idea that the most momentous changes in human societies often occur as a result of unforeseen events, this landmark case raises questions that go far beyond Sweden's (or any other society's) borders. Some people may be tempted to dismiss the Swedish decision as an anomaly, as nothing more than a part of Sweden's unusual experiments in public welfare and sexual freedom.

But the probable Swedish decision to repeal criminal laws against incest cannot be regarded so lightly; this simple step reflects a trend in human society that has been developing for several thousand years. When we arrange human societies along a continuum from the least to the most complex, from those with the smallest number of interacting social groups to those with the highest number of groups, from those with the simplest technology to those with the most advanced technology, we observe that the incest taboo applies to fewer and fewer relatives beyond the immediate family.

Though there are exceptions, the widest extension of incest taboos beyond the nuclear family is found in the least complex societies. In a few societies, such as the Cheyenne of North America and the Kwoma of New Guinea, incest taboos extend to many remote relatives, including in-laws and the in-laws of in-laws. In modern industrial societies, incest taboos are usually confined to members of the immediate household. This contraction in the range of incest taboos is reaching the point at which they may disappear entirely.

The source of these changes in incest taboos lies in changing patterns of external trade. Trade is a society's jugular. Because every group lives in a milieu lacking some necessities that are available in other habitats, the flow of goods and resources is a society's lifeblood. But it is never sufficient merely to encourage people to form trade alliances with others in different areas. Incest taboos force people to marry outside their own group, to form alliances and to maintain trade networks. As other institutions—governments, business organizations—begin to organize trade, incest taboos become less necessary for assuring the flow of the society's lifeblood; they start to contract.

Other explanations of the incest taboo do not, under close examination, hold up. The most common assumption is that close inbreeding is biologically deleterious and will lead to the extinction of those who practice it. But there is strong evidence that inbreeding does not materially increase the rate of maladies such as albinism, total color blindness, or various forms of idiocy, which generally result when each parent carries the same recessive gene. In most cases these diseases result from chance combinations of recessive genes or from mutation.

According to Theodosius Dobzhansky, a geneticist, "The increase of the incidence of hereditary diseases in the offspring of marriages between relatives (cousins, uncle and niece or aunt and nephew, second cousins, etc.) over that in marriages between persons not known to be related is slight—so slight that geneticists hesitate to declare such marriages disgenic." Inbreeding does carry a slight risk. The progeny of relatives include more stillbirths and infant and early childhood deaths than the progeny of unrelated people. But most of these deaths are due to environmental rather than genetic factors. Genetic disadvantages are not frequent enough to justify a prohibition. Moreover, it is difficult to justify the biological explanation for incest taboos when many societies prescribe marriage to one cousin and prohibit marriage to another. Among the Lesu of Melanesia, a man must avoid sexual contact with his parallel cousins, his mother's sisters' daughters and his father's brothers' daughters, but is supposed to marry his cross cousins, his mother's brothers' daughters and his father's sisters' daughters. Even though both types of cousins have the same genetic relationship to the man, only one kind is included in the incest taboo. The taboo is apparently a cultural phenomenon based on the cultural classification of people and cannot be explained biologically.

Genetic inbreeding may even have some advantages in terms of natural selection. Each time a person dies of a hereditary disadvantage, his detrimental genes are lost to the population. By such a process of genetic cleansing, inbreeding may lead to the elimination, or at least to reduced frequencies, of recessive genes. The infant mortality rate may increase slightly at first, but after the sheltered recessive genes are eliminated, the population may stabilize. In-breeding may also increase the frequency of beneficial recessive genes, contributing to the population's genetic fitness. In the end, inbreeding seems to have only a slight effect on the offspring and a mixed effect, some good and some bad, on the gene pool itself. This mild consequence hardly justifies the universal taboo on incest.

Another explanation of the incest taboo is the theory of natural aversion, first produced by Edward Westermarck in his 1891 book, *The History of Human Marriage*. According to Westermarck, children reared in the same household are naturally averse to having sexual relations with one another in adulthood. But this theory has major difficulties. First, it has a basic logical flaw: If there were a natural aversion to incest, the taboo would be unnecessary. As James Frazer pointed out in 1910, "It is not easy to see why any deep human instinct should need to be reinforced by law. There is no law commanding men to eat and drink or forbidding them to put their hands in the fire . . . The law only forbids men to do what their instincts incline them to do; what nature itself prohibits and punishes, it would be superfluous for the law to prohibit and punish . . . Instead of assuming, therefore, from the legal prohibition of incest that there is a natural aversion to incest, we ought rather to assume that there is a natural instinct in favor of it."

Second, the facts play havoc with the notion of natural aversion. In many societies, such as the Arapesh of New Guinea studied by Margaret Mead, and the Eskimo, young children are betrothed and raised together, usually by the boy's parents, before the marriage is consummated. Arthur Wolf, an anthropologist who studied a village in northern Taiwan, describes just such a custom: "Dressed in the traditional red wedding costume, the bride enters her future husband's home as a child. She is seldom more than three years of age and often less than a year . . . [The] last phase in the marriage process does not take place until she is old enough to fulfill the role of wife. In the meantime, she and her parents are affinally related to the groom's parents, but she is not in fact married to the groom."

One of the examples commonly drawn up to support Westermarck's theory of aversion is the Israeli *kibbutz*, where children who have been raised together tend to avoid marrying. But this avoidance has been greatly exaggerated. There is some tendency among those who have been brought up in the same age group in a communal "children's house" to avoid marrying one another, but this arises from two regulations that separate young adults from their *kibbutz* at about the age when they might marry. The first is a regulation of the Israel Defense Forces that no married woman may serve in the armed forces. Conscription for men and women is at 18, usually coinciding with their completion of secondary school, and military service is a deeply felt responsibility for most *kibbutz*-reared Israelis. Were women to marry prior to 18, they would be denied one of their principal goals. By the time they complete their military service, many choose urban spouses whom they have met in the army. Thus the probability of marrying a person one has grown up with is greatly reduced.

The second regulation that limits intermarriage on a *kibbutz* is a policy of the federations to which almost all *kibbutzim* belong. Each of the four major federations reserves the right to transfer any member to any other settlement, especially when a new one is being established. These "seeds," as the transferred members are called, are recruited individually from different settlements and most transfers are made during a soldier's third or fourth year of military service. When these soldiers leave the army to live on a *kibbutz*, they may be separated from those they were reared with. The frequency of marriage among people from working-class backgrounds who began and completed school together in an American city or town is probably higher than for an

Israeli *kibbutz*; the proclivity among American college graduates to marry outside their neighborhoods or towns is no more an example of exogamy or incest avoidance than is the tendency in Israel *kibbutzim* to marry out.

Just as marriage within a neighborhood is accepted in the United States, so is marriage within a *kibbutz* accepted in Israel. During research I conducted in Israel between 1967 and 1969, I attended the wedding of two people in a *kibbutz* who supposedly were covered by this taboo or rule of avoidance. As my tape recordings and photographs show, it would be difficult to imagine a more joyous occasion. When I questioned members of the *kibbutz* about this, they told me with condescending smiles that they had "heard of these things the professors say."

A third, "demographic," explanation of the incest taboo was originally set forth in 1960 by Wilson Wallis and elaborated in 1959 by Mariam Slater. According to this theory, mating within the household, especially between parents and children, was unlikely in early human societies because the life span in these early groups was so short that by the time offspring were old enough to mate, their parents would probably have died. Mating between siblings would also have been unlikely because of the average of eight years between children that resulted from breast feeding and high rates of infant mortality. But even assuming this to have been true for the first human societies, there is nothing to prevent mating among the members of a nuclear family when the life span is lengthened.

A fourth theory that is widely subscribed to focuses on the length of the human child's parental dependency, which is the longest in the animal kingdom. Given the long period required for socializing children, there must be regulation of sexual activity so that children may learn their proper role. If the nuclear family's members are permitted to have unrestricted sexual access to one another, the members of the unit would be confused about their roles. Parental authority would be undermined, and it would be impossible to socialize children. This interpretation has much to recommend it as far as relationships between parents and children are concerned, but it does not help explain brother-sister incest taboos or the extension of incest taboos to include remote relatives.

The explanation closest to my interpretation of the changes in the taboo is the theory of alliance advocated by the French anthropologist Claude Levi-Strauss, which suggests that people are compelled to marry outside their groups in order to form unions with other groups and promote harmony among them. A key element in the theory is that men exchange their sisters and daughters in marriage with men of other groups. As originally propounded, the theory of alliance was based on the assumption that men stay put while the women change groups by marrying out, moved about by men like pieces on a chessboard. But there are many instances in which the women stay put while the men change groups by marrying out. In either case, the result is the same. Marriage forges alliances.

These alliances freed early human societies from exclusive reliance on their own limited materials and products. No society is self-sustaining or self-perpetuating; no culture is a world unto itself. Each society is compelled to trade with others and this was as true for tribal societies as it is for modern industrial nations. North America, for instance, was crisscrossed with elaborate trade networks before the Europeans arrived. Similar trade networks covered aboriginal New Guinea and Australia. In these trade networks, coastal or riverline groups gave shells and fish to hinterland people in exchange for cultivated foods, wood, and manufactured items.

American Indian standards of living were quite high before the Europeans destroyed the native trade networks, and the same seems to have been true in almost all other parts of the world. It will come as no surprise to economists that the material quality of people's lives improves to the extent that they engage in external trade.

But barter and exchange do not automatically take place when people meet. Exchange involves trust, and devices are needed to establish trust, to distinguish friend from foe, and to assure a smooth, predictable flow of trade goods. Marriage in the tribal world established permanent obligations and reciprocal rights and privileges among families living in different habitats.

For instance, when a young Cheyenne Indian man decided on a girl to marry, he told his family of his choice. If they agreed that his selection was good, they gathered a store of prized possessions—clothing, blankets, guns, bows and arrows—and carefully loaded them on a fine horse. A friend of the family, usually a respected old woman, led the horse to the tepee of the girl's elder brother. There the go-between spread the gifts for everyone to see while she pressed the suitor's case. The next step was for the girl's brother to assemble all his cousins for a conference to weigh the proposal. If they agreed to it, the cousins distributed the gifts among themselves, the brother taking the horse. Then the men returned to their tepees to find suitable gifts to give in return. Within a day or two, each returned with something roughly equal in value to what he had received. While this was happening, the bride was made beautiful. When all arrangements were completed, she mounted one horse while the return gifts were loaded on another. The old woman led both horses to the groom's camp. After the bride was received, her accompanying gifts were distributed among the groom's relatives in accordance with what each had given. The exchanges between the two families did not end with the marriage ceremony, however; they continued as a permanent part of the marriage ties. This continual exchange, which took place periodically, is why the young man's bridal choice was so important for his entire family.

Marriage was not the only integral part of external trade relationships. Another was ritualized friendship, "blood brotherhood," for example. Such bonds were generally established between members of different groups and were invariably trade partnerships. Significantly, these ritualized friendships often included taboos against marriage with the friend's sisters; sometimes the taboo applied to all their close relatives. This extension of a taboo provides an important key for understanding all incest taboos. Sexual prohibitions do not necessarily grow out of biological ties. Both marriage and ritualized friendships in primitive societies promote economic alliances and both are associated with incest taboos.

Incest taboos force people into alliances with others in as many groups as possible. They promote the greatest flow of manufactured goods and raw materials from the widest variety of groups and ecological niches and force people to spread their social nets. Looked at another way, incest taboos prevent localism and economic provincialism; they block social and economic inbreeding.

Incest taboos have their widest extensions outside the nuclear family in those societies in which technology is least well developed and in which people have to carry their own trade goods for barter or exchange with members of other groups. Often in these small societies, everyone in a community is sexually taboo to the rest of the group. When the technology surrounding trade improves and shipments of goods and materials can be concentrated (as when people learn to build and navigate ocean-going canoes or harness pack animals), fewer and fewer people have to be involved in trade. As this happens, incest taboos begin to contract, affecting fewer and fewer people outside the nuclear family.

This process has been going on for centuries. Today, in most industrial societies, the only incest taboos are those that pertain to members of the nuclear family. This contraction of the range of the

taboo is inseparable from the fact that we no longer engage in personal alliances and trade agreements to get the food we eat, the clothes we wear, the tools and materials we use, the fuels on which we depend. Goods are brought to distribution points near our homes by a relatively tiny handful of truckers, shippers, merchants, entrepreneurs, and others. Most of us are only vaguely aware of the alliances, negotiations, and relationships that make this massive movement of goods possible. When we compare tribal and contemporary industrialized societies, the correspondence between the range of incest taboos and the material conditions of life cannot be dismissed as mere coincidence.

Industrialization does not operate alone in affecting the degree to which incest taboos extend beyond the nuclear family. In the history of societies, political institutions developed as technology advanced. Improvements in packaging and transportation have led not only to reductions in the number of people involved in external trade, but also to greater and greater concentrations of decision making in the hands of fewer and fewer people. Trade is no longer the responsibility of all members of a society, and the maintenance of relationships between societies has become the responsibility of a few people—a king and his bureaucracy, impersonal governmental agencies, national and multinational corporations.

To the extent that trade is conducted and negotiated by a handful of people, it becomes unnecessary to use incest taboos to force the majority of people into alliances with other groups. Treaties, political alliances, and negotiations by the managers of a few impersonal agencies have replaced marital and other personal alliances. The history of human societies suggests that incest taboos may have outlived their original purpose.

But incest taboos still serve other purposes. For social and emotional reasons rather than economic ones, people in modern industrial societies still need to prevent localism. Psychological well-being in a diversified society depends largely on the ability to tap different ideas, points of view, life styles, and social relationships. The jugulars that must now be kept open by the majority of people may no longer be for goods and resources, but for variety and stimulation. This need for variety is what, in part, seems to underlie the preference of Israelis to marry outside the communities in which they were born and brought up. The taboo against sex within the nuclear family leads young people to explore, to seek new experiences. In a survey of a thousand cases of incest, Christopher Bagley found that incestuous families are cut off from their society's social and cultural mainstream. Whether rural or urban, he writes, "the family seems to withdraw from the general community, and initiates its own 'deviant' norms of sexual behavior, which are contained within the family circle." "Such a family," he continues, "is an isolated cultural unit, relatively untouched by external social norms." This social and cultural inbreeding is the cause of the profound malaise represented by incest.

To illustrate the correspondence between incest and social isolation, let me describe an incestuous family reported by Peter Wilson, an anthropologist. Wilson sketched a sequence of events in which a South American family became almost totally isolated from the community in which it lived, and began to practice almost every variety of incest. The decline into incest began many years before Wilson appeared on the scene to do anthropological research, when the father of five daughters and four sons made the girls (who ranged in age from 18 to 33) sexually available to some sailors for a small sum of money. As a result, the entire household was ostracized by the rest of the village. "But most important," Wilson writes, "the Brown family was immediately cut off from sexual partners. No woman would have anything to do with a Brown man; no man would touch a Brown woman."

The Brown's isolation and incest continued for several years, until the women in the family rebelled—apparently because a new road connecting their hamlet to others provided the opportunity for social contact with people outside the hamlet. At the same time the Brown men began working in new light industry in the area and spending their money in local stores. The family slowly regained some social acceptance in Green Fields, the larger village to which their hamlet belonged. Little by little they were reintegrated into the hamlet and there seems to have been no recurrence of incest among them.

A second example is an upper middle class, Jewish urban American family that was described to me by a colleague. The Erva family (a pseudonym) consists of six people—the parents, two daughters aged 19 and 22, and two sons, aged 14 and 20. Mr. Erva is a computer analyst and his wife a dentist. Twenty-five years ago, the Ervas seemed relatively normal, but shortly after their first child was born, Mr. and Mrs. Erva took to wandering naked about their apartment, even when others were present. They also began dropping in on friends for as long as a week; their notion of reciprocity was to refuse to accept food, to eat very little of what was offered them, or to order one member of their family not to accept any food at all during a meal. Their rationale seemed to be that accepting food was receiving a favor, but occupying

a bed was not. This pattern was accompanied by intense family bickering and inadvertent insults to their hosts. Not surprisingly, most of their friends wearied of their visits and the family was left almost friendless.

Reflecting Bagley's general description of incestuous families, the Ervas had withdrawn from the norms of the general community after the birth of their first child and had instituted their own "deviant" patterns of behavior. They thereby set the stage for incest.

Mr. Erva began to have intercourse with his daughters when they were 14 and 16 years old. Neither of them was self-conscious about the relationship and it was common for the father to take both girls into bed with him at the same time when they were visiting overnight. Mrs. Erva apparently did not have intercourse with her sons. The incest became a matter of gossip and added to the family's isolation.

The Erva family then moved to the Southwest to start over again. They built a home on a parcel of land that had no access to water. Claiming they could not afford a well of their own, the family began to use the bathrooms and washing facilities of their neighbors. In the end these neighbors, too, wanted nothing to do with them.

Mr. and Mrs. Erva eventually separated, he taking the daughters and she the sons. Later the younger daughter left her father to live alone, but the older daughter still shares a one bedroom apartment with her father.

Social isolation and incest appear to be related, and social maturity and a taboo on incest are also related. Within the modern nuclear family, social and emotional relationships are intense, and sexuality is the source of some of the strongest emotions in human life. When combined with the intensity of family life, sexually stimulated emotions can be overwhelming for children. Incest taboos are a way of limiting family relationships. They are assurances of a degree of emotional insularity, of detachment on which emotional maturity depends.

On balance, then, we can say that legal penalties for incest were first instituted because of the adverse economic effects of incestuous unions on society, but that today the negative consequences of incest affect only individuals. Some will say that criminal penalties should be retained if only to protect children. But legal restraints alone are unlikely to serve as deterrents. Father-daughter incest is regarded by many social workers, judges, and psychiatrists as a form of child abuse, but criminal penalties have not deterred other forms of child abuse. Moreover, incest between brothers and sisters cannot be considered child abuse. Some have even suggested that the concept of abuse may be inappropriate when applied to incest. "Many psychotherapists," claims psychologist James McCary in *Human Sexuality*, "believe that a child is less affected by actual incest than by seductive behavior on the part of a parent that never culminates in any manifest sexual activity."

Human history suggests that the incest taboo may indeed be obsolete. As in connection with changing attitudes toward homosexuality, it may be maintained that incestuous relations between consenting mature adults are their concern alone and no one else's. At the same time, however, children must be protected. But questions still remain about how they should be protected and until what age.

If a debate over the repeal of criminal laws against incest is to begin in earnest, as it surely will if the Swedish Parliament acts on the proposed reversal, one other important fact about the social history of sexual behavior must be remembered. Until about a century ago, many societies punished adultery and violations of celibacy with death. When it came time to repeal those laws, not a few people favored their retention on the grounds that extramarital sexual relationships would adversely affect the entire society. Someday people may regard incest in the same way they now regard adultery and violations of celibacy. Where the threat of punishment once seemed necessary, social and emotional dissuasion may now suffice.

References

Bagley Christopher, "Incest Behavior and Incest Taboos," *Social Problems*, Vol. 16, 1969, pp. 505–519.

Birdsell, J.B., *Human Evolution: An Introduction to the New Physical Anthropology*, Rand McNally, 1972.

Bischof, Norbert, "The Biological Foundations of the Incest Taboo," *Social Science Information*, Vol. 11, No. 6, 1972.

Fox, Robin, *Kinship and Marriage*, Penguin Books, 1968.

Slater, Mariam, "Ecological Factors in the Origin of Incest," *American Anthropologist*, Vol. 61, No. 6, 1959.

Wilson, Peter J., "Incest: A Case Study," *Social and Economic Studies*, Vol. 12, 1961, pp. 200–209.

"THE DISAPPEARANCE OF THE INCEST TABOO"

Yéhudi Cohen

1) What is the incest taboo, and what relatives does it cover?

2) What are the various theories suggested to explain the origin of the incest taboo, and what are their strengths and weaknesses?

3) Cohen suggests that incest taboos force people to forge alliances. What purposes do such alliances serve in human culture?

4) What are the major problems caused by incest, in Cohen's view?

5) Why does Cohen suggest that the need for the incest taboo is disappearing? Do you agree or disagree with his thesis and conclusions?

NAYARS: TRADITION AND CHANGE IN MARRIAGE AND FAMILY[1]

N. Prabha Unnithan

Anthropologists and sociologists have often remarked on the unique features of marriage and family during the nineteenth century among the Nayars, a caste group who inhabit what is now the state of Kerala in southwestern India.[2] Social scientists describe the Nayars of old as an "exception" to general definitions of marriage and family because sex was separated from economic relations in marriage.[3] Among certain regional Nayar communities, a woman did not have a "regular" husband and a man usually did not help much to support his wife and children. In recent times, however, many changes have taken place that have blurred and even overturned those distinctive features of former domestic life.[4]

In this reading, the Nayars as a group are described in historical, geographic, and cultural terms. The traditional and current forms of Nayar marriage, family, and household arrangements are discussed in detail so that changes that have taken place can be identified. Most of these changes occurred in the late nineteenth and twentieth centuries, and in a final section I discuss the factors that brought change about. I begin, however, with a personal note.

I am a Nayar, but I was born and brought up in Malaysia where my parents had migrated before the Second World War. Other than the language we spoke at home (Malayalam, the language of Kerala) my childhood and family life in multi-ethnic Malaysia carried no trace of anything systematically different from that of other immigrant families from India (mainly from the states of Tamil Nadu and Andhra Pradesh). On a visit to India as a ten-year-old, it appeared to me that my mother and I were spending more time at her family *taravad* (ancestral home based on descent group), which was described to me as "my home." I preferred my father's place where there were more children of my age but I remember suggestions from my mother's family that I did not "really belong" to my father's family. I thus recall wondering why my two brothers and I were encouraged to identify more with my mother's family and my maternal uncles. At the time, I thought this was because there were more members of my mother's family among those who had migrated to Malaysia.

My first perception of the uniqueness of my heritage came as a college student in other parts of India in the 1970s. Visiting Kerala for extended periods of vacation time, reading a series about the various communities of India (including the Nayars) carried by a leading magazine, *The Illustrated Weekly of India,* and discussing similarities and differences among various states and groups of India with students of anthropology (I was a criminology major) formed my first exposure to the exceptional traditions of the Nayars. What I learned awoke a degree of curiosity that led me to read as much as possible about the Nayars, and to discuss these matters with other Nayars. This interest was sustained and enhanced after coming to the United States. My wife and I discovered we could attract the respectful and fascinated attention of any anthropologist around by merely stating that we were Nayars. However, as a criminologist/sociologist my own background has not been particularly relevant even in semi-autobiographical writing[5] and this is the first time I have explored it professionally. Thus I hope that the combination of familiarity and distance (in both personal and professional senses) that I bring to these issues will help illuminate this fascinating topic.

Kerala and the Nayar

Evans-Pritchard declares, "The people of Kerala in South Western India are amongst the most fascinating ethnic groups of the world. Their traditional claim to anthropological eminence rested on the once flourishing institution of matriliny among the Nayars and a special ritual bond of caste between the Nambudiri Brahmins and the martial Nayars."[6] The Indian state of Kerala where these groups have traditionally lived has a history and culture that "is one of the major streams that have enriched the composite culture of the country."[7]

Kerala is a state that was created in 1956 on the basis of a common language among its inhabitants following the linguistic reorganization of states in India. It immediately gained prominence when in 1957 the local Communist Party was elected to form the state government, the first time that this had happened anywhere in the non-Communist world.[8] Besides for its scenic beauty, in recent times Kerala has attracted attention because of its performance on various indicators of "development." Remarkably, for a state with significant levels of poverty and unemployment, it has achieved high rates of life expectancy and literacy combined with low rates of birth and infant mortality.[9]

Geographically, Kerala consists of "a long fish-shaped land squeezed between"[10] the thickly forested Western Ghats on the east and a 360-mile coastline on the Arabian Sea on the west. The resulting geographic isolation from the rest of the Indian sub-continent and extensive contact with other countries across the seas have facilitated the growth of a distinctive culture. For example, at various times, Christianity, Judaism, and Islam have all found a home in Kerala; and trade with Greek, Roman, and Arab states has been historically documented.

Kerala's geography also provided a religio-mythical rationale for the ritual bond between Nayars and Nambudiris that Evans-Pritchard commented on.[11] Jeffrey describes the creation of Kerala according to Brahminical tradition as resulting from:

> . . . the banishment from India of the god Parasurama. Having nowhere to live, he won the permission of Varuna, the god of the sea, to reclaim all the land within a throw of his axe. Parasurama threw his axe from Cape Comorin to Gokarnam, the sea receded and Kerala was formed. To populate the new area, Parasurama introduced a special race of Brahmins, the Nambudiris, and gave them ownership of all the land and unique customs which prevented their return to the India on the other side of the Western Ghats. Next, he brought Sudras—the Nayars—to act as servants and bodyguards of the Nambudiris. He bestowed on the Nayars the *marumakkattayam* or matrilineal system of family and inheritance, and decreed that Nayars should have no formal marriage and that their women should always be available to satisfy the desires of the Nambudiris.[12]

Jeffrey considers this legend to be an attempt to justify the most important features of the seventeenth-century social structure of certain areas of Kerala.[13] Namboodiripad however, dismisses it as "obviously invented" by those who benefited from it.[14] This legend illustrates the point that unlike the caste stratification system (based on birth/occupation) of the rest of India the traditional configuration in Kerala had different connotations and consequences. Traditionally, Hindu society has been divided into four major categories. The Brahmins were priests and pursued religious learning; the Kshatriyas were soldiers and kings; the Vaisyas were traders, and the Sudras performed various occupations of service to the castes above them. In Kerala, the Nayars, although Sudras, also carried out the functions of Vaisyas and Kshatriyas.

Before I describe the place of the Nayars in the traditional caste structure of Kerala, one further characteristic of various regions of Kerala needs to be pointed out. In the scholarly literature and based on traditional descriptions, Kerala has been divided into three major geographic/cultural areas: North Kerala, Central Kerala, and South Kerala.[15] Nayar marriage, family and kinship patterns have varied roughly along these regional lines. Politically, during the period of British domination of India, most of North Kerala was directly controlled by the British government in Madras, while Central and South Kerala operated as kingdoms that were (nominally independent) British protectorates.

The traditional Hindu caste system of Kerala, which Puthenkulam refers to as "the citadel of caste rigidity and orthodoxy," came into being around the tenth century and is extremely complicated.[16] Woodcock comments, "There were no less than five hundred castes and sub-castes, divided from each other by rigorous rules against inter-marriage and by an extraordinary pattern of pollution taboos."[17] He goes on to identify the nine principal categories, in descending order, in the caste hierarchy as follows:[18]

1. Brahmins, the priestly caste (originally only Nambudiris, but by extension Brahmins who migrated from neighboring states);
2. Kshatriyas, the rulers (mainly members of a few kingly families of the smaller kingdoms from which Kerala was formed);
3. Ambalavasis, the temple attendants and musicians (believed to be a pre-Brahmin priesthood);
4. Samantans, the local chieftains;
5. Nayars, the traditional warriors and feudal landholders;
6. Kammalans, the artisans and craftsmen (believed to have migrated from the Tamil areas east of the Ghats);
7. Ezhavas, originally those who tapped toddy from palm trees, but subsequently agrarian tenants;
8. Mukkuvans, the fisherman castes; and

9. the "outcastes," such as astrologers, washermen, and agricultural laborers (who toiled under conditions of servitude for the Nayars).

The historical and contemporary significance of Nayars in Kerala can be understood when we consider the following. The Nayars were "simultaneously the backbone of the military system, stratum of the cultivating population and did service to the Brahmin and ruling families."[19] The nominal Kshatriyas and the Samantans identified above are also thought to have originally been Nayars. The Nayars dominated Kerala earlier through force as "a class of professional warriors who developed to a high level the art of swordsmanship, who formed themselves at time of battle into suicide squads"[20] in the service of various kings and local chieftains.[21] More recently, their importance is based on ownership of land and distribution all across Kerala. Historically, the Nambudiri Brahmins were "never more than a thin insecure top crust on society."[22]

Traditional Nayar Marriage, Family, and Kinship Patterns

Rules of descent connect individuals with particular sets of kin because of a presumed common ancestry. Traditionally, Nayars with minor exceptions were matrilineal (*marumakkatayam* or, literally, descent traced through sister's children). This meant that in terms of succession the females carried the family name and their children also had claims to family property. In contrast the Nambudiri Brahmins were patrilineal (*makkatayam* or, literally descent traced through own children); males carried the family name and their children were the ones who had claims to the family property.

Among the Nayars, two patterns of marriage and family life have been identified. In Central Kerala and the upper region of South Kerala, the first and (to social scientists) more well-known pattern was practiced. Here, every Nayar girl before puberty underwent a *talikettu-kalyanam* (literally, *tali*-tying ceremony) as part of an elaborate celebration, which Fuller indicates died out in the 1920s.[23] Following a short period of seclusion (supposedly indicating menstruation) a *tali* (a small leaf-shaped locket worn on a string or gold chain) was tied around the girl's neck by an "adult male who is a member of a superior caste, an unrelated member of the same caste, a cross-cousin, an aunt or the shaman of a local goddess."[24] Among Hindus in other parts of India the tali indicated that a woman was married. This ceremony was followed by the girl and the man who tied the

tali spending a short time (hours or days) together after which they separated. There were no sexual connotations to this event. A lively debate exists in the anthropological literature as to what the talikettu-kalyanam meant.[25] Recent views appear to be that it should be considered an elaborate prepuberty rite of passage rather than (as previously thought) a form of sham marriage and divorce (between the girl and the man who tied the tali) or a full-dress marriage rehearsal.

Some time following the talikettu-kalyanam, when the female in question had attained maturity, she became eligible to form more or less permanent sexual relationships with other men each known as *sambandham* (literally, alliance). Puthenkulam defines it as "the socially recognized alliance constituting matrimony among matrilineals."[26] The sambandham was initiated without elaborate associated ritual. A proposal from either the parents or friends of either sambandham partner was followed by consultations with the *karanavan* (the eldest male who usually was the head) of each ancestral home (taravad). Males eligible to be considered had to be of equivalent or higher caste status. On an auspicious day, the man went in procession to the woman's house followed by a brief ceremony with minimal religious connotations. The couple then spent the night together and the man left for his taravad in the morning. A gift of clothes for the woman was sent by the man's family if this was not a part of the ceremony. A woman could consent to receive several men as sambandham partners with the approval of the head of her taravad although it is highly unlikely a separate ceremony was held each time. The various partners took turns visiting the Nayar woman at night. At the same time, men in that woman's taravad would be visiting their own sambandham partners. The men were also permitted to have more than one sambandham partner but the children of such unions belonged in the mother's taravad. The man and woman in a sambandham partnership did not live together and the man did not have any say in the upbringing of his biological children.

Ceremonial gifts such as clothes, betel-nut, as well as hair and bath oil were given by the man to his sambandham partner during important festivals. The only other obligation of the man to his sambandham partner was to acknowledge paternity of his children and to assume a minimal portion of the expenses of the midwife during the delivery. The relationship could be broken off at any time by either partner without any formality.

In attempting to account for this rather unique form of marriage, anthropologists have observed that there is symmetry between the Nayar matrilineal and

Nambudiri Brahmin patrilineal systems. In most Nambudiri *illams* (the equivalent of the Nayar taravads), only the oldest son was allowed to marry (sometimes, and particularly if no male heir was born, he could marry more than one wife) and inherit property so that ancestral land and wealth would not be sub-divided away. Thus, younger Nambudiri men were allowed to form sambandhams with Nayar women who were lower in caste status. At the same time, given the matrilineality of the Nayars, these Nambudiri men had no responsibility towards their biological children or their Nayar sambandham partners. The Nayar taravad in question gained some status in being associated with Brahmins (and by extension, Kshatriya upper castes) although the Nambudiri Brahmin community considered the relationship nothing more than concubinage. This explanation comes close to suggesting that matrilineality was a system imposed on the Nayars by the Nambudiris for the latter's convenience. However, as the Nambudiris were historically a small minority, their ability to impose cultural patterns would have been limited. Further, such an imposition if true could have affected only a small proportion of Nayar families whose female members would be needed as sexual partners.

Fuller suggests that this form of marriage, "developed in response to the problems caused by their [Nayars'] military role."[27] Matrilineality and sambandhams can also be viewed as solving some of the problems of soldiers and mercenaries who had to be away from home for extended periods of time and who could die in battle. This form of marriage "inhibited the development of close attachments between Nayar men and women in their native villages and, at the same time, permitted them sexual access to Nayar women throughout the land."[28]

The second and less well-known pattern of marriage and family life was practiced mainly in North Kerala.[29] Here the talikettu-kalyanam was not considered an important rite although it was carried out. The sambandham relationship was similar to Hindu marriages in other parts of India and was meant to be a stable one. Gough describes the ceremony as follows:

> The giving of the cloth by the husband which marked the start of a sambandham was carried out with ceremony in the girl's ancestral house and was the occasion for a large feast to relatives of both parties. After the marriage had been consummated in the girl's house the couple were ceremonially conducted to the bridegroom's taravad and the girl was formally received into it by her husband's mother and his karanavan's wife.[30]

The man and woman lived together in his matrilineal taravad along with his brothers and all of their children or the woman would live in a separate house with her own children where she would be visited by her husband. In the latter case, the man split his time between both houses. Women who were divorced or widowed moved back to their own taravad where they (and their married sisters who may have been living elsewhere) retained property rights. Divorce and remarriage were permitted but rare.

The two traditional patterns described above are somewhat simplified and not quite as clearcut in terms of regions. Apparently, many local or minor variations—such as preference for cross-cousin sambandham, and a few cases of brothers having a common wife—existed.[31] What did not vary as far as Nayar families were concerned were three features. First, there was matrilineality of descent and inheritance, whereby female members and their (both male and female) children possessed property rights; the children of male members did not have such rights. Second, there was a professed identification with one's own taravad whose members were considered blood relatives (this obviously excluded the father's family who belonged to a different taravad) and were therefore ineligible to marry each other. Finally, a great deal of importance was attached to the whims and wishes of the eldest male karanavan who acted as head, manager as well as representative (in public) of the taravad.[32]

In comparison to other Hindus, the traditional arrangements of Nayars provided relatively greater freedom and status for their female members. Women had a say in consenting to the initiation or termination of marriage relationships. Children, as long as their paternity had been acknowledged, had to be taken care of by their taravad. Property rights were guaranteed for females. A certain amount of respect for women and "intensity of concern for mothers and sisters"[33] as carriers of the taravad name existed among Nayar men. At the same time, under most circumstances all of the above depended on the responsible management of taravad affairs by the karanavan and the good graces of other older males.

Contemporary Nayar Marriage, Family, and Kinship

A number of factors that affected Kerala and its people in the nineteenth and early twentieth centuries (to be discussed in detail later) resulted in the dying out or extreme modification of the ceremonies, marriage patterns, and family relationships described above. In this section, I will describe the current versions of these practices so that a sharp contrast can be made with the traditional forms. The contemporary situation can be summarized as including a decline in identification with the taravad; the expansion and increased importance attached to the sambandham ceremony; and the second also signifying an almost absolute conversion by Nayars to the ideal of a "strong" or stable monogamous marriage.

The Decline of the Taravad

One of Puthenkulam's respondents remarked that with regard to family relationships and descent, Nayars "had left the mother's house but have not yet reached the father's home."[34] This implies that while the transition to a more patrilineal system is ongoing, there continue to linger remnants of identification with matrilineality and the taravad. A number of manifestations of this state of transition can be identified.

The most remarkable of these is the changed nature of property ownership within the taravad. Property used to be held jointly by the taravad and administered by the eldest male in the matrilineal group (the karanavan). It was difficult, though not impossible, for the property to be divided against the wishes of the *karanavan* and older males in the matrilineal family. Historically, in the nineteenth and early twentieth centuries a number of reports and court cases accusing karanavans of financial mismanagement, extravagance, waste and transfer of property on the sly to their own children came up. This led to more legal equality among members of a taravad with regard to property. Now, such property is owned jointly by individual members who may ask for their share of it on attaining adulthood. Puthenkulam notes that given the legal bias towards individual property division, "it is not surprising that the vast majority of Nayar taravads have made use of it and partitioned their taravads."[35] Thus ancestral property that belonged to my own taravad through my maternal grandmother has been subdivided as follows: roughly equally among eleven people, her seven children (my mother, her sister and five brothers) and the four grandchildren of her two daughters (my two brothers, me, and a cousin-sister, who is my mother's sister's surviving daughter). Note that matrilineality continues with the children of female members receiving shares, while those of male members do not. Often even unborn babies of pregnant women are given shares in the property. This arrangement pertains only to taravad property. Obviously, after a few generations of division and sub-division and

given the increasing role of the father in Nayar households, there is not likely to be any matrilineal property left. Individual property owned by a father is now divided equally among his sons and daughters, where previously it would have reverted back to the father's matrilineal taravad.

A second measure of the decline of the taravad can be found in the increased influence of the father in the affairs of his children and the corresponding decrease in that of the karanavan. Or as Puthenkulam puts it, "The father has come to his own and the karanavan has been supplanted."[36] Previously, as noted, children had very little to do with their fathers. They may have not even seen much of him, particularly if he continued to live in his own taravad, and only visited at night. Given the changed pattern of residence and consequent economic arrangements, this is perhaps inevitable. Still, certain attachments to the karanavan and/or mother's brother continue. For example, my older brother spent much of his childhood with one of my maternal uncles who also lived in Malaysia (because better educational facilities were available nearby). My uncle was accepting of his guardianship role, and this was accepted by others in the extended family as "proper."

Finally, consider the current expectation regarding residence following marriage. It is assumed now that the wife will move permanently into her husband's home and live there along with any children that may ensue. In terms of the transitional state of Nayar customs, ironically, the house she moves into may sometimes be his ancestral taravad. A married son may thus bring his wife to live with his parents if he cannot afford a separate home. With employment opportunities mainly in the more urbanized areas of Kerala, elsewhere in India or abroad, the couple is more likely to establish a new residence apart from kin (neolocal residence). Thus, the nuclear family I was a member of (my parents, brothers and myself) lived in Malaysia where my father found employment in rubber plantations in the 1930s. Similarly, my wife, our two children and I live together in the United States. Neither of these middle- and late-twentieth century living arrangements is looked upon as anything unusual among Nayars today.

However, the influence of the taravad does persist in some matters. First, it continues to be expected and followed that Nayars take their surnames from their mother's side of the nuclear family and often also include their taravad name. Clearly, this is an expectation that I have violated. For purposes of convenience (having spent a large part of my life in patrilineal or bilateral descent societies and not being very good at snappy explanations of my matrilineal heritage) I have taken my father's surname (Unnithan) rather than my mother's (Nair); and I also do not use the name of my taravad (Payanimvilayil). This has led to rather bemused questioning among some of my relatives as to how and when I had turned into an Unnithan!

Second, although supplanted otherwise, the karanavan continues to command formal and deferential respect. For example, it is expected that his nephews and nieces stand, as a mark of respect, in his presence. His formal consent is sought on matters involving younger siblings, nephews and nieces. He is the first to be invited for weddings and often presides over family ceremonies. The honor accorded to the karanavan in contemporary times can be viewed as resulting from a combination of expectations: remnants of the Nayar past and traditional Indian respect for elders.

The Expansion and Importance of the Sambandham

Both Fuller and Puthenkulam suggest that the word sambandham is not in use anymore to describe Nayar marriage, because of what many reformers from within the community felt was its "immoral" connotations.[37] I continue to hear it used, though less often than *vivaham* (originally, the Nambudiri Brahmin word for wedding) and *kalyanam* (literally, ceremony). While the talikettu-kalyanam and associated rituals have all but disappeared, those surrounding the sambandham have expanded. However, in comparison to marriage ceremonies of other Hindu groups, that of the present-day Nayars tends to be very short and simple.

The actual marriage ceremony is the culmination of a number of steps taken in advance that represent a close approximation of what social scientists have described as the "arranged" form of marriage. Marriages based on notions of romantic love do take place but are to a large extent subject to family approval. Marriages are mostly intra-caste, with marriages to upper (including Nambudiris) and lower castes rare. The preference for intra-caste marriage often causes middle-class Nayar families to look for potential partners in places far beyond the local village or district. Photographs of "eligible" young men and women are exchanged utilizing professional matchmakers or friends and relatives to see if there is any interest on either side in a potential sambandham. Horoscopes are matched to consider whether the couple is astrologically compatible. The young man may make a short visit to the woman's home along with his relatives for what is referred to as a *pennukaanal*

(literally, seeing the young woman). Based on the consent of both the young man and woman and their respective families, arrangements are made for the wedding ceremony itself. Often a ceremony that is meant to determine an astrologically auspicious date and time for the marriage ceremony is also held. Invitations are mailed out by both families, or personally handed to close relatives who live nearby. Among some Nayars, wedding invitations are issued in the name of the karanavan, another vestige of the prestige that position once commanded.

Marriage ceremonies may be conducted at the bride's home or in an area built and used for that purpose at a temple nearby. The bridegroom, who arrives in a procession of his family and friends, is greeted at the entrance by members of the bride's family. His feet are washed and he is garlanded. The actual ceremony itself follows and consists of these rites: The couple sit next to each other facing (among other objects that signify auspiciousness and fertility) a pot full of rice and a lighted oil lamp. The couple exchange rings and garlands (previously blessed by placing in front of a temple idol). The bridegroom places and/or ties the tali around the neck of the bride. The bridegroom then gives the bride a piece of cloth (almost always a *saree*). The bride and groom clasp hands and walk around the lighted lamp three times. They are then blessed by elders of both families. The ceremony is followed by a vegetarian feast in which both families participate. As noted above, the bride accompanies the groom to live with his family or (perhaps, later) to a new residence.

Let me point out a few features of contemporary Nayar marriage that indicate continuity and change. In terms of continuity, although a marriage may be solemnized at a temple, religious connotations are still minimal and the ceremony is often conducted by a fellow Nayar in the community. The giving of clothing also survives from the traditional Nayar sambandham ceremony. Tremendous changes can also be detected. The tali-tying rite has been shifted from the talikettu-kalyanam to the sambandham ceremony. The sambandham ceremony itself and the process leading up to it have expanded and taken on features that serve to underline the desirability of monogamy and stability of marriage. In addition, there are now elements suggesting increasing male dominance. For example, the male's family goes to view the bride-to-be and the bridegroom's party is respectfully received at the wedding site. Increasingly, the groom's family demands from the bride's family a "groomprice" or "direct payments to the family of the groom"[38] as a condition of marriage. This was previously unknown among Nayars. Finally, the expansion of rites associated with the sambandham and the receiving of blessings from elders signify the encouraging of stability in the marriage partnership being entered into.

Stable Monogamy as an Ideal

The importance of the sambandham relationship among contemporary Nayars is associated with the promotion of a family ideology based on stable monogamy. Three expressions of this ideal can be found in contemporary marriage and family patterns. The traditional pattern identified in Central Kerala and upper regions of South Kerala involving multiple visiting husbands and relationships with Nambudiri Brahmins is not operative any longer. In its place, Nayars have substituted endogamy (as in restricting the selection of marriage partners from within the caste and sub-caste group) and long-term monogamy. The practice of allowing Nambudiri sambandham partners has also died out. This can be attributed to the cessation of military service as the common occupation of Nayars; to changes within Nambudiri households that allowed all males (not just the oldest) to marry Nambudiri women; and to criticisms from Nayar reformers who berated Nambudiris harshly on their "religious" pretensions in separating sex and responsibility for its consequences (children).

The second aspect of this ideal can be found in the contemporary expectation that a husband and wife be sexually faithful to each other over the period of marriage. Not surprisingly, divorce is strongly discouraged. This focus on sexual exclusivity has also resulted in scrutiny of a potential bride's "character" (premarital virginity) before moving forward with the steps towards an arranged marriage. There is some, though less intense, attention paid to a potential groom's "character."

A third expression of the stable, monogamous family ideal is the rise of essentially neolocal (living apart from kin) nuclear family living arrangements especially when work locations are far away.[39] Biological parents and children live together over a long period of time with the former having responsibility and authority over the latter. In the twentieth century, Nayar men in search of employment (Kerala being a state with high levels of both education and unemployment) have migrated to and lived in other parts of India (e.g., my father-in-law), Southeast Asia (e.g., my father), the Middle East (e.g., my wife's cousin, i.e., her mother's sister's son), and the West (e.g., me). It has become customary and accepted for their wives to live with them and raise their children

in nuclear family units. If the couple returns to Kerala, they continue to live together.

It is difficult to find remnants of the old order "weak" marriage ties among the Nayars. It is my observation that in comparison to other Hindu groups, Nayar women have greater degrees of freedom in consenting or turning down potential marriage proposals. Whether this is the result of Nayar traditions or because Nayar women possess relatively high levels of education and are more likely to work outside the home is open to question. Relative to other Hindu women, it also appears that Nayar women may also choose to remain unmarried for longer periods of time. Further, female children are not looked upon with disfavor even in the face of the creeping in of practices such as "groomprice." Billig predicts that these practices "may actually enhance female autonomy and economic independence in Kerala by forcing women even further to pursue educational and career opportunities outside of marriage."[40] If so, given their traditionally higher status, such effects should be more pronounced for Nayar women.

Change Factors in Nayar Marriage and Family Practices

Having identified the traditional and contemporary forms of Nayar marriage and family, let us turn our attention to accounting for some of the influences that have propelled the remarkable changes documented. It is possible to discern factors that can be subsumed under either materialist, ideological or other types of explanation for social change. It should be recognized that any categorization of change factors is somewhat artificial and that causal interactions may exist between them. It is possible to identify three sets of influences—economic, reform movements, and legal—that helped move Nayars away from their traditional patterns of marriage and family.

Economic Influences

Two major economic factors have been identified by observers. The first is the end of the traditional military occupational roles of Nayars. After the British established effective and actual control in the early nineteenth century over the regions that constitute the present Kerala, they demobilized the armies of the local kings and chieftains. The Nayar men who controlled lands that had been given to them earlier by these rulers turned their attention to agriculture and supervision of those who worked for them producing rice, coconuts, pepper, and so on. There was more stability in their lives and more contact of a permanent nature with their sambandham partners, relatives and their biological children. This may have led to greater identification with their family of procreation rather than their family of orientation. This may also be the reason why many men began to ignore traditional norms with regard to property accumulated on their own. Earlier, on a man's death his property reverted to his matrilineal taravad. Instead, many Nayar men wished to transfer such property to their wives and children.

The second of these economic factors is the increasing role of manufacturing and service industry sectors in India, and Kerala in particular. Nayars, given their elite status, had greater opportunities to achieve the educational qualifications needed for these new jobs. At the same time, the last century saw population growth and tough competition from Ezhavas (a lower caste group) and Syrian Christians who were also rapidly "modernizing." These groups also began to aggressively buy up land that Nayar taravads and Nambudiri illams had owned. This resulted in the migration of Nayars (as mentioned earlier) to more urban areas, elsewhere in India and other parts of the world. All this meant that the rural agricultural feudal economy that supported the caste structure and the place of Nayars in it was being dismembered. Puthenkulam observes, "Neither the taravad nor its kinship system or the sambandham could be imagined outside a village set-up. When the village economy crumbled, systems built on it had to follow suit."[41]

Reform Movements

The economic changes should not obscure the importance of reform movements from among the Nayars themselves that agitated for an end to matrilineality and the regularization of sambandham unions. Groups such as the Malayali Sabha and, later, the Nayar Service Society and their leaders were instrumental in developing forceful arguments and agitating to end features of traditional Nayar life of which they disapproved.[42] They disliked the grip of the karanavan on the property and affairs of the younger members of a taravad. The reformers wanted to end what they considered wasteful celebrations such as talikettu-kalyanam. They had nothing but bitter scorn for the "status" associated with sambandhams that involved Nayar women and Nambudiri men, particularly since the latter did not have any further responsibility towards the children they fathered. They also wished for sambandham

relationships to be recognized as legal marriages whereby the husband could leave property accumulated by him during his lifetime to his children.

Fuller suggests that the scathing attacks these reformers launched on the old order through newspapers, books (the first Malayalam novel dealt with Nayars and matrilineality), and speeches, were "undoubtedly . . . due to the spread of Western ideas" most of it through education in English.[43] To this we should also add that Kerala during this period was becoming less isolated from the rest of India. Contacts multiplied with other (mostly patrilineal) Hindu and non-Hindu groups through the migration patterns described above (assisted by the spread of rail travel). In addition, the work of Christian missionaries (who though they may have failed to convert the Nayars were able to instill Christian ideas regarding morality and monogamy) was also among the influences on these reformers. Some observers suggest that cumulatively Nayar reformers were ashamed of their traditional way of life and its implied "immorality" and wished to substitute for it one that had a higher moral tenor. As Aiyappan puts it, "We grew ashamed of our matriliny and this affected even the thinking of scholars. . . ."[44]

Legal Changes

The reformers, perhaps aided by changing economic and political circumstances, were successful in challenging almost every feature of traditional Nayar life that they disapproved of. These legal changes hastened the decline of taravad and matrilineality. In South Kerala, this took the form of two pieces of legislation called the Nair Acts of 1912 and 1925. Although there were significant differences between the two, taken together they had the effect of allowing for the division and bequeathing of individually acquired property to any individual's children, and made the practice of multiple spouses illegal. Similar legislation in Central Kerala enacted in 1920 and 1938 severely curtailed the powers of the karanavan, legalized the sambandham relationship, prohibited multiple spouses, and declared the wife and children of a man as his heirs. Most of North Kerala, which was ruled directly by the British provincial government in Madras, enacted the legislation in 1933 with similar provisions. These laws resulted in the many court cases brought against karanavans alluded to earlier, charging them with mismanagement. It should also be noted that legislation was also brought forward that allowed all Nambudiris to inherit their joint family property and for all Nambudiri men (not just the eldest) to be able to marry. This was the result of efforts from within the Nambudiri community as well, and effectively ended the era of Nayar sambandhams with Nambudiris.

While these pieces of legislation were frontal attacks on the traditional structure, at the same time other laws subverting the economic basis that sustained it were coming into effect. Land reforms that allowed tenants (primarily of the lower castes) to become owners of the lands that they had cultivated for generations began to be enacted in the early twentieth century. As Nayars and to a lesser extent Nambudiris were the landholders, such legislation was clearly inimical to their interests. Related reforms protected tenants from arbitrary eviction and from being required to pay excessive rents. The pace of these reforms picked up considerably after India's independence in 1947, and as a result of a string of communist and leftist governments that have ruled Kerala since 1957. More recent legislation has given existing tenants the right to buy the land they have tilled, banned the creation of new tenancies, and proposed limits on the amount of land that can be owned by any one family.

Political Factors

Although at one time the "dominant caste"[45] of Kerala, Nayars do not occupy elite positions automatically anymore. "The traditional Kerala society in which the caste of a person and the extent of the landed property owned by him determined his standing in the social scale is now a thing of the past."[46] Instead, the disappearance of their patrons (rulers and local chieftains), democratization and preferential policies favoring lower castes (implemented all over India) have eroded the powerful position that Nayars once held. They now have to compete with other groups or form coalitions with them to achieve power, wealth and prestige. Caste, taravad, and matrilineality matter less in the public sphere than what can be gained or lost through interpersonal and intergroup transactions. Thus, while there exist political parties claiming to represent the interests of Nayars, Ezhavas and other caste groups, the major parties in Kerala are shifting coalitions of various castes, classes, and religious groups. The leadership of the government and these parties also varies among all of these groups. The structures that propped up Nayars and their particular way of life have been dismantled, making them, at least politically, not very different from other groups around them.

Conclusion

Under attack from the outside through economic, legal, and political changes and from within through the efforts of Nayar reformers, it is not surprising that the traditional Nayar system of marriage and family that so captivated social scientists began to change. As we have seen, there are a few lingering remnants of their matrilineal past and it has not been replaced by a completely male-dominated system. For example, although matrilineal inheritance has all but disappeared, Nayar women have more to say about their lives than do other Hindu women. Currently, Nayars can best be described as possessing stable, monogamous marriages, with a tendency for families to live with the husband's family or alone.

Notes

1. I gratefully acknowledge the help of Robert Theodoratus with the anthropological literature on the Nayars as well as the comments and clarifications of Gopi Nair and Raman R. Nayar.

2. Kathleen Gough, "Nayar: Central Kerala" and "Nayar: North Kerala," in David M. Schneider and Kathleen Gough, eds., *Matrilineal Kinship* (Berkeley, CA: University of California Press, 1961).

3. Carol R. Ember and Melvin Ember, *Cultural Anthropology,* 7th ed. (Englewood Cliffs, NJ: Prentice Hall, 1993).

4. Kathleen Gough, "Nayar: Central Kerala" and "Nayar: North Kerala," in David M. Schneider and Kathleen Gough, eds., *Matrilineal Kinship* (Berkeley, CA: University of California Press, 1961).

5. N. Prabha Unnithan, "Marginality, Credibility, and Impression Management: The Asian Sociologist in America," *The American Sociologist* 19 (1988): 372–377.

6. Edward Evans-Pritchard, "Foreword," in K. E. Verghese, *Slow Flows the Pampa: Socio-Economic Changes in a Kuttanad Village in Kerala* (New Delhi, India: 1982), p. 5. The Nambudiri Brahmins engaged in religious occupations were, as we will see, at the top of the caste ladder.

7. A. Sreedhara Menon, *A Survey of Kerala History* (Kottayam, India: National Book Stall, 1967), p. 1.

8. P. M. Mammen, *Communalism vs. Communism: A Study of the Socio-Religious Communities and Political Parties in Kerala, 1892–1970* (Columbia, MO: South Asia Books, 1981).

9. Richard Franke and Barbara Chasin, "Development without Growth: The Kerala Experiment," *Technology Review* (April 1990): 43–51.

10. George Woodcock, *Kerala: A Portrait of the Malabar Coast* (London: Faber and Faber, 1967).

11. Edward Evans-Pritchard, "Foreword."

12. Robin Jeffrey, *The Decline of Nayar Dominance: Society and Politics in Travancore, 1847–1908* (New York: Holmes and Meier, 1976), p. xv.

13. Ibid.

14. E. M. S. Namboodiripad, *Kerala Society and Politics: An Historical Survey* (New Delhi, India: National Book Centre, 1984), p. 25.

15. Kathleen Gough, "Nayar: Central Kerala" and "Nayar: North Kerala," in Christopher J. Fuller, *The Nayars Today* (Cambridge, England: Cambridge University Press, 1976), suggests that there are further differences in the local cultures of the upper and lower regions of South Kerala.

16. J. Puthenkulam, *Marriage and the Family in Kerala: With Special Reference to Matrilineal Castes* (Calgary: University of Calgary, 1977), p. 22.

17. Woodcock, *Kerala: A Portrait of the Malabar Coast*, p. 58.

18. Ibid., pp. 5–69.

19. Namboodiripad, *Kerala Society and Politics*, p. 28.

20. Woodcock, *Kerala: A Portrait of the Malabar Coast*, p. 60.

21. Jeffrey, *The Decline of Nayar Dominance*, provides a historical account.

22. Woodcock, *Kerala: A Portrait of the Malabar Coast*, p. 59.

23. Fuller, *The Nayars Today*.

24. A. Aiyappan, *The Personality of Kerala* (Trivandrum, India: University of Kerala, 1982), p. 226.

25. Puthenkulam, *Marriage and the Family in Kerala*, pp. 35–54, summarizes the debate.

26. Ibid., p. 74.

27. Fuller, *The Nayars Today*, p. 121.

28. Ibid., p. 124.

29. Ibid., p. 100.

30. Gough, "Nayar: Central Kerala," and "Nayar: North Kerala," p. 398.

31. Puthenkulam, *Marriage and the Family in Kerala*, pp. 73–117.

32. For a more conventional way of defining matrilineality, see Ember and Ember, *Cultural Anthropology*.

33. Aiyappan, *The Personality of Kerala*, p. 192.

34. Puthenkulam, *Marriage and the Family in Kerala*, p. 216.

35. Ibid., p. 157.

36. Ibid., p. 162.

37. Fuller, *The Nayars Today*; Puthenkulam, *Marriage and the Family in Kerala*.

38. Michael S. Billig, "The Marriage Squeeze and the Rise of Groom-price in India's Kerala State," *Journal of Comparative Family Studies* 23 (1993): 197–216.

39. Gough, "Nayar: Central Kerala" and "Nayar: North Kerala"; Fuller, *The Nayars Today*.

40. Billig, "The Marriage Squeeze," pp. 211–212.

41. Puthenkulam, *Marriage and the Family in Kerala*, p. 245.

42. Jeffrey, *The Decline of Nayar Dominance: Society and Politics in Travancore, 1847–1908*.

43. Fuller, *The Nayars Today*, p. 130.

44. Aiyappan, *The Personality of Kerala*, p. 222.

45. See Jeffrey, *The Decline of Nayar Dominance: Society and Politics in Travancore, 1847–1908*.

46. A. Sreedhara *Menon, A Survey of Kerala History* (Kottayam, India: National Book Stall, 1967), p. 393.

Suggested Readings

Aiyappan, A. *The Personality of Kerala.* Trivandrum, India: University of Kerala, 1982. Based on a series of lectures, it provides some detailed discussion of matrilineality and Kerala in general.

Fuller, Christopher J. *The Nayars Today.* Cambridge, England: Cambridge University Press, 1976. Somewhat argumentative, but provides probably the best account of Nayar traditions and practices.

Jeffrey, Robin. *The Decline of Nayar Dominance: Society and Politics in Travancore, 1847–1908.* New York: Holmes and Meier, 1976. Historical account of changes in South Kerala society at the turn of the twentieth century.

Menon, A. Sreedhara. *A Survey of Kerala History.* Kottayam, India: National Book Stall, 1967. Provides a basic overview of Kerala history from ancient to contemporary times.

Namboodiripad, E.M.S., *Kerala Society and Politics: An Historical Survey.* New Delhi, India: National Book Centre, 1984. Written by a prominent Communist Party leader from Kerala, it attempts to weave Marxist analysis into a discussion of the state's history.

Puthenkulam, J. *Marriage and the Family in Kerala: With Special Reference to Matrilineal Castes.* Calgary: University of Calgary, 1977. Based on survey research, it provides a comprehensive (though unevenly written) discussion of marriage and family practices in Kerala.

Woodcock, George. *Kerala: A Portrait of the Malabar Coast.* London: Faber and Faber, 1967. An impressionistic account of Kerala in the 1960s shortly after its three regions were reconstituted into one state.

"Nayars: Tradition and Change in Marriage and Family"

N. Prabha Unnithan

1) What is the traditional caste hierarchy of Kerala State in India, and what role did the Nayar play in this system?

2) What is the *sambandham* marriage pattern found in central and upper South Kerala?

3) What role did the Nayar's traditional profession as mercenaries play in establishing and perpetuating the *sambandham*?

4) What is the taravad, and what is its function in traditional Nayar culture?

5) What changes have occurred in Nayar culture that have reduced the function and cohesion of the taravad?

6) What changes have occurred in Nayar culture to change the functions and role of the *sambandham* in Nayar society?

FAMILY AND HOUSEHOLD: WHO LIVES WHERE, WHY DOES IT VARY AND WHY IS IT IMPORTANT?

Burton Pasternak

And Ruth said: "Entreat me not to leave thee, or to return from following after thee; for whither thou goest, I will go; and where thou lodgest, I will lodge; thy people shall be my people, and thy God my God." (*Ruth*: 1:16)

One consequence of the incest taboo is that people everywhere must find mates outside the immediate family. Because wives and husbands most often live together, one or both must move from the home of their parents. When Ruth married, in accordance with custom she went to live with the family of her husband. Even after his death, as the citation indicates, she remained with her mother-in-law. Why should Ruth have been the one to inconvenience herself? Why didn't her husband leave everything and everyone to join her family? Or, for the sake of fairness, why didn't they simply go off to live independently when they married, as we do?

Because our custom is for married couples to live on their own, we tend to think that ours is the natural way. But in societies where people are more dependent on kin than on employers or government when it comes to making a living, defense, and support in old age, newlyweds more commonly live with or near close relatives.

In most societies (Table 1), custom recommends the way of Ruth—a bride leaves home to live with her husband with or near his family (*patrilocality*). In fewer societies, men live with or near the families of their wives (*matrilocality*), and even less often do couples live with or near *either* set of parents (*bilocality*). Our own preference for independence of the married couple (*neolocality*) is actually rarer still. Nearly as common as neolocality is a custom that has newlyweds live with or near the groom's mother's brother (*avunculocality*). There are even a few societies in which *duolocality* is the preference, where husband and wife live apart after marriage. Although we might imagine still other arrangements, they do not occur. There are no societies in which residence at marriage is with the groom's father's

sister, for example. Why do people marry the way they do, why are some practices more common than others, and what difference does it make if people marry one way rather than another?

TABLE 1: Prevailing Rules of Residence, by Frequency*

Rule of Residence	Percent of All Societies Coded for Residence
Patrilocality	68.5
Matrilocality	13.1
Bilocality	8.5
Neolocality	4.7
Avunculocality	4.3
Duolocality	0.9
Total No. Societies	*858*

*Sample includes all societies coded for residence in George P. Murdock, Ethnographic Atlas (Pittsburgh: University of Pittsburgh Press, 1967).

Marital Residence: Causes and Consequences

What have we learned about the factors likely to induce people to adopt one residence option rather than another? If we can answer that general question, will we better understand why the majority of societies prefer patrilocal residence? Whatever one might think of male chauvinism, we can hardly suppose that our remote male ancestors, at some regular cave meeting, conspired to inconvenience women, and that the decision then passed from generation to generation and people to people. The mere existence of other practices argues against that. Why, indeed, do some people reject patrilocality?

And why should we care? Because the decision we make on this issue may shape the composition of our families, determining who the insiders and outsiders are. Which kin live together or nearby in turn affects the nature of whatever larger kin groups we might form—and indeed most societies organize functional groups on the basis of descent from a common ancestor. Further, the nature of residence can even influence the status of women and gender relations.

Residence, Family, and Kin Group

If men stay put at marriage, over time the local group comes to include a core of men related through their fathers. If families coalesce into groups based on common descent, they are likely to trace descent through males since only they have a common ancestor. Women are outsiders from different places and blood lines. But if men live with or near the parents of their wives, descent will more likely be traced through women because the men come from different localities and blood lines. Avunculocality, like patrilocality, localizes males (a maternal uncle and his sisters' sons) who are related through their *mothers* rather than their fathers. When avunculocal peoples form descent groups (and most do), they trace descent through *females*.

Because bilocality and neolocality create local groups in which some people are related through females and others through males, these customs are not conducive to tracing descent exclusively through one sex. In bilocal societies people trace descent through either sex, or provide some other basis for organization apart from common descent. Neolocal residence by its nature emphasizes independence of the married couple, and societies with that preference rarely have descent groups of any sort.

Even kinship terms are affected by marital residence because they reflect the kinds of families and descent groups people have. In our own society, for example, we refer to the brothers and sisters of our parents as uncles and aunts, without distinguishing those on our father's and mother's side. Similarly, we distinguish cousins from brothers and sisters without regard to whether they are on our father's or mother's side. But in many more societies people refer to uncle on the father's side as father, and mother's sister as mother. The children of such fathers and mothers are, as we might expect, brothers and sisters.

Such usages are not the product of misunderstanding. Even when paternity is uncertain, people usually know who their mothers are. The terms have sociological rather than purely biological meaning; they signal the presence (or past presence) of extended families and descent groups. Thus, *father* may simply indicate a male in father's generation and descent group, and *mother* can be any woman of mother's generation and descent group, or a woman eligible to marry one of one's fathers.

It is because kinship terms reflect kinship organization that anthropologists are attentive to them. In some cases they may even provide a window on the past. If rule of residence has changed, for example, it may have produced adjustments in family composition and descent but not yet in kinship terms. In that event unexpected terms can provide a hint about forms of organization now superseded.

Residence and the Status of Women

Apart from its impact on family, descent, and kinship terms, there is another reason to be attentive to marital residence, and especially to the circumstances that account for a predominance of patrilocality. So long as women leave their families (and often their communities as well) when they marry, they are considered losses. Their labor and reproductive contributions ultimately belong to others. Patrilocal residence thus has profound implications for the status and well-being of women. There is also cross-cultural evidence suggesting that women enjoy higher status in some respects in matrilocal, matrilineal societies.[1]

In most societies people rely on offspring for care in old age. Rarely can they count on welfare, pensions, or public institutions like old age homes, nursing facilities, or hospices. If marriage transfers daughters to others, parents have little motivation for investing heavily in them. They are more likely to favor sons when it comes to food, attention, and education and, if resources are in short supply, females may even be at higher risk of early death.

Norma Diamond highlighted the problem in a study of early Communist transformation in China.[2] From the outset the Communists had promised to liberate women and break the constraints that the traditional patriarchal family and descent group imposed on modernization. But the Communists fell far short of their goals; their failure was commonly attributed to wrong thinking—to the persistence of "feudal patriarchal ideology." The hope was that enlightened reeducation would correct the situation. Yet, despite many campaigns designed to alter traditional notions, preference for sons has persisted and people still commonly assert that "boys are precious, girls worthless." It is not that they do not want daughters (they do), but sons still constitute "large happinesses," daughters only small ones.

Ultimately, the problem has less to do with ideology than with economic reality. Despite all the transformations—land reform, collectivization, drawing women into the labor force, etc.—the rule of post-marital residence remained unchanged. Ironically, when land was collectivized—transferred from families to collectives and then later to teams, brigades, and communes—the persistence of patrilocality meant that land was still vested in groups of men related through the male line. Despite their concerted attempt to undermine descent groups and to politically emasculate their wealthy leadership, the Communist transformation actually recreated and incorporated *de facto* patrilineal descent groups. Even with recent privatization of the economy, women continue to be losses. Without altering the rule of postmarital residence the situation is unlikely to change in China, and wherever else marriage requires the bride to move. The popularity of patrilocality in human societies is a matter of considerable consequence.

Why One Way Rather Than Another?

What does cross-cultural research tell us about the circumstances that lead people to adopt one residence practice rather than another, and why is patrilocality especially preferred in so many societies? Are we to suppose that it reflects a basic and inevitable human condition—male dominance? Were that the case, wouldn't all societies be patrilocal? As it turns out, moreover, beyond the family itself males are politically dominant in all societies, even in matrilocal and avunculocal ones.

Some have proposed that perhaps the societal propensity for patrilocality reflects the fact that, in most societies, men do most of the subsistence work. Another suggestion has been that the popularity of patrilocality may have something to do with the fact that male activities more often require cooperation, especially where there is a potential for violence. Perhaps that provides a reason for keeping men who know each other and their territory well together.

Cross-cultural research indicates that neither the division of labor by sex nor male cooperation in hunting or war help us predict whether people will be patrilocal or matrilocal. We find no relationship between contribution to subsistence and residence, or between frequency of fighting and likelihood of patrilocality over matrilocality.[3]

How then might we effectively anticipate the likelihood of patrilocality or matrilocality? One suggestion is that we must simultaneously consider the nature of warfare and the division of labor. Indeed, it turns out that where fighting occurs only among people with different cultures and languages (external warfare), the division of labor alone predicts quite well whether patrilocality or matrilocality will prevail. If men contribute most to subsistence the society will be patrilocal; where women contribute most it will be matrilocal. But if people fight among themselves, even occasionally (internal warfare), residence

will likely be patrilocal *regardless of the division of labor.*[4]

Why should the division of labor be relevant when warfare is purely external but not if fighting is internal? Since men normally do the fighting, it may be particularly advantageous to localize them, regardless of the division of labor, if there is a possibility of sudden attack from nearby (more likely with internal warfare). But where the enemy provides earlier warning (more commonly the case with purely external warfare), keeping sons together may be less vital and the division of labor might then be more important.

Perhaps because childbearing and menstruation periodically remove women from labor outside the home, men normally have principal responsibility for crucial tasks that must be completed at specific times. But if fighting periodically requires men to be away when those tasks need doing, women may assume a greater role and localizing them may be preferred. This would explain why matrilocality is so rare—we expect it only in relatively rare situations where we find purely external warfare of a sort that imposes heavier obligations on women.

Internal warfare discourages matrilocality regardless of the division of labor, and there may even be a structural incompatibility between matrilocal residence and internal warfare. Consider some salient characteristics of matrilocal societies. When they form larger kin groups they are likely to trace descent through women. While succession and property pass through females, however, authority is still vested in men (their brothers). Because they play an important authoritative role in matrilocal, matrilineal societies, brothers rarely move far when they marry. The situation is quite different in patrilocal societies, where women are neither channels for descent nor sources of authority. Daughters are dispensable; there is no need for them to remain close after marriage.

Consider now what might happen were neighboring matrilocal communities to begin fighting among themselves. The danger of sudden raids would increase, as would the desirability of keeping brothers together. And since men exercise authority in their sisters' homes and villages even after marriage, they might have to defend a sister's group in a conflict involving members of their own local group! We might well expect people in that situation to change to a post-marital residence option that localizes males rather than females.[5]

There are only two ways that could be accomplished. A matrilocal people without important matrilineal descent groups could simply shift to patrilocality. To do that might be highly destabilizing if they had functional matrilineal descent groups, however. In that case it would be better to find a way to localize males without disturbing the matrilineal descent groups. Only avunculocality meets the need, by localizing men related through the female line.

We can appreciate now why patrilocality is so much more common than matrilocality. Rarely do people fight only externally and never among themselves, and even more rarely is the division of labor matridominant. We can now understand also why avunculocality is even less common than matrilocality. To produce it you would have to confront a matrilocal society with conditions that favor keeping brothers together (like the development of internal warfare), and there would also have to be important matrilineal descent groups. This is an uncommon combination, since matrilocality is not that common. Not all such societies have matrilineal descent, and even fewer will develop internal war.

Thus far we have only discussed factors that might predispose societies to patrilocal or matrilocal residence. But what conditions might favor bilocal or neolocal residence? Comparative research indicates that bilocality results from a recent and dramatic depopulation, which brings local groups or kin groups below optimal size for organizing work.[6] They must reconstitute to survive. So couples may move to the most viable group. Many technologically simpler peoples have found themselves in this position. All too often contact with more developed societies has brought disease and death, and in many instances the victims have found themselves displaced and forced into marginal environments. The linkage between bilocality and depopulation has evolutionary implications. If bilocality is mostly a product of contact, it could be a relatively recent phenomenon, one less familiar to our ancient hunting-gathering ancestors.

The same may be true of neolocality. This is a residential pattern particularly common in complex industrial-commercial societies like our own, where conditions encourage independence of the nuclear family, the conjugal unit consisting of husband, wife, and children.[7] In these societies opportunity is particularistic and the nuclear family is pretty much on its own. Individuals, not families or larger kin groups, find employment. Education and ability are usually more important than kinship when it comes to finding work. When work requires movement, people take their spouses and children along but rarely their brothers and sisters. Many burdens of the extended family in simpler societies—education, defense, welfare, and care of the elderly—pass to public institutions in complex societies.

Family and Household

The rule of post-marital residence influences the form of family as well as its composition. It says something not only about who remains, but also about the kind of families that result. Our own nuclear families are small and simple, but in other societies families are commonly larger and more complex, in part because of the rule of post-marital residence. Neolocality produces independent nuclear families. But by bringing newlyweds to live with or near relatives, the other rules provide greater potential for family extension.

Most societies allow family enlargement through polygamous marriage, but more often extension involves some combination of married couples. In *stem* families, for example, there are two married couples in different generations—parents and a married child. Even more complex are *joint* families, which contain two or more married couples in the same generation. What might encourage such family extension and, apart from the rule of post-marital residence, what factors influence the form of extended family?

The Extended Family and Its Variants

Comparative research indicates that extended families (stem and joint) prevail in more than 50 percent of societies.[8] They are less common in very simple and very complex societies than in mid-range agricultural societies, however. We find them less often among hunter-gatherers or in commercial-industrial-urban contexts than in nonintensive agricultural societies. Various explanations have been offered for this curvilinear relationship between family and societal complexity.[9] According to one view, families are simpler (and kinship in general less important) in urban-industrial contexts for much the same reasons that neolocality becomes more common. Public institutions assume many functions performed by extended families and kin groups in simpler societies, while the economy encourages nuclear family independence. Hunter-gatherers may less often form extended families because their way of life encourages mobility and because food production is limited or stored less often. Families may be more complex in simple agricultural societies because cultivation encourages a sedentary way of life, while land ownership discourages family division.

But there are problems with these speculations, empirical as well as logical. For one thing, while mid-range (nonintensive) agricultural societies are more likely to have extended families (and descent groups) than simple or very complex societies, it is not easy to predict which mid-range societies will have them.

Some hunter-gatherers and some complex societies have them as well, and the curvilinear hypothesis will not anticipate those cases.

If simple societies have extended families less often it is probably not because they cannot produce sufficient food to sustain them. Hunter-gatherers have not always inhabited only the marginal areas in which we now find them, and even contemporary representatives in areas unsuited for cultivation produce enough to support multi-family groups. If they can feed collections of families, why not extended families?

In a demographic sense, cultivators certainly have a greater potential for large, complex families. Hunter-gatherers have lower fertility, perhaps because women cannot leave babies home alone. They carry their infants as they work, nursing on demand, a practice that inhibits the resumption of ovulation and hence conception. Cultivators can leave their infants home in the care of another woman, often a mother-in-law in the same extended family. Nursing is therefore less frequent, birth spacing shorter, and fertility higher. But we cannot conclude that cultivators have larger families simply because they have more children. More offspring could as well translate into more conflict, earlier family division and, therefore, more simple families.

How then can we account for the greater likelihood of extended families in mid-range cultivating societies? Is there some way we might even anticipate which societies are more likely to have them? Cross-cultural evidence suggests that extension is most likely when the various activities of women or men regularly require them to be in two places at once, which is more often the case in cultivating contexts where women tend home and children and also work in fields. Family extension resolves the problem by providing a second woman—a mother-in-law or mother, and/or a sister-in-law or sister. Indeed, task incompatibility effectively predicts which societies of any complexity are more or less likely to have many extended families.[10]

Chinese Clues

Cross-cultural research thus explains why some societies are more likely than others to favor family extension. But we also observe considerable variation within societies. Why are joint families more often found in certain villages than in others? Why do some families resist division longer than others, even in the same community? Why are joint families more common at one time than at another? Focusing on how labor is used may also help us anticipate

particular forms of family extension within societies and communities.

Many have noted that joint families are especially common among the wealthy. For example, Nimkoff & Middleton proposed that, cross-culturally, differences in land ownership may be crucial—the more land owned the more family members needed.[11] But why should family extension be necessary if land can be rented out or labor hired? Since many scholars have similarly observed some connection between class and family extension we need to consider, in specific contexts, why the wealthy might be more likely to have joint families than the poor. Further, we should consider cases in which even poor families have them.

Joint families have been highly valued but actually rare in China. There is abundant evidence of a class linkage there; the wealthy achieved the ideal more often than the poor. It is speculated that this is because they had more land and therefore needed more labor, or because the wealthy were better educated and more familiar with Confucian virtues. Their value system thus encouraged family extension. Sons of the wealthy were especially likely to obey their parents, and younger brothers to defer to older brothers. Filial piety delayed family division.

But not all wealthy families were joint, while even some poor ones were. More land does not necessarily demand more *family* labor if workers can be hired or land rented out. Nor can differences in education, ideology, or values really account for joint families, or for the linkage between wealth and their maintenance. However, studies conducted in specific Chinese communities do indicate how specific technological and economic considerations may discourage family division, especially among the wealthy.

Chinese commonly attribute family division to arguments among women, an explanation not without some merit. It is important to keep in mind that, in traditional Chinese contexts, property passes in the male line. It is divided equally among sons, so women have access to it only through husbands and sons. The situation pits mothers-in-law against daughters-in-law and sisters-in-law against each other. It poses a threat to family harmony and, thus, discourages family extension, especially to joint form.

For her well being, that of her children, and even that of her husband, a woman must influence those who control property. When she marries she seeks to assure the loyalty of her husband. Since she will likely outlive him, security in old age will also depend on the control she can exert over her sons. But in that regard she has competition from her daughters-in-law, which is why, in traditional contexts, marriage so often unites people from different communities who have never met. A conjugal bond otherwise formed could more readily constitute a threat to the parent-child bond.

Whereas a mother-in-law has reason to keep her sons together, daughters-in-law have good reason to press for family division, to pull the men apart. Each looks to the interests of her own conjugal unit, her own children. Their interests often do not coincide with those of the parents-in-law. A few hypothetical situations make the contradiction clear.

Mr. Hwong, head of a joint family, decides to send the son of his eldest son to college. The boy is the smartest, most capable of his grandsons, the one most likely to bring rewards to the larger family by virtue of advanced education. But his younger son's wife resents this decision. Why should the labor and resources of her conjugal unit be used to subsidize the well being of people who will eventually be independent? She therefore becomes what the Chinese sometimes call a "pillow ghost." In bed at night she presses her husband to seek a family division.

To take another case, suppose one daughter-in-law has a child while another does not. The childless one might well agitate for family division on the grounds that her labor, and that of her husband, are subsidizing food for an unproductive family member, one who could well depart before matching their contribution. Her position will likely change when she has her own infant and when her nephew is old enough to work a plow. Her sister-in-law will become the pillow ghost then.

Given the potential for conflict that patrilocal residence and patrilineal inheritance provide, it is hardly surprising that, despite the praise lavished upon them, joint families rarely endure long, if they are formed at all. Although most people may spend some part of their lives in such families, at any given time there are likely to be few of them in any Chinese farming village—perhaps not more than five percent of all families. However, in some cases we do find more of them. Why in those villages, or in those families, are the usual centrifugal tendencies repressed? What factors suppress conflict and, thus, delay family division?

In one village, dependence on rainfall rather than canals for irrigation discouraged family division even in poor families by putting a premium on adult male labor.[12] People could break soil and prepare their fields for rice only when it rained and the ground was wet. The work had to be done quickly and, since it rained on all fields at the same time, there was little opportunity for cooperation among families. Only men plowed, so it was important that every family try to have more than one. Under the circumstances

there was good reason to resist the pillow ghost and, in that village, the frequency of joint families was unusually high. This is consistent with our cross-cultural finding that activity incompatibility is likely to encourage family extension.

Confucian virtue had little to do with it. In fact, while there were many joint families, there were also many marriages of a less than filial, virtuous sort. In response to the need for males, parents without adult sons often brought husbands in for their daughters, deviating from the customary and more valued patrilocal pattern. The situation changed later, when there was a reservoir to store water and irrigation canals to deliver it. Access to water could then be controlled and water allocated over a longer period. Families no longer had to accomplish tasks at the same time—in fact they could not do so. Cooperation then became possible and commonplace. From that time, the frequency of joint families and of matrilocal marriages dropped precipitously.

This case indicates yet another way in which the rule of residence, the way marriage is contracted and why, can influence other things we do. Before the shift to canals, matrilocality had demographic effects—compared to patrilocal marriage, and to matrilocal marriage elsewhere, it was here associated with relatively high fertility, low divorce, and relatively infrequent female adoption.

When Chinese deviate from the patrilocal ideal by bringing in a husband for a daughter, they normally do so to ensure family continuity. Matrilocality is most often a resort of poor couples who lack an heir (male) to carry on their family line. The husband, usually also poor, allows his children to take their mother's surname in exchange for access to her family's land. Although poverty has driven him to this concession, people pity him because he has turned his back on his ancestors and married in like a woman, leaving his family and community.

The likelihood of discord and dissatisfaction is great in such marriages. Anticipating that, parents try to find a husband far away, someone their daughter has never seen. It is especially important in such cases to compromise the conjugal bond for the sake of the parent-child bond. That increases the likelihood that a daughter will remain behind with her children even if her husband departs. People therefore anticipate that matrilocal marriages arranged to carry on the family will be fragile, with relatively high divorce rates and perhaps lower fertility.

But in this particular community, where an unusual dependence on rainfall rather than canals put a premium on male labor, matrilocality had little to do with family continuity and much to do with an exaggerated need for labor. These marriages were, therefore, arranged quite differently. Every effort was made to attract a man within the community, possibly a long-term laborer, someone already familiar to their daughter.

Parents were prepared to compromise the parent-child bond here because their intention was to ensure an enduring union—to lock the husband in. If he lived in their village and already knew their daughter he might be less likely to leave. Their daughter would likely be content since marriage did not require that she leave family and community to join strangers elsewhere.

As we might expect, matrilocal marriage had lower divorce rates than patrilocal marriages in this village, and also lower rates than matrilocal marriages in other Chinese villages. Given the familiarity upon which matrilocal marriages were based, it is no surprise that marital fertility (and the rate of premarital conception) was higher than for patrilocally married women. It was also higher than for matrilocally married women in villages where family continuity was the motive. The fertility of these marriages declined, however, once canals reduced the need for males, and matrilocal marriages were once again arranged for more traditional purposes.

The need for male labor also discouraged early female adoption, commonplace in other Chinese villages. Given high infant mortality rates, one could never be certain that a son would survive to adulthood. Better, then, to hold daughters longer as potential lures for matrilocal husbands should the need arise.

This case shows how technology can alter marital residence and the form of family by creating an unusual need for men. Data from another Chinese village illustrates how technology can discourage family division by putting a special premium on the labor of women.[13] When some rice-growing families began to cultivate and process tobacco as a profitable cash crop, most of the work was given to women. The men continued to concentrate on rice. Women picked tobacco leaves as they ripened, carried them to the drying house, regulated fires there day and night, and sorted the leaves when dried. Their skills were so crucial that tobacco growers married only tobacco growers.

While rice farmers had few joint families, those that also cultivated tobacco were almost invariably joint. For them family division created special problems. Which son, for example, would inherit the very profitable drying house, and how would his brothers be compensated? More important, any family division would mean a diversion of female labor from tobacco to separate kitchens, pigs, and child care.

We have seen how technology can delay family division by encouraging men or women to remain together. These two Chinese examples actually illustrate our more general cross-cultural finding— namely, that activity or task incompatibility encourages family extension. In one case a single male could not accomplish on his own all the work that needed to be done, in the other the different tasks of women were at issue.

There are also certain economic conditions, especially characteristic of the wealthy, that may have a similar effect. In the Chinese context, the wealthy have been able to delay family division longer than the poor because they enjoy a greater potential for multienterprise family investment. To the extent that a family invests human and capital resources in different enterprises (i.e., puts its eggs in many baskets), it improves security, ability to withstand economic fluctuations, and long term wealth. Consider the following case: Mr. Lin manages a substantial family estate and heads a joint family consisting of four married sons and their respective children. He lives on the family farm with one son. Another son runs the family brothel in town, one manages the family brick factory, and yet another runs a family trucking firm. The family is invested in a number of enterprises, each of which operates on its own schedule. While the joint family is the minimal corporate kin group, the brothers live apart in different households. That short-circuits some of the conflict that might otherwise emerge were they living together. But there are also powerful economic reasons to avoid family division in this case.

By keeping the family intact, Mr. Lin can shift family labor and capital around in the most profitable way, an advantage that would be lost were his sons to divide. When the crop is brought in, he directs sons and grandsons to help. Men and women are diverted from other family enterprises as needed. Once the crop is in, assuming a good yield, the brothel gets busy. Family members then help there. In winter, during the slack, the brick factory needs workers. Mr. Lin can meet that need as well without having to hire outsiders. He can shift capital, too, from one enterprise to the other, reducing the need to borrow at high rates of interest.

His brothel, very profitable in good years, can be a serious drain on family resources when harvests are poor and farmers less free with their money. A family that can move labor and capital between enterprises is better able to weather fluctuations of this sort. The advantage would be lost were Mr. Lin's sons to divide. Further, it would not be easy to divide the family estate. How does one assess the value of a brothel compared to a brick factory or farm? They have different values, potentials, and risks.

Conclusions

Several lessons emerge from this discussion of marital residence and family. Clearly, how and why people marry the way they do and where they live after marriage are not inconsequential matters of accident. Some practices are more common than others. Cross-cultural research has suggested some conditions that usually favor one pattern over another. The task is of more than casual interest, given that these choices have ramifications elsewhere—they influence the nature of our families and kin groups, have implications for gender relations, and even for demographic performance.

One of our Chinese examples suggests that something will be lost if we think about residence patterns exclusively in terms of general social patterns. It illustrated how, in the Chinese case, matrilocal marriage can be contracted for very different purposes, in dissimilar ways, with varied consequences. Clearly we have much to learn about how technology and economy shape motivation, residence, and family form in particular contexts, and about how these in turn affect demographic behavior.

We learned from these Chinese examples, too, that predicting post-marital residence, or the likelihood and form of family extension in terms of shared values, level of development, or class is not very effective. Consistent with our cross-cultural findings we should, in specific contexts as well, look for technological and/or economic conditions likely to produce task incompatibilities, or that might especially encourage keeping men and/or women together.

The case of Mr. Lin warns us to avoid confusing families and households, especially in complex societies. The minimal corporate kin group or family in his case consisted of several residential units, or households. If we confuse the two we run a serious risk of underestimating the incidence of extended families, especially in complex societies.

An Indian grocery store owner in Hoboken, New Jersey, living with his wife and children, might well be only one segment of a larger family corporation centered in Bombay, India. They may merely be one egg in a basket. The illegal Chinese boat person in New York, whose voyage was paid for by his relatively wealthy family in China, may similarly represent another family investment. If we fail to recognize the connections between households, we may underestimate family complexity and mystify our understanding of family dynamics.

Notes

1. Martin K. Whyte, *The Status of Women in Preindustrial Societies* (Princeton, NJ: Princeton University Press, 1978), pp. 132–134.

2. Norma Diamond, "Collectivization, Kinship, and the Status of Women in Rural China," in Rayna R. Reiter, ed., *Toward an Anthropology of Women* (New York: Monthly Review Press, 1975), pp. 372–395.

3. See Melvin Ember and Carol R. Ember, "Conditions Favoring Matrilocal versus Patrilocal Residence," *American Anthropologist* 73 (1971): 571–594; and William T. Divale, "Migration, External Warfare, and Matrilocal Residence," *Behavior Science Research* 9 (1974): 75–133. However, one study of only hunting-gathering societies does indicate a relationship between division of labor and marital residence. Where men contribute most to subsistence in such societies, residence is more often patrilocal; where women predominate, the rule is more likely to be matrilocal. The matter becomes far more complicated if we include other sorts of societies, however. On hunter-gatherers, see Carol R. Ember, "Residential Variations among Hunters-Gatherers," *Behavior Science Research* 10 (1975): 199–227.

4. Ember and Ember, "Conditions Favoring Matrilocal versus Patrilocal Residence."

5. Melvin Ember, "The Conditions That May Favor Avunculocal Residence," *Behavior Science Research* 9 (1974): 203–209.

6. Some suggest that bilocality reflects sexual equality. Another proposal is that scarce, fluctuating resources encourage greater residential flexibility, and thus bilocality. Although these are reasonable expectations, the ethnographic record indicates that not all bilocal peoples have these characteristics. Depopulation is a better predictor. It accounts for most bilocal cases, and perhaps for the environmental marginality of many of them as well. See Carol R. Ember and Melvin Ember, "The Conditions Favoring Multilocal Residence," *Southwestern Journal of Anthropology* 28 (1972): 382–400.

7. Melvin Ember, "The Emergence of Neolocal Residence," *Transactions of the New York Academy of Sciences* 30 (1967): 291–302.

8. Allan D. Coult and Robert W. Habenstein, *Cross Tabulations of Murdock's World Ethnographic Sample* (Columbia: University of Missouri Press, 1965).

9. Ray Lesser Blumberg and Robert F. Winch, "Societal Complexity and Familial Complexity: Evidence for the Curvilinear Hypothesis," *American Journal of Sociology* 77 (1972): 898–920; M. F. Nimkoff and Russell Middleton, "Types of Family and Types of Economy," *American Journal of Sociology* 66 (1960): 215–225.

10. Burton Pasternak, Carol R. Ember, and Melvin Ember, "On the Conditions Favoring Extended Family Households," *Journal of Anthropological Research* 32, no. 2 (1976): 109–123, reprinted in Melvin Ember and Carol

R. Ember, *Marriage, Family, and Kinship: Comparative Studies of Social Organization* (New Haven: HRAF Press, 1983), pp. 125–150.

11. Nimkoff and Middleton, "Types of Family and Types of Economy."

12. Burton Pasternak, *Kinship and Community in Two Chinese Villages* (Stanford: Stanford University Press, 1972); Burton Pasternak, *Guests in the Dragon: Social Demography of a Chinese District, 1895–1946* (New York: Columbia University Press, 1983).

13. Myron L. Cohen, *House United, House Divided: The Chinese Family in Taiwan* (New York: Columbia University Press, 1976).

Suggested Readings

Pasternak, Burton. *Introduction to Kinship and Social Organization*. Englewood Cliffs, NJ: Prentice-Hall, 1976. General overview with coverage of marital residence and family organization.

Ember, Melvin, and Carol R. Ember. *Marriage, Family, and Kinship: Comparative Studies of Social Organization*. New Haven: HRAF Press, 1983. Collection of cross-cultural studies of variation in social organization, including marital residence and family.

"Family and Household: Who Lives Where, Why Does It Vary and Why Is It Important?"

Burton Pasternak

1) What are the different types of post-marital residence found around the world?

2) How are residence and kinship organization interrelated?

3) What are the possible influences of warfare and the division of labor on a culture's preference for certain residence patterns?

4) What circumstances or factors influence a society to choose bilocality or neolocality as a preferred residence pattern?

5) What is a "joint family" and what practical purposes does it serve for Chinese society?

FAMILY AND KINSHIP IN VILLAGE INDIA

David W. McCurdy

On a hot afternoon in May, 1962, I sat talking with three Bhil men in the village of Ratakote, located in southern Rajasthan, India.[1] We spoke about the results of recent national elections, their worry over a cattle disease that was afflicting the village herds, and predictions about when the monsoon rains would start. But our longest discussion concerned kin—the terms used to refer to them, the responsibilities they had toward one another, and the importance of marrying them off properly. It was toward the end of this conversation that one of the men, Kanji, said, "Now sāb (Bhili for sāhīb), you are finally asking about a good thing. This is what we want you tell people about us when you go back to America."

As I thought about it later, I was struck by how different this social outlook was from mine. I doubt that I or any of my friends in the United States would say something like this. Americans do have kin. We have parents, although our parents may not always live together, and we often know other relatives, some of whom are likely to play important parts in our lives. We grow up in families and we often create new ones if we have children. But we also live in a social network of other people whom we meet at work or encounter in various "outside" social settings, and these people can be of equal or even greater importance to us than kin. Our social worlds include such non-kin structures as companies and other work organizations, schools, neighborhoods, churches and other religious groups, and voluntary associations, including recreational groups and social clubs. We are not likely to worry much about our obligations to relatives with the notable exceptions of our children and grandchildren (middle-class American parents are notoriously child-centered), and more grudgingly, our aging parents. We are not supposed to "live off" relatives or lean too heavily on them.

Not so in Ratakote. Ratakote's society, like many agrarian villages around the world, is kinship-centered. Villagers anchor themselves in their families. They spend great energy on creating and maintaining their kinship system. This actually is not so surprising. Elaborate kinship systems work well in agrarian societies where families tend to be corporate units and where peoples' social horizons are often limited to the distance they can walk in a day.

For the same reasons, families in the United States were also stronger in the past when more of them owned farms and neighborhood businesses.

What may come as a surprise, however, is how resilient and strong Indian kinship systems such as Ratakote's have been in the face of recent economic changes, especially the growth of wage labor. Let us look more closely at the Bhil kinship system, especially at arranged marriage, to illustrate these ideas.

Arranging a Marriage

If there is anything that my American students have trouble understanding about India, it is arranged marriage. They cannot imagine sitting passively by while their parents advertise their charms and evaluate emerging nuptial candidates. The thought of living—to say nothing of have sex with—a total stranger seems out of the question to them. In our country, personal independence takes precedence over loyalty to family.

Not so in India. There, arranged marriage is the norm, and most young people, as well as their elders, accept and support the custom. (They often find it sexually exciting, too.) There are many reasons why this is so, but one stands out for discussion here. Marriage constructs alliances between families, lineages, and clans. The resulting kinship network is a pivotal structure in Indian society. It confers social strength and security. People's personal reputations depend on the quality and number of their allied kin. There is little question in their minds about who should arrange marriages. The decision is too important to leave up to inexperienced and impressionable young people.

As an aside I should note that young Indians play a greater part in the process than they used to. Middle-class boys often visit the families of prospective brides, where they manage to briefly "interview" them. They also tap into their kinship network to find out personal information about prospects. Young women also seek out information about prospective grooms. Bhils are no exception. They often conspire to meet those to whom they have been betrothed, usually at a fair or other public event where their contact is likely to go unnoticed. If they don't like each other, they will begin to pressure their parents to back out of the arrangement.

The importance of arranging a marriage was brought home to me several times during fieldwork in Ratakote, but one instance stands out most clearly. When I arrived in the village for a short stay in 1985, Kanji had just concluded marriage arrangements for his daughter, Rupani.[2] What he told me about the process underscored the important role kinship plays in the life of the village.

Kanji started by saying that he and his wife first discussed Rupani's marriage the previous year when the girl first menstruated. She seemed too young for such a union then so they had waited nine months before committing to the marriage process. Even then, Rupani was still only 15 years old. Kanji explained that everyone preferred early marriage for their children because young people were likely to become sexually active as they grew older and might fall in love and elope, preempting the arrangement process altogether. Now they figured that the time had come, and they began a series of steps to find a suitable spouse that would eventually involve most of their kin.

The first step was to consult the members of Kanji's *lineage*. Lineage is an anthropological term, not one used by Bhils. But Bhils share membership in local groups of relatives that meet the anthropological definition. Lineages (in this case, patrilin-eages) include closely related men who are all descended from a known ancestor. Kanji's lineage consists of his two married brothers, three married sons of his deceased father's brother (his father is also dead), and his own married son when the latter is home. All are the descendants of his grandfather who had migrated to Ratakote many years earlier. He had talked with all of them informally about the possibility of his daughter's marriage before this. Now he called them together for formal approval.

The approval of lineage mates is necessary because they are essential to the marriage process. Each one of them will help spread the word to other villages that Rupani is available for marriage. They will loan money to Kanji for wedding expenses, and when it comes time for the wedding ceremony, they will provide much of the labor needed to prepare food and arrange required activities. Each family belonging to the lineage will host a special meal for the bride (the groom is similarly entertained in his village) during the wedding period, and one or two will help her make offerings to their lineal ancestors. The groom will also experience this ritual.

The lineage also has functions not directly related to marriage. It has the right to redistribute the land of deceased childless, male members, and it provides its members with political support. It sees to memorial feasts for deceased members. Its members may cooperatively plow and sow fields together and combine their animals for herding.

With lineage approval in hand, Kanji announced Rupani's eligibility in other villages. (Bhils are village exogamous, meaning they prefer to marry spouses from other communities.) Kanji and his lineage mates went about this by paying visits to feminal relatives in other villages. These are kin of the women, now living in Ratakote, who have married into his family. They also include the daughters of his family line who have married and gone to live in other villages, along with their husbands and husbands' kin.

Once the word has been spread, news of prospective candidates begins to filter in. It may arrive with feminal kin from other villages when they visit Ratakote. Or it may come from neighbors who are acting as go-betweens in Ratakote for kin who live in other villages and who seek partners for their children. Either way, a process of evaluation starts. Does the family of the suggested boy or girl have a good reputation? Are they hospitable to their in-laws? Do they meet their obligations to others? What is the reputation of the boy or girl they are offering in marriage? Is he or she tall or short, light or dark, robust or frail, cheerful or complaining, hard working or lazy? What about their level of education? Does the family have sufficient land and animals? Have they treated other sons- and daughters-in-law well?

The most fundamental question to ask, however, is whether the prospective spouse is from the right clan. In anthropology, the term *clan* refers to an aggregate of people who all believe they are descended from a common ancestor. In Ratakote this group is called an *arak*. Araks are named and the names are used as surnames when Bhils identify themselves. Kanji comes from the pargi *arak* and is thus known as Kanji Pargi. There is Lalu Bodar, Naraji Katara, Dita Hiravat, Nathu Airi—all men named for one of the 36 araks found in Ratakote. Women also belong to their father's clan, but unlike many American women who adopt their husband's surname at marriage, they keep their arak name all their lives.

Araks are based on a rule of patrilineal descent. This means that their members trace ancestry through males, only. (Matrilineal descent traces the line through females only, and bilateral descent, which is found in U.S. society, includes both sexes.) Patrilineal descent not only defines arak membership, it governs inheritance. (Sons inherit equally from their fathers in Ratakote; daughters do not inherit despite a national law giving them that right.) It says that the children of divorced parents stay with the father's family. It bolsters the authority of men over their wives and children. It supports the rule of patrilocality. It even defines the village view of conception. Men plant the "seeds" that grow into children; women provide the fields in which the seeds germinate and grow.

The arak symbolizes patrilineal descent. It is not an organized group, although the members of an arak worship the same mother goddess no matter where they live. Instead it is an identity, an indicator that tells people who their lineal blood relatives are. There are pargis in hundreds of other Bhil villages. Most are strangers to Kanji but if he meets pargis elsewhere, he knows they share a common blood heritage with him.

It is this sense of common heritage that affects marriage. Bhils, like most Indians, believe that clan (arak) mates are close relatives even though they may be strangers. Marriage with them is forbidden. To make sure incest is impossible, it is also forbidden to marry anyone from your mother's arak or your father's mother's arak, to say nothing of anyone else you know you are related to.

This point was driven home to me on another occasion when a neighbor of Kanji's, Kamalaji Kharadi, who was sitting smoking with several other men, asked me which *arak* I belonged to. Instead of letting it go at "McCurdy," I said that I didn't have an *arak*. I explained that Americans didn't have a kinship group similar to this, and that was why I had to ask questions about kinship.

My listeners didn't believe me. After all, I must have a father and you get your arak automatically from him. It is a matter of birth and all people are born. They looked at each other as if to say, "We wonder why he won't tell us what his *arak* is?", then tried again to get me to answer. My second denial led them to ask, "OK, then what is your wife's *arak*?" (If you can't get at it one way, then try another.) I answered that she didn't have an *arak* either. This caused a mild sensation. "Then how do you know if you have not married your own relative?", they asked, secretly (I think) delighted by the scandalous prospect.

The third step that occurred during the arrangement of Rupani's marriage came after the family had settled on a prospective groom. This step is the betrothal, and it took place when the groom's father and some of his lineage mates and neighbors paid a formal visit to Kanji's house. When they arrive, Kanji must offer his guests a formal meal, usually slaughtering a goat and distilling some liquor for the occasion. The bride, her face covered by her sari, will be brought out for a brief viewing, as well. But most of the time will be spent making arrangements—when will the actual wedding take place?; who will check the couple's horoscopes for fit?; how much will the bride price (also called bride wealth by many anthropologists) be?

Bride price (*dapa*) deserves special comment. It is usually a standard sum of money (about 700 rupees in 1985), although it may also include silver ornaments or other valuables. The dapa is given by the groom's father and his line to the parents of the bride. Bhils view this exchange as a compensation for the loss of the bride's services to her family. It also pays for a shift in her loyalty.

The exchange points up an important strain on families in patrilineal societies, the transfer of a woman from her natal family and line to those of her husband. This transfer includes not only her person, but her loyalty, labor, and children. Although she always will belong to her father's arak, she is now part of her husband's family, not his.

This problem is especially troublesome in India because of the close ties formed there by a girl and her parents. Parents know their daughter will leave when she marries, and they know that in her husband's house and village, she will be at a disadvantage. She will be alone, and out of respect for his parents her husband may not favor her wishes, at least in public. Because of this, they tend to give her extra freedom and support. In addition, they recognize the strain she will be under when she first goes to live with her new husband and his family. To ease her transition, they permit her to visit her parents frequently for a year or two. They also may try to marry her into a village where other women from Ratakote have married, so that she has some kin or at least supporters.

After her marriage, a woman's parents and especially her brothers find it hard not to care about her welfare. Their potential interest presents a built-in structural conflict that could strain relations between the two families if nothing were done about it.

A solution to this problem is to make the marriage into an exchange, and bride price is one result. Bride price also helps to dramatize the change in loyalty and obligation accompanying the bride's entrance into her new family.

Bhils have also devised a number of wedding rituals to dramatize the bride's shift in family membership. The bride must cry to symbolize that she is leaving her home. The groom ritually storms the bride's house at the beginning of the final ceremony. He does so like a conquering hero, drawing his sword to strike a ceremonial arch placed over the entrance while simultaneously stepping on a small fire (he wears a slipper to protect his foot), ritually violating the household's sacred hearth. At the end of the wedding, the groom, with some friends, engages in a mock battle with the bride's brothers and other young men, and symbolically abducts her. The meaning of this ritual is a dramatic equivalent of a father "giving away the bride" at American weddings.

One additional way of managing possible tension between in-laws is the application of respect behavior. The parents of the bride must always treat those of the groom and their relatives with respect. They must not joke in their presence, and they must use respectful language and defer to the groom's parents in normal conversation. In keeping with the strong patrilineal system, a groom may not accept important gifts from his wife's family except on ritual occasions, such as weddings, when exchange is expected. A groom may help support his own father, but he should not do so with his in-laws. That is up to their sons.

Bride price exchange also sets in motion a lifelong process of mutual hospitality between the two families. Once the marriage has taken place, the families will become part of each other's feminal kin. They will exchange gifts on some ritual occasions, open their houses to each other, and, of course, help one another make future marriages.

The Future of Indian Kinship

On our last trip to India in 1994, my wife and I learned that Rupani had delivered three children since her wedding. Kanji had visited them a few months before we arrived, and he said that Rupani was happy and that he had wonderful grandchildren. But he also mentioned that her husband now spent most of his time in the nearby city of Udaipur working in construction there. He sent money home, but his absence left Rupani to run the house and raise the children by herself, although she did so with the assistance of his parents and lineage mates.

Rupani's case is not unusual. Every morning 70 or 80 men board one of the 20 or so busses that travel the road, now paved, that runs through Ratakote to the city. There they wait to be recruited by contractors for day labor at a low wage. If they are successful, gain special skills, or make good connections, they may get more permanent, better-paying jobs and live for weeks at a time in the city.

The reason they have to take this kind of work is simple. Ratakote has more than doubled in population since 1962. (The village had a population of 1,184 in 1963. By 1994 an estimate put the number at about 2,600.) There is not enough land for everyone to farm nor can the land produce enough to feed the growing population, even in abundant years. Work in the city is the answer, especially for householders whose land is not irrigated like Kanji's.

Cash labor has a potential to break down the kinship system that Bhils value so highly. It frees men and women from economic dependence on the family (since they make their own money working for someone else). It takes up time, too, making it difficult for them to attend the leisurely eleven-day weddings of relatives or meet other obligations to kin that require their presence. With cash labor, one's reputation is likely to hinge less on family than on work. For some, work means moving the family altogether. Devaji Katara, one of Kanji's neighbors, has a son who has moved with his wife and children to the Central Indian city of Indore. He has a good factory job there, and the move has kept them together. By doing so, however, he and they are largely removed from the kinship loop.

Despite these structural changes, kinship in Ratakote and for India as a whole remains exceptionally strong. Even though they may live farther away, Bhil sons and daughters still visit their families regularly. They send money home, and they try to attend weddings. They talk about their kin, too, and surprisingly, they continue the long process of arranging marriage for their children.

Perhaps one reason for kinship's vitality is the use to which kinship is put by many Indians. The people of Ratakote and other Indians have never given up teaching their children to respect their elders and subordinate their interests to those of the family. Family loyalty is still a paramount value. They use this loyalty to help each other economically. Family members hire each other in business. They take one another in during hard times. They offer hospitality to each other. Unlike Americans who feel guilty about accepting one-sided help from relatives, Indians look to the future. Giving aid now may pay off with a job or a favor later. Even if it doesn't, it is the proper thing to do.

Instead of breaking up the kinship network, work that takes men and families away from the village has simply stretched it out. An Indian student I know has found relatives in every American city he has visited. He knows of kin in Europe and southeast Asia too. Anywhere he goes he is likely to have relatives to stay with and to help him. When he settles down he will be expected to return the favor. Another Indian acquaintance, who went to graduate school in the United States and who continues to work here, has sent his father thousands of dollars to help with the building of a house. This act, which would surprise many Americans, seems perfectly normal to him.

Kanji is not disturbed by the economic changes that are overtaking the quiet agricultural pace of

Ratakote. I last left him standing in front of his house with a grandson in his arms. His son, who had left the village in 1982 to be a "wiper" on a truck, returned to run the farm. He will be able to meet the family's obligation to lineage and feminal kin. For Kanji, traditional rules of inheritance have pulled a son and, for the moment at least, a grandson, back into the bosom of the family where they belong.

Notes

1. Ratakote is a Bhil tribal village located 21 miles southwest of Udaipur, Rajasthan, in the Aravalli hills. I did ethnographic research in the village from 1961 to 1963, and again in 1985, 1991, and 1993 for shorter periods of time.

2. Kanji and Rupani are not real people. Their experiences are a composite of several life histories.

"FAMILY AND KINSHIP IN VILLAGE INDIA"

David W. McCurdy

1) What is an arranged marriage?

2) Why are arranged marriages the norm in India, and what purposes do such marriages serve?

3) What characteristics do Indian families look for in a potential spouse in arranging marriages for their children?

4) What pressures are being placed on the institutions of marriage and kinship in India, and what problems can these pressures potentially cause?

SECTION TEN

The Old and New in Cultures and Anthropology

CONFRONTING CREATIONISTS

Michael Shermer

Late in his life, Charles Darwin received many letters asking for his views of God and religion. On October 13, 1880, for example, he answered a letter from the editor of a book on evolution and free thought who was hoping to dedicate it to him. Knowing that the book had an antireligious slant, Darwin dissembled: "Moreover though I am a strong advocate for free thought on all subjects, yet it appears to me (whether rightly or wrongly) that direct arguments against christianity & theism produce hardly any effect on the public; & freedom of thought is best promoted by the gradual illumination of men's minds, which follow from the advance of science. It has, therefore, been always my object to avoid writing on religion, & I have confined myself to science" (in Desmond and Moore 1991, p. 645).

In classifying the relationship of science and religion, I would like to suggest a three-tiered taxonomy:

> The *same-worlds model:* Science and religion deal with the same subjects and not only is there overlap and conciliation but someday science may subsume religion completely. Frank Tipler's cosmology (1994), based on the anthropic principle and the eventual resurrection of all humans through a supercomputer's virtual reality in the far future of the universe, is one example. Many humanists and evolutionary psychologists foresee a time when science not only can explain the purpose of religion, it will replace it with a viable secular morality and ethics.

> The *separate-worlds model:* Science and religion deal with different subjects, do not conflict or overlap, and the two should coexist peacefully with one another. Charles Darwin, Stephen Jay Gould, and many other scientists hold this model.

> The *conflicting-worlds model:* One is right and the other is wrong, and there can be no reconciliation between the two viewpoints. This model is predominantly held by atheists and creationists, who are often at odds with one another.

This taxonomy allows us to see that Darwin's advice is as applicable today as it was a century ago. Thus, let us be clear that refuting creationists' arguments is not an attack on religion. Let us also be clear that creationism is an attack on science—all of science, not just evolutionary biology—so the counterarguments presented in this chapter are a response to the antiscience of creationism and have nothing whatsoever to do with antireligion. If creationists are right, then there are serious problems with physics, astronomy, cosmology, geology, paleontology, botany, zoology, and all the life sciences. Can all these sciences be wrong in the same direction? Of course not, but creationists think they are, and, worse, they want their antiscience taught in public schools.

Creationists and religious fundamentalists will go to absurd lengths to protect their beliefs from science. The Summer 1996 issue of the National Center for Science Education's *Reports* notes that in Marshall County, Kentucky, elementary school superintendent Kenneth Shadowen found a rather unique solution to a vexing problem with his fifth- and sixth-graders' science textbooks. It seems that the heretic textbook *Discovery Works* claimed that the universe began with the Big Bang but did not present any "alternatives" to this theory. Since the Big Bang was explained on a two-page spread, Shadowen recalled all the textbooks and glued together the offending pages. Shadowen told the *Louisville Courier-Journal,* "We're not going to teach one theory and not teach another theory" and that the textbook's recall "had nothing to do with censorship or anything like that" (August 23, 1996, A1, p.1). It seems doubtful that Shadowen was lobbying for equal time for the Steady State theory or Inflationary Cosmology. Perhaps Shadowen found his solution by consulting librarian Ray Martin's "Reviewing and Correcting Encyclopedias," a guide for Christians on how to doctor books:

> Encyclopedias are a vital part of many school libraries. . . . [They] represent the philosophies of present day humanists. This is obvious by the bold display of pictures that are used to illustrate painting, art, and sculpture. . . . One of the areas that needs correction is immodesty due to nakedness and posture. This can be corrected by drawing clothes on the figures or blotting out entire pictures with a magic marker. This needs to be done with care or the magic marker can be erased from the glossy paper used in printing encyclopedias. You can overcome this by taking a razor blade

and lightly scraping the surface until it loses it glaze. . . . [Regarding evolution] cutting out the sections is practical if the portions removed are not thick enough to cause damage to the spine of the book as it is opened and closed in normal use. When the sections needing correction are too thick, paste the pages together being careful not to smear portions of the book not intended for correction. (*Christian School Builder*, April 1983, pp. 205–207)

Fortunately, creationists have failed in their top-down strategy of passing antievolution, pro-creationism laws (Ohio, Tennessee, and Georgia recently rejected creationist legislation), but their bottom-up grassroots campaign bent on injecting Genesis into the public school curriculum has met with success. In March 1996, for example, Governor Fob James used a discretionary fund of taxpayers' money to purchase and send a copy of Phillip Johnson's antievolution book, *Darwin on Trial*, to every high school biology teacher in Alabama. Their success should not be surprising. Politically, the United States has taken a sharp turn to the right, and the political strength of the religious right has grown. What can we do? We can counter with our own literature. For example, the National Center for Science Education, Eugenie Scott's Berkeley-based group specializing in tracking creationist activities, countered Governor James's mailing with a mailing that included a critical review of Johnson's book. We can also try to understand the issue thoroughly so that we are prepared to counter procreationist arguments wherever we meet them.

The following is a list of arguments put forth by creationists and answers put forth by evolutionists. The arguments are primarily attacks on evolutionary theory and secondarily (in a minor way) positive statements of creationists' own beliefs. The arguments and answers are simplified due to space constraints; nonetheless, they provide an overview of the principal points of the debate. This list is not meant to substitute for critical reading, however. While these answers might be adequate for casual conversation, they would not be adequate for a formal debate with a well-prepared creationist. Numerous books offer fuller discussions (e.g., Berra 1990; Bowler 1989; Eve and Harrold 1991; Futuyma 1983; Gilkey 1985; Godfrey 1983; Gould 1983a, 1991; Lindberg and Numbers 1986; Numbers 1992; Ruse 1982; and, especially, Strahler 1987).

What Is Evolution?

Before reviewing creationists' arguments against evolution, a brief summary of the theory itself might be useful. Darwin's theory, outlined in his 1859 *On the Origin of Species by Means of Natural Selection*, can be summarized as follows (Gould 1987a; Mayr 1982, 1988):

Evolution: Organisms change through time. Both the fossil record and nature today make this obvious.

Descent with modification: Evolution proceeds via branching through common descent. Offspring are similar to but not exact replicas of their parents. This produces the necessary variation to allow for adaptation to an ever-changing environment.

Gradualism: Change is slow, steady, stately. *Natura non facit saltum*—Nature does not make leaps. Given enough time, evolution accounts for species change.

Multiplication of speciation: Evolution does not just produce new species; it produces an increasing number of new species.

Natural selection: The mechanism of evolutionary change, co-discovered by Darwin and Alfred Russel Wallace, operates as follows:

A. Populations tend to increase indefinitely in a geometric ratio: 2, 4, 8, 16, 32, 64, 128, 256, 512, ...

B. In a natural environment, however, population numbers stabilize at a certain level.

C. Therefore, there must be a "struggle for existence" because not all of the organisms produced can survive.

D. There is variation in every species.

E. In the struggle for existence, those individuals with variations that are better adapted to the environment leave behind more offspring than individuals that are less well adapted. This is known in the jargon of the trade as *differential reproductive success*.

Point E is crucial. Natural selection, and thus evolutionary change, operate primarily at the local level. It is just a game of who can leave behind the most offspring, that is, who can most successfully propagate their genes into the next generation. Natural selection has nothing to say about evolutionary direction, species progress, or any of the other teleological goals, such as human inevitability or the necessary evolution of intelligence, which are commonly attributed to it. There is no ladder of evolutionary progress with humans at the top, only a richly branching bush with humans as one tiny twig among millions. There is nothing special about humans; we just happen to be extremely good at differential reproductive success—we leave behind lots of offspring and are good at getting them into adulthood—a trait that could eventually cause our demise.

Of the five points of Darwin's theory, the most controversial today are gradualism, with Niles Eldredge (1971, 1985; Eldredge and Gould 1972) and Stephen Jay Gould (1985, 1989, 1991) and their supporters pushing for a theory called *punctuated equilibrium*, which involves rapid change and stasis, to replace gradualism; and the exclusivity of natural selection, with Eldredge, Gould, and others arguing for change at the level of genes, groups, and populations in addition to individual natural selection (Somit and Peterson 1992). Ranged against Eldredge, Gould, and their supporters are Daniel Dennett (1995), Richard Dawkins (1995), and those who opt for a strict Darwinian model of gradualism and natural selection. The debate rages, while creationists sit on the sidelines hoping for a double knockout. They will not get it. These scientists are not arguing about *whether* evolution happened; they are debating the *rate* and *mechanism* of evolutionary change. When it all shakes down, the theory of evolution will be stronger than ever. It is sad that while science moves ahead in exciting new areas of research, fine-tuning our knowledge of how life originated and evolved, creationists remain mired in medieval debates about angels on the head of a pin and animals in the belly of an Ark.

Philosophically Based Arguments and Answers

1. Creation-science is scientific and therefore should be taught in public school science courses.

Creation-science is scientific in name only. It is a thinly disguised religious position rather than a theory to be tested using scientific methods, and therefore it is not appropriate for public school science courses, just as calling something Muslim-science or Buddha-science or Christian-science would not mean that it requires equal time. The following statement from the Institute for Creation Research, which must be adhered to by all faculty members and researchers, is a powerful illumination of creationist beliefs: "The scriptures, both Old and New Testaments, are inerrant in relation to any subject with which they deal, and are to be accepted in their natural and intended sense . . . all things in the universe were created and made by God in the six days of special creation described in Genesis. The creationist account is accepted as factual, historical and perspicuous and is thus fundamental in the understanding of every fact and phenomenon in the created universe" (in Rohr 1986, p. 176).

Science is subject to disproof and is ever-changing as new facts and theories reshape our views. Creationism prefers faith in the authority of the Bible no matter what contradictory empirical evidence might exist: "The main reason for insisting on the universal Flood as a fact of history and as the primary vehicle for geological interpretation is that God's Word plainly teaches it! No geological difficulties, real or imagined, can be allowed to take precedence over the clear statements and necessary inferences of Scripture" (in Rohr 1986, p. 190). Here is an analogy. Professors at Caltech declare Darwin's *Origin of Species* dogma, the authority of this book and its author absolute, and any further empirical evidence for or against evolution irrelevant.

2. Science only deals with the here-and-now and thus cannot answer historical questions about the creation of the universe and the origins of life and the human species.

Science does deal with past phenomena, particularly in historical sciences such as cosmology, geology, paleontology, paleoanthropology, and archeology. There are experimental sciences and historical sciences. They use different methodologies but are equally able to track causality. Evolutionary biology is a valid and legitimate historical science.

3. Education is a process of learning all sides of an issue, so it is appropriate for creationism and evolution to be taught side-by-side in public school science courses. Not to do so is a violation of the principles of education and of the civil liberties of creationists. We have a right to be heard, and, besides, what is the harm in hearing both sides?

Exposure to the many facets of issues is indeed a part of the general educational process, and it might be appropriate to discuss creationism in courses on religion, history, or even philosophy but most certainly not science; similarly, biology courses should not include lectures on American Indian creation myths. There is considerable harm in teaching creation-science as science because the consequent blurring of the line between religion and science means that students will not understand what the scientific paradigm is and how to apply it properly. Moreover, the assumptions behind creationism comprise a two-pronged attack on all the sciences, not just on evolutionary biology. One, if the universe and Earth are only about ten thousand years old, then the modern sciences of cosmology, astronomy, physics, chemistry, geology, paleontology, paleoanthropology, and early human history are all invalid. Two, as soon as the creation of even one species is attributed to supernatural intervention, natural laws and inferences about the workings of nature become void. In each case, all science becomes meaningless.

4. There is an amazing correlation between the facts of nature and the acts of the Bible. It is therefore appropriate to use creation-science books and the Bible as reference tools in public school science courses and to study the Bible as a book of science alongside the book of nature.

There is also an amazing correlation between acts in the Bible for which there are no facts in nature and between facts in nature for which there are no acts in the Bible. If a group of Shakespeare scholars believe that the universe is explained in the bard's plays, does that mean science courses should include readings of Shakespeare? Shakespeare's plays are literature, the Bible contains scriptures sacred to several religions, and neither has any pretensions to being a book of science or a scientific authority.

5. The theory of natural selection is tautological, or a form of circular reasoning. Those who survive are the best adapted. Who are the best adapted? Those who survive. Likewise, rocks are used to date fossils, and fossils are used to date rocks. Tautologies do not make a science.

Sometimes tautologies are the beginning of science, but they are never the end. Gravity can be tautological, but its inference is justified by the way this theory allows scientists to accurately predict physical effects and phenomena. Likewise, natural selection and the theory of evolution are testable and falsifiable by looking at their predictive power. For example, population genetics demonstrates quite clearly, and with mathematical prediction, when natural selection will and will not effect change on a population. Scientists can make predictions based on the theory of natural selection and then test them, as the geneticist does in the example just given or the paleontologist does in interpreting the fossil record. Finding hominid fossils in the same geological strata as trilobites, for instance, would be evidence against the theory. The dating of fossils with rocks, and vice versa, could only be done *after* the geological column was established. The geological column exists nowhere in its entirety because strata are disrupted, convoluted, and always incomplete for a variety of

reasons. But strata order is unmistakably *nonrandom*, and chronological order can be accurately pieced together using a variety of techniques, only one of which is fossils.

6. There are only two explanations for the origins of life and existence of humans, plants, and animals: either it was the work of a creator or it was not. Since evolution theory is unsupported by the evidence (i.e., it is wrong), creationism must be correct. Any evidence that does not support the theory of evolution is necessarily scientific evidence in support of creationism.

Beware of the either-or fallacy, or the fallacy of false alternatives. If A is false, B must be true. Oh? Why? Plus, shouldn't B stand on its own regardless of A? Of course. So even if evolutionary theory turns out to be completely wrong, that does not mean that, ergo, creationism is right. There may be alternatives C, D, and E we have yet to consider. There is, however, a true dichotomy in the case of natural versus supernatural explanations. Either life was created and changed by natural means, or it was created and changed by supernatural intervention and according to a supernatural design. Scientists assume natural causation, and evolutionists debate the various natural causal agents involved. They are not arguing about whether it happened by natural or supernatural means. And, again, once you assume supernatural intervention, science goes out the window—so there can be no scientific evidence in support of creationism because natural laws no longer hold and scientific methodology has no meaning in the world of creationists.

7. Evolutionary theory is the basis of Marxism, communism, atheism, immorality, and the general decline of the morals and culture of America, and therefore is bad for our children.

This partakes of the reductio ad absurdum fallacy. The theory of evolution in particular or science in general is no more the basis of these "isms" and Americans' so-called declining morals and culture than the printing press is responsible for Hitler's *Mein Kampf* or *Mein Kampf* is responsible for what people did with Hitler's ideology. The fact that the atomic bomb, the hydrogen bomb, and many even more destructive weapons have been invented does not mean we should abandon the study of the atom. Moreover, there may well be Marxist, communist, atheistic, and even immoral evolutionists, but there are probably just as many capitalist, theist, agnostic, and moral evolutionists. As for the theory itself, it can be used to support Marxist, communist, and atheistic ideologies, and it has; but so has it been used (especially in America) to lend credence to laissez-faire capitalism. The point is that linking scientific theories to political ideologies is tricky business, and we must be cautious of making connections that do not necessarily follow or that serve particular agendas (e.g., one person's cultural and moral decline is another person's cultural and moral progress).

8. Evolutionary theory, along with its bedfellow, secular humanism, is really a religion, so it is not appropriate to teach it in public schools.

To call the science of evolutionary biology a religion is to so broaden the definition of religion as to make it totally meaningless. In other words, religion becomes any lens that we look through to interpret the world. But that is not what religion is. Religion has something to do with the service and worship of God or the supernatural, whereas science has to do with physical phenomena. Religion has to do with faith and the unseen, science focuses on empirical evidence and testable knowledge. Science is a set of methods designed to describe and interpret observed or inferred phenomena, past or present, and aimed at building a testable body of knowledge open to rejection or confirmation. Religion—whatever it is—is certainly neither testable nor open to rejection or confirmation. In their methodologies, science and religion are 180 degrees out of phase with each other.

9. Many leading evolutionists are skeptical of the theory and find it problematic. For example, Eldredge and Gould's theory of punctuated equilibrium proves Darwin wrong. If the world's leading evolutionists cannot agree on the theory, the whole thing must be a wash.

It is particularly ironic that the creationists would quote a leading spokesman against creationism—Gould—in their attempts to marshal the forces of science on their side. Creationists have misunderstood, either naively or intentionally, the healthy scientific debate among evolutionists about the causal agents of organic change. They apparently take this normal exchange of ideas and the self-correcting nature of science as evidence that the field is coming apart at the seams and about to implode. Of the many things evolutionists argue and debate within the field, one thing they are certain of and all agree upon is that evolution has occurred. Exactly how it happened, and what the relative strengths of the various causal mechanisms are, continue to be discussed. Eldredge and Gould's theory of punctuated equilibrium is a refinement of and improvement upon Darwin's theory of evolution. It no more proves Darwin wrong than Einsteinian relativity proves Newton wrong.

10. "The Bible is the written Word of God . . . all of its assertions are historically and scientifically true. The great Flood described in Genesis was an historical event, worldwide in its extent and effect. We are an organization of Christian men of science, who accept Jesus Christ as our Lord and Savior. The account of the special creation of Adam and Eve as one man and one woman, and their subsequent Fall into sin, is the basis for our belief in the necessity of a Savior for all mankind" (in Eve and Harrold 1991, p. 55).

Such a statement of belief is clearly religious. This does not make it wrong, but it does mean that creation-science is really creation-religion and to this extent breaches the wall separating church and state. In private schools funded or controlled by creationists, they are free to teach whatever they like to their children. But one cannot make the events in any text historically and scientifically true by fiat, only by testing the evidence, and to ask the state to direct teachers to teach a particular religious doctrine as science is unreasonable and onerous.

11. All causes have effects. The cause of "X" must be "X-like." The cause of intelligence must be intelligent—God. Regress all causes in time and you must come to the first cause—God. Because all things are in motion, there must have been a prime mover, a mover who needs no other mover to be moved—God. All things in the universe have a purpose, therefore there must be a purposeful designer—God.

If this were true, should not nature then have a natural cause, not a supernatural cause? But causes of "X" do not have to be "X-like." The "cause" of green paint is blue paint mixed with yellow paint, neither one of which is green-like. Animal manure causes fruit trees to grow better. Fruit is delicious to eat and is, therefore, very unmanure-like! The first-cause and prime-mover argument, brilliantly proffered by St. Thomas Aquinas in the fourteenth century (and more brilliantly refuted by David Hume in the eighteenth century), is easily turned aside with just one more question: Who or what caused and moved God? Finally, as Hume demonstrated, purposefulness of design is often illusory and subjective. "The early bird gets the worm" is a clever design if you are the bird, not so good if you are the worm. Two eyes may seem like the ideal number, but, as psychologist Richard Hardison notes cheerfully, "Wouldn't it be desirable to have an additional eye in the back of one's head, and certainly an eye attached to our forefinger would be helpful when we're working behind the instrument panels of automobiles" (1988, p. 123). Purpose is, in part, what we are accustomed to perceiving. Finally, not everything is so purposeful and beautifully designed. In addition to problems like evil, disease, deformities, and human stupidity which creationists conveniently overlook, nature is filled with the bizarre and seemingly unpurposeful. Male nipples and the panda's thumb are just two examples flaunted by Gould as purposeless and poorly designed structures. If God designed life to fit neatly together like a jigsaw puzzle, then what do you do with such oddities and problems?

12. Something cannot be created out of nothing, say scientists. Therefore, from where did the material for the Big Bang come? From where did the first life forms that provided the raw material for evolution originate? Stanley Miller's creation of amino acids out of an inorganic "soup" and other biogenic molecules is not the creation of life.

Science may not be equipped to answer certain "ultimate"-type questions, such as what there was before the beginning of the universe or what time it was before time began or where the matter for the Big Bang came from. So far these have been philosophical or religious questions, not scientific ones, and therefore have not been a part of science. (Recently, Stephen Hawking and other cosmologists have made some attempts at scientific speculations on these questions.) Evolutionary theory attempts to understand the causality of change after time and matter were "created" (whatever that means). As for the origin of life, biochemists do have a very rational and scientific explanation for the evolution from inorganic to organic compounds, the creation of amino acids and the construction of protein chains, the first crude cells, the creation of photosynthesis, the invention of sexual reproduction, and so on. Stanley Miller never claimed to have created life, just some of its building blocks. While these theories are by no means robust and are still subject to lively scientific debate, there is a reasonable explanation for how you get from the Big Bang to the Big Brain in the known universe using the known laws of nature.

Scientifically Based Arguments and Answers

13. Population statistics demonstrate that if we extrapolate backward from the present population using the current rate of population growth, there were only two people living approximately 6,300 years before the present (4300 B.C.E.). This proves that humans and civilization are quite young. If the Earth were old—say, one million years—over the course of 25,000 generations at a 0.5 percent rate of population growth and an average of 2.5 children per family, the present population would be 10 to the power of 2,100 people, which is impossible since there are only 10 to the power of 130 electrons in the known universe.

If you want to play the numbers game, how about this? Applying their model, we find that in 2600 B.C.E. the total population on Earth would have been around 600 people. We know with a high degree of certainty that in 2600 B.C.E. there were flourishing civilizations in Egypt, Mesopotamia, the Indus River Valley, and China. If we give Egypt an extremely generous one-sixth of the world's population, then 100 people built the pyramids, not to mention all the other architectural monuments—they most certainly needed a miracle or two . . . or perhaps the assistance of ancient astronauts!

The fact is that populations do not grow in a steady manner. There are booms and busts, and the history of the human population before the Industrial Revolution is one of prosperity and growth, followed by famine and decline, and punctuated by disaster. In Europe, for instance, about half of the population was killed by a plague during the sixth century, and in the fourteenth century the bubonic plague wiped out about one-third of the population in three years. As humans struggled for millennia to fend off extinction, the population curve was one of peaks and valleys as it climbed uncertainly but steadily upward. It is only since the nineteenth century that the rate of increase has been steadily accelerating.

14. Natural selection can never account for anything other than minor changes within species—microevolution. Mutations used by evolutionists to explain macroevolution are always harmful, rare, and random, and cannot be the driving force of evolutionary change.

I shall never forget the four words pounded into the brains of the students of evolutionary biologist Bayard Brattstrom at California State University, Fullerton: "Mutants are not monsters." His point was that the public perception of mutants—two-headed cows and the like at the county fair—is not the sort of mutants evolutionists are discussing. Most mutations are small genetic or chromosomal aberrations that have small effects—slightly keener hearing, a new shade of fur. Some of these small effects may provide benefits to an organism in an ever-changing environment.

Moreover, Ernst Mayr's (1970) theory of *allopatric speciation* seems to demonstrate precisely how natural selection, in conjunction with other forces and contingencies of nature, can and does produce new species. Whether they agree or disagree with the theory of allopatric speciation and punctuated equilibrium, scientists all agree that natural selection can produce significant change. The debate is over how much change, how rapid a change, and what other forces of nature act in conjunction with or contrary to natural selection. No one, and I mean no one, working in the field is debating whether natural selection is the driving force behind evolution, much less whether evolution happened or not.

15. There are no transitional forms in the fossil record, anywhere, including and especially humans. The whole fossil record is an embarrassment to evolutionists. Neanderthal specimens, for example, are diseased skeletons distorted by arthritis, rickets, and other diseases that create the bowed legs, brow ridge, and larger skeletal structure. *Homo erectus* **and** *Australopithecus* **are just apes.**

Creationists always quote Darwin's famous passage in the *Origin of Species* in which he asks, "Why then is not every geological formation and every stratum full of such intermediate links? Geology assuredly does not reveal any such finely graduated organic chain; and this, perhaps, is the gravest objection which can be urged against my theory" (1859, p. 310). Creationists end the quote there and ignore the rest of Darwin's chapter, in which he addresses the problem.

One answer is that plenty of examples of transitional forms have been discovered since Darwin's time. Just look in any paleontology text. The fossil *Archeopteryx*—part reptile, part bird—is a classic example of a transitional form. In my debate with Duane Gish, I presented a slide of the newly discovered *Ambulocetus natans*—a beautiful example of a transitional form from land mammal to whale (see *Science*, January 14, 1994, p. 180). And the charges about the Neanderthals and *Homo erectus* are simply absurd. We now have a treasure trove of human transitional forms.

A second answer is a rhetorical one. Creationists demand just one transitional fossil. When you give it to them, they then claim there is a gap between these two fossils and ask you to present a transitional form between these two. If you do, there are now two more gaps in the fossil record, and so on ad infinitum. Simply pointing this out refutes the argument. You can do it with cups on a table, showing how each time the gap is filled with a cup it creates two gaps, which when each is filled with a cup creates four gaps, and so on. The absurdity of the argument is visually striking.

A third answer was provided in 1972 by Eldredge and Gould, when they argued that gaps in the fossil record do not indicate missing data of slow and stately change; rather, "missing" fossils are evidence of rapid and episodic change (punctuated equilibrium). Using Mayr's allopatric speciation, where small and unstable "founder" populations are isolated at the periphery of the larger population's range, Eldredge and Gould showed that the relatively rapid change in this smaller gene pool creates new species but leaves behind few, if any, fossils. The process of fossilization is rare and infrequent anyway, but it is almost nonexistent during these times of rapid speciation because the number of individuals is small and the change is swift. A lack of fossils may be evidence for rapid change, not missing evidence for gradual evolution.

16. The Second Law of Thermodynamics proves that evolution cannot be true since evolutionists state that the universe and life move from chaos to order and simple to complex, the exact opposite of the entropy predicted by the Second Law.

First of all, on any scale other than the grandest of all—the 600-million-year history of life on Earth—species do not evolve from simple to complex, and nature does not simply move from chaos to order. The history of life is checkered with false starts, failed experiments, local and mass extinctions, and chaotic restarts. It is anything but a neat Time/Life-book foldout from single cells to humans. Even in the big picture, the Second Law allows for such change because the Earth is in a system that has a constant input of energy from the Sun. As long as the Sun is burning, life may continue thriving and evolving, automobiles may be prevented from rusting, burgers can be heated in ovens, and all manner of other things in apparent violation of the Second Law may continue. But as soon as the Sun burns out, entropy will take over and life will cease and chaos come again. The Second Law of Thermodynamics applies to closed, isolated systems. Since the Earth receives a constant input of energy from the Sun, entropy may decrease and order increase (although the Sun itself is running down in the process). Thus, because the Earth is not strictly a closed system, life may evolve without violating natural laws. In addition, recent research in chaos theory suggests that order can and does spontaneously generate out of apparent chaos, all without violating the Second Law of Thermodynamics (see Kauffman 1993). Evolution no more breaks the Second Law of Thermodynamics than one breaks the law of gravity by jumping up.

17. Even the simplest of life forms are too complex to have come together by random chance. Take a simple organism consisting of merely 100 parts. Mathematically there are 10 to the power of 158 possible ways for the parts to link up. There are not enough molecules in the universe, or time since the beginning, to allow for these possible ways to come together in even this simple life form, let alone to produce human beings. The human eye alone defies explanation by the randomness of evolution. It is the equivalent of the monkey typing *Hamlet*, or even "To be or not to be." It will not happen by random chance.

Natural selection is not random, nor does it operate by chance. Natural selection preserves the gains and eradicates the mistakes. The eye evolved from a single, light-sensitive cell into the complex eye of today through hundreds if not thousands of intermediate steps, many of which still exist in nature (see Dawkins 1986). In order for the monkey to type the thirteen letters opening Hamlet's soliloquy by chance, it would take 26 to the power of 13 trials for success. This is sixteen times as great as the total number of seconds that have elapsed in the lifetime of our solar system. But if each correct letter is preserved and each incorrect letter eradicated, the process operates much faster. How much faster? Richard Hardison (1988) wrote a computer program in which letters were "selected" for or against, and it took an average of only 335.2 trials to produce the sequence of letters TOBEORNOTTOBE. It takes the computer less than ninety seconds. The entire play can be done in about 4.5 days.

18. Hydrodynamic sorting during the Flood explains the apparent progression of fossils in geological strata. The simple, ignorant organisms died in the sea and are on the bottom layers, while more complex, smarter, and faster organisms died higher up.

Not one trilobite floated upward to a higher stratum? Not one dumb horse was on the beach and drowned in a lower stratum? Not one flying pterodactyl made it above the Cretaceous layer? Not one moronic human did not come in out of the rain? And what about the evidence provided by other dating techniques such as radiometry?

19. The dating techniques of evolutionists are inconsistent, unreliable, and wrong. They give false impressions of an old Earth, when in fact it is no older than ten thousand years, as proven by Dr. Thomas Barnes from the University of Texas at El Paso when he demonstrated that the half-life of the Earth's magnetic field is 1,400 years.

First of all, Barnes's magnetic field argument assumes that the decay of the magnetic field is linear when geophysics has demonstrated that it fluctuates through time. He is working from a false premise. Second, not only are the various dating techniques quite reliable on their own but there is considerable independent corroboration between them. For example, radiometric dates for different elements from the same rock will all converge on the same date. Finally, how can creationists dismiss all dating techniques with a sweep of the hand except those that purportedly support their position?

20. Classification of organisms above the species level is arbitrary and man-made. Taxonomy proves nothing, especially because so many of the links between species are missing.

The science of classification is indeed man-made, like all sciences, and of course it cannot prove anything about the evolution of organisms absolutely. But its grouping of organisms is anything but arbitrary, even though there is an element of subjectivity to it. An interesting crosscultural test of taxonomy is the fact that Western-trained biologists and native peoples from New Guinea identify the same types of birds as separate species (see Mayr 1988). Such groupings really do exist in nature. Moreover, the goal of modern cladistics—the science of classification through nested hierarchies of similarities—is to make taxonomy less subjective, and it successfully uses inferred evolutionary relationships to arrange taxa in a branching hierarchy such that all members of a given taxon have the same ancestors.

21. If evolution is gradual, there should be no gaps between species.

Evolution is not always gradual. It is often quite sporadic. And evolutionists never said there should not be gaps. Finally, gaps do not prove creation any more than blank spots in human history prove that all civilizations were spontaneously created.

22. "Living fossils" like the coelacanth and horseshoe crab prove that all life was created at once.

The existence of living fossils (organisms that have not changed for millions of years) simply means that they evolved a structure adequate for their relatively static and unchanging environment, so they stopped once they could maintain their ecological niche. Sharks and many other sea creatures are relatively unchanged over millions of years, while other sea creatures, such as marine mammals, have obviously changed rapidly and dramatically. Evolutionary change or lack of change, as the case may be, all depends on how and when a species' immediate environment changes.

23. The incipient structure problem refutes natural selection. A new structure that evolves slowly over time would not provide an advantage to the organism in its beginning or intermediate stages, only when it is completely developed, which can only happen by special creation. What good is 5 percent of a wing, or 55 percent? You need all or nothing.

A poorly developed wing may have been a well-developed something else, like a thermoregulator for ectothermic reptiles (who depend on external sources of heat). And it is not true that incipient stages are completely useless. As Richard Dawkins argues in *The Blind Watchmaker* (1986) and *Climbing Mount Improbable* (1996), 5 percent vision is significantly better than none and being able to get airborne for any length of time can provide an adaptive advantage.

24. Homologous structures (the wing of a bat, the flipper of a whale, the arm of a human) are proof of intelligent design.

By invoking miracles and special providence, the creationist can pick and choose anything in nature as proof of God's work and then ignore the rest. Homologous structures actually make no sense in a special creation paradigm. Why should a whale have the same bones in its flipper as a human has in its arm and a bat has in its wing? God has a limited imagination? God was testing out the possibilities of His designs? God just wanted to do things that way? Surely an omnipotent intelligent designer could have done better. Homologous structures are indicative of descent with modification, not divine creation.

25. The whole history of evolutionary theory in particular and science in general is the history of mistaken theories and overthrown ideas. Nebraska Man, Piltdown Man, Calaveras Man, and *Hesperopithecus* are just a few of the blunders scientists have made. Clearly science cannot be trusted and modern theories are no better than past ones.

Again, it is paradoxical for creationists to simultaneously draw on the authority of science and attack the basic workings of science. Furthermore, this argument reveals a gross misunderstanding of the nature of science. Science does not just change. It constantly builds upon the ideas of the past, and it is cumulative toward the future. Scientists do make

mistakes aplenty and, in fact, this is how science progresses. The self-correcting feature of the scientific method is one of its most beautiful features. Hoaxes like Piltdown Man and honest mistakes like *Hesperopithecus* are, in time, exposed. Science picks itself up, shakes itself off, and moves on.

Debates and Truth

These twenty-five answers only scratch the surface of the science and philosophy supporting evolutionary theory. If confronted by a creationist, we would be wise to heed the words of Stephen Jay Gould, who has encountered creationists on many an occasion:

> Debate is an art form. It is about the winning of arguments. It is not about the discovery of truth. There are certain rules and procedures to debate that really have nothing to do with establishing fact—which they are very good at. Some of those rules are: never say anything positive about your own position because it can be attacked, but chip away at what appear to be the weaknesses in your opponent's position. They are good at that. I don't think I could beat the creationists at debate. I can tie them. But in courtrooms they are terrible, because in courtrooms you cannot give speeches. In a courtroom you have to answer direct questions about the positive status of your belief. We destroyed them in Arkansas. On the second day of the two-week trial, we had our victory party! (Caltech lecture, 1985)

References

Berra, T.M. 1990. *Evolution and the Myth of Creationism: A Basic Guide to the Facts in the Evolution Debate*. Stanford, Calif.: Stanford University Press.

Bowler, P.J. 1989. *Evolution: The History of an Idea*, rev. ed. Berkeley: University of California Press.

Darwin, Charles. 1859. *On the Origin of Species by Means of Natural Selection: Or the Preservation of Favored Species in the Struggle for Life. A Facsimile of the First Edition*. Cambridge, Mass.: Harvard University Press, 1964.

Dawkins, R. 1986. *The Blind Watchmaker*. New York: Norton.

——— 1995. Darwin's Dangerous Disciple: An Interview With Richard Dawkins. *Skeptic* 3(4): 80–85.

——— 1996. *Climbing Mount Improbable*. New York: Norton.

Dennett, D.C. 1995. *Darwin's Dangerous Idea: Evolution and the Meaning of Life*. New York: Simon & Schuster.

Desmond, A., and J. Moore. 1991. *Darwin: The Life of a Tormented Evolutionist*. New York: Warner.

Eldredge, N. 1971. The Allopatric Model and Phylogeny in Paleozoic Invertebrates. *Evolution* 25: 156–167.

————— 1985. *Time Frames: The Rethinking of Darwinian Evolution and the Theory of Punctuated Equilibrium*. New York: Simon & Schuster.

Eldredge, N., and S.J. Gould. 1972. Punctuated Equilibria: An Alternative to Phyletic Gradualism. In *Models in Paleobiology*, ed. T.J.M. Schopf. San Francisco: Freeman, Cooper.

Eve, R.A., and F.B. Harrold. 1991. *The Creationist Movement in Modern America*. Boston: Twayne.

Futuyama, D.J. 1983. *Science on Trial: The Case for Evolution*. New York: Pantheon.

Gilkey, L. ed. 1985. *Creationism on Trial: Evolution and God at Little Rock*. New York: Harper & Row.

Godfrey, L.R. ed. 1983. *Scientists Confront Creationism*. New York: Norton.

Gould, S.J. 1983a. *Hens's Teeth and Horse's Toes*. New York: Norton.

————— 1985. *The Flamingo's Smile*. New York: Norton.

————— 1989. *Wonderful Life*. New York: Norton.

————— 1991. *Bully for Brontosaurus*. New York: Norton.

Hardison, R.C. 1988. *Upon the Shoulders of Giants*. New York: University Press of America.

Kauffmann, S.A. 1993. *The Origins of Order: Self-Organization and Selection in Evolution*. New York: Oxford University Press.

Lindberg, D.C., and R.L. Numbers. 1986. *God and Nature*. Berkeley: University of California Press.

Mayr, E. 1970. *Populations, Species, and Evolution*. Cambridge, Mass.: Harvard University Press.

————— 1982. *Growth of Biological Thought*. Cambridge, Mass.: Harvard University Press.

————— 1988. *Toward a Philosophy of Biology*. Cambridge, Mass.: Harvard University Press.

Numbers, R. 1992. *The Creationists*. New York: Knopf.

Rohr, R. ed. 1986. *Science and Religion*. St. Paul, Minn.: Greenhaven.

Ruse, M. 1982. *Darwinism Defended*. Reading, Mass.: Addison-Wesley.

Somit, A., and S.A. Peterson. 1992. *The Dynamics of Evolution*. Ithaca, NY: Cornell University Press.

Strahler, A.N. 1987. *Science and Earth History: The Evolution/Creation Controversy*. Buffalo, NY: Prometheus.

Tipler, F. 1994. *The Physics of Immortality*. New York: Doubleday.

"CONFRONTING CREATIONISTS"

Michael Shermer

1) What are the three models that Shermer suggests are representative of the range of beliefs that people have regarding the relationship between science and religion?

2) What tactics have creationists used to protect their beliefs from the impact of science?

3) Does Shermer consider refuting creationist ideas to be an attack on religion? Do you believe this? Why or why not?

4) Discuss in broad outline evolutionary theory using Shermer's summary.

5) Select one or two arguments employed by creationists and using Feder's "Epistemology . . ." article ask the following questions about the arguments:

   a) Does the argument follow the four operating principles of science that Feder defines?

   b) What are the scientific, social, legal, and religious issues involved?

   c) Does this creationist argument (and thus creationism) fit the definition of a *theory* as employed in science?

THE PRICE OF PROGRESS

John Bodley

Until recently, government planners have always considered economic development and progress beneficial goals that all societies should want to strive toward. The social advantages of progress—as defined in terms of increased incomes, higher standards of living, greater security, and better health—are thought to be positive, *universal* goods, to be obtained at any price. Although one may argue that tribal peoples must sacrifice their traditional cultures to obtain these benefits, government planners generally feel that this is a small price to pay for such obvious advantages.

Evidence demonstrates that autonomous tribal peoples have not *chosen* progress to enjoy its advantages, but that governments have *pushed* progress upon them to obtain tribal resources, not primarily to share with the tribal peoples the benefits of progress. It has also been shown that the price of forcing progress on unwilling recipients has involved the deaths of millions of tribal people, as well as their loss of land, political sovereignty, and the right to follow their own life style. This chapter does not attempt to further summarize that aspect of the cost of progress, but instead analyzes the specific effects of the participation of tribal peoples in the world-market economy. In direct opposition to the usual interpretation, it is argued here that the benefits of progress are often both illusory and detrimental to tribal peoples when they have not been allowed to control their own resources and define their relationship to the market economy.

Progress and the Quality of Life

One of the primary difficulties in assessing the benefits of progress and economic development for any culture is that of establishing a meaningful measure of both benefit and detriment. It is widely recognized that *standard of living*, which is the most frequently used measure of progress, is an intrinsically ethnocentric concept relying heavily upon indicators that lack universal cultural relevance. Such factors as GNP, per capita income, capital formation, employment rates, literacy, formal education, consumption of manufactured goods, number of doctors and hospital beds per thousand persons, and the amount of money spent on government welfare and health programs may be irrelevant measures of actual *quality* of life for autonomous or even semiautonomous tribal cultures. In its 1954 report, the Trust Territory government indicated that since the Micronesian population was still largely satisfying its own needs within a cashless subsistence economy, "Money income is not a significant measure of living standards, production, or well-being in this area" (TTR, 1955:44). Unfortunately, within a short time the government began to rely on an enumeration of certain imported goods as indicators of a higher standard of living in the islands, even though many tradition-oriented islanders felt that these new goods symbolized a lowering of the quality of life.

A more useful measure of the benefits of progress might be based on a formula for evaluating cultures devised by Goldschmidt (1952:135). According to these less ethnocentric criteria, the important question to ask is: Does progress or economic development increase or decrease a given culture's ability to satisfy the physical and psychological needs of its population, or its stability? This question is a far more direct measure of quality of life than are the standard economic correlates of development, and it is universally relevant. Specific indication of this *standard* of living could be found for any society in the nutritional status and general physical and mental health of its population, the incidence of crime and delinquency, the demographic structure, family stability, and the society's relationship to its natural resource base. A society with high rates of malnutrition and crime, and one degrading its natural environment to the extent of threatening its continued existence, might be described as at a lower standard of living than is another society where these problems did not exist.

Careful examination of the data, which compare, on these specific points, the former condition of self-sufficient tribal peoples with their condition following their incorporation into the world-market eco-nomy, leads to the conclusion that their standard of living is *lowered*, not raised, by economic progress—and often to a dramatic degree. This is perhaps the most outstanding and inescapable fact to emerge from the years of research that anthropologists have devoted to the study of culture change and modernization. Despite the best intentions of those who have promoted change and improvement, all too often the results have been poverty, longer working hours, and much greater physical exertion, poor health, social disorder, discontent, discrimination, overpopulation, and environmental deterioration—combined with the destruction of the traditional culture.

Diseases of Development

> Perhaps it would be useful for public health specialists to start talking about a new category of diseases . . . Such diseases could be called the "diseases of development" and would consist of those pathological conditions which are based on the usually unanticipated consequences of the implementation of development schemes [Hughes & Hunter, 1972:93].

Economic development increases the disease rate of affected peoples in at least three ways. First, to the extent that development is successful, it makes developed populations suddenly become vulnerable to all of the diseases suffered almost exclusively by "advanced" peoples. Among these are diabetes, obesity, hypertension, and a variety of circulatory problems. Second, development disturbs traditional environmental balances and may dramatically increase certain bacterial and parasite diseases. Finally, when development goals prove unattainable, an assortment of poverty diseases may appear in association with the crowded conditions of urban slums and the general breakdown in traditional socioeconomic systems.

Outstanding examples of the first situation can be seen in the Pacific, where some of the most successfully developed native peoples are found. In Micronesia, where development has progressed more rapidly than perhaps anywhere else, between 1958 and 1972 the population doubled, but the number of patients treated for heart disease in the local hospitals nearly tripled, mental disorder increased eightfold, and by 1972 hypertension and nutritional deficiencies began to make significant appearances for the first time (TTR, 1959,1973, statistical tables).

Although some critics argue that the Micronesian figures simply represent better health monitoring due to economic progress, rigorously controlled data from Polynesia show a similar trend. The progressive acquisition of modern degenerative diseases was documented by an eight-member team of New Zealand medical specialists, anthropologists, and nutritionists, whose research was funded by the Medical Research Council of New Zealand and the World Health Organization. These researchers investigated the health status of a genetically related population at various points along a continuum of increasing cash income, modernizing diet, and urbanization. The extremes on this acculturation continuum were represented by the relatively traditional Pukapukans of the Cook Islands and the essentially Europeanized New Zealand Maori, while the busily developing Rarotongans, also of the Cook Islands, occupied the intermediate position. In 1971, after eight years of work, the team's preliminary findings were summarized by Dr. Ian Prior, cardiologist and leader of the research, as follows:

> We are beginning to observe that the more an islander takes on the ways of the West, the more prone he is to succumb to our degenerative diseases. In fact, it does not seem too much to say our evidence now shows that the farther the Pacific natives move from the quiet, care-free life of their ancestors, the closer they come to gout, diabetes, atherosclerosis, obesity, and hypertension [Prior, 1971:2].

In Pukapuka, where progress was limited by the island's small size and its isolated location some 480 kilometers from the nearest port, the annual per capita income was only about thirty-six dollars and the economy remained essentially at a subsistence level. Resources were limited and the area was visited by trading ships only three or four times a year; thus, there was little opportunity for intensive economic development. Predictably, the population of Pukapuka was characterized by relatively low levels of imported sugar and salt intake, and a presumably related low level of heart disease, high blood pressure, and diabetes. In Rarotonga, where economic success was introducing town life, imported food, and motorcycles, sugar and salt intakes nearly tripled, high blood pressure increased approximately ninefold, diabetes two to threefold, and heart disease doubled for men and more than quadrupled for women, while the number of grossly obese women increased more than tenfold. Among the New Zealand Maori, sugar intake was nearly eight times that of the Pukapukans, gout in men was nearly double its rate on Pukapuka, and diabetes in men was more than fivefold higher, while heart disease in women had increased more than sixfold. The Maori were, in fact, dying of "European" diseases at a greater rate than was the average New Zealand European.

Government development policies designed to bring about changes in local hydrology, vegetation, and settlement patterns and to increase population mobility, and even programs aimed at reducing certain diseases, have frequently led to dramatic increases in disease rates because of the unforeseen effects of disturbing the preexisting order. Hughes and Hunter (1972) published an excellent survey of cases in which development led directly to increased disease rates in Africa. They concluded that hasty development intervention in relatively balanced local cultures and environments resulted in "a drastic deterioration in the social and economic conditions of life."

Traditional populations in general have presumably learned to live with the endemic pathogens of their environments, and in some cases they have evolved genetic adaptations to specific diseases, such as the sickle-cell trait, which provided an immunity to malaria. Unfortunately, however, outside intervention has entirely changed this picture. In the late 1960s, sleeping sickness suddenly increased in many areas of Africa and even spread to areas where it did not formerly occur, due to the building of new roads and migratory labor, both of which caused increased population movement. Large-scale relocation schemes, such as the Zande Scheme, had disastrous results when natives were moved from their traditional disease-free refuges into infected areas. Dams and irrigation developments inadvertently created ideal conditions for the rapid proliferation of snails carrying schistosomiasis (a liver fluke disease), and major epidemics suddenly occurred in areas where this disease had never before been a problem. DDT spraying programs have been temporarily successful in controlling malaria, but there is often a rebound effect that increases the problem when spraying is discontinued, and the malarial mosquitoes are continually evolving resistant strains.

Urbanization is one of the prime measures of development, but it is a mixed blessing for most former tribal peoples. Urban health standards are abysmally poor and generally worse than in rural areas for the detribalized individuals who have crowded into the towns and cities throughout Africa, Asia, and Latin America seeking wage employment out of new economic necessity. Infectious diseases related to crowding and poor sanitation are rampant in urban centers, while greatly increased stress and poor nutrition aggravate a variety of other health problems. Malnutrition and other diet-related conditions are, in fact, one of the characteristic hazards of progress faced by tribal peoples and are discussed in the following sections.

The Hazards of Dietary Change

The traditional diets of tribal peoples are admirably adapted to their nutritional needs and available food resources. Even though these diets may seem bizarre, absurd, and unpalatable to outsiders, they are unlikely to be improved by drastic modifications. Given the delicate balances and complexities involved in any subsistence system, change always involves risks, but for tribal people the effects of dietary change have been catastrophic.

Under normal conditions, food habits are remarkably resistant to change, and indeed people are unlikely to abandon their traditional diets voluntarily in favor of dependence on difficult-to-obtain exotic imports. In some cases it is true that imported foods may be identified with powerful outsiders and are therefore sought as symbols of greater prestige. This may lead to such absurdities as Amazonian Indians choosing to consume imported canned tunafish when abundant high-quality fish is available in their own rivers. Another example of this situation occurs in tribes where mothers prefer to feed their infants expensive and nutritionally inadequate canned milk from unsanitary, but *high-status,* baby bottles. The high status of these items is often promoted by clever traders and clever advertising campaigns.

Aside from these apparently voluntary changes, it appears that more often dietary changes are forced upon unwilling tribal peoples by circumstances beyond their control. In some areas, new food crops have been introduced by government decree, or as a consequence of forced relocation or other policies designed to end hunting, pastoralism, or shifting cultivation. Food habits have also been modified by massive disruption of the natural environment by outsiders—as when sheepherders transformed the Australian Aborigine's foraging territory or when European invaders destroyed the bison herds that were the primary element in the Plains Indians' subsistence patterns. Perhaps the most frequent cause of diet change occurs when formerly self-sufficient peoples find that wage labor, cash cropping, and other economic development activities that feed tribal resources into the world-market economy must inevitably divert time and energy away from the production of subsistence foods. Many developing peoples suddenly discover that, like it or not, they are unable to secure traditional foods and must spend their newly acquired cash on costly, and often nutritionally inferior, manufactured foods.

Overall, the available data seem to indicate that the dietary changes that are linked to involvement in the world-market economy have tended to *lower* rather than raise the nutritional levels of the affected tribal peoples. Specifically, the vitamin, mineral, and protein components of their diets are often drastically reduced and replaced by enormous increases in starch and carbohydrates, often in the form of white flour and refined sugar.

Any deterioration in the quality of a given population's diet is almost certain to be reflected in an increase in deficiency diseases and a general decline in health status. Indeed, as tribal peoples have shifted to a diet based on imported manufactured or processed foods, there has been a dramatic rise in malnutrition, a massive increase in dental problems, and a variety of other nutrition-related disorders. Nutritional physiology is so complex that even well-meaning dietary changes have had tragic consequences. In many areas of Southeast Asia, government-sponsored protein supplementation programs supplying milk to protein-deficient populations caused unexpected health problems and increased mortality. Officials failed to anticipate that in cultures where adults do not normally drink milk, the enzymes needed to digest it are no longer produced and milk *intolerance* results (Davis & Bolin, 1972). In Brazil, a similar milk distribution program caused an epidemic of permanent blindness by aggravating a preexisting vitamin A deficiency (Bunce, 1972).

Teeth and Progress

There is nothing new in the observation that savages, or peoples living under primitive conditions, have, in general excellent teeth . . . Nor is it news that most civilized populations possess wretched teeth which begin to decay almost before they have erupted completely, and that dental caries is likely to be accompanied by periodontal disease with further reaching complications [Hooton, 1945:xviii].

Anthropologists have long recognized that undisturbed tribal peoples are often in excellent physical condition. And it has often been noted specifically that dental caries and the other dental abnormalities that plague industrialized societies are absent or rare among tribal peoples who have retained their traditional diets. The fact that tribal food habits may contribute to the development of sound teeth, whereas modernized diets may do just the opposite, was illustrated as long ago as 1894 in an article in the *Journal of the Royal Anthropological Institute* that described the results of a comparison between the teeth of ten Sioux Indians and a comparable group of Londoners (Smith, 1894:109–116). The Indians were examined when they came to London as members of Buffalo Bill's Wild West Show and were found to be completely free of caries and in possession of all their teeth, even though half of the group were over thirty-nine years of age. Londoners' teeth were conspicuous for both their caries and their steady reduction in number with advancing age. The difference was attributed primarily to the

wear and polishing caused by the traditional Indian diet of coarse food and the fact that they chewed their food longer, encouraged by the absence of tableware.

One of the most remarkable studies of the dental conditions of tribal peoples and the impact of dietary change was conducted in the 1930s by Weston Price (1945), an American dentist who was interested in determining what caused normal, healthy teeth. Between 1931 and 1936, Price systematically explored tribal areas throughout the world to locate and examine the most isolated peoples who were still living on traditional foods. His fieldwork covered Alaska, the Canadian Yukon, Hudson Bay, Vancouver Island, Florida, the Andes, the Amazon, Samoa, Tahiti, New Zealand, Australia, New Caledonia, Fiji, the Torres Strait, East Africa, and the Nile. The study demonstrated both the superior quality of aboriginal dentition and the devastation that occurs as modern diets are adopted. In nearly every area where traditional foods were still being eaten, Price found perfect teeth with normal dental arches and virtually no decay, whereas caries and abnormalities increased steadily as new diets were adopted. In many cases the change was sudden and striking. Among Eskimo groups subsisting entirely on traditional food he found caries totally absent, whereas in groups eating a considerable quantity of store-bought food approximately 20 percent of their teeth were decayed. The figure rose to more than 30 percent with Eskimo groups subsisting almost exclusively on purchased or government-supplied food, and reached an incredible 48 percent among the Vancouver Island Indians. Unfortunately for many of these people, modern dental treatment did not accompany the new food, and their suffering was appalling. The loss of teeth was, of course, bad enough in itself, and it certainly undermined the population's resistance to many new diseases, including tuberculosis. But new foods were also accompanied by crowded, misplaced teeth, gum diseases, distortion of the face, and pinching of the nasal cavity. Abnormalities in the dental arch appeared in the new generation following the change in diet, while caries appeared almost immediately even in adults.

Price reported that in many areas the affected peoples were conscious of their own physical deterioration. At a mission school in Africa, the principal asked him to explain to the native school children why they were not physically as strong as children who had had no contact with schools. On an island in the Torres Strait the natives knew exactly what was causing their problems and resisted—almost to the point of bloodshed—government efforts to establish a store that would make imported food available. The government prevailed, however, and Price was able to establish a relationship between the length of time the government store had been established and the increasing incidences of caries among a population that showed an almost 100 percent immunity to them before the store had been opened.

In New Zealand, the Maori, who in their aboriginal state are often considered to have been among the healthiest, most perfectly developed of peoples, were found to have "advanced" the furthest. According to Price:

> Their modernization was demonstrated not only by the high incidence of dental caries but also by the fact 90 percent of the adults and 100 percent of the children had abnormalities of the dental arches [Price, 1945:206].

Malnutrition

Malnutrition, particularly in the form of protein deficiency, has become a critical problem for tribal peoples who must adopt new economic patterns. Population pressures, cash cropping, and government programs all have tended to encourage the replacement of traditional crops and other food sources that were rich in protein with substitutes high in calories but low in protein. In Africa, for example, protein-rich staples such as millet and sorghum are being replaced systematically by high-yielding manioc and plantains, which have insignificant amounts of protein. The problem is increased for cash croppers and wage laborers whose earnings are too low and unpredictable to allow purchase of adequate amounts of protein. In some rural areas, agricultural laborers have been forced systematically to deprive nonproductive members (principally children) of their households of their minimal nutritional requirements to satisfy the need of the productive members. This process has been documented in northeastern Brazil following the introduction of large-scale sisal plantations (Gross & Underwood, 1971). In urban centers the difficulties of obtaining nutritionally adequate diets are even more serious for tribal immigrants, because costs are higher and poor-quality foods are more tempting.

One of the most tragic, and largely overlooked, aspects of chronic malnutrition is that it can lead to abnormally undersized brain development and apparently irreversible brain damage; it has been associated with various forms of mental impairment or retardation. Malnutrition has been linked clinically with mental retardation in both Africa and Latin America (see, for example, Mönckeberg, 1968), and this appears to be a worldwide phenomenon with serious implications (Montagu, 1972).

Optimistic supporters of progress will surely say that all of these new health problems are being overstressed and that the introduction of hospitals, clinics, and the other modern health institutions will overcome or at least compensate for all of these difficulties. However, it appears that uncontrolled population growth and economic impoverishment probably will keep most of these benefits out of reach for many tribal peoples, and the intervention of modern medicine has at least partly contributed to the problem in the first place.

The generalization that civilization frequently has a broad negative impact on tribal health has found broad empirical support (see especially Kroeger & Barbira-Freedman [1982] on Amazonia; Reinhard [1976] on the Arctic; and Wirsing [1985] globally), but these conclusions have not gone unchallenged. Some critics argue that tribal health was often poor before modernization, and they point specifically to tribals' low life expectancy and high infant mortality rates. Demographic statistics on tribal populations are often problematic because precise data are scarce, but they do show a less favorable profile than that enjoyed by many industrial societies. However, it should be remembered that our present life expectancy is a recent phenomenon that has been very costly in terms of medical research and technological advances. Furthermore, the benefits of our health system are not enjoyed equally by all members of our society. High infant mortality could be viewed as a relatively inexpensive and egalitarian tribal public health program that offered the reasonable expectation of a healthy and productive life for those surviving to age fifteen.

Some critics also suggest that certain tribal populations, such as the New Guinea highlanders, were "stunted" by nutritional deficiencies created by tribal culture and are "improved" by "acculturation" and cash cropping (Dennett & Connell, 1988). Although this argument does suggest that the health question requires careful evaluation, it does not invalidate the empirical generalizations already established. Nutritional deficiencies undoubtedly occurred in densely populated zones in the central New Guinea highlands. However, the specific case cited above may not be widely representative of other tribal groups even in New Guinea, and it does not address the facts of outside intrusion or the inequities inherent in the contemporary development process.

Ecocide

"How is it," asked a herdsman . . . "how is it that these hills can no longer give pasture to my cattle? In my father's day they were green and cattle thrived there; today there is no grass and my cattle starve." As one looked one saw that what had once been a green hill had become a raw red rock [Jones, 1931].

Progress not only brings new threats to the health of tribal peoples, but it also imposes new strains on the ecosystems upon which they must depend for their ultimate survival. The introduction of new technology, increased consumption, lowered mortality, and the eradication of all traditional controls have combined to replace what for most tribal peoples was a relatively stable balance between population and natural resources, with a new system that is imbalanced. Economic development is forcing *ecocide* on peoples who were once careful stewards of their resources. There is already a trend toward widespread environmental deterioration in tribal areas, involving resource depletion, erosion, plant and animal extinction, and a disturbing series of other previously unforeseen changes.

After the initial depopulation suffered by most tribal peoples during their engulfment by frontiers of national expansion, most tribal populations began to experience rapid growth. Authorities generally attribute this growth to the introduction of modern medicine and new health measures and the termination of intertribal warfare, which lowered mortality rates, as well as to new technology, which increased food production. Certainly all of these factors played a part, but merely lowering mortality rates would not have produced the rapid population growth that most tribal areas have experienced if traditional birth-spacing mechanisms had not been eliminated at the same time. Regardless of which factors were most important, it is clear that all of the natural and cultural checks on population growth have suddenly been pushed aside by culture change, while tribal lands have been steadily reduced and consumption levels have risen. In many tribal areas, environmental deterioration due to overuse of resources has set in, and in other areas such deterioration is imminent as resources continue to dwindle relative to the expanding population and increased use. Of course, population expansion by tribal peoples may have positive political consequences, because where tribals can retain or regain their status as local majorities they may be in a more favorable position to defend their resources against intruders.

Swidden systems and pastoralism, both highly successful economic systems under traditional conditions, have proven particularly vulnerable to increased population pressures and outside efforts to raise productivity beyond its natural limits. Research in Amazonia demonstrates that population pressures and related resource depletion can be created indirectly by official policies that restrict swidden peoples to smaller territories. Resource depletion itself can then become a powerful means of forcing tribal people into participating in the world-market economy—thus leading to further resource depletion. For example, Bodley and Benson (1979) showed how the Shipibo Indians in Peru were forced to further deplete their forest resources by cash cropping in the forest area to replace the resources that had been destroyed earlier by the intensive cash cropping necessitated by the narrow confines of their reserve. In this case, a certain species of palm trees that had provided critical housing materials were destroyed by forest clearing and had to be replaced by costly purchased materials. Research by Gross and others (1979) showed similar processes at work among four tribal groups in central Brazil and demonstrated that the degree of market involvement increases directly with increases in resource depletion.

The settling of nomadic herders and the removal of prior controls on herd size have often led to serious overgrazing and erosion problems where these had not previously occurred. There are indications that the desertification problem in the Sahel region of Africa was aggravated by programs designed to settle nomads. The first sign of imbalance in a swidden system appears when the planting cycles are shortened to the point that garden plots are reused before sufficient forest regrowth can occur. If reclearing and planting continue in the same area, the natural pattern of forest succession may be disturbed irreversibly and the soil can be impaired permanently. An extensive tract of tropical rainforest in the lower Amazon of Brazil was reduced to a semi-arid desert in just fifty years through such a process (Ackermann, 1964). The soils in the Azande area are also now seriously threatened with laterization and other problems as a result of the government-promoted cotton development scheme (McNeil, 1972).

The dangers of overdevelopment and the vulnerability of local resource systems have long been recognized by both anthropologists and tribal peoples themselves, but the pressures for change have been overwhelming. In 1948 the Maya villagers of Chan Kom complained to Redfield (1962) about the shortening of their swidden cycles, which they correctly attributed to increasing population pressures. Redfield told them, however, that they had no choice but to go "forward with technology" (Redfield, 1962:178). In Assam, swidden cycles were shortened from an average of twelve years to only two or three within just twenty years, and anthropologists warned that the limits of swiddening would soon be reached (Burling, 1963:311–312). In the Pacific, anthropologists warned of population pressures on limited resources as early as the 1930s (Keesing, 1941:64–65). These warnings seemed fully justified, considering the fact that the crowded Tikopians were prompted by population pressures on their tiny island to suggest that infanticide be legalized. The warnings have been dramatically reinforced since then by the doubling of Micronesia's population in just the fourteen years between 1958 and 1972, from 70,600 to 114,615, while consumption levels have soared. By 1985 Micronesia's population had reached 162,321.

The environmental hazards of economic development and rapid population growth have become generally recognized only since worldwide concerns over environmental issues began in the early 1970s. Unfortunately, there is as yet little indication that the leaders of the now-developing nations are sufficiently concerned with environmental limitations. On the contrary governments are forcing tribal peoples into a self-reinforcing spiral of population growth and intensified resource exploitation, which may be stopped only by environmental disaster or the total impoverishment of the tribals.

The reality of ecocide certainly focuses attention on the fundamental contrasts between tribal and industrial systems in their use of natural resources. In many respects the entire "victims of progress" issue hinges on natural resources, who controls them, and how they are managed. Tribal peoples are victimized because they control resources that outsiders demand. The resources exist because tribals managed them conservatively. However, as with the issue of the health consequences of detribalization, some anthropologists minimize the adaptive achievements of tribal groups and seem unwilling to concede that ecocide might be a consequence of cultural change. Critics attack an exaggerated "noble savage" image of tribals living in perfect harmony with nature and having no visible impact on their surroundings. They then show that tribals do in fact modify the environment, and they conclude that there is no significant difference between how tribals and industrial societies treat their environments. For example, Charles Wagley declared that Brazilian Indians such as the Tapirape

are not "natural men." They have human vices just as we do. . . . They do not live "in tune" with nature any more than I do; in fact, they can often be as destructive of their environment, within their limitations, as some civilized men. The Tapirape are not innocent or childlike in any way [Wagley, 1977:302].

Anthropologist Terry Rambo demonstrated that the Semang of the Malaysian rain forests have measurable impact on their environment. In his monograph *Primitive Polluters*, Rambo (1985) reported that the Semang live in smoke-filled houses. They sneeze and spread germs, breathe, and thus emit carbon dioxide. They clear small gardens, contributing "particulate matter" to the air and disturbing the local climate because cleared areas proved measurably warmer and drier than the shady forest. Rambo concluded that his research "demonstrated the essential functional similarity of the environmental interactions of primitive and civilized societies" (1985:78) in contrast to a "noble savage" view (Bodley, 1983) which, according to Rambo (1985:2), mistakenly "claims that traditional peoples almost always live in essential harmony with their environment."

This is surely a false issue. To stress, as I do, that tribals tend to manage their resources for sustained yield within relatively self-sufficient subsistence economies is not to make them either innocent children or natural men. Nor is it to deny that tribals "disrupt" their environment and may never be in absolute "balance" with nature.

The ecocide issue is perhaps most dramatically illustrated by two sets of satellite photos taken over the Brazilian rain forests of Rôndonia (Allard & McIntyre, 1988:780–781). Photos taken in 1973, when Rôndonia was still a tribal domain, show virtually unbroken rain forest. The 1987 satellite photos, taken after just fifteen years of highway construction and "development" by outsiders, show more than 20 percent of the forest destroyed. The surviving Indians were being concentrated by FUNAI (Brazil's national Indian foundation) into what would soon become mere islands of forest in a ravaged landscape. It is irrelevant to quibble about whether tribals are noble, childlike, or innocent, or about the precise meaning of balance with nature, carrying capacity, or adaptation, to recognize that for the past 200 years rapid environmental deterioration on an unprecedented global scale has followed the wresting of control of vast areas of the world from tribal groups by resource-hungry industrial societies.

Deprivation and Discrimination

Contact with European culture has given them a knowledge of great wealth, opportunity and privilege, but only very limited avenues by which to acquire these things [Crocombe,1968].

Unwittingly, tribal peoples have had the burden of perpetual relative deprivation thrust upon them by acceptance either by themselves or by the governments administering them—of the standards of socioeconomic progress set for them by industrial civilizations. By comparison with the material wealth of industrial societies, tribal societies become, by definition, impoverished. They are then forced to transform their cultures and work to achieve what many economists now acknowledge to be unattainable goals. Even though in many cases the modest GNP goals set by development planners for the developing nations during the "development decade" of the 1960s were often met, the results were hardly noticeable for most of the tribal people involved. Population growth, environmental limitations, inequitable distribution of wealth, and the continued rapid growth of the industrialized nations have all meant that both the absolute and the relative gap between the rich and poor in the world is steadily widening. The prospect that tribal peoples will actually be able to attain the levels of resource consumption to which they are being encouraged to aspire is remote indeed except for those few groups who have retained effective control over strategic mineral resources.

Tribal peoples feel deprivation not only when the economic goals they have been encouraged to seek fail to materialize, but also when they discover that they are powerless, second-class citizens who are discriminated against and exploited by the dominant society. At the same time, they are denied the satisfactions of their traditional cultures, because these have been sacrificed in the process of modernization. Under the impact of major economic change family life is disrupted, traditional social controls are often lost, and many indicators of social anomie such as alcoholism, crime, delinquency, suicide, emotional disorders, and despair may increase. The inevitable frustration resulting from this continual deprivation finds expression in the cargo cults, revitalization movements, and a variety of other political and religious movements that have been widespread among tribal people following their disruption by industrial civilization.

References

Ackermann, F. L. 1964. *Geologia e Fisiografia da Região Bragantina, Estado do Pará.* Manaus, Brazil: Conselho Nacional de Pesquisas, Instituto Nacional de Pesquisas da Amazônia.

Allard, William Albert, and Loren McIntyre. 1988. Rôndonia's settlers invade Brazil's imperiled rain forest. *National Geographic* 174(6):772–799.

Bodley, John H. 1983. The World Bank tribal policy: Criticisms and recommendations. *Congressional Record,* serial no. 98–37, pp. 515–521. (Reprinted in Bodley, 1988.)

Bodley, John H., and Foley C. Benson. 1979. Cultural ecology of Amazonian palms. *Reports of Investigations,* no. 56. Pullman: Laboratory of Anthropology, Washington State University.

Bunce, George E. 1972. Aggravation of vitamin A deficiency following distribution of non-fortified skim milk: An example of nutrient interaction. In *The Careless Technology: Ecology and International Development,* ed. M. T. Farvar and John P. Milton, pp. 53–60. Garden City, N.Y.: Natural History Press.

Burling, Robbins. 1963. *Rengsanggri: Family and Kinship in a Garo Village.* Philadelphia: University of Pennsylvania Press.

Crocombe, Ron. 1968. Bougainville!: Copper, R. R. A. and secessionism. *New Guinea* 3(3):39–49.

Davis, A. E., and T. D. Bolin. 1972. Lactose intolerance in Southeast Asia. In *The Careless Technology: Ecology and International Development,* ed. M. T. Farvar and John P. Milton, pp.61 –68. Garden City, N.Y.: Natural History Press.

Dennett, Glenn, and John Connell. 1988. Acculturation and health in the highlands of Papua New Guinea. *Current Anthropology* 29(2):273–299.

Goldschmidt, Walter R. 1952. The interrelations between cultural factors and acquisition of new technical skills. In *The Progress of Underdeveloped Areas,* ed. Bert F. Hoselitz, pp. 135–151. Chicago: University of Chicago Press.

Gross, Daniel R., and Barbara A. Underwood. 1971. Technological change and caloric costs: Sisal agriculture. *American Anthropologist* 73(3):725–740.

Gross, Daniel R., et al. 1979. Ecology and acculturation among native peoples of Central Brazil. *Science* 206(4422):1043–1050.

Hooton, Earnest A. 1945. Introduction. In *Nutrition and Physical Degeneration: A Comparison of Primitive and Modern Diets and Their Effects* by Weston A. Price. Redlands, Calif.: The author.

Hughes, Charles C., and John M. Hunter. 1972. The role of technological development in promoting disease in Africa. In *The Careless Technology: Ecology and International Development*, ed. M. T. Farvar and John P. Milton, pp. 69–101. Garden City, N.Y.: Natural History Press.

Jones, J. D. Rheinallt. 1934. Economic condition of the urban native. In *Western Civilization and the Natives of South Africa,* ed. I. Schapera, pp. 159–192. London: George Routledge and Sons.

Keesing, Felix M. 1941. *The South Seas in the Modern World.* Institute of Pacific Relations International Research Series. New York: John Day.

Kroeger, Axel, and Françoise Barbira-Freedman. 1982. *Culture Change and Health: The Case of South American Rainforest Indians/* Frankfurt am Main: Verlag Peter Lang. (Reprinted in Bodley, 1988:221–236).

McNeil, Mary. 1972. Lateritic soils in distinct tropical environments: Southern Sudan and Brazil. In *The Careless Technology: Ecology and International Development*, ed. M. T. Farvar and John P. Milton, pp. 591–608. Garden City, N.Y.: Natural History Press.

Mönckeberg, F. 1968. Mental retardation from malnutrition. *Journal of the American Medical Association* 206: 30–31.

Montagu, Ashley. 1972. Sociogenic brain damage. *American Anthropologist* 74(5):1045–1061.

Price, Weston Andrew. 1945. *Nutrition and Physical Degeneration: A Comparison of Primitive and Modern Diets and Their Effects.* Redlands, Calif.: The author.

Prior, Ian A. M. 1971. The price of civilization. *Nutrition Today* 6(4):2–11.

Rambo, A. Terry. 1985. *Primitive Polluters: Semang Impact on the Malaysian Tropical Rain Forest Ecosystem.* Anthropological Papers no. 76, Museum of Anthropology, University of Michigan.

Redfield, Robert. 1962. *A Village That Chose Progress: Chan Kom Revisited.* Chicago: University of Chicago Press, Phoenix Books.

Reinhard, K. R. 1976. Resource exploitation and the health of western arctic man. In *Circumpolar Health: Proceedings of the Third International Symposium, Yellowknife, Northwest Territories,* ed. Roy J. Shephard and S. Itoh, pp. 617–627. Toronto: University of Toronto Press. (Reprinted in Bodley, 1988.)

Smith, Wilberforce. 1894. The teeth of ten Sioux Indians. *Journal of the Royal Anthropological Institute* 24:109–116.

TTR: *See under* United States.

United States, Department of State. 1955. *Seventh Annual Report to the United Nations on the Administration of the Trust Territory of the Pacific Islands* (July 1, 1953, to June 30, 1954).

_____. 1959. *Eleventh Annual Report to the United Nations on the Administration of the Trust Territory of the Pacific Islands* (July 1, 1957, to June 30, 1958).

_____. 1973. *Twenty-Fifth Annual Report to the United Nations on the Administration of the Trust Territory of the Pacific Islands* (July 1, 1971, to June 30, 1972).

Wagley, C. 1977. *Welcome of Tears: The Tapirape Indians of Central Brazil.* New York: Oxford University Press.

Wirsing, R. 1985. The health of traditional societies and the effects of acculturation. *Current Anthropology* 26:303–322.

"THE PRICE OF PROGRESS"

John Bodley

1) How do western cultures define the term *progress*?

2) How do western and traditional cultures compare in terms of quality of life, and how do you define this quality?

3) What diseases has Bodley defined as "diseases of development" and how have they impacted traditional societies?

4) Has a change in diet from traditional foods to western foods had a beneficial or deleterious effect on the health and well-being of traditional peoples?

5) According to Bodley, what have been the ecological impacts of development and westernization?

6) What other social ills has impact with western society brought to traditional peoples?

MUCH ADO ABOUT NOTHING: THE "FATEFUL HOAXING" OF MARGARET MEAD

James E. Côté

In 1983, Derek Freeman published *Margaret Mead and Samoa: The Making and Unmaking of an Anthropological Myth,* a book-length critique of the late Margaret Mead's *Coming of Age in Samoa.* Freeman, an emeritus professor at the Australian National University, had done considerable fieldwork in Samoa and weighed in on Mead's work with great authority. His critique of Mead was picked up in the popular media, and, almost overnight, the Mead-Freeman controversy was born. The title of Freeman's book conveyed his belief that Mead's *Samoa* was a myth, and her book a deceptively bad piece of research authored by a young anthropologist who did a minimum of real fieldwork, had little understanding of Samoan culture, and naively believed Samoan lies about their private lives. Was Mead, one of anthropology's great pioneers, duped into thinking that Samoa was a sexual paradise when, according to Freeman, it was a sexually repressive society?

The response to Freeman's attack on Mead's work was immediate. Anthropologists for the most part were critical. Unfortunately, the public has heard mostly Freeman's side of the controversy, and many people find his argument believable. Freeman has responded to his critics within anthropology with harsh words, and now he has a new book allegedly demonstrating that Mead was "hoaxed" by Samoans. As recently as 1997, Freeman published an article on his view of the controversy. However, scholars James E. Côté and Paul Shankman make a strong case that Freeman's argument against Mead is deeply flawed and that the public, and even respectable journals, have been taken in.

Derek Freeman's polemical arguments about Margaret Mead's Samoan research fail to stand up to tests of evidence based on examination of Mead's book, her field notes, and her correspondence. His claimed "smoking gun" is itself a misrepresentation based on selective quotation and omission.

Derek Freeman wants the world to believe that Margaret Mead was "fatefully hoaxed" about the sexual behavior of Samoan adolescents. He also wants people to think that this purported hoaxing is of tremendous significance to the history of ideas. The link, in his mind, is that Mead's book *Coming of Age in Samoa* (1928) was based on this hoaxing, and

that it subsequently had a profound influence on the way people throughout the twentieth century have thought about human behavior.

In his efforts to convey these ideas, Freeman has managed to have his say in a documentary film (Heimans 1988); get a play written and performed about his life, titled *Heretic: Based on the Life of Derek Freeman* (Williamson 1996); present his "story" to academic colleagues on numerous occasions (for example, Freeman 1989, 1991a, 1991b, 1992, 1997); and convince someone to publish an entire book on the matter (Freeman 1998). He also has been successful in gulling many intelligent people about the validity of his "story," including Martin Gardner (1993, 131) who reported in *Skeptical Inquirer* that Freeman had "irrefutable evidence" that Mead was "the gullible victim of a playful hoax." Unfortunately, Gardner based his report entirely on Freeman's version of events, and was apparently unaware of the notorious unreliability of Freeman's representation of the work of others.

Freeman's first book claiming to refute Mead's Samoan research created a great stir when it came out in 1983, but has been dismissed in numerous scholarly examinations (see Côté 1994 for a review). Not finding acceptance or adulation in the scholarly community, Freeman has gone to extraordinary lengths to present his complaint with Mead to the general public. He has managed, through years of work, to weave together miscellaneous details—some accurate, some not, and others exaggerated—into an easily conveyed melodramatic plot.

His story is much simpler than the truth, though, which gives him an advantage over those scholars who attempt to fully represent Mead's research in Samoa. In fact, the simplistic storyline he has managed to concoct provides the basis of the play about his life now running in Australia and New Zealand. As Monaghan (1996, 8) argues in a *Lingua Franca* review, this play "appears to have been culled largely from the Movie-of-the-Week playbook." But, forget the play, the plot contrived by Freeman in his ostensibly academic version of events has all the elements of a made-for-TV movie: a hero and villains, a conspiracy, deception, a smoking gun, and a motive and an opportunity.

I am an academic who has been attempting to accurately represent the complexity of Mead's research in Samoa (Côté 1992, 1994, 1995). Although I am somewhat handicapped by the necessary brevity of the present article, I hope to provide enough factual information for readers to judge for themselves the accuracy of Freeman's construction of events surrounding Mead's research in Samoa.

The Plot

A Hero and Villains

Throughout the Mead-Freeman controversy, as it is called, Freeman portrayed himself as a hero simply searching for truth in a world of dogmatists, ideologues, and Philistines. The villains include Margaret Mead (who is portrayed as a sycophant of Franz Boas), Franz Boas (who is portrayed as a dogmatist insisting on exclusively cultural explanations of human behavior), and the social anthropology establishment (which is portrayed as consumed by a "cult of culture"). In Freeman's world, these villains are not malicious; rather, they are "cognitively deluded," as he likes to put it.

A Conspiracy

In his iterative renditions of this plot, Freeman has woven together disparate events, linking conversations from one day in 1926 with the shaping of intellectual history for the remainder of the century. This is true melodrama indeed! One of Freeman's practiced accounts of this intrigue is worth citing in detail, if only for the sense of importance he ascribes to his "find." The following is from the most recent version of his "paradigms in collision" essay (the latest subtitle is "Margaret Mead's mistake and what it has done to anthropology"):

> We are here dealing with one of the most spectacular events of the intellectual history of the 20th century. Margaret Mead, as we know (sic), was grossly hoaxed by her Samoan informants, and Mead in her turn, by convincing others of the 'genuineness' of her account of Samoa, completely misinformed, and misled virtually the entire anthropological establishment, as well as the intelligentsia at large. . . . That a Polynesian prank should have produced such a result in centers of higher learning throughout the Western world is deeply comic. *But* behind the comedy there is a chastening reality. It is now apparent that for decade after decade in countless textbooks, and in university and college lecture rooms throughout

the Western world, students were misinformed about an issue of fundamental importance, by professors who by placing credence in Mead's conclusion of 1928 had themselves become cognitively deluded. Never can giggly fibs have had such far-reaching consequences in the groves of Academe. (1997, 68)

Sex and Deception

The stir created by Freeman's 1983 book, *Margaret Mead and Samoa: The Making and Unmaking of an Anthropological Myth*, lasted for several years. Serious scholars had been aware for years of the limitations of Mead's book,[1] but few endorsed Freeman's polemic on Mead, or his skewed reconstruction of how she supposedly shaped twentieth century social anthropology and intellectual history (Côté 1994). Not one to be daunted, though, Freeman has capitalized on the opprobrium of his critics, claiming victim status as a "heretic" who is ahead of his time (Freeman 1992, 1997). The strategy of claiming victim status at the hands of a dogmatic anthropology community has generated considerable support from a public that is unaware of the complexities of the controversy. His support is mainly from Australia, however, where it has been fuelled recently by the play about him showing there. More than one Australian colleague has told me that his cause strikes a chord with the longstanding anti-Americanism among some Australians, whereby he is seen by some as a brave Aussie standing up to bullying Yanks.

It appeared that the controversy would die out in academia until Freeman announced in the late 1980s that he had "crucially important new evidence" that resolved the controversy (Freeman 1989, 1017). This evidence, not coincidentally, also promised to rescue his failed attempt to convince fellow anthropologists that they should take a similarly scornful view of Mead's work in Samoa, and consign her work to "the trash cans of human error" (Freeman 1992, 23). What he referred to were statements made by Fa'apua'a Fa'amu, an elderly woman who had been one of Mead's age-mate Samoan friends during her 1925–1926 study. These statements have become the key issue in the controversy as it has dragged on into the 1990s.

Freeman (1996) presented the following scenario, hinging upon Fa'apua'a's statements, to the Australian public in a magazine article titled "False Paradise." According to Freeman's reconstruction of events, on Saturday, March 13, 1926, Margaret Mead was hoaxed by Fa'apua'a and a friend, Fofoa, when they were "on an outing" together. Conversations from this day, according to Freeman, led Mead to believe that she had discovered a free love society where the community did not attempt to curb the sexual activity of adolescents. Giving tremendous significance to the events of that day, Freeman specifically claims that "having been comprehensively hoaxed, she relied on what she had been told by Fofoa and Fa'apua'a, and *made this the information on which she based* her best-selling *Coming of Age in Samoa*" (emphasis added).

It is not quite clear exactly what Freeman would have us believe here. Certainly he cannot want us to believe that Mead's 297-page book is based on one day of conversation with two people, including Fa'apua'a. The ludicrous nature of this claim can be evaluated by simply reviewing Mead's book. Particular attention should be paid to the five detailed Appendices, especially Appendix V in which the results of her personal interviews are tabulated. When this is done, it is clear that she provided extensive details about her twenty-five adolescent informants and many others. Surely, Freeman cannot expect anyone who can read to believe that this highly detailed information was collected on one day.

When we look more deeply into Mead's book, we find a mass of information about dozens of people and little about a character resembling Fa'apua'a. However, if Freeman's claim about the hoaxing is correct, we should end references to a character resembling Fa'apua'a throughout Mead's fieldnotes and book.[2] But we do not. So, even if information about, or obtained from, Fa'apua'a made it into the book and is false, Fa'apua'a's current recanting has little bearing on the other material in Mead's book.

The spuriousness of Freeman's argument is clearly evident when we compare the information that Freeman alleges Mead obtained from Fa'apua'a with what Mead actually wrote in her fieldnotes and book. The following, taken from the film *Margaret Mead and Samoa*, is what the elderly Fa'apua'a claimed in 1987 to have said sixty-one years earlier to Mead in 1926:

Galea'i Poumele: Did she ever ask what you did at nights?

Fa'apua'a: Yes, she asked us what we did after dark. We girls would pinch each other and tell her that we were out with the boys. We were only joking but she took it seriously. As you know Samoan girls are terrific liars and love making fun of people but Margaret thought it was all true. [In another account of this same interview, Freeman (1989) cites her as saying "We spend the night with boys"]

Galea'i Poumele: So you answered Margaret Mead with lies?

Fa'apua'a: Yes, we just lied and lied.

In evaluating the possible link between these statements by Fa'apua'a and the contents of *Coming of Age in Samoa*, we can first consult Mead's fieldnotes. Martin Orans (1996) has carefully examined these and her correspondence with Franz Boas. On the basis of this evidence, he concludes several things about the unlikeliness of Freeman's argument. For example, Orans argues that "not only was Fa'apua'a unlikely to have been Mead's principal informant, as Freeman reports, but she appears to have been regarded by Mead as no kind of informant for there is not a single bit of information in the field materials attributed to Fa'apua'a" (152). In addition, Orans found in these fieldnotes that "the alleged testimony of Fa'apua'a hardly compares in detail, never mind seriousness, with the evidence that Mead compiled from acknowledged informants including the adolescent girls themselves" (152).

In evaluating the relevance of Fa'apua'a's statements for Mead's book, we also can examine the book itself. If *Coming of Age in Samoa* is based on what Fa'apua'a said to Mead, where is this character in the book? Based on my many readings of the book, I found only two people who come even close to matching Fa'apua'a's identity. These are characters Mead called Manita and Pana. However, the description of Manita comprises less than one page of text spread over pages 166 and 167 and that of Pana only a few descriptive sentences on page 52. From his reading of the fieldnotes, Orans has concluded that Fa'apua'a is Pana, but he found no reference to a Manita (personal communication, April 16, 1998). It is possible that Mead split Fa'apua'a into the two characters in an attempt to disguise Fa'apua'a's identity, but this would still amount to only about a page of text about Fa'apua'a. In short, had Mead based the book on what she was told by Fa'apua'a, Fa'apua'a would have figured prominently in the fieldnotes and as a character in the book, and she does not.

Freeman could perhaps present a more convincing argument if he claimed only that Fa'apua'a influenced the direction Mead took her book, leading her to depict a free love society in general. However, this argument fails several tests of logic.

First, Mead could not have gone into the field unaware of the reports of Polynesian sexual practices that date back to Cook. For example, while on her way to Samoa she stopped at the Bishop Museum in Honolulu from August 11 to 24, 1925. During that visit she met with officials of the museum who "did their utmost to persuade her to undertake ethnological research in Samoa on behalf of the Bishop museum"

(Freeman 1996, 9). They were very helpful in preparing Mead for her research. This is indicated in a letter to Boas of August 29, 1925, including a note that while there she "went through the literature on Samoa which [she] had not seen." On the issue of whether Fa'apua'a might have misled Mead into portraying Samoan society as one of free love, then, it is highly unlikely that Mead needed Fa'apua'a to introduce her to such ideas; because evidence of sexual promiscuity can be found in many of the early writings on Polynesia in general, and Samoa in particular (Côté 1994). Mead was not the first to capitalize on Western sexual stereotypes about Polynesians, and she certainly would not have needed Fa'apua'a to introduce her to these.

But Freeman's notion that Mead's book is some sort of a handbook for a free-love society based on Fa'apua'a's fibs fails the test of scrutiny (this is a crucial scene in the play about Freeman that suggests why he decided to begin his life-long crusade against Mead). In *Coming of Age,* we find extensive references to restrictions on adolescent sexual behavior, particularly by the family. Readers can check this for themselves, and they can consult Orans (1996) with respect to her fieldnotes. Mead was aware of, and wrote about these restrictions. Although Mead did provide misleading embellishments when it came to writing the book for the general public,[3] anyone who has read her book knows that she did not describe a free love society and her book is not some sort of free love manual. The type of first-hand knowledge gained from actually reading Mead is lost on those who rely only on Freeman's account. Orans (99) draws a similar conclusion:

> When one compares the data on sexuality that Mead had collected from sources other than Fa'apua'a and Fofoa with the paltry data to which Fa'apua'a testifies, it is evident that such humorous fibbing could not be the basis of Mead's understanding. Freeman asks us to imagine that the joking of two women, pinching each other as they put Mead on about their sexuality and that of adolescents, was of more significance than the detailed information she had collected throughout her fieldwork.

And finally, in an attempt to create high drama, Freeman put all his eggs in one basket by claiming that the hoaxing took place on one day (March 13, 1925). What Freeman is remiss in reporting, though, is that during subsequent interviews with Fa'apua'a, evidence of a sudden hoaxing vanished. In May 1993, for example, she told a follow-up interviewer that "the hoaxing occurred over a long period of time" (Orans, 1996, citing *The Samoa Times,* May 21, 1993).

From every angle considered, Freeman's attempt to use Fa'apua'a as a foil to foment controversy and resolve it in his favor fails decisively. The only plot that thickens concerns his motivations to misrepresent and conceal reality. This plot may not have sex, but it appears to have deception.

The Smoking Gun

Freeman must have realized that the vague recollections of an elderly woman who swears on a bible that she is a liar lack credibility. In his search for better evidence, he eventually reviewed Mead's fieldnotes and personal letters. From among the letters Mead wrote to Boas, he claims to have found the "smoking gun." This "hard evidence" is from a letter written by Mead to Franz Boas on March 14, 1926, the day after the supposed "fateful hoaxing" took place. According to Freeman, "she wrote elatedly to Boas describing Samoa . . . as a place where 'the community' did not attempt to 'curb' the sexual activity of adolescence" (1996, 9).

Fortunately, Freeman is not the only one with access to these letters. Orans (1996, 96–97) also has examined this letter (and other letters between Mead and Boas), to discover that Freeman has seriously distorted its contents. The truth is that Mead wrote something quite different in that letter. Four sentences before the line Freeman cites, she wrote that it is "the family and not the community (except in the case of the taupou) which attempts to preserve a girl's virginity and this attempt is usually secretly frustrated rather than openly combatted by the adolescent." In the sentence that Freeman cites, Mead actually wrote that when the community recognizes the stress caused if it interferes with adolescent sexual behavior, "and does not attempt to curb it there is no conflict at all between the adolescent and the community." In other words, Mead wrote to Boas saying that the Samoan *family,* not the community, curbed female adolescent behavior, except in the case of *taupou* (who are the ceremonial virgins representing the village). Freeman cites only the part about the community not curbing sexual behavior, making it sound like she was telling Boas there were no restraints at all. Freeman portrays Mead as claiming that she found a free love society, when in fact she was reporting that adolescents do not encounter conflict with the community when people stay out of their personal lives.

I am also in possession of these letters and I can verify that Orans' citation is accurate and complete. Freeman's selective account, however, is a gross misrepresentation of the letter's content. Freeman ought to know what the truth is, for the following reasons: (a) he has claimed throughout the controversy that he is a meticulous scholar and this is not something that can be easily missed; (b) he knows that Orans has pointed out the true contents of the letter because he read a prepublication draft of Orans' book (Orans 1996, vii); and (c) he is in possession of a copy of the letter himself. Yet, Freeman continues to misrepresent Mead on this matter. Is this an oversight or fraud? Whatever it is, there is no "smoking gun." However, there does appear to be misrepresented evidence proffered by Freeman that constitutes a form of academic perjury in its published form.

The Motive and the Opportunity

A good detective story would not be complete without a well-rounded plot. To put flesh on the bones of his plot, Freeman ascribes a motive to Mead for being so ready to accept the "giggly fibs" of Fa'apua'a and Fofoa. Freeman claims that several months into her study Mead was delinquent in undertaking her investigation of "the sexual life of the adolescent girl." In his view, this was in part because a hurricane hit the villages she was studying and in part because she was collecting ethnographic information for the Bishop Museum of Honolulu. Freeman claims that the collection of ethnographic data was done against Boas' wishes, and that this put Mead's "study of heredity and environment in relation to the adolescent . . . in a state of acute crisis" (Freeman 1996, 9).

With this purported motive, Freeman has seized upon the following events as a concoction of Mead's opportunity to commit the intellectual crime of the century. Freeman frames this as follows: "It was this parlous situation, with very little time left to her in Samoa, that Mead turned to insistently questioning Fofoa and Fa'apua'a about the sexual behavior of Samoan girls and young women. . . . As Fa'apua'a confessed it was during this time that, as a prank, she and Fofoa told their American inquisitor the very antithesis of the truth" (Freeman 1996, 9).

Freeman would have us believe that Mead was in such a panic to present findings that would please Boas that she desperately believed some "giggly fibs" about spending nights with boys. However, as we saw above, Freeman is remiss in reporting that upon further questioning Fa'apua'a thought that "the hoaxing occurred over a long period of time." This revelation devastates Freeman's theory of opportunity.

As for motive, we can turn to Orans' book to see how poorly Freeman's gumshoe account accords with the actual content of Mead's fieldnotes and letters, which provide a log for her investigations. Orans (1996, 97–99) lays these events out quite clearly. He begins by noting that Mead had in fact been working

for some time on the aspect of her study dealing with sexual behavior. One account was based on five weeks of detailed work. In a letter of January 6, 1926, she reported a conclusion similar to the March 14 letter.[4] This was two months before the supposed "fateful hoaxing." And again on February 15, one month before the alleged hoaxing, we find her discussing sexual matters in a letter to Boas. Orans concluded from his examination of these primary sources that "Mead's conclusions regarding sexuality were changed in no way by the alleged fibbing of Fa'apua'a and Fofoa."

Freeman's evidence that Mead planned to undertake "a special investigation of sexual behavior," but did not undertake it, is from a letter she wrote to Boas on February 15. However, once again, Freeman is selective in his citation of a source because Mead also wrote in this letter that "and of course I have a good deal of material on both subjects already," referring to her respondents' sexual lives and philosophical conflicts. Thus, Mead was intending to complete these investigations, not begin them as Freeman would have us believe. Freeman also omits the portion of Mead's February 15 letter that states: "I have been taking stock of the amount of material which I have accumulated and I think I can report that my work is going nicely." Indeed, Orans found evidence in Mead's fieldnotes that her "inquiries on adolescent sexuality continued after February 15." So much for motive.

Much Ado About Nothing . . . Except Perhaps Freeman's Attempt to Bully His Way into Intellectual History

With so many holes in his "fateful hoaxing" theory, just why would Freeman press the issue? Might it be that the public acclaim from the documentary film, the play, and the various articles about him provide Freeman with a sufficient gratification for his efforts? And, might it be that it is the general public that is being hoaxed with a "discovery" that has a half-life of credibility far shorter than the "discovery" of Piltdown Man? When the facts are known, and common sense prevails in the matter, I believe the general public will realize that his "fateful hoaxing" claim is much ado about nothing, and that it is Freeman who has hoodwinked the public, not some Samoan women or Margaret Mead. I also believe that Freeman's quest to create an esteemed place for himself in the history of ideas at the expense of his colleagues is ill-fated, and that conscientious scholars will not let his misrepresentations go uncorrected.

References

Côté, J. 1992. Was Mead wrong about coming of age in Samoa? An analysis of the Mead/Freeman controversy for scholars of adolescence and human development. *Journal of Youth and Adolescence* 21:499–527.

———. 1994. *Adolescent Storm and Stress: Art Evaluation of the Mead/Freeman Controversy.* Hillsdale, NJ: Lawrence Erlbaum Associates.

———. 1995. A tempest in a teapot? (letter to the editor regarding Freeman's "Paradigms in collision"). *Academic Questions* Winter:5–6.

Freeman, D. 1983. *Margaret Mead and Samoa: The Making and Unmaking of an Anthropological Myth.* Cambridge, MA: Harvard University Press.

———. 1989. Fa'apua'a Fa'amu and Margaret Mead. *American Anthropologist* 91:1017–1022.

———. 1991a. There's tricks i' th' world: An historical analysis of the Samoan researches of Margaret Mead. *Visual Anthropology Review* 7:103–128.

———. 1991b. On Franz Boas and the Samoan researches of Margaret Mead. *Current Anthropology* 32:322–330.

———. 1992. Paradigms in collision: The far-reaching controversy over the Samoan researches of Margaret Mead and its significance for the human sciences. *Academic Questions Summer:* 23–33.

———. 1996. False paradise. *The Australian* April 3:9.

———. 1997. Paradigms in collision: Margaret Mead's mistake and what it has done to anthropology. *Skeptic* 5(3): 66–73.

———. 1998. *Franz Boas and the "The Flower of Heaven" Coming of Age in Samoa and the Fateful Hoaxing of Margaret Mead: An Historical Analysis.* Boulder, CO: Westview Press.

Gardner, M. 1993. The great Samoan hoax. *Skeptical Inquirer* 17, Winter, 131–135.

Heimans, F. 1988. *Margaret Mead and Samoa.* (film) New York: Brighton Video. Howard, J. 1984. Margaret *Mead: A Life.* New York: Simon and Schuster.

Lewis, A. 1938. *They Call Them Savages.* London: Methuen.

Mead, M. 1928. *Coming of Age in Samoa: A Psychological Study of Primitive Youth for Western Civilization.* New York: Morrow Quill Paperbacks.

———. 1972. *Blackberry Winter: My Earlier Years.* New York: Morrow.

Monaghan, P. 1996. Fantasy island. *Lingua Franca* July/August, 7–8.

Orans, M. 1996. *Not Even Wrong: Margaret Mead, Derek Freeman, and the Samoans.* Novato, CA: Chandler and Sharp.

Williamson, D. 1996. *Heretic: Based on the Life of Derek Freeman.* Melbourne: Penguin Books.

Notes

1. In writing the book for the general public, Mead did simplify and over-generalize in places, providing some misleading accounts to those who would undertake only a surface reading of the book. In her Appendix II, however, she explains the problems she faced in describing a culture in transition (see Côté, 1994, for a detailed discussion of this). It is also apparent in her correspondence with Boas that she was unsure how to provide convincing generalizations based on nonstatistical methods.

2. Mead (1972, 154) wrote that she "carefully disguised all the names, sometimes using double disguises so that the actual individuals could never be identified." While this is laudable, obvious details like someone being a *taupou* (the ceremonial virgin of a village) limit the disguise considerably, and given this is a nonfictional book, the factual elements of characters could not have been extensively fabricated. At the same time, because of her attempt to disguise characters, we should not expect a total correspondence between details of the characters in her book and the details about the lives of the people she discussed.

3. The embellishments were apparently encouraged by her publisher, who was obviously interested in selling as many of her books as possible. They can be found mainly in Chapters 2, 13, and 14, which were added at her publisher's request. But even these chapters contain only a few questionable phrases that intelligent readers would identify as being targeted at the general public in an attempt to maintain their interest in the book. The issue of the book's reputation as being some sort of Kama Sutra of the South Seas appears to stem from the publisher's promotion of the book, and the suggestive cover designs of various editions. Mead's biographer, Jane Howard, gives us a glimpse of the events surrounding the publication of the book: A professor in Tennessee wrote her to suggest that she expurgate her final two chapters, which, following her publisher's suggestion, connected her Samoan conclusions with her view of America. Mead replied that out of a total of 297 pages, there were exactly 68 which dealt with sex" (1984, 128).

4. And, even before meeting Fa'pua'a, Mead wrote in her November 29, 1925, report to Boas, that on "the problem of the adolescent girl," there were "two sets of ideals, one the Taupou Concept and the other the missionary one of the Good Christian Girl." She went on to note that the taupou tradition had been passing away there, but that it provided "vicarious virtue for the rest of the village" and since there was virtually no chance of the rest of the girls of the village becoming a taupou, "none of the requirements of modesty, dignity, chastity, were made on the other girls in the village." The exception to this were the girls who attempted to follow the Good Christian life and live in the household of the pastor, sometimes at the urging of their parents who wanted them "to appear virtuous." They were strictly supervised, and constituted a control group for Mead in comparison to the other girls in the community.

"Much Ado About Nothing: The 'Fateful Hoaxing' of Margaret Mead"

James E. Côté

1) According to Côté, what are Freeman's claims about the quality and the accuracy of Margaret Mead's work in Samoa?

2) What information does Freeman claim to base his contentions about Mead on?

3) In Côté's analysis, what is the problem with Freeman's evidence about Mead and her work? What contradictions does Côté point out between what Freeman claims and the evidence from Mead's published material and her fieldnotes?

4) What motives does Côté suggest are behind Freeman's attempted debunking of Mead's work?

MARGARET MEAD, DEREK FREEMAN, AND THE ISSUE OF EVOLUTION

Paul Shankman

After reading a recent article by Derek Freeman, I had a curious sense of déjà vu. The article was entitled "Paradigms in Collision: Margaret Mead's Mistake and What It Has Done to Anthropology" (1997), and it reminded me that Freeman had published an article with almost the same title and similar content five years earlier (1992). But then Freeman has been relentlessly criticizing the work of Margaret Mead for the past fifteen years. And he shows no signs of tiring.

One of the most interesting aspects of Freeman's critique is that a number of intelligent people have come to believe it. Initially, Freeman argued that a young, gullible Mead mistook Samoan jokes about sexual conduct for the truth, and that this alleged mistake led to the false doctrine of absolute cultural determinism, which in turn had profound intellectual consequences. Recently, Freeman has given more attention to the issue of evolution, which he believes is at the heart of the controversy. Specifically, he holds Mead responsible for the anti-evolutionary paradigm in which only cultural variables are important and in which "all human behavior is the result of social conditioning." For Freeman, evolution has become the ultimate issue in his critique of Mead and is the central focus of "Paradigms in Collision."

Freeman rejects the "Mead paradigm" in favor of an interactionist one that recognizes biological as well as cultural variables. Freeman also deplores the dominance of the "Mead paradigm" which, due to a cult-like loyalty to her, has perpetuated a "tabula rasa anthropology" from which the discipline has yet to recover. He believes that only when anthropologists recognize Mead's initial error and its disastrous intellectual consequences will the discipline have a promising future.

There is high drama in Freeman's account: A lone dissenter from the conventional wisdom uncovers a great anthropologist's original sin in his search for truth. Her reputation is tarnished. What ensues is an epic struggle for the soul of a discipline held hostage by the ghost of a legendary figure. Margaret Mead, symbol of American anthropology, was anti-evolutionary. What could be worse?

Unfortunately, like so much of his critique of Mead, Freeman relies on a caricature of Mead's views and her influence on anthropology. Granted that it is an entertaining caricature full of implications about Freeman's own place in intellectual history. Yet a closer look at this argument demonstrates that on the fundamental issues of biology, culture, and evolution, Mead and Freeman are in substantial agreement. Mead was not anti-evolutionary; she held what are now conventional views on evolution, just like Freeman. So there are no "paradigms in collision." Freeman has simply omitted much of what Mead actually wrote on evolution. In this article, Freeman's and Mead's views on biology, culture, and evolution are reviewed. Freeman's misrepresentation of Mead's views raises questions about his scholarship, which is now the real issue in this long-running "controversy."

Mead's View of Biology, Culture, and Evolution

Mead's views on the interaction of biology and culture were complex, not simplistic, and developed over her long career. Early on, she emphasized the importance of culture, stating that differences between cultures arose from a common biological basis. This was the crux of *Coming of Age in Samoa* (1928), in which Mead argued that adolescence was a universal biological process, but that there were differences in the way that this process was handled by different cultures. Cultural differences arose from a common biological basis, yet they could not be explained by biology alone. These differences suggested to Mead that there was no single way to manage adolescence. Americans could therefore make choices about handling this stage in the human life cycle.

In her early work, Mead did argue that human nature was extremely malleable. However, as historian Carl Degler (1991) found in his comprehensive review of Darwinian thought in the twentieth century, Mead's views on human nature developed over four decades during which the political and intellectual climate was changing. Thus, when she argued against racial and biological explanations, she emphasized culture; when she was discussing sex roles, biology received more attention. For example, in *Male and Female* (1949), Mead discussed the significance of biological differences in sex roles and sexuality.[1]

Far from naively embracing the *"tabula rasa"* point of view, Mead specifically pointed out its weaknesses in the 1940s (1942, 1947), while noting the importance of the interaction of biology and culture in the human maturation process. Furthermore, in her presidential address to the American Anthropological Association in 1960, Mead stated that genetics is "enormously relevant to problems absolutely central to our discipline" and was concerned that research on genetics had been largely confined to physical anthropology (1961, 480). She also urged her colleagues to take advantage of "the opportunity provided by the new upsurge of interest in the whole field of evolution, in which human evolution is one part and cultural evolution a smaller one" (1961, 481). And she reminded anthropologists that Theodosius Dobzhansky, George Gaylord Simpson, and other natural scientists were interested in communicating with them about evolution (1961, 481). Given such public statements, can anyone take seriously Freeman's assertion that Mead believed that "all human behavior is the result of social conditioning" or that she was anti-evolutionary? Of course not. Freeman has simply neglected those parts of Mead's work that do not support his current views.

Freeman's View of Biology Culture, and Evolution

Freeman's views are, in fact, very similar to Mead's. He often emphasizes the importance of culture. Like Mead, Freeman believes that because humans can learn non-genetically and transmit information symbolically, culture often gives meaning to behavior. He notes that people may attribute different cultural meanings to the same genetically prescribed behaviors. As an example, he cites the genetically prescribed behavior known as the eyebrow flash which means "yes" in Samoa while meaning "no" in Greece. According to Freeman, "It is the existence of such conventional behaviors, in great profusion, in all human populations, that establishes, indubitably, the *autonomy of culture*" (1980, 215; my emphasis).

On the issue of choice, Freeman is as much a cultural determinist as Mead. He states that "because cultural phenomena are particular alternatives, created by human agency in the course of history, it is always possible for these alternatives to be rapidly, and even radically changed . . . [T]he choice of new alternatives, is, in many instances, not connected in any significant way with the process of genetic evolution, or, for that matter, with human physiology"

(1980, 215). He concludes that humans, "with their biologically given and culturally nurtured capacity for alternative action, cannot be said to have any kind of 'ultimate' nature" (1981, 99–100).

Evolution

In "Paradigms in Collision, " Freeman stresses our primate heritage, our evolutionary history, and the emergence of culture as a biologically based means of allowing choices to be made and transmitted through non-genetic mechanisms. This view of culture, based on a common biological heritage, is one he shares with Mead. She stated that "Cultural systems will be treated as extensions of the power to learn, store, and transmit information, and the evolution of culture as dependent upon biological developments of these abilities and the cultural developments that actualize them" (1964, 31).

The emphasis on cultural variables at one point in time and biological variables at another may give the appearance of the existence of two very different paradigms, but Freeman seems to have no problem embracing the "autonomy of culture" when criticizing sociobiology (1980), while invoking evolution in his critique of Mead (1997). For Mead, this was a matter of emphasis, not one of irreconcilable differences. In her book *Continuities in Cultural Evolution*, she stated that:

> At some points in the history of anthropology it has been important to stress the discontinuity between man as a culture-building animal and all other living creatures. It has also been important to stress that man is a mammal with certain types of behavior appropriate to mammals and to identify these behaviors which can be recognized as related between monkeys, apes, and man (1964, 25).

Mead, along with most anthropologists, would no doubt have agreed with Freeman when he asserts that "humans, like our chimpanzee cousins, far from being empty tablets at birth, are born with a phylogenetically given primate nature, components of which remain with us throughout our lives beneath all of the conventional behaviors that we acquire by learning from other members of the society to which we belong" (1997, 70).

Interactionism

What of the modern interactionist paradigm that Freeman advocates? Freeman believes in a view of human evolution in which the genetic and exogenetic (that is, cultural) are distinct but interacting parts of a single system (1983, 299) and that genetic factors combine with environmental factors to influence behavioral differences among individuals (1997, 71). Mead anticipated this position in 1935 when discussing the role of innate temperament and its interaction with culture. In *Behavior and Evolution,* edited by Anne Roe and George Gaylord Simpson, she stated that "We can get some picture of how change occurs only when each individual is fully specified in his genetic and experiential peculiarity . . . " (1958, 496).

Given Mead's interactionist views of the relationship of biology and culture, and her interest in evolution, articulated *long before* Freeman developed his current views on these subjects, one might expect Freeman to review and discuss Mead's actual positions as they developed over her fifty-year career, especially because he is willing to discuss how his own views have changed over the course of his career. Yet Freeman cites Mead selectively and omits mention of her interest in evolution. He does not even pretend to review Mead's work on this subject.

This omission raises an important question. If evolution is not at the heart of Freeman's critique of Mead, if indeed both Freeman and Mead hold similar views of the relationship of biology and culture, then what is the point of Freeman's "Paradigms in Collision"? Freeman attempts to enlist the legitimacy of evolution and interactionism as a weapon in his effort to cast doubt on the work of Mead, but there are no "paradigms in collision."[2] Indeed, the so-called central issue in Freeman's critique is not an issue at all.

By misrepresenting Mead's views and by presenting himself as the guardian of evolution and interactionism, Freeman asks his readers to dismiss Mead's work as mistaken, misguided, and anachronistic, and accept Freeman's position as accurate, responsible, and thoroughly scientific. The choice, however, is not between Mead on the one hand and Freeman on the other. It is between wondering whether Freeman has read what Mead said and, for whatever reasons, omitted passages that do not support his argument, or whether he did not carefully read Mead and therefore is not fully aware of what she has written. Neither of these choices reflects well on Freeman's scholarship.

The World View of Derek Freeman

Freeman's own discovery of evolution's importance came rather late, in the 1960s. And there is little that is new or original in Freeman's discussion of the worthwhile topics of evolution and interactionism.

Evolution is part of most general textbooks in anthropology in the U.S., despite Freeman's insistence on the negative influence of the so-called "Mead paradigm." Nevertheless, Freeman portrays himself as a victim in the lonely struggle for truth. He sees himself as the voice of reason among "irrational" anthropologists following the "prescientific ideology" of a "totemic mother." Freeman even asserts that a top professional journal, the *American Anthropologist,* has suppressed his work in "the interests of a ruling ideology" (1997, 73). He does not mention that this same journal has published more exchanges on his critique of Mead than any other. This fact is irrelevant: The rhetoric has served its purpose.

The general approach that Freeman has employed to promote his argument and himself was described in broad terms by anthropologist Marshall Sahlins (1979) well before the Mead/Freeman controversy existed. At the outset, Sahlins comments, Professor X publishes a theory despite evidence to the contrary. When scholars familiar with the evidence question Professor X's work, he denounces them in "the highest moral tones" and engages in attacks on them personally. The battle lines are drawn, and he has now become "the controversial Professor X." His ideas are discussed seriously by nonprofessionals, especially journalists. Soon he has become a familiar figure in the media where nonprofessionals have difficulty challenging him and demonstrating the weaknesses in his argument. It is through this process that Professor X, like Freeman, has gained popular respectability.

With each new version of his critique of Mead, Freeman has escalated the rhetoric and his importance in this self-made controversy. What began fifteen years ago as a critique of the "Boasian paradigm" has become a critique of the "Mead paradigm." Mead's alleged "mistake" in Samoa has become her "fateful hoaxing." Freeman himself has gone from a critic of Mead to a self-styled "heretic" in pursuit of truth against the conventional wisdom of a discipline. The title of a new edition of *Margaret Mead and Samoa* (1983) released in Australia reflects Freeman's increasing sense of stature in relation to Mead; it is now *Margaret Mead and the Heretic* (1996). And the title of Freeman's recent article, "Paradigms in Collision," implies near-mythic proportions of Freeman's critique.

Yet *Coming of Age in Samoa* was not the intellectual disaster of momentous consequence that Freeman believes. The book posed important questions for the general public at the time it was written in 1928 and for about four decades thereafter. That is why it became a popular classic, not because it is a model for professional scholarship today. *Coming of Age in Samoa* was never a sacred text for most anthropologists. Although Mead and *Coming of Age in Samoa* were enormously popular with the general public, within the profession neither she nor her book led generations of anthropologists to embrace the so-called "Mead paradigm." Her very popularity led academic anthropologists to treat her work with caution, recognizing its limitations as well as its strengths. Like so much of the anthropology from the early part of the century, ideas proposed by Mead in the 1920s, 1930s, and 1940s were later criticized, modified, and revised. Thus Mead is not the central theoretical figure in anthropology that Freeman suggests, although she did make a number of important contributions.

No wonder that most professional anthropologists have lost interest in Freeman's argument. His critique of Mead and his history of the discipline are deeply flawed. Yet the same style of argument that has turned off anthropologists has attracted the media, and intelligent people have been drawn to Freeman's appeals to truth, science, and evolution. This is unfortunate because these are not the real issues involved. The truth about the controversy is more mundane. Evolution and interactionism are old news. *Coming of Age in Samoa* was written in 1928. Mixing these ingredients together in Freeman's intellectual Cuisinart and adding words like "hoax" and "paradigm" may be enticing, but it does not make for good scholarship. By exaggerating Mead's theoretical place in academic anthropology, Freeman implicitly magnifies his own importance and neglects her real contributions. By relying so heavily on caricature, omission, and overstatement, Freeman, far from saving anthropology, has become an intellectual speedbump in the way of our understanding Samoa, the work of Margaret Mead, and the state of anthropology today.

Remembering Margaret Mead

When the dust eventually settles on this never-ending controversy, how will Mead and Freeman be remembered? Freeman will be remembered for his tireless assault on Mead, which has received widespread attention, in part because his misrepresentations are so boldly stated that relatively few people have bothered to check the historical record. But Freeman's proverbial fifteen minutes of fame will expire, and his contributions are limited.

Anthropologists will remember Mead as more than the object of Freeman's critique simply because, over the course of her long career, she did make a number of lasting contributions. Mead was a pioneer.

In a span of fifteen years between 1925 and 1939, she made five field trips to the South Pacific, studied eight different cultures, and published popular and professional works on most of them. Although these works are not particularly important today, they became part of the foundation on which future anthropologists built. Mead was also among the first anthropologists to focus on childhood, adolescence, and gender as important topics of research; today anthropologists approach these issues more wisely because of her work. Mead's efforts to bring teams of male and female anthropologists to the field, instead of only individuals, improved data collection and analysis. She was among the first to use still photography and film in the field. Most importantly, Mead almost single-handedly popularized anthropology for the general public, putting the discipline on the map. And, whatever her shortcomings, she did all of these things at a time when women were not expected to be professionals. It is for these reasons, and many more, that Mead deserves recognition as the pioneering figure that she was.

References

Degler, C. 1991. *In Search of Human Nature.* New York: Oxford University Press.

Freeman, D. 1980. Sociobiology: The "antidiscipline" of anthropology. In *Sociobiology Examined.* A. Montagu, editor. New York: Oxford University Press.

————. 1981. The anthropology of choice: An ANZAAS presidential address. Given in Aukland, New Zealand on 24 January 1979. *Canberra Anthropology* 4(1): 82–100.

————. 1983. *Margaret Mead and Samoa: The Making and Unmaking of An Anthropological Myth.* Cambridge, MA: Harvard University Press.

————. 1992. Paradigms in collision: The far-reaching controversy over the Samoan researches of Margaret Mead and its significance for the human sciences. *Academic Questions* (Summer):23–33.

————. 1996. *Margaret Mead and the Heretic: The Making and Unmaking of an Anthropological Myth.* Ringwood (Australia). Penguin Books.

————. 1997. Paradigms in collision: Margaret Mead's mistake and what it has done to anthropology. *Skeptic* 5(3):66–73.

Ehrenreich, Barbara and Janet McIntosh. 1997. The new creationism: Biology under attack. *The Nation* (June 9, 1997): 11–16.

Mead, M. 1928. *Coming of Age in Samoa.* New York: William, Morrow & Company.

————. 1935. *Sex and Temperament in Three Primitive Societies.* New York: Morrow.

———. 1942. Anthropological data on the problem of instinct. *Psychosomatic Medicine* 4:396–397.

———. 1947. On the implications for anthropology of the Gesell-Ilg approach to maturation. *American Anthropologist* 49:69–77.

———. 1958. Cultural Determinants of Behavior. In *Behavior and Evolution*. A. Roe and G. G. Simpson, editors. New Haven: Yale University Press.

———. 1961. Anthropology among the sciences. *American Anthropologist* 63:475—82.

———. 1964. *Continuities in Cultural Evolution*. New Haven: Yale University Press.

Sahlins, M. 1979. Cannibalism: An exchange. *New York Review* of Books. March, 22, 1979, pp. 46–47.

Wilson, E. O. 1994. *Naturalist*. Washington, D.C.: Island Press.

Notes

1. Degler concludes that Mead's changing views on the biological differences between men and women were a "harbinger of things to come: the emergence of the sociobiological approach to the ancient question of the nature of the sexes, and the rediscovery by a reinvigorated feminist movement of the human values of differences between men and women" (1991, 138).

Mead did become involved in the controversy over sociobiology. In his autobiography, E. O. Wilson, a founder of sociobiology, recalls that at the 1976 American Anthropological Association meetings, a motion was made to formally censure sociobiology and to cancel two symposia on the subject that had been previously scheduled. "During the debate on the matter Margaret Mead rose indignantly, great walking stick in hand, to challenge the very idea of adjudicating a theory. She condemned the motion as a "book-burning proposal." Soon afterward the motion was defeated—but not by an impressive margin" (1994, 331).

The following year, at a conference on human behavior, Mead invited Wilson to dinner to discuss sociobiology. He remembers, "I was nervous then, expecting America's mother figure to scold me about the nature of genetic determinism. I had nothing to fear. She wanted to stress that she, too, had published ideas on the biological basis of social behavior" (1994, 348). Thus, at the very end of her career, Mead's interest in the role of biology in human behavior was apparent.

2. There is such a cultural determinist school/social constructionist school of thought, and here there are "paradigms in collision," but this school draws on a different intellectual ancestry than Margaret Mead (Ehrenreich and McIntosh 1997).

"MARGARET MEAD, DEREK FREEMAN, AND THE ISSUE OF EVOLUTION"

Paul Shankman

1) In Shankman's analysis, what appears to be one of the major "mistakes" of Mead's work that Freeman says greatly influenced the course of development of anthropological theory?

2) What does Shankman say was Mead's ideas regarding the interrelationship between biology, culture, and evolution? How does Shankman suggest that Freeman's views on these issues are actually close to those of Mead's?

3) How do both Côté and Shankman claim Freeman has distorted Mead's views and writings to support his own position?

4) According to Shankman, how does Freeman portray himself in the purported "intellectual struggle" against the so-called "Mead Paradigm"?

5) What does Shankman say about Mead's real contributions to the overall field of anthropology?